INDUSTRIAL APPLICATIONS OF ARTIFICIAL INTELLIGENCE

INDUSTRIAL APPLICATIONS OF ARTIFICIAL INTELLIGENCE

Proceedings of the IFIP TC5/WG5.3 International Conference on
Artificial Intelligence in CIM
Leningrad, USSR, 16-18 April, 1990

Edited by

JAMES L. ALTY
Department of Computer Studies
University of Loughborough
Loughborough, Leicestershire, UK

LEONID I. MIKULICH
Institute of Control Sciences
Moscow, USSR

1991

NORTH-HOLLAND
AMSTERDAM • LONDON • NEW YORK • TOKYO

FOREWARD

J. L. ALTY+ and L. I. MIKULICH*

+Dept. of Computer Studies,
University of Loughborough,
Loughborough,
UK

*Institute of Control Sciences,
Moscow,
The USSR.

The IFIP sponsored International Conference on the Industrial Applications of Artificial Intelligence was held in Leningrad early in April 1990. It was attended by many contributors from the USSR, Bulgaria, Czechoslovakia, Poland, The GDR, The FDR, China, The UK, The USA, Italy, France, and Japan. It was held at a time of great change, both in the world perception of the usefulness of Artificial Intelligence and in the USSR. The introduction of Glaznost has opened up a window on the USSR, and the conference provided not only a welcome meeting point for scientists from all over the world, but also a broad look at what is currently interesting and active in science in the Soviet Union.

The conference was organised by

- The Scientific Board for Artificial Intelligence of the USSR Academy of Sciences.
- The Leningrad Institute for Informatics and Automation of the USSR Academy of Sciences (LIIAN)
- The Association of Foreign Economic Cooperation "NAUKA-SERVICE"

The International Program Committee consisted of the Chairman, G.S. Pospelov (SU), together with J.S. Gero (Australia), G. Guiho (F), D. Kochan (GDR), L. Nemes (Australia), G. Olling (USA), V. M. Ponomaryov (SU), D.A. Pospelov (SU), B. Prasad (USA), Y Shirai (Japan), E.H. Tyugu (SU) and M. Vucobratovic (Yug).

Particular thanks are due to the Organising Committee: G. S. Pospelov, V.M. Ponomaryov, I.P. Podnozova and Yu. N. Ivanov.

Because of the time required to pass documents backwards and forwards to the Soviet Union, the editors took it upon themselves to make some corrections to the English translations of the papers presented. Most of these were minor stylistic corrections, but if we have erred more substantially from the authors intentions we pray forgiveness from authors.

The conference was a great success and we hope that the reader finds this collection of papers stimulating and thought-provoking.

CONTENTS

Industrial Applications of Artificial Intelligence
J.L. Alty and L.I. Mikulich (Editors)
Elsevier Science Publishers B.V. (North-Holland)

ARTIFICIAL INTELLIGENCE AND INDUSTRY

J. L. ALTY+ and L. I. MIKULICH*

+Dept. of Computer Studies,
University of Loughborough,
Loughborough,
UK

*Institute of Control Sciences,
Moscow,
The USSR.

ABSTRACT: The lack of acceptance of Artificial Intelligence solutions in industry is briefly discussed. It is argued that there is now a more realistic approach to the application of AI techniques in industry. We have better tools and a better understanding of the types of problems which can be solved. Some new paradigms are briefly discussed.

1. INTRODUCTION

Since 1984, the fortunes of Artificial Intelligence have moved through the seasons. It has had its spring, its high summer and its winter of discontent. However, there are now signs that it is moving out of the disappointing stage and is being re-appraised more realistically. The possible applications of Artificial Intelligence are expanding again and there is a general feeling that, in the right circumstance, with the right problem, it can offer really useful solutions to the difficult problems of industry. The Leningrad Conference is a particularly interesting one, coming as it does, at what appears to be the start of renewed interest in Artificial Intelligence solutions.

2. WHY A WINTER OF DISCONTENT ?

There is no doubt that we have just moved through a period of disillusionment and this was probably inevitable. The idea of mimicking human intelligence in machines was bound to raise false hopes for quick solutions to difficult problems. The idea was a good one, and still is, but a great deal of work remains to be done to bring the idea to reality in many problem areas. The cause was not helped in the early days by an over-zealous selling of the concepts. It was all too easy for people to go on television and promise near-instant solutions. As a consequence the field was misunderstood and hopes were raised too high. There was another more important reason, however, for failure. We simply did not have the right tools for the job. At the high end of the market were Symbolics and Texas Instruments systems running software such as KEE or ART. Such systems cost a lot of money and there were problems of delivering their solutions on smaller systems. At the lower end of the market we had small expert system shells promising (so they said) to solve all major knowledge based problems.

Today these two extremes have begun to merge, and powerful but affordable toolkits are coming onto the marketplace. We now understand much more about the problems which are amenable to our current techniques. We understand the limitations of our methods and we have more paradigms to address problems. New paradigms involving Deep Knowledge Representation, Qualitative Modelling and Case Based Reasoning are beginning to be used effectively. Thus Artificial Intelligence workers now present themselves as more-realistic, better equipped and better armed to deal with the complex problems that industry presents. These problems are indeed complex and Schuett [15] presents a set of eight powerfully argued theses in which Artificial Intelligence will play a major role.

3. DIAGNOSIS AND FAULT FINDING

Diagnosis and Fault Finding appear to be particularly fruitful areas for study and were, of course, areas where the early successes in rule-based systems were achieved. We know why this was so. One of the well-recognised problem areas in Artificial Intelligence is the representation of common sense knowledge. Such knowledge is so wide-ranging that it is beyond our present capabilities to represent it (even human beings take about 15 years to acquire it, and it is said that some never do !). It does not conveniently break down into neat fragments, so we cannot even solve subsets of it. The early expert systems were successful because they attacked highly specialised fields of knowledge which did not require an understanding of common sense.

An attractive feature of a piece of industrial equipment is that its workings also do not depend upon common sense knowledge, indeed, a knowledge of common sense alone does not enable an operator to successfully diagnose problems. Equipment also has the advantage that it can be modelled. We think that the model-based reasoning approach offers really interesting possibilities and can enable us to build upon the early rule-based successes. An example of such an approach is that of Menexiades and Soenen [1] who have constructed an expert system for the diagnosis of failures in vibrating machinery. Storr et al [4] also utilise a model of a machine tool in their expert system and have an inferencing process which switches between two points of view - a general one and a specific one.

Another interesting advantage with machine diagnosis is that the machine itself can be used to assist in the problem solving process. This is illustrated in the paper by Sgurev et al [2] on Diagnostic Expert Systems for Digital Electronics, where the expert system, machine and operator, work together to locate the fault.

A different combination of model based reasoning and shallow reasoning is exemplified in the paper by Alty and Pearce [3] where a model is constructed from which failure examples are generated and rules are induced from these examples. The approach also provides a mechanism for attacking the difficult problem of validation in expert systems. The theme of Validation is also addressed by Rousset [22] in the COVADIS system where a definition of rule base consistency is put forward.

The importance of having good approximate reasoning systems should not be lost sight of, as discussed by Gorodetsky [9] who has proposed a new approach to the construction of decision algorithms based on a model of binary random string distribution.

There was a time when argument raged over the difference between Expert Systems and Decision Support Systems. Where Decision Support Systems and and Expert Systems begin, however, is a moot point. Barnikow et al [28], for example, describe a DSS system which aims to determine decision variants in industrial development planning with different time horizons.

4. MACHINE LEARNING

Machine learning techniques have provided useful solutions to the problems of knowledge acquisition in industry, but one difficulty has resulted from the lack of a framework in which to compare Learning Algorithms. Ganascia et al [5] have described a model of behaviour for machine learning in which they contrast ID3 and the PRODIGY system within a common architecture and show that their proposed architecture can be used as a basis for comparing learning systems.

There are large amounts of data lying in databanks or filing cabinets which might contain important rules of behaviour. Lasek and Peczkowski [6] use machine induction to analyse the financial standing of an enterprise. The problem is classified and then data from 500 companies is used as a set of examples to tease out the rules. There must be many more such data collections waiting to be unravelled by inductive techniques. Matskin [7] describes a system where learning by example is combined with knowledge representation by concept. More theoretical aspects of inductive inference are discussed by Lyashenko [8].

Zebrowski [19] uses inductive techniques to derive the rules for an expert system which enables a designer to define the structure of a process dispatching system taking into account such features as the type of production flow, stability of production output, the organisational structure of the production facilities, the degree of automation and engineering features such as product mix, specific labour demands and the number of operations.

It is important to note that operating logs are also a form of example set and can be used to determine the hidden rules of a device. Naidenova and Polegaeva [23] describe an induction system for deriving rules from such known facts - the SIZIF system.

5. AUTOMATED MANUFACTURING

This is an area which has received a lot of attention recently and the possibilities for industry are very promising. One of the important (though now obvious) points being brought out is the proposition that successful approaches will combine traditional engineering approaches with those based in Artificial Intelligence. Dwivedi and Lanka [12] propose a harmonious blending of Artificial Intelligence techniques (with a proven potential for planning) with what they call "Concurrent Engineering", a technique which addresses all the product life-cycle disciplines with the objective of getting it "right first time".

Michelini et al [13] make the point about mixing Artificial Intelligence techniques with algorithmic efficiency with respect to deep knowledge. As they point out "it would certainly be foolish to build 'intelligent' systems based only on heuristics, with no regard for experienced engineering models, acknowledged physical principles, or governing equations, that have been tested and known for many years". Laurent and Ayel [16] describe a Manufacturing Management Monitoring System (a 3-M System) which proposes an architecture based upon "islands" of Production Management Activities controlled by Unit Controllers which are knowledge based systems.

Tsarevsky [14] describes the AMIGO planning system which allows a user to describe a manufacturing object, to experiment with a numerical model and to improve dynamic features of the object in terms of productions.

The mathematical modelling of robot dynamics and robotized flexible cells is an important issue in Flexible Manufacturing. Vukobratovic [17] in a comprehensive paper discusses these aspects and the adaptability features are examined by Timofejev [18].

6. REASONING AND META KNOWLEDGE

Ohsuga [10] makes the case for the development of a conceptual framework to aid human problem solving in its totality. He stresses the importance of meta-knowledge or a multilevel architecture. For example, Learning, scheduling, evaluation and the handling of ambiguous information and model operations all need meta-level operations. A key feature of trial and error operations in a model based world is the possibility of contradictions with existing knowledge. Provided that consistency can be maintained in any particular "local" world, they can conflict across local worlds. Ohsuga also stresses the importance of mirroring the multiple meta-levels in any interface provided to the user, in this case there is a window for every meta-level.

The CASS system [11] for example uses three meta levels - conceptual, formal and implementational, and it accesses global meta-knowledge.

7. REPRESENTATION AND INFERENCE ISSUES

In order to fully exploit Artificial Intelligence techniques in industry, we need to extend the range and versatility of our representation techniques. One of the most important of these is temporal reasoning. Most industrial process involve a progression of time. One example of an approach is the Calculus of Metric Temporal Reasoning put forward by Kirillov [20] where a generalisation of the Production Rule framework is proposed from which a prototype system has been constructed. Yakovlev and Petrov [21] attempt to model event oriented knowledge using a subclass of Petri nets and put forward an efficient framework for event oriented knowledge.

Petri Nets (with variable markings) are also the representation mechanism used by Maltsev [24] for representing different grammar constructions which may form a basis for representing concurrent systems and by Capkovic [26] who constructs a system by analogy with Petri Nets to describe both the structure of knowledge about a problem in question and the dynamic behaviour of the deductive reasoning process.

An interesting dual representation approach is addressed by Ilyin and Ignatova [25]. A formalism is developed for describing a robot vision scene. The system can then take a description in Russian and reconstruct a visual scene using a graphical planner to produce the patterns of output in the scene taking into consideration the number of objects and the relationships between them.

Polyakov [27] proposes a management expert system which uses techniques of non-verbal communication. The system uses a toolset of cognitive graphic and simulation game techniques to implement peoples visual abilities. Ming et al [29] propose modifying inference procedures in order to make them more suitable for a CAD environment.

Finally, Holden [30] shows how to combine a knowledge based approach with a massively parallel neural net to control a dynamic robot system. The Knowledge is provided in a hierarchy of contexts. The paper also shows how the use of hints can considerably speed up the learning process.

8. CONCLUSIONS

This brief, and incomplete, survey of the papers in the 1990 Leningrad Conference show, we think that, many new ideas central to the problems of industry are being explored both theoretically and practically. The winter is over, but has the spring begun ?

9. REFERENCES

[1] Menexiades, D., and Soenen, R., "An Expert System for Maintenance Diagnosis", Proc. of the International Conference on the Industrial Applications of Artificial Intelligence (Leningrad 1990), Alty, J.L., and Mikulich, L.I., (eds.), Section 5, pp 243-247 . (1991)

[2] Sgurev, V., Dochev, D., Agre, G., Dichev, Ch., and Markov, Z., "Diagnostic Expert Systems for Digital Electronics, Proc. of the International Conference on the Industrial Applications of Artificial Intelligence (Leningrad 1990), Alty, J.L., and Mikulich, L.I., (eds.), Section 5, pp 220-224 . (1991).

[3] Alty, J.L. and Pearce, D., "Artificial Intelligence and Fault Diagnosis: An Approach to the Validation Problem", Proc. of the International Conference on the Industrial Applications of Artificial Intelligence (Leningrad 1990), Alty, J.L., and Mikulich, L.I., (eds.), Section 3, pp 121-129 . (1991).

ELSEVIER SCIENCE PUBLISHERS B.V.
Sara Burgerhartstraat 25
P.O. Box 211, 1000 AE Amsterdam, The Netherlands

Distributors for the United States and Canada:
ELSEVIER SCIENCE PUBLISHING COMPANY INC.
655 Avenue of the Americas
New York, N.Y. 10010, U.S.A.

ISBN: 0 444 88981 7

Printed in The Netherlands

[4] Storr, A., Hardtner, M., and Wiedmann, W., "An Expert System for Technical Diagnosis", Proc. of the International Conference on the Industrial Applications of Artificial Intelligence (Leningrad 1990), Alty, J.L., and Mikulich, L.I., (eds.), Section 5, pp 267-275 (1991).

[5] Ganascia, J.G., Puget, J.F., and Helft, N., "A Model of Behaviour for Machine Learning", Proc. of the International Conference on the Industrial Applications of Artificial Intelligence (Leningrad 1990), Alty, J.L., and Mikulich, L.I., (eds.), Section 1, pp 33-39, (1991).

[6] Lazek, M., and Peczkowski, M., "Knowledge Acquisition Method of Expert System for Analysis of Financial Standing of an Enterprise, Proc. of the International Conference on the Industrial Applications of Artificial Intelligence (Leningrad 1990), Alty, J.L., and Mikulich, L.I., (eds.), Section 2, pp 81-86, (1991).

[7] Matskin, M.B., "Intelligent Programming Environments for CAD", Proc. of the International Conference on the Industrial Applications of Artificial Intelligence (Leningrad 1990), Alty, J.L., and Mikulich, L.I., (eds.), Section 4, pp 209-212, (1991).

[8] Lyashenko, N.N., "Inductive Inference Algorithms and their Applications", Proc. of the International Conference on the Industrial Applications of Artificial Intelligence (Leningrad 1990), Alty, J.L., and Mikulich, L.I., (eds.), Section 6, pp 302-307, (1991).

[9] Gorodetsky, V.I., "Bayes Inference and Decision Making in Artificial Intelligence Systems", Proc. of the International Conference on the Industrial Applications of Artificial Intelligence (Leningrad 1990), Alty, J.L., and Mikulich, L.I., (eds.), Section 6, pp 276-281, (1991).

[10] Ohsuga, S., "Multiple Meta-level Architectures and Man-machine interaction in a Knowledge Based System, Proc. of the International Conference on the Industrial Applications of Artificial Intelligence (Leningrad 1990), Alty, J.L., and Mikulich, L.I., (eds.), Section 1, pp 67-77, (1991).

[11] Chekmenev, S.E., and Krasnikova, O.V., "CASS: The Knowledge Based System for Selecting Expert System Building Tools", Proc. of the International Conference on the Industrial Applications of Artificial Intelligence (Leningrad 1990), Alty, J.L., and Mikulich, L.I., (eds.), Section 5, pp 239-242, (1991).

[12] Dwivedi, S.N., and Lanka, R., "AI and Concurrent Engineering in Factories of the Future", Proc. of the International Conference on the Industrial Applications of Artificial Intelligence (Leningrad 1990), Alty, J.L., and Mikulich, L.I., (eds.), Section 1, pp 20-32, (1991).

[13] Michelini, R.C., Acaccia, G.M., and Molfino, R.M., "Computer Intelligence Options in Flexible Manufacturing", Proc. of the International Conference on the Industrial Applications of Artificial Intelligence (Leningrad 1990), Alty, J.L., and Mikulich, L.I., (eds.), Section 8, pp 344-349, (1991).

[14] Tsarevsky, N.A., "Scheduling in the Intelligent System AMIGO", Proc. of the International Conference on the Industrial Applications of Artificial Intelligence (Leningrad 1990), Alty, J.L., and Mikulich, L.I., (eds.), Section 8, pp 355-360, (1991).

[15] Schuett, D., "Theses on Information Technology in the Nineties", Proc. of the International Conference on the Industrial Applications of Artificial Intelligence (Leningrad 1990), Alty, J.L., and Mikulich, L.I., (eds.), Section 1, pp 8-19, (1991).

[16] Laurent, J-P., and Ayel, J., "Real Time Supervision for Production Management Activities", Proc. of the International Conference on the Industrial Applications of Artificial Intelligence (Leningrad 1990), Alty, J.L., and Mikulich, L.I., (eds.), Section 1, pp 40-50, (1991).

[17] Vukobratovic, M., "Applied Robotics in Robotized Flexible Manufacturing Cells", Proc. of the International Conference on the Industrial Applications of Artificial Intelligence (Leningrad 1990), Alty, J.L., and Mikulich, L.I., (eds.), Section 1, pp 51-66, (1991).

[18] Timofejev, A.V., "The Adaptive Intelligent Control of Robots and Technological Equipment for Intelligent Manufacturing", Proc. of the International Conference on the Industrial Applications of Artificial Intelligence (Leningrad 1990), Alty, J.L., and Mikulich, L.I., (eds.), Section 9, pp 442-445, (1991).

[19] Zebrowski, W., "An Expert System for Selection of Dispatching Systems to be Used in Flexible Automation of Production", Proc. of the International Conference on the Industrial Applications of Artificial Intelligence (Leningrad 1990), Alty, J.L., and Mikulich, L.I., (eds.), Section 9, pp 420-425, (1991).

[20] Kirillov, V.M., "The Calculus of Metric Temporal Relations as a Knowledge Representation Framework for Rule Based Expert Systems", Proc. of the International Conference on the Industrial Applications of Artificial Intelligence (Leningrad 1990), Alty, J.L., and Mikulich, L.I., (eds.), Section 3, pp 106-110, (1991).

[21] Yakovlev, A.V., and Petrov, A.I., "A Process Event Knowledge Model for Industrial Expertise", Proc. of the International Conference on the Industrial Applications of Artificial Intelligence (Leningrad 1990), Alty, J.L., and Mikulich, L.I., (eds.), Section 3, pp 115-120, (1991).

[22] Rousset, M-C., "On the Validation and Consistency of Knowledge Bases: the COVADIS System", Proc. of the International Conference on the Industrial Applications of Artificial Intelligence (Leningrad 1990), Alty, J.L., and Mikulich, L.I., (eds.), Section 3, pp 111-114, (1991).

[23] Naidenova, K.A., and Polegaeva J.G., "SIZIF: The System of Knowledge Acquisition from Experimental Facts", Proc. of the International Conference on the Industrial Applications of Artificial Intelligence (Leningrad 1990), Alty, J.L., and Mikulich, L.I., (eds.), Section 2, pp 87-92, (1991)

[24] Maltsev, P.A., "The Simulation of Formal Grammar Constructions by Algebraic Petri nets with Variable Marking (Variable Structure)", Proc. of the International Conference on the Industrial Applications of Artificial Intelligence (Leningrad 1990), Alty, J.L., and Mikulich, L.I., (eds.), Section 3, pp 146-151, (1991).

[25] Ilyin, G.M., and Ignatova V.N., "A System for Describing a Scene which a Robot Observes and Displays it According to Text in Natural Language", Proc. of the International Conference on the Industrial Applications of Artificial Intelligence (Leningrad 1990), Alty, J.L., and Mikulich, L.I., (eds.), Section 3, pp 130-134, (1991).

[26] Capkovic, F., "Analytical Forms for Describing a Class of Knowledge Representation and Related Inference Mechanisms of a Reasoning Process", Proc. of the International Conference on the Industrial Applications of Artificial Intelligence (Leningrad 1990), Alty, J.L., and Mikulich, L.I., (eds.), Section 3, pp 135-140, (1991).

[27] Polyakov, V.G., "Management Consulting Expert System (MCES)", Proc. of the International Conference on the Industrial Applications of Artificial Intelligence (Leningrad 1990), Alty, J.L., and Mikulich, L.I., (eds.), Section 4, pp 213-217, (1991).

[28] Barnikow, A., Behrendt, U., Hartmann, K., and Scharni, M., "Decision Support System for large Scale Development planning in the Chemical Industry", Proc. of the International Conference on the Industrial Applications of Artificial Intelligence (Leningrad 1990), Alty, J.L., and Mikulich, L.I., (eds.), Section 7, pp 323-328, (1991).

[29] Ming, W., Guofang, J., and Shenqian, L., "An Intelligent CAD System for Structure Design", Proc. of the International Conference on the Industrial Applications of Artificial Intelligence (Leningrad 1990), Alty, J.L., and Mikulich, L.I., (eds.), Section 7, pp 336-341, (1991).

[30] Holden, A.D.C., "Intelligent Neural Networks for Robotic Control", Proc. of the International Conference on the Industrial Applications of Artificial Intelligence (Leningrad 1990), Alty, J.L., and Mikulich, L.I., (eds.), Section 8, pp 361-365, (1991).

Industrial Applications of Artificial Intelligence
J.L. Alty and L.I. Mikulich (Editors)
Elsevier Science Publishers B.V. (North-Holland)

SECTION 1: PLENARY PAPERS

THESES ON INFORMATION TECHNOLOGY OF THE NINETIES

D. SCHUETT

Information and Knowledge Processing,
Siemens AG, Munich

"We regard the brain as an apparatus, an organ which generates images of the world, and because of the great usefulness of these images for the maintenance of the species in accordance with Darwin's theory this function has developed to particular perfection in the human being, just like the unusual length of the giraffe's neck or the stork 's beak. We now seek to represent the material processes taking place in the brain by means of the images we have created to understand matter and at the same time to obtain a better idea of the mental realm, as well as some idea of the mechanism which has developed in the human head to allow the representation of such complex and relevant images. "
Ludwig Boltzmann (Popular writings)

1. FIRST THESIS

Information technology of the nineties requires broad-based and future-oriented research and investigation into new software techniques and systems. Knowledge based techniques in particular will gain greatly in importance.

Starting in the eighties, major applications such as integrated mailing services, CAD electronics or distributed office or production operations have obliged us to introduce new methods into the software life cycle.

In the utilization of computer systems, it is becoming of increasing importance to model more comprehensive object spheres and their semantic aspects. To these we must add modified application conditions: extensive, open networks are now replacing single installations; the computer is losing its significance as an automatic system and is increasingly becoming an interactive tool. This last point is well illustrated by an example from the sector of knowledge processing (see Fig. 1 A,B C).

CONSHEL/K - Configuration of industrial automation systems
Background:
High engineering cost in automation technology
Task:
Support the custom design of an automation system
Approach:
Automation system knowledge: object model
Configuration knowledge: Strategy description language
Consistency checking

Figure 1A The CONSHEL/K

DIWA - Diagnosis tool with knowledge acquisition
Background: Increase up-time of machines **Task:** Experts should develop diagnosis expert systems **Approach:** Diagnosis knowledge: Model of a faulty machine graphical knowledge editor

Figure 1B DIWA Diagnosis Tool

Real-time expert systems in power distribution
Background: Increase up-time of power distribution network **Task:** Operator support with failure diagnosis **Approach:** Knowledge base development by power distribution experts Real-time architecture development by Corporate Research and Development

Figure 1C Real Time Expert System Projects

1.1 DIWA, a Knowledge-based Dialogue System for Semiconductor Processing

When a machine fails in the late and night shifts, the relevant expert is usually not present. Although the staff at hand have the technical capabilities to handle frequently occurring problems, they lack the experience required to cope with a specific machine. So fault localization takes longer and leads to expensive machine dead times and production losses. The problems occurring during the late and night shifts can be largely handled with the aid of an expert system which contains and makes available an expert's experience-based knowledge. The advantages of an expert system are the easy extendibility of its knowledge base and the explicitness of the knowledge it contains.

The following targets were specified for the development of a system of this kind: - Increase of machine operation times

- Minimizing staff intervention in the late and night shifts
- Help / advisory function of the expert system in the night shift
- Use of cost-effective hardware, namely a PC of the AT category.

The first machine to be selected was the plasma etcher. The aim was to develop a prototype expert system for one of its components, the high-frequency generator. The viability of this approach was confirmed by a practical test with various users.

The next step: Since the range of machines used in the factories is very large and diverse, there is a need to implement such expert systems for as many different machines as possible.

A tool is now being developed which translates the structures developed in the process of organizing knowledge on the basis of a model of the "faulty" machine into a knowledge base capable of execution. This allows

- a dramatic reduction of the development time for an expert system
- the expert system to be applied very much earlier than is possible for a conventional

development
- the expert to build up the knowledge for a machine incrementally with increasing levels of qualification.

The expert can use this tool to enter, modify or delete - in graphical form - the knowledge he has structured according to the model of the 'faulty' machine. If he approves the structure to be entered, the tool generates the associated knowledge base which can then be executed. This can be used with the relevant executable system in the night shift. The behaviour of the system corresponds to that of the prototype already developed.

2. SECOND THESIS

The main emphasis in the software technology of the nineties will be placed on software design, validation and implementation procedures, new software architectures, safety standards as well as software distribution concepts.

Security of access to dp systems will become important. The opening up of new IT application sectors as well as the decentralization of computer power means that increasing significance will be placed on protecting data and programs from unauthorized access.

Security requirements of the kind originally existing only in the military sector are being increasingly placed on commercial applications too. A definable security level for future dp systems must therefore be ensured.

The worldwide activities in the sector of access protection comprise protection mechanisms for individual components of a dp system as well as for computer networks.

To create a standardized measure for evaluating systems, the DoD published the first version of its "Trusted Computer System Evaluation Criteria" (Orange Book) in 1983. It contains criteria for the evaluation of protective mechanisms with respect to their effectiveness and quality. These make provision for a subdivision into four main classes (D-A) and up to 3 subclasses.

Class D contains either minimal protection or none at all. This class comprises the majority of today's existing operating systems. Class A means "verified design" and requires that the protective mechanisms were already specified and verified formally at the system design stage as well as confirmation that the specification was adhered to during the entire development process.

To do justice to the importance of secure computer networks, in 1987 the DoD published the "Trusted Network Interpretation of the Trusted Computer System Evaluation Criteria" (Red Book), containing guidelines for security criteria in computer networks.

For the Federal Republic of Germany, the IT Security Criteria (previously National Criteria Catalogue) which was commissioned by the national evaluation authority, the Central Office for Security in Information Technology (ZSI, previously ZfCh), was officially approved in the spring 1989 and is thus binding. In contrast to the Orange Book, the IT security criteria form classes of security functions, which describe the extent of the security offered by a dp system. The quality stages define a measure of trustworthiness for each functional class which can be expected of the dp systems to which the defined security functions have been assigned.

2.1 Security in the BS2000

The BS2000 V10.0 is one of the first large computer operating systems whose operational security is to be investigated and evaluated according to IT security criteria by the national evaluation authority.

The developers of this operating system receive support in attaining the targetted security classification by means of the "Security in BS2000" project. The support relates to the design and implementation of concrete security functions on the one hand and to the complete documentation of the operational security on the other. This latter represents a necessary precondition for the successful implementation of the evaluation.

2.2 Security in UNIX

In the "Security in UNIX" project, the security aspect is considered from the viewpoint of the UNIX operating system The requirements defined in the "IT security criteria" as well as in the Orange Book are taken as a basis for the criteria required for security. In this project, mechanisms are firstly developed which enhance the security of UNIX systems and secondly flanking measures are implemented which relate to the trustworthy operation of UNIX systems.

3. THIRD THESIS

> **Innovation in systems (hardware, software, applications) represents the effect of cumulative processes. Research and development for very large systems can no longer be implemented in the artificial world of the laboratory.**

An example:

For transmission in today's and future networks as well as for archiving on digital storage media, the massive data volumes required for images and video scenes must be highly compressed. This process should neither impair the image quality nor lose important information. Applications include the video telephone, the video conference, image services in narrow and broadband ISDN (Integrated Services Digital Network), medical picture archiving and communication systems (PACS), image transmission in local networks such as in office and industrial networks and image storage.

Image coding procedures allow cost-effective utilization of transmission channels and storage media. The availability of corresponding systems is thus of great importance in order to include images and scenes in future communication and information systems.

Objectives of the R&D activities:

- Coding systems play a key role in the application of image-based information in telecommunications. The aim of these activities is therefore to make available coding systems for a broad spectrum of application types.

- Coding systems for image transmission and archiving are developed and simulated as software prototypes and are tested on critical original images for each application. The result is a detailed specification for the hardware implementation. The aim of the algorithms is to achieve optimal reduction of the data volume for images and video scenes by the reduction factor required for the application in hand. In this process, procedures for motion recognition, image enhancement, segmenting of specific image parts and image analysis are developed which also can be used to handle other problems arising in digital image processing.

Current state of the activities:

Various coding systems were developed for the image telephone in the ISDN transmitted at 64 kbits with a reduction factor of 2000 and were presented successfully to the standardization committees. The algorithms form the basis for further developments.

For high-definition TV (HDTV), where a reduction factor of 8 is demanded, we could enhance the image quality significantly by coding strategies adapted to the image contents.

In coding medical image sequences, we attain a reduction factor of 3 for a procedure totally free of losses and a factor of 8 without detectable information loss.

The next steps:

- Coding procedure for packet-switched transmission in broadband networks (ATM)
- Testing of new image services in broadband networks
- Coding of high-definition TV (HDTV) at 140 Mbits (reduction factor 8) and 3D
- Coding for transmission and archiving of medical image sequences without detectable loss of information
- Coding for industrial networks
- Algorithms for content-oriented coding with additional applications in image and scene analysis

In the major " broadband ISDN" project, these research and development activities are integrated into the objective of implementing a pilot system for field trials by 1993. The project comprises the 3 function complexes: a B-ISDN pilot system, a connectionless server and preliminary activities. The pilot system requires the development of the ATM network and system technology, the design of interactive communications services and finally the implementation of entire system design in hardware and software. The connectionless server should couple local area networks (LANs) together and with the ATM broadband network; this requires the development of the corresponding switching and control software. The preliminary activities are devoted to future-oriented applications relating to broadband communications via ATM networks, but which do not yet play any direct part in the pilot system: voice and image coding, intelligence in the network, security aspects and the investigation of new services.

4. FOURTH THESIS

Existing media clashes between paper-bound and electronic information processing will be overcome.

Our document analysis system today offers the following (see Fig. 2):

1. Connectivity component analysis and text/graphics separation
2. Layout analysis by means of the geometrical context
3. Knowledge-based analysis of the layout and classification of the document and its parts.

Objectives of the R&D activities:

- Intelligent interface between paper and computer (inverse printer or scanner with intelligence)
- Automatic acquisition and interpretation of any paper documents: from business letters via reports and newspaper articles up to manual sketches and technical drawings
- Recognition of contents, layout and logical structure of documents

The next steps: Extension of the models in the direction of content components such as key words, syntactic and semantic constraints, utilization of linguistic knowledge. Greater integration of the graphics (office graphics, technical drawings). Error tolerance by more profound representation and inference procedures of the kind underlying the human reading process.

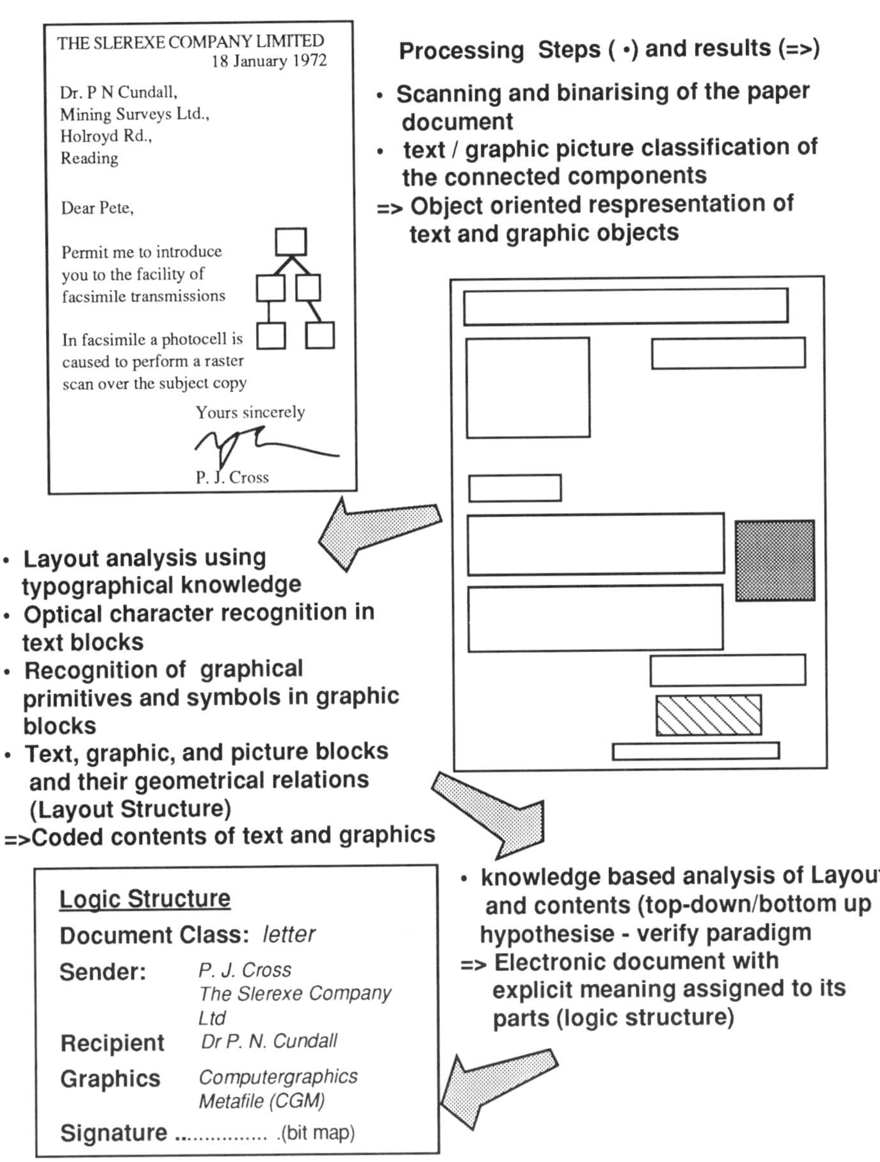

Figure 2 Office Document Analysis

5. FIFTH THESIS

Information is often "fuzzy", i.e. vague, distributed, multilayered, incomplete or even contradictory. Today we assume that human beings are able to handle such information by the collective interworking of

highly-networked intercommunicating nerve nodes (neurons).

Artificial neural networks will be able to cope with the typical weaknesses of today's information processing systems in specific application sectors. They represent a significant leap forwards in the development of information technology toward non-programmed, adaptive information processing. Fuzzy information presents today's computers with major problems. At the hardware level, where the computer's actions are performed purely by means of exactly defined sequences of calculations and storage operations, there is "no room for fuzziness". Where fuzzy information occurs in a limited or systematic way, it is suitable "prepared" with the aid of software for evaluation by the computer. In the case of massive, unsystematic occurrence of fuzziness in data, the required computing and memory expenditure goes beyond the limits of available systems.

Neurobiological considerations of the human processes of perception as well as investigations of interactive phenomena in certain materials (spin glasses) in solid state physics have, astonishingly, led to similar models for the underlying "hardware" and the communication (interaction) executed on it. These models - neural networks - have inspired the design of architectures also known as neural networks for information processing systems, which are characterized by the following properties:

- Information is stored in connections between network nodes. The network "learns" this information (learning capability)
- Information processing takes place collectively by the interworking of all network nodes (parallelism)
- Since its information is stored in a distributed way, the network is insensitive toward failure of subnetworks and is thus capable of suppressing "noisy information" (robustness)

5.1 The ZFE Neurodemonstrator Project

Within a few years, the neural approach to artificial intelligence has mobilized a research sector of unusual dynamics. If only a modest part of the hopes placed today in neural networks is fulfilled, they will certainly be used in information technology systems. In its dual role as a software house and as a user of information technology, Siemens is called upon to exploit this development in an optimal way. Neural networks must therefore be integrated into the company's hardware and software environment.

The Corporate Research and Technology Division of Siemens AG has consequently initiated a 3-year project known as the "neurodemonstrator" which combines and extends individual activities in the field of neural networks. The project started in October 1988 and provides for a staff requirement of approximately 60 man years. The activities involved aim at evaluating the potential uses of neural networks for information technology by developing a system which combines conventional and neural approaches for recognizing industrial scenes:

The methods, principles and algorithms for the design and analysis of neural networks are developed under the real boundary conditions of a specific industrial application. In this particular application, workpieces are to be identified. This process comprises the recognition of parts, their exact location and orientation as well as the recognition of details such as stamped numbers. The task can be arranged to be as complex as required.

The software simulation of neural networks is made possible by creating a powerful software development environment for neural networks. Its first extension stage comprises a simulator based on a C library, which contains various models and algorithms. Flexibility and the generation of fast codes is possible through the development of a C-based programming language for neural networks.

In addition to zoom techniques for observing and controlling the network dynamics, useful essentially for small networks, global observation parameters are further developed and implemented to supply useful information for large networks too. In this application, fundamental considerations relating to the stability of neural networks have proved to be valuable. A co-processor is being developed for the fast emulation of large networks. With the aid of a systolic architecture, it combines chip implementations of the fully networked neurons possible in state-of-the-art technology within a modular system.

6. SIXTH THESIS

> **For both management and staff, IT research and development in the nineties requires an extended conception of R & D oriented toward both the requirements and the market. The key to this idea is the concept of the "researcher as entrepreneur" .**

This approach requires research marketing which derives today's important research tasks from the needs of tomorrow's markets, and which provides marketing strategies oriented to today's sales with information about the state of the art of tomorrow's technology. Exploratory and feasibility studies must be performed to generate results which can be transferred directly to product development. What we need is an active, perhaps even an aggressive transfer policy borne by a team spirit which will ensure that the team's own research activities flow into the project.

To sell the results of research means to transfer know-how. This is done much more effectively by individuals than on the basis of reports, exhibitions and workshops. A number of individual approaches are available here. Concrete project agreements require a binding framework which also defines the transfer of persons. A systematic R & D approach must be introduced which dovetails exactly with the phase planning activities within the product development sectors in the divisions.

However, the transfer aspect must be taken into account as early as the stage of defining the core technologies in terms of strategies and when planning the exploration and feasibility activities. The technical risk potential and the complexity of a process or (planned) product define the role of universities, corporate R & D and operating divisions in the transfer procedure (see Fig. 3).

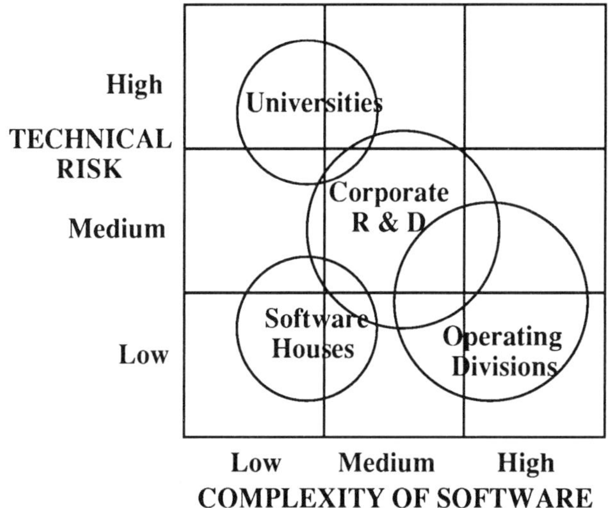

Figure 3 Roles and Risks

7. SEVENTH THESIS

Research in the precompetitive sector leads increasingly to the founding of institutions with direct participation by industrial companies (see Fig. 4).

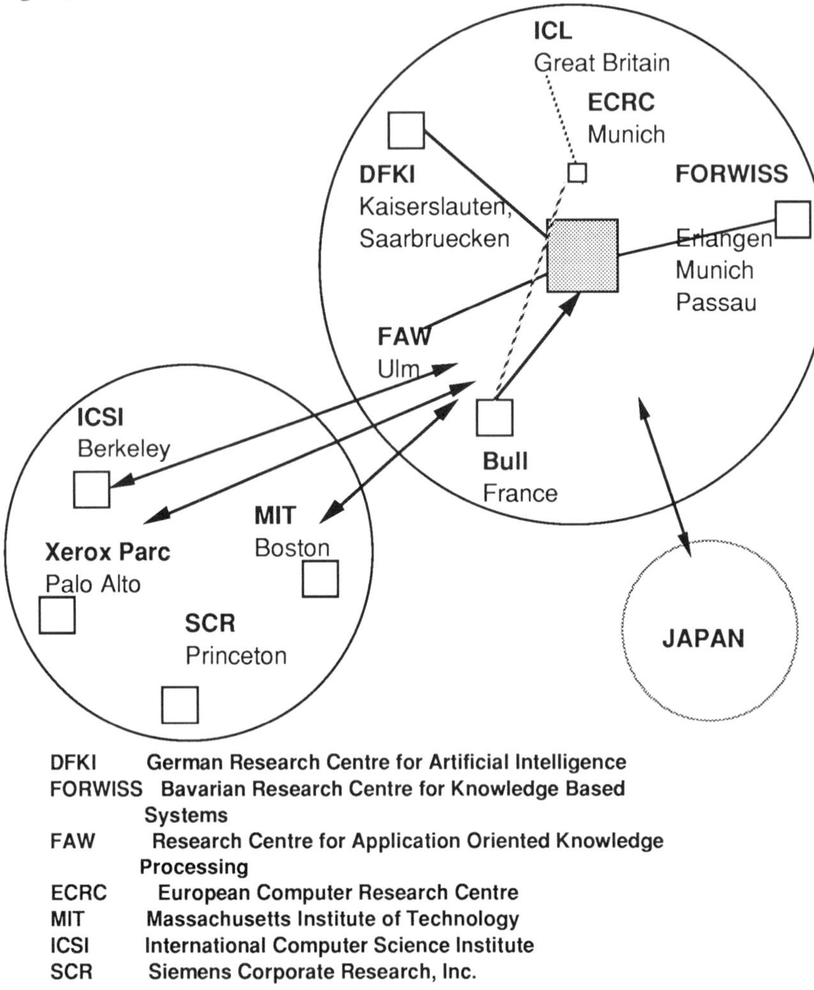

Figure 4. Siemens Corporate R&D, Informatics and Knowledge Processing: Scientific Connections.

7.1 ECRC

ECRC is an industrial research centre supported as a common resource by the European computer manufacturers Bull, ICL and Siemens. It was founded in 1984 and is owned equally by the shareholders.

The creation of ECRC reflects current industrial European thinking, which aims at consolidating Europe's presence in the electronic data processing market. This consolidation is being achieved by addressing such topics as scientific cooperation, standardization, implementation of technical standards, etc.

The aim of ECRC is to develop fundamental know-how. The Centre's field of activity includes technologies needed to improve the process of computer-assisted decision-making.

The program encompasses the set of techniques - and the necessary software tools or machine architectures to support them - needed to resolve the issues of

- knowledge description and acquisition, where knowledge comprises both basic information and situation-specific decision rules;
- reasoning mechanisms which build on the aforementioned knowledge;
- interaction models and tools to enlarge the involvement of both the user and the computer in the decision-making process.

The program of ECRC is currently centred around the following four areas: Logic programming and problem solving techniques, Knowledge Bases, Computer Architecture, Human-Computer Interaction.

An example of a cooperative project between the shareholder companies and ECRC is the Knowledge Crunching Machine (KCM).

KCM is a high performance PROLOG co-processor attachable to different UNIX workstations. The host workstation at Siemens is the MX 300. The software development environment is completely resident, including an incremental PROLOG compiler. KCM is a single task co-processor with private memory (32-256 Mbyte). I/0 operations are handled by the host. KCM is optimized concerning the execution of declarative languages like PROLOG and LISP. The architecture especially supports unification, de-referencing, backtracking, co-routining, and stack manipulation. The instruction set is micro-coded and implements an enhanced WAM (Warren Abstract Machine).

KCM executes PROLOG at 600-800 kLIPS (k Logical Inferences Per Second). Compared to standard workstations this means an average performance improvement of a factor of 25 for typical PROLOG benchmarks. KCM is one of the world fasted PROLOG machines.

KCM-Sepia is an implementation of ECRC SEPIA PROLOG-System on KCM. SEPIA is already available on several different workstations (e.g. VAX, SUN, MX 300) and stands out for the following features:

- advanced PROLOG system, contains Clocksin-Mellish Standard as a subset
- incremental compiler
- interrupt processing for real time applications
- supports global variables and arrays
- mechanism for delayed execution of predicates
- module concept
- external language interface.

KCM is dedicated to complex applications of logic programming, not feasible with the performance of conventional workstations, for example expert systems, natural language systems (e.g. translating systems) and -interfaces (e.g. to data bases), manufacturing control, circuit-/program verification, and operations research.

7.2 FAW

In 1987, at the initiative of the Federal State of Baden- Wurttemberg, the Research Centre for Application-Oriented Knowledge Processing (FAW) was founded in Ulm. FAW is organized as a foundation under German law with the State of Baden-Wurttemberg and six sponsoring companies, including Siemens AG.

In accordance with the statutes of the foundation, the functions of FAW include the implementation of research and development projects commissioned by the founders, the European Community, the Federal Government, the other Federal States, of research institutes and other third parties, as well as the further development of the scientific foundations of knowledge processing.

Siemens staff also work on site in the application sectors of office automation and environmental information systems.

7.3 ICSI

The International Computer Science Institute strives to maintain ongoing basic research projects of the highest standard in selected areas of computer science and engineering. Only by maintaining research projects in the forefront of technology can ICSI have the strength to meet its other goals in international cooperation. All of the research at the Institute is open and its results are made publicly available. The particular areas of concentration are chosen for their fundamental importance and their compatibility with the competence of the Institute and the UC Berkeley staff. Current emphasis is on distributed and parallel computation with particular attention to massive parallelism. A more detailed description is available as ICSI Research Plan 1990-1992.

It has been clear for some years that parallel computation is the key to many desirable applications. Distributed and parallel systems of moderate scale are now fairly well understood and widely employed. But the problems involved with millions or billions of independent computations appear to be different and to require new techniques. ICSI is currently addressing issues in four key areas: Theory of parallel computation, realization of massively parallel systems, applications of such systems, and very large distributed networks.

Siemens is a member of the Association for the Promotion of the International Cooperation in the Field of Computer Science and Related Applications ('Foerderverein'). A Siemens researcher was elected to join in the ICSI Postdoctoral Exchange Program.

8. EIGHTH THESIS

> **Information technology is not value free. Its agents bear the responsibility for their investigations and the consequences of their results. This is at the same time a task for politics and society as a whole.**

An example:

WIFEX is an expert system for determining the point of application and the active substance in combating fungus disease in grain. Its domain is located within the field of integrated plant protection in the overlap area between applied environmental protection and plant cultivation. The knowledge base of the current prototype (approx. 150 rules) is still incomplete, but a system is already available which allows a complete consultation for root rot in winter wheat (see Fig. 5).

WIFEX was set up in spring 1989 in conjunction with ZFE and the University of Munster. The prototype was completed in only four and a half man-months with the aid of an expert system tool implemented with an object-oriented extension of PROLOG-XT.

A representative of the Westfalen-Lippe Chamber of Agriculture in Munster was available to act as an agricultural expert from whom the specialist knowledge could be acquired.

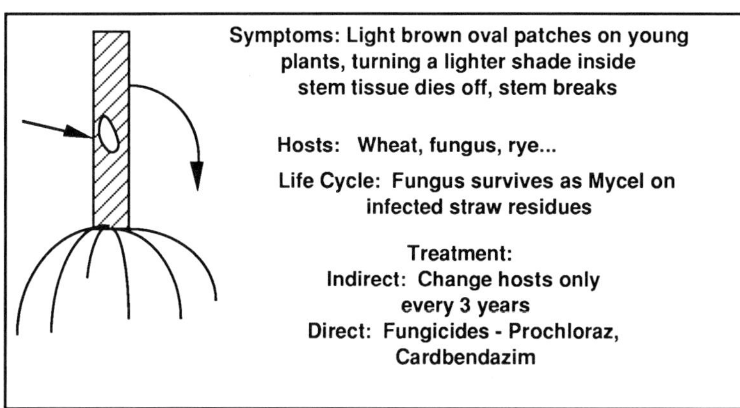

Figure 5 Root Rot: Symptoms and Treatment

9. ACKNOWLEDGEMENTS

The author would like to thank Klaus Estenfeld, Peter Moeckel, Cornelia Persy, Hans-Rainer Schuchmann, Heinz Schwaertzel, Klaus Wimmer, Klaus Winkelmann and Walter Woberschil for their helpful discussions in connection with this paper.

Industrial Applications of Artificial Intelligence
J.L. Alty and L.I. Mikulich (Editors)
Elsevier Science Publishers B.V. (North-Holland)

AI AND CONCURRENT ENGINEERING IN FACTORIES OF THE FUTURE

S. N. DWIVEDI and R. LANKA
Department of Mechanical and Aerospace Engineering,
West Virginia University,
Morgantown,
WV 26506, USA.

1. INTRODUCTION

The manufacturing industry is moving from the equipment and labor intensive stage to the knowledge and information intensive stage. Consequently, the methodology of product development needs to be changed. A strong, dependable product development methodology coupled with potential techniques in planning and controlling the manufacturing process, which emulates human expertise containing sufficient knowledge and inference mechanism to make intelligent decisions, has to developed. A dependable product development methodology is provided by the implementation of Concurrent Engineering, and the potential techniques for planning and controlling the manufacturing processes is addressed by Artificial Intelligence.

An AI system which uses expertise in a particular domain can solve problems in that domain in a similar way as an expert does. The computer-based methods which are good at data processing for information-intensive problems are not sufficient to support the knowledge-intensive manufacturing tasks. The new computer techniques should generate, record, retrieve and digest information into knowledge and represent the knowledge to support decision making.The AI technique addresses the problem at the knowledge level to change the plethora of information into useful knowledge and use it effectively to make a better knowledge-intensive industry [1,2]. The evolution of the manufacturing industry is shown in Figure 1.

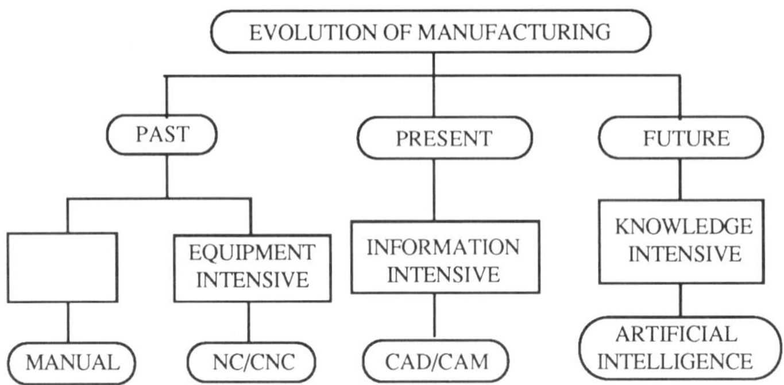

Figure 1. Evolution of Manufacturing

Concurrent Engineering (CE) is the methodology which leads to a significant reduction in costs and development time without sacrificing any of the desired product specifications. It is a combination of all the facets of product-life cycle to minimize modifications in the prototype i.e. to decrease the design iterations performed during product design.

The harmonious blending of the AI techniques with their proven potential for planning and control of manufacturing processes with CE, which addresses all the product life-cycle disciplines with the objective of getting it "right the first time", paves the way for attaining the BEST in future. This paper addresses the role AI in planning and controlling various manufacturing processes and the various CE tools which aim at a sharp reduction of life cycle costs, and short design cycles with improved quality.

2. METHODOLOGY OF AI IN MANUFACTURING

2.1 Knowledge-Based Expert Systems and Manufacturing Automation

Manufacturing automation is the goal and a knowledge-based expert system is the vehicle to achieve this goal.The approach is practical and emphasizes the applicability of knowledge based expert systems to the specific problem of manufacturing automation. Manufacturing is a complex task that involves people, machines, computers and proper interaction among them. Manufacturing activities consist of three different constraints namely facility, information and decision. Every manufacturing activity involves some kind of equipment, or device facility to accomplish specific tasks. The information level is a decision level that uses information gathered from facilities to reach the proper conclusions [1,3].

A fully autonomous manufacturing system needs automation at all levels. Computer graphics, integrated engineering data bases and multi-machine interfaces are examples of manufacturing information automation. These have made a significant impact on manufacturing productivity, and have resulted in high quality and low cost. Since knowledge-based expert systems are computer-based decision making systems, they are most predominantly used. The main reasons for applying knowledge-based expert systems to the manufacturing domain are:

1. Computer-based methods give only information and data, not knowledge for decision making.
2. Manufacturing knowledge is a combination of science-based principles with experience-based heuristics. Traditional deterministic models are not suitable for handling heuristic models.
3. Manufacturing activities cover many factors that are changing constantly and this, therefore, calls for decision making tools which can easily adapt to these changes.

2.2 Model Development For Manufacturing Process

The success of computer automation for a manufacturing process largely depends on the availability of a comprehensive model of the process. If a reliable model is implemented on the computer, analysis and prediction of the process performance could be performed before the operation. The goal is to develop an AI-based methodology which can automatically transform knowledge existing in different forms into a uniform representation for easy integration [3,5].

The methodology is represented by:

i. Mechanistic Knowledge

A model, which could be modelled by physical laws, is chosen as the knowledge source. This can be done through simulation, and process examples are chosen to provide an inductive learning program to transform the knowledge to a qualitative form .

ii. Heuristic Knowledge

Problem solving strategies are extracted from human-experts and a goal-oriented structure is constructed to solve the problem.

iii. Empirical Knowledge

Empirical relations are used in places where the knowledge induced from mechanistic model fails to address the model. The knowledge hidden in empirical data and tables is extracted through an inductive learning process, and it is organized as a part of the hierarchical knowledge representation in the comprehensive model development.

2.3 Decision Making

Engineering decision making requires analysis and synthesis with a combination of science-based and experience-based knowledge. Analysis involves deductive types of reasoning while the synthesis involves inductive inference. Computer-aided engineering addresses the analysis phase of decision making and expert systems for experience-based knowledge. Although engineering analysis is highly computerized, engineering synthesis is still based on human experience. To improve decision making, we need to integrate mechanistic process simulation with knowledge-based expert systems [3].

2.4 AI in Product Development

The various activities in manufacturing are product development, process planning, scheduling, control and maintenance. Since it requires vast knowledge in all the activities of manufacturing, which is impossible using a single human expert, various expert systems are developed to analyze and provide information for every activity in manufacturing. A well designed expert system provides flexibility and can easily be updated.

The various parameters involved in designing a product include definition of the product, definition of its functions and its physical parameters, and the details and complexity of the shape. A design process passes through stages from a rather vague and abstract model to the complete description by way of a drawing

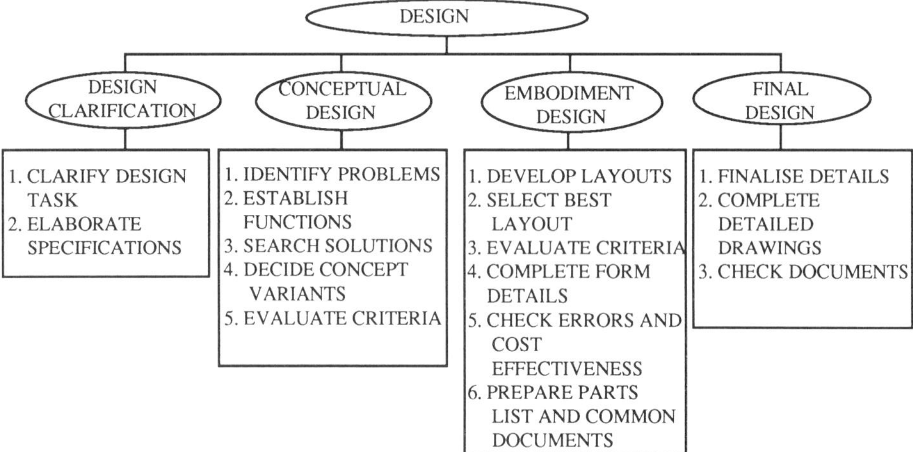

Figure 2. Different states of the design process

information about similar designs and other parameters. It provides alternative solutions to the problem and helps to reduce trial-and-error. The expert systems play a significant role in conceiving the product, for they affect up to 70% of the total cost of a product (See Figure 3). They helps the designer in the concurrent development of the product by providing manufacturing details [4,10].

Process planning involves selection of raw materials, process and operational sequence, selection of machine tools and manufacturing procedures etc. AI systems are used for any method, either variant or generative, of process planning. In the variant method, from the dimensional and physical parameters of the variant or the work piece, the machining processes and sequence of processes are analyzed. An expert system helps in generating the whole process plan from the details provided from the computer data base about similar parts. It also provides considerable flexibility of process planning. In addition, it helps in developing a generative process plan from the knowledge and rules provided from the strategies for machining a part, for which a limited number of tools and fixtures are available [4,6].

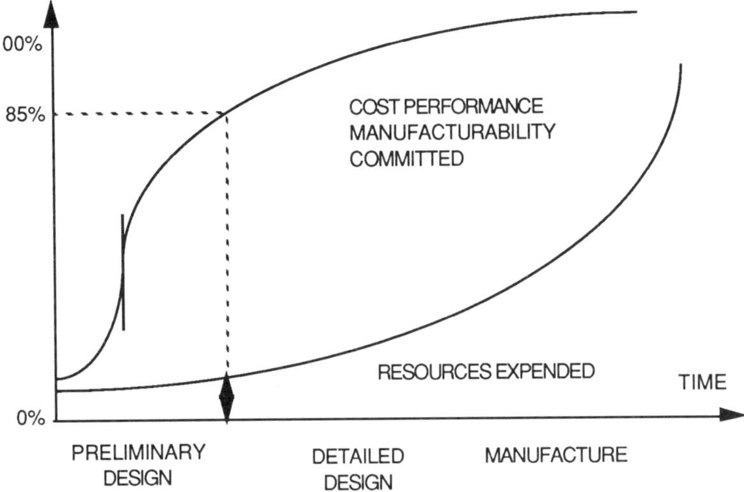

Figure 3. Conceptual Design In Manufacturing

Scheduling requires capacity planning to provide for manufacturing resources, to ensure that manufactured parts meet the deadlines and to enable thorough utilization of production equipment. Scheduling involves the consideration of a great number of alternatives and arriving at a solution which is difficult to optimise totally. With AI tools, a scheduling problem can be considered within a longer time frame and, through various steps, it is then decomposed into smaller intervals until the required plan is attained. Knowledge-based systems are capable of assisting conventional Operations Research and related methods in critical situations [4,7].

Quality is defined as the attainment by the product of all its functional objectives. Any deviations require immediate correction of the manufacturing process. For any complex product, expert systems provide the details of the parameters to be tested, procedures selected, hardware specified and data required in attaining the required Quality [4].

2.5 AI in a Manufacturing Process

AI Tools are used in different manufacturing processes and in every stage of the process, for this ensures the reduction of product development time, reduced design iterations and produce quality products. The sequence of steps followed in the analysis of a process using an expert system are:

1) Analysis of the component design by generic rules
2) Definition of the product for any CAD/CAE/AI system
3) Analysis of the process design by design rules
4) Analysis of the process functioning by the simulation rules and recommending modifications
5) Analysis of the process automation by dimensional rules
6) Analysis of the tooling by manufacturing rules
7) Analysis of the quality

A detailed expert system procedure for investment castings is shown in Figure 4. A similar expert system for machining operation provides details in selecting a machine tool, describing the work piece material, describing machining operations, selecting a tool, recommending passes, determining parameters like speed, feed and economics for each pass and check for process constraints, etc..

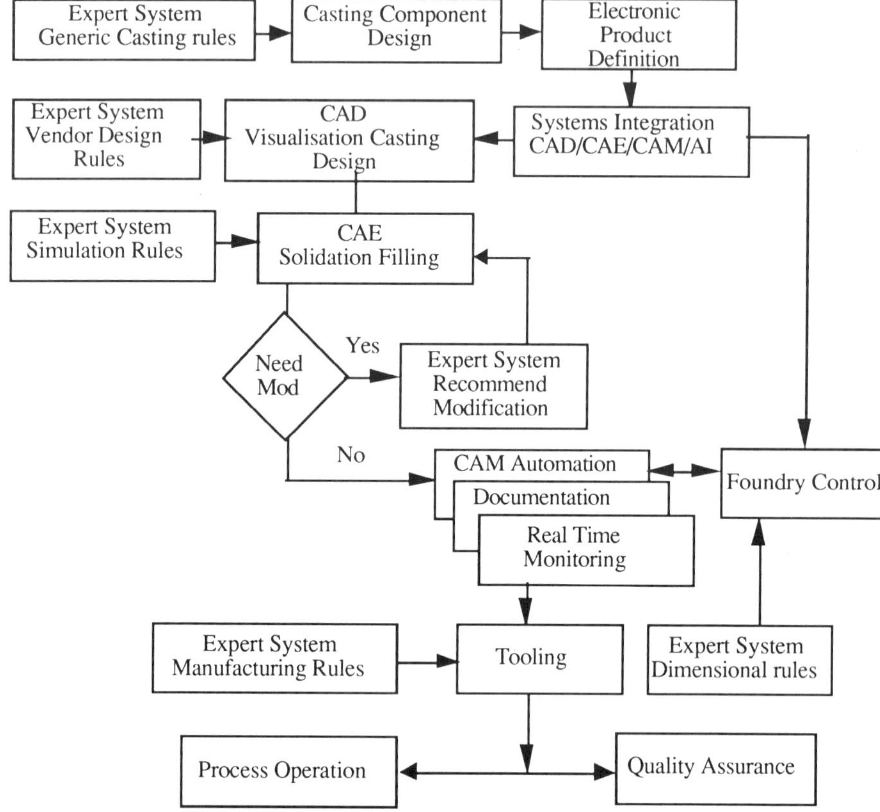

Figure 4. Expert System Development of Castings

3. AI AND CONCURRENT ENGINEERING

Concurrent Engineering is defined as the systematic approach to the integrated concurrent design of products and related processes including manufacture and support. This approach is to enable the developer, from the outset, to consider all the elements of product life cycle from conception through disposal including quality, cost schedule and user requirement.

4. CONCURRENT ENGINEERING

As defined above, CE, or Simultaneous Engineering, as the name suggests, is the approach of performing all activities at the same time. It is a combination of all the facets of a product's life cycle to minimize modifications in the prototype i.e to decrease iterations performed during product design. The CE approach is characterized by focusing on the customer's requirement; it embodies the belief that quality is built in the product, and it (quality) is a result of continuous improvement of a process. Integrated, parallel product and process design are the keys to concurrent design. The CE approach, as opposed to the sequential approach, advocates a parallel design effort. The objective is to ensure that serious errors do not go undetected and that design intent is fully captured. An analogy of series and parallel circuits of electrical resistors are given to emphasize the above point. Figure 5 depicts the cross-functional integration scheme used in the CE approach [12].

The above-mentioned integrated design process should have the following features:

a) There must be a strong information sharing system which will enable the design teams to have access to all corporate facilities and work done by individual teams.

b) Any design is necessarily an iterative process requiring successive redesigns and modifications. The CE process attempts to ensure that the effects of a change incorporated by one team on other design aspects are automatically analyzed. Moreover, the affected functions should be notified of the changes.

c) The CE process must facilitate an appropriate trade-off analysis leading to process design optimisation. Conflicting requirements and constraint violations must be identified and resolved concurrently.

d) All the relevant aspects of the design process must be recorded and documented for future reference.

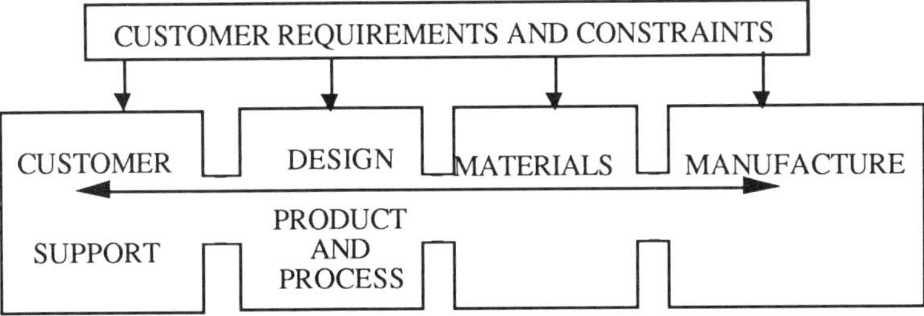

Figure 5 . Integration Scheme in Concurrent Engineering

5. IMPLEMENTATION TOOLS FOR CONCURRENT ENGINEERING

To understand the behavior of any process, product, or mechanism certain tools are required. Correct usage of these tools effectively aid design, production, and engineering aimed at sharp reductions in life cycle costs and short design cycles with improved quality. Implementation of these tools requires:

1) Identifying and analyzing the problem
2) Choosing the right tool for implementation to create order and regularity

Implementation of any of these tools depends upon the ability of the company to foresee the above-mentioned advantages. A few of these implementation tools for CE, shown in Figure 6, are discussed in detail below.

5.1.1 Design For Assembly (DFA)

According to Sandy Manro, "Design for Assembly is a methodology which optimises the relation between various functions such as materials, technology, process and cost at the conceptual stage."

The product functions, cost and quality, result from the combined efforts of engineering and manufacturing. Design for Assembly, as a CE tool, offers a structural approach for incorporating objectives into the design optimisation process even though design accounts for only 5% of the total product cost but determines at least 70% of the total cost of a product [17, 20]. The implementation of DFA needs [17]:

1) Commitment and support of top management
2) Knowledge of materials and manufacturing practices
3) Knowledge of state-of-the-art design principles and tools
4) Knowledge of geometric dimensioning and tolerancing requirements

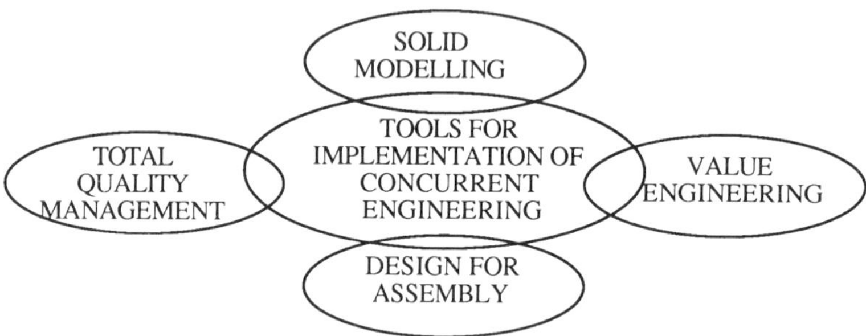

Figure 6 Tools for Concurrent Engineering

DFA focusses on the definition of a part as well as basic design principles. Certain rules and guidelines are applied to the product and process design for significant improvements and they are [14, 17]:

1) Design for minimum number of parts
2) Design for part handling and presentation
3) Evaluation of assembly methods
4) Design for ease of assembly
5) Selection of fasteners for ease of assembly
6) Design for vertical assembly
7) Design for modular assembly
8) Elimination or simplification of adjustments
9) Minimization of product variations
10) Elimination of electrical cables

Various design assessment tools can be used to quantify the extent to which a product meets DFA objectives. This help to determine the ease of product assembly, material handling and parts feeding and orientation [13,17]. They are:

The Boothroyd and Dewhurst analysis program
The Assemblability evaluation method
Assembly insights for designs
The manufacturing rating system

The various benefits through the implementation of DFA technique are [15,17]:

Elimination of non-functional parts and reduced inventory
Reduction of engineering changes
Reduction of assembly time and costs
Shortening of product cycle time and better product produced
Improved quality Increased customers satisfaction and value

5.1.2 Value Engineering (VE)

"Value Engineering is an organized effort directed at analyzing the functions of system, equipment facilities, procedures, and supplies for the purpose of achieving required function(s) at the lowest cost of effective ownership, consistent with requirements for performance, reliability, quality, maintainability and safety" [24] - (from a Defense management course).

VE identifies areas of excessive or unnecessary costs and attempts to improve the value of the product. The successful application of VE requires creativity to innovate alternate designs, and system methods or processes that will perform the necessary functions at the lowest possible costs [22,24]. The methodology of VE involves:

1) Evaluation of a function through various means by preparing a functional flow block diagrams and secondary functions.
2) Synthesis of various alternatives that will perform the basic function and determination of the cost of alternatives
3) Representation of the alternative having lowest overall cost, without sacrificing the basic function

The implementation of the above steps requires a phase-wise study, where each phase will contribute toward establishing the following requirements [22,23]:

Functional Phase-	In-depth understanding of the project and determination of functions
Creative Phase -	Conceiving new designs, development of alternatives and evaluation of alternatives
Development Phase -	Developing action plans and identification of potential problems
Recommendation phase-	Information and implementation of product development improvements

The implementation of VE provides the following major benefits:

1) Reduces the risk of new product development
2) Reduces the overall cost per unit of the new product by reducing the sunk costs development and reduction of the recurring cost of manufacturing the product
3) Helps in fostering team approach for identifying functions and designed especially to improve intergroup performance
4) Application of VE at the conceptual stage helps in achieving optimum engineering changes and reduction of overall costs.

5.1.3 Solid Modelling

In formulating a solution for a real engineering problem, the creative art of conceiving a physical means of achieving an objective comes first and an analysis of the possible solution is next. Solid Modelling plays an effective role in the conceptual design phase both in conceiving and analyzing the solution. The ability to form a visual image of geometrical and physical configurations offers a tremendous advantage in creating a physical means of achieving a technological objective. The development of Solid Modelling has provided this "thinking through" process of judgement, conception and reflection in searching for a conclusion [25, 26].

While the other tools of CE are the means by which the objective is attained, Solid Modelling gives a visual representation of the object. Lack of ambiguity in the displayed images is the key benefit of Solid Modelling, for this promotes tighter integration of design and manufacturing functions as it is easier to master and manipulate.

The development of various solid modellers which incorporate features, simulation packages and AI techniques has allowed the systems to acquire knowledge to design the part, plan the manufacturing process, make the part and inspect the finished product on its own. During the conceptual stage, this helps with a thoroughly understanding of the various degrees of difficulty in its development and gives a clear direction in the evolution of the part. It allows engineers to become productive more quickly because the flexibility of their design options minimizes the weaknesses [26].

The Solid Modelling technique provides the following benefits:

1) Complete, unambiguous picture that can be understood by all the team members easily and helps in better coordination, communication and assimilation of the objectives.
2) Helps in reduction of costs and lead times with 100% improvement in quality
3) Helps in providing the Design Engineers with flexibility to quickly create, modify and iterate the conceptual design and Manufacturing Engineer with precise geometry needed to drive automated equipment and processes.
4) Helps in the study of relationships governing the part geometry and also the interaction of the parts making the assembly thereby. It also helping the vendors in developing precise parts.
5) Helps in accelerating design and manufacturing processes, thus increasing the product development cycles.

5.1.4 Total Quality Management (TQM)

Quality consists of those product features which meet the requirements of customers and therefore provide cash-inflow, profitability, and are free from repair and replacement of defective parts. Total Quality Management is defined as

> the attitude that produces a comprehensive, company-wide system for achieving the desired product characteristics [33,34]

The various elements of TQM are:

Statistical Process Control (DEWING)
Quality Improvement Techniques (JURAN)
Company-Wide Quality Control (ISHIKAWA)
Quality Engineering (TAGUACHI)
Quality Function Deployment (CLAUSING)

A discussion of Quality Engineering and Quality Function Deployment is presented in detail below.

5.1.5 Quality Engineering by Design (Taguachi Method)

A range of values of a process characteristic which are acceptable are said to be within specified limits. If the dimensions of the individual components were made to conform to certain "optimal values" within the tolerance limits, product performance is better. Dr.Taguachi's recommends statistically designed experiments that help in setting up parameters which will result in a product whose characteristics are consistently close to the ideal target [29, 36]. He therefore underscores the importance of three design steps:

1) System design -	The best production equipment and tentative production processes.
2) Parameter design -	The values of the parameters which optimises the product loss.
3) tolerance design -	Selection of tolerance that should be implemented in manufacturing to assure minimum loss of product

manufactured and used by customer.

Various steps involved in the robust design are shown in Figure 7.

The implementation of Dr.Tagauchi's quality engineering methods led to the following accomplishments:

1) Reduction of performance variations about a target value.
2) Fewer engineering changes after product is designed.
3) Reduction of scrap and rework and increased customer satisfaction.

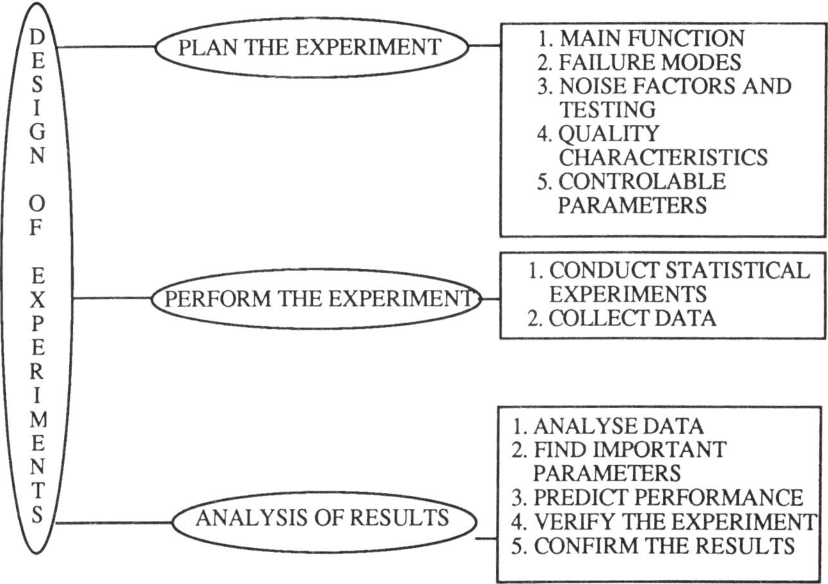

Figure 7 Tagauchi's Design of Experiments

5.1.6 Quality Function Deployment (QFD)

QFD is a means or way to connect customers' needs into many activities that can be deployed through such stages as product planning, engineering, manufacturing, assembly and service. The foundation of QFD is the belief that products should be designed to reflect customers' desires and tastes. This therefore compels marketing, design and manufacturing divisions to work closely together from the time a product is first conceived [40]. QFD uses team work for creative brainstorming and identification of customers' demands through market research data, dealers input, sales department needs, special customers' opinion surveys such as placing their products in public areas and encouraging potential customers to examine them etc.

Different parameters such as various functions, mechanisms, failure modes, parts and assemblies, and critical manufacturing steps are crucial in fulfilling customers' requirements, and these parameters are converted into engineering characteristics by using matrices. These characteristics are evaluated by multifunctional teams based on their engineering experiences, customers' responses and statistical studies to show positive results, and these parameters lead to the establishment of target values to be achieved [36, 40].

Realization of QFD yields:

1) Product development based on customers requirements, hence that objective is carried through all the stages.
2) Various strategies do not become vague or lost throughout its implementation from marketing, planning and finally manufacturing.
3) Even the minute details based on the customers requirements are not overlooked.
4) High efficiency is achieved as the number of changes required at each stage are reduced (totally eliminated) giving clear direction to the objectives.

REFERENCES

[1] Lee, S.C.Y "Knowledge-Based Expert Systems: A New Horizon Manufacturing Automation", Proceedings of the Winter annual meeting of the ASME Anaheim, CA ,Dec. 7-12, 1986.

[2] Turner, F., Carter, D.L. "Manufacturing Influence on the Design and Importance of Successful Automation", Proceedings of Autofact European Conference, pp.1-20 to 1-25

[3] Schutzer, D, "Artificial Intelligence: An Application Oriented Approach ", Van Nostrand Reinhold Company, New York

[4] Rembold, U., " The Role of Artificial Intelligence in the Factories of the Future ", University of Karlsruhe, FRG

[5] Kusiak, A " Flexible Manufacturing Systems ", Int. J. of Production Research, 23(6), pp.1057-1073

[6] Requicha, A.A.G., Vandebrande, J., " Automated Systems for Process Planning and Parts Programming ", Al & CIM Systems, pp. 302-305

[7] Kusiak, A., " Scheduling Flexible Machining and Assembly Systems ", Elsevier, New York, pp. 521-532

[8] Suzaki, Kiyoshi, " The New Manufacturing Challenges -Techniques for Continuous Improvement ", Collier Macmillan Publisher, London

[9] Vaughn, R.L " A Today's Look at the Automated, Integrated Factory of Tomorrow " Proceeding of Autofact Conference, pp 3-112 to 3-126.

[10] Cutkosky,M.R., and Tenenbaum, J.M., " CAD/CAM Integration Through Concurrent Process and Product Design ", ASME Symposium on Intelligent and Integrated Manufacturing Winter annual meeting, Dec 1987

[11] Kuvin, B.F., " Expert Systems for Fabricators ", Welding Design and Fabrication, March 87, p.56-58

[12] Ravi, L., Garg, R., Dwivedi, S.N.," Concurrent Engineering - Why and What", Proceedings of IEEE Conference, April 1990, Arizona

[13] Boothroyd, G., "Making it Simple - Design for Assembly, Mechanical Engineering, Feb. 1988

[14] Boothroyd, G., Dewhurst, P, "Design for Assembly: Selecting the Right Method".

[15] Whitney, D.E., "Manufacturing by Design", Harvard Business Review, July-August 1988

[16] "Design for Automation in Assembly", Datapro Manufacturing Automation Series, Feb. 1988

[17] Dwivedi, S.N and Klein, B.R., "Design for Manufacturability: Makes Dollars and Sense", CIM Review, Spring, 1986, pp. 53-59.

[18] Crow, K.A., "Design for Manufacturability: Its Role in World Class Manufacturing", Proceedings of Second International Conference on DFM, Nov. 1989.

[19] Wallach, J.M., "Design for Manufacturing and Solid Modelling", Proc. of the Second Int. Conf. on DFM, Nov. 1989

[20] Manro, S., "Simultaneous Engineering for Improved Product Design and Manufacturing Interface", Proceedings of Seminar of Society of Manufacturing Engineers, Oct 11-13, 1988.

[21] "The Philosophy of Value Added Manufacturing", Datapro Manufacturing Automation Series, Dec. 1988

[22] "Potential Applications of Value Engineering in a Simultaneous Engineering Concept", Proceedings of 1986 SAVE Conference, pp. 1-87 to 1-93

[23] Wixson, J.R., "Improving Product Development with Value Analysis / Value Engineering", Proceedings of 1987 SAVE Conference, pp. 51-66

[24] "Principles and Applications of Value Engineering", U.S. Army Management Training Activity Course Book

[25] Lexans, A.S., "Graphics- Analysis and Conceptual Design", Mechanical Engineering, April 1989

[26] Daniel, D. ,"The Power of Parameters", Mechanical Engineering, Jan. 1989

[27] Schraft, R.D and Bassler, R, "Possibilities to Realize Assembly Oriented Product Design", 90th International Conference on Assembly Automation, Paris, May 1984, pp. 243-261.

[28] IDA Report R-38 "The Role of Concurrent Engineering in Weapons System Acquisition", December 1988

[29] Ryan, T., "Statistical Methods for Quality Improvement, John Wiley & Sons.

[30] Tribus, M., "Quality - Deming Way", Mechanical Engineering, Jan. 1988.

[31] Box, G. and Bisguard, S., "Statistical Tools for Improving Designs", Mechanical Engineering, Jan. 1988.

[32] "Search for Quality: From Taguachi to Customers", Datapro Manufacturing Automation Series, Oct. 1988

[33] "Quality First", Datapro Manufacturing Automation Series, Oct. 1988.

[34] "Quality: A Continuing Revolution", Datapro Manufacturing Automation Series, June 1989.

[35] "Establishing Total Quality Control", Datapro Manufacturing Automation Series,

March 1987

[36] Ross, P.J., "The Role of Tagauchi Methods and Design of Experiments in QFD", Quality Progress, June 1988, pp. 41-47.

[37] Sullivan P. L., " The Beginning, The End and The Problem In-Between", A Collection of Presentations and QFD case studies, American Suppliers Institute, Inc

[38] "The Quality Function", Datapro Manufacturing Automation Series, Dec. 1988.

[39] Hauser, R.J., & Clausing, D., "The House of Quality", Harvard Business Review, May-June 1988, pp. 63-73.

[40] Sullivan, L.P., "Quality Function Deployment", Quality Progress, June 1986, pp. 39-50.

[41] Sink, D.S, "Management of Quality and Productivity in the Organization of the Future", Proceedings of 1989 IIE Integrated Systems and Society for Integrated Manufacturing Conference, pp. 21-26.

Industrial Applications of Artificial Intelligence
J.L. Alty and L.I. Mikulich (Editors)
Elsevier Science Publishers B.V. (North-Holland)

A MODEL OF BEHAVIOUR FOR MACHINE LEARNING

J-G. GANASCIA
Equipe Apprentissage et Acquisition de Connaissances,
Laforia, URA 1095 du CNRS,
Tour 46-0, 4 Place Jussieu,
75252 Paris, France

J-F. PUGET,
Equipe Inference et Apprentissage,
Laboratoire de Recherche en Informatique,
URA 410 du CNRS,
Bat. 490, Universite Paris-Sud,
91405 Orsay, France.

N. HELFT,
Institute for New Generation Computer Technology,
Mita Kokusai Bldg., 21F,
4-28 Mita, 1-chome, Minato-ku,
Tokyo 108, Japan.

ABSTRACT: This paper presents a survey of major research topics in the area of machine learning. A main motivation behind this work is that of building a behavioural model of Machine Learning systems with the help of which, systems can be analysed and compared.

1.INTRODUCTION

In building our model, we have three goals in mind:

- a didactic one, i.e. describe the characteristics and limitations of some major Machine Learning programs
- a technical one, i.e. isolate the different components of Machine Learning programs, and thus build a frame work to analyse and compare them
- a scientific one, i.e. discover the missing or weak features of present systems in order to open up new research avenues.

The work is based on a collaboration between many research groups in France [3,4], who contributed to the development of the model.

2. THE MODEL

We can roughly classify problems related to Machine Learning (ML) in two broad areas: problems related to the *inference* an ML system does, that is, define and justify the conclusions a system may draw given some initial information; and problems related to the *architecture* of the system itself, that is, how the knowledge of a system evolves, under what conditions is learned information kept or retracted, and how is this information used by the system.

We will progressively show representative examples of both concerns, and use them to build our model.

2.1 The Learning Inference

2.1.1 Generalisation

A major topic of research in learning has been generalisation. Its main application is the detection of regularities amongst data, a process that takes place both in induction and analogy, the two main reasoning patterns studied in machine learning. These regularities may produce the rules needed for a Knowledge Based System. First consider a propositional language, and suppose that we are given examples that take the form of conjunctions of propositional symbols. The first approach to generalisation is to compute the intersection of the common properties. For example, if we know an object is *red and square*, and another is *red and triangle*, we might generalise both to *red.*

In the predicate logic, we can add a generalisation rule, that of turning a constant into a variable. This rule would generalise p(a,b) and p(a,c) in p(a,X) (X being a universally quantified variable).

We thus have two popular generalisation techniques, eliminating a conjunctive factor, and turning constants into variables [5,6].

2.1.2 Bias

It was soon realised how important the role of the representation language is for induction. Consider the following example.

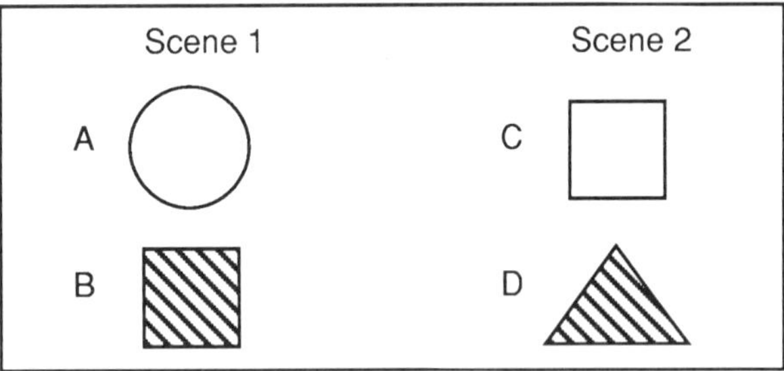

Figure 1 An Example

Even in such a trivial situation, there are many possible generalisations we might intuitively want to conclude:

- there are two objects, one over the other
- the object at the bottom is striped
- there are two objects and one of them is a square
- one of the objects is white
- etc..

Although facing this large number of possibilities, people generalise very fast and accurately. The examples and description of the space of possible generalisations is thus not enough for a generalisation program to do its job. Some additional constraints are needed to reduce the search. Mitchell [8] has called learning bias the set of all additional information provided to a system in order to assist it in learning the desired information. This is an extremely important component of a learning system, and a number of different approaches exist to introduce bias [11].

2.1.3 Domain knowledge

The examples given to a system concern a certain domain of interest. Providing information about a domain enables a program to improve its generalisations. Consider the following example

E1 = (Size = 3) & (Shape = square)

E2 = (Size = 5) & (Shape = triangle)

The examples have no common descriptor. However they share many properties they are both polygons and their size varies between 3 and 5. These regularities are "hidden" in the domain knowledge, and thus cannot be discovered without it. The following are two well-known rules used by generalisation programs.

- **Climbing a Generalisation Tree:** these trees are hierarchies defining generality relationships between descriptors. For example, $polygon \leq square$ [1]. With the help of such a hierarchy, we can conclude for example that (Shape = polygon) & (Shape = square) ≤ (Shape = square) & (Size = 3)

- **Extension of Intervals:** for attributes taking examples on ordered sets. If SIZE is such an attribute, we have that (SIZE ≥ 7) ≤ (SIZE > 5) and thus, (SIZE ∈ [-7 , 7] ≤ (SIZE ∈ [-5 , 5].

We now present the first simplified model in which the basic input/output relationships appear clearly (Figure 2)

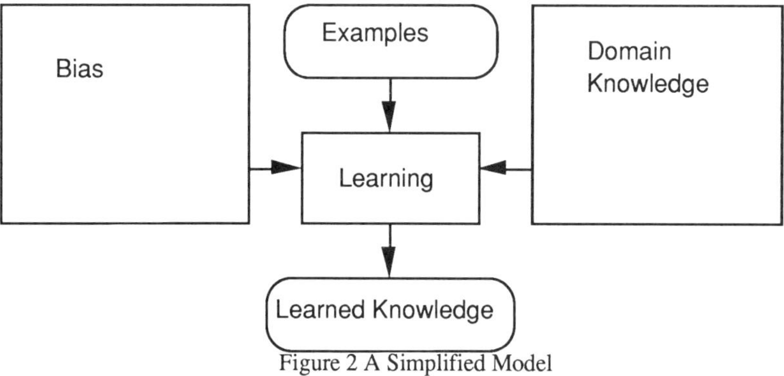

Figure 2 A Simplified Model

Basically, all generalisation programs have the above structure and they can be distinguished by their use of different encoding of the information specified in the above boxes.

2.2 The Learning Architecture

Learning systems are intended to work as part of a reasoning system, typically coupled with a problem solver. Problems arise concerning the evolution of the knowledge the learning system produces. ```we consider now two of those basic problems, namely incrementality and evaluation.

[1] P ≤ Q denotes that P is more general than Q

2.2.1 Incrementality

Obviously, any Learning system should use the knowledge it learns. When this freshly induced knowledge is used to learn new information, the learning system is incremented. However, two situations have to be distinguished and handled differently by a learning system. In the first one, the knowledge grows *monotonically* learning new things never invalidates previous knowledge. A more difficult situation arises if we allow *non-monotonicity*, that is, we consider the case in which we may reconsider previous conclusions in the light of new information. Very little research has been done on this topic although some exceptions are [2].

2.2.2 Evaluation

Learned information is by nature conjectural, no way exists to prove its validity. Every learning architecture thus incorporates some evaluation mechanism. The evaluator decides whether to accept or not knowledge induced by the system, and has thus a role similar to the learning bias. It is in fact a dynamic form of bias.

The evaluation mechanism can be internal to the system - generally called *critic* - or external - called an *oracle*. In fact, this oracle can be thought of as a "professor", who programs the machine with examples, learning bias and domain knowledge.

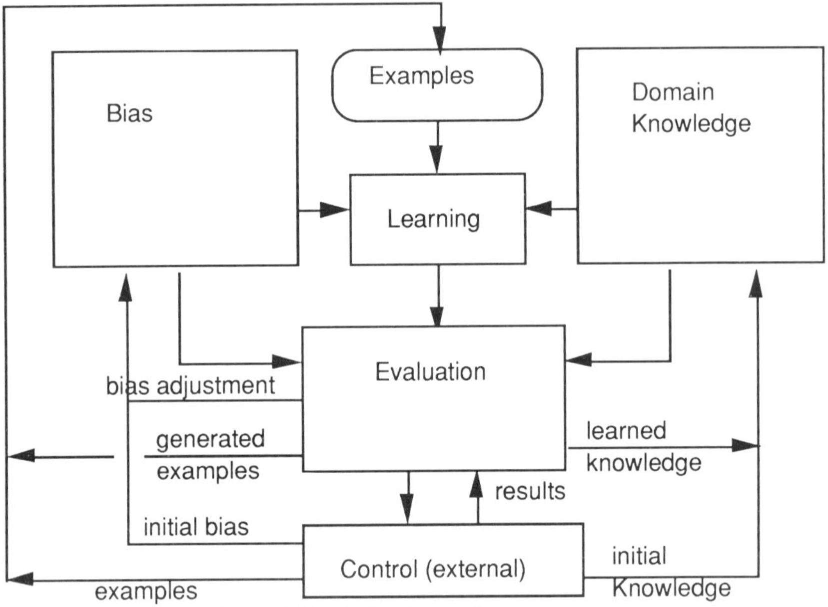

Figure 3 The Evaluation mechanism

3. Examples

This section shows how the model can be instantiated to current learning systems and generalisation theories.

We first describe ID3, the well-known decision tree builder [10]. There is no background knowledge. The bias consist in an information gain measure.

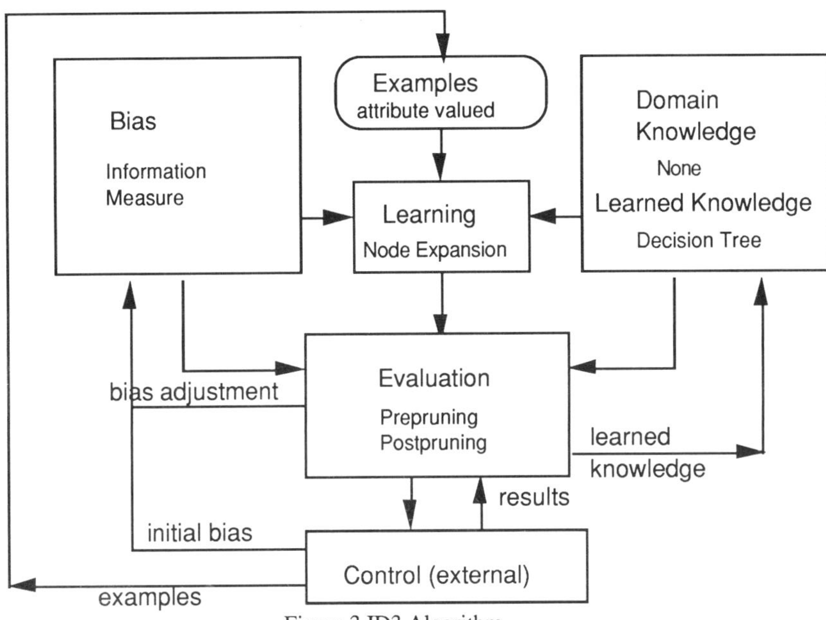

Figure 3 ID3 Algorithm

The figure below describes an Explanation Based Learning System called PRODIGY [7]. The purpose of this system is to learn preference rules (of the form "if the current goal is of this kind, then try this operator") to guide a Strips-like problem solver.

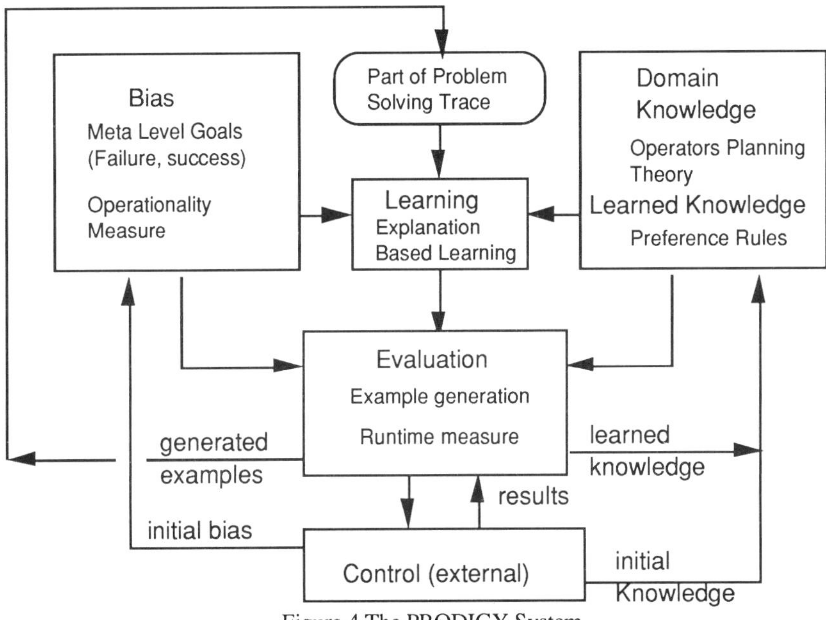

Figure 4 The PRODIGY System

The learning method consist of the following steps:

1) a problem is solved
2) the track is analysed to recognise meta-level goals, such as successes and failures
3) a theory of the planner is used to prove that the meta level goal is achieved
4) the proof is generalised by a method similar to EBG [9,1], resulting in a preference rule
5) the rule is evaluated. It is added to the domain knowledge if the problem solver performs better on a set of test problems when using the new rule.

4. Conclusions

We have actually used the above model to test and compare several learning systems. An interesting feature of the model is that it can cover very different approaches to learning, as for example, data analysis and connectionism. Basic questions which the author of such a system should answer are the following:

Concerning the generalisation process

What is the size the representation language induces on the search space for possible generalisations ?
How is this search space explored ?
How is bias used to constrain that space ?

The learning algorithm should be evaluated with respect to the answers to such questions. Particular care should be taken in defining different ways to introduce bias, as this can be either "programmed" in the learning algorithm or declaratively stated.

Concerning research on Learning Architectures the basic question is

How many of the interactions between evaluation, control, and the generalisation module a system includes ?

The answer to such a question should uncover basic limitations of learning systems and open new research areas.

5. References

[1] Dejong, J., and Mooney, R., (1986), "Explanation-Based Learning: An alternative View", Machine Learning, 2.

[2] Emde, W., (1987), "Non-cumulative learning in Metaxa", Proc. 10th Int. Conf. on Artificial Intelligence, Milan, Italy, Morgan Kaufman.

[3] Ganascia J, -G., and Helft, H., (1988), "Evaluation des systemes d'apprentissage", 3emes Journees Francaises de l'Apprentissage, Cassis, 5-6 Mai, pp 1 - 20.

[4] Ganascia J, -G., and Puget, J-F., (1989), "Modele comportemental D'apprentissage: representation de modeles existants", 4emes. Journees Francaises de l'Apprentissage, San Malo.

[5] Kodratoff, Y., Ganascia, J.G., "Improving the Generalisation Step in Learning", in Machine Learning: An Artificial Intelligence Approach, Vol II, R.S.Michalski, J. G. Carbonnel, T. M. Mitchell (Eds.), Morgan Kaufman, pp 215 - 244.

[6] Michalski, R.S., (1983), "A Theory and Methodology of Inductive Learning", in in Machine Learning: An Artificial Intelligence Approach, R.S.Michalski, J. G. Carbonnel, T. M. Mitchell (Eds.), Morgan Kaufman, pp 83 - 134.

[7] Minton, S., and Carbonnel, J.G., "Strategies for Learning Search Control Rules: An Explanation-based Approach", Proc. 10th Int. Conf. on Artificial Intelligence, Milan, Italy, Morgan Kaufman, pp 228 - 235.

[8] Mitchell, T., (1982), "Generalisation as Search", Artificial Intelligence, 18, pp 203 - 226.

[9] Mitchell, T., Keller, R., and Kedar-Cabelli, S., (1986),"Explanation-based Generalisation: a unifying view", Machine Learning, 1.

[10] Quinlan, J.R.,(1983), "Learning Efficient ~Classification ~Procedures and their application to Chess End Games", in in Machine Learning: An Artificial Intelligence Approach, R.S.Michalski, J. G. Carbonnel, T. M. Mitchell (Eds.), Morgan Kaufman, pp 463 - 482.

[11] Utgoff, P.E., (1986), "Shift of Bias for Inductive Learning Concept Learning", in Machine Learning: An Artificial Intelligence Approach, Vol II, R.S.Michalski, J. G. Carbonnel, T. M. Mitchell (Eds.), Morgan Kaufman, pp 107 - 148.

Industrial Applications of Artificial Intelligence
J.L. Alty and L.I. Mikulich (Editors)
Elsevier Science Publishers B.V. (North-Holland)

REAL-TIME SUPERVISION FOR PRODUCTION MANAGEMENT ACTIVITIES

J-P. LAURENT and J. AYEL

Laboratoire d'Intelligence Artificielle,
Universite de Savoie,
BP 1104 - 73011,
CHAMBERY (FRANCE)

ABSTRACT: The problem of integration in CIM (Computer Integrated Manufacturing) is often posed at the manufacturing process level. But the same problem arises at the production management level, as production management activities must be coordinated and synchronized with each other and with the production system. This coordination should be the responsibility of a specific system: A Manufacturing Management Monitoring System (3M-System). Such a system should not only be able to deal with changes in the environment with reflexive replies. It should also be capable of reasoning and of choosing among the actions it could undertake, according to the time constraints the system is faced with. We propose an architecture in which the supervision task is distributed at the level of "islands" of Production Management Activities under the control of software called unit-controllers. All the unit-controllers together make up the 3M-System. Each unit-controller is a knowledge-based real-time system using a blackboard mechanism and communicates with the other unit-controllers. They are obtained by instantiation of a generic unit-controller shell.

1. INTRODUCTION

The problem of integration in CIM (Computer Integrated Manufacturing) is often posed at the level of the manufacturing process only. But such a problem should also be posed at the production management level. Indeed, production management activities cannot remain isolated islands of automation. They must be coordinated and synchronized with each other and with the production system. This temporal and logical coordination should be the responsibility of a specific system: a production management supervisor,which we call a Manufacturing Management Monitoring System (3M-System).

The production management system is made up of a set of software modules (traditional software or artificial intelligence software) whose role is to set up and to update the decisions at the various levels of the plant relative to the different functions in the plant (production, maintenance, quality control, resource management, ...). The 3M-system has to control and to keep the global consistency of the different decisions made in the plant. It should continuously manage the conflicts between the various decisions made by the production management system's activities working in parallel and trigger decision updatings.

This task implies:

- continual analysis of the partial decisions set up by the production management activities in order to coordinate and synchronize them,
- detection of contradictions between the decisions (or between these decisions and the current state of the production system),
- triggering production management activities for updating decisions.

It is a system that cannot simply answer to changes in the environment with reflexive responses. It must also be able to choose between the actions it can undertake according to the time constraints it must respect.

We have defined a conceptual model of the supervision function called the Conceptual Supervision Model (CSM), in order to specify the concepts taking part in the description of the supervision behaviour of a 3M-System.

One of the fundamental concepts in the CSM has been to look at supervision as an activity partially distributed at the level of small groups of production management activities, that we called islands. Each group of management activities therefore contains a module called a unit-controller whose responsibilities are, on the one hand, to coordinate and synchronise the production management activities of the island, and on the other hand, to coordinate and to synchronise the activity of its island with those of the other islands.

Another fundamental concept in the CSM has been to assume that it is possible to define a taxonomy of behaviours between the unit-controllers resulting from the nature of the relations that may exist between islands of activities. Thus a set of behaviour models for the unit-controllers can be defined in terms of the need for coordination with the other unit-controllers and the need for coordination of the management activities inside its supervision unit. The definition of unit-controller behaviour models allows us to develop not just a supervision shell but a unit-controller shell. Using an acquisition tool it is then possible to use this unit-controller shell to create each of the unit-controllers which at the end will make up the 3M-System.

The second part of this article will briefly present the domain and the supervision task. The third part contains a description of the Conceptual Supervision Model (CSM). Part 4 is devoted to presenting the generic blackboard architecture for implementing a unit-controller, justifying the idea of a unit-controller shell.

2 THE SUPERVISION IN CIM

Satisfactory production management requires a certain number of decisions to be made on various levels of the factory. These decisions concern the various functions that play a role in the plant: production planning, product management, maintenance, resource management, quality control. The concept of Computer Integrated Manufacturing promotes the idea that if such functions are strongly interconnected, decisions can be made more rapidly and in a more coherent way leading to better flexibility and to significant reduction of production costs.

When designing a CIM supervision system for a particular plant, it is thus very important to identify decision centres and their inter-actions. The GRAI method [7], [8] provides an analysis of the decision-making network in a plant and reveals the various activities taking part in decision-making in production management as well as the interaction between these activities. It is those activities that our supervision system is meant to coordinate and synchronise, taking into consideration the interaction between them.

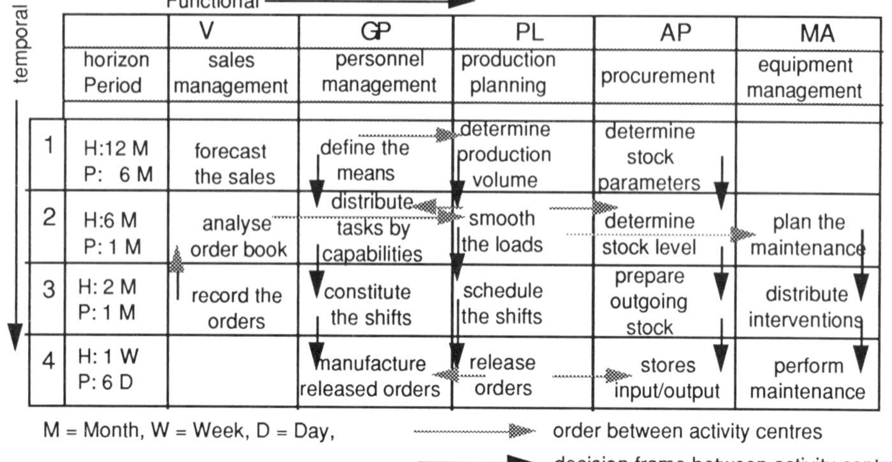

Figure 1 - Example of a GRAI grid

The GRAI method was designed by the "Groupe de Recherche en Automatisme Integre" at the University of Bordeaux. It consists first of a break-down of the production management system of a given plant into "activity centres". This break-down follows two poles: one functional (the production management functions) and the other temporal (horizon and period). Horizon represents the time interval concerned with the activity centre while period indicates how often the decisions are updated. This break-down into activity centres is represented on a grid (figure 1) on which most of the interaction and temporal constraints between activity centres are shown.

Each activity centre is itself broken down into activities. This second break-down is represented by a "macro-network" on which the interaction between activities is represented.

The supervision function implicitly follows the results of the GRAI analysis. It consists in coordinating and synchronising the activities revealed by this analysis as well as other activities, which help in making decisions, e.g. simulation activities.The supervision system must organize cooperation between these activities and control their synchronisation.

Thus the supervision function consists of:

- planning the production management activities to be triggered at a given time,
- triggering these activities appropriately,
- controlling their action,
- reacting to changes in the environment (machine break downs, labour trouble, stock shortages...).

This requires information about the activities themselves, as well as knowledge specific to supervision (that is, the behaviour to adopt in any situation that may come up).

The supervision function may be considered to be a function that not only plans actions (planning which activities to trigger) and carries out the planned actions (triggering the activities) but that can also change the plan according to the results of the actions it has triggered and to changes in its working environment. Furthermore, all this must be carried out "in real time", which means that the supervision function must consider constraints on acceptable response times .

3 . THE CONCEPTUAL SUPERVISION MODEL

The definition of this model aims to set up the concepts taking part in the supervision function of the management activities in a plant. One of its objectives is to formalize the dynamic behaviour of a supervision system. Such a formalization allows us to take out a set of general behaviours of a supervision system, leading us to some notion of supervision shell which will be described later on.

3.1. Organisational aspects

We will use act_k to stand for the activities the system has to supervise. SA will represent the supervision of all activities act_k.

The first question to set up before modelling the supervision function SA, is how to organize the activities act_k and the supervision activity SA on top of all act_k activities. One of the basic concepts in the CSM is to consider supervision activity SA as neither centralized nor totally distributed, but as partially distributed. Indeed, organising supervision in the form of a centralized system would not allow easy evolution and flexibility. A completely distributed organisation would create too many links between the act_k activities which would have to be managed.

This choice of organization implies grouping act_k activities into "activity islands" denoted by $island_i$. It entails defining criteria for this grouping. It also implies that a set of activities SA_i should be able to carry out the supervision activity SA:

Each SA_i activity is associated with an island and carries out supervision on two levels:

- at its own island's level, by controlling cooperation and synchronisation of the islands activities,
- at the level of all the islands together, by controlling cooperation and synchronisation of the islands with its own responsibilities.

Each SA_i activity is carried out by a module, called the unit-controller of the $island_i$, denoted by UC_i. We will use the term "Supervision Unit" denoted by SU_i to represent the set of act_k activities inside of the island plus the unit-controller UC_i .

$$\mathbf{SU_i = \{ \{ act_k\}_i, UC_i\}}$$

In this way, each unit-controller UC_i has two roles which it must carry out concurrently in real time:

- supervising the act_k activities of SU_i, (centralized supervision),
- taking part in the supervision of SU_i supervision units, (distributed supervision).

The supervision function is carried out by all the UCI unit-controllers together.

The break-down into activity islands must satisfy a certain number of constraints. In particular, it must allow for each island to be associated with a clearly defined, limited role in production management and for the islands to be organized in a hierarchy corresponding to the hierarchy of responsibility actually observed in the factory.

The GRAI analysis of a given plant makes it possible to define the set of activities act_k which take part in the elaboration of production management decisions as well as the links between these activities. Criteria for the break-down into islands are taken from the GRAI method and they will make it possible to define the activities of a supervision island on the basis of the results of the GRAI analysis of a plant and the analysis of its physical set-up.

A supervision unit in a plant is made up of:

- a set of software modules capable of carrying out the act_k activities of the island,
- a unit-controller that supervises the action of these modules in the process of making a decision.

It has a very specific role in production management, which is to elaborate a decision at a certain level of the plant.

There are hierarchical links between the supervision units. This hierarchy structure comes from the GRAI concept of the decision frame. In GRAI formalism, each activity centre receives from another activity centre decisional information that it uses as a decision frame for its own decision making process. In the same way, each supervision unit has its scope of responsibility limited by another single supervision unit which gives it objectives (decision frame) under the form of a set of constraints to be respected. For example, a supervision unit, the role of which is to schedule the production in a given workshop, has its responsibility limited by the supervision unit which has to plan the production in all the workshops at once.

This type of hierarchical relation between two supervision units is represented by a semantic link, called a control link. It represents the fact that a supervision unit provides a decision frame to the supervision unit it controls. Furthermore, it is associated with a set of behaviours of a supervision unit towards its controlling supervision unit and towards the supervision unit it controls. The tree of control links between the supervision units allows us to define a hierarchical structure of responsibility in the production management system. This hierarchical structure allows the supervision system to solve the conflicts between supervision units at the right level of responsibility in this hierarchy.

3.2. Dynamic aspects

By dynamic aspects we mean the supervision behaviour of each unit-controller. Firstly, there is the behaviour of unit-controllers towards the cooperation between supervision units, secondly there is the behaviour of unit-controllers toward the activities inside their supervision unit.

3.2.1 Interaction between supervision units and associated behaviour

One of the important principles of the CSM is that it is possible to defined a taxonomy of behaviours associated with different kinds of interactions between supervision units. These kinds of interaction are expressed through semantical links.

We have identify three types of links: **control** (described above), **dependency and triggering.**

In the GRAI formalism, an "order" arrow between two activity centres indicates that the first one provides the second one with constraints which are of the same kind as the objectives, but must be also respected. A dependency link between two supervision units implies a relational behaviour between these supervision units which is the translation of an order arrow between the two corresponding activity centres. Thus the dependency link may represent the dependency of decision associated with one function on other functions (Maintenance, production, resources managements,...). For example, it may model the behaviour associated with the fact that production is considered as having priority over maintenance.
The triggering links represent temporal constraints between supervision units.

The interaction network can be represented by a semantic network, called **a supervision** network whose nodes are the supervision units and each arc represents any link (control, dependency or triggering) between two supervision units. This network (figure 2) is in fact the result of superposing the three following networks: the control link network, the dependency link network, and the triggering link network.

The supervision network is defined at the initialisation phase of the supervision system building and it is used by the set of unit-controllers to determine their cooperation and synchronization behaviour when they are running. The supervision network gives the set of supervision units with which each one cooperates, and the communication needs between the supervision units.

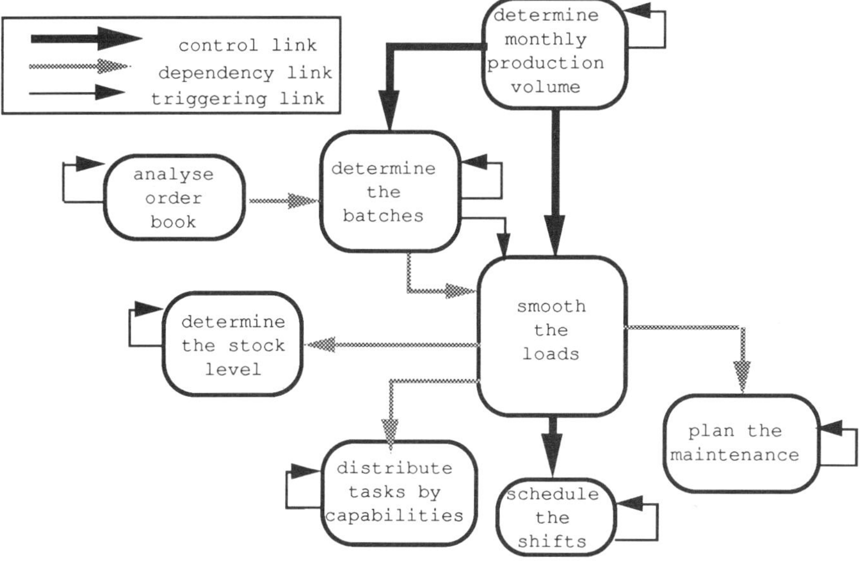

Figure 2 - A part of an external supervision network

With each type of link is associated a generic script that expresses the dynamic behaviour of the supervision units linked by such a link. This means that the script associated with the control link defines in a general way, the cooperation and synchronization behaviour for any pair of supervision units linked by a control link. This script must be instantiated on a particular supervision unit to become a behaviour script of its unit-controller. In the same way, a general script is associated with the dependency link and with the triggering link.

Each supervision unit SU_i, in the neighbour of a supervision unit SU_o, is viewed by SU_o through the link existing between SU_i and SU_o. Thus the representation that a unit-controller has from the other supervision units with which it cooperates, is structured by the taxonomy of links. The unit-controllers are responsible for automatically achieving the various kinds of behaviours corresponding to these links.

3.2.2 Dynamic aspects within a supervision unit

The dynamic aspects of supervision within a supervision unit concern:

- taking into account the decision-making strategies concerning the decision that the supervision unit is responsible for, as well as the constraints imposed by the synchronization and by the availability of the resources required to scheduling activities,

- time-dependent activity triggering and function management,
- following up on the inside activities so as to know exactly what the situation is when a decision must be made.

The fact that a specific goal is associated with each island means that the activities of an island are a set of activities that cooperate to reach a common objective. For example, the common objective of the island's activities may be to smooth the workshop's loads for one week. In this case the island's activities will be carried out by all the software modules available in the plant that can participate in "load smoothing". This set of modules should allow the unit-controller to choose dynamically between several methods (through module chaining) for smoothing loads, as some methods may sacrifice to a greater or lesser degree the quality of smoothing to the speed in setting up the decisions.

The common objective of an activity island is to solve a specific problem. For example, for the smoothing load, the unit-controller sets up a solving process for this problem. It has the role of a problem solving control mechanism for managing its island's activities. Because the problem it has to solve is always the same (updating a particular decision) and as the modules it can use are predefined, we can represent by a graph all the possible chainings of modules allowed to be carried out in the problem solving process.

A graph called the "strategy-by-default graph" (figure 3) is thus attached to each SU. The vertices of this graph are the modules which carry out the internal activities of the SU and the arcs indicate possible series of activities due to the "and/or" links between arcs arriving in or going out of the vertices. In this way the strategy-by-default graph shows the strategies which may be used by the unit-controller in the decision-making process which its supervision unit is periodically responsible for. For any given problem, the unit-controller has only to be able to decide which "problem-solving path" it will follow on this graph. Setting up a problem-solving path must be a dynamic process in order to take into account any evolution in the situation while the problem-solving process is going on.

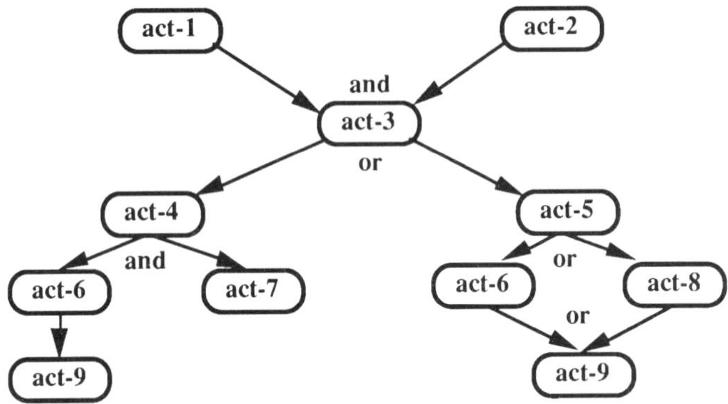

Figure 3 - The "Strategy by default" graph of a supervision unit

Therefore two kinds of criteria for choice have been defined, criteria for choosing between arcs going out of a node and linked by an "or" link, and criteria for resuming the problem-solving process in different nodes, which would allow the unit-controller to resume decision-making when a change in the current situation makes the previous process (on-going or not) obsolete.

4. GENERIC ARCHITECTURE FOR IMPLEMENTING THE UNIT-CONTROLLERS

A unit-controller must have several capabilities: reasoning about the actions it can undertake to set up the partial decision it is in charge of, and, continuously analyzing the evolution of the whole system, conversing with the other unit-controllers.

From the point of view of all the unit-controllers, the unit-controller is a relatively autonomous intelligent agent that interacts with the other ones according to three predefined kinds of script. From the point of view of the activity island the unit-controller is a problem solving control mechanism.

The unit-controller must therefore have several types of interacting capabilities:

- control of the problem solving process,
- management of the dialogues with other unit-controllers by means of messages,
- reasoning that takes into account asynchronous events (execution reports from internal modules and messages from other unit-controllers).

The computer architecture which we felt the best adapted to set up all these capabilities in a single system was a blackboard architecture ([9], [10], [11], [12]). The blackboard model is a model convenient for distributed problem solving which consists of three main entities:

- the blackboard data structure which allows storing the state of the problem solving process,
- the knowledge sources, each one containing knowledge which makes it possible to solve a part of the problem,
- the control mechanism (called here selector) which decides at a given time which knowledge source has to be chosen according to the content of the blackboard.

The blackboard data structure allows the storing of the situation the unit-controller has to reason about, i.e the state of the problem-solving process and the state of the dialogues with the other unit-controllers.

We have split up the blackboard data structure into four blackboard data structures: Result Blackboard, Control Blackboard, External I/O Blackboard and Internal I/O Blackboard, according to the kinds of data to store respectively: state of the solving process, state of control decisions for the problem solving process, state of dialogues with the other unit-controllers and the state of triggering orders for the inside activities of the supervision unit.

The knowledge sources will make it possible to express the behaviour of the unit controller towards the situations described by the state of the blackboards. They translate:

- the general supervision behaviour defined in the Conceptual Supervision Model towards the other supervision units by the behaviour scripts associated with control dependency and triggering links,
- the behaviour of the solving process control mechanism towards the modules inside of a supervision unit by using the "strategy-by-default" graph.

The classic control loop of the blackboard mechanism is modified in order to be also capable firstly, to receive and to send asynchronous messages from, and to, other unit-controllers, and secondly to send triggering orders to inside activities and to receive execution follow up from them.

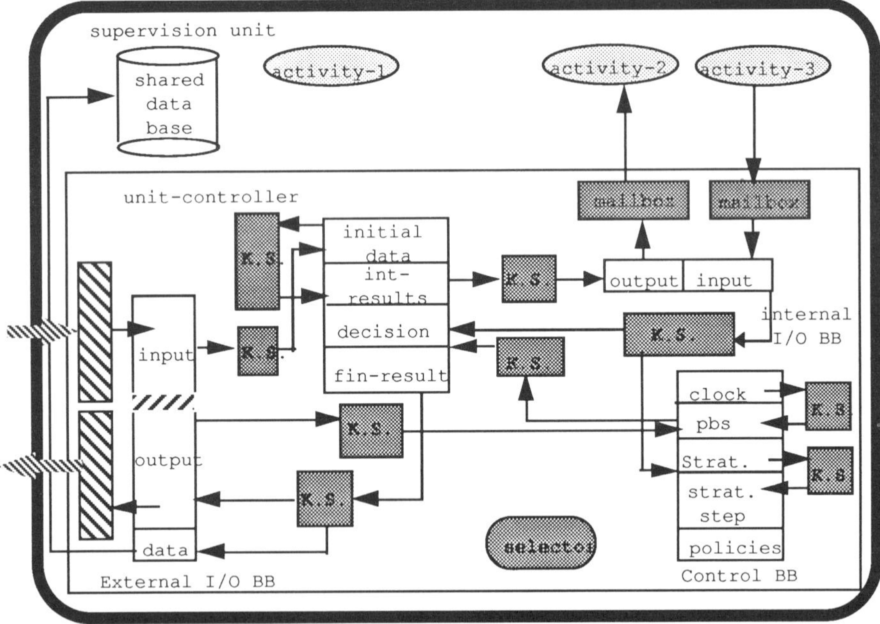

Figure 4 - The unit-controller's generic architecture

At each loop, the selector examines the situation inside and outside the supervision unit through the state of the blackboards and it can choose which knowledge source to trigger in response to the situation.

A protocol for exchanging messages has been developed and implemented in order to ensure that the blackboard can interface with the physical network. This protocol allows the contents of one SU's mailbox to be transferred to another SU's mailbox or to one of the SU's internal modules. The selector is in charge of the transfer of the messages from the mailboxes to the blackboard data structure and reciprocally.

As the internal activities triggered by the unit-controller run in parallel with the unit-controller itself and as a knowledge source translates a very elementary behaviour step, the execution time of a knowledge source is very short and so it is for the selector loop. This feature allows the unit-controller to react very rapidly to changes since the unit-controller re-analyses the situation at each selector loop.

All the above mentioned features of the required unit-controller behaviour and of the blackboard architecture have led us to build a **unit-controller shell,** which includes a supervision control mechanism, a general knowledge base and an acquisition tool.

The supervision control mechanism is the implementation, by means of the blackboard mechanism described above, of the general supervision behaviour of a unit-controller. The general knowledge base makes it possible to describe the features of each group of activities of a supervision unit in terms of supervision and to infer the cooperation behaviour of this supervision unit from the general behaviours associated to its links with the others. The acquisition tool makes it possible to instantiate the general knowledge base.

Each unit-controller is software made up of the supervision control mechanism and of the instantiation of the general knowledge base on the group of activities the unit-controller is responsible for.

5 . CONCLUSION

We have implemented a simplified mock-up of the 3M-System (a supervision subnetwork centred on a supervision unit whose task is to "smooth the loads") writing in Common LISP with Flavors and running on a SUN3 workstation. The only supervision unit to be implemented is "smooth the loads". The other supervision units are simulated through the arrival of various kinds of messages which the unit-controller of the "smooth the loads" supervision unit reacts to.

The unit-controller of this supervision unit has been built from the unit-controller shell, by recopying the supervision control mechanism and by instantiating the general knowledge sources of the unit-controller shell.

This mock-up has allowed us to check the opportunistic behaviour of our system and that it is reacting appropriately and in real time to various messages from other supervision units. The next stage in our work will be to implement in the same way a whole supervision system on two industrial application sites which are PHILIPS and PIRELLI .

ACKNOWLEDGEMENT

This work has been carried out with the support of the European Community, within the ESPRIT Project 932: "Knowledge-Based Real-Time Supervision in CIM", led by Philips. The French firms GRAPHAEL, TITN and CEA have contributed to the work described in this paper. The French Program "GRECO-PRC Intelligence Artificielle" has also supported this research.

REFERENCES

[1] J.F. Allen, "Towards a General Theory of Action and Time"", Artificial Intelligence (23) pp. 123-153 (1983)

[2] J.F. Allen ,"Maintaining Knowledge about Temporal Intervals", Communications of A.C.M. (26) (1983)

[3] J. Ayel , "A Conceptual Supervision Model in Computer Integrated Manufacturing", European Conference on Artificial Intelligence, ECAI Munchen, pp 427- 432, (1988).

[4] J. Ayel, J.P. Laurent et al "Distributed Artificial Intelligence: A necessary paradigm for supervision production management activities", Second International Conference on Industrial & Engineering Applications of Artificial Intelligence & Expert Systems (IEA/AE). UTSI Tullahoma, Tennessee USA, pp 326-335

[5] J. Ayel, J.P. Laurent, andB.P. Panet , "D.A.I. for Production Supervision", Conference invitee, AAAI Spring Symposium, Stanford (USA), March 1989.

[6] D.D. Corkill and V.R. Lesser , "The Use of Meta-Knowledge Control for Coordination in a Distributed Problem-Solving Network" 8th IJCAI pp 747-756, (1983).

[7] G. Doumeingts , "Methodology to Design CIM and Control of Manufacturing Units", Methods and Tools for CIM, Lecture notes in Computer Science pp.138-194, Springerverlag, Berlin (1984).

[8] G. Doumeingts , " How to Decentralize Decisions Through GRAI Model in Production Management" I.F.I.P.W.G. 5.7 International Working Conference, Munich, March (1985).

[9] E,H, Durfee and V.R. Lesser ,"Incremental Planning to Control a Blackboard-Based Problem-Solver", AAAI, pp 58-64, (1986).

[10] R. Englemore and T. Morgan , "Blackboard Systems", Addison- Wesley Publishing Company, (1988).

[11] L.D. Erlman et al, "The HEARSAY II Speech Understanding System: Integrating Knowledge to Resolve Uncertainty", ACM Computing Surveys ,,Vol. 12 pp 212-253, (1980)

[12] B. Hayes-Roth , " A Blackboard Architecture for Control ", Artificial Intelligence 26 pp. 251 361, (1985)

[13] S. Smith, M. Fox and P. Ow, "Constructing and Maintaining Detailed Production Plans: Investigations into Development of Knowledge-Based Factory Scheduling Systems", AI Magazine, (1986).

[14] S. Smith, and P. Ow, " The Use of Multiple Problem Decomposition in Time Constrained Planning Tasks", Proc 9th IJCAI, Los Angeles, (1985).

Industrial Applications of Artificial Intelligence
J.L. Alty and L.I. Mikulich (Editors)
Elsevier Science Publishers B.V. (North-Holland)

APPLIED ROBOTICS IN ROBOTIZED FLEXIBLE MANUFACTURING SYSTEMS

M. VUKOBRATOVIC

Robotics and Flexible Automation Laboratory,
Mihailo Pupin Institute,
Beograd,
Yugoslavia.

ABSTRACT: In the paper, recent results of user-oriented software for mathematical modelling of manipulation robot dynamics and robotized flexible cells are presented. Based on the dynamic models of robots and robotized systems, the results of the dynamic control synthesis of manipulation robots, and the synthesis of multilevel control of robotized flexible cells are also presented. The simulation of robots within the flexible manufacturing cells is considered in the paper. A software package has been developed for the simulation of flexible manufacturing cells which include robotic systems. In order to improve the benefits of such a package, various models of robotic systems are provided. These are, complete dynamic models, kinematic models of robots, and simple model in the form of finite automata.

1. CUSTOMIZED SOFTWARE FOR THE DYNAMIC ANALYSIS AND CONTROL SYNTHESIS OF ROBOTIC MANIPULATORS

1.1. Introduction

Adequate study of robotic mechanisms starts with the development of computer oriented methods for forming the mathematical models of the kinematics and dynamics of spatial active mechanisms. The rise in the development of robotic mechanism mathematical modeling began with numerical-iterative computer methods, continued through numeric-symbolic ones and, finally, arrived at the forming of mathematical models in symbolic form. Whilst the first approach, and even the second, are predominantly research approaches towards computer procedures for forming mathematical models of robotic mechanisms, the third one, symbolic model form, is a typical implementation version. Mathematical models of robot kinematics and dynamics are not the goal, but tools for the synthesis of dynamic control of these mechanisms. Thus, customized software for the synthesis of dynamic control laws of various complexity is a significant step towards the realization of the control system, the performances of which satisfy the ever more complex tasks of industrial manipulation, as well as the manipulation required in some unconventional working environments. Further and ever more complex roles for robots should be possible using flexible production cells, and broader, of intelligent technological systems. Hence customized software should be expanded towards the simulation and control of flexible models, by means of which a specific, new and more extensive promotion of the robotic technology can be carried out. In the course of the last few years, a great number of papers have been published, giving an important contribution to the development of computer methods for the forming of mathematical models of robotic mechanisms, as well as computer synthesis of non-adaptive and adaptive dynamic control of robotic systems of various complexity and dedication. The modelling methods may be classified with respect to the laws of mechanics on the basis of which motion equations are formed. One may distinguish methods based on Lagrange, Newton-Euler, Appel and other formalisms for dynamic modelling of interconnected multibody systems. The other criterion is whether the method yields the solution to both the direct and the inverse problem of dynamics or only to the inverse problem (computation of driving forces for a given desired motion of the manipulator). The number of multiplications/additions is yet another criterion for comparing methods. This criterion is the most important one from the point of view of their real-time applicability.

1.2. Lagrangian Formalism

The first result in the class of Lagrange methods, which are used to solve either the direct or the inverse problem of dynamics, was reported by Uicker [1]. Kahn elaborated an algorithm for modelling open kinematic chains [2]. The method was modified and reformulated by Woo and Freundenstein through introducing screw calculus [3]. Improved versions of this method in the sense of a reduced number of numerical operations were developed by Mahil and Renaud [4, 5]. A property common to these algorithms is that they do not employ recursive relations but closed form expressions for the elements of model matrices. The number of multiplications/additions in these methods depends on n^4 (n-number of joints) and is very large for microprocessor implementation.

1.3. Newton-Euler Formalism

The application of Newton-Euler dynamic equations to modelling of interconnected rigid bodies may be found in papers by Kane [6]. Huston adapted Kane's results to robotic systems [7]. These algorithms solve both the direct and the inverse problem of dynamics, using closed form expressions for the elements of dynamic model matrices. A more efficient computer method in the basic version was elaborated by Stepanenko [8] and in the extended form by Stepanenko and Vukobratovic [9] by introducing recursive relations into the algorithm and reduced the number of operations to n^3. Walker and Orin [10] reorganized the computations and reduced the number of operations to n^2. A special case of Newton-Euler method that yields the solution to the inverse problem of dynamics was treated by Walker and Paul [11]. They reduced the number of multiplications to 150n-48, i.e. 852 multiplications for a 6 joint manipulator.

The Recursive Lagrangian formalism developed by Vukobratovic and Potkonjak[12] improves the computational efficiency several times comparing to Kahn-Uicker's method. However, it is still difficult for real-time applications since it requires more than two thousands multiplications for a standard 6-joint manipulator. The above methods that yield the solution to both the direct and the inverse dynamic problem, are obviously not suitable for real-time applications. Thus, Waters and Hollerbach [13] developed algorithms for solving only the inverse problem of dynamics on the basis of Uicker-Kahn's method, and reduced the number of operations to n^2, or even n. Here the inertia matrix is not explicitly calculated.

1.4. Single Step Customized Algorithms

The common property of the described methods is that they do not depend on specific manipulator design. They employ general laws of kinematics and the dynamics of joint-interconnected rigid bodies. For real-time applications it is suitable to customize the algorithm for specific manipulator design. This was first recognized by Aldon [14], Vukobratovic and Kircanski [15], and Renaud [16]. The method by Vukobratovic and Kircanski is fully automatic from the standpoint of computer generation of model source code. As surveyed by Neuman and Muray [17] several papers dealing with computer symbolic models generation appeared in 1984. Most of them were based on Lagrangian formalism. It should be also pointed out that Soviet authors have also significantly contributed to the computer approach in forming mathematical models of robotic mechanisms dynamics. We stress one of the most developed, that of A.F. Vereschagin [18], who, with his co-authors, has developed general models of manipulation robots dynamics.

1.5. Multi-step Optimizing Customized Algorithms

Single-step methods represent actually the first step of the multi-step optimizing customized algorithms. The output of the first step is the source program of the robot model customized for a specific manipulator design. This source code is the input for the second step. In the second step we introduce the optimization process to minimize the number of numerical operations. The output of the second step is the source code of the optimized model. Existing results show that the number of operation is at least 2 times less comparing to one step customization. Preliminary results of a multi-step optimizing algorithm based on global optimization of symbolic polynomials are currently being developed [19].

Table 1. The reduction in numerical complexity

Manipulator	d o f	single-step		two-step	
		mult.	add.	mult.	add.
PUMA	4	135	108	78	45
SCARA	4	40	33	14	14
STANFORD	4	101	80	61	44

One F.P. operation takes about 20 ms on a low-cost microcomputer. About 100 F.P. operations are distributed to be processed on one processor board. Thus, the dynamic model computations takes about 2 ms on a 6-processor computer. Much lower computing times are achievable by the use of array processor oriented controllers. Preliminary results [20] of an implementation on a FRT-300 array processor for a PUMA-560 robot shows that the computing time is reduced to 0.1 ms.

2. DYNAMIC CONTROL OF ROBOTS

The main problem with the control of robotic systems is: to what extent it is necessary to include dynamic terms in the control law?

2.1. Non-adaptive Dynamic Control of Robots

The requirements for a dynamic control are: most accurate tracking of "fast" trajectories, simplest control structure and control robustness to robot parameters variations.

The dynamic approach can be realized via: optimal control synthesis of which is realized via minimization of some criterion (minimization of movement execution time) [21], control by linear optimal controller (synthesis based on a linearized model) [22, 23], control via "inverse method" demanding "on-line" calculation of the complete robot dynamics model [24], control via force feedback, using the fact that by means of force measurement on the robot, direct information about the robot dynamics is obtained [25, 26, 27], decoupled control, via "on-line" calculation of robot dynamics compensates the same and decouples it into subsystems [28], decentralized control stabilizing each joint (subsystem) of the robot independently from the rest of system; stability of the whole system is investigated and, if necessary, global (crosscoupling) feedback loops are introduced [29, 30].

2.2. Computer-aided Control Synthesis [31]

Modules of general software are: nominal trajectories forming block, kinematic constraints block, mechanism dynamic parameters setting block, actuators parameters setting block, synthesis of nominal dynamics, control quality setting, local control synthesis, nonlinear model analysis, global control synthesis, synthesis of control in discrete form simulation block, control laws choice of microcomputer realization.

A global flow-chart of the package for control synthesis is presented in Figure 1. (spread over the next three pages).

Mechanism parameters (number of members and degrees of freedom, masses, lengths, moments of inertia, joint types, etc..) and actuator parameters (types, model order, data, constraints)

Task setting: trajectory and object angles in the absolute coordinate system; requirements concerning the tracking quality (stability regions)

STAGE OF NOMINAL DEVICES

Option: choice of the nominal states synthesis

Optimal calculation of the tip velocity and orientation, calculation of nominal trajectory

Suboptimal synthesis of nominal trajectories via decoupling in two functional subsystems

Calculation of nominal driving torques

Option: choice of the nominal programmed control

Synthesis of nominal control on the centralised model

Synthesis of nominal control on decoupled subsystem models

STAGE OF PERTURBED DYNAMICS-
-SYNTHESIS OF LOCAL CONTROL

1

Option: Distribution of model in subsystems and coupling; choice of inertial and gravitational factors assigned to subsystems

Option: choice of local control

local output feedback

Local optimal regulator

2

3

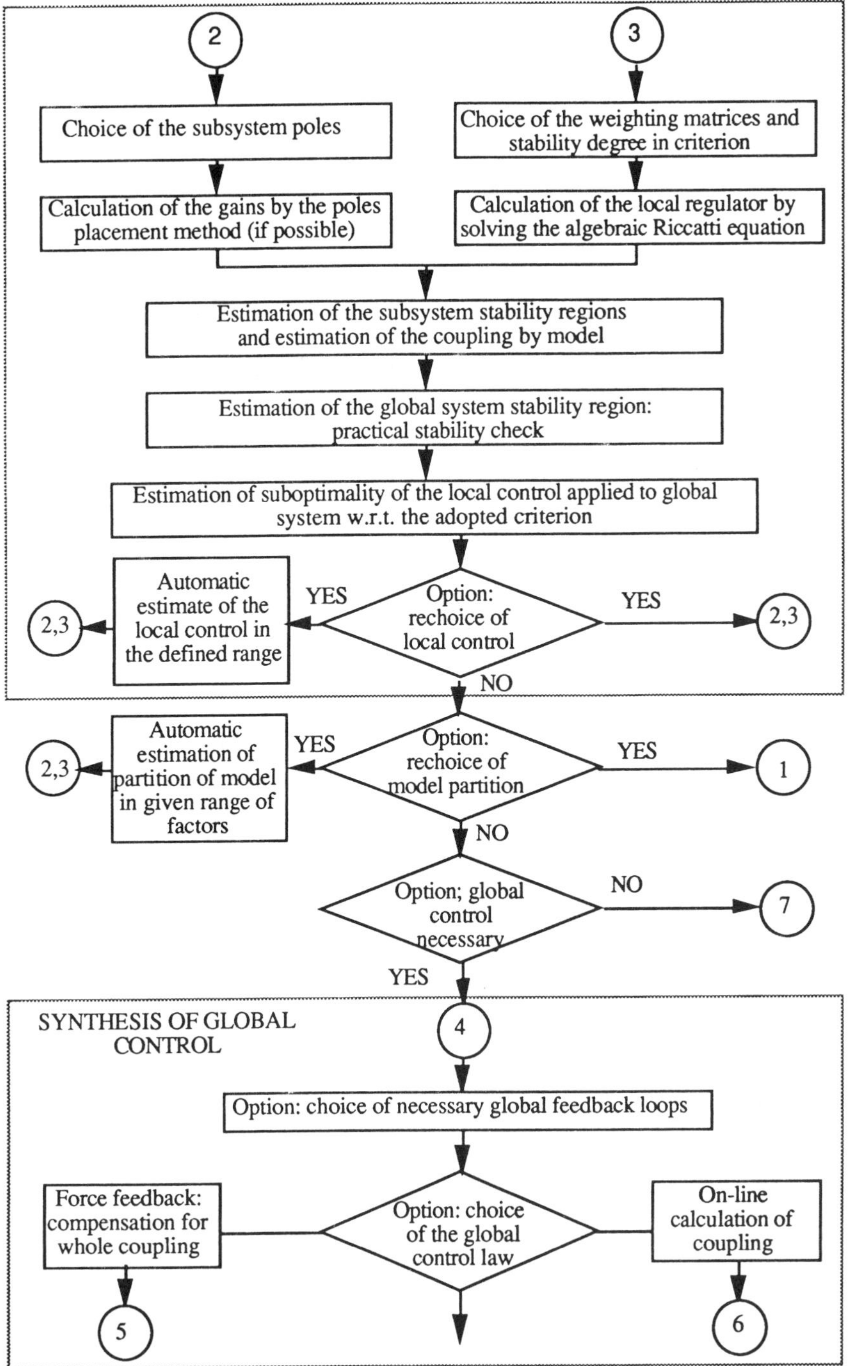
2
3
Choice of the subsystem poles
Choice of the weighting matrices and stability degree in criterion
Calculation of the gains by the poles placement method (if possible)
Calculation of the local regulator by solving the algebraic Riccatti equation
Estimation of the subsystem stability regions and estimation of the coupling by model
Estimation of the global system stability region: practical stability check
Estimation of suboptimality of the local control applied to global system w.r.t. the adopted criterion
Automatic estimate of the local control in the defined range
YES
Option: rechoice of local control
YES
2,3
2,3
NO
Automatic estimation of partition of model in given range of factors
YES
Option: rechoice of model partition
YES
1
2,3
NO
Option; global control necessary
NO
7
YES
SYNTHESIS OF GLOBAL CONTROL
4
Option: choice of necessary global feedback loops
Force feedback: compensation for whole coupling
Option: choice of the global control law
On-line calculation of coupling
5
6

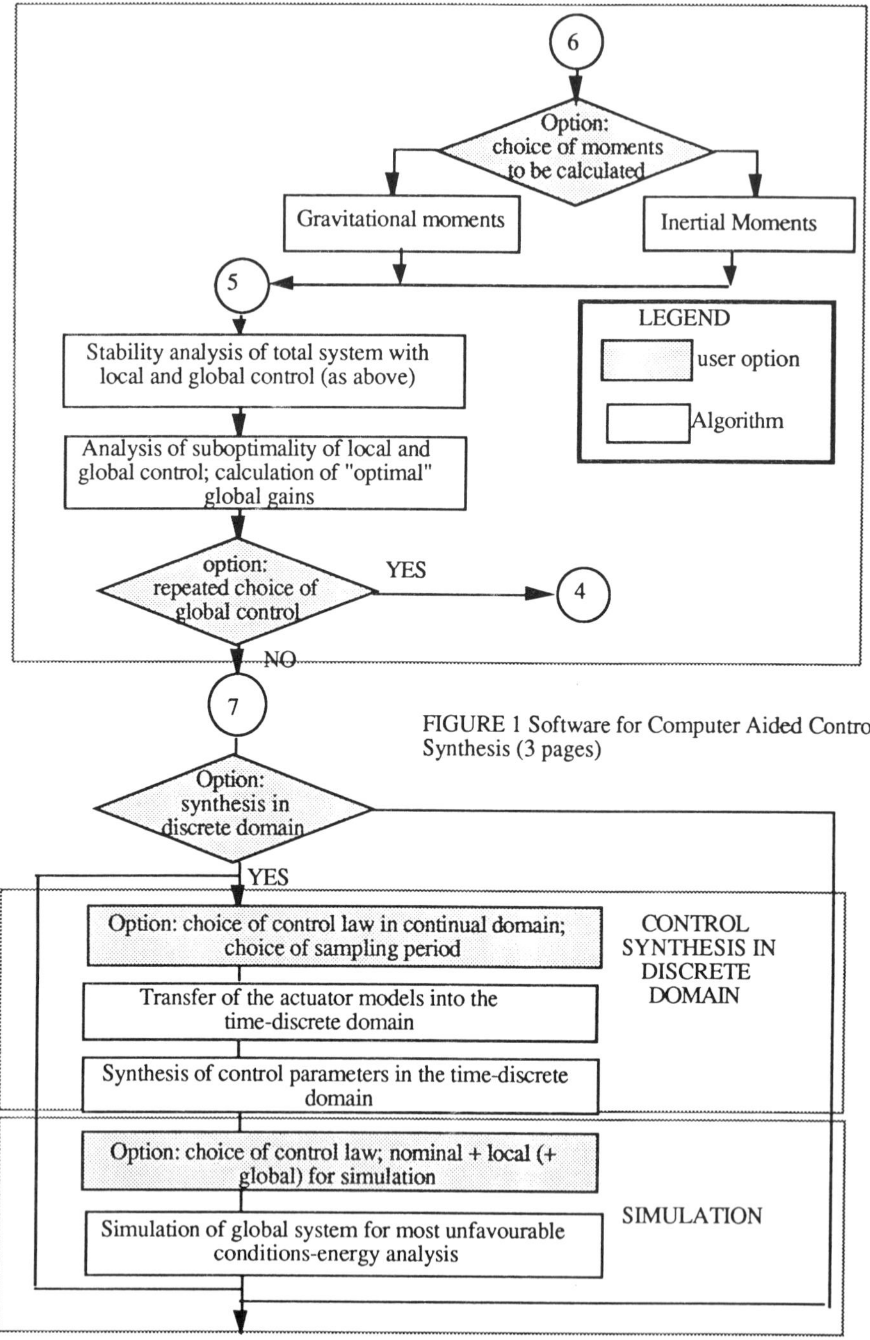

FIGURE 1 Software for Computer Aided Control Synthesis (3 pages)

The algorithm enables the control synthesis for an arbitrary manipulator configuration and arbitrary manipulator type. Thus, the user can synthesize control either for: a) an already built manipulator (evaluation of manipulator), or b) for a manipulator which is under design. In case a) the algorithm can help to improve control for the existing manipulator and can determine the equipment necessary for this improvement. In case b) the user can investigate the influence of the choice of various manipulator parameters upon the control synthesis and the performance of the manipulator, in order to find out the best solution.

2.3. Hierarchical Control Structure

The usual approach in the control of manipulation robots included in flexible manufacturing cells is by hierarchical decomposition of the control task. This means that the robot control system is decomposed into hierarchical levels. This control structure comprises three control levels [32]:

The *Strategical* control level concerns the problem of trajectory planning in the given complex environment. Using the information from various sensors (visual, tactile etc.) the strategical control has to plan the trajectory of the robot hand in order to accomplish the robotic task given by the higher control level or from the operator. Output of this control level is a specified path in external (hand) coordinates.

The *Tactical* control level has to perform the mapping from external (hand) coordinates into internal (joint) coordinates of the robot, i.e. to compute the joint trajectories of the robot. In doing this the tactical control level has to take into account the state of the sensors.

The *Executive* control level has to ensure the tracking of the joint trajectories specified by the tactical control level. This level might include control algorithms which take into account various dynamic effects of the robotic system, in order to compensate for the dynamics of the robot. The output signals of this level are sent to actuators which drive joints of the robot.

2.4. The Software Development System (SDS) for Robotic Controllers [33]

The software development system for robotic controllers (RC) is primarily aimed at generating robot models appropriate for implementation on microprocessors. The SDS is usually located on the host computer, although it might also be put directly to the controller itself. In the latter case, on imposing robot parameters, the robot programs would become "self-generated", implying that such a robot controller may be called "universal". The global SDS organization is shown in Fig. 2. Upon imposing initial requirements, such as kinematic configuration and dynamic parameters, the model "design" begins. It involves the generation of symbolic expressions describing the kinematic and dynamic models of the robot. In addition, the model "design" includes the optimization of the trigonometric expressions in order to evaluate the minimal number of numeric operations. The last part of the SDS is the model "coding" module. It produces an output source program appropriate for compilation, linking and location in the robot controller. The SDS provides for the generation of the linearized dynamic model and the sensitivity model, in addition to the kinematic and the nonlinear dynamic model. Linearized models are important in the application of highly developed linear control theory, while the models of sensitivity with respect to the variation of robot parameters are directly applicable in adaptive control algorithms and examination of the control robustness.

The tactical control level involves the transformation of external (world) coordinates into the joint coordinates using the kinematic model. The execution level usually performs the function of digital servosystems enabling the tracking of the desired trajectories. This level, however, usually includes compensation of the robot model nonlinearities, and therefore requires an approximate or even exact dynamic model. The time-distribution analysis (TDA) module determines the kinematic models, taking into account parameters of the mechanism and the actuators, as well as representative manipulation tasks (with given payload mass, velocities and accelerations). The space-distribution analysis (SDA) module determines how to distribute the model components on several parallel processor units. The inputs of this module are the elements of dynamic model matrices generated in symbolic form as subroutines, which are called "subtasks". Since the subtasks are independent each on the other, the search problem (which subtask to adjoin to which processor unit) is not very complicated. Given the number of processors n_p and the execution time of each subtask t_l (l=l,...,L) with L being the number of relevant model elements), the SDS determines the optimal distribution of subtasks among processors so that their execution times become as equal as possible.

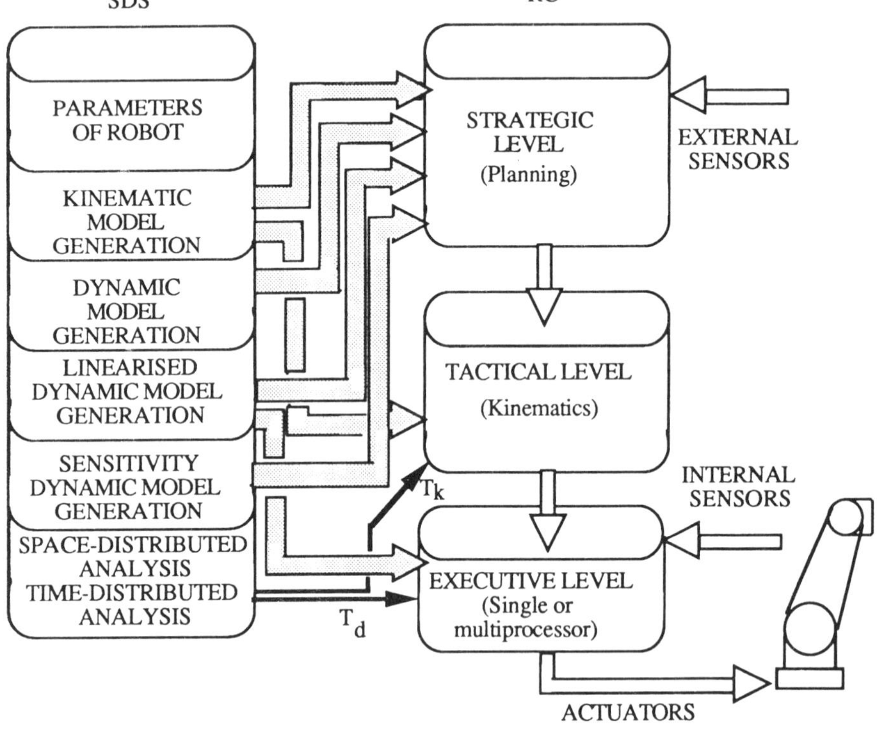

Figure 2 Software Development System

2.5. Adaptive Control Algorithms [34, 35, 36, 37]

Recently a number of papers have been published dealing with the problem of dynamic control of manipulation robots with variable parameters. Two general approaches are well known: robust nonadaptive control and adaptive control. Particularly, in last few years, many papers has been published on adaptive control for robotic systems. These adaptive controls have to solve the problem of parameter variation i.e. to ensure satisfactory performance of the robotic system if its parameters change.

An analysis of the various forms of adaptive indirect algorithms from the standpoint of numerical complexity and quality of trajectories tracking yields: local adaptive decentralised feedback with various forms of adaptive (decentralised or centralised) feedback control, local non-adaptive decentralised feedback control (fixed feedback gains) with adaptive feedforward control, and the development of implicit self-tuning control strategies as one possibility for simplified and efficient procedures for adaptive control synthesis

Indirect decentralised adaptive control includes:

a) An estimation of unknown dynamic parameters of the robot payload using recursive least square methods

(i) a complete estimation model using the sensitivity robot model with fast symbolic computations
(ii) a complete estimation model using dynamic models of robot terminal-link with fast symbolic computations,

b) The synthesis of decentralised self-tuning control

- main control structure:
dynamic compensator ("feedforward" control) + local feedback control

(i) decentralised adaptive control with adaption in feedback loop
(ii) decentralised adaptive control with adaption in feedforward loop
(iii)decentralized adaptive control with simultaneous adaptation in feedback and feedforward loop

- the synthesis of feedforward and local feedback control is accomplished with:

(i) a calculation of the regressive matrix in the estimation model depending on real-time sensor data
(ii) a calculation of the regressive matrix in the estimation model depending on nominal data.

The implementation of decentralized adaptive control:

- the possibility of using two different methods for the compensation of driving torques: driving torque measurement in terminal-link by torque sensor and calculation of approximative control variation.

- the alternative possibility of calculating internal robot accelerations: using approximation by nominal acceleration, accelerometer, velocity signal differentiation with filtration, filtration of estimation model by stable first-order filter.

- Algorithms of decentralized adaptive indirect control (specially with driving torque measurement and off-line calculation of regression matrix) absolutely satisfying real-time conditions for implementation on modern microprocessor control systems.

Except in very special tasks, we can conclude that recent industrial applications do not require adaptive controllers of industrial robots.

3. SIMULATION AND DYNAMIC CONTROL OF ROBOTIZED MANUFACTURING CELLS

3.1. Introduction

Many software packages for the simulation of flexible manufacturing cells have been developed in the past few years. The benefits of using such software packages are numerous. For example the simulation of flexible manufacturing cells (FMC) may be used to speed up the design of FMC, selecting NC machines and robots, the simulation is also used to test control of the FMC at the higher control level, i.e. to test synchronization of all subsystems in the FMC and so on. In the majority of existing software packages for the simulation of FMC, robots and NC machines are usually modelled in the form of finite automata [38, 39]. Such models of subsystems are useful for fast testing of the highest control level of FMC, i.e. by using such models we may relatively simply check synchronization of all machines, conveyers, buffers and robots. This approach is usually satisfactory for NC machines, conveyors etc., since their dynamics do not have significant influence upon the complete system performance. However, this does not hold for robotic systems, due to their highly nonlinear dynamic behaviour. Actually, robot behaviour highly depends on the dynamic regime and it varies for various positions, speeds and accelerations of the robot joints [40]. On the other hand, it is often required that the software package for simulation of FMC can answer to the following questions: could each robot in the particular FMC reach all desired positions in the working space (i.e. are all subsystems properly located in the FMC), are structure of the robots properly selected, could each robot find its paths, etc. This means that the software packages for simulation of FMC have to include kinematic models of the robots and geometric models of all subsystems. Many packages enable testing of FMC's "geometry", but there are quite a few which include kinematic models of robots [38, 41].

3.2. Hierarchical Control of Flexible Manufacturing Cells

The control of an FMC is always hierarchical. The basic hierarchical control levels are as follows [32]:

a) The highest control level has to distribute the tasks (operations) to subsystems in the FMC: to robots, NC machines, conveyors etc. The task of the highest control level is to synchronize all machines and robots in time and in space. One of the tasks of this control level might be to coordinate two or more robots in the space if they share the common work space, but often this task is associated with lower control levels. The output of the highest control level are the tasks which have to be implemented by robots and NC machines in FMC.

b) The strategical control level of robots has to plan the robot paths in such a way as to realize the task imposed by the highest control level. The strategical level has to ensure robot motion between the obstacles in its work space. Practically the strategical control level has to plan the paths of the robot gripper. One of the tasks of the strategical control level is to minimize the time required for the travel of the robot hand between two imposed positions in the work space or along the desired path. This level also plans the motion of the robot in some complex tasks, e.g. in assembling tasks. The strategic control level also plans the forces which the robot has to apply upon the objects in the work space and so on.

c) Tactical control level of robots has to realize the mapping of the desired trajectory of the robot given in external coordinates into so-called internal coordinates of the robot (the internal coordinates represent coordinates of the robot joints). Namely, the desired motion of the robot is realized by movements of the robot joints driven by corresponding actuators. Therefore, it is necessary to compute the movements of the robot joints which correspond to the imposed motion of the gripper (which has been defined at the strategical control level).

d) The executive control level has to realize the trajectories imposed by the tactical control level. At this control level, based on the imposed trajectories of the joint coordinates and on information on the actual state of the robot (obtained via corresponding sensors at the robot), the control signals for the actuators are generated.

This hierarchical control structure is simulated in the software package as a control of any FMC imposed by the user.

3.3. Description of Software Package

The software package for the simulation of FMS enables the simulation of various FMSs consisting of up to two robots, several NC machines, conveyors, buffers and various sensors. In the so-called initialization phase, the user has to prepare input data on all the subsystems which he wants to include in a particular FMC. The software package for the simulation of the FMS consists of several modules. Here we shall briefly describe these modules.

(a) The programme module for the simulation of the highest control level simulates the control of the complete FMC i.e. synchronization of all subsystems in the FMC. In the first phase of simulation package development, we have adopted the concept of so-called non-dynamic control of an FMC which is realized by Petri-nets. Using Petri-nets it is possible to achieve synchronization of all the subsystems within the FMC in a relatively simple way. However, in future work we intend to include the so-called dynamic control of the FMC at the highest control level, i.e. we shall include control of the FMC which takes into account the dynamic characteristics of subsystems (specially robots). However, other modules are independent from the module for simulation of the highest control level.

(b) The programme module for the simulation of NC machines, conveyers, and buffers simulates these subsystems in a simple manner using models in the form of finite automata. Actually, NC machines are simulated by the time periods which they require for the execution of the various programs and operations within each program. The package allows the imposition of an arbitrary number of varying NC machines and conveyers with arbitrary locations for these subsystems in the working space. During simulation the user may impose the various failures of each machine.

(c) The programme module for the simulation of sensors allows arbitrary location of the sensors at the working scene. In the first phase of the simulation package development we have included three types of so-called external sensors (sensors which are not mounted on robots and NC machines): tactile sensors, proximity sensors and cameras. We have also included various types of so-called internal sensors, e.g. potentiometers or shaft-encoders in robot joints, tachometers, accelerometers, tactile sensors, on-off sensors etc. The user also may introduce failures on each sensor in the system to test the behaviour of the control system in such situations.

(d) The package includes the programme module for the graphic presentation of FMC. By this model the users get a visual presentation of the scene in 3-D graphics. Each subsystem (e.g. robot, NC machine, conveyer, etc.) may be represented by a set of regular geometric bodies. The user controls the drawing of a scene at arbitrary moment during the simulation, or he may require graphical representation of the scene in discrete moments (e.g. the scene may be represented each 0.5 sec during simulation).

(e) The main programme module in the package is the module for the simulation of robots. The package enables the simulation of up to two robots of arbitrary type and structure. The module for the simulation of robots consists of several sub-modules. Actually, the package enables the simulation of the complete control unit for each robot. Each submodule simulates one level in hierarchical control [42] of manipulation robots:

(i)The package includes various algorithms for path planning of the robot hand at the strategical control level [43]. By these algorithms the robot controller (i.e. its strategic control level) plans the paths of the robot hand in the presence of obstacles in the working space. The output of this control level is the path of the hand which has to be realized by the lower control levels.

(ii)The next submodule simulates the so-called tactical control level of a robot controller. At this control level, the hand trajectory is mapped into joint trajectories. This control level has to solve the so-called inverse kinematic model of a particular robot. For the selected structure of the robot the package generates a kinematic model in symbolic form and automatically solves the inverse kinematic problem [44]. The output of the tactical control level are the desired trajectories of robot joints.

(iii)The submodule for the simulation of executive control level enables the simulation of various non-dynamic and dynamic control laws for manipulation robots. The task of the executive control level is to realize the desired trajectories of the robot joints which are imposed by the tactical control level. Using the separate programme package

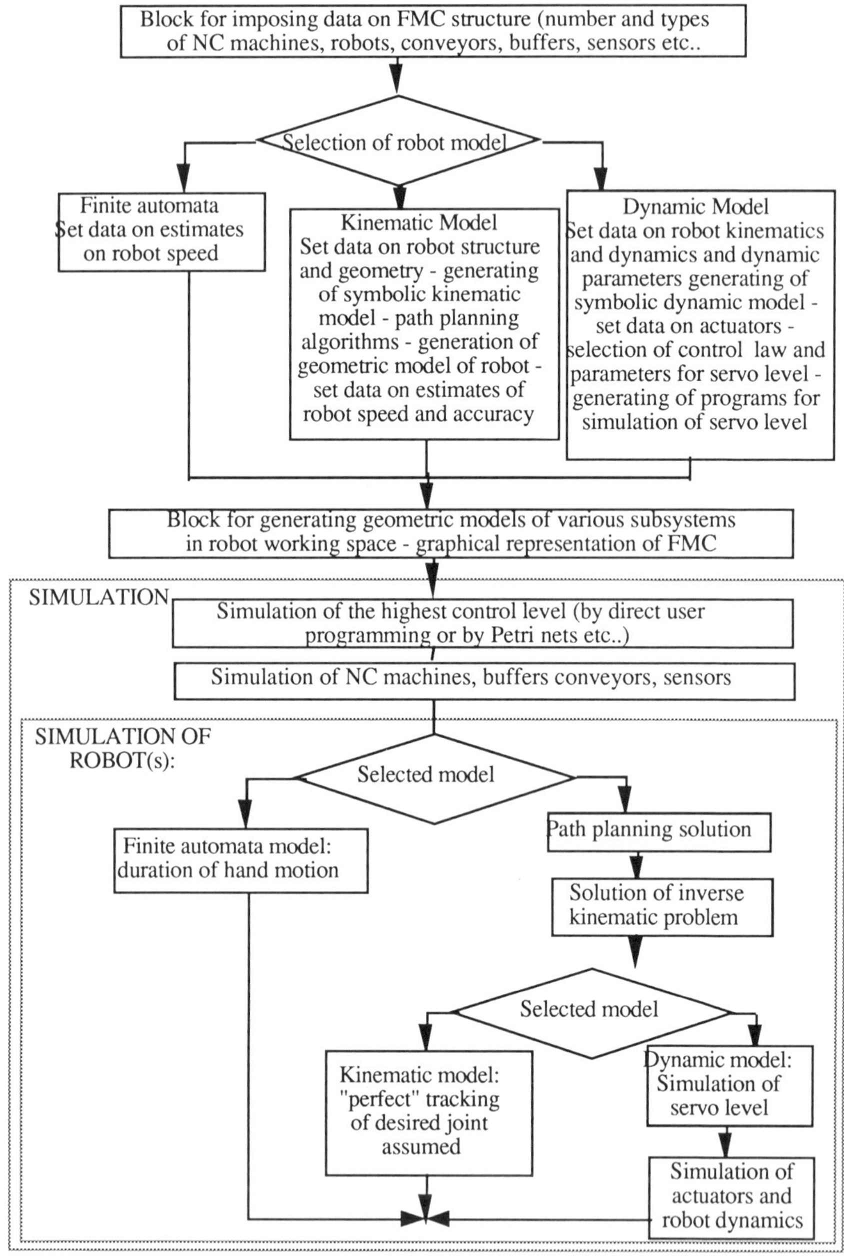

Figure 3 Global Flowchart of Simulation of Robotic FMC

for the synthesis of control for manipulation robots [45], the user may synthesize various control laws for his particular robot and then, simulate robot performance with the selected control law and control parameters within the particular FMC (in which the robot should be implemented). The package includes the synthesis and simulation of non-dynamic control laws consisting of local servos around the robot joints [42]. However, various dynamic control laws, i.e. control laws which take into account robot dynamics, may be synthesized and simulated. For example, the synthesis and simulation of global control in the form of force feedback or on-line computation of robot dynamics is included [40, 46], as well as the so-called controller-based-on-computed-torque method [47], robust control [48], etc In Fig. 3. a global flowchart of the described software package is given.

3.4. Conclusion

The developed software system offers some obvious advantages over existing software tools for the simulation and design of an FMC [49, 50]. As already mentioned this package maybe used either for the design of various FMCs (selection of robots and other subsystems, allocation of robots in working space, etc.), or for the synthesis of appropriate control at both top control level (programming of FMC) and at lower levels of robots controllers. It is obvious that the simulation of robots using their dynamic models requires much longer processor time than simulation by finite automata model and by kinematic modelling. Also the simulation of dynamic models requires knowledge on all the parameters of the robotic systems which may complicate the user's job. The more precise the applied model, the more specific data on robotic systems have to be supplied, but the benefits that should be expected from the simulation are also increased.

The user may use these model options step by step. First he may test only the highest control level using the finite automata model of the robot. This simulation is relatively fast and the user can test whether he can roughly coordinate all subsystems within his FMC. Actually, the user can program the sequence of subtasks (operations, movements of the robot hands etc.), and then the parallel actions are recognized and better synchronization and coordination of subsystems may be achieved, taking into account only rough estimates of the robot capabilities. Next, the user has to specify all the relevant data for modelling the FMC geometry: geometric models of all subsystems, their locations on the scene, data on robot kinematics and so on. The execution of the FMC's tasks is simulated using robot models of type b). Through this, the path planning algorithms can be tested as well as trajectory generation level in the robot controllers and the coordination between the robots and other subsystems may be improved.

Finally, the user has to impose data on the robot dynamic parameters and actuators, as well as on the executive (servo) control level. Then the user can simulate the performance of the FMC using the dynamic model of the robots. Through this a complete insight in the robot capabilities may be obtained, for example how fast and how accurate can the robotic system perform each particular movement. In this way one can test whether the selected robot and its controller are capable of satisfying all requirements in a specific FMC. The control at both path planning level and at the servo level may be improved in order to meet these requirements. On the other hand, synchronization and coordination of the robot(s) with the other subsystems can be significantly improved. In fact, such simulation enables the programming and control at the highest control level of FMC in such a way that the actual dynamic capabilities of the robots are taken into account.

REFERENCES

[1] Uicker J.J., "On Dynamic Analysis of Spatial Linkages Using 4x4 Matrices", Ph.D. Dissertation, Northwestern University, Evanstone, (1965).

[2] Kahn M.E., "The Near Minimum Time Control of Open Loop Articulated Kinematic Chains",Ph.D. Thesis, Stanford University, MEMO AIM. 106,(1969).

[3] Woo L.S., and Reundenstein F., "Dynamic Analysis of Mechanisms Using Screw Coordinates", ASME J. of Engineering for Industry, (1971).

[4] Mahil S.S., "On the Application of Lagrange's Method to the Description of Dynamic Systems", IEEE Trans. SMC, Vol. SMC-12, No. 6, pp. 877-890, (1982).

[5] Renaud M., "Contribution a l-Etude de la Modelisation et de la Commande des Systemes Mechaniques Articules", These de Doc. - Ing., Toulouse, (1975).

[6] Kane T.R., Wang C.F., "On the Derivation of Equations of Motion", J. Soc. for Ind. and Appl. Math., Vol. 13, pp. 487-492, (1965).

[7] Huston R.L., Passerello C.E., Harlow M.W., "Dynamics of Multi-Rigid-Body Systems", ASME J. Appl. Mechanics, Vol. 45, pp. 889-894, (1978).

[8] Stepanenko Yu., Dynamics of Spatial Mechanisms, (in Russian), Mathematical Institute, Beograd, (1974).

[9] Vukobratovic M., and Stepanenko Y., "Mathematical Models of General Anthropomorphic Systems",Math. Biosc.,Vol. 17, pp. 191-242, (1973).

[10] Walker M.W., and Orin D.E., "Efficient Dynamic Computer Simulation of Robotic Mechanisms", JACC, Charlotteville, (1981).

[11] Luh J.Y.S., Walker M.W., and Paul R.P.C., "On-Line Computational Scheme for Mechanical Manipulators", ASME J. Dynamic Systems, Meas. and Control, Vol. 102, No. 2, pp. 69-76, (1980).

[12] Vukobratovic M., and Potkonjak V., "Contribution to Automatic Forming of Active Chain Models via Lagrangian Form", ASME J. Appl. Mech., No. 1, (1979).

[13] Hollerbach M., "A Recursive Lagrangian Formulation of Manipulator Dynamics and a Comparative Study of Dynamics Formulation Complexity",
IEEE Trans. on SMC, 10, No. 11, pp. 730-736, (1980).

[14] Aldon M.J., and Liegeois A., "Generation et Programmation Automatique des Equations de Lagrange des Robots et Manipulators", Rapport de Rechearche, INRIA, (1984).

[15] Vukobratovic M., and Kircanski N., Real-Time Dynamics of Manipulation Robots, Series: Scientific Foundations of Robotics, Springer-Verlag, (1984).

[16] Renaud N., "An Efficient Iterative Analytical Procedure for Obtaining a Robot Manipulator Dynamic Model", Proc. 1st Int. Symp. Robotics Research, Bretton Woods, New Hampshire, USA, (1983).

[17] Neuman P.Ch., and Muray J.J., "Computational Robot Dynamics: Foundations and Applications", J. Robotic Systems, Vol. 2, No. 4, pp. 425-452, (1985).

[18] Popov P.E., Vereschagin A.F., and Zenkevitch L.S., Manipulation Robots: Dynamics and Algorithms, (in Russian), Nauka, Moscow, (1978).

[19] Timcenko A., Vukobratovic M., and Kircanski N., "A Multistage Algorithm for Manipulator Efficient Symbolic Model Generation", The International Journal of Robotic Research, (to appear in 1990).

[20] Kircanski N., Timcenko A., Jovanovic Y., Kircanski M., Vukobratovic M., and Milunov R., "Computation of Customized Symbolic Robot Models on Peripheral Array Processors", IEEE Journ. for Robotics and Automation, (to appear in 1990).

[21] Kahn M.E. and Roth B., "The Near Minimum Time Control of Open Loop Articulated Kinematic Chains", Trans. of the ASME Journal of Dynamic Systems, Measurement and Control, Sept. pp. 164-172, (1971).

[22] Vukobratovic M., and Stokic D., Control of Manipulation Robots: Theory and Application, Series: Scientific Fundamentals of Robotics, Vol. 2, Monograph, Springer-Verlag, Berlin, (1982).

[23] Vukobratovic M., and Stokic D., "Contribution to the Decoupled Control of Large-Scale Mechanical Systems", Automatica, No. 1, (1980).

[24] Paul R.C., Modelling, Trajectory Calculation and Servoing of a Computer Controlled Arm, A.I. Memo 177, Stanford Artificial Intelligence Laboratory, Stanford University, Sept. 1972, also in Russian, Nauka, Moscow, (1976).

[25] Vukobratovic M., and Stokic D., "Dynamic Control of Manipulators via Load-Feedback", Journal of Mechanism and Machine Theory, Vol. 17, No. 2, pp. 107-118, (1982).

[26] Luh Y.S.J., Fisher D.W., and Paul I.P.R., "Joint Torque Control by a Direct Feedback for Industrial Robots", IEEE Trans. on Automatic Control, Vol. AC-28, No. 2, (1983).

[27] Raibert H.M., and Craig J.J., "Hybrid Position/Force Control of Manipulators", Journal of Dynamic Systems, Measurement and Control, Trans. of the ASME, Vol. 103, No. 2, pp. 126-133, 1981.

[28] Roessler J., "A Decentralized Hierarchical Control Concept for Large-Scale Systems", Proc. of the II IFAC Symp. on Large-Scale Systems, pp. 171-179, Toulouse, (1980).

[29] Miyazaki F., Arimoto S., Takegaki M., and Maeda Y., "Sensory Feedback Based on the Artificial Potential for Robot Manipulators", Preprint of the 9th IFAC World Congress, Vol. 6, pp. 27-32, Budapest, July, (1984).

[30] Stokic D., and Vukobratovic M., "Robustness of Decentralized Robot Control to Payload Variation", Journal of Robotic Systems, Vol. 7, No. 2, (1988).

[31] Vukobratovic M., Stokic D., and Kircanski N., Non-Adaptive and Adaptive Control of Manipulation Robots, Series: Scientific Fundamentals of Robots, Vol. 5., Monograph, Springer-Verlag, Berlin, (1985).

[32] Medvedov V.S., Leskov A.G., and Yuschenko, Control Systems of Manipulati- on Robots (in Russian), Nauka, Moscow, (1978).

[33] Vukobratovic M., "General Structure of Software for Modelling and Control of Manipulation Robots" (in Russian), Technical Cybernetics, AN SSSR, No. 3, Moscow, (1987).

[34] Vukobratovic M., Stokic D., and Kircanski N., "Towards Non-Adaptive and Adaptive Control of Manipulation Robots", IEEE Trans. on Automatic Control, Vol. AC-29, No. 9, 841-844, (1984).

[35] Vukobratovic M., and Kircanski N., "An Approach to Adaptive Control of Robotic Manipulators", Automatica, Vol. 21, No. 6, (1985).

[36] Timofeev A.V., and Ekalo Yu.V., "Stability and Stabilization of Programmed Motions of Robots", (in Russian), Automatica and Remote Control, No. 20, (1976).

[37] Kiovo A.J., and Guo T.H., "Adaptive Linear Controller for Robotic Manipulators", IEEE Trans. on Automatic Control, Vol. 28, No. 20, (1983).

[38] Vojnovic M., et.all. "An ESPRIT Project in Advanced Robotics", 3rd International Conference on Advanced Robotics, '87 ICAR, Versailles, October, (1987).

[39] Zenkevich L.S., and Dimitriev A.A., "Mathematical and Program Support for Adaptive Robots for Assembling", The Second Yugoslav-Soviet Symposium on Applied Robotics and Flexible Automation, Arandjelovac, (1984).

[40] Vukobratovic M., and Stokic D., "Is Dynamic Control Needed in Robotic Systems and if so, to what Extent?", International Journal of Robotic Research, No. 2, (1983).

[41] Spur G., et all., "Planning and Programming of Robot Integrated Production Cells", ESPRIT Technical Conference, Brussels, (1987).

[42] Vukobratovic M., and Stokic D., Applied Control of Manipulation Robots: Analysis, Synthesis and Exercises, Textbook, Springer-Verlag, Berlin, (1989).

[43] Stokic D., Vukobratovic M., and Devedzic V., "Expert System for Synthesis of Dynamic Control of Manipulation Robots", CISM-IFToMM Conference on Robots and Manipulators. "Romansy 88", Udine, Italy, (1988).

[44] Kircanski V.M., Vukobratovic K.M., Kircanski M.N., and Timcenko M.A., "A New Program Package for Generation of Efficient Manipulator Kinematic and Dynamic Evaluations in Symbolic Form", Robotica, July, (1988).

[45] Vukobratovic K.M., and Stokic M.D., "A Procedure for Interactive Dynamic Control Synthesis of Manipulators", Trans. on Systems, Man, and Cybernetics, Sept./Oct. issue, (1982).

[46] Vukobratovic K.M., and Stokic M.D., Control of Manipulation Robots: Theory and Application, Series: Scientific Fundamentals of Robotics, No. 2, Monograph, Springer-Verlag, Berlin, (1982).

[47] Paul R.C., "Modelling, Trajectory Calculation and Servoing of A Computer Controlled Arm", A.I. Memo 177, Stanford Artificial Intelligence Laboratory Stanford University, September, (1972).

[48] Asada H., and Slotine E.J.J., "Robot Analysis and Control", John Wiley and Sons, New York, (1986).

[49] Vukobratovic K.M., and Stokic M.D., "Software Package for Simulation of Flexible Manufacturing Systems", Technical Cybernetics, Moscow, (in Russian), No. 3, (1989).

[50] Stokic M.D., Vukobratovic K.M., and Lekovic D.J., "Modelling of Robots and their Environment in Simulation of Flexible Manufacturing Cells", IFAC Symp. on Information Control Problems in Manufacturing Technology, Madrid, (1989).

Industrial Applications of Artificial Intelligence
J.L. Alty and L.I. Mikulich (Editors)
Elsevier Science Publishers B.V. (North-Holland)

MULTIPLE META-LEVEL ARCHITECTURE AND MAN-MACHINE INTERACTION IN A KNOWLEDGE-BASED SYSTEM

S. OHSUGA

Research Centre for Advanced Science and Technology
The University of Tokyo,
4-6-1 Komaba, Meguro-ku,
Tokyo 153,
Japan.

ABSTRACT: A conceptual framework for a knowledge-based system named KAUS (Knowledge Acquisition and Utilization System) is discussed. Because of the nature of problem solving, flexibility and evolutionality are required for knowledge-based systems as support tools, and the systems must have multiple meta-level architectures to meet these conditions. The role of the meta-level operation and the method of man-machine interaction in KAUS are discussed.

1. INTRODUCTION

In this paper we discuss first, the conceptual framework of a knowledge-based system which we designed to aid human problem solving. The system is named KAUS (Knowledge Acquisition and Utilization System) [6].

Because of the nature of problem solving, flexibility and evolutionality are required for knowledge-based systems as support tools and the systems must have a multiple meta-level architecture to meet these conditions. We discuss then the role of meta-level operation and finally a method of man-machine interaction with the meta-level system. This leads us to a new interpretation of display organization such as multi-window systems. As, among various types of problems, design is a typical one that needs knowledge processing technology, we focus our attention on the design problem and intelligent CAD systems in this paper.

2. META-LEVELS IN INTELLIGENT CAD SYSTEMS

In the paper [4], the author asserted, with a few examples, that in order for CAD systems to be able to support total design, they must be able to represent a total design activity explicitly, where the design activity is represented typically as shown in Fig. 1. The objective of design is to create a model of an object that satisfies a set of requirements presented in the form of functionalities. Here, in this paper, we mean by functionality a property, function, and behavior in the given environment, in relation to other entities, etc. of this object. Both model analysis/evaluation and model modification involve model transformations in the computer. Thus, to represent total design activity, a CAD systems must be able to represent:

(1) an object model,
(2) various model transformation rules, and
(3) a design process.

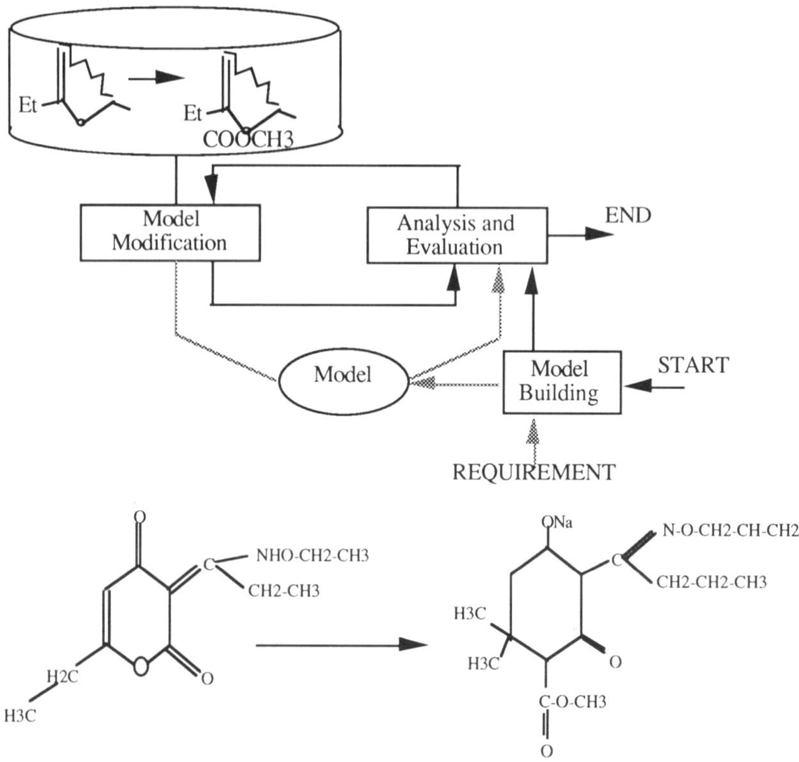

Figure 1 Typical Problem Solving Process

Each of these representations must be defined at different levels. A transformation rule includes the object model as the object of transformation and therefore it is at a higher level than the object model. A design process representation contains a set of transformation rules because a design process can be represented by an ordered set of different knowledge sources, each of which is composed of a set of transformation rules. Hence the design process representation is at a still higher level than the transformation rules.

If we intend to represent all of them by the same language, we need a higher order logic [1]. A higher order logic involves higher order predicates which include some other predicate(s) as the objects of description. But it is not easy to implement higher order logic in computers. It is difficult to assure the processing efficiency and completeness. It makes the system complicated.

In [4] we tried another method. We intended to represent the first two items of the requirements presented above by means of a knowledge representation language. It is possible to design a language that meets every necessary condition for representing these two items while ensuring their processibility. We actually designed such a language named Multi-Layer Logic (MLL) [3]. We used first order predicate logic as the basis of the language but we expanded it to represent any data structure explicitly because an ordinary design object has a very complex structure as well as a set of functionalities. A complex object structure needs to be represented in the form of predicates. MLL has such a syntax such that every variable included in MLL formula is given a domain set. The set is defined in mathematics axiomatically [2]. The definition of this axiomatic set is very wide and includes data structures (as used in computer science).

Hence, the domain set can be a data structure. Let a predicate be $P(x_1, x_2, x_n)$. Then $[Qx_i / x_i]$ $P(x_1, x_2,.... x_n)$ is an MLL formula where Q is the quantifier to denote either A (for all) or E (for some) and X_i is a domain of the variable x_i, (i = 1,2,...,n) and can be a data structure. For example, a set of all n-level hierarchical structures that are generated from the given base set Z is represented as *nZ where * is a reserved symbol to denote an operation to generate a power set (of Z) and *n means to repeat the operation n times. Thus $[Ex_i/ {*nZ}]$ $P(x_i)$ means that some n-level hierarchical structure in the set generated from Z has the property P. In the case when the data structure X is a specific hierarchical structure, [Qx/X] means 'for some x in a set of nodes immediately lower the node X'. The data structure is combined with the description in the form of predicates in this way.

Thus an object model is a set of MLL formulas that contain the data structures representing the object structure or its components. A model transformation rule is also an MLL implicative formula composed of a special predicate to apply a specific structure transformation rule and the predicates including the data structures before and after the transformation. The structural transformation rules are defined outside of the system and can be added at anytime to the system.

The third item, that is, the representation of a design process, requires us to use another method of representation. We introduce the meta-level architecture. This is equivalent to the use of a limited class of higher order logic. This class is defined by restricting the use of some part of the syntax of higher order logic that makes the implementation of the logic difficult. Concretely speaking, it inhibits using such a representation which includes variables appearing both in the inside and in the outside of an inner predicate at the same time. Here the inner predicate is a predicate included in a higher order predicate. Let a high order predicate be of the form, $P(x_1, \ldots, x_k, R(y_1, \ldots, y_m))$. In MLL, it is inhibited to use a predicate in which some x_i, (i = l,...,k) is the same as some y_j, (j = l,...,m) when y_j is a free variable in R. A predicate of the form P(...,x,.... [Ax/X] R(...,x,...)) is permitted because x within R is bounded. The meaning of this restriction is discussed in the next section.

With this restriction, the evaluation of the inner predicate can be performed independently from that of the outer predicate. Thus it is possible to separate the inner predicates and the outer predicates. The set of predicates that contain only terms, (that is, constants, variables, and functions) but don't contain the other predicate are located in the object-level while those that include some object-level predicate(s) are arranged in a different level that is immediately above the object level. This upper level forms a meta-level. Each object-level predicate that need to describe something via meta-level knowledge can be represented by an identifier (ID) in the meta-level, for example, by a rule number, while the predicate body is located in the object-level. A predicate that includes these ID's is the meta-predicate and arranged in the meta-level.

With this representation, meta-level knowledge appears the same as the object level knowledge, that is, meta-level knowledge is also represented in the form of first order MLL. There can be some predicates that are used at any level in the same form. For example, a predicate that finds a path between two nodes in the given graph is used both in the object-level and in the meta-level. Let it be represented by GRAPH-PATHFINDING (graph, init-node, term-node, path). It produces, however, different effects in different levels because the graphs have different meanings in different levels. For example, the graph in the object-level may represent a road map in the physical world while the graph in the meta-level shows the relations of the rules that manipulate this object-level graph.

3. REPRESENTATION AND CONTROL OF DESIGN PROCESSES

The meta-level organization plays various important roles in a knowledge-based system.

Learning, scheduling, evaluation and handling of ambiguous information, model operations, and so forth, need the meta-level operations because these functions need the descriptions of, and the operations to, the object-level knowledge. But representation and control of the problem solving process which also requires meta-level operations is one of immediate importance for an intelligent system to assure its capability to cope with the large scale problems which arise in the real world. We focus our attention in this issue in this paper.

Any design activity, or in the more general sense, any problem solving activity, has a specific way of solving the problem. It forms a problem solving process. The third item in the requirement discussed in section 2 is to represent it explicitly.

Let a knowledge base be composed of a set of rules and/or facts that are concerned with the object problem. If the system does not have any information at all to control the use of these operations, it can be very inefficient and in some cases where the knowledge base is large we can not obtain a solution in finite time. Moreover, it is not easy to define rules and facts to assure the correct operation of the system, nor easy to manage the knowledge base. This is the reason why we need to represent the problem solving process as discussed in section 2. In order to reduce the time that would be spent by the system in vain, that is, to avoid the selection of less significant knowledge at run time for problem solving, it is necessary to provide a mechanism to classify the knowledge properly into different set of rules/facts and control the selection of these sets. It is desirable that each subset is as small as possible but, as the matter of course, must include all the necessary knowledge to assure the correct operation of the system. There must be some knowledge to classify the knowledge base and methods to represent the classification of the knowledge base. Meta-level organization can be used here. In the following section, each subset of knowledge base is called a knowledge source.

Some expert systems use the frame structure for representing the problem solving process. This structure is decided by the user and once it is decided, restructuring by the system itself is difficult. It is inconvenient because, for some problems, the process structure should be an object of modification. It is discussed in section 5. We need a more flexible system.

Using the capability of MLL to manipulate any data structure, a control structure can be represented as shown in Fig. 2 in the meta-level. It represents the subset of the object-level rules/facts, i.e. knowledge sources, and also their order of application to the object model. Let an ID corresponds to a rule/fact in the object-level and each ID be interpreted as a constant in the meta-level. These ID's form the leaves of the control structure and each intermediate node represents a knowledge source. Attached to any node in this structure is some meta-level knowledge that specifies the use of these knowledge sources. Thus, let problem solving be started from the meta-level (by issuing some question to the meta-level). At the meta-level the proper knowledge source is selected in the proper sequence based on this control structure. Then the control is passed to the object level. The author showed an example of meta-knowledge to perform this operation in [5].

Before closing this section, we need to discuss the effect of restricting the syntax of higher order logic. One of the important characteristics of the meta-level operation is in its capability to define any number of local worlds in the object level. A local world is a unit of activation of object rules/facts in which logical consistency is ensured. In fact, each separate knowledge source forms an independent local world. The independence of the world assures the easy management of the system. Also, with this independence even contradicting rules/facts can be put into the system unless these are put into the same local world. This is quite important because the model-based trial-and-error operation is achieved on the assumption that any hypothetical model can be defined even though it can be contradictory with the existing system. It means also that the different models must belong to the different worlds.

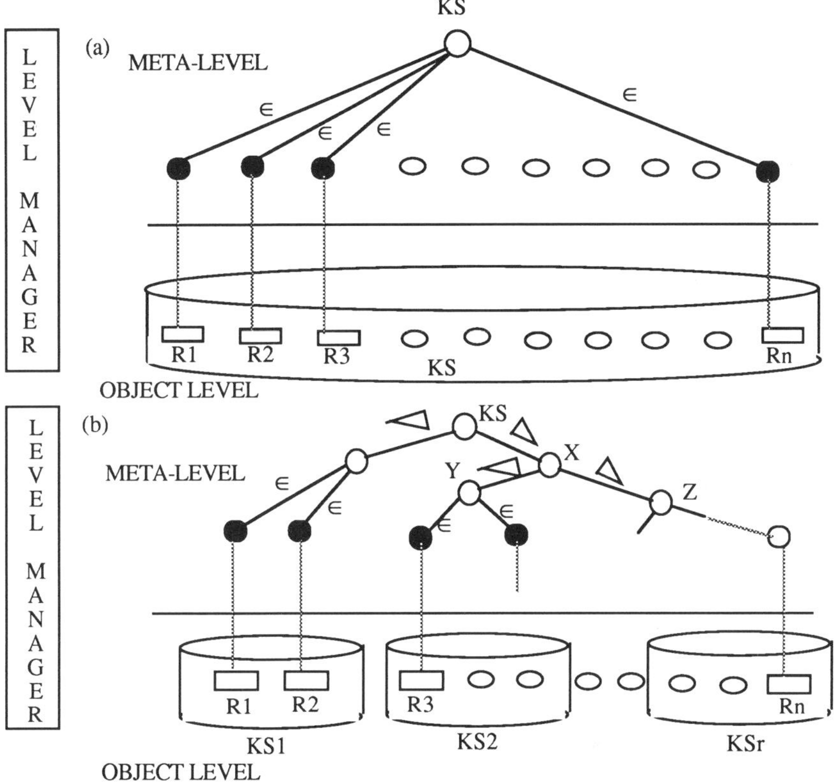

Figure 2 Meta-level Organisation

The independence of any world can be ensured unless information from the outside invades into the world unnoticed. By restricting the syntax of higher order logic as mentioned before, we can prevent information from propagating directly across the border of levels. Without this restriction, the same values may be substituted in the variables appearing both in the inside and outside of inner predicates. It is equivalent to the case, in our KAUS system, that the same value is substituted in the predicates in the object-level and meta-level at the same time. Thus by the inference operation it can happen that some information propagates to the different worlds in the object-level via meta-knowledge and it is very difficult to control. MLL cuts the propagation path by restricting the syntax.

It does not mean that each world is completely isolated but rather these local worlds can be closely related each other under the control of the management system discussed in section 5. The control structure in the meta-level can be the hierarchical structure of which the second lowest nodes defines the local worlds as the set of ID's of object rules/facts and the next higher nodes represent the larger worlds that comprise these local worlds and so on. It extends upward to any level. Through the meta-knowledge that is linked to the next higher nodes in this structure, any local world is related each other but it is under the complete control of the system.

With this independence and controllability, it become possible to check the knowledge base for consistency. Also it makes addition, deletion, and updating of rules/facts easy thus ensuring the evolutionality of the system.

The expressive power of the language becomes lower than ordinary higher order logic because of the restriction in syntax but, as far as the representation and the control of design processes are concerned, there is no inconvenience with this system.

4. ANOTHER EXAMPLE OF THE META-LEVEL OPERATION

In the following we show another example in which the design process is controlled by human being directly which is a different operation mode from that of [3,4]. The system of this example is also being developed and partly running.

This system is an application of KAUS to the design of new chemical materials. The objective of this system is to create new chemical compounds that have an expected biological property. This system is designed to generate a hypothetical chemical structure and to test it for the required property. It starts from an existing compound structure as an incipient model and if the property of the current model is not satisfactory, the chemical structure is modified. The new structure is generated by applying the conversion rules given to the system (Fig. 1). These conversion rules have been created by analyzing the existing instances of chemical reactions collected by chemical experts. Figure 3 shows some examples of the structural conversions that have been made.

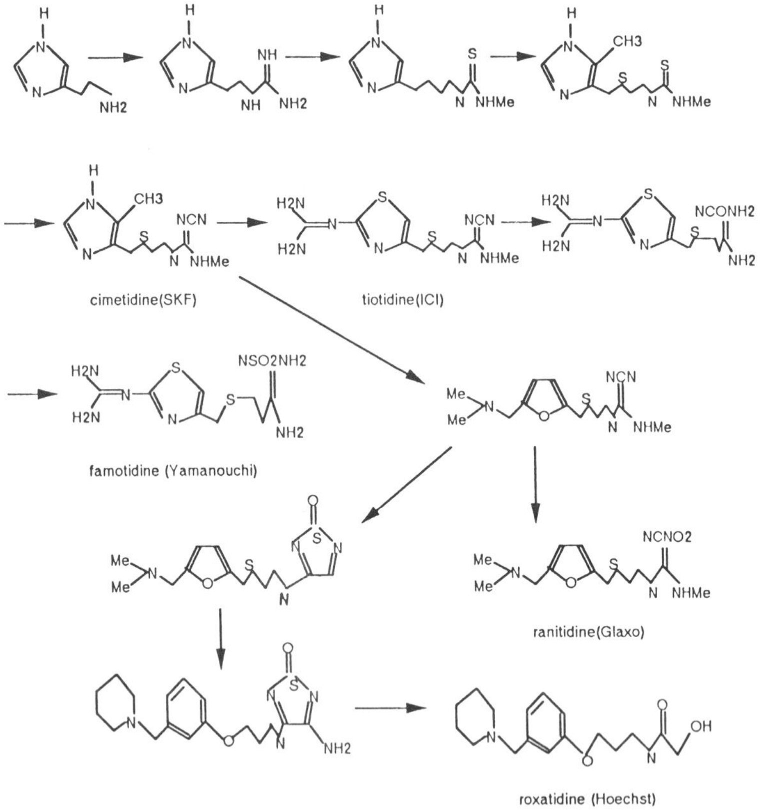

Figure 3 An example of history of conversion of chemical structure (Lead evolution in Histamine-H2 Antagonists, From Y. Inoue) (This figure was given by Prof. Fujita of Kyoto Univ.)

This figure shows two things. First, it shows us the original data from which the human expert (automatically in future) extracts conversion rules and, second, it shows the way that some chemists wish to look for new chemical compound using a knowledge-based system. The total system is a network system in which different computers are involved. Some large computer programs have been developed, in different computer sites, to evaluate the electro-chemical or biological characteristics, such as the biological toxicity of the given chemical structure and are to be involved in the total system. In this system, KAUS is used to generate a new chemical structure as the candidate using the knowledge base and then send the candidate to the other computers to evaluate its characteristics. The result of this evaluation is sent back to KAUS and displayed. The chemical engineer watches the monitor and judges what should be done next .

It is possible in some cases to give the system some rules that decide automatically what to do next based on the results of the evaluation. Then the design activity proceeds automatically to the next cycle as far as the rule is effective. But it is impossible to create all the necessary knowledge for the purpose and chemists wish to keep control in their hands in many cases. Thus cooperation of the knowledge system and human being is necessary and is expected to be effective.

Our colleagues in the chemical group of this project have already collected more than 1,500 such conversion rules. There can be many thousands conversion rules in the future and it is a very time consuming operation to generate chemical structures to come to the final model that meets the requirements. It would be impossible to do this without some control of this operation. We use the meta-level organization here. Each conversion rule is given some properties in relation to the properties of the product structure it generates. For example some conversion rules augment a specific electrochemical or biological property possessed by the prior structure. This is the property of the rule. Thus it is possible to classify the conversion rules into different sets by the properties and to represent it by the data structure in the meta-level. These properties can be represented in MLL formulae in the meta-level and linked to the related nodes of this structure.

On the other hand, the display is created. A lowest level window is created to show the current model together with the prior model to show designers a conversion process. Each model is presented as a combination of a chemical structure and its property. The list of properties corresponding to the different subset of conversion rules is shown in the other window. Thus this window corresponds to the meta-level. Fig. 4 shows an example. If the designer picks up one item in the list, it is issued to the meta-level of the system as the request to apply the conversion rules to affect the specified property. The system responds and specifies the scope of search to the object-level inference mechanism. This mechanism is described in [4,5]. In brief, it is achieved as follows: the inference operation is performed in the meta-level and decides what set of conversion rules (knowledge source) to use in the object-level. It sends the knowledge source name (a subtree node of the control structure) to the inference mechanism in the object-level. This is composed of the searcher and deducer. The former, receiving the knowledge source name from the meta-level inference mechanism, restricts the scope of search in inference in this knowledge source. The object-level system generates a set of candidate chemical compounds and shows them on the screen. If there is more than one candidate, then the designers select one of them for the next operation.

When a query is issued by the human designer through the display, it is possible to perform some deductive operations in the meta-level before selecting the set of object knowledge source instead of linking the query directly with the selection of knowledge sources .

Thus there is a close relationship between the levels in the system and the windows of the multi-window system of the display. In this case, each window is created not for mere convenience sake but with a clear meaning.

5. MULTIPLE META-LEVEL AND LEVEL MANAGER

So far we have discussed operations that extend over only two levels: object-level and metalevel. But the mechanism of KAUS to define the meta-level is completely the same as that of the object-level. Hence it is easy to extend this idea upward any number of levels. In fact, there are many functions, such as learning, that require much higher level operations. What is necessary here is a management system that manages the operation of overall system. It watches the level in which the system is running and controls it. KAUS is designed in this way. In this system, every level

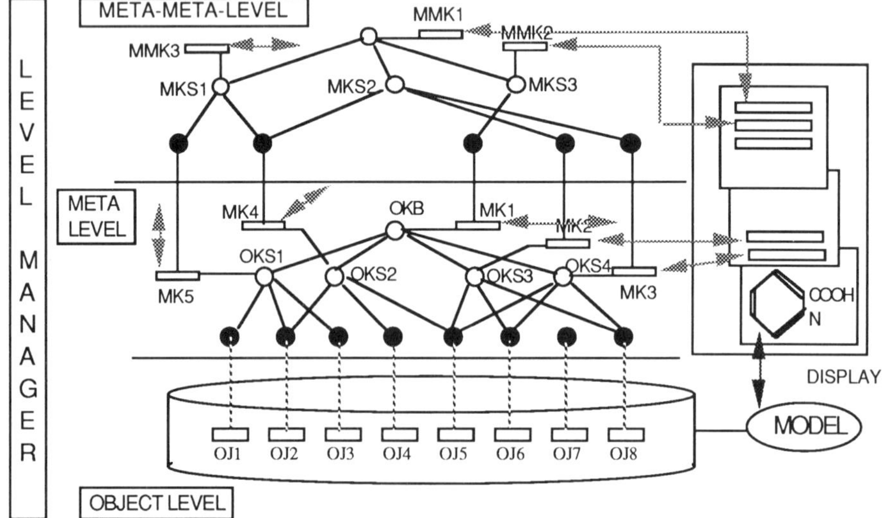

MMKi: Meta Level Knowledge MKi: Meta-level knowledge OJi: Object Level Knowledge
MKSi: Meta Level Knowledge Source OKSi: Object Level Knowledge Source
MKB: Meta Level knowledge Base OKB: Object Level Knowledge base

Figure 4 Interface between man and multi-meta-level system

is the same and, therefore, only a set of functions including an inference mechanism is provided and is shared by all levels.

Figure 4 shows the case of using the meta-meta-level. In the last section, we assumed that the human designer intervenes every repetitive cycle in the design process. But it is possible to let the system to do longer steps by specifying the order of using knowledge sources. It is specified in the meta-meta-level as shown in Figure 4. A longer sequence is specified as the (ordered) set of meta-level rules.

As an extension of the design process representation, we are going to develop a scheduling system and real time control system. These are to design the control structure in the meta-level. Substantially the same system as the design system in the object level will be used for this purpose but the system must work expanding meta-level and meta-meta levels because, in this case, the design object is the control structure. The same technique as the design in the object-level is expected to be used. The object level must be used to evaluate the control structure created as a hypothesis. As a further extension of these projects, we are intending to proceed to software design.

6. CONCLUSION

We have discussed in this paper the conceptual framework of a knowledge-based system which we designed to aid human problem solving in its totality. We have discussed that, because of very the nature of real problem solving requiring support systems flexibility and evolutionality, knowledge-based systems must be of the multiple meta-level architecture. We have discussed the role of meta-level operation and finally a method of man-machine interaction with the meta-level systems based on an example. Finally we have discussed that this idea extends quite naturally to real time control problem and software design.

REFERENCES

[1] Enderton,H.B. Mathematical Introduction to Logic Academic Press (1972).

[2] Krivine J.L. Introduction to Axiomatic Theory D.Reidel Pub. Co. Dordrecht, Holland (1971).

[3] Ohsuga,S. and Yamauchi,H. "Multi-layer logic - a Predicate Logic including Data Structure as Knowledge Representation Language", New Generation Computing Vol.3 No.4 (Special Issue on Knowledge Representation) (Ohmsha, Ltd and Springer-Verlag, 1985) pp.403-439.

[4] Ohsuga,S. 'Toward Intelligent CAD Systems ' Computer Aided Design Vol.2l,No.5 (1989) pp.315-337.

[5] Ohsuga,S. "Knowledge Representation and AI System Architecture'", Proc. 2nd Scandinavian Conference on Artificial Intelligence (June, 1989).

[6] Yamauchi,H. and Ohsuga,S. "KAUS as a Tool for Model Building and Evaluation", Proc. 5th International Workshop on Expert Systems and Their Applications (Avignon, France, May 13-15, 1985).

Industrial Applications of Artificial Intelligence
J.L. Alty and L.I. Mikulich (Editors)
Elsevier Science Publishers B.V. (North-Holland)
1991 IFIP

SECTION 2: EXPERT SYSTEMS: KNOWLEDGE ACQUISITION

TOPOLOGICAL KNOWLEDGE ACQUISITION IN CHEMICAL DATABASES

K.BIEDKA
Central Institute of Cybernetics and Information Processes (CICIP),
Academy of Sciences of the G.D.R.

ABSTRACT: Exploration and design of molecular structures are very important for modern chemical research and industrial application. In chemical laboratories computer systems are used increasingly in this matter. By applying rule-based programs, the prediction and the synthesis of molecules may be automated to a large extent. These programs are implementations of the Artificial Intelligence approach for automated learning, hierarchical planning and geometric reasoning. Such computer systems are necessary to handle the large amount of available information concerning more than six million organic molecules. In the discourse of organic molecular prediction and design, the process of knowledge acquisition must be related to existing electronic documentation of chemical knowledge in such operational systems as SPRESI, STN, Beilstein online, the Brookhaven database and others. These database systems reflect the results of many generations of chemists during the last 160 years.

This paper deals with a recognition method, based on topological information about changing objects, which can be represented in the form of graphs. There exists a widespread class of such objects (situations, semantical terms, process states and many others). An impressive demonstration can be given in the field of organic reaction equations. The recognition method is implemented as the knowledge acquisition part in the knowledge based system for organic synthesis RDSS [1].

1. CHEMICAL SYNTHESIS KNOWLEDGE ACQUISITION BY PATTERN RECOGNITION AND CONTEXT DESCRIPTION

Synthesis rules for the chemical knowledge base are acquired from pattern recognition in topological information fields of large reaction databases. The approach to knowledge synthesis in RDSS is the concept of reaction centre transformation, called by its author synthon transformation [2]. In this concept the reaction educts and products are represented as estimated graphs with

node value: atomic number in the Periodic system together with other properties of the atom (hydrogen value, charge, radical,...)

edge value: kind of bond between the two connected atoms and other properties of connection (geometrical direction, strength,...)

In the process of a chemical reaction a subgraph in the educt graph changes to give a new subgraph in the product graph. This change of subgraphs, the essential part of a reaction, is the searched transformation.

educt subgraph ---------> product subgraph transformation
educt graph ----------> product graph

A transformation can be considered as a rule, converting an educt graph to the product graph. The rule is related to a concrete context.

context: unchanged part of both graphs

When a reaction educt and reaction product are given as estimated undirected graphs, an analysing algorithm can be set up to recognize a greatest common subgraph (GCSG). Therefore the GCSG may be considered as the context for the corresponding transformation.

Because of the same reaction mechanism in several realized chemical syntheses, the amount of synthon transformations is less than the amount of the reaction equations itself. Only the context of the same transformation differs in the reactions, based on the same mechanism.

The application of synthon transformations as rules for synthesis purposes seems to be possible when the information about the context can be considered as a constraint. Therefore a context estimation is introduced, based on the interconnections of the changing subgraph with the context. The recognition method considers only the nearest surroundings of this subgraph as the essential constraint for the validity of the transformation.

constraint: description of interconnections between transformation and context.

Transformations (rules) and their corresponding constraints are stored together in the knowledge base. The set of recognized transformations from a database with changing graph objects can be considered as some kind of learned abstracts. In the case of the SPRESI database, with about 2 million chemical reaction equations, there are about 110,000 synthon transformations and context constraints.

2. RECOGNISING ALGORITHM

An effective algorithm is required for recognizing transformations from a large database in a permissible time limit. Three steps must be done:

1. Recognise a greatest common subgraph (GCSG) on both reaction sides,
2. minimise the amount of interconnections between the changing subgraph and the context to get the synthon transformation,
3. Calculate an estimation of the nearest surroundings for the synthon transformation as a context constraint.

In the first step several methods are available for the recognition of GCSG in molecular structures. The RDSS system uses the Clique algorithm [3] with some modifications. The essential features of these modifications are as follows:

- Topological patterns for the correspondence set are all triples <node1 value, edge value, node2 value> in both educt and product graphs,
- Educt and product graphs are split into skeleton and cycling substructures for the application of a decomposition method,
- Recognition of partial GCSG in each combination of split substructures and derivation of the searched GCSG as a greatest clique based on partial ones.

The decomposition method leads to an efficient algorithm, especially for large graphs with many symmetries. The recognizing algorithm will be demonstrated through the example of the Diels-Alder reaction (see below).

Diels - Alder reaction A --> B	Ordered Set of Topological Patterns

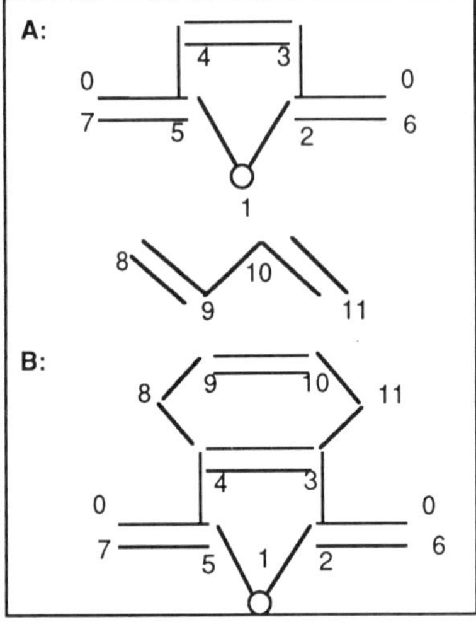

A:

B:

Element No.	Graph A Triple Symb.	Nodes	Graph B Triple Symb.	Nodes
1	C-CH	2/3	C-CH	2/3
2	C-CH	5/4	C-CH	5/4
3	C-O	2/1	C-O	2/1
4	C-O	5/1	C-O	5/1
5	C=O	2/6	C=O	2/6
6	C=O	5/7	C=O	5/7
7	CH-CH	9/10	CH-CH	3/4
8	CH=CH	3/4	CH-CH2	4/8
9	CH=CH2	9/8	CH-CH2	9/8
10	CH=CH2	10/11	CH-CH2	10/11
11			CH-CH2	3/11
12			CH=CH	9/10

For graphs A and B the set of topological patterns is derived. The compatibility matrix for the correspondence set of members (corresponding patterns) is analyzed to give a clique with a greatest number with all compatible members. Due to decomposition of that matrix according to special markers for pattern pairs, a set of partial cliques for each part can be collected by means of [3]. The partial cliques build a new set of members with a new compatibility matrix. Finally, a clique with all compatible partial cliques with the greatest number of corresponding patterns is the result. The compatibility of two given members is evaluated according to the following rule:

- Two members ml(p1A, p1B) and m2(p2A, p2B) are compatible, if and only if their corresponding patterns plA and p2A in graph A and plB and p2B in graph B satisfy two conditions

  1. (p1A is not p2A) and (p1B is not p2B)

  2. ((p1A has a common node with p2A)
     and
     (p1B has a common node with p2B)
     and
     (common node value in A = common node value in B)
)
     or
     ((p1A has no common node with p2A) and (p1B has not common node with p2B)
)

The compatibility matrix for partial cliques in the final step of the decomposition method is built up in an analogic manner . Two partial cliques are compatible, if and only if they belong to partial sets and if all their members are compatible.

Correspondence Set			**Compatibility Matrix with Clique #**													
Mem ber No.		**Pair of Triples <A,B>**	1	2	3	4	5 #	6	7	8 #	9 #	10	11	12 #	13	14 #
1	CC	<2/3 , 2/3>	0	0	0	1	1	0	0	1	1	0	0	1	0	0
2	CC	<2/3 , 5/4>	0	0	1	0	0	1	1	0	0	1	1	0	0	0
3	CC	<5/4 , 2/3>	0	1	0	0	0	1	1	0	0	1	1	0	0	0
4	CC	<5/4 , 5/4>	1	0	0	0	1	0	0	1	1	0	0	1	0	0
5	CC	<2/1 , 2/1>#	1	0	0	1	0	0	0	1	1	0	0	1	1	1
6	CC	<2/1 , 5/1>	0	1	1	0	0	0	1	0	0	1	1	0	1	1
7	CC	<5/1 , 2/1>	0	1	1	0	0	1	0	0	0	1	1	0	1	1
8	CC	<5/1 , 5/1>#	1	0	0	1	1	0	0	0	1	0	0	1	1	1
9	SS	<2/6 , 2/6>#	1	0	0	1	1	0	0	1	0	0	0	1	1	1
10	SS	<2/6 , 5/7>	0	1	1	0	0	1	1	0	0	0	1	0	1	1
11	SS	<5/7 , 2/6>	0	1	1	0	0	1	1	0	0	1	0	0	1	1
12	SS	<5/7 , 5/7>#	1	0	0	1	1	0	0	1	1	0	0	0	1	1
13	SC	<9/10 , 3/4>	0	0	0	0	1	1	1	1	1	1	1	1	0	1
14	CC	<3/4 , 9/10>#	0	0	0	0	1	1	1	1	1	1	1	1	1	0

Decomposition Markers:
CC - cycling part A with cycling part B (9 members)
SS - skeleton part A with skeleton part B (4 members)
SC - skeleton part A with cycling part B (1 member)
CS - cycling part A with skeleton part B (none members)

The GCSC for the Diels-Alder reaction as given in the clique # is not yet the context for the main changing substructure in this reaction. The triple 3/4 in A and the corresponding triple 9/10 in B are excluded from the GCSG because of their isolated position (reduction of interconnections). Due to pattern definition, the triples 4/5 and 2/3 in A are not compatible with 4/5 and 2/3 in B because the node values 3 and 4 in A differ with node values 3 and 4 in B. But the node values of the other atoms and the edge values of this triples are equal and belong therefore to the main context. Such kinds of consideration are undertaken to derive synthon transformations in the second step (graphs with node numbers of the changing subgraph):

transformation: A(3,4,8,9,10,11.) --> B(3.4,8,9,10,11.)

In the final step, the nearest surroundings of the synthon transformation must be described. This evaluation must be based on the concrete application domain. In our case it reflects some properties of bonded atoms and results in a sequences of node values for each interconnection. The first node value in such a sequence belongs to the neighbour atom of the boundary atom in the synthon. Then node values for the other context atoms are followed, which are connected with this neighbour atom. In the case of conjugate pi-bonds, this sequence is extended to such atoms, deeper in the context. Conjugate groups are represented in the sequence by a donator or acceptor marker. That means, that some topological and reactivity informations of the nearest surroundings will be related to the synthon transformation. The last picture shows the recognized synthon transformation and its context description constraint @.

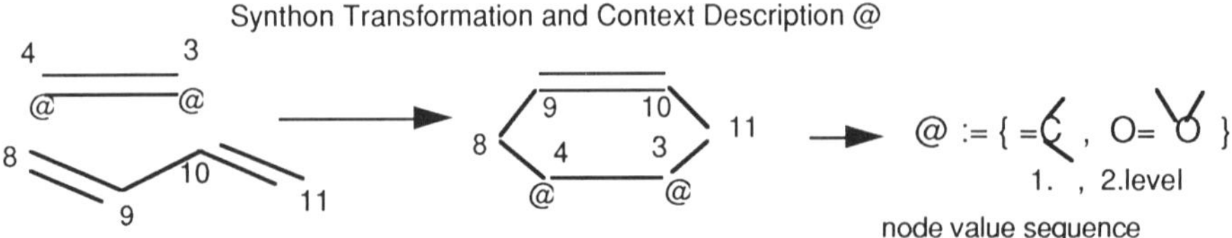

The application of transformation rules and context constraints in RDSS is based on the substitution of matching fragments in initial molecule by the other side of the transformation rule, so giving a new molecule.

REFERENCES

[1] Biedka,K., "Projektkonspekt Expertensystem Syntheseplanung, Arbeitsbericht, Zentralinstitut fuer Kybernetik und Informationsprozesse, Berlin, (1989).

[2] Weise,A., Journal der Praktischen Chemie 322(5), S., pp. .761-768 (1980).

[3] Bron, C., Kerbosch, T,, "Algorithm 457: Finding all Cliques of an Undirected Graph", Comm. ACM, 16, pp 575-577, (1973).

Industrial Applications of Artificial Intelligence
J.L. Alty and L.I. Mikulich (Editors)
Elsevier Science Publishers B.V. (North-Holland)

KNOWLEDGE ACQUISITION METHOD OF EXPERT SYSTEM FOR ANALYSIS OF FINANCIAL STANDING OF AN ENTERPRISE.

M. LASEK and M. PECZKOWSKI
Department of Cybernetics and Operational Research,
University of Warsaw,
Warsaw,
Poland

ABSTRACT: In the paper a knowledge acquisition method for expert systems is presented. The method is aimed at the analysis of the financial standing of an enterprise and includes construction of the decision tree from the data contained in balance sheets and the generation of the rules from the decision tree. The theory of the method is described and illustrated by an example.

1. INTRODUCTION

One of the barriers in the use of expert systems for the analysis of the financial standing of an enterprlse is the difficulty in developing a suitable knowledge base. This barrier can be overcome by elaboration and using the proper knowledge acquisition methods. In this paper we present such a method. Knowledge acquisition in this method is based on the data from balance sheets, which are conventionally used in practice in Polish enterprises. Balance sheets are usually prepared twice a year - at the beginning, and towards the end of the year. They are statements, in monetary terms, of the assets and liabilities relating to an enterprise. In a balance sheet, any particular enterprise aggregates its assets and liabilities into 84 assets and 84 liability items. In the method, knowledge is acquired from a large set of data - balance sheets obtained from 500 Polish enterprises - stored in standard dBASE III+ data base. These data are based upon the activities of each particular enterprise during the last few years.

2. FORMULATION OF THE PROBLEM

The problem can be formulated as follows. It is assumed that we are given a set of enterprises E={El,E2,... En} and every enterprise is characterized by multiple attributes Al, A2, . . . Am. These attributes may be either items in the balance sheet or indicators which are created on the basis of items (for example assets or liability structure indicators). Values of attributes are given for each enterprise from our set of data contained in the balance sheets. It is also assumed that each enterprise can be classified into a particular class: Cl,C2,...Ck, using overall financial or economic situation criterion.

In the proposed method we attempt to find a decision tree [1, 2, 3], which represents relationships between values of items in balance sheets and classes of enterprises. In the decision tree, items of balance sheet, Al, A2, . . . Am, are the nodes of the tree, classes of enterprises Cl,C2,... Ck are the leaves. The branches give the possible values for the items of a balance sheet . From the decision tree, rules in the form of "IF . . . THEN" clauses can be generated directly. In these rules, values of items from the balance sheet are conditions and conclusions indicating the class to which the enterprise belongs.

3. PROCEDURE OF THE METHOD

The procedure consists of the five following steps.

Step 1

The enterprises from a set E are categorized into classes Cl, C2, . . . Ck. As a distinguishing criterion of this categorization an indicator is used that describes an overall financial or economic status of an enterprise, such as profit rate or net worth of a business.

Step 2

The attributes Al,A2,... Am, are selected to describe particular enterprises. For the purposes of our research, the overall analysis of the financial standing of an enterprise, we propose to use as attributes not only items of assets and liabilities but also indicators, which characterize the structure and dynamics of assets and liabilities. Indicators which characterize assets and liability structures are defined as ratios of various asset items to total assets and ratios of liability items to total liabilities. Indicators which characterize assets and liability dynamics are defined as ratios of the same assets and liabilities from balance sheets prepared at a different time. The ratios between different positions of assets to different positions of liabilities and vice versa can also be used as attributes, but they have not been the subject of our analysis as yet.

Step 3

The decision tree is constructed from the data which specifies associations between each of attribute values and the classes to which the enterprises belong . The data, showing the associations between attribute values and classes, are set out in a contingency table [2]:

		Classes of Enterprises C1, C2, C3,..... Cl		Totals
Attribute Values	V1	x11 x12		x1.
	V2	x21 x22		x2.
			xij	
	Vr			xr.
Totals		x.1 x.2	x.k	N

where xij is the number of enterprises in class j with attribute value i. The last row of the contingency table contains the numbers of enterprises in class j (x.j). In the last column of the table there are numbers of enterprises with attribute value i (xi.) . N is the number of elements in the set E - the set of enterprises with known classes and attributes values, from which a decision tree is developed.

In the process of construction of the decision tree, Quinlan' s algorithm is used [1, 4, 5]. In this algorithm the information measure (IM) is employed. The information measure is a statistic for the contingency table based on information theory. It is defined as the gain in information resulting from the knowledge of the attribute. This can be calculated from the data in the contingency table as:

$$I(A) = M(C) - B(C \mid A)$$
$$= (\Sigma \Sigma\, xij \log xij - \Sigma\, xi.\log xi. - \Sigma\, x.j \log x.j + N \log N) / N$$

where $M(C)= - (x.1 / N) (\log x.1 / N) - (x.2 / N) (\log x.2 / N) - \dots .$

$$= (\Sigma\, x.j \log x.j - N \log N) / N$$

is the information content of the class totals as a whole,

$$B(C \mid A) = (x1./N)\, M(V1) + (x2./N)\, M(V2) + \ldots\ldots$$
$$= -(\Sigma\, \Sigma\, xij \log xij - \Sigma\, xi.\log xi.)/N$$

is an average of information content for the rows weighted by the frequency of occurrence of the row totals,

$$M(Vi) = -(xi1/xi.)(\log xi1/xi.) - (xi2/xi.)(\log xi2/xi.) - \ldots$$

is the information content for the row i.

The information measure, calculated from a contingency table, is used to select an attribute which is the best discriminator within the given set of data and for this reason is selected as a succeeding node of the decision tree. Thus in the procedure, the I(A) is calculated for all attributes and the attribute with the maximum I(A) is chosen as a node of a decision tree. The possible values of the attribute specify branches leaving the decision node. The subnodes (subtree) are established in the same procedure within the attributes not yet selected in a given path in the tree and within the subset of the data representing values on the branch being examined. The process is continued and terminates for the path when values of attributes on that path indicate explicitly on the class of enterprise, setting up a leaf of the decision tree or all attributes are examined on that path. For detailed discussion of the algorithm see Quinlan [1, 5] .

The main advantages of using Quinlan' s information measure for our purposes are

(i) usefulness in extracting associations between assets and liabilities items and classes of enterprises from a very large sets of data,
(ii) ensuring the order of the attributes, which will be next conditions in the rules, from the most important to the least important
(iii) computational simplicity.

Step 4

In this step rules are generated from the decision tree. Rules are derived directly from tree in form of "IF . . . THEN" clauses . The order of the rules and the sequence of conditions in the rules are determined by the structure of decision tree.

Step 5

Rules are analysed and evaluated by the experts.

The method has an algorithmic character. For this reason its role is to draw our attention to possible relations and connections between assets and liability items and enterprise subsets or categories rather than to generate finished and completed rules ready to use in practical applications. The proposed algorithm can help experts to identify important rules. In our opinion, because the rules are obtained from statistical data in balance sheets using the statistical process of rules induction, an expert' s judgment is necessary. Experts can examine rules under heuristic conditions which are difficult to quantify.

In the step 5 the question is also considered of how to interpret the generated rules and how many cases should be included to confirm the rule and to say that the rule is significant enough to be in the knowledge base appropriate to practical application. We have assumed that only the experts - practitioners in finance and economic analysis of an enterprise - could interpret the exact meaning of any particular rule, examine each rule to see whether it should be generalized and decide whether or not it could be accepted in the knowledge base . As a result of the experts judgments, the rules can be modified and included in the knowledge base.

The process of development of the knowledge base is iterative. In the fifth step of the method we can make decision whether it is necessary:

- to change the decision tree (return to step 3.),
- to use another attributes to describe particular enterprises (return to step 2.),
- to apply another classification of the enterprises into subsets or categories (return to step 1.).

4. SOFTWARE

The method of acquiring of knowledge from the data contained in balance sheets has been coded as a program in Turbo Pascal for the PC DOS operating system. This program can be used in IBM-PC or compatibles. In the program, the decision tree is constructed from the data in the balance sheets according to Quinlan' s algorithm. Thus in the program, the IM value for attributes are computed, and the attribute with maximum IM is selected as a succeeding node of a decision tree, the tree is constructed and the rules from the tree are generated.

5. APPLICATION

We applied our method to generate the rules representing relationships between values of assets and liabilities structure indicators and profit rate which is achieved by an enterprise. Our aim was to detect whether or not the relationships existed and if they exist, to predict the overall situation of an enterprise from certain balance sheet structures (i.e. assets and liabilities ratios in balance sheet). For the analysis we used the balance sheets of 500 Polish enterprises from 1987.

According to the method procedure, in the first step we classified all enterprises from our set of 500 analysed cases to subsets or categories. The basis of the classification was a profit rate indicator of a particular enterprise. To classify enterprises with respect of profit rate values, we used cluster analysis with the CLUSTER procedure of the SPSS/PC+ statistical package. We obtained six classes of enterprises - from the class with profit rates in the interval [-0.075, 0.18] to the class with a profit rate as high as 1. 58 .

In the second step of the method, which is aimed at selecting attributes, we selected further analysis indicators which characterize the balance sheet structure, i.e. assets and liabilities structure indicators. Because in conventional balance sheets, both assets and liabilities are classified into six main categories we took into account, as attributes, ratios of these categories to total assets and to total liabilities, respectively. The categories are very specific for balance sheets used in Polish enterprises. Characterization of these categories required detailed explanations, which are not essential for the purpose of our example in this paper. For assets, attributes include ratios of such categories as fixed assets (buildings, equipment) or such categories as current assets (inventories, receivables, accumulated loss, liquid funds) to total assets. Liability attributes included ratios of such categories as equity capital or borrowed capital to total liabilities.

In the third step of the method we set out the data, translated from dBASEIII+, into a contingency tables. Balance sheet structure indicators are continuous attributes i.e they have real values in the interval [0, 1]. This was the reason that we used once again cluster analysis with the CLUSTER procedure of SPSS/PC+ to obtain clusters-groups of their values. Therefore, in our contingency table we then obtained the data which represented an association between the groups of attribute values and the classes of enterprises.

To construct the decision tree based on the data in the contingency tables we used Quinlan' s algorithm. The results are given as a tree, a fragment of which is shown in Fig. 1 below rE ∈ [0.16,0.23]:

rB ∈ [0.03,0.15]: pr ∈ [0.36,0.61] (7)

rB ∈ [0.36,0.48]:

rD ∈ [0.00,0.03]: pr ∈ [0.18,0.35] (22)

rD ∈ [0.06,0.09]: pr ∈ [0.36,0.61] (11)

rE ∈ [0.40,0.47]:

rC ∈ [0.19,0.32]: pr ∈ [0.62,0.98] (28)

rC ∈ [0.32,0.45]: pr ∈ [1.07,1.33] (3)

Legend:
rx - ratio of x category of assets to total assets (x can be A, B, C, D, E or F category of assets, conventionally used in Polish enterprises)
pr - profit rate

Figure 1. Fragment of a sample decision tree

This fragment of the tree represents relationships between assets structure indicators and classes of enterprises differing in profit rate. The tree, as mentioned above, was generated from 500 cases of enterprises. Numbers in parentheses after each leaf indicates how many of these cases are covered by that leaf. In the tree the first attribute chosen was "category E to total assets", i.e. the ratio of financial result (accumulated loss and deductions from financial result) to total assets. This attribute became a root of the tree. The branches leaving the root represent possible values of that attribute. In the fragment of decision tree which is shown in Figure 1 there are two examples of intervals [0.16 , 0.23] and [0.40 , 0.47] for category E. The next attributes chosen as succeeding nodes are different for different intervals of root attribute. For the decision tree in Figure 1 they are: "category B to total assets" and next "category D to total assets" in the case of [0.16 , 0.23] interval, and: "category C to total assets" in the case of [0.40 , 0.47] interval. The leaves of the tree are profit rate value intervals, showing the class of the enterprise. Rule generation from the tree is automatic. The rules from the sample of the decision tree presented in Figure 1 are:

IF rE ∈ [0.16 , 0.23] AND rB ∈ [0.03 , 0.15] THEN pr ∈ [0.36 , 0.61]

IF rE ∈ [0.16 , 0.23] AND rB ∈ [0.36 , 0.48] AND rD ∈ [0.00 , 0.03]
THEN pr ∈ [0.18 , 0.35]

IF rE ∈ [0.16 , 0.23] AND rB ∈ [0.36 , 0.48] AND rD ∈ [0.06 , 0.09]
THEN pr ∈ [0.36 , 0.61]

IF rE ∈ [0.40 , 0.47] AND rC ∈ [0.19 , 0.32] THEN pr ∈ [0.62 , 0.98]

IF rE ∈ [0.40 , 0.47] AND rC ∈ [0.32 , 0.45] THEN pr ∈ [1.07 , 1.33]

In such rules it is convenient to use linguistic terms instead of intervals of values. In the example, we used the following linguistic terms for the six profit rate intervals: very low, low, medium, high, very high, excellent.

As was suggested in step 5 of the method, obtained rules were the subject of an analysis by experts before they were accepted, modified or rejected from the knowledge base before practical application. Some of the rules seemed sensible or even obvious. However, a number of leaves in the tree were based on a very small number of observations, for example with only 7, 3 or even 1 observation, while in the beginning we started with a large number of enterprises. The reason is that during the construction of the tree, the number of observations - enterprises considered in lower and lower levels of the tree - becomes progressively smaller, what has also been observed in other applications of Quinlan' s algorithm [2] .

6. CONCLUSIONS

The intention of the described method was to draw experts' attention to possible relations between financial categories and the overall status of an enterprise, and to help them to discover and express rules, which they often intuitively use for the analysis of the financial standing of an enterprise .

Experiments with both test and real data sets indicate that the method is useful for this purpose. However, some problems and questions need further investigation. These include:

- which criterion should be used to classify enterprises into subsets or categories ?
- which attributes should be considered jointly in the study ?
- how to interpret the generated rules and how many cases should be included to confirm the rule and to say that the rule is enough significant to be in the knowledge base ?
- how to evaluate the fitness of the developed rules and the resulting knowledge base, i.e . how to choose test sets - cases not used in constructing the decision tree [4] ?
- what to do in the case of many attributes taking values from the set of real numbers
- how to construct the "best" decision tree and what does it mean [5] ?
- when to stop generation of the branch in the tree - for example to be less dichotomized but with more cases [2]
- how to generate the rules involving functional dependence between the attributes, i.e possible functional relationships such as equity capital to borrowed capital
- comparison of the results with other techniques such as Kullback's Information Measure, G-Statistic, Chi-Square test.

ACKNOWLEDGEMENT

This work was supported by the Polish Academy of Sciences, Grant No. CPBP-10 . 03.

REFERENCES

[1] Quinlan J. R ., "Induction of decision trees", Machine Learning 1 , pp. 81-106, (1986)

[2] Mingers J., Expert Systems - "Rule Induction with Statistical Data", J. Op. Res. Soc. 38,, pp. 39-47., (1987).

[3] Vrba J. A., Herrera J. A., "Expert System Tools: The Next Generation", IEEE Expert Spring , pp.75-76, (1989).

[4] Quinlan J. R ., "Simplifying decision trees", Int. J. Man-Machine Studies Vol. 27, pp. 221-234, (1987).

[5] Quinlan J. R., Rivest R. L., "Inferring Decision Trees Using the Minimum Description Length Principle", Information and Computation 80, 227-248, (1989).

Industrial Applications of Artificial Intelligence
J.L. Alty and L.I. Mikulich (Editors)
Elsevier Science Publishers B.V. (North-Holland)

SIZIF - THE SYSTEM OF KNOWLEDGE ACQUISITION FROM EXPERIMENTAL FACTS

Ksenja A. NAIDENOVA and Julija G. POLEGAEVA

Institute of Remote Sensing Methods
for Geology, Geology Ministry of the USSR
Leningrad

Abstract

The problem of transformation from data to knowledge is considered. The key concept of our approach to knowledge acquisition is the concept of a good test for a given classification. An algorithm is proposed for inferring all the good maximal tests for a given classification. The test inference algorithms are currently being implemented in SIZIF - the System of Knowledge Acquisition from Known Facts.

1. INTRODUCTION

The quality of expertise depends greatly on the quality of an expert`s knowledge. Content, completeness and sufficiency are the essential characteristics of expert`s knowledge to be used in inference systems. The following components are the basis of an expert`s knowledge :
. empirical experience
. generally known regularities, functional dependencies and some other interrelations produced as a result of long-lasting data analysis process in a given problem domain.
We assume that an expert obtains his knowledge by studying a lot of experimental data associated with real world objects and interrelations between them. SIZIF doesn't pretend to replace an expert but makes easier his knowledge acquisition activity in dealing with many observations and known facts. SIZIF may serve as a logical, intelligent and prompt assistant to both experts and knowledge engineers. The goal of SIZIF is to generate a complete, soundness, consistent and efficient knowledge base.

2. THE KNOWLEDGE ACQUISITION PROCESS

The knowledge acquisition activity includes the following sophisticated components of human reasoning.

2.1. Classification

The classification of knowledge plays an important part in thinking process. It is essential that the classification of the given objects should be natural with respect to the possibility of expressing and predicting the properties of these objects perfectly. The well-known examples of natural classifications are the Periodic Law of Mendeleyev and Linney's classification.

Usually natural classifications are not equivalent to any goal classification which depends on a given task.For instance, geological objects can be divided into natural groups with respect to the type of their structure but the goal classification may be given on the base of the ore content of the samples of geological objects. In this case we have to discover functional dependencies between a goal classification and some natural classifications.

Functional dependencies serve two purposes:

. to describe the problem domain knowledge by means of available sets of interrelated classifications

. to create efficient inference rules for a classification.

2.2. Discretization

The attributes are measured on scales of various types: nominal, ordinal, interval, ratio or absolute. Usually attribute values are continuous (the height above sea level, the steepness, the spectral brightness and so on). But these attributes are used practically with discrete values in inference rules. The possible approaches to discretization of data can be considered.

2.3. Finding good and natural tests

The key concept of our approach to the knowledge acquisition problem is the concept of the good test [1]. The unique role of this concept can be identified in the existence of three equivalent definitions and of three interpretations of its use as:

1) a distinguishing/identifying relation between objects,
2) a functional dependency between classifications and
3) a partition dependency [2] between partitions of a given set of objects.

Let DO be the initial database of objects. We consider a finite, nonempty set U = {A1, ..., An}.The set U is called the universe and Ai`s are called the attributes. Each attribute Ai is associated with a classification KLi of the objects to be considered and {KL1, ..., KLn} is a set of available classifications.

Let Di = {ai1, ai2, ...} be a finite set of symbols (values) called the domain of Ai. Let the attribute values be the names of classes of the corresponding classifications. We assume that Di doesn`t intersect with U for all i from {1, ..., n} and that the intersection of Di and Dj is empty for all i,j where i is not equal j. We identify objects with positive integers. Let N = {1,2, ...,m} be the set of object indices. For each j from N there is a tuple tj in DO such that tj(Ai) is in Di for all Ai in U. The tuple tj is called the description of the jth object. A relation r over U is a collection T of the object descriptions. The example of the database DO is given in Fig.1 with N = {1,2,3,4,5,6}, U = {A,B,C,D,E,F,G}, T = {t1,t2, ..., t6}. K - the attribute, corresponding to the goal classification.

	A	B	C	D	E	F	G	K
1	a1	b1	c1	d1	e1	f1	g1	k1
2	a2	b1	c2	d2	e2	f2	g1	k1
3	a1	b1	c2	d1	e1	f3	g2	k1
4	a1	b2	c3	d2	e1	f1	g1	k1
5	a2	b2	c3	d2	e1	f1	g2	k2
6	a3	b3	c3	d3	e3	f1	g3	k2

FIGURE 1.

DEFINITION 1. A subset of attributes X of U is a test for a given classification K in a relation r over U if in r the following conditions are satisfied:

(1) ti(K) ~= tj(K) ----> ti(X) ~= tj(X)

(2) ti(X) = tj(X) ----> ti(K) = tj(K)

for all ti, tj from T, i ~= j, where '~' means 'not equal'. Clearly the condition 2 is the definition of the functional dependency X ---> K.

DEFINITION 2. A subset X of U is a test for a classification K in a relation r over U if r satisfies the following dependency X ---> K.

The good test for a given classification is defined on the base of partition model for relations [2], [3]. We assume that any attribute is associated with an object classification which induces a partition on each of the given set of data (of the set of table tuples).

We shall use P(X) to denote the partition induced by a collection X of attributes on the set of data, and we use P(X)*P(Y) to denote the product of two partitions P(X) and P(Y). The relation of partial order over a set of partitions is introduced in the standard way: P(X) < or = P(Y) iff P(X) * P(Y) = P(X). By means of kl(P(X)) we denote the number of classes of the partition P(X).

DEFINITION 3.A subset X of U is a test for a given classification K in a relation r over U, if in r the following condition is satisfied: P(X)*P(K) = P(X) (P(X) < or = P(K)).

DEFINITION 4. A test X in U for a given classification K is said to be good if the following condition holds: (for all subsets Y of U) (P(Y) < or = P(K)) (P(X) < or = P(Y)) ---> P(X) = P(Y).

DEFINITION 5. A test X in U for a given classification K is to be said natural (the best test) if the following condition is satisfied:(for all subsets Y of U)(P(Y) < or = P(K)) ---> kl(P(X)) < or = kl(P(Y)).

We define the concepts of maximal subset and nonredundant subset of attributes from U.

DEFINITION 6. A subset X of U is said to be maximal if (for all A)(A doesn't belong to X) (A belongs to U) ---> P(XA) ~= P(X).

DEFINITION 7. A subset X of U is said to be nonredundant if (for all Y)(Y is a proper subset of X) (Y ~= X) ---> P(X) ~= P(Y) or (there doesn't exist Z in X such that Y ---> Z).

DEFINITION 8. A test X in U for a given classification K is said to be maximal (nonredundant) provided X is a maximal

(nonredundant) subset of U.
Given a database D0 and a classification K we shall be interested in the set of all nonredundant good or natural tests for K implied by D0. In our running example (Fig.1) the set of all good nonredundant tests for K is: {AE, BG, DG} and one of these tests - AE is the best (natural) test for K.
Indeed we have: P(K) = {{1,2,3,4}, {5,6}}; kl(P(K)) = 2;
P(AE) = {{1,3,4}, {2}, {5}, {6}}; kl(P(AE)) = 4;
P(BG) = {{1,2}, {3}, {4}, {5}, {6}}; kl(P(BG)) = 5;
P(DG) = {{1}, {2,4}, {3}, {5}, {6}}; kl(P(DG)) = 5;
and P(AE) < P(K), P(BG) < P(K), P(DG) < P(K).

2.3.2. Inference algorithm for good classification tests

Now we give without proof a test inference algorithm to produce all good maximal tests for a given classification. Let DO, U = { A1,..., An }, T = { t1,..., tm }, N = { 1,..., m} and K be determined as above. By Sh = { s1, s2, ..., sz } we shall denote a family of the subsets of N such that each subset contains exactly h elements from N, by atr-h, test-h we shall denote respectively h-th subset of attributes from U and h-th subset of tests for K, i < h < q.
Inferring tests for a given K makes sense if the functional dependency U ---> K (P(U) < P(K)) is satisfied in r.

Algorithm. Input: a database D0, K;
Output: a set of all good maximal tests for K.
Initialization: h = 1, atr-1 = {U}, S1 = {{1},{2},...,{m}}, test-1(T,K) = {{ U }}. Induction process starts from h = 2.
1. Construct S2 = { s12, s13, ..., sij, ..., }, 1 < i < j < m, the set of all subsets of N containing exactly two elements and for T, K over U form the set first(T,K) = {Fij: Fij = {A belongs to U: ti(A) = tj(A), (i,j) belongs to S2}}.
2. From first(T,K) we construct two sets:
firstIN(T,K) = {Fij belongs to first(T,K): ti(K) = tj(K)},
firstBETWEEN(T,K) = {Fij belongs to first(T,K) : ti(K) ~= tj(K)}.
3. Produce the set FM of all maximal elements of the set firstBETWEEN(T,K) with respect to the set-theoretical inclusion:FM = {A belongs to firstBETWEEN(T,K): (for all B)(B belongs to firstBETWEEN(T,K))(B is superset of A) ---> B = A}.
4. From firstIN(T,K) we construct the set: test-2(T,K) = {F belongs to firstIN(T,K):(for all F`)(F`belongs to FM)F' does not include F}.
THEOREM 1. The set first(T,K) is the set of maximal subsets of attributes (in the sense of the definition 6).
THEOREM 2. A maximal good test for K either belongs to the set test-2(T,K) or there exists q > 1 such that the intersection of exactly q tests from test-2(T,K) forms a maximal good test for K.
For our running example, we have:

{ {sij} ---> firstIN (T,K) } =
{{1,2} --> BG, {1,3} --> ABDE, {1,4} --> AEFG, {2,3} --> BC, {2,4} --> DG, {3,4} --> AE};

{ {sij} ---> firstBETWEEN (T,K) } =
{{1,5} --> EF, {2,5} --> AD, {3,5} --> EG, {4,5} --> BCDEF,
{1,6} --> F, {4,6} --> CF};

FM = { AD, EG, BCDEF };

{ {sij} ---> test-2 (T,K) } =
{{1,2} --> BG, {1,3} --> ABDE, {1,4} --> AEFG, {2,4} --> DG,
{3,4} --> AE}.
atr-2 denotes the union of all sets of attributes appearing in the tests of test-2(T,K), i.e. atr-2 = { A,B,D,E,F,G }. To continue the process we generate by induction (until it is possible) the sequences: S3, S4,.... Sq; atr-3, atr-4,.., atr-q; test-3(T,K), test-4(T,K),..., test-q(T,K). Construct the sets S3, atr-3, test-3(T,K). For this goal we form S(test-2)={{i,j} belongs to S2: Fij belongs to test-2(T,K)}.
5. Construct the set S3 = {(ijl): there exist simultaneously (i,j),(i,l),(j,l)({i,j} belongs to S(test-2) & {i,l} belongs to S(test-2) & {j,l} belongs to S(test-2)}.
6. Construct F(S3) = {Fijl, {i,j,l} belongs to S3 : Fijl is the intersection of Fij, Fil, Fjl from test-2(T,K)}.
7. Construct the set new-test = {F belongs to F(S3):(for all subsets F` of FM) F' doesn't include F}.
8. If new-test is nonempty then we form S as the union of S(test-2) and S(new-test), where S(new-test) = {(ijl), {i,j,l} belongs to S3: Fijl belongs to new-test} and now we produce the set SM of all maximal elements of S with respect to the set-theoretical inclusion: SM = {s: (for all s`) (s` belongs to S)(s` is a superset of s) ---> s` = s}.
9. We can now form the set test-3(T,K) = {Fs: s belongs to SM, Fs belongs to the union of test-2(T,K) and new-test}.
10. Now we form the set of attributes atr-3 = {A,B,D,E,G}. It is possible to create only two triples of indices for the set S3: S3 = {{1,2,4}, {1,3,4}}. Hence we have F(S3) = {G(as the intersection of BG, DG, AEG), AE (as the intersection of ABDEG,AEG,AE)}, new-test = {AE}, test-3(T,K) = {BG,AE,DG}. The tests obtained with the use of our algorithm are maximal and nonredundant, but generally it is needed to use our algorithm for inferring good maximal tests from the obtained set test-2(T,K) (as an initial table instead of T) and the set firstBETWEEN(T,K). The generating (h + 1) - element`s subsets over the family of h - element`s subsets is of great interest (see [4]).

2.4. Generalization

The inference of reasoning rules from good and natural tests is the content of generalization in SIZIF. The number of the reasoning rules obtained from good nonredundant test may be smaller than the number of the classes induced by this test on the given objects. Apart from the usual rules of the form {the values of attributes}--> {the class of a goal classification} the rules of the following form are constructed {the values of attributes} & {the class of a goal classification} ---> false. These rules are called 'forbidden rules' and can be effectivelly used within inference process to reduce the search reasoning space.

2.5. Formation of metastructures

On carrying out his usual work every expert acquires implicitely or explicitely some metarules with respect to using his knowledge. These metarules predetermines an order of drawing reasoning rules, tests, attributes into inference process. The whole complex of rules (metarules and reasoning rules) forms the proper knowledge suitable to practical tasks.
The formation of a natural mechanism for inferring with respect to human reasoning is the content of the metastructure generating in SIZIF.

3. THE CONCEPT SCHEME OF SIZIF

In the present version of SIZIF it is supposed that two initial stages of knowledge acquisition have already been made in a given problem domain, but the implementation of these steps is intended. Now SIZIF consists of the following blocks: the block of finding good tests and the block of knowledge formation.
SIZIF provides experts with the following possibilities:
. choice of attribute as a goal classification
. choice of subset of attributes as an initial set for inferring tests
. choice of algorithm of inferring good tests (inferring only one good or natural test, all good or natural tests with the given limitations on the number of classes and/or the number of the test attributes)
. choice and memorize a collection of tests.
Every test is involved into a cycle of knowledge formation: generalization, metastructure formation, decision tree inference and so on. The rules are evaluated by an expert with respect to the degree of their credibility. From the given data a decision tree can be induced directly without the stage of generalization, but in this case a difficulty arises in the evaluation of the decision tree by an expert. The nature of knowledge formation in accordance with the requests of the expert system to be planned may be selected. SIZIF is currently being developped in C for IBM PC/AT or a compatible microcomputers in the MS DOS environment.

REFERENCES

[1]. Naidenova, K.A., Polegaeva, J.G. An Algorithm of Finding the Best Diagnostic Tests, in: Application of Mathematical Logic Method, (Tallin, 1986), pp.63-67.
[2]. Spiratos, N., Cosmadakis, S., Kanellakis, P. Partition Semantics for Relations, ACM PODS, (March 1985).
[3]. Naidenova, K.A., The Relational Model of Experimental Data Analysis, Trans. of Ac. Sci. USSR, series ' Technical Cybernetics ', (4, 1982), pp. 103-119.
[4]. Megretskaya, I.A., Construction of the Classification Natural Tests for Knowledge Base Generation, in: The Problem of the Expert System Application in the National Economy, (Kishinev, 1989), pp.105-108.

Industrial Applications of Artificial Intelligence
J.L. Alty and L.I. Mikulich (Editors)
Elsevier Science Publishers B.V. (North-Holland)

NATURAL LANGUAGE PROCESSOR TUNABLE TO DIFFERENT SUBJECT DOMAINS

O. G. GRIGORYEV, N. L. REIZIN

Computer Centre,
The USSR Academy of Sciences,
Moscow,
The USSR.

ABSTRACT: NLP is based on input sentence analysis made with the help of subject domain structure. The main goals of NLP design are the structuring and verification of a subject domain. Algorithms of knowledge acquisition and their implementation are discussed in detail.

1. PRINCIPLES OF THE SYSTEM DESIGN.

It is a well-known fact that NLP designers have difficulties either with syntactic parsing of input language or with the transition from input language to subject domain description. It seems that these shortcomings are based on the fact that subject domain and input language are regarded as completely different areas. That is why an attempt has been made to treat them from the same point of view, namely, in terms of formal grammar theory. Correspondences between grammar classes and various subject domain descriptions were shown. AND/OR graphs correspond to context-free grammars, and AND/OR graphs with node dependency correspond to attribute context-free grammars. The last formalism is powerful enough to describe almost any "intelligent" system subject domain.

Thus, there is a subject domain and an attribute context-free grammar equivalent to it. Let an input language be generated by some input grammar. Then, as the equivalence problem is unsolvable even for regular and context-free grammars, it follows that there is no algorithm for the input-grammar-parse-graph to subject-domain-parse-graph transition. Hence input sentences are to be at first parsed by means of subject domain grammar. Input grammar is used only in ambiguous cases.

One of the main results of the suggested approach is that greater efforts must be directed to constructing and investigating the subject domain to which the system is tuned.

2. INPUT SENTENCE PROCESSING.

To construct a subject domain fragment corresponding to an input sentence, the following method is suggested. Each input word is replaced by subject domain references provided the word is found in the system vocabulary. For a subject domain grammar these are alphabet and grammar rule references. Each unknown word is marked and a user can teach the system this word.

If a domain is described by a graph, these are references to nodes. As a rule, each word corresponds to a set of references. There are different types of sets: compulsory, not compulsory, etc. The particular type is determined when a word is entered into the system vocabulary.

After replacement these sets serve as a basis for constructing subgraphs of the whole subject domain graph. Each subgraph must contain at least one node from each compulsory set. In addition, the whole number of one set nodes, which are contained in the same subgraph, is minimized. This coordinated construction strongly reduces the number of initially obtained nodes. After the construction is made, one or more subgraphs are obtained. In the case of a subject domain grammar this process is equivalent to the selection of all strings which can be generated by the grammar. As the membership problem for context-free grammar is solvable, then for any string, the membership to the subject domain language can be determined. Hence, for a number of sets the subgraph construction problem is also solvable i.e., the NLP can determine if the input facts are coordinated and if the user's goal is achievable. If there are several subgraphs, one of them is selected on the basis of domain knowledge. The latter includes: subgraph estimation with the help of edge weights, morphological and/or syntactical analysis, context, user model and dialogue with a user.

The connection of each new subgraph with a previous sentence subgraph is verified in order to find context dependencies. This method makes it possible to overcome some traditional difficulties, such as ellipsis or anaphora.

The overall scheme of the system performance is as follows - after word replacement by subject domain references, these serve as a basis for subgraph construction. Each subgraph is estimated with the help of the criteria described above. The subgraph with the highest estimate is accepted. Then it is passed to a module, whose function is to run the programs and database enquiries attached to the subgraph nodes. In case of any pitfalls, such as lack of the required information in a database, a dialogue with a user or backtracking to the construction module are possible.

On the basis of the described principles a model version of NLP has been implemented on IBM PC type computers. The main purpose of the version was to verify the basic principles and to reveal the most important connections between modules, which serve to construct and choose the necessary subgraphs. At present attempts are being made to design a commercial version of the system. There are two advanced modules - the module for morphological and syntactical analysis, and the module for knowledge acquisition. The latter will be described in the following sections.

3. KNOWLEDGE ACQUISITION ALGORITHMS

Knowledge acquisition requires a great deal of effort both from the expert and the knowledge engineer. It is a rule, rather than an exception, that an expert finds it difficult to classify objects or events. To point out an explicit and sufficient set of feature values is time-consuming. Let us state the problem as the way of attributing new objects to one of some given classes. In that case it is unnecessary to ask all values of features in the set. It is true even for the case of no redundancy of features (i.e., when the set is a minimal test).

The task is much easier for an expert if the conditional test is applied according to a special scheme, when following questions depend upon values already known from previous questions. This poses the problem of the best recognition scheme for a conditional test of the minimal average length. For the case when there are N different n-dimensional vectors of feature values it is possible to design a recurrent algorithm of a directed search of a conditional test, minimizing the mathematical expectation of the number of questions. It is also assumed that the probability of a certain object to be a member of a certain class is known.

Very often questions are of differing difficulty for an expert (for example, it is more difficult to choose among more alternatives). In that case it is possible to give weights to the features and to restate the problem as to design a conditional test with the minimal mathematical expectation of the summary weight of all features. The suggested algorithm can be easily modified to design such a test. The scheme of the algorithm also allows us to include limitations on a conditional test, for example, on the allowed number of features asked at a single step, on the maximum number of steps, of alternatives suggested for a choice, etc. The suggested algorithm is generalized to the case when classes are related with unintersecting n-dimensional rectangular areas in the space of features or not rectangular unintersecting areas, each of which is an amalgam of several rectangular unintersecting sub-areas.

4. IMPLEMENTATION FOR LINGUISTIC KNOWLEDGE

The described method was used for the design of a Natural Language system in a subsystem for the morphological data input of the Russian language. Russian is a highly inflectional language. This means that it has very rich system of inflections. Besides inflections, a word can have a change of letters on the borders of different morphemes both in stem, and prefix.

Our subsystem must determine the paradigmatic class of any new word. At the same time, it must minimize the mathematical expectation of a number of questions about the word, which are put to the user. Every part of speech has quite a number of paradigmatic classes, each class presented by a unique set of endings. The expert can give answers in the most natural form, that is, he has not to give values of features (that is endings, but the expert enters the whole wordform, which is easier. The subsystem itself finds the ending, which, in general, can be ambiguous). In addition, even if the ending is unique, changes in the stem and prefix can also add some ambiguity.

To solve all the above problems the design of a conditional test is done in two stages:

- all possible paradigms of a certain part of speech are analyzed and all ambiguous situations are picked out automatically;
- the conditional test is designed with the algorithm of the directed search of variants. The test has the minimal total weight of questions and excludes the possibility of ambiguous interpretations of users answers.

The input of new words can be described as a move along the tree of the conditional test from its root to its leaves. After every answer the process passes to the next level and all possible leaves are searched. The leaves, which do not satisfy the known word-forms are excluded. Thus the number of questions is decreased. As a result, an expert has to answer from three to five questions in order to input a new word. After that, the system is able to synthesize all its word-forms (there is 12 word-forms for a noun and 20 for a verb and adjective).

5. CONCLUSION.

Summing up, the proposed principles make possible the following:

- automation of system tuning to a subject domain and postcorrection of the latter 's description;
- simplification and improvment of input sentence understanding. This is achieved by input sentence primary parsing by means of a subject domain grammar. Natural language grammar is enlisted only in ambiguous cases;
- use of widely varying parsing algorithms both for subject domain tuning and for input sentence parsing.

Industrial Applications of Artificial Intelligence
J.L. Alty and L.I. Mikulich (Editors)
Elsevier Science Publishers B.V. (North-Holland)

AUTOMATIC GENERATION OF KNOWLEDGE IN EXPERT SYSTEMS

I. V. EZHKOVA
Computer Centre,
Academy of Sciences,
Moscow,
The USSR.

ABSTRACT: An automatic knowledge generation method is proposed. The method is based on the formalization of the problem area context. An experience function is defined as a main context character. A verbalization procedure is constructed.

1. INTRODUCTION

Knowledge generation is the most labour consuming phase of expert system design. A significant disadvantage of current expert systems is that they regard knowledge bases as sets of "frozen" descriptions and disregard their contexts. Actually such a knowledge base is just a set of words that cannot be "understood" by the system itself unless the context is known

A knowledge generation mechanism including the context is a pre-requisite of expert system flexibility. Only in such cases could the expert system itself solve problems such as:

A. generation of its own knowledge;

B. updating (restructuring) the knowledge base in correspondence with current changes in the problem area;

C. processing knowledge under context-dependent schemes (including analogic, metaphoric, associative, etc.).

The use of fuzzy linguistic estimates in the knowledge base is one of the reasons for context introduction. The knowledge base is often representable as a description of problem area basic concepts through fuzzy linguistic estimates of their attributes and relations. Automatic generation (verbalization) and interpretation of these estimates depend on the problem area context.

Fuzzy set theory which formalizes fuzzy linguistic estimates [1] might help in solving the problems A, B and C provided that the notion of context is introduced into the theory body. This paper suggests an approach to automatic knowledge generation and interpretation through formalization of the notion of the problem area context.

2. EXPERT SYSTEM LEARNING

Problem area context formalization can be solved by means of expert system learning. Let us take a set of learning examples for an arbitrarily large set of concepts. Each example is a vector in the semantic space S of attributes. Attribute scales are generally ordered.

Let us fix attribute p and concept o. Let D_{po} be the distribution of the values of p for o and T_{po} be the representation of the estimation of p for o as a fuzzy subset with membership function $t_{po}(x)$ obtained from D_{po} as the result of its normalising to 1.

While tuning to a concrete context a set of base concepts, $E = \{o_1, o_2, ..o_r\}$ is defined.

Let D_p be the distribution of values of p for the concept set E as a whole. An analysis of the distributions D_p allows us to correct the attribute set to a given context.

If D_p is unimodal, its maximum defines the norm of p, p_{norm}. The attribute itself can be estimated with respect to the norm by means of linguistic estimates like "large-small". Otherwise, linguistic estimation is not possible, and the attribute must be adjusted to be usable in the given context [2].

Let S^* be a space of adjusted attributes to each of which a unimodal distribution is assigned. For each attribute p define an experience function F_p:

$$F_p(x) = \begin{cases} \dfrac{D_p(x)}{2 \max\limits_x D_p(x)} & x \leq p_{norm} \\ 1 - \dfrac{D_p(x)}{2 \max\limits_x D_p(x)} & x > p_{norm} \end{cases}$$

mapping the attribute values from the semantic scale onto the universal (with respect to any contexts) scale.

3. VERBALIZATION PROCEDURE

The notion of a universal scale has been introduced in [3] for arbitrary estimates such as "large -small", "heavy-light", etc. On the universal scale these estimates are represented as fuzzy subsets in interval [0,1] that are independent of the semantics of estimated events and of the estimating subject. Let V be the set of linguistic estimates used for an attribute p.The form of their membership functions can be chosen from some analytical reasons (e.g. special simplified form such as triangular, trapesoidal,etc.).

The semantic estimate verbalization procedure consists of two following steps:

1. mapping the fuzzy set T_{po} from the semantic scale onto the fuzzy subset R_{po} of the universal scale:

$$R_{po} = F_p(T_{po})$$

$$r_{po}(F_p(x)) = t_{po}(x)$$

where $r_{po}(y)$, $y \in [0,1]$, is the membership function of fuzzy subset R_{po};

2. choosing a linguistic estimate L from the given set V, which provides the best approximation of the fuzzy subset R_{po}

$$l(y) = r_{po}(y),\ y \in [0,1],$$

where l(y) is the membership function of linguistic estimate L (the operation of best approximation is defined in [4]).

Verbalization procedures enable automatic generation of linguistic estimates of concept attributes for a given context. This procedure may be used for linguistic estimation of any attribute value against the background of a given context. The interpretation procedure which is the inverse of that of verbalization [2] allows one to interpret linguistic estimates against different contexts. This procedure relies upon value mapping from the universal scale onto the semantic one.

The mapping of the space S^* into the universal space is defined by the vector of experience

$$F = \langle F_1, F_2, ..., F_n \rangle$$

4. CONTEXT FORMALIZATION

Different attributes, obviously, are used in the context description only once. What was essential in one context may become noise in another one. Attribute estimation on the universal scale enables determination of context-dependent coefficients of attribute significance by means of the mismax operation of fuzzy subsets R_{po} [4]. The Significance Coefficient distribution D_k inside the context is used in a similar way to that above for the construction of the experience function F_p through the significance of attributes.

After modifying D_k to the unimodal form, the most frequently occurring significance threshold k_{norm} is calculated. If an attribute has a significant coefficient less than k_{norm} it may be eliminated from the universal space. The space thus obtained is called the context space.

The context C is described by the following cortege

$$C = \langle E, A, Q, F, B \rangle$$

where E is the set of base concepts, A is the set of base attributes (attributes from the context space), Q is the vector of base attribute significance, F is the vector of experience, and B = $\{L_{po}\}$ is the set of linguistic estimates of base attributes $p \in A$ for base concepts $o \in E$.

The set B actually defines the traditional knowledge base. Thus including the problem area context notion enables automatic generation of expert system knowledge and then allows consideration of this knowledge within the context frame.

5. CONCLUSION

The proposed approach is based upon the formal introduction of the context notion for verbalisation and interpretation of fuzzy linguistic estimates. With respect to the knowledge base this notion of context is a meta-notion, the knowledge base itself being one of the context elements. The other elements enable understanding of the knowledge domain and thus, open the way to the solution of problems A, B and C. The algebra and the logic of contexts are described in [2]. The approach is used as the theoretical basis to develop the technology for creating a new class of context-oriented expert systems.

REFERENCES

[1] Zadeh, L,A., "The Concept of Linguistic Variable and its Application to Approximate Reasoning", Information Science, Part I,7, Part II,8, Part III,9, (1975).

[2] Ezhkova, I.V., "Knowledge Formation through Context Formalization", Computers and Artificial Intelligence, vol 8, numb 4 (Bratislava, 1989, pp. 305.

[3] Ezhkova, I.V., "The Universal Scale for Representing Linguistic Estimates", in: Proceedings of the IFAC Symposium on AI, Leningrad, 1983. (Pergamon Press, New York, 1985) pp. 163-170.

[4] Ezhkova, I.V., "Application of Fuzzy Inference Schemes in the Tasks of Medical Diagnostics", in: Proceedings of the Second International Meeting on AI, Leningrad, 1980, (Plenum Press, New York, 1983)

Industrial Applications of Artificial Intelligence
J.L. Alty and L.I. Mikulich (Editors)
Elsevier Science Publishers B.V. (North-Holland)

SECTION 3: KNOWLEDGE REPRESENTATION AND VALIDATION

A SYMBOL-BASED APPROACH IN TERM PROCESSING

V. S. NEIMAN

Institute of Applied Astronomy,
USSR Academy of Sciences,
8, Zhdanovskaya str.
Leningrad, 197042,
The USSR.

ABSTRACT: A method is proposed to generate quickly derivable objects in calculi over terms. The method is based on the fact that inference rules may require only partial information about their premises. In this case it is proposed to apply an inference rule not to single terms (or n-tuples of terms, if the rule has n premises) but to sets of terms (sets of n-tuples) whose elements are equivalent to each other with respect to the rule. This may reduce considerably the running time of deduction algorithms. In some cases this method even turns infinite deductions into finite ones.

The proposed method is applicable to a wide range of calculi. Moreover it is usually compatible with other deduction methods which may be of use in a particular calculus.

1. INTRODUCTION

Let a calculus with terms as derivable objects be fixed. We are interested in one of the following problems:

Problem 1. Given a term T, decide whether it is derivable in the calculus.

Problem 2. Decide whether there exists a derivable term which satisfies some property P (a variant of this problem - generate all such terms).

If the number of derivable terms in the calculus is finite then both of these problems may be solved by the straightforward algorithm which generates sequentially all derivable terms by applying the inference rules. This algorithm can be used to attack these problems even in cases when infinitely many derivable terms exist, though in this case it is not guaranteed to terminate. However, in both cases the straightforward algorithm usually is not the best way to deal with these problems. A number of more efficient methods are known for different calculi. These methods may be divided into two classes:

1) A new calculus may be constructed which is better suited for automated deduction. Thus, if problem 1 is approached, it is usually a good idea to try to construct a new calculus where all deductions start with the term T. Deducibility of a special object in the new calculus means that T is deducible in the original calculus (this is the main idea underlying goal-driven deduction methods).

2) Methods of the second class leave the original calculus intact, but either forbid certain applications of inference rules, or define an order in which inference rules must be applied . Such methods are usually called strategies.

Methods of both classes are calculus-specific i.e. each one is designed for a particular calculus. One can hardly conceive of a method of the first or the second class which may be applied in a number of different calculi.

Our proposed method has another feature. It does not depend on a particular calculus. On the contrary, it utilizes a feature which a wide range of different calculi have in common. Namely, it utilizes the fact that inference rules may require only partial information about their premises, i.e. in some cases they are able to generate an answer without full examination of their arguments. For example, this is the case with inference rules based on the unification procedure. Thus, an attempt to unify P(Tl) with Q(T2), where Tl and T2 are some terms, terminates unsuccessfully without examination of Tl and T2 . An attempt to unify P(X) with P(T), where X is a variable, also terminates without examination of T, in this case successfully.

We shall call our method symbol-based because it does not process terms as single entities, but rather processes only one symbol of a term at one step. On the other hand, each step of the method serves not only for a particular term T, but for all terms which do not differ from T in the symbols processed so far. In other words, one application of an inference rule having n arguments is split into several steps consisting in processing of one symbol of the input n-tuple. Then these small steps are merged in quite a different way: steps corresponding to the processing of n-tuples which do not differ from each other in symbols processed so far are combined together.

If two terms differ only in subterms which are insignificant to an inference rule, then they may be considered as equivalent with respect to the rule The symbol-based algorithm does not process insignificant symbols at all. So, equivalent terms are not distinguished during applications of the rule.

The symbol-based approach is not dedicated to a particular calculus. Of course, it cannot yield alone the same results as efficient methods for automated deduction designed specially for a particular calculus. But an advantage of the symbol-based approach is that it is usually compatible with methods designed for particular calculi. In fact, methods of the first class consist in shifting to another calculus. If we want to combine such a method with the symbol based approach we must simply apply the symbol based approach to the new calculus rather than to the old one. Methods of the second class (strategies) may be extended to symbol-based inferences in the following way: we can forbid (postpone) an application of an inference rule to a set of n-tuples if the strategy forbids (postpones) the application of the rule to each element of the set.

The idea of the symbol based approach for one particular calculus (goal driven deductions in Horn fragments of the first-order logic) was described in [1]. Here the approach is proposed for a significantly more general situation.

2. SOME PRELIMINARIES

We assume that a signature (set of symbols together with their arities) is fixed. In a calculus these symbols may be divided into several classes (e.g. predicate symbols, functional symbols, variables, etc..), but this distinction is not significant to us.

DEFINITION. A *term* is an expression of the form F(Tl, T2, ..., Tn), where F is an n-place symbol from the signature and Tl, T2, ..., Tn are terms. If n=0 then the brackets may be omitted.

DEFINITION. A *generalized term* is either * (asterisk) or an expression of the form F(Tl, T2, ..., Tn), where F is an n-place symbol and Tl, T2, ..., Tn are generalised terms. The brackets may be omitted if n=0. Each occurrence of the asterisk in a generalized term is called a parameter. An instance of a generalized term is a term which may be obtained from it by replacing all parameters with some terms.

Informally a generalized term is a term some subterms of which are unknown; these subterms are denoted by asterisks. In some cases it is convenient to identify a generalized term with the set of all of its instances.

DEFINITION. An *inference rule* with n premises is an algorithm which transforms n-tuples of terms (premises of the rule) into finite sets of terms (conclusions of the rule). The set of conclusions may be empty. A calculus is a pair consisting of a finite set of inference rules and a finite set of terms called axioms.

One additional assumption must be made about inference rules in order to make the symbol-based approach possible. Namely, the inference rules must be able to work in a situation when some subterms of their premises are unknown. Let us formulate this requirement more precisely.

ADDITIONAL REQUIREMENT TO INFERENCE RULES. Each Inference rule with n premises must be applicable to an arbitrary n-tuple of generalized terms (Gl, G2, ..., Gn). One of the following answers must be returned.

1) Conclusions cannot be generated until the values of some parameters of the premises are specified. In this case a pointer to a desired parameter in the premises must be returned.

2) All unknown subterms are really inessential. In this case a set of generalized terms {Cl, C2, ..., Ck} (conclusions of the rule) must be generated. With each parameter in a conclusion, the pointer to a parameter in the premises of the rule must be associated. This answer must be sound in the following sense: if we apply this rule to such n-tuple of terms (T1, T2, ..., Tn) that each Ti is an instance of Gi, then the set of conclusions must coincide with the set of terms obtained from {Cl, C2, ..., Ck} by replacing all parameters with the values of the corresponding subterms of Tl, T2, ..., Tn.

3 . GENERAL OVERVIEW OF THE SYMBOL BASED METHOD

Due to the limited length of this paper we cannot provide the full description of the symbol-based method; so we confine ourselves to outlining the main data structures and algorithms.

The main data kept during the inference process are the list of waiting operations which contains operations ready to be executed, and the term tree which represents the set of derived terms. Deduction is done in the following way: whilst the list of waiting operations is not empty, its elements are selected and executed. Each operation may change global data (including the list of waiting operations). If the list becomes empty, it means that the deduction is completed and the term tree now represents the set of all deducible terms.

The order in which elements from the list of waiting operations are chosen and executed is not fixed. This means that the symbol based approach allows us to use different strategies of computation.

The term tree is a tree whose nodes are generalized terms. The root of the tree is always the generalized term *. The following condition must be satisfied. If a node T has sons Tl, T2, ..., Tk, then each Ti must be obtained from T by replacing one parameter of T with a generalized term of the form F(*,*,...,*),where F is some symbol (the asterisks are absent if the arity of F is equal to 0). The parameter of T which is replaced must be the same for all sons; it is called the *point for expansion* of T.

The terms themselves are kept at the leaves of the tree. The above mentioned condition means that when we traverse the tree from the root to a leaf, on each step one new symbol of the destination term becomes known. In order to describe how terms are represented, we need the following definition.

DEFINITION. A *term over the tree* is either a pointer to a node of the term tree or an expression of the form F(Tl, T2, ..., Tn), where F is an n-place symbol and Tl, T2, ..., Tn are terms over the tree. The brackets may be omitted if n=0. A *refinement* of a generalized term having n parameters is an n-tuple of terms over the tree. In other words, refinement associates a term over the tree with each parameter of T.

A list of refinements is associated with each leaf of the term tree. Each refinement represents one or several (in some cases even infinitely many - see figure 4 below) derived terms. Figure 1 shows an example of the term tree. This tree represents the set of terms {P(A), P(F(A)), P(F(X)), Q(A), Q(B), Q(X)}. To the right of each leaf which has at least one parameter the list of refinements is shown in square brackets (in this example each refinement is simply a term).

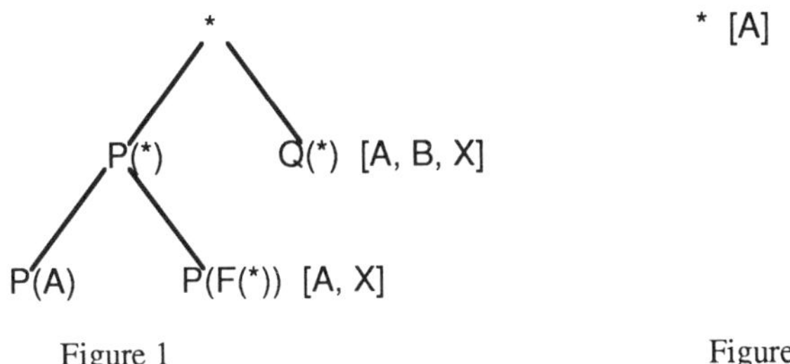

Figure 1

Figure 2

The arguments of all operations are nodes of the term tree. In other words all operations are executed on generalized terms rather than on ordinary ones. Even if a node of the tree has several refinements associated with it, inference operations would nevertheless work only with the node itself unless values of some parameters of the node are required. In this case the operation of expansion of this node is executed. This operation determines the point for expansion, then creates sons of the node and distributes its refinements among its sons. Then the operation which has required the value of a parameter is repeated with all the sons.

For each inference rule of the calculus a corresponding inference operation of the symbol-based method exists. If an inference rule has n premises, then the corresponding inference operation has n arguments, each one being a node of the term tree. The operation is executed in the following way. First it forms the n-tuple of generalized terms from its arguments and passes it to the inference rule. If the inference rule returns the set of conclusions then each conclusion is inserted in the term tree. Otherwise, if the inference rule called is unable to generate conclusions, it returns the pointer to a parameter in the premises whose value is required. This means that the inference operation must be repeated with all sons of the node to which this parameter belongs. So, if the expansion of this node has not been done yet, it is executed now. Then the inference operation is called for all sons of the node; in addition this operation is memorised in order to be executed with sons which may appear in future.

Initially, the term tree has only one node - the root *. The list of refinements of the root contains one element for each axiom A of the calculus, namely the term A. The list of waiting operations has one element for each inference rule of the calculus. All arguments of the operations are equal to the root of the term tree.

4. AN EXAMPLE

Let us consider the following calculus. The signature consists of l-place symbols F and G, 0-place symbols A and B, and the set of 0-place symbols {X, Y, Z, ...} which are marked as variables. There are three inference rules:

X --> F(X)
G(X) --> X
F(G(X)) --> G(F(X))

A rule L --> R has one premise and works in the following way: if the premise is unifiable with L, then the rule returns the answer {Rv}, where v is the most general unifying substitution. Otherwise the empty set of conclusions is returned.

The calculus has one axiom - the term A. We are interested in deducibility of the term B in this calculus.

It is clear that these inference rules and the axiom A may be regarded as Horn clauses, and our problem is equivalent to that of the deducibility of B from these clauses in the standard predicate calculus. The example is chosen in such a way that B is not deducible, but existing inference methods for Horn clauses (e.g. those described in [2] cannot prove it. Thus, the bottom up (fact driven) method would generate the infinite sequence of terms A, F(A), F(F(A)), F(F(F(A))), etc. and would never terminate. On the other hand, the top down (goal-driven) method would generate the infinite sequence of subgoals B, G(B), G(G(B)), G(G(G(B))) etc. and would also never terminate. The third clause is added in order to make it harder to determine statically the fact that the first and the second clauses cannot interact one with the other in these deductions.

The term tree in the initial moment is shown in figure 2, and the list of waiting operations includes three elements - one for each inference rule. The first inference operation terminates successfully and produces the answer {F(*)}. The second and the third operations, are unable to generate conclusions when called with the argument * . It means that the operation of expansion of the root must be executed. The term tree after the expansion is shown in figure 3 (*/1 designates the first parameter of the node *). Notice that only the second and the third operations will be repeated on the new nodes; the first inference operation, being terminated successfully on the root of the term tree, would never be executed anew.

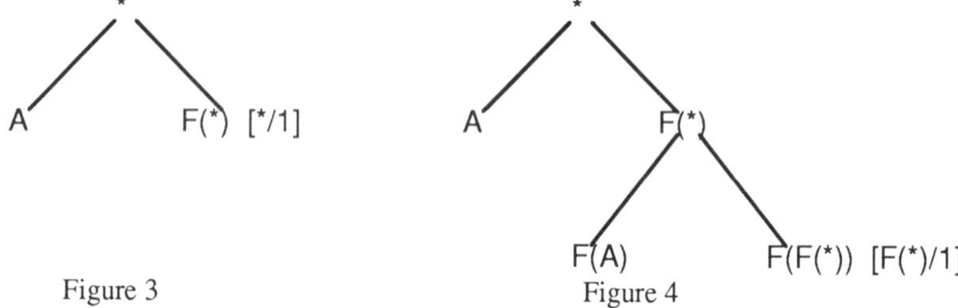

Figure 3

Figure 4

The second inference operation terminates on both new nodes with the empty sets of conclusions (because G(X) is not unifiable either with A or with F(*)). The third operation terminates on the node A with the empty set of conclusions (F(G(X)) is not unifiable with A), but cannot terminate on the node F(*). So the node F(*) also needs to be expanded. The term tree after the expansion is shown in figure 4.

Only the third inference operation must be applied to the new nodes F(A) and F(F(*)) . On both nodes it terminates with empty sets of conclusions. Now the list of waiting operations becomes empty. It means that the current term tree represents the set of all derivable terms. Notice that the infinite set of terms {A, F(A), F(F(A)), ... } is represented by the finite term tree.

Now we can answer the question whether the term B is derivable. We see that it is an instance of the root of the tree, but is not an instance of one of the sons of the root. This indicates that B is non-derivable.

REFERENCES

[1] Neiman, V.S., "Using Partially Defined Terms in Logic Inferences". In: Theory and Applications of Artificial Intelligence (Bulgaria, Sozopol, 1989), pp 241 - 248 (in Russian)

[2] Kowalski, R. "Logic for Problem Solving", (North Holland, 1979)

Industrial Applications of Artificial Intelligence
J.L. Alty and L.I. Mikulich (Editors)
Elsevier Science Publishers B.V. (North-Holland)

THE CALCULUS OF METRIC TEMPORAL RELATIONS AS A KNOWLEGE REPRESENTATION FRAMEWORK FOR RULE-BASED EXPERT SYSTEMS

Vadim P. Kirillov

Kharkov, USSR

A formal framework for knowledge representation of temporal aspect of situation recognition problems in real-time environment is proposed. The framework is a more developed version of a production-rule approach which is commonly used in expert systems.

1. INTRODUCTION

Temporal relations are of great importance in problem solving dealing with the real-time control of complex objects. Unfortunately,there are very few sutable means for formalizing temporal aspect of experts′ knowlege.

In this paper a generalization of a production rule framework is proposed. It gives a knowledge engineer a formalization tool well suited to situation recognition problems related to control in complex dynamic environment.This work is a more detailed and refined version of a previously published short note [1].

2. PRODUCTION RULE SYSTEM AS A FIRST-ORDER FORMAL THEORY

We treat a production system as a formal theory in a first order multi-valued logical calculus of a special kind. In this calculus, marked logical truth values are all real numbers of the segment [0,1], and the ′?′ symbol is a non-marked value. Terms are temporal variables t_k, constants T_k, and functions $F_k(.)$. All the terms are assumed to be fuzzy moments of time.

The formal theory is presented by two axiom schemes. The first scheme is used to represent events, which altogether characterize the state of the environment at the time of discourse:

$$\mathrm{Val}\ \{\ A(\hat{T})\ \} = \alpha, \qquad (1)$$

where $\mathrm{Val}\ \{\ \Phi\ \}$ is the truth value function of the logical formula Φ,

$A(.)$ is a predicate symbol,

$\hat{T}$ is a fuzzy estimate of a temporal constant T.

(Henceforth low-case Greek letters α, β, γ are used to denote marked truth values).

The second axiom scheme represents expert's knowledge in Horn's production rule form:

$$\mathrm{Val}\ \{\ \forall\ \vec{t}\ \exists\ t_o[A(t_1)\wedge\ldots\wedge A(t_n)\wedge \mathbb{T}(t_o,\vec{t})\ \rightarrow A_o(\ t_o)]\ \} = \beta, \qquad (2)$$

where $\vec{t} = <\ t_1,\ldots,t_n\ >$ is an ordered set of temporal variables,

$A_k(\ t_k\ )$ is the k-th premise (k>0) or the conclusion (k=0) of the production rule,

$\mathbb{T}(t_o,\vec{t})$ is a temporal relation,

$\wedge$, $\rightarrow$ are logical connectives, conjunction and implication, respectively.

At the common-sense level, expression (2) means the following. Given events $A_1,\ldots,A_n$ taking place at instants of time $\vec{t} = <t_1,\ldots,t_n>$ respectively, and if for all these instants the temporal relation $\mathbb{T}(\ t_o,t_1,\ldots,t_n)$ holds, then the value of moment of time t_o may be calculated which also is matched with this relation and at which the event A_o exists with truth value β.

A situation recognition problem is represented by a finite set of formulae given by the expressions (1) and (2), being a partially ordered set with respect to the inclusion relation of conclusions of some production rules into sets of premises in other productions. Any predicate P, which is contained in the production rules as a conclusion only, is called a target claim. Predicates, which play the exclusive role of premises in any given production rule, are called primary facts.

A situation recognition problem is stated as follows. One should infer, if it is possible, target claims from given sets of primary facts and production rules built according to axiom schemes (1), (2), respectively.

To make it possible, the following inference rules are used.

R1. Existential quantifier deletion rule:

$$\frac{\mathrm{Val}\ \{\ \forall\ \vec{t}\ \exists\ t_o\ G\ (\ t_o,\vec{t}\ )\ \} = \alpha}{\mathrm{Val}\ \{\ \forall\ \vec{t}\ G\ (\ F\ (\ \vec{t}\ ),\ \vec{t}\ )\ \} = \alpha}, \qquad (3)$$

where G(.) is a logical formula,

F(.) is the Skolem function, which semantics is discussed further.

R2. Universal quantifier deletion rule:

$$\frac{\mathrm{Val}\ \{\ A(T)\ \} = \alpha,\ \mathrm{Val}\ \{\ \forall\ t_1[A(t_1) \wedge B(t_1) \rightarrow C(t_1)]\ \} = \beta}{\mathrm{Val}\ \{\ A(T) \wedge B(T) \rightarrow C(T)\ \} = \mathbb{H}_1(\alpha, \beta)} . \quad (4)$$

R3. Conjunction injection rule:

$$\frac{\mathrm{Val}\ \{\ A\ \} = \alpha,\quad \mathrm{Val}\ \{\ B\ \} = \beta}{\mathrm{Val}\ \{\ A \wedge B\ \} = \mathbb{H}_1(\alpha, \beta)} . \quad (5)$$

R4. Modus ponens rule:

$$\frac{\mathrm{Val}\ \{\ A\ \} = \alpha,\quad \mathrm{Val}\ \{\ A \rightarrow B\ \} = \beta}{\mathrm{Val}\ \{\ B\ \} = \mathbb{H}_2(\alpha, \beta)} . \quad (6)$$

Truth functions $\mathbb{H}_1(.)$ and $\mathbb{H}_2(.)$ used in the above inference rules take their values in the segment [0,1] and should have some special properties which we do not discuss here. For convenience, one may assume that $\mathbb{H}_1(x,y) = \mathbb{H}_2(x,y) = \min(x,y)$.

3. THE ESSENCE OF THE KNOWLEGE REPRESENTATION FRAMEWORK

The essence of the framework discussed in this paper is the method of the representation of the temporal relation $\mathbb{T}(.)$ in the axiom scheme (2), and the semantics of the Skolem function represented here by an algorithm for calculating it's values in the inference rule (3).

In situation recognition problems we use stochastic treatment of fuzzy moments of time. That is, instead a crisp instant of time T_k we use a pair of real numbers $T_k = < \hat{\tau}_k, \sigma_{\tau k} >$, where $\hat{\tau}_k$ is an estimated value of time instant T_k, and $\sigma^2_{\tau k}$ is the variance of this estimate.

The structure of the temporal relation in any production rule is as follows:

$$\mathbb{T}(t_o, t_1, \ldots, t_n) \equiv \bigwedge_{k=1}^{n} \mathbb{P}(t_k, \Delta t_k, \sigma_k, t_o), \quad (7)$$

where $\equiv$ is logical eqivalence symbol.

The elementary time relation $\mathbb{P}(\hat{T}_k, \Delta t_k, \sigma_k, \hat{T}_o)$ in this expression means that for the estimated parameters of time instants T_k and T_o the following relations hold:

$$\hat{\tau}_o = \hat{\tau}_k + \Delta t_k, \quad (8)$$

$$\sigma^2_{\tau o} = \sigma^2_{\tau k} + \sigma^2_k . \quad (9)$$

In other words, the point T_o of time axis is situated to the right from the point T_k at a random distance Δt_k, the variance of the latter being equal σ_k^2. For any pair of events, $\langle A_k, A_o \rangle$, k=1,2,...n, the values of Δt_k and σ_k should be given by the expert taking part in the formalization process of a situation recognition problem.

The above mentioned assumptions allow us to treat the problem of evaluating of the time relation $\mathbb{T}(.)$ and estimating the value of the temporal parameter of a conclusion in a production rule (2) during the process of logical inference of target claims as a stochastic detection/estimation problem, i.e. as two matched subproblems.

The first one is stochastic estimating of the moment of time T_o, corresponding to the event A_o which is a conclusion of respective production rule, assuming that the time relation in this production holds.

The second subproblem deals with testing of a simple stochastic hypothesis about the agreement of estimated instances $\hat{T}_1, \ldots, \hat{T}_n$, and $\hat{T}_o$, at which premise events $A_1, \ldots, A_n$ take place, and the conlusion event A_o is assumed, with the limitations, imposed by the temporal relation $\mathbb{T}(\hat{T}_o, \hat{T}_1, \ldots, \hat{T}_n)$. The alternative hypothesis assumes that there exists at least one instance $\hat{T}_k$ for which the temporal relation $\mathbb{T}(\hat{T}_o, \hat{T}_1, \ldots, \hat{T}_n)$ does not hold.

Assuming stochastic independence and Gaussian distribution of all random variables in the stated above problem, and using a classic inference approach [2], one may get the following expression for estimating the time parameter of the conclusion event of a production rule (2):

$$\hat{\tau}_{o\$} = \frac{\sum_{k=1}^{n} (\hat{\tau}_k + \Delta t_k)/(\sigma_{\tau k}^2 + \sigma_k^2)}{\sum_{k=1}^{n} (\sigma_{\tau k}^2 + \sigma_k^2)^{-1}} . \tag{10}$$

This estimate has a Gauss an distribution with mean T_o, and its variance is given by the following expression:

$$\sigma_{\tau o\$}^2 = 1 / \sum_{k=1}^{n} (\sigma_{\tau k}^2 + \sigma_k^2)^{-1} . \tag{11}$$

Using von Neumann-Pearson's criteria of optimality, one can infer the following decision rule for hypothesis testing:

$$\mathrm{Val}\,\{\Pi(\hat{T}_0 \hat{T})\} = \left\{ \begin{array}{l} 1.\ \text{if} \sum_{k=1} \dfrac{(\tau_K + \Delta t_K - \tau_0)}{\sigma^2_{\tau K} + \sigma^2_K} < L_0 \\ ?\ \text{in the opposite case} \end{array} \right\} \qquad (12)$$

where L_0 is a threshold value, corresponding to a given probability of erroneous rejection of the simple hypothesis mentioned above.

The expressions (10) - (12) present an algorithm for evaluating the temporal relation P(.) , which is used when the inference rules (3) - (6) and applied to an axiom-production in the situation recognition problem solving process.

CONCLUSION

The knowledge representation framework proposed here may be used in expert systems intended to solve state assessment problems in a complex dynamic environment. In 1986 - 1988 an expert system shell DIRP based on this framework was developed by the author and his colleagues [3] and an experimental study of the new method proved its feasibility in real-time environments

REFERENCES

[1] Kirillov, V.P., "A Metric Model of Time for a Production Rule-Based System", (In Russian), Proc. Vsesoyuznaya Konferenciya "Problemy Razrabotky i Vnedreniya Ekspertnykh Sistem", Informiribor, (1989), pp. 61 - 63.

[2] Van Trees, H., "Detection, Estimation, and Modulation Theory", Part 1, (Wiley, N.Y., 1968).

[3] Kirillov, V.P. Majorov, V.N., Mitroshkin, V.B., Teplov, S.A., Chernozobov, Yu. V., "A Formalisation Method of Situation Recognition Problems and a Tool for Expert System Development", (In Russian), Proc. Vsesoyoznaya Konferenciya "Problemy Razrabotky i Vnedreniya Ekspertnykh Sistem", Informiribor, (1989), pp. 15 - 17

Industrial Applications of Artificial Intelligence
J.L. Alty and L.I. Mikulich (Editors)
Elsevier Science Publishers B.V. (North-Holland)

ON THE VALIDATION AND CONSISTENCY OF KNOWLEDGE BASES: THE COVADIS SYSTEM

M-C. ROUSSET

L.R.I - Universite Paris-Sud,
91405. ORSAY,
FRANCE.

ABSTRACT: The problem of detecting inconsistencies in knowledge bases is a crucial one, however, no general definition of the concept of "rule base consistency" has so far emerged. This paper deals with the general problem of knowledge validation in rule-based systems. The first part of the paper defines the concept of "rule base consistency" as a partial validation of rule bases in relation to some formal specification. The second describes a method for proving the consistency (or the inconsistency) of knowledge bases and its implementation in the COVADIS system.

It is currently held, in the rule-based systems domain, that sophisticated tools are necessary for helping an expert with the difficult task of knowledge acquisition. The problem of detecting inconsistencies is especially crucial. The risk of inconsistency increases with the size of the knowledge base. For large knowledge bases, detecting inconsistencies "by hand" is impossible.

Although some inconsistency checking tools exist, no general definition of the concept of "rule base consistency" has so far emerged; each tool implicitly defines the "consistency" concept as the absence of the type of abnormality it is intended to treat. A simplistic case, within the competence of a simple syntactic analyzer, consists of detecting some syntactic faults in rules, for instance wrong types for attributes.

Some other systems, while going further, are still only able to detect *superficial* inconsistencies, not taking into account the whole deductive potentiality of a rule base. The work on the ONCOCIN system [8] and, more recently the CHECK system [4] illustrates such an approach with its intrinsic limits; indeed, most inconsistencies are due to the interaction between several rules often via deep deductions.

The work presented in this paper deals with the general problem of knowledge validation in rule-based systems. The first part of the work consists of defining the concept of "rule base consistency" as a partial validation of rule bases *in relation to some formal specification.* The second part consists of designing a complete method to prove the consistency (or the inconsistency) of knowledge bases and implementing it in the COVADIS system.

Rule-based system validation can be seen from a software engineering point of view: the program consists of the inference engine and the rule base, and input data corresponding to the initial fact bases provided by any user. A classical validation consists, then, in testing the system on several test cases and comparing the obtained results with the expected ones. To be really rigorous and satisfactory, such an approach needs to take into account some criteria of cover of the domain by the different chosen test cases. Such a problem is not specific to rule-based systems validation: it exists and it is judged as difficult in the general domain of software testing.

Another approach consists in investigating the validation problem *in relation to some formal specification* that can be seen as a partial model of the real world which is used as reference of the validation. In the framework of this paper, these specifications are Integrity Constraints (IC) expressing some (syntactic or semantic) incompatibilities of facts in the domain.

A rule base RB is then said to be *consistent* if for any initial fact base (FB) acceptable as input to the system, the set of the deducible facts RB.FB satisfies the integrity constraints.

Definition: RB is consistent iff ∀ initial realistic FB, RB.FB IC

The notion of *realistic* initial fact bases corresponds to the notion of acceptable inputs for a program. Such a notion can be *partially* formalized by some of the integrity constraints, denoted IC_{input}, the other ones being denoted IC_{output}.

This strategy can be compared to the proving of program correctness, since it consists of proving that for any input FB of the "program" RB, satisfying IC_{input}, the corresponding output RB.FB satisfies IC_{output}; this can be denoted by $\{IC_{input}\}$ RB $IC_{output}\}$

However, the characterization IC_{input} is not necessarily complete: the existence of an initial fact base FB satisfying IC_{input} such that RB.FB does not satisfy IC_{output} does not necessarily mean that RB is inconsistent because the *potential counter example* FB may not be realistic.

An interaction mechanism can be used to display potential counter examples to the expert and to ask him whether they are realistic or not.

Before designing automatic tools to prove rule base consistency, it is necessary to pose the question of decidability of that notion, as defined above. The problem is that the number of initial fact bases can be potentially infinite; this is equally true for rule bases written in a first order logic syntax as for those written in a "attribute-operator-value" syntax. The solution comes from recognizing that a rule base has a finite number of *behaviours* . The notion of the *behaviour* of a rule base RB intuitively corresponds to the fact that different initial fact bases can activate the same set of rules (noted RB/FB). The formalization of the notion of the *behaviour* of a rule base RB is based upon the definition of an equivalence relation on the set of the initial fact bases:

FB *R* FB' iff RB/FB = RB/FB'.

Definition

- **the classes of equivalence of the relation *R* are the *behaviours* of RB**
- **any fact base belonging to a class of equivalence is called *representative* of the behaviour.**
- **a set of representative fact bases such that all the classes of equivalence are represented, is said to be a *representative set* of RB.**

According to the syntax of RB, some properties can be identified.

a) In the case of an "attribute operator value" syntax.

- The number of behaviours is finite.
- different initial fact bases having the same behaviours, produce the same set of deducible facts.

These two properties guarantee the decidability of the rule base consistency in the framework of an "attribute-value-syntax".

b) In the case of a "first order logic" syntax.

It is necessary to make some restrictions since first order logic is, by nature, not decidable.

The first restriction, which is often implicit in a rule-based system's framework, is to consider a syntax without symbols of functions. In such a framework, we have the following properties:

- the number of behaviours can a priori be infinite, but the number of *minimal* behaviours is finite. Intuitively, the notion of *minimal behaviour* means that the number of different instances of the rules defining the behaviour are minimal. Under some hypothesis on the integrity constraints, it is possible to restrict oneself to the minimal behaviours for the problem of consistency:

- the sets of deducible facts from two initial fact bases representative of the same behaviour correspond to instances of a same set of literal.

In conclusion, in the above framework of a certain type of "first order logic" syntax, the decidability of the rule base consistency property would then be guaranteed.

The second part of the work consisted of designing a method to prove rule base consistency and implementing it in the COVADIS system. The characteristics of the COVADIS system are:

- the rule bases concerned are written in the "attribute-operator-value" syntax of the expert system shell MORSE ([3]),

- the integrity constraints are expressed via "inconsistency rules" having the same syntax as the rule base but with the special conclusion INC (for inconsistency).

The method is based upon an ATMS mechanism providing a context for each potentially deducible fact, which explains it in terms of initial literals. If the special fact INC can be derived, the associated context serves to characterize the basic situations which are responsible for its deduction. The implementation of these method in the COVADIS system has proved this approach is feasible. It is, although costly, complete: once a rule base has been checked and proven consistent by COVADIS, no risk of inconsistency exists when it is used by any user. In addition to that, COVADIS has computed the contexts of all terminal facts; these can be submitted to the expert for validation. In addition to proving rule base consistency, COVADIS provides promising prospects in systematic rule base validation.

REFERENCES

[1] J.De Kleer, An Assumption-Based Truth Maintenance System. Artificial Intelligence, Vol 28 ,1, 1986.

[2] J.R. Geismann, R.D. Schultz, "Verification and Validation of Expert Systems", AI Expert, February 1988, pp 26-33.

[3] "equipe IASI du L.R.I, MORSE, manuel de reference, Rapport Interne No. 255", L.R.I, Orsay, France, Decembre 1985.

[4] T.A.Nguyen, W.A.Perkins, T.J.Laffey, D.Pecora. "Checking An Expert Systems Knowledge Base For Consistency And Completeness", . Proceedings of IJCAI 1985, pp 375-379.

[5] R.M O'Keefe, O. Balci, and E.P.Smith. "Validating expert system performance", IEEE Expert, Vol 2, No. 4, pp 81-90.

[6] M.C. Rousset. "On the Consistency of Knowledge Bases: the COVADIS System". Proceedings of ECAI 88.

[7] M.C. Rousset. "Sur la coherence et la validation des bases de connaissances: le systeme COVADIS", These d'Etat. Universite d'Orsay. France. Septembre 1988.

[8] M.Suwa, A.Scott, and H.Shortliffe, "An approach to verifying Completeness and Consistency in RBS". The AI Magazine, Fall 1982.

[9] D.C.Wilkins, and B.G.Buchanan."On Debugging Rule Sets When Reasoning Under Uncertainty". Proceedings AAAI 1986, August 1986, pp 448-454.

Industrial Applications of Artificial Intelligence
J.L. Alty and L.I. Mikulich (Editors)
Elsevier Science Publishers B.V. (North-Holland)

A PROCESS EVENT KNOWLEDGE MODEL FOR INDUSTRIAL EXPERTISE

Alexandre V. YAKOVLEV and Alexej I. PETROV

Department of Computing Science
Leningrad Electrical Engineering Institute
Leningrad 197022 USSR

The modelling of event-oriented knowledge is a key problem in designing intelligent support systems for industrial experts who operate in such domains as equipment assembly/repair process planning or tracing of events in the diagnosis of faulty equipment. In this context, we use labeled event nets, a subclass of Petri nets, for which two types of semantics, the event semantics and the equipment state semantics, are introduced with the examples of properties inherent to them. Finally, a prototype system architecture, called PREFIX, is briefly described.

1. INTRODUCTION. MOTIVATION OF EVENT KNOWLEDGE MODELING

One of the most crucial problems in designing intelligent support systems for the industrial process control staff involved in (Case A) the development of process technology charts for assembly-disassembly-repair of various equipment or (Case B) diagnostic activities for faulty equipment consists of modeling and representing the several kinds and levels of event-oriented knowledge [1-3], which can be regarded as a specific kind of procedural knowledge [4]. (The application domain of such knowledge mav also include analysis and design of organizational systems [5], office automation [6] to name but a few.) The importance of event knowledge stems from the following, though not all possible, factors. In Case A, the correct cost evaluation of a process operation (e.g. the "changing a car brake disk" operation requiring the "removing a wheel" operation, which in its turn requires "removing a hubcap", "unscrewing a bolt" etc.) can only be achieved if a proper estimation of the corresponding process chart is ensured. In Case B, when some device must be diagnosed, the expert should establish the course of events relevant to the fault. In doing so, he or she matches the equipment operator's "story" with some of the generic "event cliches" of potential faults.

Unlike many application domains using static knowledge representations, such as semantic networks, descriptive frames, AND-OR trees and production rules, the above paradigms require an adequate formal model for representing the system of events (the so-called "deep knowledge" [7]) which are temporally ordered by causal relationships and occur through the interaction of a set of communicating agents. An agent can be interpreted by such operations, atomic for a certain abstraction level, as "removing a wheel", "unscrewing a bolt", "switching-on a fuel pump" etc. An agent is the object (person) having a sequential, or linear, behavior (at any moment, at most one action or operation is allowed), which can be synchronized, at certain actions, with the other agent behaviors, e.g. in adjusting the ignition mechanism of a car, one of the agents operates the starter while the other agent assesses the quality of spark. Such a "joint venture" must therefore be included in the behavior of each of the participating agents.

Petri nets have been suggested [8] as a useful tool for event knowledge representation. In this paper, we use labeled event nets, which are syntactically close to occurence nets of [7]. They are a subclass of Petri nets, quite sufficient for the indicated purposes.

2. LABELED EVENT NETS

A labeled event net (LEN) is defined as a partially ordered set (poset) $< E, O, \mu, \leq >$ represented by an acyclic graph, whose vertices correspond to events in set E, labeled with "process technology" operations in set O by means of a labeling function $\mu : E \dashrightarrow O$, and arcs stand for the $\leq$ (partial order) relation.

Each operation in O is assigned to a particular technological asset - the element or component of equipment involved in the operation. Hence, each operation implies some discrete change of a state of a particular component. For a given LEN there is a partition of the set of ordered event pairs (e_i, e_j), $e_i \leq e_j$, associated with the behavior of each individual agent.

For every agent, all the events corresponding to the actions it is involved in are linearily ordered. The entire LEN is thus a superposition of the linear LENs of agents interacting on joint events.

3. EVENT SEMANTICS OF LENs

For efficient use of LEN framework in the knowledge base of an industrial expert one should clearly define the semantics of LENs. As such semantics, with which the expert can solve necessary problems, we can consider the semantics of execution sequences, also known as "interleaving semantics", and the relational event semantics, known as "causal semantics" [9]. The first is suitable for a human, who is supposed to have a sequential way of thinking, and hence, in Case A, it can be used, for example, for matching a particular schedule of actions on the process chart, executed by one of the agents, with the entire chart.

In Case B, such semantics correspond to eliciting a fact of matching between some sequence of the equipment operator's actions and equipment response observations and the poset stereotype of a "fault fabula". This matching can be mimicked as either an identity, thus being a strong form, or as "covering" by a given fault fabula, thus meaning a weaker form, i.e. the top-down similarity.

The second semantics is needed when one cannot distinguish between certain effects using the first one. These effects may pertain to concurrency between events. For example, using the interleaving semantics, one cannot precisely claim HOW the two operations marked with events e_i and e_j are executed if there are at least two such sequences have been observed that in one, "e_i precedes e_j", and in the other, "e_j precedes e_j."

Here, the concurrent execution of both e_i and e_j by the two independent agents is possible, with a possibility of either of them to be the first at finish, and the alternative execution of both e_i and e_j by the same agent ("today, I shall do e_i first and then e_j but, tomorrow, the other way round") may be realized, too.

On the other hand, the interleaving semantics may also be unsuitable in the step-wise refinement of events [10], which one may need to specify in changing the process description level, e.g. the refinement of the "removing a wheel" operation into the component actions - "removing a hubcap", "unscrewing a bolt" etc.

The extraction of the both of these semantics can be done using the efficient graph-based analysis algorithms [11]. For example, for a LEN, one can easily compute the binary relations between events which are defined as follows.

The relation of causal dependence denoted by LI is the transitive closure of $\leq$, while the relation of causal independence, denoted by CO, is given by

$$e_i \text{ CO } e_j = \text{not}(e_i \text{ LI } e_j) \ \& \ \text{not}(e_j \text{ LI } e_i) \ .$$

Using the relational semantics of LENs, the reasoning system can reply to such queries of a user as "if the specified process chart allows for executing the different actions on the same equipment component" , which is a kind of conflict checking paradigm, or "if the continuity between adjacent assembly-disassembly actions on the same component is violated", which presents a kind of interoperational consistency checking.

4. EQUIPMENT STATE SEMANTICS

In addition to the above semantics of LENs, one may also consider semantics defined in terms of the states of components which are involved in a process chart. Such semantics can be extracted by building the reachability tree, starting from the global state of the components which correspond to the set of minimal vertices of the LEN and, hence, is associated with an initial equipment status. Using the interpretation given by labeling μ, this tree allows for the transition from one global state to another global state by firing of a vertex in the LEN and thereby making a corresponding change of the local states of the involved components. Having this semantics, the user may query "if there are any closed non-efficient sequences of actions (loops), after which the equipment, within the single process chart, may return to some, already visited,states." Such checks are very useful in assessing the quality of process schedule documentation and cost evaluation. For example, this gives assurance of correctness of a price list for the various technological services with respect to avoidance of the so-called technological "add-ups". The latter can be utilized, say, by the insurance company which needs appropriate certification of the cost of repair for a damaged equipment.

When checking this semantics with respect to presence of non-efficient operation loops, one can use an alternative technique - the analysis of the dynamic coupledness of the described event structure directly on the LEN, without building a state graph. From the viewpoint of computational complexity, this may yield a crucial speed advantage. In such an analysis, one has to compute the hierarchy of the so-called coupledness relations between components and partition the set of components into coupledness classes [12]. The set of such relations presents a special kind of semantics, the relational semantics of dynamic coupledness of the equipment components.

5. THE PREFIX SYSTEM

To implement the above approach we have developed the prototype architecture of a software package, called PREFIX (from PRocess Events Framework for Industrial eXpert). It consists of the following modules: "LEN Editor", "LEN Librarian", "LEN Manipulator", "LEN Syntax Analyzer", "LEN Semantics Generator", and "LEN Verifier". The latter is loaded together with the knowledge base which supports the semantic analysis of LENs and tailors the system to a given application domain.

The modules have the following basic functions:

"Editor" supports the process of building new and modifying the library LENs, with their graphical representation and interactive inclusion of a textual interpretation of events and agents.

"Librarian" has the capability of a package database and provides necessary facilities for storing and maintaining the LENs.

"Manipulator" serves as an algebraic processor, which implements, on a user demand, the set of operators on LENs, such as "weaving" two given LENs with a possibility of having a non-empty subset of joint events, the projection of a LEN onto a set of specified events (or components), the reduction of a LEN with respect to a given subset of agents, the event refinement (stepping down to the lower abstraction levels), the encapsulation of subsets of events into a single event (steping up to the higher abstraction levels). Under certain conditions, "Manipulator" implements some target functions of the process chart analysis: for example, in Case A, when building a process chart from the set of partial subcharts (in Case B, the composition of a unified "fault history" from separate partial observations) of individual agents, we need to cohere them on joint actions. The checking of coherence is automatically provided by executing the weaving operator between the corresponding LENs, in an incrementally pairwise way.

"Syntax Analyzer" checks the syntactic correctness of the graphical and textual LEN specifications.

"Semantic Generator" extracts the semantics of the above mentioned types, the interleaving semantics, the relational event semantics, the equipment state graph, and the relational semantics of component operation coupledness, from a given LEN.

"Semantic Verifier" assumes an appropriate knowledge base, the rules of semantic analysis, which is formulated (and learned) according to the application domain defined by the user. It responds to the user queries the examples of which have been already presented.

At present, the PREFIX prototype is being implemented using Prolog and Pascal in the MS DOS environment.

6. CONCLUSION

An efficient framework for event-oriented knowledge has been developed. It is based on the labeled event net formalism. Such nets have several fundamental kinds of semantics, within which the user, an industrial expert, can reason about various properties of technological schedules and fault fabulas.

We plan further development of the methods for LEN analysis and reasoning about event knowledge:
(i) towards the capabilities of manipulating uncertain event knowledge structures, and
(ii) towards more creativity of the analysis, which means brining the analysis closer to the process of searching for most adequate process charts or most appropriate "fabulas" of faults.

This being so, one of the important methodological concepts can be the concept of distinction systems and dystinction dynamics [13], which may help to realize real-time reasoning in the PREFIX software.

REFERENCES

[1] Williams, T.P. and Kraft,R., COGSYS: an expert system for process control, Proceedings of the Fifth International Conference on Expert Systems, London, 1989.

[2] Gallanti, M., Guida, G., Spampinato, L. and Stefanini, A., Representing procedural knowledge in expert systems: an application to process control, Proceedings of the IJCAI 9, Los Angeles, 1985.

[3] Gallanti, M., Gilardoni, L., Guida, G. and Stefanini, A., Exploiting physical and design knowledge in the diagnosis of complex industrial systems, Proceedings of the ECAI 7, Brighton, 1986.

[4] Bullock, H., et al., A "bee-hive" model for heterogenious knowledge in expert systems, Proceedings of the ACM 14th Annual Computer Science Conference, Cincinatti, Ohio, 1986.

[5] De Cindio, F., De Michelis, G. and Simone, C., GAMERU: a language for the analysis and design of human communication pragmatics within organizational systems, Lecture Notes in Computer Science, No. 266 (Springer-Verlag, Berlin, 1987).

[6] De Cindio, F., De Michelis, G. and Simone, C., CHAOS as a coordination technology, Proceedings of the Conference on Computer Supported Cooperative Work, Austin, Texas, 1986.

[7] Bandini, S., Carniel, B. and Pomello, L., Narrative context model for representing deep knowledge, Proceedings of the 9th European Meeting on Cybernetics and Systems, Vienna (Kluwer AP, Dordrecht, 1988) Part 2.

[8] Fidelak, M., Petri nets: a formal language for knowledge representation, Proceedings of the ECAI 7, Brighton, 1986.

[9] Rosenblum, L., Yakovlev, A., and Yakovlev, V., A look at the concurrency semantics through lattice glasses, Bulletin of the EATCS, No. 37, 1989.

[10] Castellano, L., De Michelis, G. and Pomello, L., Concurrency versus interleaving: an instructive example, Bulletin of the EATCS, No. 31, 1987.

[11] Kndratyev, A. Yu., Rosenblum, L. Ya. and Yakovlev, A.V., Signal graphs: a model for designing concurrent logic, Proceedings of the International Conference on Parallel Processing, August 1988, (The Pennsylvania State University Press, University Park, 1988) Vol. 1.

[12] Rosenblum, L.Ya. and Yakovlev, A.V., Analyzing semantics of concurrent hardware specifications, in print.

[13] Heylighen, F., Formulating the problem of problem-formulation, Proceedings of the 9th European Meeting on Cybernetics and Systems, Vienna (Kluwer AP, Dordrecht, 1988) Part 2.

Industrial Applications of Artificial Intelligence
J.L. Alty and L.I. Mikulich (Editors)
Elsevier Science Publishers B.V. (North-Holland)

ARTIFICIAL INTELLIGENCE AND FAULT DIAGNOSIS: AN APPROACH TO THE VALIDATION PROBLEM

J. L. ALTY and D. PEARCE,

Turing Institute,
George House
36 N. Hanover St.,
Glasgow, UK.

ABSTRACT: The problem of validating expert systems is discussed and a number of techniques for performing validation are examined. Two techniques are considered in more detail - knowledge integrity checking and qualitative modelling using inductive techniques. The qualitative modelling approach is explained and some limitations investigated. The qualitative modelling approach does move back the validation problem from checking the consistency of a set of rules to validating the model itself, but the problem of constructing a consistent model remains. An approach is suggested which uses SGML to define the model and then derives the model and documentation automatically. This also enables further validation checks to be carried out on the model.

1. THE VALIDATION PROBLEM

Validation of Expert Systems raises serious problems. Whilst these problems are well-known, little work as yet has been done. Usually some limited form of validation is carried out under the heading of evaluation - "evaluation by domain experts helps to determine the accuracy of the embedded knowledge and the accuracy of any advice given" (Gaschnig et al [1]). Using this approach a completed, or partially completed, system is checked by the expert for reasonableness. Although the process of evaluation normally goes beyond validation and involves measuring the utility of the system as well as its authenticity, thus far, "post" evaluation appears to be the only practical validation technique in current use.

The difficulty in validating rule-based systems results from the intimate connections between rules and data instantiations. The many possible instantiations rapidly generate a combinatorial explosion of states which cannot be explored exhaustively. The set of conflicting rules generated at any point in the consultation depends entirely upon current instantiations of variables making formal evaluation difficult. As a result the prototype approach is usually favoured. It involves a continuously interactive evaluation procedure probing for the lack of validity of the knowledge in the system by execution. However such prototyping approaches also pose a considerable problem for validation. A set of rules is only "correct" until the next rule is added. The process of validation is therefore non-monotonic. Under certain special circumstances it is possible to prove that a set of rules is correct. Niblett [2], for example, was able to prove an advice strategy for a chess end-game. However such an approach is not generally applicable.

Additional validation problems arise from other aspects of the knowledge usually stored in expert systems, such as the issue of "deep" versus "compiled " knowledge, the extensive use of heuristics (how does one prove the validity of a heuristic which depends upon current instantiations), the mix of forward and backward chaining, and, in some systems, the use of probabilities which even the domain experts do not fully understand.

In searching for a solution to the problem of validating expert systems it is useful to examine validation in more traditional areas of computer science. There are a number of techniques in the traditional language validation field which may be broadly classified into pragmatic and formal approaches. Pragmatic approaches cannot be proved and are not usually complete. They are essential since the formal methods are usually only applicable to a small sub-set of problems. Many pragmatic approaches have grown out of systems analysis and design. Examples of such approaches are Top-down Design or Step-wise refinement (Wirth [3], Constantine and Yourdon [4]), Data Driven design (Warnier [5]) and Testing strategies (Myers [6]). The former two are classed as design methodologies and are used during the design process. The latter approach is more concerned with constructing appropriate testing sets.

Formal verification has been attempted using three main techniques:

- the operational approach (Berg et al [7]).An abstract machine is defined and the language semantics expressed in terms of this machine.
- the denotational approach (Strachey and Milne [8]).Constructs are mapped onto an abstract value space.The values in this space are mathematical objects so that mathematical techniques may be used to reason about them.
- The axiomatic approach (Hoare [9]). In this approach each program construct has associated axioms which state what may be asserted after the execution of the construct.

A formal approach usually involves a formal notation and a proof theory. The most promising approaches at present appear to be those based upon the Floyd-Hoare inductive assertion method using inductive invariants (Hoare [10]). Unfortunately the formal specification technique does not work well for the complex high level abstractions used in Software Engineering. For example the proof of a string search algorithm involving one page of code requires quite a deep proof.

It is reasonable to assume that formal methods are not yet powerful enough to be of any immediate use and there are two sub-optimal approaches which can be used:

- the construction of knowledge checkers which can examine particular aspects of consistency. Examples of such approaches include KIC (Pearce [11]), Type Checking (Mycroft and O'Keefe, [12] and Stachowitz et al [13])

- approaches using qualitative modelling and inductive techniques (Mozetic et al, [14])

Knowledge Checkers can operate at many different levels. The highest level would verify that a complete system was correct and would produces the appropriate outputs under all conditions. From the discussion above it is clear that this is not possible so checking is limited to one or more levels including:

- verification of the syntax of individual statements (as in the conventional compiler approach)
- verification of the logic of individual statements
- verification of semantic aspects of the whole, or parts of the system
- verification of the logic of subsets of the system
- variable binding analyses

Two examples of knowledge checkers are KIC and EVA. In the Knowledge Integrity Checker KIC (Pearce, [11]) checks are made for unreachable clauses, dead-end clauses, cyclic clauses, type checking, incompleteness and subsumption on a set of rules in PROLOG format. The Expert System Validation Associate EVA (Stachowitz et al [13]) which is written in LISP, comprises a logic checker, structure checker, semantics checker, omission checker, rule proposer, behaviour verifier and control checker. Such knowledge checkers are very useful but they can miss vital errors.

In the qualitative modelling approach, a model is created which can then be progressively failed across all components. This provides a series of examples which form the input for an inductive algorithm which generates the rules to be used in the expert system. This approach changes the validation problem from validating a set of rules to validating the qualitative model itself.

2. THE QUALITATIVE MODELLING APPROACH AND FAULT DIAGNOSIS

The use of the qualitative modelling approach for fault diagnosis has already been reported by Pearce [15]. The area of application was the electrical power sub-system of a satellite. This consisted of a set of solar arrays, switching circuits, two batteries and an electrical bus for connecting with the payload. Thirty seven telemetry points provided information for ground control and from such information the ground based operators had to determine faults and suggest error correction procedures. A model of the subsystem was constructed in PROLOG. It consisted of a set of predicates which defined the interconnectability of the constituent components and their initial states. Behaviour rules were then specified for each component to define how a change of state of one particular component affected another. By running these heuristic behaviour rules the performance of the satellite can be simulated. In particular, its behaviour (and the corresponding values of the thirty seven telemetry points) when one or more components fail can be generated.

The procedure is as follows. A component is failed. The model is run until it reaches a steady state. All the possible measuring points (in the satellite's case the set of telemetry points relayed to ground control) are read-off. These together with the introduced fault form an example of failure, the result being the introduced fault and the telemetry points being the attributes. A second component is then failed and the process repeated yielding a second example. The process is repeated until all components have been individually failed. At this point an induction algorithm is applied to induce a set of rules which summarise the complete set of behaviour represented by the example set. These rules can then be used for diagnosing all single faults in the subsystem. The above process can be repeated for all combinations of two faults to give the rules for two-component failure and so on.

The important point about the above process is that the induction is carried out over a complete set of examples and thus avoids the usual problems of completeness when inducing rules from an incomplete set of examples. Thus if our original model is correct our rules should be correct so the validity problem reduces to ensuring that the model itself is correct.

In the case reported by Pearce, an expert system had already been constructed for the power subsystem by traditional means. This had been constructed using the Expert System Shell "Envisage", had taken about 6 man-months to construct and had resulted in a 110-rule system. By comparison, the induction approach yielded 75 rules and required only 3 to 4 man-months to construct. When both sets of rules were tested on a real-time simulator the induced rules achieved a 100% success rate as compared with 75% for the Envisage rules. The superiority of the qualitative modelling approach is clearly evident in this particular example. It is also interesting to note that Pearce also ran both sets of rules (the Envisage rules and the induced rules) through the Knowledge Integrity Checker KIC. Whilst the induced rules passed without any identified error, six faults were found in the rules derived by conventional knowledge engineering techniques.

3. WHY IS THE QUALITATIVE MODELLING APPROACH BETTER ?

In order to understand why the qualitative modelling approach yields superior results it is necessary to examine how each rule set was created. In the Envisage case, standard Knowledge Engineering techniques were used to extract the rules from the engineers. This is a difficult process and checking the validity of a set of 110 rules is problematic. In the qualitative modelling case the model was developed from discussions with the engineers and a key feature of the process was the construction of a visual simulation of the model. The

PROLOG model was used to drive a schematic representation on a colour SUN workstation using the HYPERNEWS graphics interface software (Van Hoff, [16]). Engineers were therefore able to play with the model and verify (by experience) its "correctness". Whilst this is no guarantee of its validity it is certainly much easier to do than verify a set of rules. Thus we have pushed back the validation problem into one of validating a visual model (a much easier process).

4. COMBINATORIAL EXPLOSION PROBLEMS

Because example creation involves the systematic failing of each component in turn it might be said that the above approach will be similarly limited by the combinatorial explosion problem. In particular two- and three- simultaneous component failure will involve large amounts of computation. Furthermore, the satellite problem described above only had 61 functional components under 8 payload conditions and 3 solar phases. A complete example set therefore covered 1464 examples in all. A justifiable criticism would be that such an approach would not scale-up for "real" problems.

In fact, the induction process is reasonably fast and the time taken for the ID3 algorithm to induce rules is roughly linear with respect to the number of examples. The above example required about 20 seconds on a SUN/3 workstation so increasing the number of components to, say, 2,000 or 3,000 would not be serious particularly as the induction process only has to be done once and so could be left running overnight if necessary.

A more serious problem, however, is the generation of the examples. To generate each example the model has to be run until it reaches a steady state. In the 1464 example mentioned earlier, this took nearly one hour. Although this process is effectively linear with respect to the number of components, a 2,000 or 3,000 component model might require 30 to 40 hours. Although, once again this is a one-off process, it does suggest that such a size of model might pose a real upper limit for the technique.

There are two other ways of reducing the combinatorial complexity - by introducing real world constraints in order to limit the number of examples, and by decomposing the problem hierarchically and solving each subsystem separately. In the heart modelling case (Mozetic et al) some faults simply could not exist simultaneously so that the number of possible examples was considerably reduced. Whilst it is undoubtedly true that some faults will be mutually exclusive in the electric circuit case it is unlikely that there will be a significant reduction in problem complexity, so this is not an option in our case. We are therefore examining the possibility of using the hierarchical nature of collections of components to reduce problem complexity.

Two- and three-simultaneous fault rule induction would place prohibitive demands on computing requirements, however, it should be noted that no other attempts have been made, by other means, to solve problems of such complexity.

5. USE OF SGML IN DEFINING AND BUILDING THE MODEL

There are two aspects to model building which would greatly improve the usefulness of the technique. These are

- specifying the model in a more fundamental way (rather than simply building it in PROLOG).
- using such a specification as the basis for automatic model generation.

Such an approach would have two benefits. Firstly, one cannot expect engineers to become proficient in PROLOG so without automatic generation from a more readable specification the technique requires continuous assistance from a proficient PROLOG programmer. Secondly, as we have already mentioned, we have only pushed back the validation problem one stage to validation of the model rather than validation of the rule-set. A specification would enable us to verify some (if not all) aspects of the model. We thus require a specification technique which is readable by engineers and yet is formal enough to yield to some form of analysis. This dual requirement led us to consider the use of the Standard Generalised Mark-up Language (SGML) for model specification.

SGML [17] [18], [19] was developed by publishers to ease to problems of document interchange. It is an attempt to formalise and standardise the process of marking-up a document before publication defining such features as layout, style, font, format etc.. by inserting marks (or tags) in the document. Such mark-ups are concerned with defining the appearance of the document to a fine level of detail. SGML is a meta-language which can be used to define an arbitrary number of mark-up languages in a standardised way [19]. Since one can define one's own mark-up language using SGML the mark-up need not be restricted to publication features such as paragraphs, fonts, titles etc.. but can be extended to include semantic features as well and it is in this regard that we have found SGML useful for defining our models.

In SGML the format of a document is defined in a Document Type Definition (DTD). For example, a simple article DTD might be defined as (not is strict SGML language):

```
REPORT ::=            OPENING , MAIN_SECTION , CLOSE
OPENING::=            TITLE, ABSTRACT?
MAIN_SECTION ::=      PARA+
CLOSE ::=             REFERENCE*
ABSTRACT ::=          PARA+
PARA ::=              #PCDATA
REFERENCE ::=         #PCDATA
TITLE ::=             #PCDATA
```

Where "," means "followed by", ? means "optional", + and * have their usual meanings of "at least one" and "none or more", and #PCDATA means "character data" (i.e. the actual text of the document containing no further subdivisions of layout). When the document is created using an SGML editor under this DTD, marks are inserted into the text (with these names) to preserve the document structure. Once a document has been created using a DTD, the marked version can then be translated into other formats using a translator which parses the document using the DTD and then translates the marked-up sections to other formats defined by a set of translation rules. In publishing terms this could mean translating documents from MacWrite to Word to LaTex etc.. The above example is a very simple DTD. In SGML tags can have attributes and these can be used to cross reference within the document.

Although not the original intention of SGML, marks can also be defined of a semantic nature, and we have defined our model using such a mark-up. Furthermore, we can express the model in normal text which is readily readable by engineers and yet contains the mark-up for defining the relevant aspects of the model. Translators can then use the mark-up to create the actual PROLOG model from the original text, and other translators could be used to extract model information for consistency checking.

6. AN EXAMPLE MODEL

A DTD has been constructed to illustrate how the technique can be applied to qualitative modelling. As an example we model the Freddy3 robotics environment at the Turing Institute. The DTD looks like this:

MODEL ::= DOC* , COMP+ , INDTYPE* , IND+
a model consists of some documentation, a number of components possibly some indicator types and at least one indicator. Indicators are interface control options for starting, stopping, single-stepping etc..
INDTYPE ::= #PCDATA

an indicator type is described in text
IND ::= SIMPLE | COMPLEX
visible indicators are either simple or complex
COMP ::= DOC^* , $SUBCOMP^*$, ATT^* , $RESP^*$, $FUNC^*$
a component consists of some documentation, a number of subcomponents, a set of attributes for the component , a set of message responses to other components and a set of functions
SUBCOMP ::= COMP
a subcomponent is the same as a component
ATT ::= DOC^*
an attribute is some documentation
RESP ::= DOC^* , RL^+
a response is some documentation and one or more response lines
FUNC ::= DOC^* , RL^+
a function (user defined) is documentation and one or more response lines
DOC ::= REFATT | REFCOMP | REFRESP | #PCDATA
documentation is a reference defined later or just text
RL ::= SETTO | SETPAR | GEN | ADD | SEND | FOWD | EXE |
REPEAT | IFELSEIF | IFELSE | IFTHEN | EOR
setto - set an attribute value to something, setpar - set a parameter, ...
fowd - forward a message, exe - execute code, ...
REFATT has attributes NAME, UNIT
REFRESP has attributes NAME, UNIT
REFCOMP has attributes NAME
these last three definitions show that you can give attributes to tags.
The definition carries on but we will stop here

The documentation is created under the control of this DTD which prevents the user from inputting information in the wrong position. As a result a marked document is created. Here is an actual example of a marked document produced with this DTD. Each mark has an open mark <mark> and a close mark </mark> to delimit the marked area. Labels and parameters are placed in [] .

<MODEL> [NAME = Freddy3] Freddy3 is the advanced robotics environment located at the Turing Institute. It consists of an overhead
<REFCOMP> [NAME = "camera"] </REFCOMP>
<REFCOMP> [NAME = "vision system"] </REFCOMP>
<REFCOMP> [NAME = "conveyor"] </REFCOMP>
belt and a single
<REFCOMP> [NAME = "puma"] </REFCOMP>
200 series robot with its own
<REFCOMP> [NAME = "controller"] </REFCOMP>
all controlled by application software running on a Sun workstation, and driven through a
<REFCOMP> [NAME = "vax"] </REFCOMP>
computer.

<COMP> [NAME = "application"] The application runs on a Sun workstation and has been deliberately designed to perform as an integral part of any automated application. It is divided into five separate logical steps each representing.... </COMP>
<COMP> [NAME = "camera"] An overhead camera is used to scan the
<REFCOMP> [NAME = "conveyor"] </REFCOMP> belt it can operate in one of two modes: either scanning a long thin strip on the moving conveyor ....when the belt is stationary.
<ATT> [NAME = "look_image" VALUE = "false" TYPE = "STD"] Look.image holds true if the object is currently visible on the conveyor belt whilst in scan mode. Values are (true, false). </ATT>

<ATT> [NAME = pick_position" VALUE = "empty" TYPE = "STD"] Pick.position holds the visible object's qualitative position on the conveyor belt. Values are (empty, entering, inside, leaving) </ATT>
<ATT> [NAME = "pick_clarity" VALUE = "normal" TYPE = "STD"] Pick.clarity describes the general form of the image the camera sees, values are (normal, blurred, bright, dark, black) </ATT>
....
<RESP> [NAME = "conveyor_look"] initiates the action of scanning the conveyor to detect an object. Result is passed back through the vax as the attribute
<REFATT> [NAME = "look_image" UNIT = "camera"] </REFATT>
<RL> <SETTO> [ATT = "scan_region TYPE = "LIT" VALUE = "look"] </SETTO> </RL>
<RL> <FOWD> [UNIT = "conveyor" </FOWD> </RL>
<RL> <SEND> [ID = "return_look_image UNIT = "vax" PARS = "[look_image]"] </SEND> </RL>
</RESP>
....

<INDTYPE> [TYPE = "B"] true false </INDTYPE>
<INDTYPE> [TYPE = "PP"] empty entering inside leaving </INDTYPE>
<INDTYPE> [TYPE = "CM"] stopped forward backward </INDTYPE>
......
<IND> <SIMPLE> [NAME = "time_period" TYPE = "TP" UNIT = "application" ATT = "time_period"] under which time period is the application performing </SIMPLE> </IND>
<IND> <COMPLEX> [NAME = "object_position" TYPE = "OP"] what is the objects current position
<INDCOND> [VALUE = "at_goal"]
<COND> <ATTVAL> [ATT = "object_released" VALUE = "true" COMP = "gripper" TYPE = "IS"] </ATTVAL> </CONDl </INDCOND>
<INDCOND> [VALUE = "off_end"]
<COND> <ATTVAL> [ATT = "object" VALUE = "off_end" COMP = "conveyor" TYPE = "IS"] </ATTVAL> </COND> </INDCOND>
<INDCOND> [VALUE = "dropped"]
<COND> <ATTVAL> [ATT = "object_dropped" VALUE = "true" COMP = "gripper" TYPE = "IS"] </ATTVAL> </COND> </INDCOND>
....

One translator which we have written simply converts this into a readable document.

> MODEL
> Freddy3 is the advanced robotics environment located at the Turing Institute. It consists of an overhead camera, vision system, conveyor, belt and a single puma 200 series robot with its own controller all controlled by application software running on a Sun workstation, and driven through a vax computer.
>
> APPLICATION
> The application runs on a Sun workstation and has been deliberately designed to perform as an integrated part of any automated application. It is divided into five separate logical steps each representing ... (rest of description omitted)
>
> COMPONENTS
>
> CAMERA
> An overhead camera is used to scan the conveyor belt. It can operate in one of two modes: either scanning a long thin strip on the moving conveyor simply to detect an object, or alternatively to determine the exact coordinates of an object when the belt is stationary.
>
> > ATTRIBUTE DEFINITIONS
> > Look.image holds true if the object is currently visible on the conveyor

belt whilst in scan mode, values are (true, false)
Pick.position holds the visible object's qualitative position on the conveyor belt, values are (empty, entering, inside, leaving)
Pick.clarity describes the general form of the image the camera sees, values are (normal, blurred, bright, dark, black)......

MESSAGE RESPONSES
Conveyor.look initiates the action of scanning the conveyor to detect an object. Result is passed back through the vax as the attribute camera (look.image)
Conveyor.pick initiates the action of examining the pick region on the conveyor once the conveyor is stationary and an object has been recognised. Result is passed back through the vax as the attributes camera (pick.position) and camera(pick.clarity)....

INDICATOR TYPES
Type BB has values true,false
Type PP has values empty, entering, inside, leaving
Type CM has values stopped, forward, backward....

INDICATOR DEFINITIONS
Time Period indicator indicates under which time period the application is performing.
Object Position indicator indicates the objects current position
Value is "at_goal" if "object_released" at gripper is true
Value is "off_end" if "object" on conveyor has value "off_end"
Value is "dropped" if "object_dropped" at gripper is true.
....

Another translator produces a hypertext version so that where-ever there are cross references in the SGML the user can switch in the text to the appropriate place.

A third translator produces automatically the actual PROLOG code which comprises the qualitative model. The designer then has only to connect the PROLOG with the actual screen images to produce a working model. Since the model and the documentation are both produced directly from the same SGML document there is always consistency between them. Extra validation can be performed upon the original document. For example connectivity of components and possible message response sequences can be checked.

7. CONCLUSION

The qualitative modelling approach when used with inductive techniques to extract the rules required for a diagnostic expert system provides a powerful approach for attacking the problem of validating expert system rules. It pushes back the problem to one of validating the qualitative model itself. The use of SGML to define the model enables a normal textual description to be produced which is completely consistent with the model description and the actual qualitative model derived automatically from it. It also offers extra possibilities for further validating the model.

The acceptance of SGML as an international standard and its current use by many influential organisations means that we will soon have a plethora of good SGML tools in the market place. These should greatly improve the ease with which our descriptive models are produced.

8. ACKNOWLEDGEMENT

We wish to acknowledge support from the European Space Research and Technology Centre.

9. REFERENCES

[1] Gaschnig J., Klehr P., Pople H., Shortliffe E., and Terry A, "Evaluation of expert systems: issues and case studies", in Building Expert Systems, (ed. Hayes-Roth F., Waterman D. A., and Lenat D. R) , Chapter 8, Addison-Wesley, (1983).

[2] Niblett T, "A provably correct advice strategy for the end game King and Pawn versus King", Machine Intelligence 10, (ed. Hayes J., Michie D. and Pao Y-H), pp 101 - 120. (1984)

[3] Wirth N., "Systematic programming, an introduction", Englewood Cliffs, NJ: Prentice Hall, (1976)

[4] Constantine L. L., and Yourdon E., "Structured Design" , Englewood Cliffs, NJ: Prentice Hall (1979).

[5] Warnier J. D., "Logical construction of programs", New York: Van Nostrand, (1977)

[6] Myers G., "The art of software testing", New York:Wiley, (1979).

[7] Berg H.K., Boebert W.E., Franta W.R. and Moher T.G, "Formal methods of program verification and specification" , Englewood Cliffs, NJ: Prentice Hall (1982).

[8] Strachey C., and Milne R. "A theory of programming language semantics", London: Chapman and Hall, (1976)

[9] Hoare C. A. R.,, "An axiomatic basis for computer programming", Comm. A.C.M. Vol 12, No 10, pp 576 - 583, (1969).

[10] Hoare C. A. R.,Communicating sequential processes, Comm. A. C. M. Vol 21, pp 666 - 677, (1978).

[11] Pearce, D., "KIC: A knowledge integrity checker", Turing Institute Report TIRM-87-025, Available for the Turing institute, Glasgow, UK, (1987).

[12] Mycroft, A., and O'Keefe, R., "A polymorphic type system for PROLOG", Artificial Intelligence, Vol 23, pp 295 - 307, (1984)

[13] Stachowitz, R.A., and Combs, J.B., "Validation of expert systems", Proc. 20th Hawaii Int. Conf. on Systems Sciences, pp 686 - 695, (1987).

[14] Mozetic, I., Bratko, I., and Lavrac, N., "Automatic synthesis and compression of cardiological knowledge", Machine Intelligence 11, (1988).

[15] Pearce, D., "The induction of fault diagnosis systems for qualitative models", In AAAI-88, Proc. of 7th. Int. Conf. on Artificial Intelligence, St. Paul, Minnesota, pp 353 - 357, (1988)

[16] Van Hoff, A., "HyperNeWS 1.3 User Manual", available from the Turing Institute, Glasgow, UK., (1989)

[17] International ISO Standard 8879: information processing - text and office systems - Standard Generalised Mark-up Language (SGML) British Standards Institute, (1986)

[18] Smith, J. M., and Stutely, R., "SGML: The users guide to ISO 8879", Ellis Horwood Ltd., Chichester, (1988).

[19] Barron, D., "Why use SGML ?", Electronic Publishing, Vol 2, No. 1, pp 3 - 24, (1989)

Industrial Applications of Artificial Intelligence
J.L. Alty and L.I. Mikulich (Editors)
Elsevier Science Publishers B.V. (North-Holland)

A SYSTEM FOR DESCRIBING A SCENE WHICH A ROBOT OBSERVES AND DISPLAYS IT ACCORDING TO TEXT IN NATURAL LANGUAGE

G.M. ILYIN and V.N. IGNATOVA

Institute of Mathematics and Mechanics,
The Leningrad University,
Petrodvoretz,
Leningrad,
The USSR.

ABSTRACT: The problem here discussed grew out of research in constructing a system that, on the one hand, perceives a three-dimensional static scene and generates its description in natural language, and, on the other hand, displays a scene according to its description in Russian.

One part of this system may be regarded as a system of scene recognition, but this part is not considered in the paper.

The system contains a mechanism (a robot) that can perceive objects of the scene (comparing them with the given pattern) and discern elementary relations between them. Here two types of relations can be discerned : binary relations that indicate the correlation of two different objects; and unary relations that indicate the position of the object in the given scene in a system of coordinates fixed by the computer. The results obtained in the process of scene perception can be represented as a list of objects participating in the scene and as a set M of triplets x R y, where x and y are the objects of the scene and R is a relation between them in the given scene.

Note that the set M is composed in such a way that for every pair of objects participating in the scene, all the relations linking the objects in the scene are enumerated, i.e. the set M contains all the information about the scene. It is obvious though that the text describing the situation should contain not all the information available in M. The text contains only a portion of the information considered essential for the reconstruction of the initial scene in its main features. This essential portion will be referred to as the "content" of the scene.

Certain conventions of the text describing the scene serve as a basis for revealing the content. A study of such texts showed that a certain sequence of elements of the set M may serve as an approximation (a so-called "deep" representation) of the text. In this case it is considered that every sentence of the text corresponds the statement about the relation of one object to another. At the same time it is supposed that every sentence introduces a new object through objects already introduced. At the start of the text there is a sentence introducing the object independently from other objects. Such a technique of text generation gives a good approximation - the obtained texts can be regarded as an acceptable description of the scene observed by the robot. It is necessary to determine the rules of the selection out of set M of the elements that will be included in the resulting sequence S and the rules for ordering these elements.

Formally the conditions for the sought-for sequence can be formulated in the following way.

Let $S = (S_1, S_2, \ldots\ldots, S_n)$ be regarded as the content of the scene, if:

a) $S_1 = Px$, where P is the predicate introducing object x for consideration. In natural language it is an expression like "there is", "is situated" and other synonymous expressions specific for every object, for example "a tree grows", "the sun is shining", "a bird is flying" etc;

b) $S_i(1 < i \leq n) = x R y$, where the triplet x R y is an element of the set M;

c) if $S_i = x R y$ AND $S_k = x' R' Y'$, then $x \neq x'$;

d) if x is an object participating in the scene then there is a $S_k = x' R' y'$, where $x' = x$; in other words the number of objects in the scene coincides with that of elements in S,

e) if $S_i = x R y$ AND $S_k = y R' z$, then $i > k$, i.e. any element x is introduced through the element already introduced.

In order to build such a sequence it is necessary to determine the rules of selection of some subset of M meeting the conditions c) and d). For that, for every object but one (belonging to S_1) only one triplet should be found where this object has the position of the left member.

In the suggested system the process of revealing the sought-for subset is based on the technique of attributing ranks to objects and relations. The ranks are the numbers that order the objects and the relations according to their importance for description. The introduction of the concept of "rank of object" allows us to select out of pairs of opposite relations linking the same objects, the relation which introduces the object with a higher rank through the lower rank object. The study of language constructions serves as the basis for attributing ranks. So, phrases like "a man on the truck" or "a man under the truck" are quite natural in the language, whereas "a truck above the man" or "a truck under the man" are not. In the initial set M (in the description of certain scenes) there are both types of elements, but in the resulting sequence S there should be only the elements that are natural in the language. The introduction of the concept of "rank of relation" allows us to select out of all triplets x R y introducing object x, the one that expresses the closest link of x with another object. It is this link that is preserved in the resulting text, it being the most informative one.

The experimental variant of the system deals with situations describing outdoor scenes with objects like "man", "bicycle", "house", "truck", "car", "fir", "lime", "hat", "spade" etc. (Though the list of objects is a fixed one, the system was built to be independent of a specific set of objects as far as possible. The introduction of new objects requires additional coding of the initial data, but does not lead to any alteration of the program). Each object is introduced by the number of the corresponding reference and the referencial index indicates the number of the object among other objects with the same reference.

Each reference is attributed a certain rank, independent from the concrete scene. Note two peculiarities. Firstly, some objects perceived by the computer as belonging to the same reference may get different ranks. For example the reference "fir" obtains its rank depending on the position of the object corresponding to it in the given scene. If the object corresponds to the reference directly, it gets one rank and in the resulting text is named "a fir". If the object corresponds to the reference with a turn 90° or 270° (which is stated in a set M with the help of a certain unary relation) then another rank is attributed to the object and in the resulting text it is named "a lying fir". The different ranks are attributed because of the different functions of these objects. Compare the texts: "There is a fir-tree. A truck is near the fir-tree" and "A fir-tree is lying. A truck is under the fir-tree". In the second case it is more natural to say: "There is a truck. A fir is lying on the truck" that is:

r ("a fir-tree") < r ("truck") < r ("a lying fir-tree").

The symbol r(x) designates the rank of the element x .

Secondly, there may be some objects the perception of which is complicated. For example, there is an object "a fence" in the analysed scenes which is perceived by the computer as two different objects (as in case when the fence is on different sides of the house, or there is a gate in the fence). Special rules of identification are needed for the perception of such objects.

In the collection of relations the following binary space relations between objects were employed:

"above" < "under" < "behind" < "in front of" < "near" < "to the left of" <"to the right of".

The symbol < shows the order of these relations, set with the help of ranks,- that is, the closest relation is the relation "above", then "under" and so on. In certain cases we should consider the most informative relation as the one which reflects the so-called "semantic valency" of one object to another most significantly, but not the relation with the lowest rank. For example, in the situation described by the text "A man with a spade stands in the truck" the relation "near" links the objects "a man" and "a spade" more closely than the relation "above" does the objects "a spade" and "a truck". Such contextual dependencies of the objects are stated by the special conditions for the situations. When these conditions are met, a special relation (it is also named a spec-relation) is established between the corresponding objects, and this relation is given the rank of the closest link. The conditions for the spec-relation are formulated in such a way that every object has a special relation with no more than one other object.

The basic data of the text generation facility are the results obtained in the process of scene analysis which can be represented as a list of objects participating in the scene and as a set M of triplets x R y, where x and y are the objects of the scene and R is a relation between them in the given scene. In addition the objects are also characterized by a set of unary relations.

The above mentioned considerations were the foundation of the algorithm which builds a sequence S corresponding the text of the scene description according to the given set M. At the outset certain corrections of the initial set M are carried out. Firstly, the objects depending on unary relations (like "a lying man", "a lying tree") are introduced. Secondly, the identification of different objects is carried out if they correspond to the same semantic equivalent ("a fence"). Finally, if the stated conditions are met, "special" relations between objects are introduced. Then the objects are arranged according to their ranks, and for every object x the triplets x R y are revealed, that contain R with the lowest rank among other triplets of the same type, and where $r(x) > r(y)$. The minimum number of these triplets is selected taking into account the following considerations:

a) if $x R y_1$ AND $x R y_2$ AND $y_1 R y_2$ then the triplet $x R y_2$ is not considered (i.e. out of the two objects y_1 and y_2 we choose the one that is linked directly with x by R).

b) if $x R y_1$ AND $x R y_2$ AND $r(y_1) < r(y_2)$ then the triplet $x R y_2$ is crossed out. If at the same time only one triplet corresponds the object x, then this triplet is included in the resulting sequence. If there are more than one triplet for the object x: $x R y_1$, $x R y_2$, ... , $x R y_n$(note that here $r(y_1) = r(y_2) = ... = r(y_n)$), then a new object of the type y_1 & y_2 & ...... & y_n is constructed (in its content this object will correspond the sum total of objects y_1 ,y_2 , ..., y_n) and a triplet x R (y_1 & y_2 & ...... & y_n) is included in the resulting sequence.

After the subset of triplets which include the sequence sought for has been chosen, these triplets are arranged in a succession meeting the conditions of coherency - every object can be introduced only through the object that has already been introduced. This is achieved through the output of the elements of the graph. In the beginning there is an object for which there is no triplet (the object with the lowest rank), then for each of the objects which depend on it, each of them is given with its own objects depending on it.

Experiments show that the resulting sequences can be regarded as a satisfactory approximation to the texts describing visual situations (scenes).

A more concise version of the algorithm for revealing "content" from a description in a special language was presented by us at the International AI Conference in Repino, 1977. It should be noted here that the content revealing algorithm uses ranks of objects and relations in a means of content graph constructed with a nodes-object and arcs-relation representations. Object ranks may be treated as a kind of common knowledge formalization. The content graph is used then for generating text in natural language describing the scene being processed, that is, research is made to transform the "deep" representation of generated texts into a more customary form meeting the requirements of good Russian, which is an interesting linguistic problem in itself.

Here we use a dictionary for objects and relations and take into consideration certain linguistic regularities such as the communicative perspective of the sentence being generated; introducing attributes ("{There is} a hat above a man" --> "a man in a hat"); selecting a fellow-verb for an object ("the sun shines", "a cloud moves", "there is a house", "a fir grows"); forming a complex sentence with a "which-clause"; denoting referential indexes for different objects belonging to the same class; conceptualization nets. At the same time the resulting text is subjected to automatic editing.

The second part of our system is the "question - answer" system for the content of the scene.

Any description of the scene will not contain all the information that is at the computer's disposal. That is why it is possible that the operator may sometimes feel like clarifying some details in the scene having some specific ideas in mind.

Consider for example a description: "There is a house with a fence. A fir grows behind the fence". The text does not display the relation between "a fir" and "a house" though it is surely included in the initial table. The relation can be extracted from the table with the help of the appropriate question ("How is the fir situated regarding the house?"). In Figure 1 you can see a scene displayed according to the following text (translated from the Russian ed. note)

Figure 1 A scene

"There is a house with a fence and a chimney which smokes. Two fir trees are growing behind the fence. In front of the fence a man is walking with the dog. A car is in front of the house. A bench with three men on it is near the house. Two limes are growing near the bench, a cyclist is going in front of them"

We certainly have not been striving for thorough questioning and answering. Accordingly we consider the three types of questions:

general questions ("is it true that X is related to Y by R-relation?")
relation-questions ("how X is related to Y?") and
object-questions ("which X is related to Y by R-relation? ").

However, the lexicon is broader than that. Basic objects X and Y can be expressed not only by a single word but also by a word combination with a sufficiently complex structure. It is also possible to couple questions of basic types using logical operators AND, OR and NOT.

The analysis of a question is based on a dictionary with stem entries producing a semantic description for a word and on structural rules applying to the questions of the three above-mentioned types. The answer generating procedure finds basic objects X and Y in the scene, defines the relations between them and generates an answer in a form corresponding to that of the question.

The third and the last component of the system is intended for the transformation a natural (Russian) text describing a scene into its visual match. The processing consists of three phases.

The first one is a linguistic analyzer which is based on a dictionary and a comparatively simple grammar (automaton type). The analyzer forms a list of objects participating in the scene and indicates space relations between them. During the processing the system can put some questions for clarifying the situation.

The second phase is a graphics planner. In accordance with the results of the analysis and taking into consideration a number of objects and the relations between them, an arrangement, size and order of the output of patterns corresponding to the objects of the scene are defined.

The third phase is visual scene reconstruction per se. The picture can be both of multi-coloured and of monochromatic type.

The software package is written in Turbo-C.

Similar systems can be applied to various domains dealing with teaching (including teaching foreign languages); facing the problem of drawing a scheme, map etc. matching its textual description; in different robot controlling tasks and in some other applications.

Industrial Applications of Artificial Intelligence
J.L. Alty and L.I. Mikulich (Editors)
Elsevier Science Publishers B.V. (North-Holland)

ANALYTICAL FORMS FOR DESCRIBING A CLASS OF KNOWLEDGE REPRESENTATION AND RELATED INFERENCE MECHANISMS OF A REASONING PROCESS

František ČAPKOVIČ

Institute of Technical Cybernetics
Slovak Academy of Sciences
Bratislava, Czechoslovakia

The main idea consists in a suitable modification of an abstract discrete dynamic system generally describing (see [1]) both the structure and the dynamic behaviour of discrete production processes. The abstract system was constructed by means of an analogy with ordinary regular Petri nets. After a small modification the system is able to describe analytically both the structure of knowledge about a problem in question and the dynamic behaviour of the deductive reasoning process based on rules. A new algorithm realizing the inference mechanism of the reasoning process is developed to improve the algorithms presented in [4], [5].

1. INTRODUCTION

Generally, the Petri net (PN) can be characterized as an oriented bigraph with two types of nodes (positions and transitions) and two types of edges (connections oriented from the positions to the transitions and connections oriented in the opposite direction) - see [2]. Hence, the structure of the PN can be symbolically described by the quadruplet

$$\langle P, T, F, G \rangle \quad , \quad P \cap T = \emptyset \quad , \quad F \cap G = \emptyset \tag{1}$$

where $P = \{p_1, \ldots, p_n\}$ is a set of the positions

$T = \{t_1, \ldots, t_m\}$ is a set of the transitions with

n, m being, respectively, the number of the positions and the transitions

$\emptyset$ is an empty set

$F \subseteq P \times T$ is a set of arbitrary connections oriented from the positions to the transitions

$G \subseteq T \times P$ is a set of arbitrary connections oriented from the transitions to the positions

$\times$ symbolizes the Cartesian product of the sets

The PN "dynamics" can be represented by other quadruplet

$$\langle X,\ U,\ \delta,\ x_o \rangle \tag{2}$$

where $X = \{x_1, \ldots, x_{N_x}\}$ is a set of states of the PN positions

$U = \{u_1, \ldots, u_{N_u}\}$ is a set of states of the PN transitions

$\delta : X \times U \longrightarrow X$ is the transition function of the PN

x_o is the initial state of the PN positions

N_x, N_u are some integers

$x_s = (\sigma^s_{p_1}, \ldots, \sigma^s_{p_n})^t$, $s = \overline{1, N_x}$

$u_r = (\gamma^r_{t_1}, \ldots, \gamma^r_{t_m})^t$, $r = \overline{1, N_u}$

t symbolizes the vector or matrix transposition

$\sigma^s_{p_i} \in \{0, 1\}$, $i = \overline{1, n}$, are the states (0 - passive, 1 - active) of the elementary positions

$\gamma^r_{t_j} \in \{0, 1\}$, $j = \overline{1, m}$, are the states (0 - closed, 1 - open) of the elementary transitions

More details can be found in [1], [2].

2. MODELLING DISCRETE PLANTS ON THE BASIS OF THE PETRI NETS

On the basis of the general PN formalization mentioned above the analytical descriptive model of the discrete plants can be created - see [1] , [2] . Thus, the following abstract dynamic system can be obtained

$$x_{K+1} = x_K + B.u_K \quad , \quad K = \overline{0, N} \tag{3}$$

$$x_K \big|_{K=0} = x_o$$

$$B = G^t - F \tag{4}$$

$$F.u_K \leqq x_K \tag{5}$$

where K is the discrete step of the system "dynamics" development

x_K is the (n x 1)-dimensional state vector of the system in the discrete step number K

u_K is the (m x 1)-dimensional control vector of the system in the discrete step number K

F is the (n x m)-dimensional matrix. Its element f_{ij} represents existence (when $f_{ij} = 1$) or absence (when $f_{ij} = 0$) of the connection directing out of the position p_i into the transition t_j, $i = \overline{1, n}$, $j = \overline{1, m}$

G is the (m x n)-dimensional matrix. Its elements analogically represent the connections oriented from the transitions to the positions

B is the (n x m)-dimensional matrix given by G, F

The principle of the dynamic development of the system (3) and that of the control vector synthesis in each step K are given in [2]. The step-by-step analysis of the model represents a theoretical background of the decision support algorithm at the control actions synthesis - see [1].

3. THE PETRI NETS IN THE KNOWLEDGE REPRESENTATION AND THE MODELLING OF THE RULE-BASED TYPES OF REASONING

In order to automatize the process of decisionmaking an automatic mechanism of reasoning must be found. The PN seem to be suitable for this aim - see [3] where the relation between the logical PN (LPN) or fuzzy PN (FPN) and the rule-based decisionmaking was described. However, the approach described there seems to be somewhat dependent on particular features of a problem to be dealt with. Hence, handling the rules can be awkward, especially in the case of a large number of the rules.
of the approach Alternatively we can think of an analytical approach. A suitable modification of the system approach to the description of the ordinary regular PN behaviour enables us to apply this powerful analytical tool to the study of the LPN and FPN. It consists of two simple steps. In the first of them we replace the arithmetical operations of multiplying and additioning that occur in the relationships (3) - (5) by the logical or fuzzy ones. In the second step we realize the related modification of the decision support algorithm mentioned above.

Let us introduce the following quadruplet

$$\langle S, R, F, G \rangle \tag{6}$$

for formal representation of the LPN or FPN structure. The "dynamics" of the LPN or FPN can be symbolically expressed by the quadruplet as follows

$$\langle {}^{S}X, {}^{R}U, \delta, x_o \rangle \tag{7}$$

The meaning of the particular symbols is the following

$S = \{S_1, \ldots, S_n\}$ is a set of statements. They correspond to the positions of the LPN or FPN. They represent some pieces of knowledge about a process.

$R = \{ R_1, \ldots, R_m \}$ is a set of rules. They correspond to the transitions of the LPN or FPN. They express our experience concerning the process operation.

$S_X = \{ x_1, \ldots, x_{N_x} \}$ is a set of states of the statements truth propagation. They correspond to the states of the positions of the LPN or FPN.

$R_U = \{ u_1, \ldots, u_{N_u} \}$ is a set of states of the rules evaluation. They correspond to the states of the transitions of the LPN or FPN.

$$x_s = (\sigma^s_{S_1}, \ldots, \sigma^s_{S_n})^t \ , \ s = \overline{1, N_x}$$

$$u_r = (\gamma^r_{R_1}, \ldots, \gamma^r_{R_m})^t \ , \ r = \overline{1, N_u}$$

$\sigma^s_{S_i} \in$

- $\{0, 1\}$, $i = \overline{1, n}$, when the LPN are used. They are the states (0 - false, 1 - true) of the elementary statements
- $\langle 0, 1 \rangle$, $i = \overline{1, n}$, in the case of using the FPN. They represent a subjective certainty in the truth of the elementary statements.

$\gamma^r_{R_j} \in$

- $\{0, 1\}$, $j = \overline{1, m}$, in the case of using the LPN. They are the states (0 - no, 1 - yes) of the elementary rules evaluation
- $\langle 0, 1 \rangle$, $j = \overline{1, m}$, when the FPN are used. They represent a measure of the elementary rules evaluation.

More details can be found in [4], [5]. The rules can be expressed either in the form of implications or in the form of IF--THEN structures. On the basis of the formalization introduced above, taking the relationships (3) - (5) into account, we can obtain the abstract dynamic system for the knowledge representation in the form

$$x_{K+1} = x_K \ \underline{\text{or}} \ B \ \underline{\text{and}} \ u_K \quad , \quad K = \overline{0, N} \tag{8}$$

$$x_K \big|_{K=0} = x_o$$

$$B = G^t \ \underline{\text{or}} \ F \tag{9}$$

$$F \ \underline{\text{and}} \ u_K \leq x_K \tag{10}$$

where <u>or</u> symbolizes alternatively the operator of the logical additioning either in the well known bivalued /Boolean/ logic (when the LPN are used) or in the fuzzy logic - in the case of using the FPN

<u>and</u> symbolizes alternatively the operator of the logical multiplying in such the types of logic

To be familiar with particulars see [4], [5].

4. THE INFERENCE MECHANISMS OF THE REASONING PROCESS

Let us introduce the algorithm for the reasoning process as the final result of this paper. Because of its automatic character we can speak about the inference mechanism of reasoning. The algorithm alternatively realizes either the logical inference mechanism - when the bivalued logic is used - or the fuzzy one - when the fuzzy logic is used. The algorithm is very simple. It automatically finds such transitions of the LPN or FPN which are able to be opened in the step K. As to the complexity it represents an important improvement in comparison with both the algorithm of the logical reasoning process presented in [5] and the fuzzy one presented in [4]. The improvement concerning the uniformity of the expression both of those algorithms is important too. The algorithm has the following form

START

- $K = 0$
- $x_K = x_o$

Label 1:

- $\bar{x}_K = \underline{neg}\ x_K$ (11)
- $v_K = F^t\ \underline{and}\ \bar{x}_K$ (12)
- $u_K = \underline{neg}\ v_K$ (13)
- $x_{K+1} = x_K\ \underline{or}\ B\ \underline{and}\ u_K$
- IF ($x_{K+1} = x_K$) THEN GO TO Label 2
- $K = K + 1$ (i.e. $x_K = x_{K+1}$)
- GO TO Label 1

Label 2:

- output of the histogram (x_K, u_K), $K = \overline{0, N_D}$
- realization of the decision on the basis of the results of the reasoning process

END

where v_K is the (m x 1)-dimensional auxiliary vector

<u>neg</u> is the operator of negation in the alternative type of logic. It is well known in Boolean logic. The negation of an operand $a \in \langle 0, 1 \rangle$ in the fuzzy logic is given by a fuzzy value

$$\bar{a} = \underline{neg}\ a = 1 - a \quad , \quad \bar{a} \in \langle 0, 1 \rangle .$$

N_D is a number of needed steps - i.e. the length of the reasoning process. It may be unknown at the start.

The kernel of the inference mechanism is given by relationships (11) - (13).

5. CONCLUSIONS

The improved algorithm of the automatic development of the reasoning process dynamics is presented in this paper. It represents the inference mechanisms of both the logical and the fuzzy rule-based deductive types of reasoning in the uniform way. The inference mechanisms have an analytical origin. They are based on the automatic analysis of the analytical description of the related rule-based types of knowledge representation. The structure and the dynamics both of the alternative types of the representation are described by the abstract discrete dynamic system in the uniform way.

Because of its simplicity and the ability to cover a wide class of processes, the presented approach is suitable especially for users who want to build up their own intelligent control system.

REFERENCES

[1] Čapkovič, F., A Decision Support Algorithm for Flexible Manufacturing Systems Control, Computers in Industry, Vol. 10, No 3, 1988, pp. 165-170

[2] Čapkovič, F., An Analysis and Modelling of Operating the Flexible Manufacturing Systems on the Basis of Petri Nets, lecture presented on the "Summer School for Scientific Workers in the Area of Robotics and FMS", Sozopol, Bulgaria, 1986, 20 pages, in Russian

[3] Looney, C.G., Fuzzy Petri Nets for Rule-Based Decisionmaking, IEEE Trans. on Syst., Man, and Cybern., Vol. SMC-18, No 1, 1988, pp. 178-183

[4] Čapkovič, F., A Representation of Rule-Based Types of Reasoning by Means of an Abstract Dynamic System Development, lecture presented on the international conference "Systems Science X", Wroclaw, Poland, 19-22 September 1989, 32 pages, to appear in the journal "Systems Science" in Poland

[5] Čapkovič, F., An Analytical Model of Rule-Based Types of Reasoning and Decisionmaking, in: Plander, I., ed. , Artificial Intelligence and Information-Control Systems of Robots - 89, Proceedings of the Fifth International Conference on Artificial Intelligence and Information-Control Systems of Robots, Štrbské pleso, Czechoslovakia, 6-10 November, 1989, (North-Holland, Amsterdam, 1989) pp. 369--372

Industrial Applications of Artificial Intelligence
J.L. Alty and L.I. Mikulich (Editors)
Elsevier Science Publishers B.V. (North-Holland)

MULTI-LANGUAGE PROCESSORS FOR COMPUTER SYSTEMS

A. E. VOEVUDKO and V. I. TSURKOV

Geotechnical Mechanics Institute,
UkrSSR Academy of Sciences,
Dniepropetrovsk.,
The USSR.
and
Computer Centre,
USSR Academy of Sciences,
Moscow,
The USSR.

ABSTRACT: Multi-language processors for the Parametric Statements Language and the Message Language are proposed. They will provide computer systems with many contact languages: Russian, English, French, etc. Industrial application areas include: Operating Systems, DBMS, Expert Systems. Scientific and Engineering packages, etc. Processors (especially as hardware) are able to unite many categories of system languages, e.g. data and knowledge representation and manipulation, commands, messages and dialogues.

1. INTRODUCTION

There are two types of languages which have a widespread use in all spheres of computer technology, parametric-oriented languages and message-oriented languages. As was shown in [1-4], all implementations of these languages which are used in various computer systems are distinguished only by "cosmetic" peculiarities. Therefore, they can be generalized and it is possible to create unified support tools.

Many benefits can be expected from universal processors. The first is that duplication will be greatly reduced. The second is that a simple way to internationalise computer systems can be realised. Users will make contact with computers in their native languages.

2. THE PARAMETRIC STATEMENT LANGUAGE

The parametric statement concept is well-known and widely used. Its many different approaches and peculiarities were analysed and resulted in the development of the generalized Parametric Statements Language (PSL) [1,4]

Positional Parameters (PP) and keyword parameters (KP) are the basis of the PSL. In accordance with [5] the formal syntax definition of PSL is as follows:

High Level Rules

1. <statement> --> <PP-list> ; | <KP-list> ; | <PP-list> , <KP-list>;
2. <PP-list> --> <PP> | <PP> , <PP-list>
3. <KP-list> --> <KP> | <KP> , <KP-list>
4. <PP> --> e ! <value>
5. <value> --> <name> | <text> | <integer> | <real> | <byte>
6. <name> --> <base name> | <synonym>
7. <KP> --> <name> = <KP-value>

8. <KP-value> --> <value> | (<value-list>) | '< string >'
9. <value-list> --> <value> | <value> , <value-list>

Regular Tokens Definitions

<delimeter>= , | = | (|) | ' | ;
<base name>= (<character>-<delimeter>)$^{+}$
<synonym>=<base name>
<text>=<base name>
<string>= (<character>-')$^{+}$
<number>=0 | 1 | 2 | 3 | . . . | 9
<sign>=e | + | -
<integer>=<sign><number>$^{+}$
<decimal>=<integer>|<sign>(<number>*.<number>$^{+}$|<number>$^{+}$
. <number>*)
<exponent>=e | E <integer>
<real>=<decimal><exponent>
<bit>=O | 1
<byte>=<bit>$^{+}$

Lexical Variable

<character>

From its definition it follows that PSL is a context-free language. It should be stressed that "delimiters" are variables. Thus, " , = ( ) ' ; " are a short form of lexical variables as follows: <parameters delimeter>, <KP-delimeter>, ... , <statement delimeter>. Moreover, it is possible to add any new tokens, both to rules and definitions (e.g, packed decimal and hexadecimal numbers)

The general purpose Processor (Translator) of PSL (PPSL) was implemented on an ES computer (similar to an IBM/370). It uses an operating memory of about 1 KB.

PPSL is a syntax-directed and table-controlled processor. There are three tables that control translation [4]; the Delimeter Table (DT), the Parameter Quantity Table (PQT) and the Parameter Description Table (PDT). The PDT has a complicated structure and consists of 12 blocks: B11, B12, ... B34. The contents and characteristics of each block are summarized in table 1.

	Base Names	Synonyms	Index of Synonyms	Classifier / Default Values
	8	8	4	1
PP	B11	B12	B13	B14
	K4	K6	K6	K1
	8	8	4	1
KP	B21	B22	B23	B24
	K2	K7	K7	K2
	8	8	4	1
KP value	B31	B32	B33	B34
	K5	K8	K8	K1+K2

Table 1. The Parameters Description Table (PDT)

In the block corners are the byte-size (upper) and the quantity (lower) of elements. The Index of Synonyms concerns the "base name", Classifier is an integer. e,.g. 0 - "text" 1 - "name" etc...

DT and PQT are vectors. The PQT structure is presented in Table 2.
After translation the results are output to the Parameter Value Table (PVT) which consists of 8-byte elements. The PVT structure is presented in Table 3

Element	Quantity of...
K1	PP
K2	KP
K3	KP-value in a list
K4	PP base names
K5	KP-value base names
K6	PP synonyms
K7	KP synonyms
K8	KP-value synonyms

Table 2 Parameter Quantity Table (PQT)

Values	Quantity
PP	K1
KP	K2
Size of list	
classifier index	1
From KP-values list	K3
String	10
String Index	1

Table 3 Parameter Value Table (PVT)

Such a non-traditional approach allows translation of all kinds of statements both with a different quantity of parameters and with variable main tokens, names, synonyms and delimeters. That is why PPSL is a general-purpose processor. Thus, there are two multi-language aspects of the PPSL. First, synonyms allow the support of many contact languages such as Russian. English, French, etc. Secondly, many Integrated languages both non-procedural and procedural could be developed. It is a simple approach - one PPSL and many DT, PQT and PDTs

Many different applications of the PSL to both well-known and original languages have been illustrated. [1 - 4].

It should be noted that a "cosmetic" front-end processor should be used to change or delete any delimiters, carry over any statements. etc. Only the statement form is interesting for us in the examples. That is why we do not need to explain them.

Operating Systems:

a) OS IBM / 370

```
//Task1 JOB  MSGLEVEL=(1,0), REGION=100K
//Step1  EXEC  PGM=A, PARM = 'A,B,C'
```

b) MS-DOS

```
DIR dd/ABC\W
ASSIGN A=B, B=A
```

c) UNIX

```
ls/abc/own>tf
ls ch[2-9]
```

d) DBMS Network Model

DDL

```
SCHEMA NAME=A1
LOCMODE  CALC=PROCI, USING=P1, DUPL=NO
O2 B I ;  PICTURE = A(50)
```

DML

```
READY AREA=A1,  COND= (EXCLUS,  UPDATE )
FIND FIRST, RECORD=B, SETA1B
```

e) DBMS (relational model)

Refreshing

```
ADD SHED,FLIGHT=117,FROM=MOSCOW, TO=TOKYO, TIME=9.15
        FINISH=17.25
        or in short form
ADD SHED,117,MOSCOW,TOKYO, 9.15, 17.25
```

SQL

```
SELECT SUPPLIER,STATE
FROM          S
WHERE CITY=PARIS
AND       STATE= 20,OR=>
```

f) Knowledge representation:
Frames

```
TOUR WHO='IVANOV  I . I .' WHERE=(TOKYO,OSAKA), WHEN=110990
        PERIOD= 10, WITH PETROV P.P. "
IF A=X1, B=5, C=YES
OR A=X2, B=7, C=NO
THEN P=M1, %=75.2
ELSE P=M2,%=61.1
```

g) graphics

```
CIRCLE CENTER = (5.,5.), RADIUS = 1.2
SHIFT UP=2., LEFT =1.3
```

h)calculations

```
A = 1. + 2. * 3. / 4.
E = A + B * C
E = A & B | C
```

Even these examples show that the PPSL can be used to unify many integrated languages. Their design and development could be stimulated and accelerated.

3. THE MESSAGE LANGUAGE

There are many kinds of message languages. But practically (with the exception of illustrations) only two languages dominate: parameter based and natural.

It is easy to make an "echo" of the PPSL statements. However, more interesting is to design the retranslator of PSL from PVT, DT, PQT, PDT, - to PSL statements. It will be very useful in many respects not only for mesages.

Four main forms of message language were picked out [4]:

<MPF> *<MO>* <MT>
<MPF> <MT>
<MT>
<MT>

where the meaning is <MPF> - message prefix (3 symbols), <MT> - message text (50 symbols), <MO> - message object or "mini-window" (8 symbols).

It should be emphasised that other forms can be used.

All these forms are supported by the Message Processor (MP) which works with the Message Quantity Table (MQT) and the Message Description Table (MDT) [4]. MQT is a vector and set a quantity of languages and messages. MDT consists of structurally equal blocks: one block for one language. A structure of one block is shown in Table 4.

Element Number	Value
1	Message prefix
2	1st Message
3	2nd Message
...	...
K	(K-1)th message

Table 4 A block of MDT for one language

The Processor is elementary. It operates in two environments: with RAM (institutional messages) and with a disk memory (ad- hoc messages).

4 . CONCLUSIONS

The PSL/ML and their processors provide a very simple and effective way of solving the problem of international computer systems. They can provide language support functions on any computer system. perhaps alternatively.

Because the industrial application area is wide, it is very important to implement these processors via hardware. Parallelism during translation of PP and KP is possible. That is why the PPSL can be a multiprocessor with a high-speed response

REFERENCES

[ll Voevudko, A.E., "Language tools of the DBMS BAMAS and their use for applied packages and systems", Dniepropetrovosk, 1986. pp. 11 Dep. 9063-V86.

[2] Voevudko, A. E., and Tsurkov. V. I ., "Implementation of the DBMS. BAMAS and applied aspects", 1zv. AN SSSR Tekhn. Kib. , 1988 1, p. 191.

[3] Voevudko, A.E.,. and Tsurkov, V. I ., Knowledge Representation Tools of the DBMS, BAMAS, Izv. AN SSSR. Tekhn. Kib., 1988, 3 . pp. 212-215

[4] Voevudko. A..E., "The Database Management System for applied Package Development ", (Moscow 1988, p. 196 . Thesis)

[5] Aho, A.V. and Ullman, J.D., " The Theory of Parsing, Translation and Compiling", (Prentice-Hall Inc., 1972, v. I)

Industrial Applications of Artificial Intelligence
J.L. Alty and L.I. Mikulich (Editors)
Elsevier Science Publishers B.V. (North-Holland)

THE SIMULATION OF FORMAL GRAMMAR CONSTRUCTIONS BY ALGEBRAIC PETRI NETS WITH VARIABLE MARKING (VARIABLE STRUCTURE)

Pavel A. MALTSEV

Institute of A. F. Mojayskyi
Leningrad , USSR

ABSTRACT
Different grammar constructions have a wide utilization in decision support systems for the inference of strings. The description of concurrent components in formal grammar constructions by the algebraic Petry net language decreases the inference time for strings. The analysis methods of algebraic Petri nets allow problems connected with the inference possibility of concrete strings by fixed grammar to be solved.

1. INTRODUCTION

The purpose of this text is to present an approach to the description of different grammar constructions by algebraic Petri nets tool and the application of specific methods to some problems of syntactic analysis. At first we introduce the basic notation and terminology to be used in the paper, in particular the formal notion of algebraic Petri nets and context grammars.

1.1. Algebraic Petri nets

The papers [1,2,3] develop the foundation of the algebraic Petri nets theory. Further developments [4] permitted the creation of a powerful tool for the modelling discrete dynamic systems. Algebraic Petri nets are described by the following definition.

DEFINITION 1. The algebraic Petri net N is defined by : $N=(P\cup F,T,A,V,M_0)$, where $P=\{p_1,..,p_n\}$ is a finite nonempty set of "p" type places; $F=\{f_1,..,f_m\}$ is a finite nonempty set of "f" type places; $T=\{t_1,\cdots,t_r\}$ is a finite nonempty set of transitions; A- is the finite alphabet; $V:[(P\cup F)\times T]\cup[T\times(P\cup F)\rightarrow A^*$

is a mapping marking arcs between places and transitions (or transitions and places), where A^* is a set of all finite strings over A, including the empty string γ;

M_0: $P \cup F \to A^*$ is an initial marking of places.

For every place $a \in P \cup F$ let $\Gamma^-(a)$, $\Gamma^+(a)$ be

$\Gamma^-(a) = \{b \in P \cup F \cup T \mid V(a,b) \neq \gamma\}$,

$\Gamma^+(a) = \{b \in P \cup F \cup T \mid V(b,a) \neq \gamma\}$.

The desire to model FIFO and LIFO processes has resulted to a requirement for places of two types: p and f. With this aim we describe the words in places of types p and f by strings over A. If we denote words going from places by direct and mirror strings, then places of f type will model FIFO processes and places of p type will model LIFO processes.

Now we describe the function rules of algebraic Petri nets. The general state of a net is defined by words in places. The words in places $\Gamma^-(t) \cup \Gamma^+(t)$ are modified after the firing of some transition t. The function rules of transitions provide the dynamics in the algebraic nets. The state of every net is defined by the marking $M : P \cup F \to A^*$.

The word $M(a)$, $a \in P \cup F$ marks the place a. The vector M represents the marking of the net :

$M = (M(f_1), \ldots, M(f_m), M(p_1), \ldots, M(p_n))$, $card\ M = card\ (P \cup F) = m+n$.

We now define the fire condition of the transition t, $t \in T$.

DEFINITION 2. The transition t has a concession at the marking M, if for all places of f type, $f_i \in \Gamma^+(t)$, $V(f_i, t)$ is the left multiplier of $M(f_i)$, and for all places of p type, $p_j \in \Gamma^+(t)$, $V(p_j, t)$ is the left multiplier of $\tilde{M}(p_j)$, where $\tilde{M}(p_i)$ is the mirror string relatively to $M(p_i)$.

DEFINITION 3. The fire of transition t, having a concession at the marking M, results in the marking M_1, $M\ (t\rangle\ M_1$,

$M_1(f_i) = g(V(f_i,t), M(f_i)) \cdot V(t, f_i)$, $f_i \in F$, where $g(a, ab) = b$;

$M_1(p_i) = d(\tilde{V}(p_i,t), M(p_i)) \cdot V(t, p_i)$, $p_i \in P$, where $d(a, ba) = b$.

We put on the set $X = \{V(a, t_i) \mid t_i \in \Gamma^-(a)\}$, $a \in P \cup F$ one condition: X^* is the free monoid, or X is the codex (see[4]). This condition in some cases may be reduced: the subset $X_1 \subset X$ is codex, $X_1 = \{V(a, t_i) \mid t_i \in \Gamma^-(a)$ and t_i have concession$\}$.

1.2. Formal grammars

In the paper three types of context grammar are considered: regular, context-free and phrase-structured. From the formal viewpoint a context grammar is $G=(N,T,P,S)$, where
N is the finite set of nonterminal symbols with $S \in N$;
T is the finite set of terminal symbols;
P is the finite set of productions $a \to b$, $a \in (N \cup T)^* \setminus \{\gamma\}$, $b \in (N \cup T)^*$.
The type of context grammar is defined by the nature of its productions. The regular grammars include the following productions:

$A \to a$, where $A \in N$, $a \in T$, or $A \to aB$, where $A,B \in N$, $a \in T$. Every context-free grammar has production: $A \to b$, where $A \in N$, $b \in (N \cup T)^*$. The phrase-structure grammars have more general productions: $a \to b$, where $|a| \leqslant |b|$, $a, b \in (N \cup T)^*$.

2. THE SIMULATION OF FORMAL GRAMMARS BY ALGEBRAIC PETRI NETS

In the definition of algebraic Petri nets the places are marked by strings over A. If the alphabet A includes sets of terminal and nonterminal symbols of context grammar G, $N \cup T \subset A$, then we may reproduce the formal grammars and their words by using the direct form without any recording by algebraic Petri net language. In the book [4] four fundamental operations of arithmetic are represented by concrete algebraic nets, since the algebraic net model is equivalent to the Turing machine. Consider some examples of concrete grammars in particular those which are not described by ordinary Petri nets.
Notice, that the vagueness of the production choice for the formal grammars in the algebraic Petri nets is ensured by the transitions with the front conflict.

At first we show the example of a regular grammar: $G_1=(N_1,T_1,P_1,S_1)$, where $N_1=\{A,B,S\}$, $T_1=\{a,b\}$, the set of productions are $S \to A|B$, $A \to a|aA$, $B \to b|bB$. The grammar G_1 is connected with the language $L(G_1)=\{a^n, b^m | n,m \geqslant 0\}$. The algebraic Petri net modelling this language is shown in Figure 1. The initial marking in the inference of the new word is:
$M(p_1)=S$, $M(p_7)=l$, $M(p_i)=\gamma$, $i=2,..,6,8,9$.

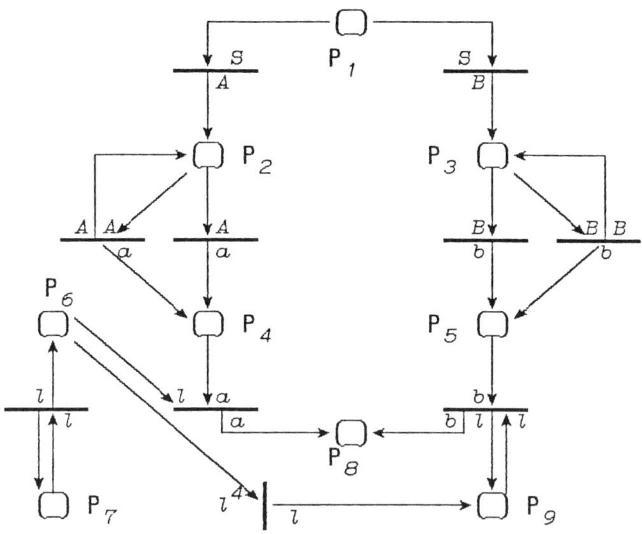

FIGURE 1

The algebraic net modelling the context-free language $L(G_2)=\{ww^r|r\geqslant 0\}$, $w\in A^*$ is shown in Figure 2. The initial marking of net is: $M(p_1)=w$; $M(p_2)=k^r$; $M(p_6)=t$;

$M(p_i)=$; $i=3,4,5,7,\dots,11$, $A=\{a,b\}$, $w\in A^*$.

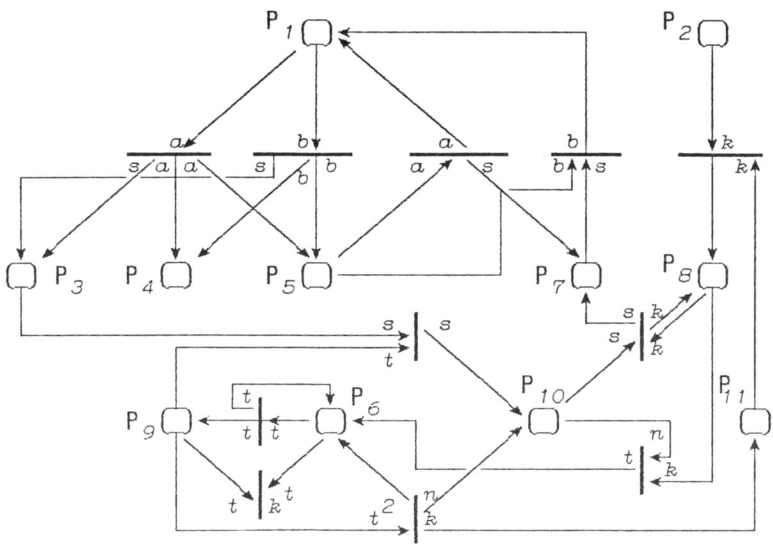

FIGURE 2

These examples show that the description of formal constructions is too sophisticated. The development of this approach consists in the enlargement of algebraic Petri nets features, which permit the description of grammars with a limited subset of productions in fixed time. That is why the arcs of the algebraic net, whch model the grammar, are marked by the words from the position of second additional algebraic net. The joint function of main and additional algebraic nets reproduce the process of the sentence inference in grammar with variable production. In the paper [5] the theoretical research on algebraic Petri nets with variable marking (variable structure) is presented .

Consider now the syntactic analyse of fixed sentences by an algebraic net. In order to achieve it, we shall construct the net, that reproduce inverse productions of our grammar. For example inverse productions in the grammar G_i are:

$b \rightarrow B$, $bB \rightarrow B$, $a \rightarrow A$, $aA \rightarrow A$, $B \rightarrow S$, $A \rightarrow S$.

The algebraic net verifying the truth of the inference in the language $L(G_1)$ of words is shown in Figure 3. In the position p_1 we write verifying word and the grammar G_1 infers this word if the final marking is be $M(p_1)=S$.

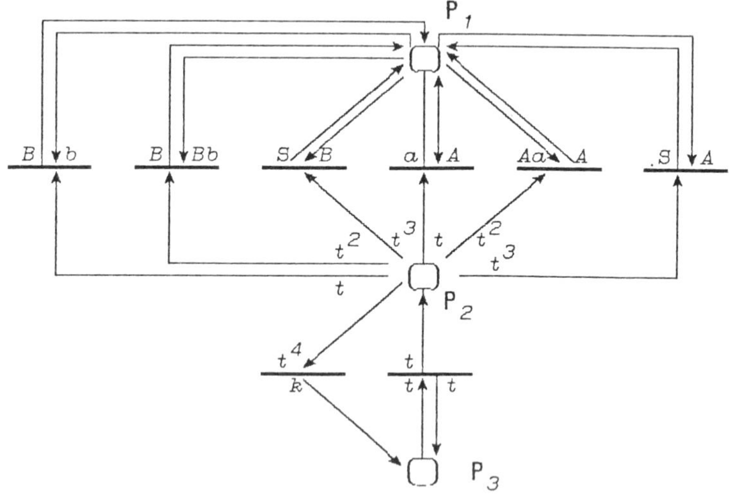

FIGURE 3

3. CONCLUSION

The aim of this paper is twofold: firstly it was intended to suggest some formal techniques describing and analysing the context grammars. secondly, our intention was to construct united language for the techniques mentioned. It gives us more knowledge how to design concurrent systems modelled by algebraic Petri nets.

REFERENCES

[1] Finkel A., Blokage et vivacite dans les reseaux a pile-file, LNCS 176, (Springer, 1984) pp. 151-162.

[2] Finkel A., About Monogenous FiFo Petri Nets, in 3 European Workshop on Applications and Theory of Petri Nets, (Varenna, 1982).

[3] Valk R., Vidal-Naquet G., Petri Nets and Regular Languages, JCSS, V. 23, 3, 1981.

[4] Maltsev P. A., Leskin A. A., Spiridonov A. M., Petri nets in simulation and control, (Leningrad, Nauka, 1989), In Russian.

[5] Maltsev P. A., Leskin A. A., Algebraic Petri nets with variable marking, in the problems of information and integration automation manufacturing, (Leningrad, Nauka, 1990), In Russian.

Industrial Applications of Artificial Intelligence
J.L. Alty and L.I. Mikulich (Editors)
Elsevier Science Publishers B.V. (North-Holland)

DATA MODELLING IN A TYPE SYSTEM

Nicolas SPYRATOS

Laboratoire de Recherche en Informatique
Université de Paris-Sud
91405 Orsay Cedex, France

In order to integrate programming languages and databases, it is first necessary to unify the programming language concept of *type system* and the database concept of *data model*. In this paper, we present a model that, we believe, can serve as a basis for such a unification. Our main objective is to recast some basic database concepts in the context of a type system.

1. INTRODUCTION

Traditionally, the main concern of programming languages has been in expressing operations on data, whereas the main concern of databases has been in the structuring of data. However, over the past twenty years, programming languages have emphasized more and more the structuring of data, whereas databases have evolved towards more expressive ways of modelling reality. As a result, many researchers have suggested that there should be a systematic integration, and this has resulted in the development of systems such as Pascal/R[Sch77], PS-Algol[ACC81], and Galileo[ACO85].

Two main concepts that have emerged from these experiments are the programming language concept of *type system* and the database concept of *data model*. In order to integrate programming languages and databases, it is first necessary to unify these two concepts. In this paper, we present a model that, we believe, can serve as a basis for such a unification. In our model, types are modelled as sets (with a certain structure) and data are modelled as finite functions between such sets. Our main objective is to recast some basic database concepts, including schemes and queries, in the context of a type system. In the remaining of this section we motivate and explain informally our approach.

Roughly speaking, a type is a set of elements with common properties. We refer to the elements of a type as *objects*, and we write t:T to denote that object t is of type T. Types can be combined, using type constructors, in order to form more complex types. The type constructors that we use in our model are the *cartesian* constructor and the *arrow* constructor. Given types U and V, UxV denotes the set of all pairs (u,v), where u is an object of type U and v is an object of type V, and $U \rightarrow V$ denotes the set of all functions from U to V. In an arrow type $U \rightarrow V$, U is called the *source* of the type and V is called the *target* of the type; we also refer to V as the *attribute* of U.

Objects of arrow type are functions, and functions can be either finite or infinite. (A function $f: U \rightarrow V$ is called finite if f is defined only on a finite set of points in U, i.e. f is finite if its graph is a finite set of pairs.) If the function is finite then we may store it explicitly (i.e. extensionally), by storing its graph. However, if the function is infinite, then we can only store it implicitly (i.e. intentionally), by storing a definition of the function using formulas, or by storing a procedure that computes argument-value pairs of the function. We refer to objects of arrow type that are stored explicitly as *data*.

In our model, a *scheme* is specified by giving
- a set of *atomic types*, for example, EMP, NAME, SAL, DEPT, and
- a set of *data*, for example, f : EMP → NAME, g : EMP → SAL, h : EMP → DEPT

Roughly speaking, an atomic type is a set of simple objects, and a data is a finite function. For example, we can think of EMP as a set of integer identifiers for employees, of NAME as a set of character strings, and of f : EMP → NAME as a finite function associating employees with names.

Figure 1(a) shows a PASCAL-like definition of the above example of a scheme. Let us call this scheme the EMP-scheme, for later reference. Figure 1(b) shows a graph representation of the EMP-scheme, according to the following convention: each data t : U→V in the scheme is represented by an arrow from U to V with label t. A scheme, like the EMP-scheme, in which all data have common source is called a *context*. The common source is called the source of the context, and the attributes of the source are called the attributes of the context. For example, in the EMP-context, EMP is the source whereas NAME, SAL, and DEPT, are the attributes.

Figure 1(c) gives examples of graphs for the data f, g, and h, of the EMP-context. The graphs show how the objects of EMP are associated with their attributes, that is, with objects of NAME, SAL and DEPT, respectively. These graphs constitute the *state* of the context. We note that the association between objects and attributes is *functional*. That is, in every state, an

scheme EMP-scheme;

atomic types EMP, NAME, SAL, DEPT; **(a)**

data f : EMP → NAME, g : EMP → SAL, h : EMP → DEPT

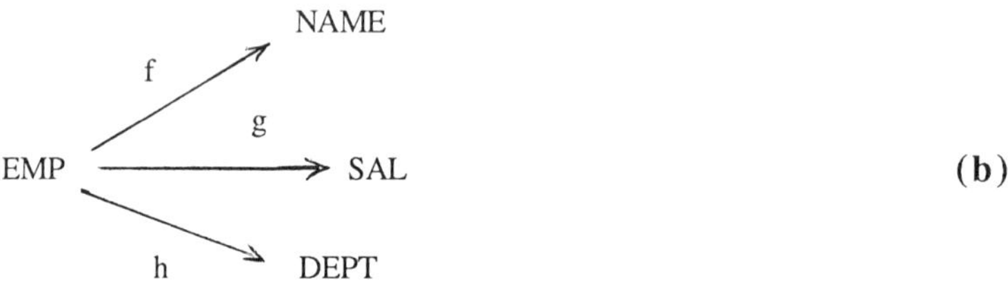

(b)

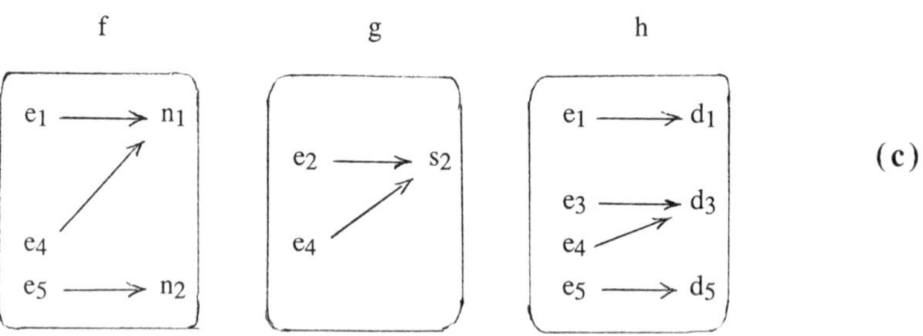

(c)

EMP	NAME	SAL	DEPT
e_1	n_1		d_1
e_2		s_2	
e_3			d_3
e_4	n_1	s_2	d_3
e_5	n_2		d_5

(d)

Figure 1: The EMP- scheme

object of a given type is associated with at most one object of any other type. In this respect, we follow along the lines of [Spy85] (see also [Spy84]).

We can conveniently represent both, the definition of a context and its state, by means of a table as shown in Figure 1(d). The first column of the table (leftmost column) is headed by the source of the context, here EMP, and the remaining columns are headed by the attributes of the context (in any order), here NAME, SAL, DEPT. Now, let def(f), def(g) and def(h) denote the domains of definition of the functions f, g and h, respectively. First, we represent the finite set $def(f) \cup def(g) \cup def(h)$ in the column headed by EMP. Then, in order to represent a function, say f, we simply consider each element e in def(f), and we place next to it (in the column headed by NAME) the value f(e). In this way the column headings EMP and NAME indicate the type of f, and the pairs (e, f(e))

that appear under these headings constitute the graph of f. The values of g and h are represented in a similar manner.

Notice that the table of Figure 1(d) can be regarded in two different ways. First, it can be regarded as a relational table where null values of the kind "value doesn't exist" are permitted in nonkey fields. (Clearly, if def(f) = def(g) = def(h) then we have no null values and the table looks like a usual relational table.) Second, it can be regarded as a file, where the source of the context is the set of identifiers for the records of the file, and where the attributes are the fields of the file. Indeed, in the table representation of Figure 1(d), the entries e_1, e_2, e_3, e_4 and e_5 can be regarded as record identifiers, where e_1 identifies the record <NAME: n_1, SAL: null, DEPT: d_1>, e_2 identifies the record <NAME: null, SAL: s_2, DEPT: null>, and so on. As we shall see later, the construction of this file corresponds to the construction of a function <f, g, h>: EMP $\rightarrow$ NAMExSALxDEPT from functions f: EMP $\rightarrow$ NAME, g: EMP $\rightarrow$ SAL, and h: EMP $\rightarrow$ DEPT.

The scheme of Figure 2, called the EMP/DEPT-scheme, consists of two contexts, one with source EMP and one with source DEPT. (Accordingly, its state is represented by two tables, also shown in that figure.) The first context is the EMP-context that we have just seen, whereas the second context (which is the DEPT-context) gives information about departments, namely, their telephone numbers and their locations. As this example shows, (a) scheme definition can be done inrementally, by concentrating on one context at a time, and (b) scheme modification, i.e. addition or deletion of functions (or even of whole contexts), is a straightforward matter (at least conceptually). We note that, in the EMP/DEPT-scheme, EMP is a source but *not* an attribute, and that DEPT is both, a source with attributes TEL and LOC *and* an attribute of EMP.

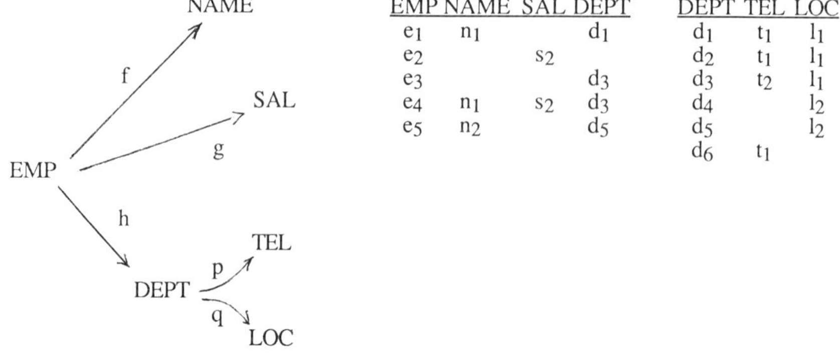

EMP	NAME	SAL	DEPT
e_1	n_1		d_1
e_2		s_2	
e_3			d_3
e_4	n_1	s_2	d_3
e_5	n_2		d_5

DEPT	TEL	LOC
d_1	t_1	l_1
d_2	t_1	l_1
d_3	t_2	l_1
d_4		l_2
d_5		l_2
d_6	t_1	

Figure 2: The EMP/DEPT-scheme and a database over this scheme

Notice that, in the EMP/DEPT-scheme employees can be associated with telephone numbers (via departments, by composing the functions f and p), and with locations (via departments, by composing the functions f and q).Thus, TEL and LOC can be considered as *derived* attributes of EMP, as opposed to NAME, SAL and DEPT that are "direct" attributes of EMP.

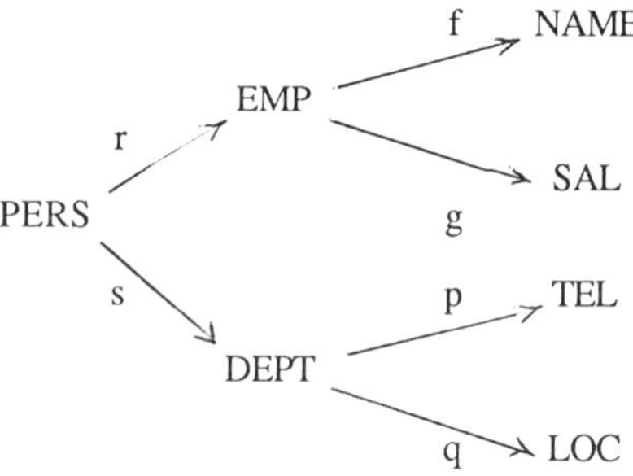

Figure 3: The PERS-scheme

It is important to remember that a scheme describes a real world situation and, therefore, its definition is influenced by the nature of the relationships between real world objects. For example, consider again the EMP/DEPT-scheme of Figure 2. This scheme describes a real world in which employees are related to departments *funtionally,* that is, DEPT is an attribute of EMP. A similar situation would arise if EMP were an attribute of DEPT. Assume now a situation where DEPT is not an attribute of EMP and where EMP is not an attribute of DEPT (that is, assume that employees and departments are in a one-to-many relationship, in both directions). In this case we can assume that there are objects (say persons, of type PERS) (that is, assume that employees and departments are in a one-to-many relationship, in both directions). In this case we can assume that there are objects (say persons, of type PERS) associated functionally with employee numbers and with department numbers. The scheme that describes this situation is given in Figure 3, above.

To summarize, a scheme is specified by giving a set of atomic types and a set of data. The atomic types represent sets of objects of interest, and the data represent functional relationships between these objects. The graphs of the data constitute the state of the scheme and we shall refer to it as a *database* over the scheme. Since a scheme can also be regarded as a collection of contexts, a database over the scheme can be regarded as the set of states of these contexts. Moreover, as a context and its state can be represented by a table, a scheme and a database over the scheme can be represented by a collection of tables, one for each context (in much the same way as a relational database can be represented by a collection of tables, one table for each relation scheme).

In the rest of the paper, we present first a simple typed calculus (in Section 2) and then a data model based on this calculus (in Section 3).In Section 4, we offer some concluding remarks and suggestions for further research.

2. THE TYPE SYSTEM

2.1 Syntax

The *types* of the system are constructed from a set of atomic types T1, T2, ... , Tn, using the type constructors 'x' and ' $\rightarrow$ '. More precisely:

1. Atomic types T1, T2, ... , Tn are types.
2. If U and V are types, then UxV and U $\rightarrow$ V are types.
3. The only types are those obtained by means of 1 and 2.

Each type is assumed equipped with a set of variables. The variables can be combined to form *typed terms*, following a set of rules. More precisely:

1. If x is a variable of type T then x is a term of type T.
2. If u and v are terms of types U and V, respectively, then <u,v> is a term of type UxV.
3. If t is a term of type UxV then π_1t and π_2t are terms of types U and V, respectively.
4. If x is a variable of type U and v is a term of type V then λ x.v is a term of type U$\rightarrow$V.
5. If t and u are terms of types U $\rightarrow$ V and U, respectively, then tu is a term of type V.

2.2 Semantics

The types and terms just defined can be given denotational semantics using a novel kind of domain theory based on the notions of *coherence space* and of *stable function* between coherence spaces. According to this semantics, a type is interpreted by a coherence space C and a term of this type by a point of C. The usual types, can be represented as coherence spaces. A discussion of this subject is outside the scope of the present paper and the interested reader is referred to [GLT89].

In order to simplify the presentation we shall often confuse syntactic objects and their denotations. In particular, we shall often use indifferently the phrases "type T" and "set T", or "term t of type $U \to V$" and "function t from U to V".

3. THE DATA MODEL

In this section, we define our data model, namely, we define a database scheme and its associated query language.

3.1 Schemes

A scheme describes the types of objects of interest in an application, as well as the relationships of interest among these objects.

Definition 3.1 A *scheme* is defined by giving
a set of *atomic types* $T_1, T_2, \ldots, T_n$ and
a set of *data* $f_1 \colon U_1 \to V_1$, $f_2 \colon U_2 \to V_2, \ldots, f_m \colon U_m \to V_m$.
The types U_i, V_i are constructed from the atomic types, using the type constructors. ❑

We note that the source and the target of a data can be the same type, and that two data may have the same type. We also note that the process of choosing the atomic types and the data to be included in a scheme (for a specific application) is known as "scheme design". Although this is an important aspect of data modelling, scheme design lies outside the scope of the present paper and will not be discussed any further here.

A *database* over a scheme is an assignment of values to the data of the scheme. Thus, a database over a scheme is a set of finite functions. Figure 1(b) shows a database over the EMP-scheme. Of course, the fact that all data in a database are functions must be verified at database update time.

3.2 Queries

The data of a scheme can be combined in order to form more complex data. We use two operations for doing this: composition and pairing. What we call query language of a scheme is actually the closure of the scheme under these operations. So let us first define them formally.

Given functions f: U → V and g: V → W, such that the target of f is the source of g, the *composition* of f and g is a function gf: U → W such that: for all u in U, gf(u) = g(f(u)). Clearly, g(f(u)) is defined iff f(u) is in def(g).

Given functions f: U → V and g: U → W, with common source U, the *pairing* of f and g consists of a function <f, g>: U → VxW, such that: for all u in U, <f,g>(u) = <f(u), g(u)>, together with two functions π_1: VxW → V, and π_2: VxW → W, called its *projections*, such that: for all v in V and w in W, π_1(<v, w>) = v and π_2(<v,w>) = w. Clearly, <f, g>(u) is defined iff f(u) and g(u) are both defined. It is interesting to note that the pairing <f, g> can be regarded as a file in which every object u is the 'identifier' of 'record' <f(u), g(u)> (see also Figure 1), and in which the projections π_1 and π_2 are the field selectors. Finally, we note that π_1<f,g>(u)=f(u) and π_2<f,g>(u)=g(u), for all u for which <f,g> is defined, that is, the following diagram commutes:

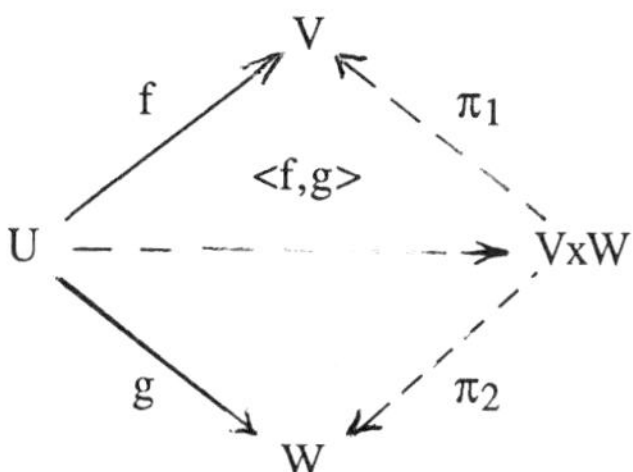

We are now ready to define queries over a given scheme. Roughly speaking, a query is a well-formed expression whose operands are data and whose operations are composition and pairing:

Definition 3.2 A *query* over a scheme is defined recursively as follows:

1. If f is data in the scheme then f is a query.
2. If f: U → V and g: V → W are queries, then their composition is a query.
3. If f: U → V and g: U → W are queries, then their pairing is a query.

4. The only queries are those obtained from 1,2, and 3.

The set of all queries over a scheme is called the *query language* of the scheme ❑

It is important to note that all queries are of arrow type, thus we can represent the query language in the form of a graph. This graph is obtained from the scheme graph, by adding recursively all arrows suggested by Definition 3.2. In the resulting graph each path from a node U to a node V corresponds to a query of type U → V whose components (and their order of composition) are defined by the arrows of the path. We shall refer to this graph as the *query graph* of the scheme. For example, the query graph of the EMP/DEPT-cheme (see Figure 2) contains the following path:

$$\text{EMP} \xrightarrow{h} \text{DEPT} \xrightarrow{\langle p,\, q\rangle} \text{TELxLOC} \xrightarrow{\pi_2} \text{LOC}$$

This path corresponds to a query of type EMP → LOC whose components are h, <p, q> and π_2 (applied in the order of writing).

It follows from Definition 3.2 that, for every query and for every assignment of values to the data, we can obtain a value by simply performing the calculations indicated in the query. It is this value that we call the answer of the query (for the given assignment). If we recall that a database over a scheme is precisely an assignment of values to data, then we have the following definition:

Definition 3.3 The *answer* of a query with respect to a database is computed as follows: substitute data from the database in the query and perform the calculations. ❑

The type of a query can be regarded as a specification of *what* the query (abstractly) does, whereas, the path of its components can be regarded as a specification of *how* it does it. For example, consider the following query over the EMP/DEPT-scheme of Figure 2: EMP, DEPT, TEL. The type of this query is EMP → TEL, and this says what the query does: it associates employees with telephone numbers. The path of its components says how it does it: if an employee is associated with a department and if this department is associated with a telephone number, then the employee is associated with that telephone number.

To summarize, we have seen that every scheme is associated with a query language and that the answers of queries are computed based on the values of the data. For the purposes of this paper, we have used only certain terms of arrow type in order to represent queries. Clearly, one can define more expressive query languages, for example, by including terms of the form fx (where f is of type, say, U → V and x is of type U), or by defining a *selection* operation on data variables [Spy90].

4. CONCLUDING REMARKS

We have seen a database model defined in the context of a type system. In doing so our objective was to recast some basic database concepts in a formalism akin to programming languages. The type system that we have used is a simple typed calculus based on 'x' and '→'. Within this type system, we have seen the definition of a database scheme and its associated query language.

Scheme definition can be enriched by adding to the scheme isa relationships and data dependencies [Spy90]. The resulting model presents several advantages over the relational model and can serve as the basis of an object-oriented database model. Investigations under way include a closer look into the concepts of method and inheritance, algorithms for deciding database consistency and performing data completion, and the study of scheme and database updating.

BIBLIOGRAPHY

[ACC81] Atkinson M.P., Chisholm K.J., Cockshot W.P., "PS-Aigol: AN Algol with a Persistent Heap", ACM SIGPLAN Notices 17-7, July 1981

[ACO85] Albano A., Cardelli L., Orsini R., "Galileo: A Strongly Typed, Interactive, Conceptual Language", ACM TODS 10-2, 1985

[GL89] Girard J.Y., Lafont Y., Taylor P., "Proofs and Types", Cambridge University Press, 1989

[Sch77] Schmidt J.W., "Some High-level Language Constructs for Data of Type Relation", ACM TODS 2-3, 1977

[Spy84] Spyratos N., "The partition model: A deductive database model", INRIA Research Report No 286, April 1984 (Also In: ACM-TODS 12-1, March 1987)

[Spy85] Spyratos N., "The partition model: A functional approach", INRIA Research Report No 430, July 1985

[Spy90] Spyratos N., "A Functional Database Model and its Query Language", To appear.

Industrial Applications of Artificial Intelligence
J.L. Alty and L.I. Mikulich (Editors)
Elsevier Science Publishers B.V. (North-Holland)

KNOWLEDGE BASED SYSTEMS: DYNAMIC ASPECT MODELLING

V. E. WOLFENGAGEN and V. J. YATSUK

Department of Cybernetics,
Moscow Engineering Physics Institute,
Kashirskoe Schosse 31,
115409 Moskva,
The USSR.

ABSTRACT: The lambda-calculus and its relating theories have been introduced by several authors to provide the right framework for applicative computational systems (ACS). In this contribution ACS are combined with a model theoretic approach giving rise to a new kind of knowledge base: the conceptual base with switching concepts. The basic ACS-evaluation technique in this paper goes further and is presented as a 'knowledge assembler'. Its mechanisms are applied to the embedding of variable concepts depending upon the laws of "evolving events". Both the Assembler and the conceptual base are implemented as a part of general knowledge kit Expandable Programming Environment (EPE).

1. INTRODUCTION

Knowledge representation systems arise for many reasons, sometimes for special applications and often more general inspirations. Periodically we ought to ask ourselves where these representation systems should have come from. Our remarks here can be treated as a way of how to integrate diverse representation models in a general framework of conceptual modelling. The target is to obtain in a mixed environment, the possibilities of LISP, relational data bases and conceptual bases. The language LISP, relational algebra and conceptual algebra are the first stage in this general consideration. The next step is in defining a knowledge assembler, extentional algebra and intensions (concepts) definition and manipulation facilities at the fixed "stage of knowledge'. After that we take into account the laws of evolution for the initial problem domain. Then we establish the dynamical entities and relationships: variable objects, variable concepts, variable domains etc. Note that the static entities correspond to the neutral (identity) laws of evolving events as the $1^1 : 1 \text{-->} 1$ (here "-->" is symbol of mapping).

2. KNOWLEDGE ASSEMBLER KIT

Before saying where the knowledge assembler comes from let us consider the role of the data base in the Knowledge System : the DataBase can be empty for a long time only becoming nonempty in the future. Hence data objects in the knowledg system can be partial.

Using the Knowledge Assembler we are going to evaluate expressions of the knowledge representation language of the form "expert i believes the restriction F is evaluated as true". This is formally express //F//i. The definition of semantics in this case is rather complicated but its natural adaptation is straight-forward if we use applicative computational systems (ACS) and LISP. The real situation is rather complex when we take into account applicative relational algebra and its dynamical properties for knowledge representation.

So applicative computations (LISP-like) save expert effort in the case of knowledge representation. These computations are based on some principle outlined below.

2.1 Applicative Evaluation Principles

The 1st principle is formulated as following.

(1) The evaluation of application is the application of the evaluations.

This principle must be refined. Taking into account the fixed assignment we obtain:

//MN//i = (//M//i) (//N//i)

for any terms M, N.

Using Curry's combinators and principle (1):
I=lambda x.x,
S=lambda xyz.xz(yz),
C=lambda xyz.xzy,
(x,y)=lambda r.rxy,
$=CIS

it is possible to conclude that

//MN//i = (//M//i)(//N//i)
= CIS(lambda r.r//M// //N//)i
= $(//M//,//N//)i

Hence the extentional version of lambda-convertion makes it possible to introduce the following rule:

(Rule 1) //MN// = $(//M//,//N//)

The 2nd principle is due to the ordered pairs properties:

//(M,N)//i = (//M//i,//N//i)

for any terms M,N and assignment i:

(2) The evaluation of the ordered pair is the ordered pair of the evaluation.

Adding the categorical combinatory logics (CCL) notations we can infer the following rule:
(Rule 2) //(M,N// = ⟨ //M//,//N// ⟩
for any f , g and ⟨ f , g ⟩= lambda t. (ft , gt).

These principles and rules give the framework for the semantical needs and reasons of the target computational model (CM).

2.2. Computational Model

We complete the KA-building by adding practical rules of the lambda-expressions evluation. The following rules follow from principles (l) and (2).

(Rule 3) // (lambda . M) d̂//i = //M// (i,d)

Because of the validity of equalities : // (lambda . M) d//î = A//M//id = //M//(i,d), where //d̂// = d,A - currying function (Abstractor).

(Rule 4) //MN// = App ^{0} ⟨ //M// , //N// ⟩

is an immediate corollary of the principle (1) (here: App is an application operator, or applicator).

(Rule 5) //c// = lambda i.c

for individual constants in the extention of the equality //c// = c

The modified set of rules include the dynamical properties when assignments are treated as the functions f : B --> I from "stages of knowledge" I to "later stages of knowledge" B.

3. KNOWLEDGE BASE MANAGEMENT SYSTEM

3.1. Data Object Models

Data object models arise for many reasons, often in connection with applications in knowledge systems, or expert systems. Periodically we ought to ask ourselves what the ground generic "building blocks" of the expert system are. The concepts (intentionals) and the relations between them are in our view the vital point.

Another case in point gives the expert system implementation 'in' LISP (not 'on') environment. We suppose that our contribution is mainly in setting up the 'conceptual' surrounding ideas and LISP-programming in this order.

3.2. Implementation

Our practical experience with the Expert System is based upon the Expansible Programming Environment (EPE) - our original kit for building knowledge systems of different classes and purposes. It contains both standard and additional LISP-media, applicative relational algebra and user friendly interfaces. In usage EPE promotes the facilities of the knowledge base management system. Our originality lies in some solutions concerning the knowledge base in the conceptual base for supporting such knowledge base facilities.

3.3. Conceptual Base and 'Switching' Concepts

The conceptual base is defined as the set of the concepts and conceptual relations that vary along the transitions f : B --> I between the "stages" I and the "later stages" B.

The main procedure is written as follows:

1) set up a collection of functions (restrictions) by means of the data definition language (DDL);
2) select the relatively self contained sets of individuals that are identified by the assignments;
3) build (declare) the concepts using the restriction functions;
4) set up the relations between the concepts using the assignments.

The Conceptual Base flexibility is due to assignments in accordance with the following procedure:

1) Set up the concepts with the assignments as indicies;
2) supposing the events evolve along f : B --> I take into account the transitions between events;
3) set up concepts depending on f;
4) set up relations between concepts depending on f;
5) supposing that transitions between the events do not vary the asgignment set up the 'static' concepts;
6) maintain the resulting system of concepts in accordance with functorial properties.

The concept description; have being given by the expression

C (⟨i⟩) = 'I' y 'All" h (yi (hi) <---> //(lambda . F)h//i)

where i is the assignment,
C the concept,
'I' the description,
'All' the universal quantifier,
F the DDL formula,
<--> the one-to-one correspondence,
(⟨....⟩) the pointer of the set.

3.4. Dynamical Aspects

We have defined the concept C [[i]] which is originally the 'variable concept' with the parameter i. Now suppose that the events evolve along the law f : B --> I , i.e. take into account the transition from the possible world I into the possible world B. In fact, the application (lambda.F)h is evaluated as

$$\text{(CSR)} \qquad //(\text{lambda} . F)\, h // i = //F//_f (b, (h\,^{o} f)\, b) = //F//_f\,^{o} \langle J, h\,^{o} f \rangle)\, b$$

in accordance with (Rule 3) (here: i is an element of I, b belongs to B, J=lambda x.x, F is the DDL expression).

The previous equation is the 'concept suitching rule', denoted as (CSR).

3.5. Dynamic Principle

The concept switching rule (CSR) contains the essence of conceptual base evolution and its life-time cycle:

substitution of an individual h into lambda-abstraction body F is not the membership check of

'h belongs to //F//', but the following: the image of h when events evolve along the transition f in the "subworld" b (from B) must belong to the image of //F//, i.e.

$$h \circ f \text{ belongs to } //F//_f$$

That is the matching of the main dynamical property of those variable concepts that are defined in the DDL framework.

3.6. Static Principle

And what can we do when transitions do not influence the knowledge base ? We conclude that the knowledge is the same as in the previous stage .So our variable concept has the 'constant' behaviour, a static one. Our conclusion is the following:

The 'static concept' is identified by the mapping

$$f : I \dashrightarrow I \text{ when } f=1_I \text{ and } //(\text{lambda}. F)h // i = //F//_{1_I} (i.hi)$$

3.7. Modified Membership Procedure

Now we discuss a very interesting concept C_f that is assigned not to worlds but to transitions f between them. The modified membership procedure for the dynamic concept C_f time evolving along f : B --> I is

1) set up the new assignment b as the alternative for the old assignment i supposing the events evolve along f;

2) set up the type symbol T of the individual image h from the data base image according to the mapping f;

3) support the restriction P for the individual image h in the world b;

4) select the individuals $\hat{h} = h \circ f$ for establishing the extension of the concept $C'_f(b)$; this leads to the inclusion C'_f (b) ISA T.

5) the pairs $(b, \hat{h}b)$ identify the individuals $\hat{h}$ in the world b from the set B; these pairs create the extension of the variable concept $C_f(B)$;

6) set up the natural inclusion $C_f(B)$ is in $H_T(B)$ for the variable domain $H_T(B)$,

where $H_T(B) = \{ \hat{h} / \hat{h} : B \text{ ---> } T \}$.

4. CONCLUSIONS

The main constructions reviewed and stressed here have been rather lengthy. In summary, the main results we have obtained are:

1) The 'knowledge assembler' is linked to the dynamic models of lambda-calculus . The first proposition was due to D.Scott research in his variants of the theory of computations (combinatory logics and cartesian closed category approach).
2) In the 'knowledge assembler' a variable domain provides an interpretation of the vital constructs.
3) Variable concepts are implemented using type/subtype discourse. For instance, the frames with the ISA-dimension give the rough ground that would be modified by the assignments and the transitions between assignments.
4) We have omitted discussion of the dynamical variant of the relational languages and their usage by 'conceptual modelling style'.
5) The authors hope that the present version of EPE will stimulate them (and others) to further research.

ACKNOWLEDGEMENTS

We wish to thank all colleagues who took part in the implementation of EPE. The long term discussions and their friendly assistance have inspired the authors.

REFERENCES

[1]. Scott, D.S. "Relating Theories of the Lambda-Calculus", in: Seldin, J.P. and Hindley, J.R. (eds.), "To H.B. Curry: Essays on Combinatory Logic, Lambda Calculus and Formalism "(Academic Press, 1980) pp.403-450 .

[2] Brodie, M.L. and Schmidt, J.W. (eds.) "On Conceptual Modelling. Perspectives from Artificial Intelligence, Data bases and Programming Languages", (Springer Verlag, 1984) 510 p.

[3] Brodie, M.L. and Mylopoulos, J. (eds.) "On Knowledge Base Management Systems. Integrating Artificial Intelligence and Database Technologies", (Springer Verlag, 1986) 660 p.

[4] Wolfengagen, V.E. "Frame Theory and Computations", in: Computers and Artificial Intelligence (1984), Vol. 3, No. 1, pp. 3-32

Industrial Applications of Artificial Intelligence
J.L. Alty and L.I. Mikulich (Editors)
Elsevier Science Publishers B.V. (North-Holland)

INFORMATION APPROACH TO DESIGN COMPUTATIONAL HEAD OF CONTROL SYSTEMS

Sergey M. Moroz and Dmitry S. Kuprik

Department of Computing Systems
Radioengineering Institute
Minsk, The USSR

The structure design problems of distributed computing systems are very complex and hard. The attempt to use both human knowledge, experience and clustering model for their decision is proposed.

1. INTRODUCTION

Rather severe requirements on reconfiguration and process speed are made to the computational head of control systems, of the real-time control systems in particular. Some problems can be solved in the computing systems with distributed data processing. However, when designing such systems a number of intractable problems arise due to a combinatorial character of synthesis' problems. Approaches to the problems of the computing system design known at the time [1] are based on narrow model representations. At the same time the control system belong to the class of complex systems, and the problem of their computional head design gets a number of specific features which fail to be taken account of by traditional methods. They are as follows :

- nonquantitative, badly formalized notions reflecting context aspects of original descriptions, quality criteria, system constraints;
- principal indefiniteness of initial information that is natural on a predesign stage;
- absence of precise recognition of all aspects of functioning of the system as a whole in accordance with the incompatibility principle.

In spite of the fact that each of the known synthesis methods is based upon rather particular approaches, being taken together they reflect a great acquired experience in system creation.

The given paper attempts to generalize the experience in the state of art taking into account all foregoing features, to integrate the achivements of particular approaches to a higher information level. Chapter 2 reveals the essence of the suggested approach, which is formulated in Chapter 3. Chapter 4 concerns the learning process.

2. THE SUGGESTED APPROACH CONCEPTION

The problem of the distributed computing system design will be treated in its traditional way: given the known characteristics of the computational unit (CU) and the algorithm of the task being executed, which has been partitioned into a set of program modules (PM) or other kinds of code units. It's necessary to define the structure of the computing systems and the initial placement of the PM with the least "cost" satisfying the given quality criteria.

In a general case, the problem is the integer optimization problem and while being NP-hard it cannot be solved by the traditional methods. One can tackle it only by heuristic procedures using nonformal research principles.

The essence of the suggested approach is the problem implication from a subject level to an information metalevel. Every object of the latter level is semantically an elementary partial solution of the structural synthesis. The matter aspect of the objects is determined by integrated estimations both computationaltask characteristics and computational unit possibilities from the point of view of system requirements as a whole. Similarity relation intuitively associated with the possibility and quality of joint partial decisions having been given in this domain, the process of groups or clusters formation will correspond to decisionmaking stages of the structure synthesis. Quality criteria on a subject level are implicitly replaced by interclustering criteria.

This transfer is not trivial because :

- structures and semantics of initial descriptions refer to different model representation levels;
- concrete relation pragmatics is defined by specific features of the synthesis problem;
- selection consequences of this or that alternative on low levels of the structure hierarchy must be extrapolated on the general system level and therefore alternatives' estimations must be defined by the system requirements as a whole.

Such transfer can be done only on a system information-logic representation based on heuristics formed by experts and on experience acquired in the course of learning.

3. THE INFORMATION APPROACH IMPLEMENTATION

We'll discuss the task of the structural synthesis in the framework of the following model.

1. Given X is the set of PM , each being characterized by the feature set, reflecting the essencial properties of PM, and the precedence relation $\mathfrak{R}_x$, describing the order of PM performing. Each element of the $\mathfrak{R}_x$ is also described by the feature

collection.
2. The collection of CU is described by analogy with the foregoing $\langle Y,\mathfrak{R}_y\rangle$, where $\mathfrak{R}_y$ describes the possibility of CU connection. The composition of the head can be represented as the multiset Y^* of the set Y.
3. Sets X,Y are connected by the relation $\mathfrak{R}_{xy}$, reflecting the permissibility of performing any of PM by any CU.
4. The objective function Q represents the superposition of the particular quality criteria, which can possess a nonquantitative nature in a general case.
5.The system of constraints F joins the requirements to the whole system, the limitations defined by technical possibility of CU, stuctrural constraints $(\mathfrak{R}_x,\mathfrak{R}_y,\mathfrak{R}_{xy})$.

Taking into account all mentioned above the synthesis problem represents the formation Y^* and the definition of the relation

$$\mathfrak{R}^* : X \rightarrow Y^*,$$

optimizing the objective function Q on satisfying the constraints F.

As $\mathfrak{R}_{xy}$ defines $\mathfrak{R}^*$, consider it as a sampled set of elementary partial decisions. Then $\mathfrak{R}^*$ may be received by forming clusters in $\mathfrak{R}_{xy}$ corresponding to some separate CU by the context. The solution of such a problem may be divided into three stages:

- the formation of the reciprocal similarity matrix on a sampled set of elementary decisions;
- the transitive connection of the similarity relation matrix;
- the hierarchy taxonomy of sampled data, directly corresponding to the structural synthesis process.

3.1. The Matrix Formation of Reciprocal Similarity.

As it was mentioned above the similarity relation in the domain of elementary decisions is associated with the possibility and quality of their joint decision in the context of the given problem. It is determined by the local characteristics of components of the computational task and by descriptions of the whole task, CU possibilities ,system requirements.Besides, des, it is necessary to take into account the interdependence and interconstrained of partial decisions. Due to this indefiniteness and necessity of taking account of the similarity value, the similarity relation will be considered in the fuzzy interpretation :

$$\mathfrak{A} : \mathfrak{R}_{xy} \times \mathfrak{R}_{xy} \rightarrow L ,$$

where L is a part of a real line.

The function $\mathfrak{A}$ is not a trivial one, its formation being possible on the basis of the fuzzy relation system, connecting the system quality criteria with its primary descriptors.

The fuzzy relations are heuristics, formed by experts on generalization of acquired skill. They are represented in the form of a multilevel hierarchy network. The latter is a information-logic deductive system, the axiomatics of which is determined on the set of global aims, that are corresponded to the system requirements as a whole. The concretization operation is applied then to the level notions, and this results in a set of networks, and the operation is reused. The generated notions correspond to local targets, particular criteria.

As a rule the low network level forms the notions corresponding to primary descriptions. The notions themselves are mutually joined by the target relations which reflect pragmatic connections. The contribution of the low level notions to the target achievement defined by the high level notions is used as a measure of these connections' estimation.

Finally, the network is represented by knowledge-base and judgement guidelines that follow from skill-based experiential reasoning.

3.2. The Transitive Connection of Similarity Relation.

The necessity of the transitive connection of the formed similarity relation is defined by a condition of fuzzy coverage of the sampled set [2]. This task can be solved by known approximation procedures of the reciprocal similarity matrix [3].

3.3. The Decisionmaking Process.

The previous task having been solved on the set $\mathfrak{R}_{xy}$ by the procedure given in [2], the cluster hierarchy can be formed, which is associated with the descisionmaking stages in the system synthesis. The path length of the connection acts as the optimization criterion.

As the sampled set $\mathfrak{R}_{xy}$ has a redundant number of elements (i.e. partial decisions) the connection process interruption is the fact that each element of the set X, being a member of the two-placed local element $\mathfrak{R}_{xy}$, has been already clustered. And the set of the formed clusters corresponds to the multiset Y^*. $\mathfrak{R}_{xy}$ elements being in the clusters define $\mathfrak{R}^*$, which is the target relation.

4. THE LEARNING PROCESS PROBLEMS

The formation of the reciprocal similarity matrix is the main and most saturated by intelligence stage described above. The design success is defined by validity of the heuristic-based rules, composing the latter. One possible approachto this problem is to use machine-learning techniques. Learning occurs, as both a direct and a feedback process, through observation of their results.

Obviously, the heuristics themselves are formed by experts, but learning is directed for revealing relation pragmatics contained in the heuristiCs. It is necessary to extract

two kinds of these relations:
- stable, defined by the essence and general principles of system functioning and designing;
- sensitive, affected by particulars of the syntesis task.

The latter needs performing of the contingent task structure diagnosis to determine the appropriate relation perspective.

5. CONCLUSION

The traditional application of clustering models in the system design based on the so-called "projection". The latter means that the alternative solution of a structure selection isprojected on the set of the known familary structures. However such an approach doesn't allow to solve the design problem as the optimized one in the above mentioned sense.

On the other hand the approach rested upon the rule-based reasoning proves to be inefficient for solving similar problems because of an extraordinary large search tree.

The suggested approache combines both approaches mentioned. It deals with the system design as a successive process, in which :
- rule-based reasoning is the means of target structurization and information-logic decomposition of the initial information;
- a clustering model is the way of revealing tendencies in the design process.

Though the suggested approach doesn't lead to an accurate optimum decision, it is a suitable intelligent means for performing predesign investigations.

REFERENCES

[1] Casavant, T.L., and Kuhl, J.G., A Taxonomy of Scheduling in General-Purpose Distributed Computing Systems, IEEE Trans. Software Eng., vol. 14, no. 2, pp. 141-154, 1988.

[2] Ruspini, E.H., Recent developments in fuzzy clustering, in: Yager, R.R., (eds.), Fuzzy Sets and Probabilitary Theory (N.Y.: Pergamon Press, 1982) pp. 133-146.

[3] Vatlin, S.I., Moroz, S.M., Effective algorithm of building *max*-Δ transitive connection of closeness relation, in Proc. All-Union seminar "Optimization of calculation", Oct. 1988, pp 99-100.

Industrial Applications of Artificial Intelligence
J.L. Alty and L.I. Mikulich (Editors)
Elsevier Science Publishers B.V. (North-Holland)

SECTION 4: EXPERT SYSTEMS: SOFTWARE TOOLS

TECHNOLOGICAL ENVIRONMENT FOR EXPERT SYSTEMS DEVELOPMENT

Anatol SLISSENKO

Leningrad Institute of
Informatics and Automation
of the USSR Academy of Sciences
the 14th liniya 39, Leningrad
199178, USSR

ABSTRACT: Knowledge based systems with diverse and complicated inner structures, large number of inference rules and intelligent user screen interface need new tools for their fast prototyping. A set of such tools based on the ideas of high modularity, simple ad hoc ideographic languages and program generation abilities, including a new design for logic knowledge processing, is outlined in the paper. The set is partly implemented, and was used to create several expert systems prototypes.

1. INTRODUCTION

The topic of the present paper concerns programming tools for fast prototyping of knowledge based systems related to certain problem domains. These domains include computer systems (with means for automated reasoning) for supporting research in mathematics or (and this is the most influential background) for dynamic situations understanding and estimating, with further decision making. Such a system may operate (in industrial versions, not in prototypes) with many tens of thousands of inference rules and may have resulting inferences up to tens of steps. In addition, such systems have a diversive and complicated structure of inner interactions, and need intelligent screen interface which play a crucial role in its total productivity; an inference rules structure, inference control setting, modules interaction structure and screen interface are to be represented in the prototype. Modifications and even some restructuring of the system are also to be done smoothly, reliably and with moderate efforts.

During recent years one could see a considerable increase of activity in the field of creating tools for fast expert systems prototyping. The earlier work on 'knowledge base management systems', similar to DBMS, was evidently doomed to have a rather limited application success. In the area of relatively small expert systems with simple logic, limited screen interface and straigtforward system organization some shells work satisfactory. But there are other cases, where these tools are unable to give even a basic prototype that could serve as a starting point for smooth development of further working versions.

The concepts and results presented in this paper arose in joint work and discussions with V.I.Gorodetsky, S.N.Baranoff and V.A.Erokhin.

2. BASIC PRINCIPLES AND MAIN COMPONENTS

No reasonable technological environment can be universal or completely created in a short period of time. Thus we design and implement our environments stepwise, putting modules into practical operation as early as possible. Modules we deal with, concern the screen interface and some ideographic language generators, tools for arranging logic knowledge engineering and processing, general purpose and ad hoc libraries. We do not discuss here problems of system programming level, computational resources management, portability problems, languages and other means of controlling the design and realization process. The latter problems are being solved on the basis of traditional tools we have at hand, namely, network diagrams (currently computer unassisted) to support design, widespread programming languages to overcome system programming problems (having started with Pascal, we now use C, and a parallel project based on Forth is being considered) etc.
In the system under discussion the following 3 parts could be distinguished: user languages (including screen interface), control subsystem and knowledge base (which, in its turn, can contain a data base, an algorithmic base and a logic/inference knowledge base).

Development of the user screen interface usually involves tools like the MS Windows Development Kit (we use our own small window generator for text windows), and on such a ground special-purpose metalanguages come into action. The latter allows quickly produce simple user languages for, say, logic inference rule input or exposing (in a form of a quasinatural language), schedule representation, or some ad hoc ideographic means, such as timing diagrams (to expose dynamic interactions) or icons and contours to represent situations on maps. More involved net-based language tool is under design. Main efforts in ideographic languages creation are spent on libraries.

Three issues are essential for control subsystem development: interaction description, query processing control and the system's general working state visualization (as we mentioned above, we do not touch traditional program control problems). The interaction description is solved by means of window development tools and appropriate algorithms libraries organization. The query processing control will be discussed in the next section. The system's current state visualization can be solved at the architectural and special iconic language level.

New features in the knowledge base organization concerns its logic part. As for data management we often use our own simple file data base because of specific demands for control opportunities. Similar demands concern algorithms libraries - they must be suitable for easy reassembling and interaction scheduling.

3. LOGIC KNOWLEDGE REPRESENTATION

We now concentrate upon the abstract structure of the knowledge base, omitting user interaction and implementation (e.g. data structure) problems. We distinguish 3 levels in our knowledge base: problem-oriented, structural and inference search control.

The problem-oriented level consists of a query language of the usual logic type (queries are of the form 'find a term x such that F(x)' where F is a formula in the problem-oriented logic language) and a set of inference rules that define its semantics. Every inference rule is an algorithm that transforms a current proof in its extension. In fact, all the rules are of 3 types: evaluation by data base reference, applying an algorithm (say, from a library or even an involved simulation subsystem) or applying a substitution-like rule.

The structural level concerns features describing structures of the problem-oriented rules. These features are essential for knowledge engineering, for improving effectiveness (e.g. by partial compilation of metarules and rules), consistency analysis and so on. So the structural level knowledge is rather diversive and needs special study. At the moment only some knowledge classification is supported by Gorodetsky's system of learning by example type, which exploits original algorithmic solutions. An advanced research and instrumental support in the field of knowledge and metaknowledge engineering has been accomplished by A.S.Klestchev [1]. We hope to use also his methods.

Our inference search control, which is now under design and implementation, is based on a separate language (whose development is accessible also to the user) which consists of features, representing various properties of a current proof and its formulas, and of simple constructions for describing proof search control.

An approach to theoretical analysis of this knowledge representation framework is given in [2]. Problems treated there include measuring similarity of formulas (queries), proofs and sets of inference rules, defining an entropy of the system, describing and localizing inconsistencies.

It is instructive to make a comment on the inference control arrangements. The common notion of the proof treats it as a list of formulas (with a information about their origin) where every formula is either an assumption or a conclusion, and every conclusion is obtained from formulas to the left of it, by some inference rule. Note that in our framework rules can be of deducing or reducing type (the empty list is a universal axiom). Firstly, we extend the notion of formula to metaformula permitting metavariables for some syntactic classes of the basic language, such as variables, terms of this or that type and so on. The set of metavariables is flexible. In a sense we embed the basic language in an appropriate occurrence language over it. Let us call it the basic metalanguage. The inference rules are usually formulated in terms of this metalanguage. Now we deliberately allow them to be of such a kind. In terms of these rules we will construct derivative metarules by some restricted set of programming means. In addition, we extend our setting for proof representation by control labels that are simple formulas in a special language treated only by inference control and ignored by inference rules. The control labels are transformed by its own separate rules. The control language is constructed from predicates and functions over generalized proofs by some simple compositions. On the basis of this machinery, inference control or interpreter can be described as a list of statements of the form

> for any sublist X of the current generalized proof L if C(Q,L,X) then assign to L new value obtained by application of R to X in L, and then go to another statement according to prescription P,

where Q is a given query, C is a formula in the inference control language, R is a rule composed from inference metarules and control labels transforming rules. Simple versions of such interpreters, free from control labels processing, can easily be written by problem solving specialists. Backtracking can be arranged with the help of control labels including some in-built ones that make its usage trivial.

REFERENCES

[1] Klestchev A.S. Expert Systems Realization Based on Declarative Models of Knowledge Representation. (In Russian.) Preprint, Vladivostok, Far-East Division of the USSR Academy of Sciences, 1988, 46 pp.

[2] Slissenko A.O. On Measures of Information Quality of Knowledge Processing Systems. Information Sciences: An International Journal, (1990), 55-56.

Industrial Applications of Artificial Intelligence
J.L. Alty and L.I. Mikulich (Editors)
Elsevier Science Publishers B.V. (North-Holland)

DESIGN AND SUPPORT SIMULATION TOOLS FOR COMPUTER AIDED SYSTEMS INFORMATION BASE (PROLOG-IMPLEMENTATION)

V.N. KHANENKO, T.N. BARANOVSKAYA,
and G.Yu. TEREMENKO

Leningrad Institute for Informatics and Automation,
USSR Academy of Sciences,
Leningrad,
The USSR.

ABSTRACT: This paper covers the design methodology and the automatic design and support system "LUCH", which assists in solving problems of Data Base conceptual schema simulation, relational Data Base structure implementation design and information base / database design control. LUCH was implemented using the Prolog language within the Russian-language system for Prolog learning (PROKOP).

1. BRIEF OVERVIEW OF THE PROBLEM

The design of the information base for any Computer Aided System, (e.g. for a research automatization system, an automated control system, or a flexible manufacturing system) is a very complicated and labour-consuming process which involves a great number of highly skilled specialists. This is equally true for the process of Computer Aided System information base support and development. Therefore, an automated design and support systems development for a Computer Aided System information base, with its system program kernel (which compromises tools for the data bases and knowledge bases which in turn determine the information base), simulation, and design and support, is of current concern and practical importance.

Work in this direction is currently under way in many countries. One of the following approaches is generally used:

1) strict orientation to a specific software environment (i.e a data base management system - DBMS, Knowledge Base generation facility) and the development of specialised software for end users;

2) the development of "universal" facilities which enable one or more stages of the information base (Data Base or Knowledge Base) generation and support to be automated.

An example of the first approach implementation is ASSIST for dBASE products, and ZIM of the ZANTHE company can be considered as an example of the second approach.

This paper contains the research and development results achieved by the authors in 1985-1989 with the aim of providing a tool ("LUCH") for the simulation, design and support of factographic Data Bases using a relational model of data as part of the Information Base for such Computer Aided Systems.

2. THE DESIGN METHODOLOGY AND "LUCH" ARCHITECTURE

The following key ingredients determined the methodology adopted in the construction of "LUCH":

1) the basic flow diagram (FD) used for Data Base construction;
2) the "LUCH" construction conceptual principles;
3) the "LUCH" program implementation principles.

The ANSI/SPARC methodology is used as the basic Flow Diagram for the Data Base construction in "LUCH"; in this case it can be formally described as follows:

$$[\{CM(DB):\ \langle CM(S): CM(Q): CM(R)\rangle\}]\ R(DB) \overset{\lim (DBMS)}{\Longrightarrow} M(DBMS)$$

where CM(DB) is the conceptual model (CM) of the Data Base to be designed, whose components are CM(S), CM(Q), and CM(R), which are CM-structures, queries and reports respectively. M(DBMS) is the result of CM(DB) transformation to the corresponding DBMS-orientated information structure, provided that the restrictions of the DBMS adopted (lim(DBMS)) are complied with.

The following principles were defined as the most important conceptual ones in the "LUCH" development:

1) the Information base modular construction principle, which is responsible for the information base hierarchical decomposition into a set of information modules (IM) and IM aggregation ("assembly") to form the information base;
2) the principle of using the IM type designs and IM unification;
3) the principle of requirements for the information base integration into the vector R(DB);
4) the principle of the cooperative heterarchy of the "LUCH" functional units which provides each of them with:
   a) an independent mode of operation with the succession of decisions made;
   b) mutual access to each other on the basis of equal rights;
   c) equal rights access to "LUCH" common system resources.

Generalization of just these two aspects of the methodology adopted enables one to justify the "LUCH" architecture, which is determined by the following functional units:

1) analysis of requirements for the designer information base and R(DB) generation;
2) conceptual simulation (construction of CM(DB);
3) DBMS selection and lim(DBMS) determination;
4) design of M(DBMS) implementation;
5) analysis of information base functioning;
6) M(DBMS) modification and editing.

For the cooperative heterarchy principle implementation, together with the introduction of common communication protocols for the functional units of the "LUCH", an information base design control unit is added. The functional units for conceptual simulation, and the implementation design and design control of the information base are given primary emphasis in this paper.

3. DB CONCEPTUAL SCHEMA SIMULATION

The simulation process is defined by the following sequence of its components:

1) an application-domain description which makes it possible to specify all entities defining the application domain under consideration, the natural language form, and the establishment of interconnections between the entities;
2) the construction of binary "trees" which defined relationships between the entities, i.e. the generation of a set of elementary entity relationship models permissible in the Application Domain under consideration;

3) the aggregation of elementary entity relationship models and the construction of the network semantic model for the given Application Domain;
4) normalisation of the network semantic model in 3-rd normal form.

An algebra was developed for implementation of the Conceptual Model generation, aggregation and modification methods. Emphasis was placed on a "morphism" operation, special cases of which are the operations "isomorphism", "homomorphism" and "design". The inverse problem of integrated conceptual model integrity support under M(DBMS) changes is emphasised. The significance of this problem is important for

1) implementation of information base support methods, when added requirements cannot be satisfied by M(DBMS) modification (editing) in the implementation design unit;
2) integration of Data Bases distributed on the network, including usage of different-types of DBMSs or different types of computer equipment.

4. RELATIONAL DATABASE STRUCTURE IMPLEMENTATION DESIGN

The use of hierarchical decomposition methods enables three design functions to be implemented in the information base implementation design unit:

1) structures;
2) queries;
3) reports.

The Structure Implementation Design architecture is determined by its four components:

1) an aggregated set of specified descriptions of DBMS-orientated Flow Diagrams for structure implementation design, the set being implemented as a Knowledge Base (the Knowledge Base segment of the implementation design unit, Knowledge Base subsegment of "LUCH").
2) DBMS expert-orientated interactive facilities for Knowledge Base completion and development;
3) Interactive Facilities for relational Data Base structure design;
4) Interactive Facilities for structure editing (modification).

To formalize knowledge in the relational data base structure implementation design process which determines the DBMS-orientated Flow Diagram, the following approach is used. In conformity with the basic points of relational data base theory, three stages are always defined in the process:

1)design of relationships (Rel);
2) design of domains (Dom);
3) design of formats (Form).

Then for any DBMS-orientated Flow Diagram a construction of the following form can be provided:

$$KI_p\ (FD) = \{Dsc\ [FDI_p];\ Pr\ [FDI_p]\},$$

where p belongs to P, KI_p is the knowledge on the p-th Flow Diagram implementation, P is the Knowledge Base capacity, (i.e. the number of DBMS for which construction is provided at a given adjustment of the Structure Implementation Design module,

$$Dsc\ [FDIp] = \langle Dsc\ [KI_p\ (Rel)];\ Dsc\ [KI_p(Form)],\ Dsc\ [KI_p\ (Dom)]\rangle,$$
$$Pr\ \ [FDI_p] = \langle\ Pr[\ KI_p\ \ (Rel)]\ ;\ Pr\ [\ KI_p\ (Form)\ ]\ ;\ Pr\ [\ KI_p\ (Dom)\ ]\ \rangle$$

$Dsc[FDI_p]$, $Dsc[KI_p$ (Rel)], Dsc [KI_p (Form)], Dsc [KI_p (Dom)] being natural language descriptions of the knowledge on the Flow Diagram and the implementation of its stages provided by DBMS experts and Pr [KI_p (Rel)],

Pr [KI_p (Dom)], and Pr [KI_p (Form)] are predicates which formalise corresponding natural language descriptions of the Flow Diagram and its stages. Then the pair < Dsc [K], Pr [K] > is a complete (from the viewpoint of knowledge base construction) specification of the experts knowledge.

The knowledge presentation method proposed enables one to suggest rational aggregation and generalization schemes for both Flow Diagram knowledge on any DBMS (KBOI completion method). The set of facilities for KBOI completion and development in the natural language relevant predicate notations is substantiated. The expediency of using a specially designed learning system for construction and completion of natural language descriptions is substantiated.

5. INFORMATION BASE DESIGN CONTROL

The problems solved by this functional unit of information base design control are localized at the hierarchical levels by the appropriate modules:

1) the project goal tree (PGT) generation and analysis design structuring;
2) determination of all kinds of information base resources required for the design and design-process scheduling;
3) on-line design-process control.

The base of the information base for this information unit is determined by the design information model. With the introduction of two types of abstract entities "task" and "executor", such an information model design is realized by an abstract network semantic structure having nodes of two types: nodes of the first type are determined by the pair <task, executor> while nodes of the second type are determined by the pair component domains, and arcs show either running in accordance with the Flow Diagram (design time) or components belonging to the abstract entity.

The approach makes it possible to construct a compact notation for the recurrent specification of the information base design at any level of refinement. For the modules of the first level as no clear-cut specification of the information base requirements is possible at early design stages, so the approach which proposes a description of the design goal space turns out to be more effective, a possible design generation trajectory being represented by the PGT. The PGT generation algorithm can be constructed as an algorithm of the project-goal set initial variants analysis for completeness, redundancy, vertical and horizontal conformity.

6. "LUCH' IMPLEMENTATION

Currently, a prototype of "LUCH" which solves a number of conceptual simulation problems, design and the implementation of relational Data base structures in such DBMSs as dBASE III, Plus, Oracle and Ingres, as well as Data Base design control, has been implemented with personal computer software which is compatible with the IBM PC. The prototype is software-supported by the Prolog language using the Russian-language program system for Prolog learning - PROKOP. The prototype is meant to be used by a Russian-speaking non-programming user, a researcher, or a production manager.

Industrial Applications of Artificial Intelligence
J.L. Alty and L.I. Mikulich (Editors)
Elsevier Science Publishers B.V. (North-Holland)

BLACKBOARD ARCHITECTURE FOR INDUSTRIAL AND MANAGEMENT EXPERT SYSTEMS

J. STAWICKI, K. OLSZEWSKI and
M. NALBACH
Institute for Organization of Machine Industry,
Warszawa,
Poland.

ABSTRACT: The characteristics and requirement of complex management and engineering problems are examined to define an expert system architecture. It is shown that the blackboard architecture is well suited for such systems. BB_POL, a blackboard expert system shell, and application areas of blackboard systems are presented.

1. INTRODUCTION

An analysis of problems associated with engineering and management in industrial enterprises reveals that many of them belong to planning (e.g. production planning and control, strategic planning), design (e.g. design of organizational structure of the industrial enterprise, layout planning) and the data analysis category of problems.

From an artificial intelligence point of view these problems may be characterised by:

- a large solution space,
- a variety of data and a need to integrate diverse sources of information,
- the need for many independent pieces of knowledge to cooperate during a solution process,
- the need for real-time problem solving,
- the need for multiple lines of reasoning.

Other expert system requirements result from peculiarities in the problem domain. They are:

- coupling of symbolic and numeric processing,
- flexibility and variance in the inference processes,
- integration with conventional management data processing techniques (data base. spreadsheet, word processing).
- integration with optimisation systems.

An adequate architecture for an expert system is required to solve problems of this kind. Experiments with rule-based expert system shells has shown that rule-based systems are inflexible and too weak, with respect to knowledge representation methods, inference engines and the user interface.They may be used only as a prototyping tool or as a testing tool for some solutions. In such situations another method of knowledge representation and a more flexible inference engine should be used.

2. MANAGEMENT EXPERT SYSTEM ARCHITECTURE

Problems connected with a management expert system architecture involve the following issues: knowledge representation, inference mechanisms and expert system environments. Management expert systems should support the following features connected with knowledge representation:

- use of the various knowledge representation methods: rules, frames and objects, inheritance, use of meta-knowledge and active knowledge in the form of methods,
- hypothetical reasoning, making possible the creation and maintenance of multiple knowledge bases,
- use of knowledge acquisition aids,
- use of few abstraction levels of problem description.

The requirements concerning the inference engine and control include:

- use of backward, forward and mixed (backward and forward) chaining,
- flexibility of the inference engine,
- use of a truth maintenance system

The expert system environment requirements cover a broad spectrum of tools from knowledge base management and debugging, to graphic interface creation etc. The basic features of a management expert system resulting from a detailed analysis of requirements connected with the above-mentioned groups of problems are:

- variety of knowledge representation methods,
- variety and flexibility of inference methods,
- hierarchical and evolutionary methods of inferencing.

The integration of expert systems with other management information systems is also desirable. It applies specially to conventional, domain oriented management information systems such as:

- computerised management tools (data base, spreadsheet, word, processors, business graphics),
- optimisation systems.

This set of requirements implies three possible architectures of management expert system:

- a blackboard architecture: an expert system in which several independent knowledge bases (knowledge sources) cooperate through a common working memory (a blackboard) and an agenda based control system continually examines all of the possible pending actions and chooses the one to try next [1,2,3],

- tandem expert systems, combining the operational research approach with the expert system approach in order to solve a problem, which can be thought of as an expert system linked to a data base of models and algorithms [4],

- an integrated expert system combining an expert system with a conventional business data processing systems (data base, word processor, business graphics, communication system), e.g. GURU [5].

3. THE BLACKBOARD ARCHITECTURE

The Blackboard Architecture is a special architecture of expert systems. An expert system conforming to its principles comprises the following parts:

- knowledge sources (thereinafter referred to as KS-s) independent procedural modules that deal with various aspects of a problem being solved by the expert system,

- the blackboard - a global data structure that is manipulated by the KS-s,

- the control unit - a single program module monitoring the problem solving processes of the system.

The blackboard architecture has several important advantages from the point of view of an expert system developer and user. It allows the combination of various knowledge representations and problem solving methods, it facilitates structural and hierarchical descriptions of the problems being solved, it may provide a way of solving a particular problem which is regarded by an expert as the most natural one, and it allows the mixing of the usual imperative programming mechanisms with those of a more declarative nature (like pattern directed procedure invocation).

The blackboard architecture can also form a basis of an intelligent system to [6] control and explain its actions and learn about its actions.

The blackboard architecture was chosen as the basis for an expert system and expert system shell for industrial and management problems because of:

1) the strong advantages of that architecture, e.g.

-the possibility of applying various knowledge representation methods
-the possibility of applying various inference strategies
-the rendition of the natural way of solving problems by human experts
-the possibility of application to complex planning and design problems and to complex problems, requiring multiple solving strategies.

2) the appropriateness of the blackboard architecture for complex industrial and management problems,

3) the need for AI methods which are more flexible than simple rule-based systems.

In comparison with rule-based systems the blackboard architecture imposes different structuring and organizational constraints upon working memory elements and its control mechanism can exhibit far greater ranges of behaviour. These points indicate that the blackboard architecture is much more powerful than other architectures.

4. BB_POL: A BLACKBOARD EXPERT SYSTEM SHELL

A blackboard expert system shell called BB_POL was designed according to the following assumptions:

- it should be a tool for a knowledge engineer supporting a description of both problem and problem solving method and generating a blackboard expert system,
- it should possess its own language for problem and problem solving method description,
- the generated expert system should be fast and portable,
- the generated expert system should be used as a stand-alone program in the absence of other parts of the expert system shell.

These assumptions influenced decisions concerning the structure and the implementation language of BB_POL as well as the method used for translation (compilation). BB_POL is written in the C language and is implemented on an IBM PC/AT. It consists of the following modules:

(1) BB EDITOR: a context editor providing functions for description - in a special Blackboard Language (BBL) - of problems and problem solving methods.
(2) BB GEN: a compiler translating BBL source programs into C source code,
(3) libraries including standard BB_POL procedures, inference engine, running system and testing-debugging programs,
(4) INTEGRATOR: a program supervising all modules of BB_POL.

The system closely cooperates with a C language compiler and a linker of object modules. BB_POL's blackboard system consists of the three main elements: blackboards, knowledge sources (KSs) and a control module. Blackboards are multidimensional structures organized in levels used to hold solution-state data. There are two blackboards in the system: a domain blackboard and a control blackboard. The current state of a problem solving process is represented by a collection of record-like objects, called units and kept in the domain blackboard. Data for the control of problem solving are kept in the control blackboard. Knowledge used by the system is partitioned into knowledge sources, which communicate only by changing the contents of the blackboard. A single knowledge source action results in a set of events causing changes in the state of a blackboard (usually of the domain blackboard).

The control module decides which knowledge source is to be chosen. It runs in the following loop: (i) determining actions possible in current situation, (ii) choosing next action, (iii) performing the selected action, until the solution is found. In the first stage of the loop trigger conditions of all KSs are checked. Knowledge source activation records (KSARs) are created for all KSs with satisfied conditions. Then preconditions of all KSARs are checked. The control module chooses a KSAR with the highest priority.

The detailed description of the BB_POL structure, its blackboard architecture and its own language (BBL)are presented in [7].

5. APPLICATIONS AREAS OF BLACKBOARD SYSTEMS AND BB_POL

5.l. Industrial applications of blackboard systems

Blackboard systems have found the following industrial applications in recent years:

- BBl a tool for building blackboard systems for production planning at the shop level in the factory producing car radios, to investigate its possibilities for production planning systems [8],
- SIGHTPLAN expert system to assist project managers in laying out temporary facilities on a construction site [9],
- AVC system for mission planning for autonomous vehicles,
- PHRED system for planning the construction process for aircraft components,
- RAPS for diagnosing electro-mechanical systems,
- OPIS for production planning 110],
- PEP38 for capacity planning for IBM System/38 [11].

5.2. The planned applications of BB_POL

There are two planned real-life applications of BB_POL.

The first application is modelling and design of an organization structure of an industrial enterprise. An expert system for that problem is being currently built in two concurrent tasks:

1. an implementation of the blackboard expert system shell,
2. an acquisition and a structuralisation of the organization structure modelling knowledge for the blackboard architecture.

The structure modelling knowledge that will be used in the first version of the blackboard system concerns only one of the several steps in the whole organization structure design procedure - developing of a function tree. Other steps will be included in the system in a further version.

Objects in a problem domain form blackboard levels and their attributes form so called units on blackboard levels. Knowledge concerning a function's development is included in

Knowledge Sources.

The second area is production planning on the shop floor level. BB POL is well adapted to production planning problems, because planning can be described as reasoning about actions to achieve goal.

6. CONCLUSIONS

The blackboard architecture is well suited for intelligent systems, solving complex management and engineering problems in the industrial enterprise. This results from the following characteristics of the architecture:

- combination of various knowledge representation and problem solving methods,
- structural and hierarchical description of the problems being solved,
- mixing of imperative and declarative programming mechanisms - a rendition of the natural way of solving problems by human experts.

Additionally the openness of the blackboard architecture allows enhancing of the expert systems with:

- the truth maintenance system,
- distributed or parallel method of problem solving,
- the hierarchy of knowledge abstractions in the form: architecture framework - application.

REFERENCES

[1] Hayes-Roth B. : "A Blackboard Architecture for Control",. Artificial Intelligence 26, (1985) pp. 251-321.

[2] Nii H.P. : "The Blackboard Model of Problem Solving and the Evolution of Blackboard Architectures". AI Magazine, vol.7, no. 3, (1986).

[3] Nii H.P., "Blackboard Application Systems and a Knowledge Engineering Perspective". AI Magazine, vol.7, no. 4, (1986).

[4] Kusiak A., Heragu S.S. "Expert Systems and Optimisation". The University of Manitoba Department of Mechanical and Industrial Engineering Working Paper 06/87. May 1987.

[5] Holsapple C.W., Whinston A.B. : Business Expert Systems. Irwin Inc. 1987.

[6] Hayes-Roth B., Garvey A., Johnson Jr. M.V., Hewett M., A., " Modular and Layered Environment for Reasoning about Action"., Stanford University, Computer Science Dept, Knowledge Systems Laboratory Report No KSL 86-38.

[7] Nalbach M., Olszewski K., Stawicki J., "BB_POL : a blackboard expert system shell for industrial applications", this volume.

[8] Isenberg R., Comparison of BBl and KEE for Building a Production Planning Expert System, in: Third International Expert Systems Conference (Learned Information, Oxford and New Jersey, 1987 pp. 407-421.

[9] Tommelen I.D., Levitt R.E., Hayes-Roth B., "Using Expert Systems for the Layout of Temporary Facilities on Construction Sites", Stanford University, Computer Science Dept, Knowledge Systems Laboratory Report No KSL 87-47.

[10] Smith S.I., Fox M.S., and Ow P.S., "Constructing and Maintaining Detailed Production Plans: Investigations into the Development of Knowledge-Based Factory Scheduling Systems", AI Magazine, Fall 1986.

[11] Stroebel G.J., Baxter R.D., and Denney M.J., "A Capacity Planning Expert System for IBM System/38", Computer 19 (1986), No 7, pp. 42-50.

Industrial Applications of Artificial Intelligence
J.L. Alty and L.I. Mikulich (Editors)
Elsevier Science Publishers B.V. (North-Holland)

BB_POL - A BLACKBOARD EXPERT SYSTEM SHELL FOR INDUSTRIAL AND MANAGEMENT APPLICATIONS

M. NALBACH,
K. OLSZEWSKI and
J. STAWICKI

Institute for Organisation of Machine Industry,
Warszawa,
Poland.

ABSTRACT: BB_POL, a tool system supporting development of blackboard expert systems, is presented. A description of BBL, a blackboard oriented programming language, and examples of BBL programming, are given. Expert systems are written in BBL and fully compiled. No kind of interpretive knowledge base is used.

1. INTRODUCTION

An analysis of industrial and management problems from an Artificial Intelligence point of view [1] has shown that the blackboard architecture [2, 3, 4] is an adequate expert system architecture for these problems.

The blackboard architecture has several advantages, important from the point of view of expert system developers and users. It allows the combination of various knowledge representation and problem solving methods, it facilitates structural and hierarchical description of the problem being solved, and it may easily allow for a way of solving a particular problem which is regarded by an expert as the most natural one.

These premises influenced the decision to start work on a blackboard expert system shell.

2. BB_POL SYSTEM STRUCTURE

A blackboard expert system shell [5] called BB_POL has been designed. It is written in the C language and is implemented on the IBM PC/AT. It consists of the following modules:

(1) BB_EDITOR: a context editor providing functions for the description of problems and problem solving methods in a special language BBL. The BB_EDITOR consists of a system editor,

- a knowledge source editor,
- a function editor,

(2) BB_GEN: a compiler translating BBL source programs into C source codes,
(3) libraries including standard BB_POL procedures, inference engine, a runtime system and testing-debugging programs,
(4) INTEGRATOR: a program supervising all modules of BB_POL.

The system closely cooperates with a C language compiler and a linker of object modules.

The development of a blackboard expert system consists of several steps. A user starts his work with BB_POL by preparing an expert system description in BBL - a blackboard oriented programming language. First he prepares a system description and all global declarations and definitions with the help of a system editor. Then he describes some separate knowledge sources using a knowledge source editor. If it is needed he may use a function editor to write some auxiliary functions and procedures.

The second step of a session with BB_POL is compilation. BB_GEN compiles a system description separately, each function and each KS, generating intermediate code in the C programming language. Then a standard C compiler is used to translate that code into object modules. A standard linker links object modules together with the system libraries mentioned above. The expert system is then ready to be tested. As soon as the user decides that his expert system is ready and does not require further testing, he may link all its modules without testing/debugging libraries, and use the resultant executable file as a stand alone tool without the BB_POL shell.

All these actions are easy to be performed because of the integrator's menu system.

3. BB_POL BLACKBOARD ARCHITECTURE

BB_POL's blackboard system consists of the three main elements: blackboards, knowledge sources (KSs) and a control module. Blackboards are multidimensional structures organized in levels used to hold solution-state data. There are two blackboards in the system: a domain blackboard and a control blackboard. The current state of a problem solving process is represented by a collection of record-like objects, called units kept in the domain blackboard. Data for control of the problem solving is kept in the control blackboard.

Knowledge used by the system is partitioned into knowledge sources, which communicate only by changing contents of the blackboard. A single knowledge source action results in a set of events causing changes in the state of a blackboard (usually of the domain blackboard).

The control module decides which knowledge source is to be chosen. It runs in the following loop: (i) determining actions possible in current situation, (ii) choosing next action, (iii) performing the selected action, until the solution is found. In the first stage of the loop, the trigger conditions of all the KSs are checked. Knowledge source activation records (KSARs) are created for all KSs with satisfied conditions. Then preconditions of all KSARs are checked. The control module chooses a KSAR with the highest priority.

There is a net-like structure dedicated to trigger satisfaction monitoring. This structure is aimed at speeding up the process of finding trigger conditions that are currently satisfied, by elimination of irrelevant conditions.

4. BBL - A LANGUAGE DESCRIPTION

BBL is an original programming language embedding conventional C-like language control instructions and data structures as well as data structures and instructions specific for the blackboard architecture. A blackboard system description in BBL consists of some separately compiled parts:

1. A blackboard system global definition.
2. Some (as much as needed) knowledge source definitions.

A blackboard system global definition consists of: symbolic constants definitions; types definitions; a blackboard definition; global variables declarations; procedures and functions declarations; and a blackboard initialisation.

All above parts are optional except a blackboard definition. A blackboard definition consists of global classes definitions,and levels definitions.

A class is a unit type. All units of a given class have the same number of the same attributes. Units of a global class may appear on any level. A class definition consists of definitions of all its fields. A field definition contains a field name and a field type.

A level definition comprises a list of global classes used on this level and definitions of local (for this level) classes.

During blackboard initialisation initial units with given attributes values are created. An initialisation process is executed before a reasoning process is started.

A knowledge source definition consists of: context variable declarations, KS description, creation, date, cost, credibility, efficiency, importance, static priority, a trigger declaration, a precondition declaration and an action declaration.

A KS describes operations performed during problem solving and two conditions that must be met for their execution. The first condition,called a trigger, deals with events from the last reasoning cycle, the second - called precondition - with the state of the blackboard.

A trigger condition is either an elementary or a complex condition. A complex trigger condition is either a conjunction or a disjunction of elementary conditions. Every elementary condition refers to a single event and must specify several characteristics of those events that are to satisfy this condition. Let us take, for example, a simple trigger condition:

(T1) mod person (age eq 18; height gt 190).

Trigger condition T1 is satisfied only by those events dealing with units of class person that result in a specific state of the modified unit: resultant value of the age field is required to be 18 and the value of height field must be greater than 190 centimeters.

When a trigger of a KS is satisfied by some events then a knowledge source activation record (KSAR) is created for this KS. Every KSAR contains references to the precondition and action of its mother KS. Moreover, references to vectors of context variables may be attached to KSAR-s. Context variables are a vehicle of parameter passing characteristic to the blackboard model for computations. They also facilitate access to blackboard units. The scope of a context variable covers the entire knowledge source in which the variable has been defined (unlike the scope of local variables, which doesn't include the trigger). Assignment of values to context variables results from the process of matching trigger conditions against events. A context variable may have different values in different KSAR-s. A value of a context variable is defined in an action of a KS ony if this variable has an occurrence inside the trigger condition of the KS. Instructions that occur in actions and preconditions are allowed to read context variables.

The next part of every KS is a precondition. A return() phrase with a boolean expression as its argument must appear inside a precondition. Tests performed by preconditions may be more sophisticated than those of triggers for two reasons. Firstly, a precondition is not syntactically constrained to be a logical combination of unit patterns – it may be as complex as any procedure. Secondly, preconditions can manipulate global and local variables and, moreover, investigate the whole content of the blackboard, not being restricted to events of the latest cycle and their associated units.

When both trigger and precondition are satisfied then the action of their KS may start.

Actions of KS-s might be compared to procedures of classical imperative programming languages or to right hand sides of production system rules (e.g. of OPS). Actions are program units made up of both commonly used instructions (e.g. variable assignement, conditional statements, loops) and instructions specific for blackboard model of computation. In BBL instructions of the former kind apply to local variables of a single KS. The scope of local variables cover its action and precondition. Blackboard oriented instructions operate on blackboard units and their fields. These instructions include creation, modification, acess and removal of units and unit selection by means of pattern matching.

The Programmer may prohibit event generation by adding the keyword noevent in front of a blackboard instruction. It does not, however, hinder the assignement instructions following with from changing field values of the bound unit.

5. EXAMPLE PROBLEM

The domain problem chosen as a test application of BB_POL is that of an automated guided vehicle (AGV) or robot, navigating along a factory plant floor [6] without colliding with any of the objects on the plant floor. Some of these objects can be discovered by the robot on the route. The Task's accomplishment requires: planning a path; moving along the path and backtracking and path re-planning when blocking objects are encountered.

The domain blackboard for robot problem consists of levels concerning path planning, storing information about the room, floor plan, movement goal, paths, segments, nodes and levels storing dynamic information about robot's current movements and its position.

The domain knowledge is partitioned between knowledge sources responsible for problem solving (e.g. path planning KS, path selection KS, backtracking KS, etc).

A fragment of the system and knowledge source description in BBL is presented:

```
/* SYSTEM DESCRIPTION : BBL SOURCE CODE */

system robot
/* type definitions */
   ......
blackboard              /* definition of the blackboard */
{
level d_problem_level   /* example of a blackboard level */
{ class d_problem
  { problem_name : symbol;
    room_no : integer;
  }
}
/* other blackboard levels */
   ...
}

/* Knowledge source code in BBL */
Ksource Movement_Finished_Ks;
var NEW_SQUARE : current_square;
desc "KS for checking if solution was found"
created "89/10/23"
cost 100
cred 100
effic 100
imp 100
prior 500
trigger {NEW_SQUARE: new current_square}
```

```
precondition
{ return(true);}
action
var coord_x,coord_y : integer;
    cur_goal : stream of current_goal;
    c_goal : current_goal;
    cur_problem : stream of c_problem;
    c_problem : c_problem;
{
access NEW_SQUARE with {coord_x = x; coord_y = y;}
match to cur_goal {(current_goal on current_goal_level :
                                             status eq open)}
c_goal = first(cur_goal);
match to cur_problem {(c_problem on c_problem_level :
                                         status eq solving)}
c_problem = first(cur_problem);
if c_goal.stop_x == coord_x && c_goal.stop_y == coord_y
then modify c_problem with {status = solved;}
}
```

6.CURRENT STATE OF IMPLEMENTATION

Currently a compiler and a runtime system are being tested on the robot example. The integrator and the context editor are being implemented. Development of an expert system for modelling and designing of an organization structure is in progress.

Planned applications of BB_POL are described in details in [1].

REFERENCES

[1] Stawicki J., Nalbach M., Olszewski K. : Blackboard Architecture for Industrial and Management Expert Systems. Artificial Intelligence - Industrial Application . Leningrad 1990.

[2] Hayes-Roth B. : A Blackboard Architecture for Control. Artificial Intelligence 26 (1985) 251-321.

[3] Nii H.P. : The Blackboard Model of Problem Solving and the Evolution of Blackboard Architectures. AI Magazine, vol.7, no. 3, 1986.

[4] Nii H.P.: Blackboard Application Systems and a Knowledge Engineering Pespective. AI Magazine, vol.7, no. 4, 1986.

[5] Velthuijsen, Lippolt B.J., Vonk J.C. : BLONDIE: a blackboard shell. Netherlands PTT. Dr. Neher Laboratories, memorandum 1404 DNL/86.

[6] Giguere Ch., Lim T., McGill R. : A Blackboard Expert System Shell. University of Toronto. Department of Electrical Engineering. ELE 1635 Project Report.

Industrial Applications of Artificial Intelligence
J.L. Alty and L.I. Mikulich (Editors)
Elsevier Science Publishers B.V. (North-Holland)

DDSS: A KNOWLEDGE-BASED ENVIRONMENT FOR COMPUTER-AIDED CONTROL SYSTEM DESIGN: CONCEPTION AND IMPLEMENTATION

J. LUNZE

Zentralinstitut fur Kernforschung der AdW der DDR,
Postfach 19,
Dresden,
DDR-8051.

H-P. SCHEFFLER

Zentralinstitut fur Kybernetik und Informationsprozesse der AdW der DDR,
Haeckelstrasse 20,
Dresden,
DDR-8027

ABSTRACT: DDSS is a knowledge-based environment for computer-aided control system design packages (CACSD packages). It performs most of the organisational work of a design engineer, (i.e. it carries out the design planning, organises the execution of the design steps, and stores the design process in a knowledge base). DDSS provides communication between the designer and the design system at a high level of abstraction. It has a component for knowledge acquisition and is applicable to large classes of CACSD packages.

1. INTRODUCTION

In the theory of automatic control, a large body of analysis and design methods has been elaborated. Based on this theoretical knowledge, computer-aided control system design packages (CACSD) have been implemented, which support the solution of practical analysis and design tasks in the following way:

- The CACSD package provides separate algorithms for solving prescribed design steps (e.g. observer design, simulation, stability analysis).

- The designer organises the design process, i.e. he chooses a specific module of the CACSD package, specifies parameters for the corresponding algorithm, and gives the names of the data files to be processed.

In the course of the design process, man and computer strongly communicate (see Figure 1) via drivers (module run commands, data file names, parameter values) and indicators (information concerning the results received by the CACSD module). This interaction is necessary because the CACSD package includes merely the algorithmic knowledge that results from the special technical topic. Knowledge concerning motivation, aims, and the results of the underlying concepts of control system design as well as the heuristics resulting from experience with the methods implemented in the CACSD package have to be contributed by the designer.

The aim of creating the environment DDSS (see Figure 1) is to enhance the CACSD package by a component that performs most of the organisational work and enables the dialogue between designer and design system to take place at the level of technical conceptions and imagination.

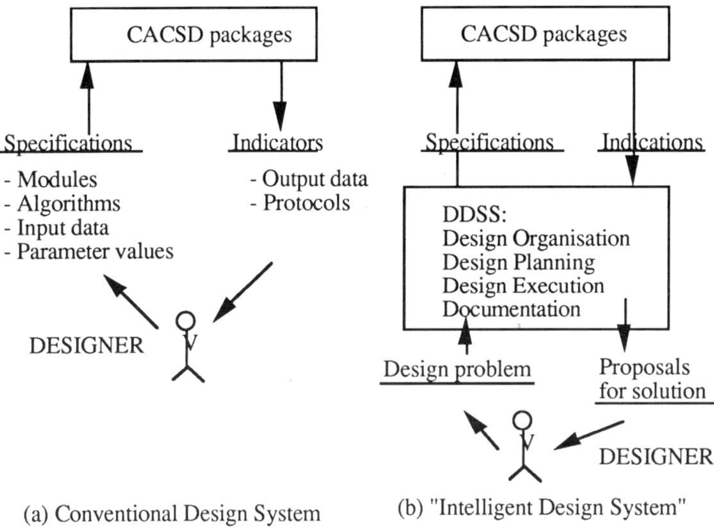

(a) Conventional Design System (b) "Intelligent Design System"

Figure 1 Communication between designer and CACSD package.

The DDSS therefore allows a considerable automation of the design process. In particular, the following tasks are supported:

- Design Planning: DDSS finds out and offers alternative plans for solving the current design problem.
- Design Execution: DDSS calls the modules of the design system and supplies them with the required data.
- Documentation of the Design Process: DDSS records the design steps in such a manner that it can inform the designer about the existing design process and thus the consistency of the input data for planning and execution can be ensured.
- Control of the Design Process: DDSS organises the coordination of planning, execution, and documentation as well as backtracking within the design tree.
- Knowledge Acquisition: DDSS has a component for supporting the adaption of the knowledge bases to special CACSD packages. Hence, DDSS is applicable to a large class of CACSD packages and, moreover, to CAD systems in general.

Concerning the second and third items, DDSS has similar goals to the CAD environment DEMAN for VLSI circuit design described by Salov [4].

2. MODEL OF THE DESIGN PROCESS

In DDSS, design processes are represented by a hierarchical *model* that distinguishes between the conceptual, the structural, and the algorithmic level of abstraction (Figure 2).

On the *conceptual level* communication between designer and CACSD package is performed in terms of concepts and ideas well-known to the control engineer (e.g.. output feedback or state feedback design). For this purpose, so-called macrosteps are introduced. The *structural level* represents the module structure of the CACSD package. Generally, each module contains several algorithms for performing one macrostep. On the *algorithmic level* design algorithms are executed. This requires that data files are selected, parameters are evaluated, and algorithms are invoked by prescribed run-time commands.

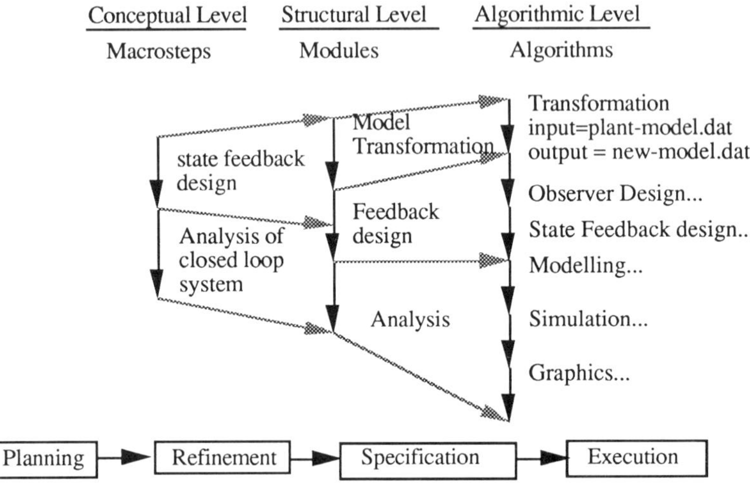

Figure 2 The three level Model of the Design Process

On each level the macrosteps, the modules, and the algorithms are considered as mappings that transform data with special properties into data with other properties. Hence, these mappings can be characterised by their input-output behaviour. This approach results in the notion of the design state (where "state" is used in the artificial intelligence sense). The design state is characterised by the set (of types) of available data and the way these data are generated. This state space representation leads to a graph-theoretical interpretation of design processes by trees (Fig. 2).

It is obviously, that different state spaces are necessary for representing design processes at the different levels of abstraction mentioned earlier. Areas of these state spaces are the search spaces, which are passed through by a design process. This, and the relations between the state spaces are examined in more detail in a forthcoming paper of the authors [1]

What are the relationships between the tasks of the environment and the different levels of the design process? The planning of the design process is performed on the conceptual level, where the technical concepts are available as macrosteps. By a process of refinement, in which each macrostep is assigned to a sequence of modules or algorithms, the structural level is reached. Then the execution of design steps begins (Fig. 2). The execution requires the choice of one algorithm included in the module and the specification of this algorithm (i.e. the determination of input data and parameter values). Now, the transition to the algorithmic level is finished. The executed design steps and the searched parts of the state spaces on each level have to be stored in the process of documentation.

3. KNOWLEDGE REPRESENTATION

The essential knowledge is derived from the state space representations of the design process as well as from the input/output behaviour of the macrosteps, the modules, and the design algorithms. In particular, knowledge of the following kinds has to be presented:

- Knowledge about the applicability and the input-output behaviour of macrosteps, modules, and design algorithms (W1).

- Knowledge about the suitability of design step sequences with respect to the current design problem. This knowledge includes the heuristic experience of the designer on the effects of certain design step sequences. It is the basis of the planning process (W2).

- Knowledge about the current state of the design process (W3).

- Knowledge about the processing of the knowledge given in (Wl) to (W3) for the organisation and execution of the design process. This knowledge is the basis for the structure of DDSS and the implementation of its supervisor.

Knowledge of this kind consist of facts (discrete events or situations) and relations between these facts. It is used for solving tasks that are mainly formulated as decision problems. Representation schemes developed in artificial intelligence are best suited for the represention of such forms of knowledge. In DDSS an object-oriented knowledge representation formalism, which is characterised by the existence of different object classes has been implemented. The following object classes are distinguished: MACROSTEP, MODULE, ALGORITHM, FILE-PREDICATE, and INFILE, OUTFILE, PARAMETER (with respect to algorithms). Each object class is characterised by special knowledge items. Therefore, the elements of these classes (the so-called *instances*) are embodied by different frame structures. The knowledge base of DDSS is formed from instances of the object classes. For each CACSD package, the same object classes are necessary, but different instances have to be created.

This approach to knowledge representation is well-suited for supporting the knowledge acquisition process. For that reason, object classes are defined by so-called *prototypes*. Prototypes are frame structures that contain descriptions about the syntax and semantics of the different knowledge aspects. In DDSS a special component for knowledge acquisition is integrated. With the aid of this component knowledge bases for different CACSD packages can be generated rapidly. In order to get a qualified behaviour of the CAD-environment the knowledge acquisition must be considered as a dynamic process. The result depends on the knowledge and the experience of the man who generates the instances. The communication between this specialist and the component is situated in the context of specific concepts of the CACSD package, (i.e. nobody has to learn the specific knowledge representation language). This component opens the possibility of applying the concept of DDSS to further CAD systems.

4. ARCHITECTURE OF DDSS

The environment of DDSS consists of a supervisor and components for design planning, the execution of design steps, and documentation (Fig. 3).

Communication between these components is controlled by the supervisor and is organised by a common working memory. The CACSD package is connected with the component for design execution that generate the drivers for the design system and organises calls of the algorithms. The CACSD package returns indicators stored in common working memory and processed by the documentation component. Each of these components is implemented as a rule-based system with separate knowledge bases and inference engines.

The knowledge bases for the supervisor and the documentation part are independent of the CACSD package. Only the knowledge bases for the planning and execution have to be changed for different CACSD packages. The generation of these knowledge bases is performed with the aid of the knowledge acquisition component. Although the design process in the DDSS environment can be performed by any designer, the process of knowledge acquisition requires cooperation between experts in automation control and the CACSD package.

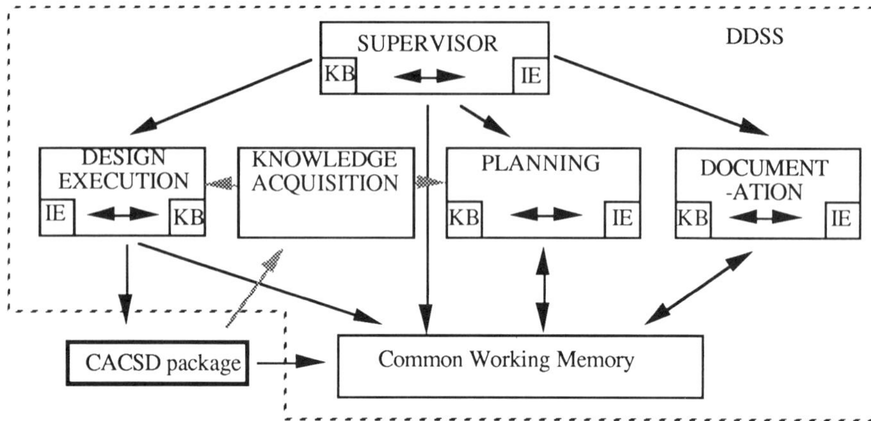

Figure 3 The Architecture of the Environment of DDSS

5. IMPLEMENTATION

As the problems to be solved and the forms of knowledge representation suitable for these tasks do not fit nicely into the framework of commercially available expert system shells and as the system DDSS has to be integrated with the CACSD package, DDSS has been implemented in Common LISP. This implementation has been performed for applications such as the logical design of VLSI circuits by MIPRE (cf. [2]). The application of DDSS to the CACSD package IMGRE (cf. [3]) has also been studied [1].

6 . CONCLUSIONS

The DDSS environment enhances the scope of functions and decisions that can be carried out by the computer. This is obviously reflected in the fact that the man-machine interaction is raised from the algorithmic level to the conceptual level of abstraction, in which the designer may think in terms of analysis and design principles known from automatic control. The communication no longer refers to drivers and indicators. Instead, the designer prescribes his design aims which the system DDSS expands into a sequence of module run commands including relevant parameters and data file names. The answers to the designer yield intermediate results (controller parameters, newly created data files, evaluations, graphic representations of step responses) which cause the engineer to finish the design process or to prescribe a new design problem (Figures 1 and 2). The documentation module frees the designer from expensive documentation of the design process, supplies the designer with information about the design process executed so far, and stores information that influences the forthcoming design steps and ensures the consistency of the data even if the design steps turn out to be useless and the design process is restarted at an earlier stage.

In this way, the DDSS environment considerably extends that part of the design process which is automatically performed. It reduces the knowledge and skill that is necessary for using the CACSD package. Moreover, since each piece of information is asked for only once, the consistency of the design process is ensured. The designer has to interact with the computer only for those tasks whose solution necessitates human creativity and intuition.

Knowledge bases for planning and execution can be easily generated with the aid of the knowledge acquisition component. This component is based on an object-oriented knowledge representation formalism with prototype and instance frames. It enables the application of the

DDSS environment to a large class of design systems, consisting of autonomously working design algorithms (cf. the introduction). In particular, DDSS is applicable to CACSD packages and the design of VLSI circuits.

REFERENCE5

[l] Lunze, J. and Sheffler J. H.-P., "A Knowledge Representation Formalism for Computer-aided Control Systems Design" submitted for publication.

[2] Franke, G. and others, "MIPRE-Nutzerdokumentation (Research Report ZKI 1988)

[3] Rudolph, H. and others, "SKR-Dialogsystem fur den Zeitbereichsbezcgenen Mehrgrossenregelungsentwurf (IMGRE)", (Research Report ZKI 1984)

[4] Salov, G.M. and Jossifov, D.K., J. "New Generation Computer Systems", Vol. 2 (1989), 2, pp. 145 - 158.

Industrial Applications of Artificial Intelligence
J.L. Alty and L.I. Mikulich (Editors)
Elsevier Science Publishers B.V. (North-Holland)
1991 IFIP

DEVELOPMENT OF A KNOWLEDGE-PROCESSING MODULE FOR INTEGRATING EMPIRICAL KNOWLEDGE

D. KOCHAN and J. OELSCHLEGEL
Technical University of Dresden,
Germany.

ABSTRACT: Within the last 30 years Artificial Intelligence has created a number of methods and software tools, which have led to an enrichment of software development. Nevertheless, using these results is still at an experimental stage. So emphasis is on the development of universal language systems with new paradigms rather than on hybrid tools and the possibility of their integration into existent systems. Object-oriented (e. g. frames) and control-oriented (e. g. production systems) systems are used for automated generation of the CAD/NC interface. But as with many other engineering decision processes, a complete automation of NC programming is not possible.

Empirical knowledge (both individual and operational) should be kept separately from generation algorithms so as to be easily traceable and hence maintainable. Such a separation is suited for verbalized explanations - e. g. for preceding and subsequent relationships of stages of operation in NC machining.

This requires language hierarchies (meta-languages) which are interpretatively mapped onto AI languages. Expert systems are to be constructed by experts, whereas the respective software tools should be developed by knowledge engineers.

1. PROBLEM SITUATION

Despite of all of the advances the integration of design data, the manufacturing engineering planning of single parts and their production (CAD/CAM of individual production) still comes under research work, from the viewpoint of optimality and functionality. A standardisation of product descriptions [1] is in the process of development, as is a CAD/CAM data base [2].

To structure data into information and knowledge is a creative process (with data being elementary components, information being data and their relations and knowledge representing the connection between information and methods of modifying information. Hence it follows that all programs represent knowledge). This process is assisted by knowledge processing; and a clearer distinction is made between processing and storage (compare Fig. 1).

This paradigm is supported by methods such as the

- trial-and-error-method in solving problems (back tracking);
- transmission of properties in class hierarchies (realised, for instance, in frames);
- symbolic manipulation and recursion;
- realisation of constraints.

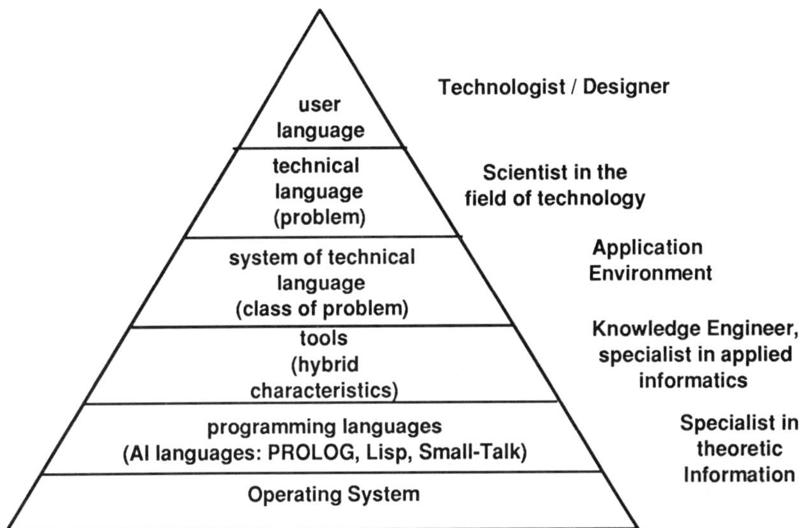

Figure 1 The Software Pyramid

Following these abstractions which form the basis of powerful AI tools (e.g. PROLOG and PL-shells in LISP) and after having prepared the problem as to its contents sufficiently, the technologist who initiated the design can start by selecting software tools using the CAD/NC interface.

Experience teaches that it is not possible for

- the technologist to have sufficient knowledge of the great variety of software tools;
- for the software tools to formally represent the problem adequately down to the last detail. So the problem will have to be "adapted" in order that the tool used may be applied throughout.

From this angle it becomes clear that AI software, too, is not able to overcome the software crisis, but continues it on a higher level. In our opinion this crisis is caused by the black-box behaviour which the user shows towards software products. Requests for software changes often lead to completely new programming of the whole product or to considerable service and maintenance requirements. [3]. So in a process of division of labour between a specialist in applied informatics, a knowledge engineer, a scientist of the specialist field, and the user, hierarchies of programming languages should be developed so as to equip each one involved with a means of expression at the appropriate level for them to express their problem.

All this requires both a change in thinking (a departure from searching solutions which are directly generalisable) and powerful hardware (for interpretative processing). Along these lines we extended an NC-part-programming system AUTOTECH/DR 43 with regard to the 4 (2 times 2) axis-controlled lathe as a CNC machining centre.

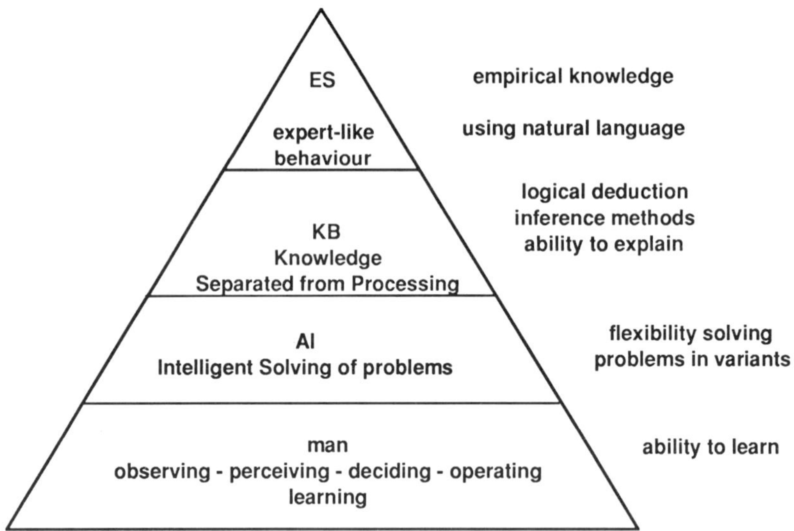

Figure 2 Relations and Properties of Artificial Intelligence (AI), Knowledge Bases (KB) and Expert Systems (ES).

2. MODULE FOR USING AND MANAGING EMPIRICAL KNOWLEDGE WITH REGARD TO 4-AXIS-CONTROLLED TURNING

The lathe of the type DF 2/2-4A is further developed towards a complete CNC machining centre. At present, a 2/2-4 axis controlled lathe is available. In single-part production it allows an increase of productivity from 30 to 60 % due to the parallel use of two tool turrets. But economical effects will be produced only on condition that all additional expenditure in work planning is reduced. For this, Hess/Bruemmer [4] extended AUTOTECH/DR 43 by four modules

- the automated variant determination of sequences of stages of operation module,
- the graphically dynamic simulation of workpiece machining module,
- the operate value determination module and
- the equipment with tool carriers module.

For the sequences of stages of operation a hierarchical regulating system was developed,

- using the empirical knowledge of the technologist;
- softening complicated design models for optimisation;
- utilizing test results.

From technical/technological and economic viewpoints, this regulating system (of about 250 rules) evaluates the suitable combination of machining units (which before were generated as possible parallel machining variants by evaluating geometric relations). The result is then offered to the NC programmer to decide on, with the respective combination of machining units being simultaneously flashed on the graphical display.

Thus it is for the technologist to decide on the selection of combinable machining units. For this he is given the opportunity of having the possible evaluations explained (explanation of the rules which generated the result of evaluation). Within the first project stage of the module, software engineering aspects are considered, for example aspects which may be reduced to the following theses:

- It will take about two weeks to program and test the regulating knowledge for instance by means of FORTRAN. But then it can be maintained by its designer only, which because of the flexible and non-closed nature of the regulating system leads to the product software crisis.

- Representing regulating knowledge in a user-adequate manner and supporting it by formalisms (e. g. automated hierarchical formation) will take one year of interpreter development by two men, which however enables the NC programmer (up to the operator) to independently accumulate empirical knowledge in the regulating system.

All this illustrates that software development always is an optimisation problem and that a "one and only" solution does not exist. We decided to approach in the following way:

1) The present regulating system (expert knowledge) is available in a "preformalised" but uncomputerisable form (mixture of decision table and graphic elements). A logical analysis showed the possibility of mapping the regulating system in three levels, namely

   a) in calculations of intermediate results which as fuzzy technological rules are "sharpened", depending on the used cutting tool and the material of the finished part,

   b) in classifying rules (which use the intermediate results) in groups of rules from the viewpoint of contents (e.g. for external-external machining in roughing on both machining units),

   c) in perceiving the relations existing between these groups of rules.

2) By analogy with [5] we have realized that empirical knowledge is not mappable directly by PROLOG, whereas a user language resulting from logical analyses with regard to contents can be functionally mapped onto PROLOG. By means of a number of "tricks", (for instance mapping the operations of a rule by the built-in predicate "assert" [2]), it is possible to save enormous expenditure in the adapted rule interpreter. Thus it is also possible to rapidly program this functional level and test it as to contents within the first project stage in order to continue with attaching a user language to generate the functional level (rapid prototyping by means of PROLOG).

3) The data are to be obtained from the interfaces of AUTOTECH/DR 43 and generated as PROLOG terms. The specific nature of the problem demands determination of the type of a term by means of a description table. (e. g. machplace (X) - machining place of the tool on the workpiece, which has the values X, e.g. (1,2,3), with 1 being the first third from the spindle; 2 being the second third ... etc.). DR 43 gives the PROLOG module only the number of the two machining units to be evaluated, from which the interface interpreter then generates the terms for both machining units (e. g. machplace A (1), machplace B (2)).

The explanatory texts to be read at the terms and rules are used for generating "why" questions, which is a first step towards explaining computer-aided decisions in a meta-linguistic way.

This shows that the simpler and easier programming shells are to operate, the greater the expenditure in regard to the software level below. But we agree with [6] that this approach is a practicable way for knowledge-processing expert systems. In this connection the prerequisite is a portable PROLOG system which in addition generates really compilable programs on efficient hardware.

REFERENCES

[1] "Eingabenormalform zur Alphanumerischen Beschrei-bung prismatischer Werkstucke; TU Karl-Marx-Stadt, (1989).

[2] "G4 - Forschungsbericht; Ein Patenmodell zur Be-schreibung von CIM-Datenbasen", TU Dresden, 1989

[3] Struss, P., "Wissensreprasentation - Abschied vom Programmieren?", In: Informationstechnik it 31, 2, pp. 91 - 94, (1989)

[4] Hess, M., and Bruenner, U., "Programmiersystem fur 2 x 2 Achsen gesteuerte CNC-Drehmaschinen", Dissertation A, TU Dresden, (1989).

[5] Krickhahn, R., and Schachter-Radig, M.-J., "Grund- konzepte der regelorientierten Programmierung", In: Informationstechnik it 30, 6, pp. 434 - 445, (1988)

[6] Lehmann, N.J., "Fachsprachen als konzeptionelle Basis fur Programm- und Expertensysteme (I)", In: GI - Mitteilungen - 3, 4, pp. 162 - 173, (1988)

[7] Geske, U., "Programmieren in PROLOG", Berlin, 1988

Industrial Applications of Artificial Intelligence
J.L. Alty and L.I. Mikulich (Editors)
Elsevier Science Publishers B.V. (North-Holland)

THE ARIES ENVIRONMENT (V4.00) FOR THE DEVELOPMENT OF KNOWLEDGE-BASED EXPERT SYSTEMS

A.V. DE LA CRUZ, J.J. VALDES, A. PEREZ, E. JOCIK, J. BALSA, A. RODRIGUES

Laboratory of Artificial Intelligence,
SOFTEL-ACC,
Calle 7ma y 194,
Siboney,
La Habana,
Cuba.

ABSTRACT: The ARIES environment and knowledge programming language for expert systems development is presented, and its main features outlined. The system is being used in a broad spectrum of complex domains and successful applications have being produced.

1. INTRODUCTION

ARIES is a general purpose environment for the development of expert systems and a language for knowledge programming. Accordingly, a problem solving conception based on heuristic and/or formal knowledge can be specified, organized, and implemented with ARIES's toolbox for knowledge representation, control strategies, inference mechanisms, man-machine interaction uncertainty processing, etc, which the knowledge engineer may use and combine at will.

Some general characteristics of ARIES are:

- ARIES does not impose a rigid way about how to do things, and usually a certain effect can be a achieved by a variety of ways, combining different tools.
- ARIES is shrinkable/expandable. Versions are tailored from a minimal one (one diskette) to a full one (more than 3 MB).
- ARIES is configurable. You can change ARIES's outlook as well as its internal way of working even within a consultation an arbitrary number of times.
- ARIES was conceived for both real world problems and experimental work in expert systems development.

The present description corresponds to version 4.00 and it is composed of a package of programs grouped into four modules:

- The Consulting System (ARIES)
- The Knowledge Acquisition and Handling System (SAMC)
- The Installator
- Utilities

2. THE CONSULTING SYSTEM ARIES 4.00

2.1. Knowledge Representation

Different knowledge representation forms can be jointly used:

2.1.1. Production Rules

The antecedent is a conjunctive or disjunctive form, and the succedent is a list of element each with two certainty factors, the first one used when the antecedent is true and the second when it is false. Thus, a single rule might contain the same knowledge far more economically than in a usual MYCIN- like system.

2.1.2. Relations of Alternative Evaluation

This is established when a given element should be considered as primary evidence, or evaluated using the knowledge base. Thus the system may exhibit a differential behaviour according to the expertise or type of user.

2.1.3. Contextual Relations

This relation express common sense knowledge, and methods for reducing the dimensionality of complex problems by heuristic pruning of the knowledge base.

2.1.4. Variables

Several kinds are present:

2.1.4.1. Quantitative

These are real valued quantities (e.g. temperature or voltage) - The following classes are considered:

a) single-valued (e.g. distance = 10 km),
b) occasional (e.g. the operating voltage of something is 20 or 50 volts),
c) interval (e.g. the voltage is between 20-50 volts),
d) time (the variable is some kind of time and the units are definable),
e) external (their values are obtained via external computer programs with optional information exchange with ARIES. This makes possible the combination of heuristic with formal knowledge in any proportion),
f) formula (the values are given by mathematical formulae with logarithms, powers, Hyperbolic, Bessel, and many other functions).

Remark: These classes of quantitative variables are not exclusive (a given variable might be declared as being of several types simultaneously). Moreover, a certainty degree may be associated with the value of the variable (e.g. "The voltage is 25 volts and I am *almost* sure about it").

2.1.4.2. Qualitative

In this case the values are non-numerical, for example, hair colour, day of the week, etc. There are several classes:

a) simple (composed by exclusive elements as day of the week, etc),
b) multiple (the variable is multi-valued such as user's hobbies: philately, alpinism,...),
c) sequence (this variable allows the expert system to make retrospective and script-like reasoning, in order to detect not only if some events effectively have occurred but also if they have appeared according to admissible sets of possible sequences of events along time/space defined in the knowledge base).

2.1.4.3. Relation of Comparison

Involves logical expressions using <, =, >, < >, and their combinations with certainties, real variables or formulae. Optionally, absolute or percentage tolerances might be included as criteria for comparison.

2.1.4.4. Question

It is a kind of variable introduced for special purposes, and several classes are considered:

a) aclaratory (used for extended questioning, via additional texts),
b) screen (allows the use of graphical screens as part of the knowledge base), and
c) external (another way for activate external programs in a consultation with more freedom).

2. 1.4.5. Re-evaluation

This variable allows a simple and practical way of implementing non- monotonic reasoning, and its scope can be specified in several ways.

2.1.5. Declared Implications

This a kind of semantic network expressing relations of membership, inclusion, taxonomy, consequence or equivalence.

2.1.6. Control base and Knowledge Programming

The control base contains knowledge programming structures and instructions for ARIES. Partitions or subproblems can be defined, as well as the conditions under which they should be analyzed, the assumptions to be made if they are not, and the goals focused by the partition, the type of output, the configuration which ARIES must adopt, and the way in which conclusions must be constructed. It is possible to mix partitions, and also to specify the order in which they should be analyzed (sequential, hierarchical, etc). Programming rules are the instructions for defining problem solving strategy and conclusion elaboration. This gives immense possibilities for the development of concrete applications in a great variety of different domains.

2.1.7. Programming Rules and Elaboration of Conclusions

These are the instructions by means of which the knowledge engineer can define precisely how the system must use its knowledge, the problem solving strategy and actions, what is a conclusion, and how to construct it. A conclusion in a real problem is not simply a list of goals ordered by their certainty or probability, but a complex structured statement (e.g. in medecine: disease-treatment- recommendations).

In ARIES, conclusions are defined by means of conclusion rules which are a kind of programming rule. The antecedent of all such rules is composed of two parts (ANTl and ANT2). The first is obligatory and the second is optional, with the semantics: "the situation described by ANTl is true and (if defined) the one described by ANT2 is unknown". The kind of rule is given by the kind of succedent, and they are the following (the first three are the conclusion rules):

a) pure (shows a given message),
b) simple (define when an element should be considered as a conclusion),
c) compound (define the condition under which some subset of elements from a given set should be included as conclusions, being the conclusion of the whole subset. How to build such a subset is specified by the rule parameters),
d) action (commands the investigation of the element given as succedent, is useful also for activation of external programs when building conclusions),
e)partial results (presents partial results of the partition under analysis in several ways),
f) interruption (establish the conditions under which the analysis of the partition

should be interrupted and how this should be done).

The number of programming rules for a given partition is in the order of tens of thousands as well as the number of partitions.

2.1.8. Complementary Rules.

In addition, a set of complementary rules exist, which can be combined with both production and programming rules. They are:

a) difference (define the conditions under which an element is sufficiently differentiated from a given set of others),
b) selection (establish that a given element is true if a certain conjunction or disjunction was previously considered as a conclusion),
c) interval (the element being the succedent of the rule is true if a set of elements is compatible with a given certainty interval). The number of complementary rules is in the order of tens of thousands.

All the knowledge representation forms described so far can be combined and jointly used when constructing a knowledge base with ARIES.

2.2. Control Mechanisms

In ARIES two main non-exclusive controls are possible: internal (backward chaining, forward chaining, dynamic forward chaining, and backward-forward combined), and external (introduced through the knowledge representation forms and the control base).

2.3. Reasoning with Uncertainty

ARIES offers 40 different logical calculi, based on Hajek's theory of combining functions. Within this theory, classical uncertainty calculi like those of MYCIN and PROSPECTOR are particular cases. Moreover, non-Archimedean calculi and a-priori reasoning are introduced.

2.4. Inference Engines

Two different inference engines working at different hierarchical levels exists in ARIES. The first takes care of the "far vision" strategy (the control base), and the second examine the details about the individual elements or "bricks" within the analysis.

2.5. Man-Machine Interaction

A large set of commands with the following functions: modification of the working regime, the answer mode, the control mechanisms, the visualisation of intermediate results, information about system's goals, and many others.

2.5.1. The Explanatory System

Groups a large number of options by means of which ARIES makes transparent the work of its inference engines.

2.5.2. Other options

Among them there are: give volunteer information, change of opinion, several ways how to quit, and several help systems.

2.6. Support Files

There are two external files which the users may optionally use when working with ARIES:

a) an information file (an ASCII file with information about a given case), and b) a trace of the consultation.

3. THE KNOWLEDGE ACQUISITION AND HANDLING SYSTEM (SAMC)

SAMC performs all operations concerning an ARIES knowledge base (creation, modification, maintenance and many others). It works with a set of screen editors, prompting mechanisms, and error controls.

Among the possibilities of SAMC there are:

3.1. Knowledge acquisition.

There are three separate modes for knowledge acquisition:

3.1.2 Knowledge Acquisition System (KAS)

Directly creates ARIES's knowledge basis in the internal representation used for consultation. This is highly interactive way, guided by the system in the necessary places.

3.1.2. Text Construction

The knowledge base is an ASCII file with a specific format make with a conventional text editor. This text must be compiled for create the internal representation with which ARIES works.

3.1.3. Machine Learning Tools

The ALV family of inductive learning algorithms is available in order to construct directly a knowledge base from a data base. Within ALV it is possible to define the learning strategy, with tens of variants (induction algorithms such as ID3 are here only particular cases). The base constructed in such a way may be directly used or complemented with knowledge from other human or data sources.

3.2. Some Knowledge Base Handling Possibilities

a) restoration of ASCII basis (it is a decompilation of the base),
b) listings (to different devices)
c) statistics (a set of tables and histograms showing the composition of the base and other informations),
d)compression (creates a compressed version of the base by intelligent elimination of all previous changes and their consequences),
e) error checkings (discovers syntactic and semantic errors as loops and many others),
f) exploration (a navigation inside the base which clarifies the relation between the different components),
g) questionnaire (operations over the questionnaire of a given knowledge base, as well as over the information files defined above),
h) orientations (a multilevel help system).

4. THE INSTALLATOR OR CONFIGURATOR

This module establishes the environmental, internal controls, and defaults for ARIES's parameters. The options available for the user are also definable, and this is convenient for setting routine applications of a concluded expert system project.

5. UTILITIES

The following programs complement the ARIES environment: a) formula (an editor, debugger, evaluator, and handler for ARIES's formulae), b) screen (a screen manager for the variables of the question-screen type), c) pre text, text (allows the preparation and display of scrolling colour text windows of variable size as part of the base, very useful for intelligent tutorials).

Industrial Applications of Artificial Intelligence
J.L. Alty and L.I. Mikulich (Editors)
Elsevier Science Publishers B.V. (North-Holland)

INTELLIGENT PROGRAMMING ENVIRONMENTS FOR CAD

Michail B. MATSKIN

Department of Software
Institute of Cybernetics
Estonian Academy of Sciences
Tallinn, USSR

The family of intelligent programming environments for personal computers and workstations designed in the Institute of Cybernetics of Estonian Academy of Sciences is described. The following problems are considered: knowledge representation, computations and architecture for programming environments, interface with users and applications.

1. INTRODUCTION

Intelligent programming tools for CAD has been a traditional research field of the Department of Software of the Institute of Cybernetics during the last 15 years. Our first systems were based on an original approach to knowledge representation and automatic program synthesis and have been developed on IBM-like mainframes [1]. During the last five years we have been investigating the problem of combining different knowledge representation methods and different models of computations. The present paper desribes some results obtained in this field and their implementation in programming systems EXPERTPRIZ and C-PRIZ for IBM-like personal computers and in the NUT system for workstations [2].

2. KNOWLEDGE REPRESENTATION IN CAD

The knowledge used in CAD can be classified as follows [3]:
- shallow and deep. Deep knowledge is based on some general formal theory. Shallow knowledge is based on experience, is not supported by formal theories and can be extracted from experts,
- hard and soft. In one and the same situation hard knowledge produces a single result, but soft knowledge can produce many variants.

The same knowledge can be classified as:
- conceptual knowledge. It describes the entities of objects, processes and situations through concepts (basic elements) of corresponding problem area. Conceptual knowledge is usually represented as frames (or classes in object-oriented programming),
-expert knowledge. It represents knowledge of experts from different problem areas and accumulates their experience.

The representation of conceptual and expert knowledge is supported by wide range of programming tools. In this paper projection of deep, shallow, soft and hard knowledge on conceptual and expert knowledge is considered.

First we consider the language for representation of conceptual knowledge. It contains constructs for description of classes (concepts of problem area) and objects that are instances of classes. A class is a carrier of the knowledge about the common properties of the objects belonging to the class. A class represents the structure of objects of this class and functions applicable to them. Functions are specified in the form of relations. A relation may be either an equation or a program (in the last case it has specification and implementation part). Besides, a class may describe the initialization of the objects´ components as well as virtual components of the objects which can be used in computations but are not contained in the objects.

Our systems provide several predefined classes representing objects which are often used in a program. The properties of these classes are predefined, i. e. the operations which are applicable to the objects of these classes are defined and implemented already in the system.

All other classes are described explicitly. Any class can be used for specifying the class of components of new classes. Classes can also be described hierarchically through inheritance.

Objects are instances of classes. All computations in systems are performed with objects. Every object belongs to a class and has a value (which may be *nil*). The class of object determines the operations which can be performed with the object. During the computations the objects can be created, deleted and changed.

The value of an object is either primitive or compound. Elements of a compound value are the values of objects which are the components of the object with the compound value. Hence, objects (and values) can have hierarchical structure.

New objects are generated explicitly (using predefined function *new*) or implicitly (as a result of operations on some other objects).

Expert knowledge is represented by means of:
- production language (NUT),
- knowledge representation by examples (EXPERTPRIZ and C-PRIZ).

Productions have a form of implications where an atomic formula consists of predicate symbol and a list of parameters. They represent facts and rules. Productions can be used for producing new facts and also for immediate computations. The connection of productions with class descriptions will be described in the next chapter.

Knowledge representation by examples is very close to [4], but has additional facilities for connection with class descriptions.

Classes, objects and productions (or examples) can be combined into knowledge units called packages. A package may contain knowledge of different levels (knowledge about a problem area, knowledge about a particular problem etc.).

3. COMPUTATIONS IN INTELLIGENT ENVIRONMENTS

The considered family of programming environments implements different approaches to computations. It covers wide spectrum of tools from traditional procedural tools (algorithmic programming languages) to nonprocedural tools (automatic program synthesis from specification and different methods of deduction). Very important feature of those systems is the combination of logic, conceptual and object-oriented approaches to programming.

The integration of conceptual and object-oriented approaches is based on semantics of relations in the class description.The relation description has two meanings:
- a pattern for procedure call (object-oriented approach),
- an axiom for program synthesis (conceptual approach).

In connection with conceptual approach to programming, the method of automatic program synthesis is considered [1]. It realizes the following schema:

problem specification ---> goal and axioms ---> proof ---> program

The first step along this way is translating a problem specification from a user friendly language into logic language. The second step is building a proof of the statement "solution of the problem exists". The last step is extraction of program from the proof.

All our systems consider a problem description written in knowledge representation language (see previous chapter) as a problem specification. Axioms are obtained from corresponding specification part of relations.

The implementation part of a relation may contain:
- the text of program,
- reference to corresponding program written in algorithmic language,
- the keyword *specification* .

Application of operation to object in the first and the second case initiates execution of corresponding program.

In the last case specification part of corresponding relation is considered as goal description for automatic program synthesis. Application of such relation to object initiates a process of program synthesis that is completely hidden from a user.

The connection between logic and conceptual approaches can be considered in a dual way.

First, conceptual approach is based on intuitionistic propositional calculus and thus on logic.

Second, it would be very useful to use first order calculus to increase the level of generality of knowledge used in the system. So production language for knowledge representation was introduced and a method of translating specification from one logic language to another was proposed. The main idea of such method is transformation of atomic formula description to class description and vice versa.

An atomic formula may contain predicates of three types:
- abstract predicates that are abstract associations between objects,
- computable predicates that are names of preprogrammed procedures,
- defining predicates that are names of classes.

In the last case atomic formula is automatically extracted from description of objects of corresponding class. List of parameters in extracted formula consists of names of objects bound with corresponding objects´ components by means of equality relation. Derived by producer atomic formulas with defining predicates can be translated into description of objects. So they can automatically extend the problem specification.

The combination of knowledge representation by examples and knowledge representation by concepts is done as follows.

First, examples may contain names of objects from problem specification. Thus values of such objects can be extracted from corresponding model and results can be returned to that model.

Second, during the processing of examples, text of model can be generated and so problem description can be extended.

4. THE ARCHITECTURE OF PROGRAMMING ENVIRONMENT

Integrated programming environments are a very convenient approach for building software for users. Systems like FRAMEWORK, SYMPHONY, MASTER etc. demonstrate that using different objects (data) and their integration increases productivity of work. The set of integrated sybsystems depends on application environment. Usually it is office automation and integrated environment in this case contains: text editor, spread sheet, data base, graphics editor etc.

Our programming environments are oriented on CAD and contain:
- knowledge base management system,
- input language compiler,
- interpreter,
- production system or tool for knowledge representation by examples,
- graphics (including graphics editor and interactive graphics tools),
- data base management system,
- text editor,
- run-time support.

The integration of those subsystems is based on common internal representation of objects or on message sending between them.

5. INTERFACE

Our programming environments have multiwindowing graphic interface and advanced graphics tools, including facilities for binding problem area objects with graphic objects on screen. That allows the user to have a convenient graphic interface with the system.

6. PRACTICE AND EXPERIENCE.

The EXPERTPRIZ system is distributed as a commercial product. At the present moment NUT and C-PRIZ systems exist as experimental versions and we hope that during this year they will become commercial products too.

We have successful experiments with application of our programming environments in following problem areas:
- design of mechanical drives,
- design of hydraulic systems,
- design of active filters,
- design and checking of gear transmissions,
- modelling of logic and alternating current circuits,
- analysis of snowload on roofs.

REFERENCES

[1] Tyugu, E.H., Knowledge-Based Programming (Addison-Wesley, 1986)
[2] Tyugu E., Matskin M., Penjam J., Eomois P., NUT - An Object-Oriented Language, Computers and Artificial Intelligence, 5 (1986), No 6, pp. 521-542.
[3] Tyugu E.H., Merging Conceptual and Expert Knowledge in CAD, Expert Systems in Computer-Aided Design (North-Holland, 1987) pp. 423-434.
[4] Hart A., Role of Induction in Knowledge Elicitation, in: Kidd A.L., (eds.), Knowledge Acquisition for Expert Systems, Plenum Press, 1987, pp. 165-189.

Industrial Applications of Artificial Intelligence
J.L. Alty and L.I. Mikulich (Editors)
Elsevier Science Publishers B.V. (North-Holland)

MANAGEMENT CONSULTING EXPERT SYSTEM (MCES)

V. G . POLYAKOV

Institute of History,
Philology and Philosophy,
Siberian Division of the USSR Academy of Sciences,
IHPP, ac, Lavrentjev's Prospect, 17,
630090, Novosibirsk,
The USSR.

ABSTRACT: The main structures and organization of the MCES (Management Consulting Expert System) are discussed. The author proposes a technique of procedural non-verbal knowledge representation. Contrary to the prevailing point of view that artificial intelligence systems are essentially verbal in nature, the present approach proposes to use the toolset of cognitive graphic and simulations game techniques to implement people's visual abilities. This overcomes the difficulty of knowledge extraction, its presentation in computer systems, and the necessity to unify rational and perceptional components of mentality.

1. INTRODUCTION

Expert systems have developed with the evolution of appropriate hardware and corresponding software (frame and rule-based systems, LISP and PROLOG specialized languages). Some expert systems built on the basis of this concept are used when the structure of problems can be determined a-priori and their solution is based on scientific data [1]. However, attempts to apply this approach to the sphere of social knowledge extraction and its presentation in a computer system were a failure [2]. Problems appears in the sphere of management, such as the bilateral and conflicting nature of management itself; the important role of the personal peculiarities of decision makers; the fact that a manager's abilities are not a goal, but rather a means; that there are no scientific rules only a knowledge of precedents and practical skills at the level of reproducing patterns; and that the system of knowledge demands the presence in MCES of incentives to Project Management Decisions, making it possible to combine actual knowledge with practical skills and the desire to use them (it means that the final goal should be included in the sphere of a manager's activities). Some ways of solving the above-mentioned problems are proposed.

2. ORGANISATIONAL PRINCIPLES AND STRUCTURE OF MCES

The main organizational principles of MCES are as follows :

- MCES uses a blackboard expert system [3] integrating a rule-based system (verbal base of knowledge) and a data base (constructed with the help of well-known techniques [l]) and a graphic base of actual knowledge, as shown in Fig. 1;

- an important element of MCES is the human intellect of a consultant, whereas non-verbal knowledge can be reproduced in the process of interaction of a decision maker (user) and consultant,
- game-simulation enables one to reproduce the non-verbal knowledge of a decision maker [4].
- cognitive computer graphics allows interaction between a decision maker and the MCES.

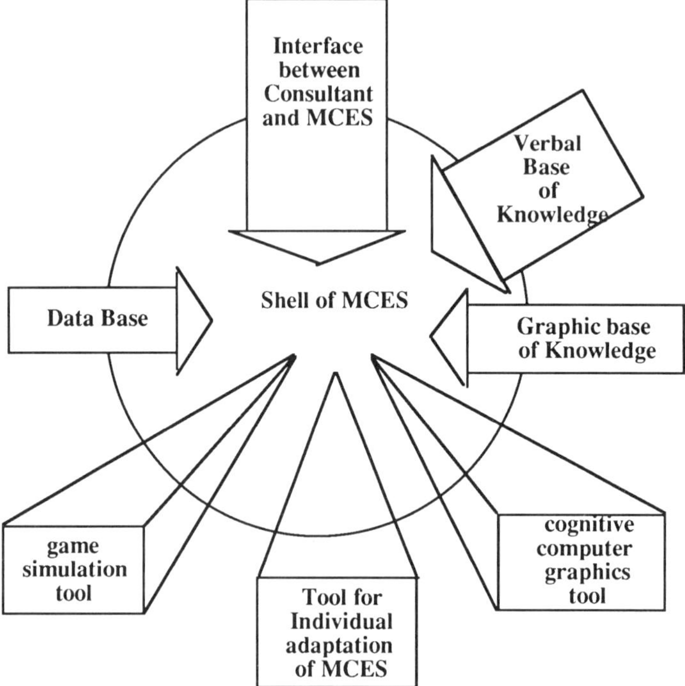

Figure 1 MCES Organisation

- custom adaptation of MCES is possible, because socio-psychological and computer graphics techniques are included in the game-simulation software.

The expert system consists of separate blocks, which allows modification and widening both of the toolset and the subject sphere (Fig.2).

The toolset of the consultant consists of the following elements:

- economic-mathematic models and heuristic algorithms,
- a formal mechanism for coordinating the economic interests of a decision maker solving the conflicts and search-for-compromise decisions on the basis of the personal preferences of the decision maker [5].

All this makes it possible to perform cognitive interaction between the user and the consultant, thus helping to collect information in MCES concerning "the principles of management" of decision making [6].

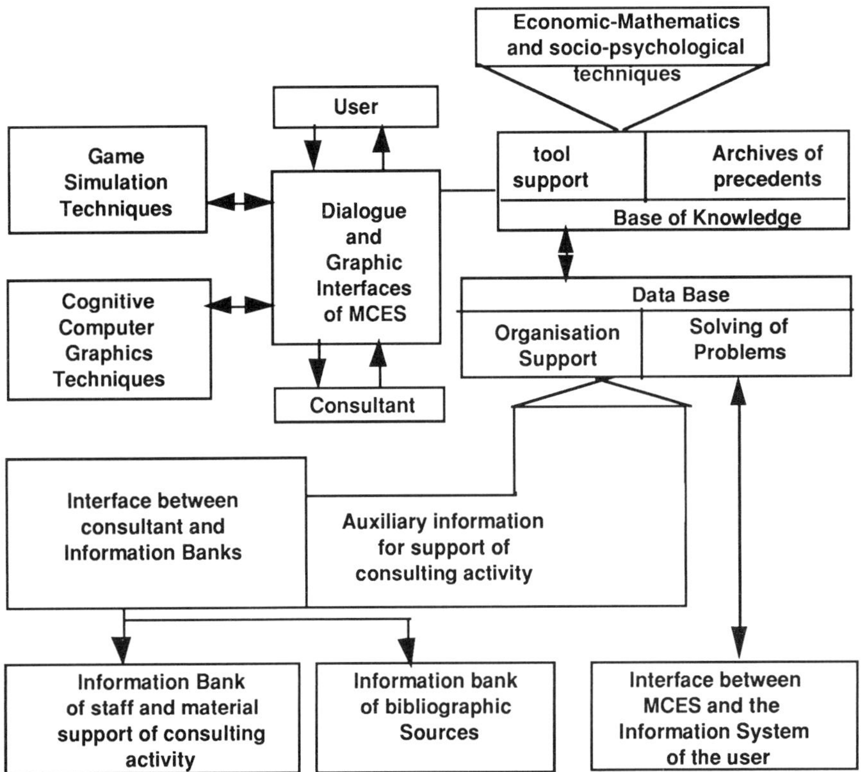

Figure 2 Interactions in MCES

3. REPRODUCTION OF GRAPHICAL KNOWLEDGE

The use of graphical images in the management sphere is based on two principal approaches. According to the first principle, definite configurations of graphical images correspond to each condition of the management system. According to the second principle, the presence of limits of admissability in the variations of economic indexes in the condition space, is ensured. The management tasks are thus to support the image conditions or to ensure the image variations over the range of assumed alterations.

The implementation this approach using PCs will be possible provided graphical presentation is adequate for the management activity. For this, four types of elementary graphical structure are elaborated. On this basis all stages of forming the graphical images are executed (Fig. 3).

The first graphical structure is formed by economic indexes (demand, supply, capacity, etc.) and by gauges (absolute and relative sizes, percent , etc.) presented, as well as the ranges of the index changes. The second graphical structure is formed by virtue of binary comparison of elementary structures of the first type united by common meaning (demand - supply, resource - production, etc.). The second structure is represented by a matrix, in which the differences between pair indices are reflected.

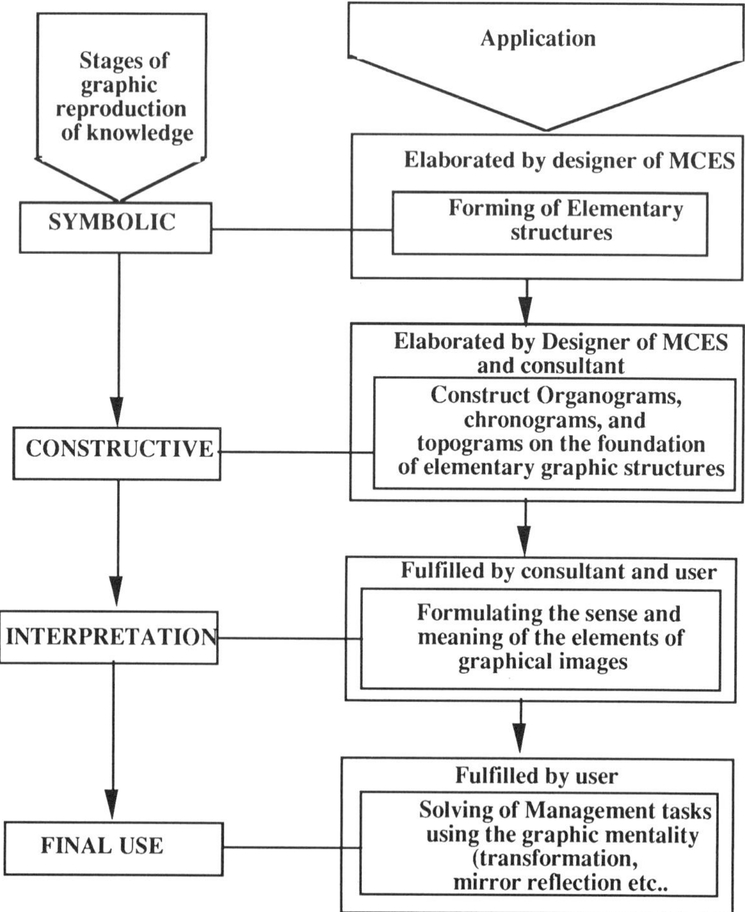

Figure 3 Graphic Reproduction of Knowledge in MCES

The third graphic structure presents a network, based on the following principles

- the possibility of using the group of economic indices united by the common unit of measurement;
- connection between indices is supposed (bilateral or unilateral);
- there exists an economic meaning for the correlation of different levels of indices.

The fourth graphic structure characterizes the case when one of the economic indices (financial conditions, fulfilment of contracts, etc.) appears to be in the range of meaning (such ranges may be fixed or changed according to certain rules). This structure shows the position of the index in units of time.

All elementary structures may be represented by some means or other in 2,3-dimensions using well-known software from computer graphics.

4. MCES APPLICATION AREAS

Some experience has been acquired using the above-mentioned approach in training methods, simulation games, consultation practice. Three forms of practical application of MCES exist

- use of MCES to solve the problem of independent consultations for enterprises on the topic of management incentives without presenting their results to the user (diagnostics and implementation)
- presenting methodical and software materials of MCES to the user for solving tasks concerning consultations and teaching of decision makers (training to make particular decisions)
- training of students according to a management programme.

REFERENCES

[1] Siegel P., "Expert systems : a Nonprogrammer's Guide to Development and Applications", - TAB Professional and Reference Books, (1986).

[2] Perrone G., "Down from the Clouds : Notes on Expert Systems, Microcomputers and Operation Research" , Comput. and Oper. Res. . Vol.13, No. 2/3, pp. 323-344 ,(1986).

[3] Hayes-Roth B., "A Blackboard Architecture for Control in Artificial Intelligence", Vol. 26 ,pp. 251-321, (1985).

[4] Polyakov V.G. "Simulation Games as Experiments in Management's World", Novosibirsk, (Preprint / IHPP). (In Russian), (1990).

[5] Isard W., and Smith C., "Conflict Analysis and Practical Conflict Management Procedures", Cambridge Ballinger Publ., (1982).

[6] Ladenko I.S., Polyakov V.G., "Problems and Methods of Representation of Knowledge in Intellectual Management Systems. Novosibirsk, (Preprint / IHPP). (In Russian), (1989).

Industrial Applications of Artificial Intelligence
J.L. Alty and L.I. Mikulich (Editors)
Elsevier Science Publishers B.V. (North-Holland)

SECTION 5: APPLIED EXPERT SYSTEMS

SPEECH INTERFACE FOR INFORMATION INPUT IN EXPERT, INFORMATION RETRIEVAL AND CONTROL SYSTEMS

A. V. KELMANOV and S. A. KHAMIDULLIN
Institute of Mathematics,
Siberian Branch of the USSR Academy of Sciences,
Novosibirsk,
The USSR.

ABSTRACT: The characteristics of a speech interface designed to be connected to an intelligent system are described. The interface is distinguished by its ability to operate under conditions of intensive external noise and speech signal non-linear distortions, as well as in the range of telephone channel frequency bandwidth regardless of vibro-interference affecting an operator.

Complex object control and operations with expert and information-retrieval systems cause rapid weariness of an operator's sight due to frequent shiftings of attention from display to control keyboard. Speech is often preferred and is sometimes the only means of transmitting control commands to an object or system. Practical experience, for example, shows that the use of speech dialogue (recognition and synthesis) usually increases control system and decision making effectiveness. However, existing systems for speech dialogue and object control are mostly intended for speech recognition under noiseless conditions. These systems are used in different spheres of management to model spoken dialogue language. However, external noises and non-linear distortions in a communication line make these systems practically useless due to the low reliability of speech recognition.

To develop a voice-controlled expert information-retrieval and control systems, which can be communicated with in a language close to a natural one, it is necessary to solve the problem of representing the knowledge of the object field language in a computer. To solve this problem, a spoken dialogue language model or a reduced language of a spoken dialogue is input into the computer's memory. The information is input into the above systems by means of discrete speech spoken phrases (by discrete speech we mean with short pauses between words). The language model supposes that linguistic, semantic-syntactical and pragmatic restrictions are available. Methods of defining these restrictions are to a large extent dictated by recognition techniques of isolated words in discrete, and continuous speech, which are input into the speech interface.

Voice data input into an intelligent system requires combining a phrase recognition operation with one for checking these phrases for permissibility (semantic-syntactical and pragmatic analyses) and this makes the speech interface software more complex. Experience of intelligent systems with speech input development shows that semantic-syntactical and pragmatic restrictions should be preferentially defined as a graph (semantic net), the arcs of which reflect the permissible possible phrase continuations. Words or equivalent semantic classes serve as nodes in this graph. The net description can be stored in a computer's memory in the form of lists with references. Each list defines a set of permissible phrases, and the combination of lists forms a net description or a language model.

Only phrases which are grammatically correct are considered permissible according to syntactical restrictions. Semantic restrictions select from the whole set of syntactically correct phrases the sensible phrases only. Pragmatic restrictions allow operation with phrases permissible in definite situations which are determined by definite object field specific features.

Speech recognition systems developed in the Institute of Mathematics of the Siberian Branch of the USSR Academy of Sciences can be used as voice interfaces for intelligent systems as well as for the speech control of various complex objects. The system base structure includes the microcomputer ELEKTRONIKA-60 (or DVK-3 or DVK-4), a band-pass feature extraction block, a speech synthesis block and software providing external noise compensation [1], insensitivity to non-linear signal distortions [2], binary-dichotomic coding of band-pass features [3] voice command recognition [4] and the dialogue itself [5]. The expanded variant allows the inclusion of additional external memory from 1 to 6 Mbytes with software which realises direct access, on the one hand, and operations with external memory without operational system control, on the other. This gives the possibility of constructing a dialogue on the basis of vocabularies of between 3-18 thousand words. Binary coding the application allows an increase in this vocabulary of approximately 4 times. These facilities are sufficient for voice data input in various applied intelligent systems.

The speech interface provides several modes: "training", "pretraining", "reference changing", "reference recoding" on an external carrier and "reference reading". "Recognition" mode is a basic one. The interface is distinguished by its ability to operate under conditions of intensive external noise and speech signal non-linear distortions, as well as in the range of a telephone channel frequency bandwidth regardless of vibro-interference effecting an operator. In addition, it can be easily adjusted to a definite object field.

A speech interface has been tested which is connected to an intelligent system intended to control a moving object, as well as to operate under conditions of vibro-interference and noises up to 110 dB. The system vocabulary includes about 100 words. Four operational modes are available ("control", "dialogue", "notification", and "request") which can be entered after the corresponding commands have been recognised. Control modes include 5 submodes (commands), each containing from 3 to 15 control commands. The dialogue mode provides synthesised answers to about 25 questions, while "request" mode allows access to reference information of 13 types. Noise intensity is 110 dB, and the subvocabulary recognition reliability is 97 %.

In conclusion we want to draw attention to the fact that the developed interface has been successfully used to input information into air control trainers simulating air conditions near the airport, into a partner expert system to make a decision concerning the directions for Novosibirsk Region agricultural development, and into an information retrieval reference system to obtain data about the Exhibition of the Siberian Branch of the USSR Academy of Sciences achievements.

REFERENCES

[l] Kelmanov A.Y., and Khamidullin S.A., "Sequential Multichannel Algorithms of Speech Signal Feature Extraction and Input under Noise Conditions", Proc 15th Soviet Workshop of Automatic Speech Recognition (ARS0-15), Tallinn, pp. 208-209, (1989).

[2] Kelmanov A.V., "Speech Analysis Algorithms by Distorted Observations", ibid., pp. 206-207.

3] Kelmanov A.V. , "Speech Recognition by Recoded Dichotomic Band-Pass Features", Proc. 13th Soviet Workshop of Automatic Speech Recognition (ARSO-13) , Novosibirsk, July, pp. 89-90, (1984).

[4] Kelmanov A.V., and Khamidullin S.A., "Large Vocabulary Recognition by Microcomputers ", Proc. 14th Soviet Workshop on Automatic Speech Recognition (ARCO-14), , Kaunas, August, p. 73, (1986).

[5] Kelmanov, A.V., and Khamidullin S.A., "A Voice Request Response Dialogue Control System Insensitive to Noise", New Information Technology Software, Proc. Soviet Scientific Technical Conference, Kalinin, pp. 59-6, (1989).

Industrial Applications of Artificial Intelligence
J.L. Alty and L.I. Mikulich (Editors)
Elsevier Science Publishers B.V. (North-Holland)

DIAGNOSTIC EXPERT SYSTEMS FOR DIGITAL ELECTRONICS

V. SGUREV, D. DOCHEV, G. AGRE, Ch. DICHEV, Z. MARKOV
Institute of Engineering Cybernetics and Robotics - BAS
Acad. Bonchev str. bl. 29A,
Sofia 1113,
Bulgaria.

ABSTRACT: The characteristics of two particular expert systems for diagnosis in the field of digital electronics are briefly outlined. Some problems of the development and use of systems for the representation and processing of diagnostic knowledge are discussed. The knowledge representation and acquisition and some features of the man-machine and instrumental interfaces are considered.

1. INTRODUCTION

This paper deals with some practical problems of the development and use of expert systems for diagnosis in the field of digital electronics. The characteristics of two expert systems, made for the producers of corresponding electronic devices are briefly outlined. The experience, acquired during their development serves as a basis for considering some implementation problems of the systems for the representation and processing of diagnostic knowledge. A generalization of this experience was used to develop an instrumental programming system, intended to automate the phases of the process of generating expert systems (ES) for technical diagnosis. The first versions of this instrumental systems have been used and tested in the development of practical expert systems.

2. FUNCTIONAL CHARACTERISTICS OF EXPERT SYSTEMS FOR THE DIAGNOSIS OF DIGITAL ELECTRONIC DEVICES

The diagnostic expert systems, described here, work on the personal computers IBM PC XT/AT and compatibles. The knowledge for the diagnostic process evolution is represented by means of a model, called a diagnostic net [1]. It reflects the causal relations between malfunctions and their manifestations.

2.1. An Expert System for the Diagnosis of 8-bit Personal Computers

This expert system is intended to help maintenance staff in searching for faults in the personal computers PRAVETS-82 and PRAVETS-8M (Apple-2 compatible). Two variants of the knowledge base were made - with texts in Bulgarian and in Russian. Each of them contains the following information:

- 498 symptoms describing the process of fault localization for the computer PRAVETS-82. 21 of them are initial symptoms - external manifestations of the faults. A diagnostic session is initiated by selecting one or more initial symptom.
- 807 symptoms, describing the process of fault localization for the computer PRAVETS-8M. 18 of them are initial symptoms.

The information in the knowledge base permits the localization of malfunctions down to a defective element - an integrated circuit or another discrete component.

The system input is organized by means of menus. The desired initial symptoms are selected from the list of all possible initial symptoms as their number is relatively small.

A module for automatic measurement is used in this expert system. It is implemented as a printed circuit board for the IBM PC and permits input automatically into the computer, the results of the following electric measurements:

- TTL voltage signals (0 - 5 V);
- pulse sequences with frequencies up to 14 Mc;
- power supply voltages.

The module for automatic measurement has direct access to the status of the address and data buses of the tested computer. This feature allows the automatic execution of test routines to check some functional units (memory, buffers etc.). Unfortunately such tests are not used in the expert system as the experts had not considered this opportunity.

A diagnostic session may be performed in two possible working modes:

- Mode 1 is a pure consultation mode. In this mode the user enters the results of the proposed test procedures via the keyboard. He usually has simply to choose the right answer from a menu of possible results.

- Mode 2 uses the module for automatic measurements. In this mode the system instructs the operator to place the testing probe on a given point of the tested device. After that the necessary measurement is executed automatically and the system proceeds with the diagnostic session according to the obtained result.

The knowledge base contains appropriate data structures to support both working modes. The operator may change the working mode before each test procedure proposed by the system. The system internally checks the proper operation of the module for automatic measurements and in case of faults automatically switches over to the consultation mode.

2.2. Expert System for Diagnosis of Hard Disk Subsystems

This Expert System is intended to help the maintenance staff in the search for faults in disk subsystems, consisting of a controller and a hard disk drive module with 300 or 600 MB capacity. The system is in experimental use. The knowledge base is at present in a phase of enrichment and testing. It contains about 10,000 symptoms and more than 300 initial symptoms.

The big size of the knowledge base together with the PC limitations in memory and processing speed require special attention to be paid to automatic knowledge base modularization. The large amount of initial symptoms makes it inappropriate to use long menus for the system input. The majority of the initial symptoms are obtained as results of the built-in microdiagnostic system of the hard disk subsystems. Therefore the system input has to ensure a convenient access to the initial symptoms by use of a short menu to determine the device and then entering 4 or 6-digit microcodes.

The expert system works in consultation mode - the operator enters the measurement results by choosing them from a menu of possible answers using the keyboard. The expert knowledge permits localization faults to the level of printed circuit boards. A specialized tester for printed circuit boards may be used for further troubleshooting. An automatic connection of the expert system with such a tester will be considered in the future.

The expert system for diagnosis of hard disk subsystems is developed by using DIGS - a programming system for generating expert systems for technical diagnostics [2]. The system DIGS contains a specialized knowledge base editor and automates all the necessary activities for creation, modification and maintenance of diagnostic expert systems for given technical devices. The knowledge base editor is based on the representation of diagnostic knowledge as a diagnostic net. The system DIGS is oriented towards experts on diagnostics in a given field, who have little experience of using complex programming systems.

3. DISCUSSION OF THE DIAGNOSTIC EXPERT SYSTEM DEVELOPMENT AND FUTURE TRENDS

3.1. Knowledge Representation and Acquisition

The work on the formalisation of the expert knowledge for diagnosis of personal computers and hard disk subsystems demonstrated the adequacy of the applied model for knowledge representation - the diagnostic net. It proved the assumption that the presence of a large quantity of expert knowledge is of more practical importance for Expert Systems than the availability of diverse and complex inference mechanisms.

In the field of technical diagnosis it is natural to consider the hierarchical structure of the tested device when describing the successive fault localization process. Most often experts just trace the signal paths. In such cases the information for the device structure reflects its logical scheme and/or physical layout and does not have a really expert character. The expert information is connected mainly with the probabilities of existence of the possible causes for a given symptom and with the determination of important "test points" when tracing a particular causal chain. Therefore the integration of functional and structural deep models of the tested device subblocks in the diagnostic expert system in the field of digital electronics may be considered highly useful. It is desirable to coordinate the diagnostic expert system with appropriate CAD systems in order to obtain data for such models. The proposed model of the diagnostic process permits a natural combination of the expert knowledge, reflecting the relations between the observed symptoms and deep models of the devices under test.

The knowledge acquisition process was realized by interviews with the experts. Two variants of this method were applied:

- the experts filled in standard forms to describe each situation in the process of successive fault localization. A standard form determines a complete fragment of the diagnostic net and contains information about a tested symptom, the corresponding testing procedure and the possible direct reasons for the presence of the tested symptom.

- the experts entered the data directly in the knowledge base by means of the specialized knowledge base editor of the system DIGS. This approach is more effective as the system checks automatically the links between different situation descriptions and does not allow the generation of syntactically incorrect knowledge base. Furthermore the specialized tools of the system for text processing and the additional opportunities to check the semantic correctness of the knowledge base considerably speeds up the creation of final versions. The experts on diagnosis of digital electronic devices are often computer specialists, so they are used to extensive keyboard operation.

3.2. Man-Machine Interface

Some problems of the man-machine interface for expert systems have been discussed in [3]. In the communications with the expert system the essential use of a limited natural language seems attractive. The natural language interface problems are at present outside the scope of the authors attention due to the following main reasons:

- the orientation towards personal computers, which current resource limitations impede considerably the implementation of complex additional programming subsystems with auxiliary functions;

- the research stage of the development of tools for a direct speech input to the computers does not encourage their direct application in expert systems.

Our experience in expert systems development has emphasized:

- that it is necessary to have elaborate functions for text editing (full screen editing in the bounds of a linked text, copying of records, use of keywords, text patterns, abbreviations etc.) with a context-dependent access

- it is desirable to use a specialized graphic editor to enter and store graphic information in the knowledge base (e.g. timecharts, fragments of principal and assembly diagrams etc.);

- special attention must be paid to the ergonomic characteristics of the screen layout of the system i.e. a well considered level of output information at every moment, economic use of multiple windows and visual effects.

3.3. Instrumental Interface

The expert system for personal computer diagnosis confirmed the expediency of the development of an instrumental interface for communications with specialized testing devices. The advantages of using such devices are obvious:

- the productivity of the service and maintenance activities is increased;
- the work of the maintenance staff is facilitated;
- the requirements of maintenance staff qualification decrease;
- the expert system obtains objectively correct data.

Digital electronics is an appropriate domain for automating the mass measurements because of the common signal types in a large range of devices, using the same generation of electronic components. It is possible to automate the following processes

- measurement of main types of electric signals;
- activation of test procedures, executed by the hardware of the tested device and analysis of their results in the expert system (e.g. by means of a direct access to the memory and/or the buses of the device under test);
- activation of the diagnostic session by automatic input of the present initial symptoms (e.g. by a connection with the built-in blocks for local diagnostics of the tested device);
- activation of specialized hardware testers and communications with them in order to diagnose particular subblocks of the tested device.

Both of the last two features are associated more tightly with the characteristics of the given class of devices.

4. CONCLUSION

The experience acquired in the development process of the discussed diagnostic expert systems as well as the study of world tendencies allows us to conclude that the current technology requires the use of automatic systems for monitoring and diagnosis of complex technical objects. In the near future such systems will evolve as results of a natural combination of the expert approach, the use of deep models and automatic testing devices.

REFERENCES

[1] Sgurev V., D. Dochev, Ch. Dichev, G. Agre, and Z. Markov, "An Approach to Building a Technical Diagnostic Expert System", In "Computers and Artificial Intelligence", Vol.5 , No. 2, pp.103-116, Bratislava, (1986).

[2] Agre G. and D. Dochev, "Problems of Diagnostic Knowledge Processing: Design and Implementation of the System DIGS", Proc. of the Expert Systems '89, London, UK, 20-22 September (1989).

[3] Sgurev V., D. Dochev, G. Agre, Ch. Dichev, and Z. Markov "Knowledge Acquisition and Man-machine Interface in the DIGS Expert System", In: Proc. of the II International Conference on Artificial Intelligence (AIMSA'86), Varna, 16-19 Sept., 1986, pp. 281-287, North-Holland, Amsterdam, (1987).

Industrial Applications of Artificial Intelligence
J.L. Alty and L.I. Mikulich (Editors)
Elsevier Science Publishers B.V. (North-Holland)

A REPRESENTATION AND A PLANNING METHOD FOR THE STARTUP OF CONTINUOUS CHEMICAL PLANTS

Didier CAUDRON* and Christian MELIN

URA CNRS 817 Dept GENIE INFORMATIQUE UNIVERSITE DE TECHNOLOGIE DE COMPIEGNE BP 649 60206 COMPIEGNE CEDEX FRANCE * D.CAUDRON is also with the Rhône Poulenc Company.

abstract: this paper addresses the problem of operating procedure synthesis during startup of continuous chemical plants. A representation for the operational states of process units and a basic planning methodology based on a means-ends analysis are presented; both are based on interviews with plant-operators and careful readings of operating manuals, they emphasize the notion of operating regions.

1.INTRODUCTION

The on line synthesis of operating procedures for complete chemical plants is one aspect of the tendency towards increased automation of control-rooms. Operations such as startup, shutdown, both routine and emergency, process change over, are generally carried out by human operators, mainly because they require the planning and scheduling of sequences of operating steps which, when applied, will lead the processes to new operating levels. Also, such tasks are done unfrequently, they require considerable expertise and errors can be very costly [1]. At such higher levels of monitoring and control, plant-wide operations extend significantly the operating space presumed for the design of control systems. Therefore, as pointed out by several researchers [2,3,4], knowledge-based systems constitute a valuable technology for the automation of such tasks. The objective of our work is to develop computationally tractable modelling and planning methodologies for the synthesis of operating procedures during startup operations of continuous chemical plants. Operating procedures synthesis can be viewed as finding an ordered or a partially ordered set of actions which would bring the process from some initial state to a goal state. It can be represented [4] as a highly constrained state space with "operators" used to move beween states. In this paper we present a representation for the operational states of process units and a basic method for planning. The representation comes from interviews with plant-operators and from careful readings of operating manuals of working plants. The planning method is based on a means-ends analysis to form intermediate goals, goals and operational states are representations of the operating regions of process units.

2 A REPRESENTATION FOR THE OPERATIONAL STATES

2.1 Modeling requirements

During a startup and depending upon the current initial operating state of a process, some processing facilities have to be connected to others, or have to be disconnected from another; moreover the process is in transient and as a consequence most of the control loops are non operating. Therefore, we need a concise framework to efficiently represent two broad classes of operations:

(i) operations which only consist of transfers of species without any transformation of their physico-chemical state (ex: establishing liquid levels in a distillation column).

(ii) operations where transformations of the state of species take place. (ex: bringing a distillation column in a complete recycle regime).

Process models should be capable of representing process behavior throughout the operating space. Moreover, the operation of chemical processes is subject to operational contraints dictated by various considerations including preconditions for units operation, production requirements, safety hazards, etc [4]. On the other hand, it has been recognized for a long time that the goal directed character of planning determines, to a certain extend, the level of abstraction of the process models. Domain independent planning as well as recent domain dependent planning methodologies [5], [3] rely heavily upon operator models used to move between states. But, we also known from [5] that "Planning is undecidable even with a finite initial situation if the action representation (operator) is extended to represent actions whose effects are a function of their situation".

2.2. Modelling operating states.

The following definitions summarizes the various kinds of knowledge and information used:

(a) - a processing unit is viewed as a finite set of equipments (pipes, valves, pumps, reactor vessel, distillation columns, heaters,...) which, properly interconnected and controlled, can move and transform fluids.

(b) - an operating state is primarily defined by a configuration of the logical states of all the used valves and pumps, which defines the routes for the fluids. Each configuration is represented by an instance of a vector VL of booleans.

(c) - the physical state of a processing unit is represented by a finite set of quantities such as pressures, temperatures, flow rates, concentrations etc. These quantities are classified into two subsets:- the manipulated or input quantities for which vector U is defined.- the dependant or ouput quantities for which vector Y is defined.

(d) - an operating state is wholly defined by the knowledge of vectors VL, U and Y whose dimensions depend only on the unit considered and are the same for all the operating states.

(e) - operating state m_i has constraints attached to it which are : - allowed range values of U and Y, which will be noted as $[U]_i$ and $[Y]_i$ - the allowed directions of change of the output quantities under the influence of some manipulated quantity. These directions of change are represented using the following qualitative symbols: "+" for increase, "-" for decrease, "0" when no change is allowed and "*" when both directions are allowed - constraints on the manipulated quantities may also be necessary when the operating state considered is known to be not completely controllable. We don't consider this possibility in this paper.

It is essential to notice that all the operating states are not disjoint with respect to the allowed range values of the output quantities (e.g vectors Y). The following planning method is based on this fact. The representation don't use the classical notion of operator [5]. The local and global constraints which are linked classically to the operators are included in the instances of vectors VL, $[U]_i$ and $[Y]_i$. In practice the number of instances is very small compared to the $2^{\dim(VL)}$ theorical possibilities.

3- THE PROPOSED PLANNING METHOD.

3-1-Assumptions.

The goal of the planning method is to find a sequence S of operating states together with the transition condition between two successive operating states. A condition is represented by an instance of the output vector Y such that:

$$(m_i, Y_i) \text{---->} (m_j, Y_i) \text{---->} (m_j, Y_j)$$

$$\text{and} \quad S = \{(m_0, Y_0),(m_1, Y_1), (m_2, Y_2), \ldots\ldots, (m_f, Y_f)\}.$$

Actually, the planning method is based on the assumption that for any couple $\{(m_j, Y_i), (m_j, Y_j)\}$, a control can be found which achieves the change from Yi to Yj. But there is no requirement on the planning method to find such a control. Figure 1 shows an illustration, a plan in the case of a two dimensionnal output vector.

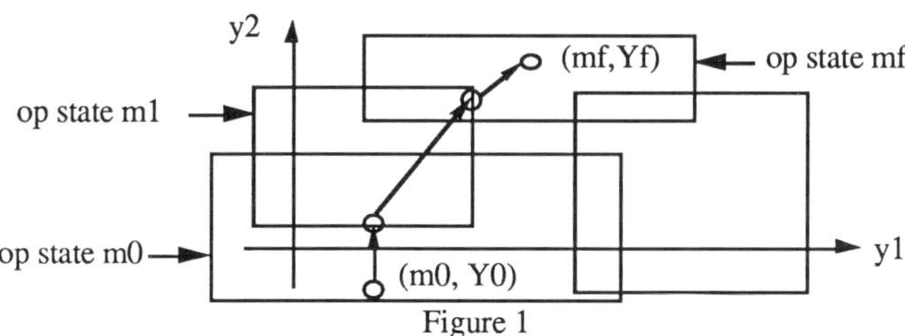

Figure 1

3-2- Method.

Let us consider an initial operating state and a prespecified final operating state, given respectively by (VL0, Y0) and (VLf,Yf). First of all, we search for operating states which are directly accessible from mo without change of Y0. Then, among the resulting subset of operating states we determine the "best" possible operating state with respect to the final goal. The selection is based on an evaluation function whose arguments are qualitative values for the differences between Yf and Y0 and the authorized directions of change of output quantities. Let (mb,Y0) stands for the best operating state at this stage. Then we proceed by searching all the reachable operating states from mb and their associated conditions of transition. This point being completed, the whole procedure is repeated until the goal is reached. In the following some details are presented about different steps of the above procedure.

- *Finding the initial operating state.*

Let LE be the list of operating states which have been used, initially LE is the empty list. A simple pattern matching between VLi and VL0 leads to LE := {m0}.

- *Finding the subset of directly accessible operating stetes.*

Let $Y0= (y_{10}, y_{20},\ldots, y_{j0},\ldots,y_{n-10}, y_{n0})$, the initial ouput vector

Let $[y_j]_i= [\min(y_j),\max(y_j)]_i$, the range value of y_j in operating state m_i

Let $L = (m_1, m_2,\ldots, m_i,\ldots,m_{k-1},m_k)$, the list of all the feasable operating state

For every component y_{j0}, one finds out the sublist LMj of operating states m_i such as: $y_{j0} \in [y_j]_i$.

Then, the sublist MI of the directly accessible operating states without change of Y0 is such that: $MI := \cap_j LM_j$.

At each operating state mi ∈ MI is attached an instance Yi of the output vector, at this step Yi:=Y0 for all i.

c- Finding a "best" operating state from MI

For each mi ∈ MI we define a qualitative vector $VQi=(vq_{1i},\ldots, vq_{ji},\ldots, vq_{ni})$ such that:
$VQi = (Sign(y_{1f}-y_{1i}),\ldots\ldots,Sign(y_{nf}-y_{ni}))$
with $Sign(x) = +$ if $x> 0$, 0 if $x = 0$, - if $x< 0$

Let $VY_i = (vy_{1i},\ldots\ldots,vy_{ji},\ldots\ldots vy_{ni})$ the vector of authorized directions of change of Y in the operating state mi, with: $vy_{ji} \in \{ +, 0, -, * \}$. The evaluation function is heuristically defined from the following application $f(vq_{ji},vy_{ji})$: { +, 0, -, *} . { +, 0, - } --> { -2, -1, 0, 2} (see figure 2).

vqj \ vyj	+	0	-
+	2	-1	-2
0	0	2	0
-	-2	-1	2
*	2	2	2

Figure 2

For every operating state m_i the following real quantity $FQi = \sum_j f(vq_j, vy_j)$ is computed. Then the resulting "best" operating state m_b is such that: $FQ_b = \max_i FQi$ and the list LE is updated LE := LE + {m_b}.

d- Finding reachable operating states from mb.

The subset of operating states which are reachable from mb is determined with respect to the allowed and desired directions of change together with the authorized range values of the output vector.

Let $VY_b = (vy_{1b},\ldots\ldots,vy_{jb},\ldots\ldots vy_{nb})$ the vector of the allowed directions of change of Y in operating state mb, with $vy_j \in \{ +, 0, - \}$.

Let $[y_j]_b= [\min(y_{jb}),\max(y_{jb})]$ the range values of y_{jb} in operating state m_b, then:
For every vy_{jb}:

if $vy_{jb} = 0$, then one finds out the list LMj of operating states m_i such as: $y_{jb} \in [y_j]_i$.
if $vy_j = +$, then one finds out the list LMj of operating states m_i such as:
$(y_{jb} < \min(y_{ji}))$ and $(\min(y_{ji}) < \max(y_{jb}))$
if $vy_j = -$, then one finds out the list LMj of operating states m_i such as:
$(y_{jb} > \max(y_{ji}))$ and $(\min(y_{jb}) < \max(y_{ji}))$

The list MR of reachable operating states is then simply deduced from: $MR := \cap_j LM_j - LE$

e- Determining the transition condition.

For every reachable operating state $m_i \in MR$ we have to find out a target output vector $Y_i = (y_{1i}, y_{2i},\ldots, y_{ji},\ldots,y_{n-1i}, y_{ni})$.

This is done by applying a set of rules which are based on the analysis of the authorized range values of $[y_j]_i$ with respect to $[y_j]_b$, the direction of change in mb and the comparison between y_{jf} and $[y_j]_i$. For example in the case depicted in figure 3, we use the following rules:

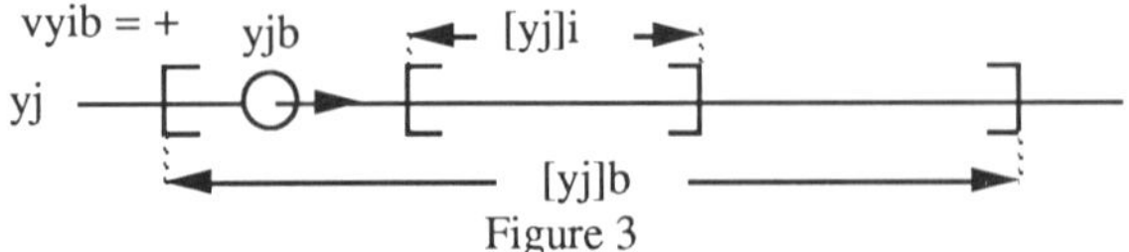

Figure 3

if y_{jf} < $\min(y_{ji})$ then $y_{ji}=\min(y_{ji})$.
if y_{jf} $\in$ $[y_j]_i$ then $y_{ji}=y_{jf}$.
if y_{jf} > $\max(y_{ji})$ then $y_{ji}=\max(y_{ji})$.

After the completion of this step we get a set of couple (mi,Yi) to which the previous steps c to e are applied, until the goal is reached.

4- EXAMPLE

To illustrate the modeling structure as well as the planning method of startup operations sythesis, consider the simple heating unit depicted in figure 4. This unit is wanted to heat a stream of specie A entering a jacketed tank. The valves Vi (i=1,5) are binary valves which be fully open (1) or fully closed (0), the two pumps P1 and P2 are running (1) or stopped (0). The operating states are defined from the following three vectors:

VL = (V1, V2, V3, V4, V5, P1, P2).
U = (F1, F2, Tc); Y = (T, L).

Figure 5 provides the complete definition of five operating states for this application.

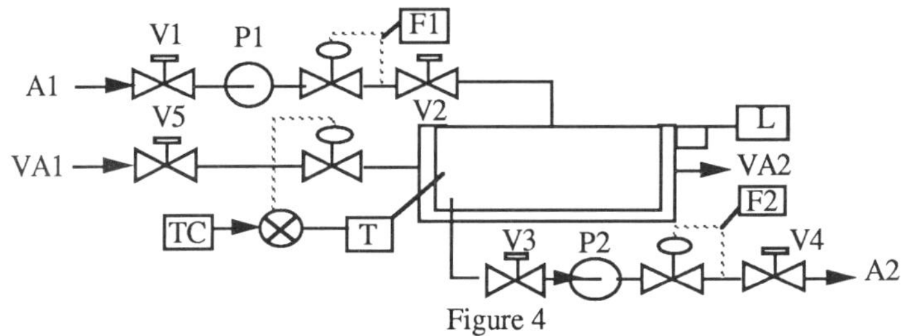

Figure 4

Operating state 1:
VL = (0, 0, 0, 0, 0, 0, 0).
[U] = ([0,0], [0,0], [0,0]).
[Y] = ([0,100], [0,100]).
VY = (0,0).

Operating state 2:
VL = (0, 0, 1, 1, 0, 0, 1).
[U] = ([0,0], [0,10], [0,0]).
[Y] = ([0,100], [0,100]).
VY = (0,-).

Operating state 3:
VL = (1, 1, 0, 0, 0, 1, 0).
[U] = ([0,10], [0,0], [0,0]).
[Y] = ([0,40], [0,80]).
VY = (0,+).

Operating state 4:
VL = (0, 0, 0, 0, 1, 0, 0).
[U] = ([0,0], [0,0], [30,60]).
[Y] = ([0,80], [40,80]).
VY = (*,0).

Operating state 5:
VL = (1, 1, 1, 1, 1, 1, 1).
[U] = ([0,10], [0,10], [40,60]).
[Y] = ([40,60], [40,60]).
VY = (*,*).

Figure 5

Let Y0 = (15, 20), VL0 = (0, 0, 0, 0, 0, 0, 0) represent the initial information and operating state 5 with Yf = (50,50) a representation of the goal. Applying the above described planning routine lead to the following sequence results:

Step a- VL0 = VL1 => The initial operating state is 1.
LE := {1}.
Step b- LM1 := {1, 2, 3, 4}; LM2 := {1, 2, 3}.
MI := LM1 $\cap$ LM2 = {1, 2, 3}; Yi := Y0 (i=1,3).
Step c1- VQi := (+,+) (i=1,3).

	FQ1 := 0; FQ2 := -2; FQ3 := 2.
	max i FQi = FQ3 => The best current operating state is 3; LE := {1 3}.
Step d1-	VY3 = (0, +); vy1 = 0 => LM1 := {1, 2, 3, 4}
	vy2 = + => LM2 := {1, 2, 3, 4, 5}
	LM1 ∩ LM2 -LE = MR := {2, 4}.
Step e1-	Conditions of transition: 3 ---> 2 Y2 = (15, 50)
	Conditions of transition: 3 ---> 4 Y4 = (15, 50)
Step c2-	FQ2 := -1; FQ4 := 4;
	max i FQi = FQ4. => The best current operating state is 4; LE = {1 3 4}.
Step d2-	VY4= (+, 0); vy1 = + => LM1 = {1, 2, 3, 4, 5}
	vy2 = 0 => LM2 = {1, 2, 3, 4, 5}
	LM1 « LM2 -LE = MR = {2, 5}.
Step e2-	Conditions of transition: 4 ---> 2 Y2 = (50, 50)
	Conditions of transition: 4 ---> 5 Y5 = (50, 50)

The desired operationnal state belonging to MR the search is stopped.
The sequence S is:

S = ((OP1, (15, 20)), (OP3, (15, 50)), (OP4, (50, 50)), (OP5, (50, 50))).

5- CONCLUSION.

In this paper we have summarized some of the issues involved in automating the synthesis of startup operating procedures for continuous chemical processing units. We have focussed on a particular modeling structure which comes from interviews with human operators and from readings of operating manuals of working plants. This modeling structure is an operating region-based representation whichdoesnot make use of the classical operator-based paradigm. The proposed representation of the operating states provides an implicit representation of local and global constraints through the instances of the vectors VL, [U], [Y], VY. Based on such a modeling structure we have derived a planning method which uses a means-end analysis approach to form subgoals.

This planning method is actually limited to single processing units, thus future work will investigate its generalization to several units. Another important point which is concerned with operation systhesis of complex feedback loops during startup, it remains to be studied.

Acknowledgement.

The authors greatly acknowledge the Rhône Poulenc company for financial and technical support during the preparation of this work, and particulary the industrial center at Decines as well as the operators and staff from the Roussillon production center.

Bibliographie.

[1]: MOORE R.L, KRAMER M.A "Expert systems in on-line process control".
Chemical Process Control CPC III CACHE ELSEVIER 86.
[2]: STEPHANOPOULOS "Intelligent systems for process operations overview"
Computer Aided Process Operation CACHE ELSEVIER 87.
[3]: R.LUKHMANAN STEPHANOPOULOS. "Synthesis of operartiong procedures for complete chemical plant." part 1&2 pp 985-1021. Computer Chemical engeneering V.12 N°9910 1988.
[4] R.H.FUSILLO G.J.POWERS "A synthesis method for chemical plant operating procedures" Computer chemical engenering vol 11, N°4 pp 369-382 1987 "Operating procedures using local models and distribued goals." Computer chemical engenering vol 12, N°9/10 pp 1023-1034 1988
[5] CHAPMAN "Planning for conjonctive Goals" Artificial intelligence N° 32 pp 333-377 1987.

Industrial Applications of Artificial Intelligence
J.L. Alty and L.I. Mikulich (Editors)
Elsevier Science Publishers B.V. (North-Holland)

THE CONCEPT OF AN EXPERT SYSTEM FOR MONITORING AND MANAGING A FLEXIBLE MODEL OF INDUSTRIAL TRAINING

S.A. KLEIMYONOV and A.I. KOROVINA

Moscow Aviation Institute,
Moscow,
The USSR.

The need for evolutionary change in technical systems and some significant changes in science and its applications have brought about the current interest in expert systems. During the development of technical systems for industry, the planning procedures become more complex as the systems themselves become more complicated. The need for a Flexible Model of Training for industry therefore arises.

A training model is flexible to the extent that it can evaluate a "training situation" and choose the best way approach amongst alternative systems. These alternative systems allow the establishment of fundamental connections between different elements in the system according to the state of evolution of the system and socio-economic parameters of the region in which it is developed. They also allow the establishment of humanitarian relationships for special training.

The elements of the model and the connections amongst them (which form the structure) should cooperate through the expert system via qualitative and quantitative descriptions. The creation of the model is necessary to solve a number of problems. Amongst these is the analysis of special purpose education dynamics with respect to the dynamic evolution of the technical system. Moreover the interconnection of humanitarian and economic monitoring can be established with the help of models as well as forming engineering cultural values which raise the level of reflection during the production planning process and operational activity (i.e. covering the whole lifecycle).

The expert system should include an information kernel which permits the following operations:

1. to determine the "training situation" connected by estimating:
   a) the dynamic state of the technical system development
   b) the state of the training model and its ability to adequately reflect current realities
2. to estimate and formulate alternative management decisions on training during the dynamic monitoring of the Flexible Model of Training

The basic system-making factors are determined by the internal amount of monitoring and management information, the technology of information processing and the universal interface. Thus, for example, internal information is found from the knowledge base where the data base is distinguished conditionally through the conceptual structure of the basis of knowledge, and on the peculiarities of the rules and procedures which help to make the decisions about alternatives in uncertain situations. Such procedures are based on specially formulated frame constructions.

It is evident that the problems of creating and using the monitoring expert system for the Flexible Training Model lie in the complexity of creating the underlying information processing technology. It is determined by the parameters of communication, the professional environment, information models, and technical and human interaction.

The usual knowledge base structures for a monitoring expert system are static. The base contains information about the specific character of the Flexible Training Model. The second component of the structure is the dynamic knowledge base used for storing information during monitoring and management of the concrete problems of training model maintenance.

The difficulties in forming the knowledge base follow from the static and dynamic information kernel which is connected with the diversity of the processes which are the essence of a training model in industry.

We can divide, say, these processes into seven groups:

1) an estimation of the results of examination of the model training introduction environment
2) the organisation of alternative training structures
3) the catalogue of possible programmes and methods for psychological and pedagogical adaptation of individuals to given problems
4) socio-economic limitations
5) the possibility of the back-connection procedures - "training process -technical object - personality"
6) innovation processes in the Training Model
7) the organisation of new qualities of Training Models. Both the knowledge structure building processes (based on facts and rules) and the management structure which permits the use of various rules are based upon the so-called information kernel or spatial algorithm of the Flexible Training Model SAFTM).

A SAFTM structure can be represented as the intersection of overlapping spheres depicting the main interconnections of the information kernel. These inter-communications are connected with the help of the shell system to the main directions - (humanitarian, social, techno-economic). The formation of the management structure can be represented as intersections of the corresponding orthogonal vectors. The forming of the information kernel takes place simultaneously with all the factors which form the intersections and relations of people, means and objects of the activity. One of the problems of creating the information kernel and Training Model using this spatial algorithm is the problem of transition from the outer shell to the inner sphere. First, the indications of innovations and demands for socio-technical resources (both object and subject) are determined. Then the rules, communication, and component elements of the static and dynamic knowledge bases (taking into account socio-economic results of the monitoring environment of the expert system of the Training Model in industry) are formed:

- production sphere: <traditional technology>; <improved technology>; <the latest technology>
- scientific sphere: <technical innovation>; <fundamental investigation>; <discoveries>; <humanitarian aspects>; <philosophical aspects>;
- training sphere: <fundamental universal engineers sphere and humanitarian>; <vocational fundamental>; <applied vocational>

The analysis of the existing principles of description of the information objects with the complex, branched structure shows that, in the condition of the monitoring of the socio-technical system, the most adequate language (which helps to describe the heterogeneous phenomena within the limits of the given problem) is frame based. Frame construction is implemented to describe the sphere of professional activity and in order to work out positive options according to the evaluation of the situation and alternative decisions for management of the Flexible Training Model.

Frame construction can present the information processing model (with the same rules) for all seven groups of training model processes in industry. The frame construction forms a net with six nodes as follows:

- innovation problems,
- psychological and pedagogical interactions (i.e. what elements help to fulfil the the action conditions ? Limitations ? What is the result ?),
- organisational and economic training principles (what does this and that structure do ? What is the aim of the organised training ? What are the conditions in which the training is implemented ?),
- contradictions (psycho-pedagogical, organisation and economic, the main principles of their elimination),
- organisational decisions and the demands on them,
- the estimation of organised decisions

The formation of the database structure, which is the key notion of the development of the technology of the expert system includes database models (the model, names of domains and relations). A unification of the great number of the names of relations and attributes, domains and attributes of the data base models of all levels, and the names of the meaning of the attributes of all the database structures are equivalent to the terminology of the inner storage of knowledge of the Flexible Training Model, and form a knowledge description theosaurus. The elementary grammar is determined with the help of well-known rules for recording the relationship schemes, including predicative forms, taking into account the development of the semantic types classifications of these schemes.

The knowledge base elements of the Flexible Training Model can be represented on the whole by

conditional rules

- P1(x,y) - with the increase of x, y decreases.
- P2(x,y) - with the increase of x, y increases
- P3(x,y) - with the x change, there is some slight change in y
- P4(x,y) - if x corresponds to A, then y corresponds to B
- P5(x,y) - if x corresponds to A, then y corresponds to B, otherwise y corresponds to C.
- P6(x,y) - x is less significant than y
- P7(x,y) - depends more on x than on y
- P8(x,y,z) - maximum x, when y is minimum on z
- P9(x,y,z) - where there is a discrepancy between x and y, then we have z

relational constants - classification, binary, temporal, dynamic, semantic, causative, prepositions

relational variables - quantificators, imperatives, notion-states, estimations, modals, modifiers

The examined structures help to form the information blocks and logical connections among them for monitoring and managing the Flexible Training Model in order to solve the following problems:

- the determination of the state indicators which have social significance for experts and political context for consumers.
- the investigation on the possibility of integrating indicators
- investigations on the types of acceptability criteria and the desirable application of these indicators, the communication load in the social context, the estimated influence on existing situations (it strengthens, weakens, remains neutral), instrumental load in the social context, estimation and forecasting of the practical results of indicator application and integration in social dynamics (strengthens, refutes, remains neutral)
- the creation and application of social technology standards which provide coordination and regulation of social interaction systems

- description rules and the application of indicators
    - rational aspects (aspects of knowledge)
    - relative estimation of reality
    - standard (normative) aspects, estimation of acceptable policy
    - behaviour aspect, the influence on people and organisation relations, the estimation of policy implementation dynamics
- estimation rules for group interactions (the attitude of the indicators of social processes)
    - the rational adequacy (knowledge adequacy)
    - standard (normative) adequacy
    - behaviour adequacy
- the estimation of indicator influence and application in economic management

It is necessary to note that the limitations based upon the results of examinations are determined with the knowledge limits about production, organisation, labour organisation, stereotype of the profile knowledge and pedagogical knowledge. The effectiveness of the work with the monitoring expert system of the Training Model in industry is determined with the conditions of natural limitations. These limitations are connected with the concrete (specific) social reality of the Training Model introduced during the evolution of the technical system in industry.

Thus the above suggested conception of the expert system permits:

- determination of "situation of training" connected with the estimation of:

    a) the state of the dynamics of the development of technical systems
    b) the state of the Training Model and the adequacy of reflection by its respective realities
- to estimate and elaborate alternative management decisions about training in the process of dynamic monitoring

Consequently, this conception of the expert system permits the creation of the parameter row of the expert modules for monitoring and managing the Flexible Training Model of engineers for industry and to solve the following problems:

- the estimation of the structure creation ideas of the engineer's training for enterprises. This estimation is based upon the results of the socio-economic and socio-ecological examination and on the results of humanitarian planning
- the estimation of the view of the training system of engineers for industry

Furthermore, the given concepts solve the following problems (during dynamic modelling of the Model):

- carrying out and monitoring of socio-economic and socio-ecological examinations
- training structures: qualification levels, and their certification, connection with examination results, organisation structure, legal security.
- The programme's content and the methods of psychological adaption
- Socio-economic model of the training system
- Humanitarian planning: structure estimation methods and monitoring
- The availability of a corresponding scientific investigation which can estimate the influence of the results on the society (the estimation of society's readiness for the application of new technologies according to the results of social examinations).

Industrial Applications of Artificial Intelligence
J.L. Alty and L.I. Mikulich (Editors)
Elsevier Science Publishers B.V. (North-Holland)

EXPERT SYSTEM FOR TECHNOLOGICAL PLANNING

Galina V. PETROVA

Leningrad Electrotechnical
Engineering Institute,
Department of Microelectronics.
Leningrad, USSR

Abstract. This paper is concentrate of advanced expert system technology in text processing (analysis and synthesis) in a product engineer - oriented language.

The design and application of expert systems are importent mainly in those fields of human activity where considerable streams of specification and reference information must be processed through analysis and synthesis of information-intensive documents.

Such a very situation is characteristic of industrial production technological planning and engineering particularly in a organization of special alphanumeric technological documents. This activity efficiency depends on the effective solution of problems related to organization and representation of technological knowledge in form satisfying compating requirements of the technological information producer and user, represented either by a human being or by a system.

The use of a product engineer-oriented language which is a subset of a natural one, provides, perhaps, the only possible approach to providing a compromise representation of information for use in both automatic and non-automatic systems.

The content of alphanumeric technological documents is described by the introduction of the concept of structured technological process declarators understood as semantic constants. Technological process declarators are considered to be structured items of alphanumeric technological documents and form some semantic-synthactic constructs.

The analysis of these constructs shows that technological process declarators consist of a number of functional elements which may be expressed in terms referring to different parts of speech. Names of concrete technological terms are minimal separated items of technological process declarators. Groups of concrete technological term names form definite semantic-syntactic constructions belonging to appropriate classes of language objects or to appropriate type of technological (professional) glossaries. Technological process declarators belonging to an appropriate type of technological (professional) glossary, is determined by a key technological concept. Key technological concepts belonging to definite parts of speech are characteristec by each type of technological (professional) glossaries.

Based on the above we can state, that usage of a structural-linguistic method of technological information analysis is an effective tool of developing knowledge models of a technological science in general and in the provision of alphanumeric technological documents representability in particular.

The theory of Chomsky formal grammars was used to model tecnological process declarators [1]. Structural-syntactic models of technological process declarators in terms of Chomsky grammars were developed . The Grammar G, is represented as a set of original concepts, based on which generalized technological concepts were formulated, a set of auxiliary elements denoting syntactic groups into which concrete technological terms, forming technological process declarators, are divided, fifty-five developed inference or production rules which describe all types of technological process declarators of a corresponding technology field for an appropriate class of language objects.

The knowledge about one or another concrete technological term's relation ship to a corresponding synthactic group was acquired using techniques of morphological analysis. This analysis enabled is to obtain the required grammatic information via identification of various conceptual forms. Morphological analysis was carried out by a word-varying approach on the basis of a developed knowledge base of a technological language. This knowledge base is a word-stem dictionary, with possible word-ending tables, characteristic inflection class tables, analysis and synthesizing morfological tables.

Structural-syntactical models of concrete terms were developed using a context-free grammar, represented by: a master terminal dictionary containing word stems which form concrete technological terms, master terminal dictionary of word inflections; auxiliary terminal dictionary of word ending concepts and finally, two production rules.

Shank's theory of conceptual relationship was used for semantic interpretation of technological process declarator structure and four rules of a conceptual syntax were used: some objects may performs actions; objects may have objects and actions may be specified (particularized) [2].

Thus, the task of automatic classification of technological information to acquire extensible knowledge base as the base of technological components was solved through sequential morphological, syntactical and semantic analysis using structural-linguistic models of product engineer knowledge representation.

It seems a reasonable statement, that if original technological process declarators are separated from technological documents with a structure conforming to adopted standards, then elements of an extensible knowledge base can derive from them technological process declarator structures, correct according to standards, with the aid of Chomsky's generative grammar.

To represent application domain knowledge in the form of technological process declarator chains specifying product manufacturing technology, a generalized model of application domain requires to be developed. In such a model a problem space representation was used.

The formalization of technological knowledge was based on semantic network constructed using the Manufacturing object classification system [3]. Such a taxonomic structural - information model is developed with the use of major network operations: intersection, complement, implication, generalization and specification. Vertexes mapping a product technology type have a complex internal structure and are modeled by reducing tasks to subtasks. Here, two levels of partition are observed: the first one is the master task of product technology classification in the form of a base network structure and the second - the task generated by a specific technology type represented by a subnetwork with technological process declarators contained in its nodes.

A particular feature of such a generalized model of technological knowledge representation is the compactness of its representation since semantic network nodes contain references to corresponding technological process declarator documents from the extensible knowledge base.

Alphanumeric technological document synthesis predetermines the way of initial decision-making in the problem space by a tree searth (from root to a target node) and node expansion for separating a subnetwork specifying process technology which is then represented in the structural form of a corresponding alphanumeric technological document.

The practical version of the expert system incorporates two subsystems: an automatic technological information classification system and an automatic alphanumeric technological document synthesis system [4]. The system requires a knowledge base of technological terms and morphological information on them, an extensible knowledge base of technological process declarators and in intensional knowledge base of processes of the corresponding technology field.

These knowledge bases in total provide the required amount of knowledge for decision making in the expert systems.

The proposed expert system is actually a system allowing for both its own extension and efficient information communication with other application-domain systems which are structured similarly.

REFERENCES.

[1] Rayward-Smith V.J., "A First Course in Formal Language Theory", Blackwell Scientific Publications, Oxford, 1983.

[2] Schank, R., (editor), "Conceptual Information Processing", North Holland, Amsterdam, (1975).

[3] Robotics and Flexible Automated Production, (in Russian), Sbornik (collection), Moskva, Vysschaya schkola, (1988).

[4] Petrova, G.V., "A System for the Automated Synthesis of Textual Technical Documents for the Functional Organisation of GPS REA", (In Russian), In: Analiz i Sintez Radiotekhnicheskikh Sistem, Leningrad, Izvestiya LETI, (1988), pp. 89 - 93.

Industrial Applications of Artificial Intelligence
J.L. Alty and L.I. Mikulich (Editors)
Elsevier Science Publishers B.V. (North-Holland)

CASS : THE KNOWLEDGE BASED SYSTEM FOR SELECTING EXPERT SYSTEM BUILDING TOOLS

Sergey E. CHEKMENEV and Oksana V. KRASNIKOVA

CAD department
MOSSTANKIN
Moscow, USSR

Abstract
This article presents the general principles of the CASS system organisation and development. CASS stands for Computer Aided Selecting System - intelligent system for supporting of hardware/software tool selecting tasks.

The perfomance of a modern CAD/CAM system depends on whether the hardware/software tools (HST) correspond to the nature of domain tasks being solved, and also on their usage by designers. Therefore the tool selecting problem at the early stages of CAD system design is most important.
The CASS project deals with some particular task: the choosing of suitable tools for intelligent CAD subsystems. CASS works with the domain expert and allows him to make a correspondence between the main properties of the domain objects and the intelligent CAD subsystem parameters.
The process of solution (that is identificaton of the tool configuration) can be subdivided into several independed steps.
1. The analysis of the *domain area* and finding classes of problems existing in it,- that is identification the *problem area* .
2. The comparison of the domain and the problem area object properties together with tool parameters. The adoption of the general solution at a conceptual level.
3. "Order" - producing the tool specification by the user.
4. "Proposal" - coordinating the specification with representatives of the tool supplier (the order refinement).
5. Tool supply.
6. Tool installation.
7. Tool maintenance.
For the solutions to the selection task some valuable systems (XCON/XSEL, DRAGON, HPCS-9370, etc.) have already been developed and new expert systems are still coming into use. As a rule they are aimed at the problem of configuring the same type of computer equipment through steps 2-6 approximately.
On the other hand, CASS is concerned with the suitable shell and hardware selection, given a domain task descriptions at the early stages of designing (i.e. at the more abstract level of representation). Such an approach can support for the growing interest towards application of artificial intelligence methods and

systems in CAD problems. A large number of the Expert System Building Tools (ESBT), a variety of knowledge representation models and methods, and the absence of sufficient knowledge engineers dealing with the designing and maintenance support of knowledge-based systems (KBS), makes the selection of adequate models and tools for KBS development of a very difficult problem. All the above support the necessity of KBS design process automation.

First version of CASS implemented currently covers steps 1 to 2. The main feature of the given system is its orientation to the end-user (a domain expert). It is based on the following general principles:

1. A concept of an "intelligent assistant":
the system should not substitute for an expert, but to be a tool for improving of the intellectual constituent of the designing process. To meet these requirements the system should have training capabilities and a didactic interface.

2. The presence of the knowledge engineer's interface is strengthened by an inductive type knowledge acquisition subsystem.

3. The hierarchically structured knowledge base includes knowledge of different types (domain, problem and meta-knowledge). The hybrid object-oriented / production rule model of knowledge representation is implemented. Production rules describe the correlation between the problem attributes and means of solution and are supplemented with a flexible object model for the presentation of the knowledge dealing with the prototype schemes of solution at various levels of abstractions (conceptual, functional, etc.).

4. "The friendliness" of the system. A convenient window, menu and graphics facilities offers visualisation of different levels of presentation of the designed configuration.

5. The ability towards extension and modification.

The conceptual organisation of CASS is based on the analysis of the *knowledge engineer's model*, which represents a knowledge structure, used for building applied itelligent systems. During the designing and realization of the applications the knowledge engineer (KE) uses various kinds of knowledge which effect differently the designing process and the completed system. This knowledge is distributed in the proposed model according to three levels: *conceptual*, *formal* and *implementational*, making up a vertical hierarchy. At each level all the knowledge is organized according to its function in the process of a knowledge engineer's mental activity and is controlled by hierarchically structured *meta-knowledge*, among which it is possible to distinguish *model*- and *problem*- types. Problem meta-knowledge describes how various solution tools and methods interact. Model meta-knowledge is used to perform model transformation,- that is conversion from one level of task representation to another (this process is based on the technique of *heuristic association*).

In the CASS knowledge structure *global meta-knowledge* is also presented. It performs two main functions:

1) preliminary problem analysis, including identification of the considered problem to the type of problem suitable for the application of the artificial intelligence methods;

2) coordination of interaction of all the knowledge groups, realization of the feedbacks and the control of the backtracking

from a lower to a higher level if the specification of the solved problem needs it.

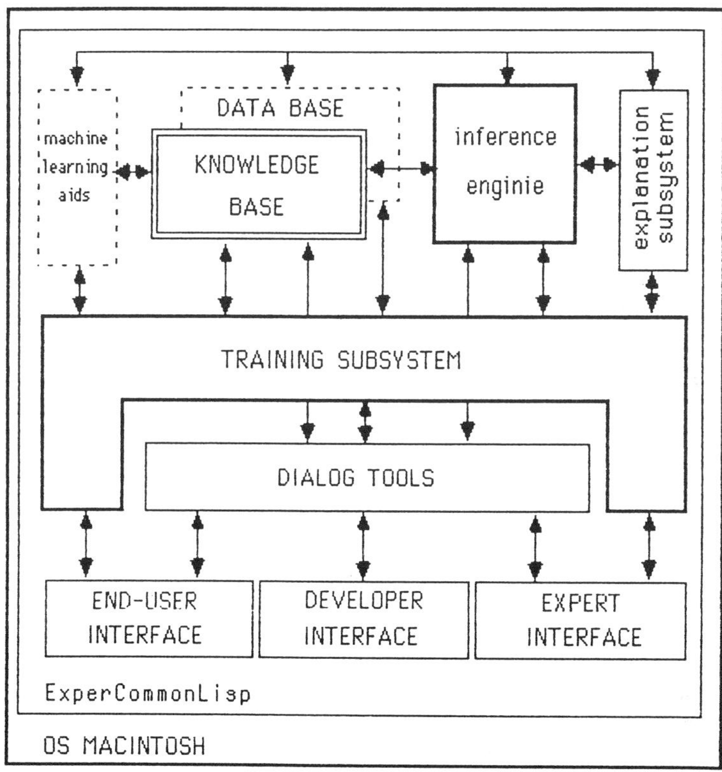

FIGURE 1
The general CASS structure

A method of *heuristic classification* [1] is used as a base method of reasoning conducted during the problem solution process.
The main CASS blocks and subsystems are given in the figure 1.
The following main modes are maintained in the system: "development", "consultation" and "learning".
The system is implemented in the Common LISP environment of the Macintosh SE personal computer.

REFERENCES

[1] Clancey W., Heuristic Classification, Artificial Intelligence, 1985, Vol. 27, pp.289-350.
[2] Gevarter W., The nature and evaluation of commercial expert system building tools, IEEE Computer, 1987, <5, pp.24-41.

Industrial Applications of Artificial Intelligence
J.L. Alty and L.I. Mikulich (Editors)
Elsevier Science Publishers B.V. (North-Holland)

AN EXPERT SYSTEM FOR MAINTENANCE DIAGNOSIS

D.MENEXIADIS and R. SOENEN

Laboratoire de Genie Industriel el Logiciel URIAH No. 1118,
Universite de Valenciennes et du Hainaut-Cambresis,
Le Mont houy. 59326,
Valenciennes Cedex,
France.

ABSTRACT: This paper describes the design of an expert system used for the diagnosis of failures in rotating machines through vibration measurements. The basic goal of the system is to assist the engineer to locate the part of the machine which might be responsible for failure without interrupting its operation. For that we use Prolog. This programming language has been proven appropriate for the implementation of production rule-like expert systems. The representation of knowledge is achieved by the use of Prolog clauses. The execution mechanism of the language is a mechanism for logical inference and is used as the basis for the definition of the inference machine. The knowledge is represented in two ways:

- -The technological part: The machine is described at this level as a hierarchical assembly of modules.
- -The vibration part: This knowledge has been structured in the form of decision trees.

The rule base can be extended by means of a rule acquisition module and a rule consistency checking module. It checks new rules asserted in the rule base against other rules and data.

1. INTRODUCTION

The economical context has led the chemical industry in efforts to decrease costs, decrease equipment failure, and unexpected production breakdowns. All these impose the installation of control and diagnosis systems that must be reliable, have fast access, and be easy to use [1].

1.1. Characteristics of the Problem

The data for the project has been taken from real problems of the Chemical Industries of Northern Greece. The availability of big rotating machines (turbogenerators, motocompressors) the subject of our application, is essential for all factory sectors.

The trouble frequency for these different machines is variable. In some cases when the fault is difficult to locate, the expert is fully mobilised. Otherwise during high production periods any stop in machine in operation is forbidden and it continues in operation. It is then necessary to follow its state and to apply expertise with a high frequency and reliability [2].

1.2.Control Procedure

The principle of these maintenance systems is built around a regular acquisition of vibration measurements according to a specified control plan, in order to detect, most rapidly, the possible significant evolution of faults, or any change in the operation conditions of the machines. When such an evolution happens. a detailed analysis of the vibration signal is necessary in order to have a successful diagnosis [3].

The vibration analysis gives us information in the form of mechanical phenomena images. The task of the instrumentation stops there. The choice of the signal treatment in order to better isolate the kinematic peaks and the diagnosis in particular are the responsibility of the engineer who performs his search from a technical report, either by looking for physical elements other than vibrations, or by means of expert knowledge associated with his own experience in signal treatment [4]

Among the different stages in the control strategy, the most complex functions are realised by the engineer. In fact the automation of these tasks represents the biggest barrier to the achievement of automatic control.

2. DEVELOPING THE SYSTEM

The vibration diagnosis is complex because numerical knowledge, such as signal treatment, and symbolic knowledge are involved at the same time. This knowledge covers different fields: vibration mechanics, equipment technology, machine history and signal treatment. And in fault diagnosis all this knowledge must be manipulated simultaneously, in the same way as is done by the human expert.

The knowledge extracted either from interviews or from documentation is written in the form of decision trees. The model we use is a motocompressor. In our implementation the user has to recognise the vibration parameters on the spectrum and to give them as input to the system.

The signal used is filtered by a low-pass filter with a cut off frequency of 20 Khz. After analysis of the spectrum, we extract from it as in Figure 1 what seems to be the most pertinent parameters to describe the signal. These parameters can be shapes events facts etc..

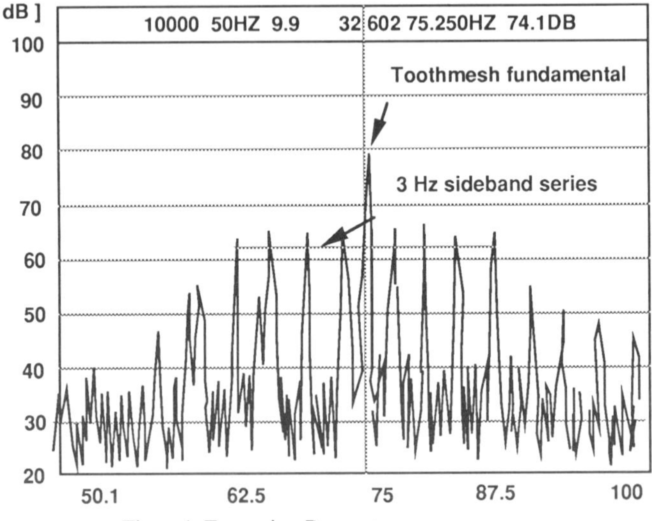

Figure1 Extracting Parameters

We use logic programming in order to describe and specify the mechanical structure of the machine [5].

A machine is composed of a set of modules, as we see in Figure 2, and links between these modules. There is a set of parts associated with every module. Between these parts there are defined connections which can be considered as inputs or outputs [6].

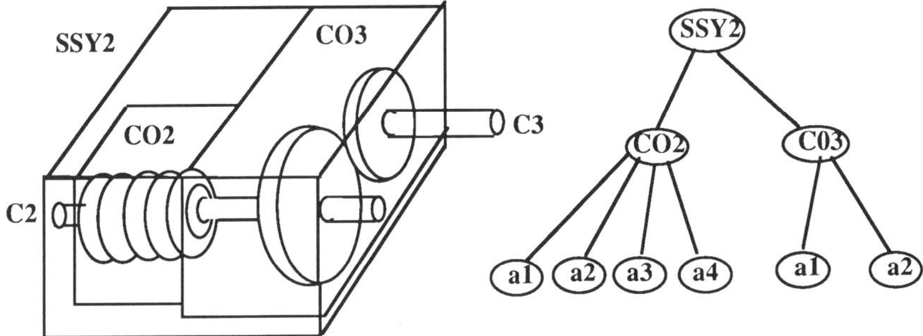

Figure 2 Modules and links

3. ARCHITECTURE OF THE EXPERT SYSTEM

The structural knowledge base is composed with the definition of every intermediate and primitive module constituting the mechanical model [7].

The meta-interpreter is a program written in prolog which together with the prolog language constitutes the inference engine of the system [8].

In addition to the knowledge base and to the inference mechanism we have created a communication interface where are principally gathered:

- a module for reasoning about explanations followed by the system.
- a consultation module for the rule base in the shape of clauses and in a form close to natural language.
- a module for the manipulation and the adjustment of the rule base
- a module for consistency checking of the rules.
- an external module specialising in the graphical representation of the inspected machine parts. These display functions become integrated into the screen management of the system.

3.1 Structure of the Knowledge Base

The machine is represented by a non elementary first order formula. The modules having n ports are represented by n-ary predicates. We represent a module by a Horn clause where the head of the clause represents the module to be defined and the body represents a module composition.

For example we have expressions such as:

```
motocompressor (Cl,C4,C5,C6):-
    sub_system1_motor(C1,C2),
    sub_system2_multiplier(C2,C3),
     sub_system3_compressor(C3,C4,C5,C6).

sub_system2_multiplier(C2,C3):-
    component2_multiplier_guide_bearing(C2,Sl),
    component3_gearing(S1,C3).
```

This representation presents numerous advantages. The machine parts are represented by prolog clauses, so the specifications can be directly executed by the Prolog system [9]. The name of the module is included in the specification increasing the readability of the machine decomposition.

This decomposition corresponds to the functional description of the machine. This model of mechanical decomposition corresponds exactly to the model implicitly considered by the human expert. during the diagnosis in addition to his expertise knowledge. This knowledge corresponds to "deep" knowledge.

At each stage of the diagnosis procedure, the system activates one of the vibration knowledge trees, which is composed of a set of nodes. For example two consecutive nodes are linked by a rule such as:

If the rotation speed is constant and
If the load is constant and
If the mesh frequency increases

Then uniform failure of gearing

3.2 Inference mechanism

The structural description of the machine is used by a program (meta-interpreter) which is a prolog procedure designed as a "layer" over the prolog language, for which we present the "Top level"

TOP-LEVEL

```
failure procedure(Machine_set):-
  test_measure_points(Machine set),
  rule(Machine_set,Machine_parts),
  failure_procedure2(Machine_parts).

failure_procedure2([First_part|Rest_of_parts]):-
  failure_procedure1(First_part),
  failure_procedure2(Rest_of_parts).
```

If there is a failure in a component, we see if this component possesses descendants and we go down of a level in the tree, then we recursively apply the search procedure on each descendant activating the corresponding expertise trees, by means of the predicate test measurement points.

If there is no rule for the identification of the trouble, the inference engine eventually allows the acquisition of a new rule through a questioning of the user if this rule is "consistent" with the data of the work memory and with the other rules of the knowledge base.

3.3 Environment

The communication interface between the system and the users is composed of several procedures. They give to the user the possibility to consult and manipulate the knowledge bases, but also to get explanations on the reasonings followed by the system.

We distinguish:

- -The actions which provide information on the knowledge base (static information).
- -The actions corresponding to the instantiation of the knowledge base (dynamic information).

During an interactive consultation, the system asks questions and the user can conversely question the system by means of key words.

He can observe the rules of the knowledge base in a form close to the natural language, or in the form of prolog assertions. The user can also obtain explanations on the reasonings followed by the system, in the form of a complete or a simplified "trace".

4. CONCLUSlON

In every industrial domain, we observe a constant automation of the equipment and therefore an increase of their complexity, leading to enormous needs in the fields of maintenance and inspection. and consequently an increased need to get specialists ("experts"). The search for reliability, rapidity, availability, led to this, an expert system prototype destined to maintenance diagnosis of the rotating machines.

The prototype uses a modelling (topological and functional) approach to industrial equipment, and aims to prove in a realistic context, the feasibility of such a system.

The prototype adopts an approach centred on using Prolog logical clauses. It allows knowledge representation on different levels of detail, by means of the recursive possibilities of Prolog and its ability to be used as a meta-language.

The representation allows also decentralisation of the vibration knowledge, so the system is more modular, facilitating the constitution and the modular adjusting of the knowledge base.

REFERENCES

[I] Shatoff, J., "Using Vibration Analysis to Determine the Dynamic Health of Turbine-Generators", Power Engines, Turbines, Generators. Instrumentation and Control, Vol.120, No 5, (1976).

[2] Dang Van, K., "Etat Actuel de la Theorie de l'Endommagement et de ses Applications", Mecanique Materiaux Electricite No. 398, (1983).

[3] Taylor, R.R., "PLAQUEMlNE: Predict Bearing Failures with Portable "Checkers", Hydrocarbon Processing, (1982).

[4] Bently, D.E., "Monitoring Rolling Elements Bearings", Bently Nevada, (1982).

[5] Davis, R.E., "Logic Programming is not Circuit Design", IEEE, ch 2017, (1984).

[6] Narain, S., "Mycin, Implementing the Expert System in Loglisp", IEEE 0740-7459, (1985).

[7] Clocksin, W.F., "Logic Programming and Digital Circuit Analysis", The Journal of Logic Programming, Vol 4, No 1, North Holland, (1987).

[8] Shapiro, E.,.Sterling, I., "The Art of Prolog: Advanced Programming Techniques", (MIT Press. 1986).

[9] Stamatsis ,D., Menextadis, D., and Soenen, R., "Expert Systems and Diagnosis of Failures for Rotating Machines: 1st Symposium National (Greece), d'automatisme et de robotique, Athenes, (1987).

Industrial Applications of Artificial Intelligence
J.L. Alty and L.I. Mikulich (Editors)
Elsevier Science Publishers B.V. (North-Holland)

ARTIFICIAL INTELLIGENCE METHODS IN PROBLEMS OF CONTROL AND TECHNICAL DIAGNOSIS

Bogomolov S.Ye.,Dmitriev A.K.,Okhtilev M.Yu.

Leningrad Institute for
Informatics and Automation
USSR Academy of Sciences
Leningrad, USSR

ABSTRACT

Structural models for constructing control and diagnosis systems of complex technical objects using the pattern recognition theory are presented. The proposed models are based on employing the mechanism of Petri nets and the concept of logic programming, the theory of formal grammars and the method of algebaic aggregation.

1. INTRODUCTION

The advanced trend of creating systems for control and diagnosis through the application of artificial intelligence methods allows us not only to accumulate new knowledge, but also to solve new problems. The methodology of pattern recognition theory can serve as a basis of producing such systems, and the control and diagnosis process reduces to the synthesis and realization of recognition algorithms for object states. The recognized object state means either individual modes of normal operation of a serviceable object (the problem of control) or its disabled states induced through failure of different functional components of the object (the problem of diagnosis). Though the above mentioned problems have much in common, their solution requires different formal schemes to be employed. Within the above methodology of pattern recognition theory the following approaches to formalizing the control and diagnosis process are possible.

2. LOGICAL SYNTHESIS OF DYNAMIC RECOGNITION ALGORITHMS OF OBJECT STATES

One can consider the process of the functioning of many complex objects as a stream of discrete events satisfying certain attribute-time relations. The latter define the time ordering of events (TOE), which characterizes the constraints of the evolution of a controlled process. "Knowledge" about different TOE descriptions is represented by rules of the form

$$(\Pi)\ G_o \leftarrow G_1 \ \&\ldots\&\ G_m,$$

where $m \geqslant 0$, $G_i \in \Gamma$. Γ is the set of TOE-atoms,given by induction:

a) if $F \in \Phi$, then $F \in \Gamma$,

b) if $F_1, F_2 \in \Phi$, then $RAN(F_1,F_2;\ \Delta,\ \Delta^1) \in \Gamma$,

c) if $F_1, F_2 \in \Phi$, then $NEOD(F_1,F_2) \in \Gamma$,

d) if $F_1, F_2 \in \Phi$, then $ODN(F_1,F_2) \in \Gamma$.

Φ denotes the set formulas-atoms of the classical logic, which are interpreted with attribute relations . RAN, NEOD, ODN are the time connectives corresponding to the time relations of the form $\tau_2 \in [\tau_1+\Delta,\ \tau_1+\Delta^1]$, $\tau_1 \neq \tau_2$, $\tau_1 = \tau_2$. The parameters Δ and Δ^1 define the variation zone at the time τ_2 with respect to τ_1.Besides the rules (Π), characterizing the particular formula descriptions of TOE´s, the knowledge base contains universal rules describing the time connective properties (transitivity, parametric transitivity and so forth), for example, of the following form:

$$ODN(F_1,F_3) \leftarrow ODN(F_1,F_2)\ \&\ ODN(F_2,F_3),$$

$$RAN(F_1,F_3;\Delta_1+\Delta_3,\ \Delta_2+\Delta_4) \leftarrow RAN(F_1,F_2;\Delta_1,\Delta_2)\ \&\ RAN(F_2,F_3;\Delta_3,\Delta_4),$$

and so on. Instead of F_i any atom in Φ can be represented. An inquiry to the knowledge base has the form (Q_o) G_1 & G_2 & ...& G_n, $G_i \in \Gamma$, and describes the TOE, for which it is necessary to prove the existence of a dynamic recognition algorithm (DRA) and then to synthesize it in case of its presence.

The proof search algorithm is similar to the SLD-resolution [1] and comes to constructing the chain of inquiries Q_o, $Q_1,\ldots,Q_k$, where $Q_\emptyset$ is the initial inquiry, Q_k is the empty unquiry. The inquiry Q_i is derived from the inquiry Q_{i-1} with the aid of the rule Π_i and the unificator Θ_i.The feature of the considered search algorithm is that not only terms and subject variables but atoms and predicate variables participate in the unification.The DRA is derived from the constructed proofas follows. The interpretation function γ unambiguously maps each rule Π_i and the TOE-net $W_i = \gamma(\Pi_i)$, which is a modification of the Petri net [2] and is represented with the graph $W_i = \langle P_i, T_i, H_i, U_i, f_i \rangle$, where H_i are nodes-places, T_i - the nodes-transitions, H_i - the arcs between P_i and T_i, U_i - the attribute-time relations which map the transitions and the places with the function f_i. The resulting TOE-net representing the structure of the desired dynamic recognition algorithm is given with the expression $W = \gamma(\Theta\Pi_1)\circ\ldots\circ\gamma(\Theta\Pi_k)$, where $\circ$ is the addition operation of TOE-nets, $\Theta = \Theta_1 * \ldots * \Theta_k$ is the unificator composition of the proof chain.The process of dynamic recognition of event streams over the TOE-nets consists in changing the marking of the net places in accordance with the certain rules φ, involving the testing of the local attribute-time relations.

3. STRUCTURE-ALGORITHMIC METHOD OF OBJECT STATE RECOGNITION

The considered method is realized in the system of structure-algorithmic recognition (SSAR) [3].A combined model is used as a model of the enterprise (ME) in the proposed SSAR. It is based on the procedural representation of the component relations of the set of parameters X characterizing an object technical state and on the declarative strategy of synthesis of the parameter calculation algorithms $C \subseteq X$ in accordance with the given objective of control and diagnosis.The propossed ME is given as a set of special CM's $M_g = \langle X, B, D \rangle$,where X is the set of technical state parameters; B is the set of applicability predicates of the corresponding CM with subject variables in X; $D \subseteq X \times X$ is the relation connecting the input X^+ and output X^- parameters ($X^+, X^- \subseteq X$). After that a constructive proof of the existence theorem of calculation program (recognition algorithm) is constructed for the predetermined parameters in the set C as follows:

$$\forall (X^+ \subseteq X)\ \exists\ (X^- \subseteq X)[(X^- = D(X^+))\ \&\ (X^- \subset C)]. \quad (1)$$

The constructive proof is performed on the basis of derivability of terminal words within the formal-deductive systems. For specifying the latter the p-grammar G is proposed which refers to the class of formal attribute grammars. This grammar can be obtained (with an accuracy to by using the homomorphic mapping $\Gamma_p : M_g \times C \rightarrow G_p$.By the proof of theorem (1), if any, first the derivation graph and then the derivation regular grammar G_υ (van Wijnguarden's grammar) are constructed $\Gamma_\upsilon : G_p \rightarrow G_\upsilon$. After that all the possible schemes of recognition algorithms A_υ are formed in accordance with $\Gamma_a : G_\upsilon \rightarrow A_\upsilon$; the duplicate branches being deleted. As a result the execution of the completeness and minimality properties (nonredundancy) of the SSAR is ensured.The calculation program, realizing the recognition algorithm in the SSAR, is given by S_g defined with the G-net. It combines the advantages of CM's and Petri nets, is an extension of the latter, and is formed as follows: $\Gamma_s : G_p \times A_\upsilon \rightarrow S_g$.The algebra allowing to form a large variety of constructions is introduced over the set of nets S_g, as well as over the set of CM's M_g.The G-net allows to organize data multithreading for achieving the objective of real time recognition. Besides, it has the maximum possible concurrency of the procedure of the measuring information processing, what is realized in an asynchronous execution of the elemenary operators of the synthesized program.

4. STRUCTURE-ALGEBRAIC APPROACH TO OBJECT STATE RECOGNITION

By the generally accepted concept of recognition the definition of an object technical state (TS) is in realizing the mapping $\eta : Y \rightarrow S$,where Y is the set (in a general case-infinite) of object states available for observation; S is the final set of patterns formed at the stage of teaching, one of which being identified as an observed state $y \in Y$. Traditionally as a basis of generating patterns $S_i \in S(i = \overline{1,m})$ one assumes the principle of partitioning the set Y into classes in accordance with some equivalence (tolerance) relation $\Sigma \subset Y \times Y$, i.e., the mapping $\vartheta : Y \rightarrow Y/\Sigma$ is realized. For each class $Y_i \in Y/\Sigma$ the corresponding pattern $S_i \in S(i =\overline{1,m})$ is formed, such that the mapping $\varkappa : Y/\Sigma \rightarrow S$ is a one-one mapping. This requirement comes from the essence of the problem considered.For substantiating the conditions, under which this requirement is held, in the proposed approach an algebraic agregation method is used [4]. It consists in defining the set S as some algebraic atructure homomorphic in relation to the structure of the initial (observed) set Y. These requirements are held if each component $S_i \in S$ represents a fixed point of the reducing mapping μ valid over the set Y/Σ, i.e., $S_i = \mu\check{Y}_i$, $\forall\ \check{Y}_i \in Y/\Sigma$, $\forall\ S_i \in S$. In this case the component $S_i \in S$ is a pattern of the corresponding class $Y_i \in Y/\Sigma$, i.e. the desired pattern of the recognized object TS. Formally it is represented with the vector $S_i = (S_{i1}, S_{i2}, \ldots, S_{in})$. The components of the vector S_i are the desired features S_{ij} describing the object state properties included into the i-th class.

The procedure of the object recognition proper does not differ, in principle, from those described above and it consists in mapping the parameter values measured on the object and the features $S_{ij}(i = \overline{1,m};\ j = \overline{1,n})$ in accordance with certain rules. These rules can be realized in different ways (deductive-logical inferece, grammar parsing and others). As a generalized model for describing the process of object TS recognition the probability-dynamic model is employed

$$M = \langle S,\ \Omega\ ,P,\ F\rangle,$$

where S is the set of possible TS's, in one of which the object can be; $\Omega = \{R\ |R \subseteq S\}$ is the algebra (or the σ-algebra) of subsets of the S, in which the components R have the meaning of phase states (PS) of the modeled recognition process; $P = \{P(R)\,|R \in \Omega\}$ is the probability measure, defined over the set Ω. F is the set of operators describing transitions from one PS of the process to another. The initial PS is the set R = S, and the final ones are the subsets R_i containing the only component S_i, where $I = \overline{1,m}$. Then the set of operators F is given by the expression

$$F = \{f_i|f_i\ :\ S \rightarrow\ R_i,\ i = \overline{1,m}\},\ \text{where}\ R_i = \{S_i\},\ i = \overline{1,m}.$$

The features obtained when teaching S_{ij} with the corresponding probability characteristics, the set of operators F, and the set of restricting conditions make up the "knowledge" base of the control system (CS). On their basis the CS is capable of synthesizing the recognition program of a particular object state automatically,In doing so, the CS itself "decides", to what part of the features available in the "knowledge" base one should refer, in what order and with what rules one should analyze them in order to define an object TS within the particular solved problem of control and technical diagnosis. The presented approach generalizes and develops the above given approaches to a certain extent. Unlike them it permits not only to control the correctness of operating the object operationally and to establish the fact of loosing its serviceability, but to discover the failure to the given depth.

5. CONCLUSION

The developed mathematical schemes allow to make automatic the process of synthesizing the recognition algorithms of an object technical state; the synthesized algorithms retaining the capability of being readjusted flexibly with regard for changing the operation conditions and the very state of an object.The proposed approaches permit to control the correctness of operating the object in real time, and in case of loosing its serviceability to discover quickly enough the failed component to the given degree of specification, no restrictions on the composition of components failed simultaneously being imposed.In spite of the differences the used algorithmic schemes are based on common methodological principles, and on the whole they allow to solve effectively the control and diagnosis problems of technical object of different structure complexity.

REFERENCES

[1] Kowalski R. Predicate Logic As a Programming Language.- Proc. of IFIP-74. North Holland Publ., Amsterdam, p.569-574.
[2] Bogomolov S.Ye. Dynamic Recognition of Temporal Orderings of Events.- Avtomatika i vychislitelnaya technika, 1988,6. - p.82-87.(Automatice and Computing Technology).-(In Russian).
[3] Okhtilev M.Yu. Structure Algorithmic Approach to Forming Applied Recognition Systems (Abstracts of the Fourth All-Union Conference "Mathematical Methods of Pattern Recognition". Part V - Riga, 1989; - p.35-37. - (In Russian).
[4] Dmitriev A.K., Maltsev P.A. Fundamentals of the Formation and Control Theory of Complex Systems. - L., Energoatomisdat. Len-d Division, 1988. - 192 p. - (In Russian).

Industrial Applications of Artificial Intelligence
J.L. Alty and L.I. Mikulich (Editors)
Elsevier Science Publishers B.V. (North-Holland)

THE INTELLECTUAL DESIGN OF THE FUNCTIONAL MUSIC

I. Y.BEREZNAYA and R. M. GRANOVSKAYA

Department of Mathematics,
Leningrad University,
Petrodvorets,
Leningrad,
The USSR.

ABSTRACT: The paper considers an algorithm for constructing a generalized portrait (a prototype) as a single visual picture which represents the rhythmical pattern of several musical compositions of the same genre and measure.

Modern science is becoming a witness to a number of evolving fields united by the Artificial Intelligence concept. Fields have already involved such issues as a picture language (to describe sensually perceived visual patterns) and algorithms of knowledge structuring which allow AI to learn. The result of a partial solution to both problems has appeared in the form of frames incorporating into them a set of pictures related to a single situation being widely used as elements of a knowledge structure.

The problem considered in this paper may be classified as related both to the formalization of the language of auditory (musical) images and to knowledge structure organization in the form of accumulated experience in describing musical rhythms.

Until recently AI dealt with problems that had been well formalized by means of logic, the algorithms of their solution being explicitly realized by humans and knowledge organization being classificational. Such problem properties and solution techniques are connected with the specificity of information processing and solution strategies used by the left cerebral hemisphere.

Today attention has shifted more and more to right hemisphere mechanisms with their analogical way of processing, situational knowledge organization and derived productions differing from the formal logics, the resulting procedures being subconscious. The solutions developed in the right hemisphere are often considered to be intuitive.

Creativity in music has always been considered as related to intuition. Based on our own experience in research into information processing in both cerebral hemispheres and in hemisphere language formalization, we have attempted to represent a musical composition's rhythmical structure as a simultaneous visual picture.

A combination of beats in a measure is defined as a rhythmical cell (a cell). E.g. in an eighth measure an octave considered as a minimal duration was designated as 1 and the durations of two, three and four eights - as 2, 3, 4 respectively. Then eight possible rhythmical cells for the measure 2/4 comprised the set (4), (3 1), (2 2), (1 3) (1 2 1), (2 1 1), (1 1 2), (1 1 1 1) So the rhythmical pattern of any musical piece might be represented as a measure sequence, the rhythmical cell sequence.

Figure 1 shows a graph of transitions between rhythmical cells in the measure 3/4 (or 6/8). There are 32 possible cells at the graph nodes with durations ranging from minimal one eight. (1) to maximal six eights (6). The transition between two cells was defined by means of the transformation D_i (i=2,3,..6). The order i transform influenced the two first cell components

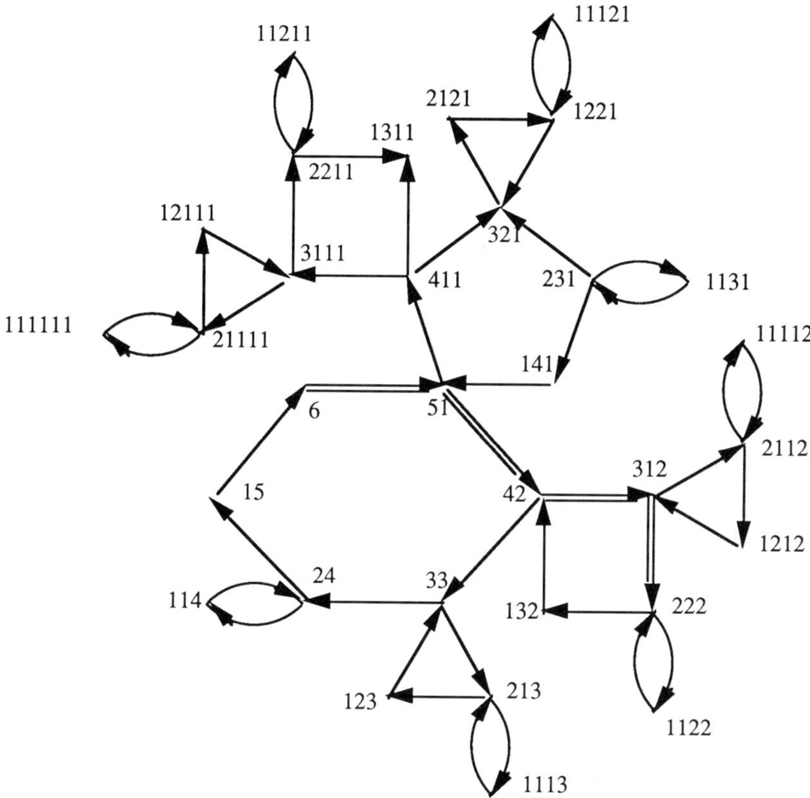

FIGURE 1 The graph of possible transitions between rhythmical cells of the measure 3/4

equalling in sum to i in such a way that a unit was substructed from the first component and added to the second one with the possibility for a zero to be inserted into the cell if necessary. E.g. the transition 51 -> 42 was described by the transform D6, 42 -> 312 by D4 (with a zero being inserted between durations 4 and 2 while transforming). Evidently, the hexagon edges in the Fig.1 graph match D6 transforms, pentagon edges - D5, squares - D4, triangles - D3, and "duangles" - D2. The transitions between the cells not adjacent on the graph were described by the Di transform superposition. So the Fig.1 graph is the simultaneous presentation of all possible rhythmical patterns in the 3/4 measure.

The graph of transitions between cells of various 8-time measures displays a complex structure with the multilevel regularity easy to trace. The graph's underlying structure is an octagon with its vertexes being attached to the subgraphs based on n-gons (n = 7, 6, 5,...2). The subgraphs with their own regular structures correspond to the widely used musical measures 7/8, 6/8 (or 3/4 Fig 1.) , 5/8, 4/8 (or 2/4), 3/8, 2/8 (or 1/4).

Such an approach has made it possible to describe rhythms of any musical composition written in a n-time measure (n=2, 4, 8, 16,. . .) in the form of a path on the graph. The graph appeared as a simultaneous visual rhythmical portrait of a musical composition as if its temporal structure is printed.

If rhythmical portraits of some compositions of the same measure are juxtaposed then their graph common parts could represent the so-called generalized rhythmical portrait (the rhythmical prototype) of the composition class. That is the way we have developed generalized rhythmical portraits of Russian, Polish and Ukranian folk songs in the measure 3/4 as well as waltzes written by various composers (Strauss, Glinka, Chaikovsky, Grieg, XX century jazz composers Brubek, Prevain, Piterson, Markin), and romances in the waltz style. The nodes and edges of the generalised rhythmical portrait obtained for all 63 musical pieces mentioned above are highlighted by circles and dual lines in the Fig.l.

Looking at the generalized portrait one can easily understand the underlying recognizability of the rhythmics of the whole musical composition class. Human beings recognise unknown languages by using a linguistic portrait, e.g. can distinguish German from French. In the same manner one can distinguish between the Chinese and Swede. In this situation, man being aware of the very fact of distinguishing (the left hemisphere process) does not consciously understand the distinction criteria since the generalized portrait which he unconsciously leaned up on (the right hemisphere process) does not contain the criteria in the form used when recognizing by the left hemisphere.

Considering the developed generalized rhythmical portraits, they include only a part of all possible graph nodes corresponding to the musical measure concerned. Thus the field for composers humans or AI systems - to make efforts to create new rhythmical patterns becomes evidently observable. In addition, the very process of forming generalized portraits produces information about changing rhythmical pattern of the composition class over time. The results obtained in the processing of musical rhythms of compositions of different epochs, cultures, peoples facilitate the constructing of algorithms of musical creativity with some properties given beforehand.

One of the industrial applications of the above algorithms is in the computer design of functional music. Physiologists and psychologists have shown that the human physical and psychical state to be controlled by law-governed changes in musical rhythm, its acceleration and slow down. The appropriate musical rhythmical structure captures human inner rhythms involving him in new work conditions, thus driving human beings into other functional states.

REFERENCES

[1] Granovskaya, R.M. , Bereznaya, I.Y. and Grigorieva, A.N., "Perception of form and forms of perception", (Lawrence Erlbaum, New Jersey, 1987)

Industrial Applications of Artificial Intelligence
J.L. Alty and L.I. Mikulich (Editors)
Elsevier Science Publishers B.V. (North-Holland)
1991 IFIP

STRUCTURE OF A KNOWLEDGE - BASED DIAGNOSIS SYSTEM FOR MODULAR DIGITAL CONTROL SYSTEMS

B. MADIGER and W. MULLER
Academy of Sciences of the GDR,
Institute of Automation,
Berlin,
GDR.

ABSTRACT: A prototype of a knowledge-based system, written in PROLOG, for failure diagnosis in machine control systems is presented. The knowledge basis consists of experiential knowledge, collected from servicers whilst repairing the control system, and special knowledge, arising during the design of the system. The system is developed by modelling the behaviour of a human expert who is searching for a failure in a sophisticated electronic device. An implementation of a knowledge base, based on the failure behaviour of a robot control system IRS 711 serves as an example.

1. INTENTION

This paper is intended to show some principles of a prototype knowledge-based system, under development in the Institute of Automation of the Academy of Sciences. The system was designed for the diagnosis of modular digital control systems. The starting point for this investigation is the fact that failures of the machine control system (CNC, robot control, PC) cause an increase in loss of production. On the other hand, these systems are very complex and hence the service and maintenance staff are often overburdened. The knowledge based System allows the possibility of wide use of the special knowledge, which the designers and the specialists of the service staff have collected in the course of time. Thus the user of a control system is able to repair small failures by himself or, if the failure is complicated, he can give detailed information to the service staff of the manufacturer to decrease repairing time. Modern control systems have a modular structure, that is why they can be repaired in the shop by changing the defective module only. That is also the reason for restricting the task of the system to the determination of the defective module. The purpose of this prototype is to make the principles and the shell of such systems known the potential users. Further, it can be used as a basis for future research on this topic.

2. CLASSIFICATION

At present the knowledge based system works like a first generation expert system. That means, the knowledge is given in form of rules and experience. The design of such systems can be done rather easily, but to form the knowledge base is not an easy task. The reason is evident, if one observes service personnel searching for a failure. They works with much intuition and often jump from one conclusion to another inexplicably . Therefore the intention for future research in a second phase has to include deeper knowledge (with models). In this way the system will be able to resolve strategies and draw conclusions itself by interpretation of common network plans. As a first step it is planned to add a second knowledge level, including causal relations. These are statements about connections with the power supply or about the bus structure for instance. The second step could be the description of fundamental principles, like interrupt chains, and global statements about the used modules. The complete modelling of a sophisticated module is too difficult and not necessary, because the servicer has only a vague idea about the modules himself. Especially, if only human experience is used, a comfortable knowledge editor is important. This component has to check the consistency of the symptom description and the possible diagnoses and subgroups. In addition this software module converts a user-convenient dialogue language for entering the knowledge into the internal computer node form, described later in this paper.

3. IMPLEMENTATION

3.1. Structure

In designing the system we tried to copy the behaviour of a human expert searching for a failure. Therefore the diagnoses take place in several phases. The definition and the variable number of these phases are stored in the knowledge base. At the moment there are the following 5 phases:

a) Analysis of starting situation (enquiry about starting symptoms). The most important symptoms, which are stated easily or which are the reasons for calling the system, are established in this phase.

b) Function-orientated diagnoses. Here the system looks for a faulty control function element, causing the failure behaviour (e. g. interrupt-pipeline, servocontroller etc..).

c) Reason-orientated diagnoses. Every faulty function is connected with a concrete faulty module. This module can be either a hardware module or a special software module (e. g. generating parameters). The task of this phase is the destination of the searched module.

d) Repairing hints. After determining the causes of the failure in general, a repair must follow, meaning that the faulty module has to be changed. A non-specialist can be guided through this phase by the system with suitable hints and explanations for the repair.

e) Final analysis. In the last phase the analysis of the attempt to repair is done and the user can decide, whether he wants to leave the system or to continue the diagnosis.

It is possible to unify these phases in groups without restrictions. Each group can be called sequentially, the phases within a group have the same level. If a phase of a group does not give a solution, the system searches for it in another phase of the same group. In the realized example the phases b) and c) are unified in one group. In the normal way the function-orientated diagnosis is carried out first and then the reason-orientated, using the solution of the first one to determine the fault, is done. Even if the function-orientated diagnosis should fail, the knowledge based system tries to get a solution from the reason-orientated diagnosis only. Every phase contains subgroups which are checked separately and alternatively. The sequence of checking is a result of the weights of every single subgroup, determined in a procedure, described later. In addition the user can favour some subgroups, selecting them directly or with the help of starting symptoms. All of the subgroups form the searching space. The decision points are described with the help of nodes which represent the real knowledge.

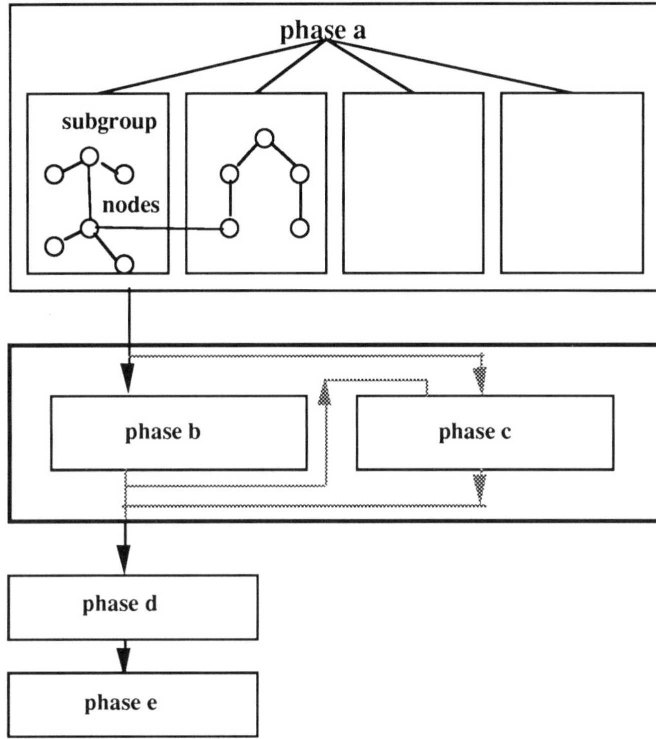

Figure. 1 System Structure

3.2. Structure of the Knowledge Base

The descriptions of the switching nodes form the knowledge base of the system. Every node is built up in the form of a frame and the size of the frame can be chosen. The structure of the frames is represented in figure 2. A frame can be divided into three parts, each containing several slots. The first part is the defining part with a slot 'structure'. It gives the possibility to structure the node, that means, one of the other parts can be omitted. If the node is the starting node for a subgroup, a slot 'sympt' determines the most important symptoms, connected with the subgroup. With a slot 'pre' (for premises) it is possible to decide, which symptoms must appear before the node is fired. The symptoms can be classified for this slot in four types with corresponding values:

type	allowed values
state	y(es)/n(o)
exact	concrete given numerical values
function	numerical values
range	values within an interval

The second part of the node frame describes the action, which has to be done by the user to fulfil this node. In the third part the user can be asked for new symptoms. For this and for the second part it is possible to give some explanations and help for the user. Depending on the user answer, the system branches to other nodes where each branch can contain various nodes or also subgroups. If the symptom is from the type 'function', the knowledge engineer has to define a function, which determines the branching nodes or subgroups in dependence on the symptom value.

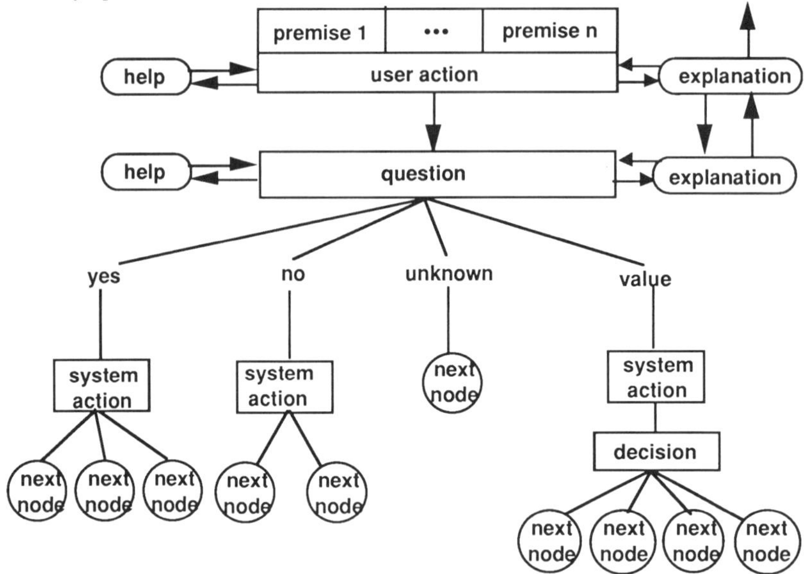

Figure 2 Structure of Nodes

3.3. Working Principles

Within the subgroups the system searches for a path from a starting symptom (beginning node) via the several switching nodes to a final node, containing the result of the diagnosis. How does the system determine the checking subgroups and the sequence within a phase? It is easy, if in a former phase a subgroup was determined. Then the system looks for the phase, containing the subgroup, and starts in this new phase with the beginning node of the determined subgroup. If there is not any starting subgroup, the system compares the appeared symptoms with the describing symptoms of all subgroups in the following phase. If there is some correspondence, this subgroup is selected. The weight value for the sequence is computed by the sum of the appeared symptoms weight. This value is weighted with the weight for the subgroups. In case of no correspondence the knowledge engineer is able to let the system ask the user for some preferred sub-groups, or, if the user cannot answer, to ask for some new appeared symptoms. Every time, if one subgroup within a phase fails, the system re-orders the other subgroups again depending on the new stated symptoms. After working off the node, various successors for each branch are possible. The working sequence is like the sequence in the corresponding frame slot left-to-right, using the PROLOG depth-first-algorithm. If one successor is a subgroup, the system looks for the subgroup in the knowledge base and, if it is allowed, the system tries to prove the subgroup. Normally the algorithm and with it the work of the system ends by finding a node with the value 'endeanf' in the slot 'structure' of a phase 'Final analysis' subgroup.

4. EXAMPLE

As an example, a knowledge base was implemented containing the descriptions of faults for the IRS 711, an 8/16 bit robot control system, produced by the VEB Numerik Karl-Marx-Stadt. The system is now in the phase of testing. The program system needs an AT/XT compatible PC with PROLOG. For the implemented system a PC-AT-286 is used, including an arithmetic coprocessor and hard disc, and S-PROLOG, containing windowing (of VEB ROBOTRON). For convenient usage a user-interface was developed, recording all appeared symptoms, investigated and failed subgroups. The user-entries take place with softkeys or can be chosen with a menu.

CONCLUSION

In our opinion the presented knowledge based system is one way to introduce such systems into practice. It needs only common hardware and is orientated towards the work of the service staff. Because of the partitioning of the knowledge base, generation and enlargement of the base can be done easily.

REFERENCES

[1] Skupping,R., and Weber,R., "PROMOTEX" In: Brauer,W., and Wahlster,W. (eds.), Wissensbasierte Systeme Proc. 2. Int. GI-Kongress Munchen 1987, Springer

[2] Trautmann,J., "Stand und Entwicklungstrends bei der Gestaltung von Diagnosesystemen fur Kleinrechner Wiss", Beitr. Inform. - IZ TU Dresden, 3 H.3, pp. 17-26, (1985).

[3] Torasso,P., and Console,L., "Causal Reasoning in Diagnostic Expert Systems", SPIE Vol.786, Appl. of AI, pp. 598-605, (1987).

[4]Cin, M.D., and Philipp,T., "Expertensysteme fur die Fehlerdiagnose Informationstechnik", it 30, 4, pp. 237-246, (1988)

Industrial Applications of Artificial Intelligence
J.L. Alty and L.I. Mikulich (Editors)
Elsevier Science Publishers B.V. (North-Holland)

EXPERT SYSTEMS SUPPORTING THE DESIGN OF THE MEASURING MODULES AND SECTIONS OF AUTOMATED RESEARCH SYSTEMS

S.I. Yeremenko, V.G. Kurbanov, A.E. Gorodetsky, A.G. Sergeyev.

LF IMASH of the USSR Academy of Scienses

ABSTRACT: Two expert systems supporting the design of measuring modules and sections are presented. The structures of the expert system (ES) are described. The ES are carried out by means of INTEREXPERT expert shell, PROLOG ahd C languages.

Recently an approach has been widely recognized to the design of measuring channels of authomated research systems which uses a set of functionally completed modules. Such an approach is called arranging design. One of the advantages of this approach is the simplicity of design process authomation. Therefore, as expert systems are being widely implemented into the various fields of science and technology, the use of them for the support of authomated research systems are becoming challenging.

Recently expert systems in the various fields of science and technology including the authomated systems designs has actually devoloped. To create an applied ES the "empty" systems are used [1]. This is one of the well - known and widely used techniques of the fast design of applied ES.

We consider an expert system with the elements of learning for the support of the design of interferial-code and raster -code analog-to-digital convertors wich uses the INTEREXPERT expert shell.

The expert system allows to choose one of two strategies of design process: a newly undertaken design and the modification of the previous design sessions.

In the "new design" case the system provides an interactive calculations of the convertor parameters while it passes on to consultation and gives advices to the user in coditions not formalized completely. During such a consultation rules sets, data bases and the results of previous design sessions are used.

In the "modification" case the system provides an interactive modification of one of the convertor types designed previously by a system user due to parameters input by the user.

If the design session is successful, its results are put into the set of data bases which is the main component of the learning part of the system.

The expert system consists of:

- the data bases on convertor components parameters (light sources and photocells characteristics, optic and electric elements);

- the data bases on convertors designed previously;

- the system control procedures (menu, calls of applied procedures etc.);

- the simulation procedures of the work of both components and system on the whole;

- the procedures of analysing the metrological characteristics of analog-to-digitals converters and their components;

- the data bases control procedures;

- the knowledge bases control procedures;

- the procedures of analising design results;

- the plot construction procedures;

- the knowledge bases of consultations in non-formalizable conditions (the choice of ADC, result analysis etc.);

- the knowledge bases of combining components.

The system is an open software and is provided with a friendly interface. The expansion of data bases and rules sets are possible during the use.

However, in the case of expert shells it is difficult to consider the specific features of the applied field in wich the "empty" ES is used. To overcome these difficulties may be a more complicated problem than to create a special ES for given application by means of a high-level language, for instance, PROLOG.

The expert system for the support of the design of the hard - software sections of measure - comptuting complexes under consideration using the CAMAC equipment is carried out in PROLOG and C.

The expert system includes the following components:

- data base on CAMAC modules;

- the procedures of choosing modules in accordance to channels parameteres required;

- the procedures of synthesizing channels;

- the procedures combining channels into sections;

- the consultation support programms: help, result interpretation, report forming, archivation.

The expert system works on the basis of information kept in the data base on CAMAC modules as well as information on and section features required wich is input by user during consultation.

The data base on modules includes information on modules arranged to their functional purpose. It represents the tables of parametrs. When browsing the tables, the varions modules of the same purpose may be compared easily. Besides, there is information on the commands of every module as well as a text comment.

On the basis of this data base an authomated "hand - book" is created which represents the information on the modules and their functional groups in interactive mode. This hand - book is available both as an independent program and through the expert system menu while the expert system is provided with the program access to the data.

Beside carefully arranged data bases the expert system includes a wide knowledge base wich consists of expert conclusions as rules of " if - then" type.

The rule system of choosing modules in accordance to channel parameteres required allows to get the modules from data base in one or several parameters (for instance, word length, conversion time, number of stations). In this case the modules choosen are arranged in accordance to the proximity of their parameteres to required values. The relative significance of parameteres may be input by user.

The rules system of channels synthesis allows to choose a typical section structure, to pick up modules for it, to calculate its extreme parameters and to estimate its efficiency. The sections obtained are arranged in efficiency factors.

The rules system of combining channels into sections integrates the available data on signals and modules then passes on simulating the work of section on the whole.

Beside procedures providing interactive consultations, data base control, rules systems change etc., the expert system concludes a big collection of procedures supporting the consultations: help, results interpretation, reports generation, archivation. Information i/o has a convenient form. The system is provided with a multy-level menu allowing to change the functions required easy, as well as with help screens supporting the menu.

At the start of consultation the data are required on sensors involved in the system designed. Then the consultation itself is carried out. The result of consultation is a section

structure recommended, its characteristics and the data on modules required with effitiency estimation.

The following consultation are provided:

- the synthesis of the measurement of the signals information parameters channels;

- the choise of modules according to characteristics required;

- the optimization according to the target functions (cost, performance, etc.) while the parameters limits are taken into account;

- the procedures combining uniform channels into sections;

One of the stages of the ES creation is the creation of rules systems choosing modules according to given metrological requirements.

For instance, in the case of the design of constant voltage section the following information processing is performed.

The sign and magnitude of sensor voltage is compared with the signs and magnitudes of ADC input voltages, and in result amplifier or divider may be included. Then the characteristics of channels obtained such as error, conversion time, the number of crate stations, cost are compared with maximal legitimate value given by user. The data on channels wich satisfy to input limitations are summarized in result table where estimate is given to every channel. This estimate is:

$F = 1 / \text{SUM } w_i * [\, p_i / p_i(\max) \,]$, where

p_i - the value of i - parameter for given channels;

$p_i(\max)$ - the maximum legitimate value of i - parameter;
w - the weight of i - parameter (from 0 to 9) given by user.

Three ways to join channels into sections are provided:

- join the channels with the same modules and the same structures;

- join the channels working not simultaneously;

- join the slow-working channels, where a polling in turn is permitted.

Corresponding examples:

_ join two channels including the same ADC into section including a two-channel ADC;

- join three channels including the same ADC into section including one ADC only with a multiplexor at its input. The information in different channels must be processed in

different time periods;

- join four slow-working channels including the same ADC into section with an ADC and a multiplexor at its input where cycle polling is performed. Information lost in every channel must not expand some input limitations.

The source texts are provided. During the use or at the customers discretion both data base and knowledge base may be exposed by introducing of new rules and data.

The following conclusions may be drown from the design and use of two expert systems described here. First, the use of empty shells may be justified in the case of the time and overcoast restrictions of concrete design. This allows to concentrate all the efforts of designer at collecting the data and knowledge to fill the shell. The described expert system of optoelectronic ADC design is filled while investigeting the applied field, and this seems a promising way of scientific researh automation. However, a considerable part of empty shell resourses may not be in use in this case.

Second, when an expert system is required such as the ES of measuring sections design a high-level programming language as a tool of working out the system manifests its advantages. This allows to create systems flexible enough for copyright and sale.

REFERENCES

[1] Pospelov G. S. Artificial intelligence as a basis of a new information technology. Moscow, Nauka (1988). (in Russian)

Industrial Applications of Artificial Intelligence
J.L. Alty and L.I. Mikulich (Editors)
Elsevier Science Publishers B.V. (North-Holland)

AN EXPERT SYSTEM FOR TECHNICAL DIAGNOSIS

A. STORR, M. HARDTNER, and H. WIEDMANN
Institut fur Steuerungstechnik der Werkzeugmaschinen und Fertigungseinrichtungen,
Universitat Stuttgart,
Stuttgart,
FRG.

ABSTRACT: This paper gives an outline of the development of an expert system shell especially adapted to the field of technical diagnosis. The necessary structuring and contents of the knowledge base are described. This involves empirical knowledge about failures and their possible reasons as well as the modelling of the functioning of a machine tool. A description is given of how both kinds of knowledge can be combined to form a so-called multi-level expert system and the strategies needed at least in the inference engine to process this knowledge are identified.

1. INTRODUCTION

The high availability of a manufacturing system is the precondition for its economical operation. However, the integration of machines into cells and systems make such systems sensitive to disturbances. Diagnosis can make an essential contribution to the shortening of stand-still time caused by faults. Thereby the availability is increased. In many areas, highly qualified service staff with their knowledge and experience are the only guarantor for an efficient diagnosis.

A basic possibility for propagating the knowledge and experience of these people and to have it at all times at one's disposal is offered by expert systems. The experience of building expert systems for technical diagnosis has shown that, at present, this is an expensive approach. There is a lack of suitable tools (shells) and engineering methods in this area. The effort which has to be undertaken to develop problem-specific tools is explained in Figure 1.

Until now, shells have been offered with basic representation facilities and inference mechanisms (e.g. rules, frames, forward/backward chaining, modus ponens etc.). It is the task of the so-called knowledge engineer to transform the experiences, strategies and models of the diagnostic experts and make these representable within the means available through the processing and representation layer. Therefore, the knowledge of a problem area must be analysed and structured first. However, these functions could be omitted if a problem-specific expert system shells containing structures, basic models and strategies of the special problem area (e.g. machine tools) were available. A requirement for building problem-specific expert systems for fault diagnosis of machine tools is the analysis of the problem area. Thus, we are in a position to define a structure and ascertain and implement the applied diagnostic methods for machine tools. When these tasks are solved the development of an expert system is reduced to the completion of the given structures.

In the following sections the requirements for the structure of a knowledge base for the diagnosis of machine tools will be worked out.

2. REASONS FOR USING A MODEL BASED APPROACH

Before we discuss reasons, we have to define what we mean when we talk about "model-based". We define: An expert system to be "model-based" if it contains the structure and correct behaviour of the technical system. This definition is in accordance with the definition of R. Davis and W. Hamscher [11], who have carried out recent work in model-based reasoning for troubleshooting in electronic circuits.

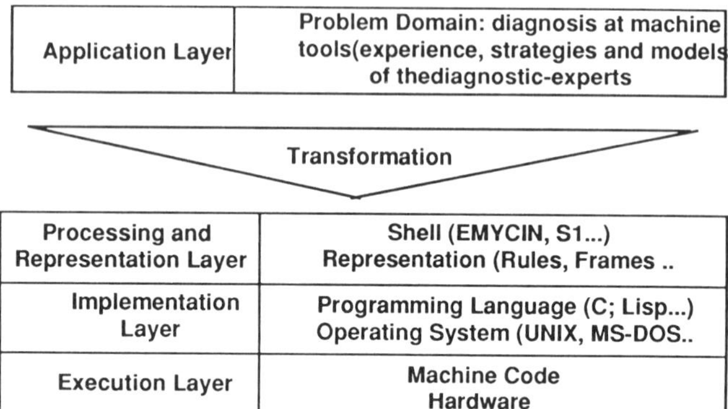

Figure 1 Layers between Problem domain and Hardware.

A model-based approach is essential for the successful solution of a diagnostic problem for the following reasons:

First reason: It is not possible to describe a complex machine tool sufficiently through its failures alone. It is obvious that the number of failures is much greater than the number of functions or components, in other words, it is easier to describe a machine tool in its nominal behaviour than in all kinds of misbehaviour or failures.

Second reason: There is not enough experience and empirical knowledge available in that critical period when a new type of machine tool is at the threshold of development towards utilisation.

The diagram in Fig. 2 illustrates the life-phases of a machine tool from development through utilisation to scrapping.

The knowledge about a machine tool can be differentiated into general knowledge, knowledge about structure and function respectively, and experience. General knowledge means basic mathematical scientific and technical laws. It does not depend on the life-phase of a machine tool or change in any major way. The knowledge about the structure and function increases from the beginning of the development until the end. During the development, a small amount of experience is attained. The greatest increase in experience is obtained during the utilisation of the machine tool, especially when it is produced in quantity. If we observe the people with this knowledge, we see that the knowledge about the structure and behaviour is obtained by the personnel of the producer of the machine tool whereas the experience is obtained by the personnel of the user of the machine tool.

This means that at the threshold of development to utilisation there is no knowledge present about the structure and function by the users of machine tools. They start at the zero-point of empirical knowledge. At the critical point between development and the beginning of utilisation it would be helpful to have the knowledge about structure and function available. In contrast to empirical knowledge, this knowledge exists.

Third reason: Human experts use models, too!

The models human experts use are circuit layouts and engineering designs for example.

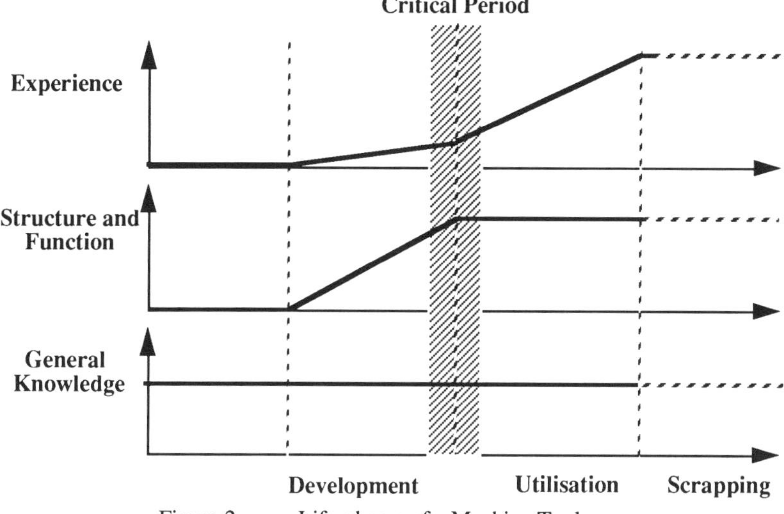

Figure 2 Life-phases of a Machine Tool.

The above reasons show that it is helpful for a diagnosis task to involve a model of a machine tool. This model is the core of the fundamental structure of the knowledge base in our expert system [2].

3. FUNDAMENTAL STRUCTURE OF THE KNOWLEDGE BASE

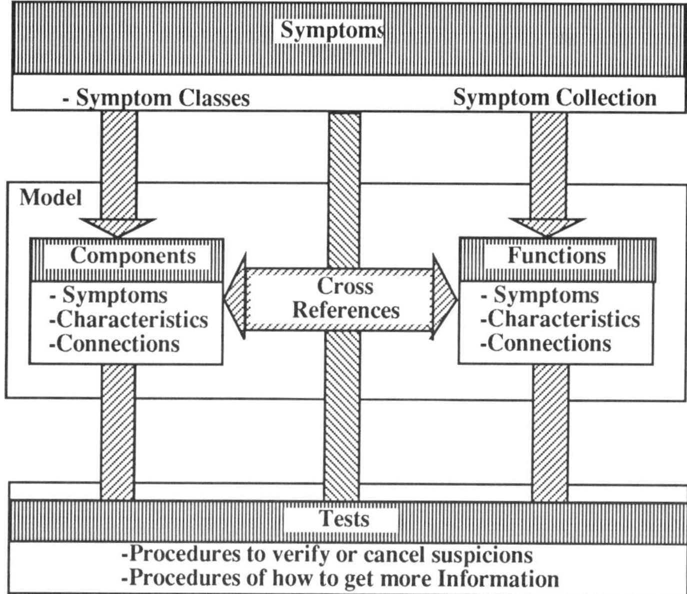

Figure 3 Fundamental Structure of the Knowledge Base.

In addition to the model we need symptoms which show us whether a failure exists or not and we need the description of tests which contain procedures to verify or cancel suspicions or show us how to get more information about the actual state of the machine tool. Figure 3 shows the fundamental structure we have chosen for our system.

It consists of four types of modules. The central modules are the components and the functions which together build the model. The components describe the physical structure of the machine tool. Each component is represented by its individual symptoms, characteristics and connections to the other components. The functions describe the logical behaviour of the machine tool. Each function is formally represented in the same way as components by its individual symptoms, characteristics and connections to other functions. These two types of modules are connected via cross-references.

The global symptoms are connected to the model, or more precisely to the components or functions via suspicions. These global symptoms describe the misbehaviour of the machine tool. They can be grouped into symptom classes and the symptom collection. In the symptom collection, previously occurring failures are stored, the symptom classes are more analytically constructed. These global symptoms cast suspicion on components or functions. Within these components or functions individual symptoms are represented. They describe typical failures of these specific elements. What we have to do to verify or to cancel the hypotheses set up by these suspicions or to show how we can attain more information about the actual state to refine the symptoms is described in test-modules.

The fundamental structure is the base on which the basic diagnostic procedure works (Figure 4).

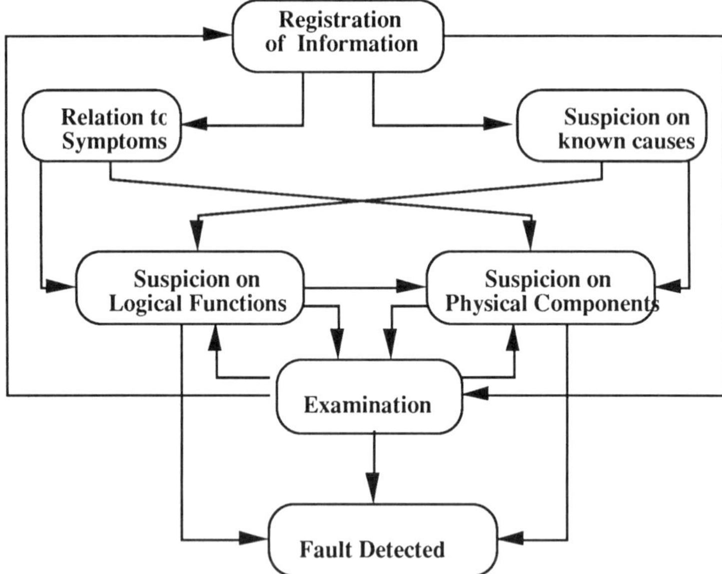

Figure 4 Basic Diagnostic Procedure.

In general we begin with the registration of some information. We either obtain this information in relation to symptoms or it casts suspicion on already known causes (symptom collection). Both parts lead us either to the suspicion of logical functions or of physical components. We examine these suspicions with the aid of tests. This examination detects the fault or makes it necessary to find out more information, in which case the procedure begins anew.

4. FUNCTIONING PRINCIPLES OF THE INFERENCE ENGINE

Because of the different procedures involved in diagnosis with empirical and causal knowledge and the benefits of modularly constructed software, two inference systems for the processing of the different knowledge types are demanded. As the two procedures should complement one another, interfaces and possible interactions between the two systems must be taken into account [3].

As far as empirical knowledge is concerned, the symptom oriented inference part takes care of the requirement to obtain measurements from the machine tool or gain other information required for diagnosis. First a little effort is applied and if this does not yield sufficient information for diagnosis or if the suspicion for some hypothesis is rising then the user is asked to pay more effort for extracting the required information from the machine. The empirical rules contained in the modules are processed in a forward-chaining manner. In order to achieve this, simple control of the system behaviour by the knowledge engineer is ensured because the processing of the rules is done locally just for those modules in current consideration. A global backward-chained processing of the rules is done each time before the user is asked to input information. With this processing, rules which conclude the required information can be found even in other modules.

The inference part, which processes the causal knowledge, consists in the main of a method for simulating the correct behaviour of the machine tool, utilising the functional description in the model and of methods for localising a fault if discrepancies between the simulated and the observed behaviour are detected. Therefore the fault localisation methods of technical diagnosis are implemented as strategies in the inference engine. These are, for example, the signal path examination, the step-by-step refinement or the functional module inspection which regards all input and output values of a module and their functional dependencies. The two inference parts must interact and exchange information for combining their problem solving capabilities. The criteria for the switch-over of the two inference parts is the state of the diagnosis which is influenced by the two examination strategies which man also uses (Fig. 5). The general view uses empirical knowledge and heuristic-based strategies implemented in the symptom oriented inference part whereas the detailed inspection is performed by the causal model driven inference part.

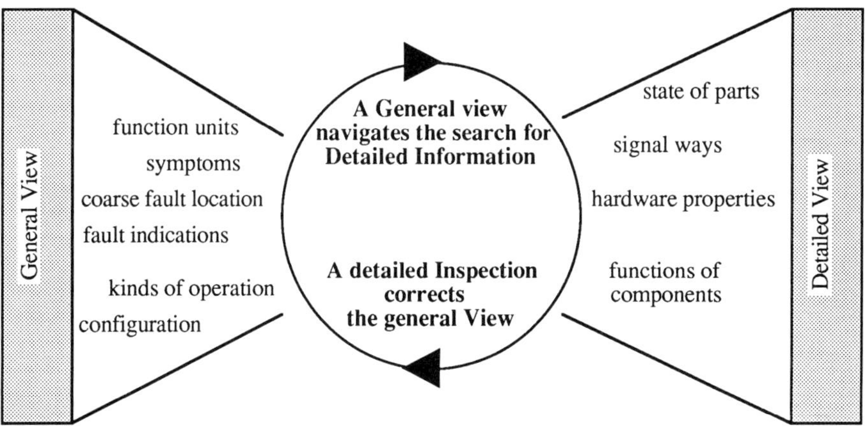

Figure 5 Control of Diagnosis through Different levels of View.

The state of the diagnosis is thereby represented as the actual state of the knowledge base. The knowledge description is the interface where information and control are exchanged by

- the hypotheses (activated components and respective function modules),
- the structuring of component and function modules and
- the input and output variables of component and function modules.

5. AN EXAMPLE

A simple example will illustrate the fundamental structure proposed before. It consists of a support which is driven by a motor via a spindle and a nut (Fig. 6). The movement to the left and to the right side is limited with cams and switches. Due to the wiring the support oscillates between the left and right position as shown in the state diagram (Fig. 7). The state diagram gives the function of this system in its entirety. This function is refined in four subfunctions (Fig. 8). Here you can see the connections between functions. A further refinement of the functions and the cross-reference to the components is shown in Fig. 9. At the function side the refinement forms the global function "oscillating support" until the primary functions like "amplification" are proposed. These primary functions give the reference to the components. One can notice that there is a different aggregation on the component and on the function side.

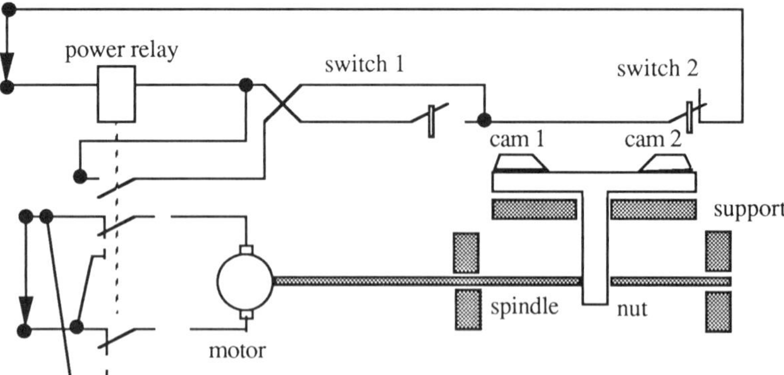

Figure 6 Example.

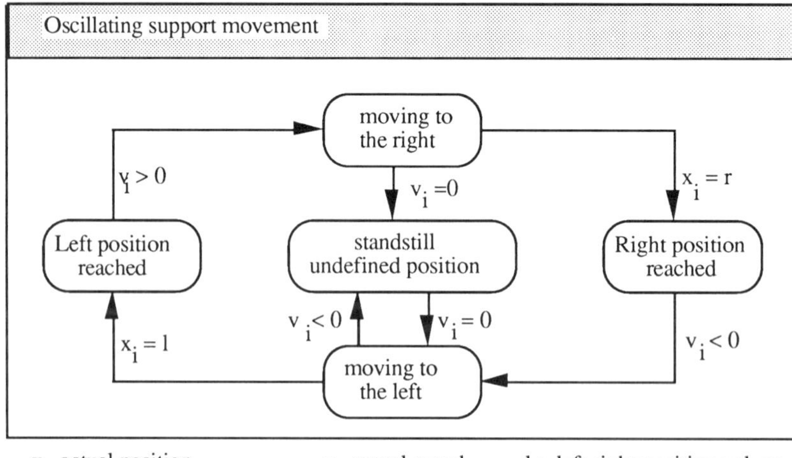

x_i actual position v_i actual speed l,r left right position values

Figure 7 State diagram.

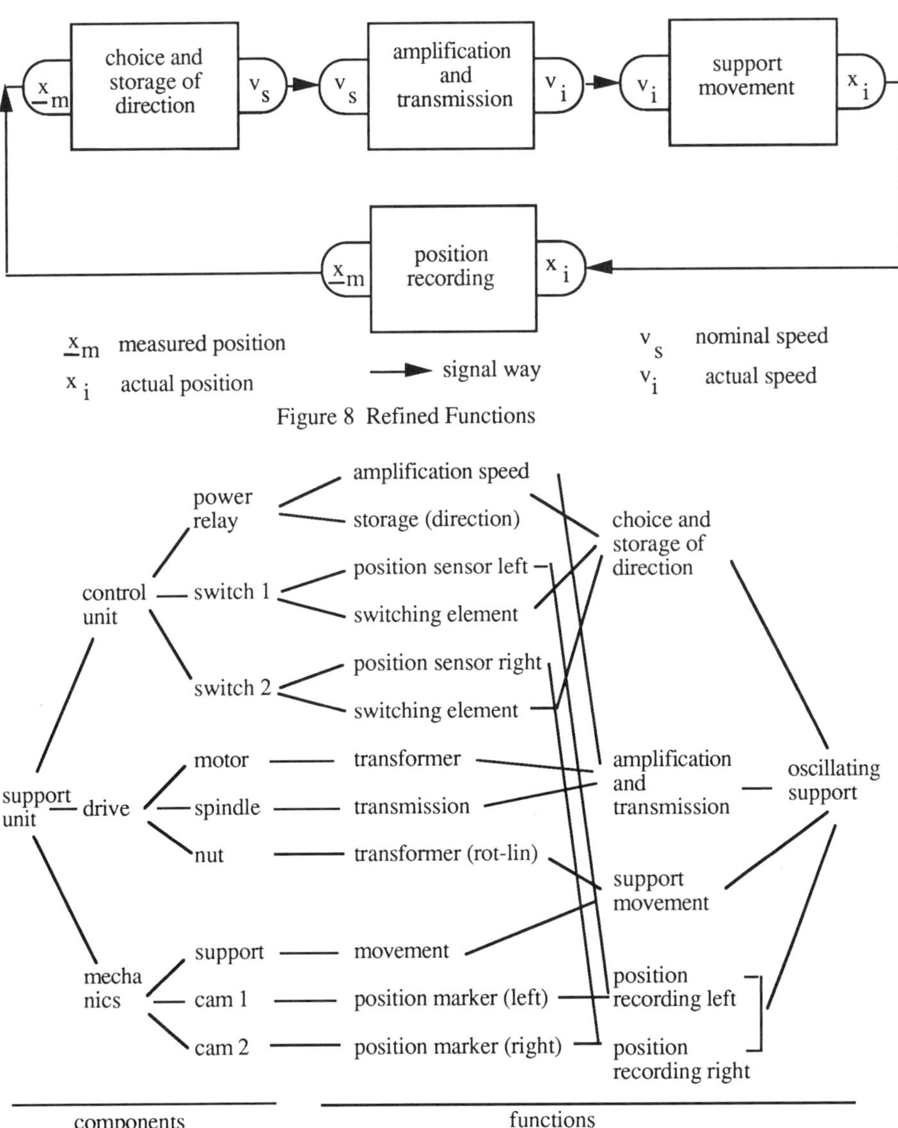

Figure 8 Refined Functions

Figure 9 Components and Functions

The symptoms and the suspicions of functions and components are illustrated in Fig. 10. The symptoms can be refined similar to the functions. Starting from the obvious symptom "oscillation" around left position. This symptom is refined and changes from a global to specific symptoms. If we have no success in defining the failure by following the symptoms the path still remains along the connections between functions or components. As you can see we are able to find the failures either via symptoms or the structure and behaviour.

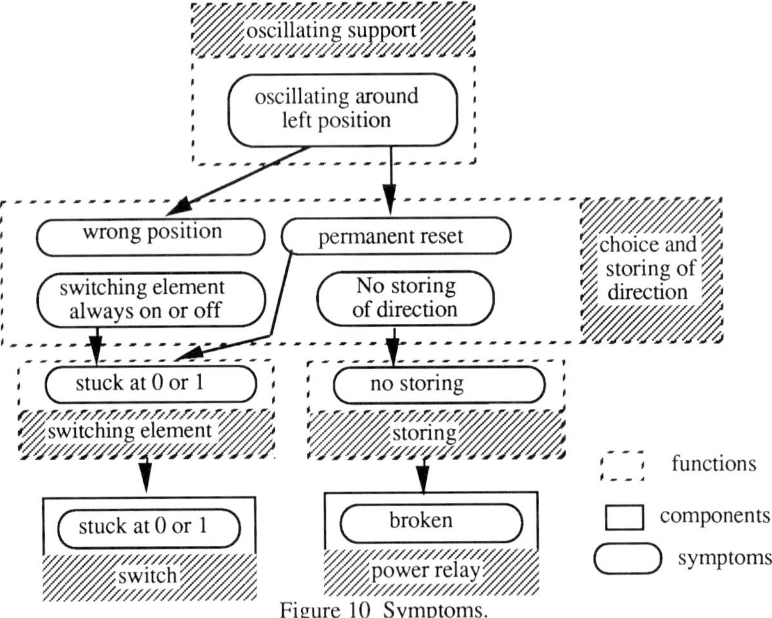

Figure 10 Symptoms.

6. THE EXPERT SYSTEM SHELL DESIS

DESIS was developed from a consideration of the requirements presented above. Further requirements for the development were a high degree of portability and a high processing speed. Both criteria were fulfilled with the implementation language COOL [4]. COOL runs on most computers under the UNIX operating system, under VAX/VMS and also, with limitations under MS-DOS. The average response time does not exceed a few seconds and is almost independent of the size of the knowledge base. Neither COOL nor DESIS limit the possible size of a knowledge base and with neat structuring as described above even large knowledge bases (500 modules, 1000 rules) can be handled easily with respect to their maintenance and service.

7. SUMMARY

The diagnosis of machine tool faults with the aid of expert systems requires a model-based approach. The essential reasons therefore are, the number of failures, the availability of knowledge depending on the life-phases of a machine tool and the fact that a human expert uses models, too. A knowledge base structure consisting of symptoms, components, functions and tests fulfils the requirements. At the same time, this can be the basis for a problem adapted expert system shell.

REFERENCES

[1] Davis, R. and Hamscher,W., "Model-Based Reasoning: Trouble-Shooting", in: Shrobe, H.E., (ed.), Exploring Artificial Intelligence (Morgan Kaufmann, San Mateo, California USA, pp. 297-346, (1988)

[2] Storr, A. and Hardtner, M., "Model-Based Expert Systems for the Diagnosis at Machine Tools", in: Proceedings of the 21st International Symposium on Automative Technology and

Automation, Wiesbaden (FRG) 6th-10th, Volume III, pp. 2381-2395, November (1989)

[3] Storr, A. and Wiedmann, H., "DESIS - Eine Expertensystemshell fur die Technische Diagnose", in: CIM MANAGEMENT, 4 (1990), in print.

[4] Hanakata, K., COOL Reference Manual, in print.

Industrial Applications of Artificial Intelligence
J.L. Alty and L.I. Mikulich (Editors)
Elsevier Science Publishers B.V. (North-Holland)

SECTION 6: DECISION MAKING SYSTEMS: ALGORITHMS AND PROCEDURES

BAYES INFERENCE AND DECISION MAKING IN ARTIFICIAL INTELLIGENCE SYSTEMS

V.I.GORODETSKY
(USSR)

1. INTRODUCTION

A new approach is discussed to algorithmization of decision-making models for solving problems such as recognition of situations, approximate inference, inference control etc., when the recognition model of an random binary sequence with a given probability distribution is an adequate means of problem model representation. A constructive method is proposed to represent information about the distribution in the form of a partially ordered set of normalized Boolean algebra (NBA) generators, on which basis an algorithm of the Bayes inference in the formalism of an attribute PDA-accepter is constructed.

2. MATHEMATICAL MODEL

By a partially defined discrete sequence (string) is meant a sequence of symbols $\hat{X}=<\hat{x}_1,\hat{x}_2,\ldots,\hat{x}_n$ (for chain $\hat{x}_1\hat{x}_2\ldots\hat{x}_n$), wherein each element $\hat{x}_i$ takes values of the alphabet $\{1,0,*\}$ which are interpreted in terms of content as "true", "false" and "unknown", respectively. Another variant of writing is one which is obtained from $\hat{X}$ by removal of symbols * and substitution of symbol x_i for symbol $\hat{x}_i$ in the i-th position, if $\hat{x}_i=1$ and x_i for $\hat{x}_i=0$. The last variant will be called the short writing.

Let $P(\hat{X})$ be a distribution function for $\hat{X}$ strings. The principal question is that of a constructive means for specifying $P(\hat{x})$ at great values of n. By a specifying means are meant a data model and a probability computation algorithm for any $\hat{X}$ string realization. Further, for the purpose of distinguishing between the string $\hat{X}$ (as an ordered sequence of argument places) and its realization (as an ordered sequence of argument values) the latter will be designated as $\tilde{X}$.

It is known that the probability model of the arbitrary sequence $\hat{X}$ can be structured in terms of NBA with the norm satisfying the probability-theory axioms. In this algebra $\tilde{X}$

realization act as basic-set elements, the relationship "string - substring" as a relationship and realization probabilities as a norm.

In terms of NBA, the problem of specifying the model is reduced to the means of specifying NBA effectively.

Let us direct our attention to the concept of the *generator system*, traditional for algebraic structures. We define it for NBA as a subset of pairs $<\tilde{X}_1, p(\tilde{X}_i)$, which knowledge enables one to calculate unambiguously the probability of any realization of the arbitrary sequence $\hat{X}$. To construct the NBA generator system, we introduce the concept of the *rigorous component dependence of the string* $\hat{X}$. Let $\tilde{X}=\tilde{x}_{i_1}\tilde{x}_{i_2}\ldots\tilde{x}_{i_k}$ be a certain random realization of the string in the short form and its probability is equal to $P(\tilde{X})$. We divide arbitrarily a set of symbols in $\tilde{X}$ into two subsets and form two substrings $\tilde{X}_1$ and $\tilde{X}_2$ of them, with their symbols arranged in the increasing order of indices, and designate their probabilities by symbols $P(\tilde{X}_1)$ and $P(\tilde{X}_2)$, respectively. Regarding $\tilde{X}$ realization, we will say that its components are rigorously dependent, if for any variant of $\tilde{X}$ division into $\tilde{X}_1$ and $\tilde{X}_2$ the condition $P(\tilde{X})\neq P(\tilde{X}_1)\cdot P(\tilde{X}_2)$ is provided.

Let $\hat{X}=\hat{x}_{i_1}\hat{x}_{i_2}\ldots\hat{x}_{i_r}$ be a certain substring of argument places with numbers $i_1, i_2, \ldots, i_r$ $(i_1<i_2<\ldots<i_r)$, and $\{\tilde{X}_1, \tilde{X}_2, \ldots, \tilde{X}_k\}$ a set of all kinds of unrepeated realizations of this substring which are obtained through designation of argument places by symbols from subsets $\{x_i, \bar{x}_i\}$ for all $i\leq\{i_1, i_2, \ldots, i_r\}$. It turns out that it is sufficient to include into the NBA generator set only one of such realizations together with all its substrings belonging to the lower cone of the NBA structure.

As a result, we will obtain such a description of the NBA generator set structure, which specifies the mathematical model of a partially defined arbitrary binary sequence: it contains all positive realizations of maximum-length strings with rigorously dependent components and all rigorously less in the NBA order.

Thus, the source information for $P(\tilde{X})$ probability computation is a set of pairs $<X_i, P(X_i)>$ belonging to the family of generators. The scheme of $P(\tilde{X})$ computation in the standard form can be presented as follows:

$$p_1=P(\tilde{x}_1),\ P_{k+1}=P_k\cdot P(\hat{x}_{k+1}/\tilde{x}_1\tilde{x}_2\ldots\tilde{x}_k),\ k=1,2,\ldots,n-1, \quad P(\tilde{X})=p_n. \tag{1}$$

The first element of the scheme is computed trivially, since the generator set includes the element $<x_1, P(x_1)>$.

Let us assume that there is an algorithm for changing the distribution generator system $P(\hat{X}_k/\tilde{x}_1\tilde{x}_2...\tilde{x}_{k-1})$ to $P(\hat{X}_{k+1}/\tilde{x}_1\tilde{x}_2...\tilde{x}_k)$, where $\hat{X}_k = <\hat{x}_k, \hat{x}_{k+1}, ..., \hat{x}_n>$, $\hat{X}_{k+1} = <\hat{x}_{k+1}x_{k+2}...x_n>$ for any $k=1(1)n-1$ and the value of p_k is known from eqn.(1).Then the generator set $P(\hat{X}_{k+1}/\tilde{x}_1\tilde{x}_2...\tilde{x}_k)$ has a pair $<x_{k+1}, P(x_{k+1}/\tilde{x}_1\tilde{x}_2...\tilde{x}_k)$, therefore the second multiplier in recurrent scheme (1) can be computed from the formula:

$$P(\tilde{x}_{k+1}/\tilde{x}_1\tilde{x}_2...\tilde{x}_k) = \begin{cases} P(x_{k+1}/\tilde{x}_1\tilde{x}_2...\tilde{x}_k), & \text{if } \tilde{x}_{k+1}=x_{k+1}; \\ 1-P(x_{k+1}/\tilde{x}_1\tilde{x}_2...\tilde{x}_k), & \text{if } \tilde{x}_{k+1}=\overline{x}_{k+1} \\ 1, & \text{if } \tilde{x}_{k+1}=*. \end{cases} \quad (2)$$

In the end, the computation of $P(\tilde{X})$ is reduced to computations with the use of (1) and conversion of sets of conditional-distribution generations generators.

The presentation of the discrete random sequence model in the form of the algorithm realizing the above operations in terms of NBA requires selection of particular data structures to present information and particular algorithm specification means.

An analysis of the model proposed shows that a convenient means for its algorithmization is a calculus in the form of the attribute translation context-free grammar which generates binary random sequences with $P(\hat{X})$ distribution. For such information presentation the algorithm of computing the random string realization probability is reduced to the procedure of establishing the string inferability, which can be realized in terms of attribute-and-syntactic analysis on the basis of the attribute PDA-accepter. The whole proposed procedure is essentially the string a posteriori probability inference according to the scheme determined by Bayes formula. It is because of this that the procedure outlined above was called the Bayes inference.

3. RECOGNITION OF SITUATIONS

By a situation is meant a state of a complex system. The content of this term can be illustrated by such examples as "emergency situation", "conflict situation". The mathematical model of a situation is characterized by a larger dimension of the alphabet of source situation statements, unpredictability of the situation information composition etc.

Models known from the recognition theory such as entity description models, teaching models and classification methods have no appropriate means for solving situation recognition problems. The apparatus of arbitrary discrete sequences proves to be an adequate means of describing situations and their classification processes.

Let $\Omega=\{\omega_1,\omega_2,\ldots\omega_m\}$ be a set of classes of situations, each of them having the a priori probability $p(\omega_k)$, $\omega_k\in\Omega$, while the situation class ω_k itself is characterized by the distribution of probabilities $P(\hat{X}/\omega_k)$, where $\hat{X}$ is a cortege of statements from the given set.

Then for some $\tilde{X}$ realization the probability of the class ω_k will be

$$P(\omega/\tilde{X})=p(\omega)\cdot P(\tilde{X}/\omega)/\left[\sum_{j=1}^{m} p(\omega_j)\cdot P(\tilde{X}/\omega_j)\right] \qquad (3)$$

To perform computations with the use of eqn.(3), one should known how to compute the values of $P(\tilde{X}/\omega_j)$. This means that the given problem is reduced to that which solution algorithm is described in par.2.

4. APPROXIMATE INFERENCE

Traditionally, the formal model of approximate inference is constructed on the basis of inference schemes with some confidence measures assigned to inference formulae and rules. These measures can be probability-treated.

Let us consider the reasoning scheme based on the use of the "modus ponens" rule: $(\alpha)P$, (β) $(R\supset Q)$ $\vdash$ $(\gamma)Q$, where α is the probability of statement R being true, β the probability of R involving Q and γ the probability of the final statement being true.

We note that although α,β and γ have a probability sense, the basis of their probability nature is different, therefore when constructing plausible reasoning schemes, one should use different procedures.

The central problem of the approximate inference is the construction of an algorithm which makes it possible to find γ from α and β for the "modus ponens" inference scheme. The schemes known from the literature, even though they do not declare it explicitly, are based by default on the following assumptions:

1. Independence of events R and Q in the knowledge model.

2. Disregard probability relations for a set of atomic formulae of the language for the description of the application area.

Such relations really exist and the structure for a set of these relations is specific for each type of the application-area states.

Let $R_1,R_2,...,R_m$ be a set of atomic formulae of the language for the description of the application area $\breve{R}_i \in \{R_i, R_i\}$ and $G_1,G_2,...,G_r$ a set of neological axioms (rule-knowledge base) of the application area, each axiom being of the form:

$$G_k=F_i \supset Q_j, \text{ where } F_i=\&\breve{R}_k,\ Q_j \in \{\breve{R}_1,\breve{R}_2,...,\breve{R}_m\}\ k \in I_i \tag{4}$$

In the construction of a knowledge base a set of formulae of the form $(\beta_k)(F_i \supset Q_j)$ is generally present as source information. In the probability structure (generator set) this information should be taken into account as a pair $<(F_i \& Q_j),\ P(F_i \& Q_j)>$. This means, that one should be able to find the probability $P(F\&Q_j)$ from $\alpha_i=P(F_i)$ and $\beta_{ij}=P(F \supset Q_J)$. The corresponding formula is of the form:

$$P(F_i \& Q_j) = p(F)-1+\beta_{ij} \tag{5}$$

Thus the information on the application-area state class is reduced to the probability model based on the NBA generator system, which has been already considered.

The second principal point in connection with algorithmization of the approximate inference scheme is the means of the generator system conversion as information of the form $p_a(R_i)=\alpha_i$ arrives. This problem is reduced to redefining probabilities $p(R_i\&F)$, $p(F)$ and $p(R_i)$ which in a new distribution have the sense of such conditional probabilities as $p(R_i\&F/p_a(R_i)=\alpha_i)$, $p(F/p_a(R_i)=\alpha_i)$ and α_i, respectively. It can be shown, that these conditional probabilities may be computed from the formulae:

$$p(R_i\&F/p_a(R_i)=\alpha_i)=p(R_i\&F)*\alpha_i/p(R_i), \tag{6}$$

$$p(\bar{R}_i\&F/p_a(R_i)=\alpha_i)=(p(F)-p(R_i\&F)*(1-\alpha_i)/(1-p(R_i)), \tag{7}$$

$$p(F/p(R_i)=\alpha_i)=p(R_i\&F/p_a(R_i)=\alpha_i)+p(\bar{R}_i\&F/p_a(R_i)=\alpha_i) \tag{8}$$

Thus, the approximate inference scheme turns out to be similar to that of situation recognition which is described in par.3.

5. INFERENCE CONTROL IN EXPERT SYSTEMS

Methods and algorithms of inference control comprise a subject of particular interest in research of expert systems (ES). Inference control means specialization of the inference strategy according to the local situation in the inference process. The inference control process constitutes recognition of local situations and selection of the next inference step, depending on the result. This scheme reduces the complex inference search procedure to a sequence of schemes, not nearly so complex as the former procedure. One can see from this that the process of decision making at the next step of inference control has local situation recognition as the main operation. The basic features of the problem which presents itself here are similar to those considered in par.3 for the problem of situation recognition.

This means that the inference-control problem in ES can be formalized in terms of the model described in par.2.

6. CONCLUSION

The key point of the given work is the model of the random binary string distribution and attribute PDA-accepter for computing the probability of a particular string realization. These results, even though they apparently refer to algorithmization of theory problems, are sufficiently widely used in the field of expert systems.

Industrial Applications of Artificial Intelligence
J.L. Alty and L.I. Mikulich (Editors)
Elsevier Science Publishers B.V. (North-Holland)

ON THE DEDUCTIVE APPROACH TO THE PROJECTING OF TECHNOLOGICAL PROCESSES IN MECHANICAL MANUFACTURING

N. K. Zamov and P. V. Pshenichny

Department of Applied Mathematics
Kazan State University
Kazan, USSR

System "Synthesis" [1], [2], [3] is applied to be automatic solution of so-called technological problems. The general idea of the construction of the system is a decomposition of the solved problem into the subproblems that in turn can be reduced to the subproblems. Rules of decomposition of each non-elementary action form a technological model of problem oriented field (TMF). Solution of the problem is a sequence of elementary actions, which are produced by the "Synthesis" on the base of the rules of TMF. User can select the several types of decomposition: complicated action can be produced from sub-activities by concatenation, simple and tabular unification, considering the variants and selection. At the unification of the actions one takes additional information, describing some requirements on the order of actions execution (contexts) into account. The process of searching the solutions of technological problems is based on the ideas of logical programming. When solving the problems one uses technological knowledge that describes problem oriented field (within formal system), and concrete facts describing a specific problem (in the tabular form).

Formally TMF should contain:
- a set of basic tables describing a set of individuals of the technological process and relations between the individuals (for instance, tables with the list of processed surfaces, elements of equipment, mutual disposition of surfaces, dimensional relations etc.);
- a set of expressions defining the derivative tables from basic ones; traditional operations under the tables (unification, intersection, cutting out etc.) are permitted;
- a set of the programs realizing elementary actions of the problem oriented fields described (external functions);
- a set of the technological rules.

"Synthesis" has a specific form of the technological knowledge, i.e. rules of the type "before execution of action A1 one must execute the action A2". Each rule of this type is defined by the following formula

k(X) = A2 bef A1

and in future we will call this as a context rule. The base of the TMF is the set of technological rules, describing non-elementary actions. Each rule is of the type

a(X) = A(X1), where

a(X) is the name of the non-elementary action, A(X1) is a defining expression, X1 is a sublist of the list X.

Let us demonstrate an approach described in the following examples. In each example names of actions start with the letter 'a', names of tables start with the letter 't', names of contexts - with the letter 'k'.
First we describe the technology of the problem of sorting the list of numbers stored in the table tab(X). We can non-strictly formulate the technology in the following way: print all the elements of the table tab(X), but before printing the elements X, print all the elements, less than X. Formally this technology consists of two rules:

1) a_sort = (tab(X) & a_print(X)) & k(X);
2) k(X) = ((tab(Y) & (X>Y)) & a_print(Y)) bef a_print(X).

The first rule shows that action a_sort is reduced to the action (tab(X) & a_print(X)) in context k(X). Action (tab(X) & a_print(X)) is equal to action a_print(X) executed for each element of the table tab(X). Action a_print(X) is elementary for this problem oriented field and is simply printing the value X. Context rule k(X) shows that before the action a_print(X) it is necessary to execute the action (tab(Y) & (X>Y)) & a_print(Y)). It means that we should execute the action a_print(Y) for each element of the table (tab(Y) & (X>Y)) which consists of the elements of the table tab(Y), less than X.

Another example describes the technology of projecting of the sequence of the actions in mechanical working of wells. We define a well as a hole in a plain part, having bottom and vertical walls. Walls of the well form its contour. On the bottom of the well there can be another well, which we will call the step, etc. TMF describes the projecting rules which permit to select the sequence of processing of the surfaces depending on their mutual disposition, choice of datum surfaces, on dimensions, requirements for tolerance and grade of fit, and also project the sequence of processing of the complicated surfaces. During processing the well is divided into subwells. Subwell is a part of the well within horizontal plains. Subwells can have several steps or can represent a part of one step. In the definition of the depth of the subwell it is necessary to take into consideration that it can not exceed the diameter of cutter and 50 mm, and depth of the subwell divided by the thickness of the base can not exceed 2. The sequence of operations consists of recursively arranged sequences of the following actions: selecting the next subwell, milling the contours of its steps, milling its base. This technique can be described in the language of the "Synthesis" system in the following way:

1) a_well(X) = t_numb(X,N) V a_subwells(X,0,N)

This rule shows that the processing of the well X is reduced to the milling of all of its subwells with numbers from 0 to N. Number N is defined from the table t_numb(X,N). This table is automatically constructed from the tables describing the dimentions of the well and its subwells and from the tables of the characteristics of the tools.

2) a_subwells(X,N1,N2) = (N1=N2) & a_empty V not(N1=N2 &
(t_seq_step(X,N1,NS1) V (t_subwell(X,NS1,N) V
(a_cut_subwell(X,NS1,N) * a_subwells(X,N,N2))))

This rule shows that the processing of the wells with numbers from N1 to N2 starts from checking the coincidence of N1 and N2. In the case of N1=N2, the removing process is not required. Otherwise the step NS1 after N1 should be defined by the table t_seq_step(X,N1,N2). The the number N of the next subwell is defined by the table t_subwell(X,NS1,N) and the actions are executed i.e. milling the subwell with number N, starting with N to N2.

3) a_cut_subwell(X,N1,N2) = a_cut_all_contours(X,N1,N2) * a_cut_base(X,N2)

This rule shows that processing of the subwell from the step N1 to the step N2 is reduced to the milling of the contours of all the steps from N1 to N2 and then milling of the base of N2.

4) a_cut_all_contours(X,N1,N2) = (t_inter(X,N1,M,N2) & a_cut_contour((X,M)
& k1(X,N1,M,N2)

This rule shows that milling of the contours with numbers from N1 to N2 is reduced to the milling of each contour with number M within N1 and N2, taking the context k1 into consideration. Number M is obtained from the table t_inter(X,N1,M,N2).

5) k1(X,N1,M,N2) = (t_inter(X,N1,M,N2) & t_seq_step(X,M1,M)
& a_cut_contour(X,M1)) bef a_cut_contour(X,M)

This context rule shows that before the action a_cut_contour(X,M) it is necessary to execute the action a_cut_contour(X,M1) for each step with number M1 whose value is located within N1 and N2 and the preceding step M.

Finally let us consider the plate with a thickness of 60 mm. It is necessary to cut out the well with the first step of 30 mm. deep, second of 5mm. deep, and third of 22 mm. deep. For such a well "Synthesis" should build the following sequence of processing:

- cut the contour of step 1 to a depth of 30 mm.
- cut the contour of step 2 to a depth of 5 mm.
- cut the base of step 2
- cut the contour of subwell 1 of step 3 to a depth of 16 mm.
- cut the base of subwell 1 of step 3
- cut the contour of subwell 2 of step 3 to a depth of 6 mm.
- cut the base of subwell 2 of step 3

REFERENCES

[1] Mikhailov V. Ju., "Solving Problems on Technological Models", Lecture Notes in Computer Science, (1987), 278, pp. 314 - 317.

[2] Zamov, N.K., and Mikhailov V. Ju., "Logical Means for the Automated Solution of Technological Tasks", (In Russian), Proc. Vsesoyuznoii Konf. po Prikladnoy Logike, Novosibirsk, (1985), pp 79 - 81.

[3] Mikhailov, V. Ju., "Solving Techological Tasks through Modelling", (In Russian), Izvestii Vuzov, Matematika, Kazan, (1988), pp. 44 - 54.

Industrial Applications of Artificial Intelligence
J.L. Alty and L.I. Mikulich (Editors)
Elsevier Science Publishers B.V. (North-Holland)
1991 IFIP

LEARNING A QUALITATIVE MODEL OF A COMPLEX SYSTEM VIA DATA ANALYSIS

D.POMOROSKI*, M. STAROSWIEKI*, and M. BARBOUCHA

*Centre d'Automatique de Lille,
Universite des Sciences et Techniques de Lille,
Flandres Artois,
59 655 Villeneuve d'Ascq Cedex,
France.

Ecole Superieure de Technologie,
Route d'El Jadida,
Oasis Casablanca,
Maroc.

ABSTRACT : The contingency table of X and Y, is used to construct rules under the form : $X=\alpha \implies Y \in B_{\sigma}(\alpha)$. According to the nature of the data (ordered or not ordered), the simplification of these rules is performed, via the clustering of certain modalities. Hierarchical and dynamic programming approaches are used.

Keywords : Learning, Data Analysis, Qualitative Model.

1. INTRODUCTION

A great number of complex industrial systems produce goods whose quality is very sensitive to variations in some production parameters. It is often the case that no model exists which relates the "quality variables" to the "production variables". However, the existence of such models would be very advantageous for process supervision. Knowledge based models can be constructed using the experience of process operators, and used for diagnosis purposes. Another approach leads to the use of data analysis methods in order to construct statistical models, since the variables which define the product's quality and the operation parameters can often be evaluated [10]. This is a learning situation, in which knowledge acquisition (model building) is made through the consideration of a set of examples (the data) [19] [14] [13]. In such a context, a precise numerical model has no meaning, and the search for a qualitative model seems to be a reasonable approach.

We use results from the structural analysis of systems by means of information theory [11] [17] [15] in order to construct a model via rule generation. We propose some algorithms for rule simplification, in both the cases where the explanatory variables take their values in non ordered as well as in ordered sets.

2. MODEL CONSTRUCTION BY RULES GENERATION

2.1. The data

The whole set of the variables describing the system is divided into two distinct parts : the set Y of variables to explain, and the set X of explanatory variables. We suppose that the joint probabilities of X and Y can be correctly evaluated, so that the analyst can construct, from the data's initial table, a contingency table $[P_{ij}]$:

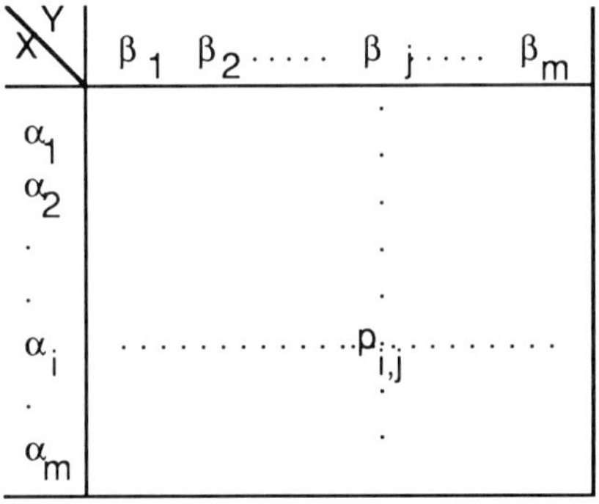

X \ Y	β_1	β_2	β_j	β_m
α_1			.	
α_2			.	
.			.	
.			.	
α_i	....	....	$p_{i,j}$	....
.			.	
α_m			.	

Where $Y = (y_1, y_2, ..., y_l)^T$ the vector of variables to explain

$X = (x_1, x_2, ..., x_p)^T$ the vector of explanatory variables

$M_X = \{ \alpha_i \; ; \; 1 \leq i \leq n \}$ the set of X's Modalities

$M_Y = \{ \beta_j \; ; \; 1 \leq j \leq m \}$ the set of Y's Modalities

P_{ij} $(1 \leq i \leq n \; ; \; 1 \leq j \leq m)$: the joint probability of α_i and β_j

2.2.Explicability

Several indices can be used to measure the explicability of certain variables (variables to explain) by means of other variables (explanatory or easily observed variables).

Using concepts from information theory, the intensity of the link between two vectorial variables X and Y can be measured by means of the conditional entropy : [2] [18] (or some generalizations [1] [17]).

$$H(Y/X) = H(X,Y) - H(X) = -\sum_{ij} P_{ij} \, \mathrm{Log} \, P_{ij} + \sum_{i} P_i \log P_i$$

However, simpler models could be obtained by considering only a subset S of the explanatory variables X. Based on H(Y/X) and H(Y/S) two explicability indexes are used. They express the feasibility of the modelisation problem and the possibility to obtain (or not) simpler models [17] [16].

2.3. Atomic Model

Each row of the contingency table $[P_{ij}]$ gives rise to a rule of the form :

$$X=\alpha \implies Y \in B_\sigma(\alpha)$$

where $B_\sigma(\alpha)$ is a subset of M_y with σ elements.

A probability distribution $R_\sigma(\alpha)$ is associated with $B_\sigma(\alpha)$ According to the type of the extracted rules, $R_\sigma(\alpha)$ is (or not) the uniform distribution.

For each rule (each couple $[\alpha, B_\sigma(\alpha)]$) a truth coefficient and an efficiency coefficient can be defined [3] [4].

2.4. Simplification of the Model

In the atomic model, the number of the rules is equal to the cardinal number of the set M_X (assuming that each row generates a rule with a satisfactory truth coefficient). When this number is important, simplification methods are welcome. Such methods rely generally on row aggregation algorithms applied to the set of the atomic rules. It can be showed that aggregation increases the truth but decreases the efficiency of the resulting rules [3].

3. CLUSTERING OF M_X AND MODEL SIMPLIFICATION

Let us suppose that a set A of rows have been aggregated. The non atomic corresponding rule is expressed in the form :

$$X \in A \Longrightarrow Y \in B_\sigma(A)$$

Such a rule expresses a (local) simplification of the model if one has :

$$X \in A \Longleftrightarrow S \in A_S$$

where S is a sub-vector of X.

So the search for a simpler model can be expressed as a clustering problem of M_X. Our approach is then the following : for given k ($k \in \{1,...,n\}$) we search for the best k-rules model (in the sense of modelisability). The clustering problem of M_X will receive different solutions when M_X is, or not, an ordered set.

3.1. Non Ordered M_X

Clustering procedures are based on exhaustive search, metric algorithms [9], hierarchical algorithms [8] [7] [12] and transfer algorithms [6].

Exhaustive search is often not feasible, taking into account the dimensions of the problems.

A metric formulation has no informational interpretation for our problem. On another hand, no optimality property can be proved using hierarchical clustering. We propose to use a group transfer algorithm based on the iterative application of two compound operators. Let IP_k be the set of the partitions of M_X into k classes. We define :

$$s : IP_k \dashrightarrow IP_{k+1} \quad \text{a splitting operator}$$
$$m : IP_k \dashrightarrow IP_{k-1} \quad \text{a merging operator}$$

A good choice of the two operators s and m leads to satisfy the two properties :

$$H[Y/ s \circ m (P_k)] \leq H(Y/P_k)$$
$$H[Y/ m \circ s (P_k)] \leq H(Y/P_k)$$

where P_k is an element of IP_k

Taking into account the contraction property and the fact that H(Y/S) is minored on IP_k the iterative application of the two compound operators " m o s " and " s o m " converges towards a k classes partition which is a local optimum.

3.2. Ordered M_X

In the case where M_X is ordered, the constraints introduced by this order relation have to be taken into account. We will first consider the case p=l where a single explanatory variable is subject to a total order relation, and then the case p>l of several explanatory variables.

3.2.1. One Explanatory Variable

The set of the modalities M_X is considered as a subset of $\Re$ and thus is ordered by the total order $\leq$. In this case, the transfer algorithm of section 3.1 applies subject to slight modification : only consecutive modalities of X can be merged: in the same way, the splitting operator must produce two convex subsets of the split set.

However, optimization approaches can be used in this case. We propose a dynamic programming algorithm which allows a direct search of the k-1 separators between the k classes. In fact, the optimality principle can be used, due to the additive nature of the entropic function, and dynamic programming easily handles the order constraints:

We consider :

$S \quad := (s_1, s_2, .. , s_{k-1})$ the (k-1) separators of the k classes
A(S) : = discretisation of M_X into k classes
$A_h \quad := \{ X_i / s_{h-1} \leq \alpha_i < s_h \}$, h=l, . . . ,k
s_o ,s_k are respectively the inferior and the superior limits of M_X.

The order constraint on the (k-l) separators is:

$$s_0 < s_1 < s_2 < ....< s_{k-1} < s_k ,$$

where s_0 and s_k are constants.

Graphically, we obtain :

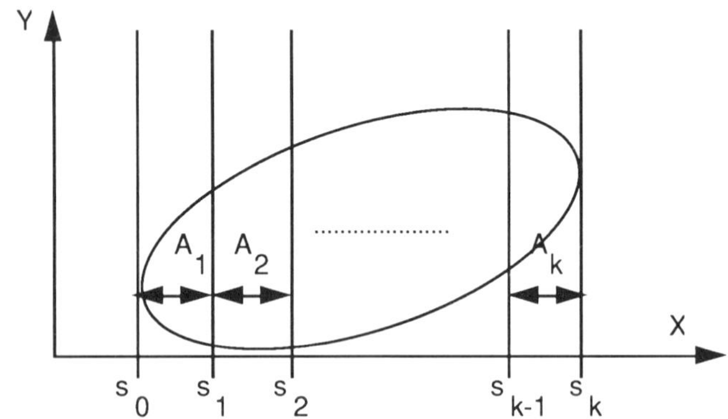

By definition :

$$H(Y/A(S)) = \sum_{i=1}^{k} p(A_i) \,.\, H(Y/X \in A_i)$$

According to the optimality principle :

$$H_k(s_0, s_k) = P(A_1) \,.\, H(Y/X \in A_1) + H^*_{k-1}(s_1, s_k)$$

where $H_k(s_0,s_k)$ is the conditional entropy of Y by X, with a partition of the segment $[s_0, s_k]$ into k classes .

$p(A_1) \,.\, H(Y/X \in A_1)$ is a function of s_1, as well as $H^*_{k-1}(s_1, s_k)$.

Then: $$H^*_k(s_0, s_k) = \min_{s_1 \in]s_0,s_k[} \left[p(A_1) \,.\, H(Y/X \in A_1) + H^*_{k-1}(s_1, s_k)\right].$$

in the same way :

$$H^*_{k-1}(s_1, s_k) = \min_{s_2 \in]s_1,s_k[} \left[p(A_2) \,.\, H(Y/X \in A_2) + H^*_{k-2}(s_2, s_k)\right].$$

....

....

$$H^*_{k-i}(s_i, s_k) = \min_{s_{i+1} \in]s_i,s_k[} \left[p(A_{i+1}) \,.\, H(Y/X \in A_{i+1}) + H^*_{k-(i+1)}(s_{i+1}, s_k)\right]. \quad (1)$$

$$H^*_1(s_{k-1}, s_k) = -p(A_k) \,.\, \sum_{j=1}^{m} p(\beta_j/X \in A_k) \,.\, \mathrm{Log}\, p(\beta_j/X \in A_k) \,.\forall\ s_{k-1} \in]s_0,s_k[\quad] \quad (2)$$

The expression (2) is the initialisation of this algorithm, and the expression (1) is the recurrence formula.

3.2.2. Several Explanatory Variables

In this case, we consider M_X as a subset of $\Re^p$ and only partial order is present on M_X. We propose an " axis by axis " method which allows successive application of the previous defined algorithms to each direction of the M_X space. Each variable x_i $(1 < i < p)$ gives rise to a k_i classes partition, and the global partition is taken as the intersection of all the "directional" partitions. The total number of rules in the model is thus given by the product of the k_i's.

4. CONCLUSION

Statistical process control is based on models learned from the analysis of the data issued from complex systems. The proposed approach allows us to obtain such models, and to search for their simplest form. In fact, the simpler the model, the easier is it's application in real time situations.

Our model construction approach makes no hypothesis on the nature of the explained and of the explanatory variables : quantitative or qualitative variables can be introduced. When variables are quantitative, the order constraint has to be considered in the algorithms.

Moreover, no hypothesis is made concerning the nature of the relationships which link the variables (linearity, ...). These two features are the result of the use of entropy based indexes ; they give to the proposed approach a great generality.

5. ACKNOWLEDGEMENT

Two authors wish to acknowledge a grant from La region Nord, Pas de Calais.

6. REFERENCES

[1] Abid Z., " Contribution a l'analyse Structurale par la Theorie des Demi-Treillis ", These de 3° cycle, Universite Claude Bernard, Lyon I, 1979.

[2] Ashby W.R., "Measuring the Internal Informational Exchange in a System", Cybernetica Namr, Belgique, Vol.8, 1965.

[3] Barboucha M., " Modelisation Structurale des Systemes Complexes - Extraction et Validation des Regles d'un Systeme Expert", These d'etat, Universite des Sciences et Techniques de Lille Flandres Artois, 26 Juin 1987.

[4] Barboucha M., StaroSwiecki M., Aygalinc P., " Generation des Regles a Partir d'un Tableau de Contingence ", 5° Journees Internationales : Analyse des Donnees et Informatique, INRIA, 29 Sept.-2 Oct. 1987, Versailles.

[5] Boudarel R., Delmas J., and Guichet P. "Commande Optimale des Processus " , Vol 3 : "Programmation Dynamique et ses Applications ", Techniques de l'Automatisme, Dunod, Paris, 1969.

[6] Bourton M. " Contribution a l'Analyse, le Traitement et la Reconnaissance des Formes Ponctuees. Application a la Classification de Couches Geologiques " These de Sciences Physique, Lille, 1975.

[7] Bruynooghe M.,"Classification Ascendante Hierarchique de Grands Ensembles de Donnees : un Algorithme Rapide Fonde sur la Construction des Voisinages Reductibles " Les Cahiers de l'Analyse des Donnees, 3, 1, 1978.

[8] Chifflet F., and Ralambondrainy H. " Optimisation d'une Classification Hierarchique " Rapport INRIA, Rocquencourt, France, 1980.

[9] Diday E. " Nouvelles Methodes et Nouveaux Concepts en Classification Automatique et Reconnaissance des Formes " Universite Paris VI, 4 dec. 1972.

[10] Diday E., Lemaire J., Pouget J., and Testu F. " Elements d'Analyse de Donnees " , Dunod, 1982.

[11] Dufour J., GillesG., and Foulard C. "Analyse Structurale et Partition des Systemes Dynamiques Complexes a l'aide de la Theorie de l'Information - Etude de l'Influence du Nombre de Classes " CRAS, tome 282, Mars 1975.

[12] Johnson S.C. " Hierarchical Clustering Schemes " Psychometrika, 32, pp. 241-254 (1967).

[13] Michalski R.S., and Stepp R.E. " Learning from Observation : Conceptual Clustering " Machine Learning : an Artificial Intelligence Approach, Tioga, Palo Alto, pp. 331-363, 1983.

[14] Perron M.C. "Learning Differential Diagnosis Rules from Numerical Knowledge " Extrait des Journees " Data Analysis, Learning Symbolic and Numeric Knowledge " , INRIA, pp. 425-432, 1989.

[15] Richetin M. "Analyse Structurale des Systemes Complexes en Vue d'une Commande Hierarchisee " These d'etat, Universite Paul Sabatier, Toulouse, No. d'ordre : 674, Juillet 1975.

[16] Sbai M. "Analyse Structurale des Systemes Complexes : Methodes d'Explication et de Partition " These de 3° cycle, Universite des Sciences et Techniques de Lille, No. d'ordre : 1087, 29 Sept. 1983.

[17] Toro Cordoba V.M. "Contribution a l'Analyse Structurale de Systemes Complexes a l'aide de l'Entropie et ses Generalisations " These de 3° cycle, Universite des Sciences et Techniques de Lille, No. d'ordre : 955, 8 mars 1982.

[18] Ventsel H. "Theorie des Probabilites " Editions de Moscou, 1973.

[19] Wille R. " Knowledge Acquisition by Methods of Formal Concept Analysis " extrait des journees " Data analysis, Learning Symbolic and Numeric Knowledge " , INRIA, pp. 365-380, 1989 .

Industrial Applications of Artificial Intelligence
J.L. Alty and L.I. Mikulich (Editors)
Elsevier Science Publishers B.V. (North-Holland)
1991 IFIP

ACCELERATED SPEECH RECOGNITION BASED ON CONTROL PRE-INFORMATION.

E. V. STRAKHOVITCH
Institute for Informatics and Automation,
USSR Academy of Sciences,
Leningrad,
The USSR.

ABSTRACT: This paper deals with a system of speech recognition which performs in a limited application domain. The levels of acoustics, syntax, semantics, and pragmatics are considered as a hierarchical system of bionical features. This approach reduces the time for information message recognition.

1. INTRODUCTION

The urgency of building speech recognition interfaces increases as society automates. The solution to this problem will enable a reduction in preliminary data preparation for computers and will approach the user's natural language. As distinct from "lively" (natural) speech, business prose always acts in a strict model situation. Rigid methods of expression economy, and other useful properties both for man and computer are inherent in business prose. Its vocabulary is limited without causing artificial restrictions for a human being, owing to the limited body of semantic relationships which need to be realised based on the application domain a-priori model.

According to linguists, the subordination tree of most Russian business prose sentences are projective or weakly projective. Essentially, this statement means that semantically close words are closely located in the text.

Psychologists have concluded that associative thinking mechanisms underly human language functioning and development and generalisation and abstraction processes ensure the formation of its grammatical structure. There are two types of associations in psychological studies. Firstly, 'external" associative links - the associations of contiguity where a given word evokes some component of an obvious situation which includes the named object; secondly, "internal" ones - those aroused by including a word in a definite category. All types of associations are factors reducing the reaction time. Associations serve as the principle of regrouping and initial vocabulary reduction. Reaction time when choosing a given alternative is determined by its probability. The higher the latter, the less is the reaction time. This has been confirmed by the fact that semantic relationships, both situational and conceptual, dominate unquestionably over sound ones.

The syntax of a sentence is closely connected with its semantics, (i.e. with its meaning) and can be considered as inferior. Every sentence has an integrated structure characterized by a certain unity; it is this semantic unity but not the principle of maximum probability of word occurrence that is the core of phrase generation. The initial word of the phrase switches on hypotheses about word-candidates, the set of hypotheses being constrained with each new succeeding word. Putting forward different words as hypotheses is not equiprobable but depends upon their semantic links.

We used the idea of the hierarchical system of bionical features [1] in which local features are primary, the relation between them are secondary and the relationships between the secondary features are tertiary ones. When considering a sentence as a whole object, the words are chosen to be primary features. The relations between words are defined through syntax and semantics. In this case, the pragmatic level defines "relationship" between meanings of sayings. Sentences with equal meanings may be attributed to one class. The recognition process begins with the classification of the entire object set under consideration into classes in accordance with the tertiary features with the primary ones being revealed simultaneously. Thus the pragmatics level is a check of the intersection of the set of given phrase words and the set of each class features (words).

The present paper concerns the syntactical, semantical, and pragmatical levels of processing speech signals in a speech recognition system, their interaction and their interaction with the acoustic level [2]. On the assumption that a phrase uttered is not meaningless, a problem has been specified for the syntactical/semantical level to reveal a meaningful phrase from a set of word alternatives revealed at the acoustical level. A word sequence on which a function depending upon links-between-words strength is a minimum has been chosen as the best alternative. At the level of pragmatics, the expression obtained is correlated with the system's resolution.

2. RECOGNITION ALGORITHM

The application domain of the system described is the control of the work of a terminal interactive system (TIS in the Academy Network) which enables one to communicate with a remote process (a TIS attached to another computer in the network), exchange messages, transfer files etc.

The pragmatics of the system are specified by a transition-and-state graph [3]. There are N control system states, each one being characterized by feasible operations performed in the network. Each arc connecting two states corresponds to the execution of a control instruction performed vocally. The control instruction is specified by the set of phrases equivalent in meaning and conveys the meaning of the transition Let q_j denote the number of instructions different in meaning and executable in a state j $(1 \leq j \leq N)$. For each instruction the set S_{jk} ($k \leq q_j$) is defined to contain all the words having instruction equivalent in meaning. For a state j we define the set

$$S_j = \bigcup_{k=1}^{q_j} S_{jk}$$

From here on it is referred to as a subvocabulary of the system in a state j_N . The total vocabulary of the system is

$$S = \bigcup_{j=1}^{N} S_j = \{ SL_i \}_{i=1}^{RSL}$$

on which all feasible instruction phrases can be generated. RSL stand for the total vocabulary size.

Some estimates are given concerning the vocabulary S . They incorporate the estimates for the word pairs in accordance with the power of the associations of contiguity and syntactical estimates reflecting word order in a sentence and such special features of the instruction language that can be represented only by a simple sentence with a simple predicate. The estimates defined in connection with word order have been brought together into the matrix

$$A = \{ a(i,j) \}_{i,j=1}^{RSL}$$

where i , j stand for word numbers in the vocabulary S . The words have been ordered according to a 5-point scale $\{p_0, p_1 .., p_4\}$ with its values increasing from the one corresponding to the strongest ("external") association up to one corresponding to the syntactical restraints. This kind of a matrix can be considered to generate the binary relation "to succeed" with the matrix elements reflecting the relation intensity. The matrix A, is not symmetric. This follows from the language properties and the values of the matrix elements allowing for semantics as well as syntax. The binary relation transitive closure generates some word sequences (phrases) on a given finite vocabulary. Proceeding from reality, a restriction has been imposed on the phrase - its length could not exceed NP. Thus a finite language described by a context-free (CF) grammar has been constructed. The use of the CF-grammar mechanism allows hypotheses to be put forward about a vocabulary subset in order to search for the acoustic standard of the next expected word of the phrase.

The recognition of an instruction is accomplished as follows. For every instant of time it is known in what state the computer network control system is and what instructions it can execute. For the first word of the instruction phrase the set M_1 is chosen, it contains numbers of certain acoustic standards from the whole subvocabulary S_j with the distances d (m_1) (m1 $< |M_1|$) between these standards and an introduced image being less than a certain threshold. Using a CF-grammar, the set

$$P_1 = \{ SL_i \mid a(i_1,i) < p4 \ , \ SL_i \in S_j \ , \ \forall \ SL_{i_1} \in M_1 \ \}$$

constructed that contains hypotheses about the succeeding expected words of the phrase. For the next uttered phrase word acoustic alternatives are defined on the set P_1 and the closest ones among them make up the set M_2. Then the set

$$P_2 = \{ SL_i \mid a(i_2,i) < p4 \ , \ SL_i \in P_1 \ , \ \forall \ SL_{i_2} \in M_2 \ \}$$

of the hypotheses for the third word of the phrase is constructed with the acoustic alternatives for this word being defined on P_3 . Thus the process continues until the phrase end. Evidently $P_1 \supset P_2 \supset ... \supset P_{NP}$. If, in the recognition of the rth word, the distances between its acoustic image and the standards-hypotheses revealed by the set $P_{(r-1)}$ exceed a certain threshold, then the search for acoustic alternatives M_r is continued on the set $S_j \setminus P_{(r-1)}$ and the hypotheses for the (r+1)th word constitute the set

$$P_r = \{ SL_i \mid a(i_r,i) < p_4 \ , \ SL_i \in S_j \setminus P_{(r-1)} \ , \ \forall \ SL_{i_r} \in M_r \ \}$$

Then the process is continued as described above.

After the acoustical and syntactical / pragmatical levels a decision about the phrase is made, according to the total function of the following form:

$$\min_{m_i \leq |M_i| \ , \ m_j \leq |M_j|} \left(\frac{1}{NP} \sum_{i=1}^{NP} d(m_i) \ + \ \frac{1}{C^2_{NP}} \sum_{j=2}^{NP} \sum_{i=1}^{j-2} d(m_i, m_j) \right)$$

where m_i is the number of the word i alternative in M_i, $d(m_i)$ is the distance between the word introduced and the m_ith alternative.

$$\text{Let } F = \{ SL_{i_1}, SL_{i_2}, ... SL_{i_{NP}} \}$$

denote the word sequence which minimizes the function. Then the control instruction corresponding to the phrase introduced is defined at the pragmatics level according to the following condition

$$\max_{k \leq q_j} |F \cap S_{jk}|$$

The instruction mnemonic code is transmitted to the Academy Network control. On receiving the answer from the network, the speech interface control program transits to a new state corresponding to the message. So the subvocabulary of a new state $S_j(J \leq N)$ is defined and the control is transferred to the program processing syntax and semantics and so forth

The present approach to natural language phrase recognition takes into account at each processing step the already obtained information on the current word sequence. So it becomes possible to rule out improbable and scarcely probable hypotheses and thus reduce the system total work time.

REFERENCES

[1] Granovskaya, R. M., Bereznaya, I.Y. and Grigorieva, A.N., "Perception of Form and Forms of Perception", (Lawrence Erlbaum, New Jersey, 1987)

[2] Vinogradov, S.Y., Kosarev, Y.A., Nikolaev, V.A., Sverdlitchenko, M.V. and Strakhovich, E.V., "The Recognition and Meaning Interpretation System of Sound Commands", in: All-union conference about speech recognition. Kiev, 1988 (Kiev, 1989).

[3] Vinogradov, S.V., Kosarev, Y.A., and Strakhovich, E.Y., "Technique Research of Sound Phrases Meaning Interpretation in Limited Object Sphere", in: Information processing problems and united mechanization of production (in print).

Industrial Applications of Artificial Intelligence
J.L. Alty and L.I. Mikulich (Editors)

Elsevier Science Publishers B.V. (North-Holland)

INTELLIGENT PROGRAMS AND METHODOLOGICAL PROCEDURES FOR DEBUGGING OF THE COMPLEX MACHINES

Eug. D. Solozhentsev, Ig. A. Korobitcin, N.N. Tkachev*

Leningrad Branch of Blagonravov's Institute of Machines Science (LF IMASH), Academy of Sciences of the USSR, Leningrad, USSR

ABSTRACT: A methodology and set of software tools for planning and performing debugging tests on prototype complex machines are considered. Intelligent software tools in the form of integrated expert system (PROLOG and C) back up the process of decision-making at each debugging stage. Software engineering facilities (SEF) are provided by using a standard IBM PC to form a problem-oriented workstation (WS) for the complex machine debugging process. This workstation is used to develop a testing program (TP) balanced with respect to engineering criterion and resources which follow by the tests proper. TP itself and a corresponding machine can be designed simultaneously with a known concurrent engineering concept.

1. INTRODUCTION

An analysis of the processes involved in machine building (engines, compressor stations, agricultural machines etc.) at various plants of this country has demonstrated that the debugging operations take as much as 80 to 90 % of the cost and time allocated to a project. The efficiency of the debugging process (equal to a ratio of testing time to the total time needed for tests recovery of the object after breakdowns, preparations for measurements to account for the failures and parameter failures and for manufacturing components implementing novel design and technological decisions) is only 5-12% [1].

Errors in complex engineering system design will occur due to the inadequacy of the mathematical models being used and complex intertwined physical processes in the object at hand. As a result, the objective of the debugging test program must consist of a search for and elimination of errors in the design. It is the purpose of the tests to remove ambiguities in the functional capabilities of the object and its components (units, mechanisms, systems, parts, processes) basing on parameter measurements.

*LF IMASH, USSR Academy of Sciences,
61, Bolshoy Av., Leningrad 199178, USSR

Practical experience is gained during debugging tests in the form of a description of tasks being solved in some design offices of aircraft construction plant or military agencies. However, the degree of formalization of this experience is far from being sufficient to be propagated on a mass scale and this operation, which is in many respects an intelligent one, needs to be computer-aided. What follows considers man-machine technology of complex engineering objects and requisite hardware to be implemented in a problem-oriented workstation (WS) comprising a personal computer and effective software tools and located at the lower level of the CAD-system local computer network.

2. DEBUGGING SYSTEM INVARIANCE

To ensure the debugging system (in informational sense) invariance to various objects (machines, technologic equipment and processes, organizational control system) the following principles have been selected:

A. A physical approach to debugging consisting in the evaluation of the machine´s functional capabilities and those of machine components to determine parameters responsible for the quality and conditions of their functioning. A consequence of the above approach is preferential use, for methodological and practical reasons, of parameter failures referring not only to a likelihood of physical breakdown (strength and wear) but also to economy, ergonomics, ecologic properties etc. The physical approach provids a speedy evalution of the functional capabilities of the machine and is an alternative to artificially speeded-up tests and estimates of the machine´s serviceability from failure statistics under conditions of long-term tests.

B. Interpretation of debugging as the known process of control of a complex object involving motion along a programmed (preselected) trajectory and correction on deviation from this trajectory for which the principal concepts of debugging procedures are singled out: Y - controlled parameters; U - controlling actions specifying test conditions; Z - corrective actions (design decision version) for returning to the program-specified trajectory; W - tests using the same or different benches starting with substandard and terminating with standard test conditions; decision making etc..

C. Uniform representation of knowledge concerning the object and its components.

D. A unified methodological and informational base for solving design, debugging and object diagnostics problems.

3. ENGINEERING KNOWLEDGE INTERPRETATION

Engineering knowledge interpretation (Fig.1) determines the informational and methodological environment for a designer . The following integrated knowledge constituents are introduced: documentation, models and technology.

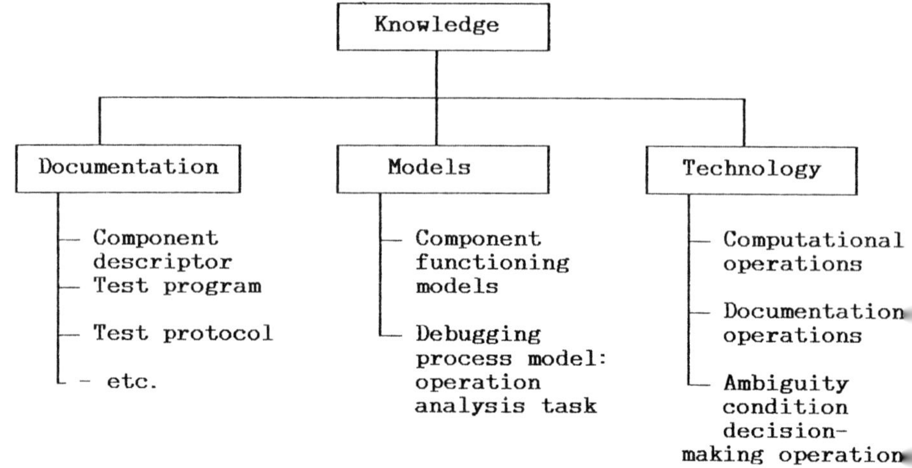

FIGURE 1
Engineering interpretation of the knowledge for objects and debugging procedures

One item of documentation, a descriptor, will be described, since program and test protocols call for no comments. The descriptor specifies the controlled parameters Y, control parameters U, correction parameters Z and test benches W for the object (component) debugging, as well as the following parameters and characteristics: permissible values of parameters Y, U, Z, W; their application costs Cy, Cu, Cz, Cw; time t and facility g losses in the case of the component´s failure. Descriptors for components are filled by design office (DO) specialists from the results of designing a particular object in accordance with investigation proposals and practical experience of similar objects.

4. DEBUGGING PROCEDURES

Technology (or debugging procedures) includes a sequence of logically closed operations:

PREDICTION of likely malfunction and failures during debugging by using functioning models and the Monte-Carlo method;

SIMULATION of the debugging process depending on the available facilities for measurement, control, test benches etc. by using models of criteria "expenses versus losses" ;

A detailed PLANNING of the debugging process using functioning models and expert system;

TESTS PERFORMANCE and decision-making during tests;

PROCESSING PROTOCOLS of the tests and actions of specialists working at the display terminal console.

The above procedures, in turn, consist of elementary operations, with total number being about a hundred. About 1/3 of the operations involve model operations, 1/3 concern documentation and 1/3 consists in decision-making under ambiguity conditions using production rules IF-THEN and BY ANALOGY formulated from the judgement and statements of competent specialists. Prompts are provided by the informational environment in which the operation is executed and includs the results of early steps of designing similar objects.

5. FUNCTIONING MODELS

The representation of a model of functioning of an object (and/or its components) is:

$$Y = F\ (U,Z,C,V)\ , \tag{1}$$

where: F - algebraic or differential equations; Y,M,Z - vectors of measurements, control and correction acts;C - vector of poorly defined coefficients of a model; V - vector of input parameters from the adjacent components or environment.

In the PREDICTION procedure the C and V vectors are assumed to be random, manifesting familiar distribution laws and the mathematical expectation and variance values of Y parameters are determined by using the Monte Carlo method. This makes it possible to establish the likelihood of Y parameters going beyond permissible limits, i.e. of their hazard.

Model (1) is used for directly determined and stochastic calculations and for solutions of inverse problems, identification (verification) of C parameters from experimental Y values, determination of U and Z parameters (given specified Y) in the course of the elaboration of the test program and decision-making during the tests. If model (1) proves too complex for computational purposes in terms of machine time, then, for debugging purposes, it may be substituted by a simpler approximating model.

6. MODEL OF CRITERIA "EXPENSES - LOSSES"

The model of criteria is intended for evaluating time T and facility Q losses for the debugging and index of the test program quality K depending on provision of the tests with checking, control and test bench facilities. The operation analysis task is solved under conditions of total ambiguity obtaining a guaranteed outcome. The test program quality criterion is evaluated by different methods. The simplest of these consists of calculating it as a ratio of the number of ambiguity factors being removed

(Y parameter hazard indices) to the total number of ambiguity factors established during the prediction of the debugging process.

The informational environment (input and output data) in the criterion model are: areas of Y, U, W; cost and consequence measures; measures of controlled parameter hazard (respectively, the index, probability and imprortance of hazard); measures of control correction and test bench efficiency; debugging program quality criteria. The informational environment is used not only for calculating debugging criteria and evaluating the test program version but also for formulating IF-THEN rules in terms of relation of parameters, measures of cost, consequences and efficiency.

7. PROBLEM-ORIENTED WORKSTATION (WS)

A prototype WS has been developed based on the aforementioned methodology for debugging complex engineering objects by using an IBM PC-AT personal computer. The invariant portion of the WS implemented in program methodological facilities includes: debugging procedures, knowledge representation methods and training courses. Particular knowledge is input by specialists in the given subject area. Software engineering facilities are intended for non-programming users who can using the system organize the knowledge autoformalization process and execution of their professional duties under CAD conditions.

The "environment-oriented" procedures for creating application systems is used. The principal tool of an SEF development engineer is not a programming language but an interactive environment with abundant built-in conversational capabilities which are properly combined and tuned. The capabilities of a Framework´s type integrated package ensure adequate visualization of practically all knowledge components. This package has sampling service facilities enabling it to be used as a system monitor. Intelligent components in the form of a microexpert system set are realised using Turbo Prolog system facilities.

Thus, from the viewpoint of traditional programming the proposed intelligent integrated program facilities represent actual specifications refined in the course of exploitation of real objects. In other words, this is a prototype specimen of a workstation. It was used to develop an engineering criterion and resourse-balanced testprogram for an actual machine (diesel engine). The quality of debugging process visualization, and the quallity and the adequacy of service facilities for specialists who are not professional programmers were evaluated. Verified specifications are used for developing an industrial (commercial) prototype WS sample through the use of Turbo C and Turbo Prolog system facilities.

Provision is made in the workstations itself for mechanism of verification of all debugging knowledge components: documents, models and rules relating to the results of actual debugging tests and console manipulations of specialists. In the general case the training mechanism includes man-machine methods of structural and parametric identification, analysis of consistency and ampleness of IF-THEN production rules.

8. CONCLUSION

The utilization of a problem-oriented workstation for debugging complex engineering objects makes it possible:

- to enhance the reliability and competitiveness of objects due to perfect debugging before manufacturing them on an industrial scale;

- to cut time and costs (by about 30%) owing to the parallel development of test programs with designing (concurrent engineering concept), early detection and elimination of errors in a design, express estimation of the functional capabilities of components of the object from measured parameters during the tests.

The methodology and software engineering facilities obtained as a result of developing debugging test procedures and relevant tools are used for construction on the basis of the same methodological and informational factors of problem-oriented WS for debugging machine-man-evironment systems, designing control and analysis system (maps) and control systems. The human factor is considered in these sytems as being an "active" component of the machine whose behaviour pattern is described by scenarios and specifications for actions and time for decision-making.

In a complex situation, the aforementioned problem-oriented WS appreciably enhances the efficiency of CAD, permits construction of safe, reliable and competitive objects and can provide a basis for knowledge engineering of industrial enterprize design offices.

REFERENCES

1. E.D.Solozhentsev. Fundamentals of construction of systems for automated debugging of complex machine building objects. Author´s Summary for Doctor of Sciences (Engineering) Thesis/ USSR AS Cybernetics Institute. Kiev, 1982. 46 pp. (In Russian).

Industrial Applications of Artificial Intelligence
J.L. Alty and L.I. Mikulich (Editors)
Elsevier Science Publishers B.V. (North-Holland)

INDUCTIVE INFERENCE ALGORITHMS AND THEIR APPLICATIONS

N.N. LYASHENKO

Leningrad Institute for Informatics
and Automation,
USSR Academy of Sciences

The paper contains a description of the inductive inference approach to different problems in data analysis (decision making, classification, diagnostics, filtering etc.).

1. INTRODUCTION

It is well known that many problems of decision making, classification, diagnostics etc. may be reduced to that of hypotheses generation from data.

Recently in the Leningrad Institute for Informatics and Automation (LIIA) fast algorithms for hypotheses generation in the sense of [1, 2] were constructed. Besides that new approaches for inference rule automation and expert choice of associative criteria were found.

The specific feature of this reasearch work is the universality of the approach and the great diversity of applications. As a result the author has an opinion that a library of program implemented inductor modules may have an instrumental meaning for different data processing systems construction.

2. INDUCTORS

At first we consider the notion of an inductor and describe two kinds of inductors. Actually we could add many other variants, so our next description must be treated as (important) examples.

2.1. Preliminary definitions

Let $E_1, \dots, E_n$ be ordered sets,

$$E = \prod_{j=1}^{n} E_j , \qquad E_0 = \prod_{j=2}^{n} E_j ,$$

M be a matrix $v \times n$ consisting of elements m_{ij} from E_j,

$$S = \{ m_{i*} \mid i \in \{ 1, \dots , v \} \}.$$

A predictor on E is a function Pred from E_0 into E_1 under the condition:

for all x from S $\mathrm{Pred}(\mathrm{proj}(x \mid E\ )) = \mathrm{proj}(x \mid E\ )$.

In the most of our cases E_j = Bool = {0, 1} (the Boolean set).

If F is a space of functions f: $E_1 \longrightarrow E_0$ and R is a metrics or a vicinity measure on F then the quantity Ac = R(Pred f, f) is called an accuracy of the predictor.

From this point of view we can consider an optimal predictor for a given R.

A process of induction is an iterative sequence of succesive improvements of predictors by data analysis. At last, an improving transformation itself is called an inductor.

2.2. Two aspects of an induction

2.2.1. Inconsistency

If E_j = Bool then we can treat data as logical assertions and interpret 1 as truth and 0 as falsehood. Particularly, an element m_{ij} may be treated as truth value of a predicate:

$$G_j(m_{i*}) \Longleftrightarrow m_{ij}$$

Then a vector m_{i*} has an interpretation

$$G_2(m_{i*})\ \&\ \dots\ \&\ G_n(m_{i*}) \longrightarrow G_1(m_{i*})\ .$$

In this case the situation when for certain i, k

$$\mathrm{proj}(m_{i*} \mid E_0) = \mathrm{proj}(m_{k*} \mid E_0)$$

and at the same time $m_{i1} \neq m_{k1}$ means a contradiction in our data. We may say that the data are inconsistent.

2.2.2. Extrapolation

Another possible feature of data is their incompleteness. It means that

$$\mathrm{proj}(S \mid E_0) \neq E_0 = \mathrm{Bool}^{n-1}.$$

If our data are incomplete then a predictor must work in some cases as an extrapolator (interpolator).

2.3. Associative inductors

Let's consider so called an associative predictor. It is defined as follows. For probabilistic criteria construction we introduce a measure mes on the algebra of all subsets of S and for every H from E put mes H = mes(H * S). Further, let be

$$G = (G_1, \ldots, G_n);$$

$$Z = G^{-1}\mathrm{Proj}(@ \mid E_1)^{-1}\{ 1 \};$$

$$W = G^{-1}\mathrm{Proj}(@ \mid E_0)^{-1}g^{-1}\{ 1 \}$$

(where g is an arbitrary Boolean function on E_0 (so it's argument is $(x_2, x_3, \ldots, x_n)$);

$$A = Z * W; \; B = Z * (E \setminus W);$$

$$C = (E \setminus Z) * W; \; D = (E \setminus Z) * (E \setminus W);$$

$$a = \mathrm{mes}\ A; \; b = \mathrm{mes}\ B; \; c = \mathrm{mes}\ C; \; d = \mathrm{mes}\ D;$$

$$J = \begin{Vmatrix} a & b \\ c & d \end{Vmatrix} \; ;$$

$$\mathrm{Matr} = \{ J \mid a, b, c, d \geq 0 \;\&\; a + b + c + d = 1 \}.$$

Now we can define so called associative statistics appropriate for introduction of probabilistic versions of thelogical equivalence. Namely, a relation $\ll$ on (Matr $\times$ Matr) is called "the relation of associative improvement" if and only if

$$J_1 \ll J_2 \Longleftrightarrow (a_1 \leq a_2) \;\&\; (b_2 \leq b_1) \;\&\; (c_2 \leq c_1) \;\&\; (d_1 \leq d_2).$$

Statistics Q is called associative if it is defined by the formula

$$Q(S, G, g) = T(a, b, c, d)$$

where $T : \mathrm{Matr} \longrightarrow R$ and T is increasing by the relation $\ll$.

The main problem in our case is a construction of the list of all Boolean functions g for which the association measure $Q > \mathrm{Level}$, where Level is a given real number. It is also important to find a function g for which Q is maximal.

The best g defines the optimal associative interpolator. So every improving transformation of g which makes Q to increase may be called an associative inductor.

2.4. Examples

As an example of an associative statistics we can take

$$\mathrm{Det}(a, b, c, d) = \det J = ad - bc;$$

another example is

$$\mathrm{Lin}(a, b, c, d) = -\ (b + c).$$

The Lin-statistics is obviously equal to (-e), where $e = b + c$ is an error of classification. One can prove that for an interesting class of associative statistics - uniform statistics (see [3]) - an improving transformation has a rather simple structure.

Our examples Det and Lin are uniform, so we get correspondingly the following two inductors.

Inductor 1 (for Det-statistics).

Let for a random s from S and z = P(Z) be

ZERO = { x | x in E, P(s = x) = 0 };

POS = { x | x in E, P(Z | s = x)≥ z } \ ZERO;

NEG = { x | x in E, P(Z | s = x)≤ z } \ ZERO.

Then the rule of induction admits:

1). Increasing of g-values on POS.
2). Decreasing of g-values on NEG.
3). Arbitrary changing on ZERO.

Inductor 2 (for Lin-statistics).

For Lin-statistics the induction rule has a similar structure where is the same set as in the previous example and

POS = { x | x ∈ E, P(Z | s = x)≥ 1/2 } \ ZERO;

NEG = { x | x ∈ E, P(Z | s = x)≤ 1/2 } \ ZERO.

These rules enable us to avoid inconsistency of data but have no extrapolation ability.

2.5. Topological inductors

Let be $E_j = \prod_{k \neq j} E_k$, Proj(x | H) be a projection of x on a partial product of E_k. Consider a topology Top on E and a family of "canonical" neighbourhoods Nb, nb(x) being a neighbourhood of point x. One of convenient principles for Nb construction is using the following rule:

$$Nb = \{ nb(x) \mid x \in E_0,\ nb(x) \in Top,\ Mu(nb(x) * S_0) = const \},$$

where $S_0 = Proj(S \mid E_0)$; Mu is a measure on E_0 induced by measure on S_0 with values in E_0.

If δ is a similarity measure on E

$$\delta : E \times E \longrightarrow R^+$$

and ξ is in E_0 then we define a "distance predictor"

$$(\xi \mid Sample,\ \delta) = \frac{\int_{nb(\xi)} \delta(\xi, x)\ Proj(x|E_0)\ \mu(dx)}{\int_{nb(\xi)} \delta(\xi, x)\ \mu(dx)}$$

The error of prediction is

$$\text{Error}(\xi \mid \text{Sample}, \delta) = f(\xi) - \text{Proj}(\xi \mid E_0).$$

Accordingly to our conception, an induction rule is a such transformation ofthe predictor which gives smaller values of Error.

For example, one of induction rules may be described as follows.

If DLT is a family of similarity measures δ (see the definition of f) then for every ξ from Sand δ from DLT let be

$$\text{Err}(\xi, \delta) = \text{Error}(\xi \mid \text{Sample} \setminus \Xi^{+})$$

where

$$\Xi^{+} = \{ x \mid x \in \text{Sample}, \text{Proj}(x \mid E_0) = \xi \}.$$

Let's suppose that $\text{Err}(\xi, \text{Dt}(\xi))$ is a solution of the minimization problem for $\text{Err}(\xi, \delta)$ for every fixed ξ. Then our inductor gives the predictor f1

$$\text{f1}(\xi \mid \text{Sample}) = f(\xi \mid \text{Sample}, \text{Dt}(\xi 1)),$$

where

ξ in E_0, and $\xi 1$ is a point from $\text{nb}(\xi)$

chosen with the help of any additional rule. For us the case in which E_j= Bool is especially interesting.

It is easy to see that topological Boolean inductors posess the property of extrapolation contrary to assotiative ones. If we use a family of predictors (as in the above example) every concrete choice of a predictor may be interpreted as an adoption of a certain axiom in addition to data (we call it a metha-axiom). From this point of view any inductor under consideration generates a new metha-axiom from the set of old ones and data.

3. MAIN PROBLEMS

Important problems are fast algorithms construction for composition of lists of empirically true assertions (for accepted confidence level), calculation of the best hypothesis under the certain criterion, consruction of empirical axioms list (i.e. the list of true and logically strongest propositions), rules automation (i.e. automatic inductor creation), expert choice of associative criteria and metha-axioms.

Many of solutions may be found in the book [3]. Besides that in the LIIA we fulfilled several applied works (see 5) in which we tried the induction ideology in the scope of a scheme described in the section 4.

4. TECHNONOGICAL SCEME

The usual application scheme for inductors may be described as follows.

Step 1. Problem formulation.
Step 2. Condition := (Data base is built).
Step 3. If Condition then go to Step 7.
Step 4. Inverse interpretation.
Step 5. Model construction.
Step 6. Data base generation.
Step 7. Induction.
Step 8. Convolution.
Step 9. System generation.

The scheme describes two situations. The first one corresponds to a really empirical approach when an experimental data base is available. The second one (occured frequently) deals with a theoretical (or partially empirical) description of the investigated object and is based on a representation of the problem as inverse one. In the latter case we have to generate data artificially using a model. The induction stage (Step 7) allows us to characterize the data base from the complexity point of view and to find

1) an appropriate segmentation;
2) a stable and reliable prediction formula.

5. APPLICATIONS

In the LIIA several versions of the inductive inference system (in the above sense) were created. These sytems were used for research works in different fields.

Our practice have convinced us in usefullness of inductors in such applications as:

- classification (therefore in diagnostics and decision making);
- transformations construction (filters, segmentations etc.) with the help of appropriate quantification of data components scales;
- data base contraction (in the case of a sufficiently accurate prediction of a datum by the rest data it may be eliminated from the data base);
- inverse problems and algorithm synthesis;
- symbolic calculations.

From a system point of view it is convenient to have a set of program implemented inductors as modules and use them for synthesis of a new data processing software.

REFERENCES

[1] Haek P., Havranek T. Hypotheses automation. Moscow. Nauka. 1984.
[2] Haek P., Havranek T., Chytil M.K. Metoda GUHA. Automaticka tvorba hypotez. Academia. Praha. 1983.
[3] Lyashenko N.N. Methods and algorithms of inductive inference. Leningrad. 1990.

Industrial Applications of Artificial Intelligence
J.L. Alty and L.I. Mikulich (Editors)
Elsevier Science Publishers B.V. (North-Holland)

DIFFERENCE ALGORITHMS ABILITIES IN DECISION SUPPORT SYSTEMS

Victor V. NIKIFOROV

Leningrad Institute for Informatics and Automation
of the USSR Academy of Sciences
Leningrad, USSR

Binary features enumeration is an ordinary method for object properties specification. Equality or inequality of feature values for a pair of objects are marked by a spesial bit scale - difference scale. A set of objects gives a difference scale table, that includes all (and only) data concerned with differences between any objects in the set. How much information about the set structure is contained in the difference scale table? This question deals with potential abilities of a special kind heuristic algorithms.

1. INTRODUCTION

There is an important step for information processing systems design - a rational choice for data formalizing rules. One way for effective data formalizing is to determine a set of binary features, that may be complete representation of actual object properties. Many heuristic ideas are often used in data processing algorithms, that support data bases with such object representation [1]. Various questions, concern with potential abilities of the heuristic algorithms have arised in this case. The abilities of special kind heuristic algorithms - difference algorithms - are discussing in this paper.

Difference algorithms may be used as implementation tools for such dicision support systems which serves for classification, pattern recognition, object identification problem solving. Appropriate conditions for difference algorithms usage depend on the set characteristics.

1.1 Representation bases

Suppose, that for actual object properties representation we use binary feature vectors (every feature vector correspond to a vertex of n-dementional cube). The feature vectors (that describes a set of objects) carry actual information about the set. However, a feature vector component value reflects not only some object pecuiarity, but also some peculiarity of the representation rules. For example, the weight of any feature vector (the number of bits, that have on-bit value), is determined by two factors: by the represented object nature, and by the description method (the definition of description basis).

There are 2^n description bases, that may be transformed one another by inversion of any feature (or any group of features) representation. Some of those bases (minimizing bases) cause minimum value of feature vectors summary weight. There is an unique minimizing basis in the case of odd objects number in the represented set.

1.2. Difference scales table

We see, that a set structure representation by binary feature vectors depends on inversion operations. It seems expedient way to use a representation method, that have no dependency on inversion operations, if we want to build various heuristic algorithms, that analyse set structure. Difference scale table (DST) is such expedient representation method: any element of DST is a difference scale for a certain pair of objects (that is a line of flags, marking differed features on a certain pair of objects). By the definition DST contents is not modified on account of description basis changing (that is on account of changing any feature representation mode). If elements of complete DST is lexicographicaly ordered, it also has not influence of any objects regulation. Hence, DST essentialy reflects pure structure peculiarity of the set.

1.3. Difference algorithms

Difference scale table includes only data, concerned with differences between objects. This circumstance justify using the term "difference algorithm" in the case, when DST data is algorithm's input. Through processing DST data difference algorithm produces information about represented set structure organization. The implementation of difference algorithm is not necessarily suppose explicit building of DST - the implementation may use initial representation of objects (binary feature vectors, corresponding to some concrete basis) as input data for dynamic computing every demanded element of DST. Difference algorithm definitial property is its independence from any inversion of feature representation and from any set of objects ordering.

The simplest examples of defference algorithms (the algorithms, that produce the most general information about the set structure) are maximum, minimum, average distance computing for vertexes of n-dementional cube, which are object representations. The distance spectrum (the spectrum of differences) and another DST features get, for example, information about set separation on any subsets (each subset includes objects, that are similar in the representation).

2. SPECTRUM OF DIFFERENCES

The weight of any object representation (on-bit features number) depends on description basis. The weight w of every DST element has no such dependence, as well as the number $D(w)$ of DST elements, which weight is w. The fnction $D(w)$ carries essential structure information about represented set of objects - it gives the spectrum of distances between objects in the set. Let us name the function $D(w)$ "D-spectrum" of the set specification. This D-spectrum keeps important structure information about the set without any connection to peculiarities of the representation basis.

2.1. Examples

Fig.1 shows three examples of D-spectrum functions. First example (fig. 1a) corresponds to set of 2^9 objects with even destribution in 9-demen-

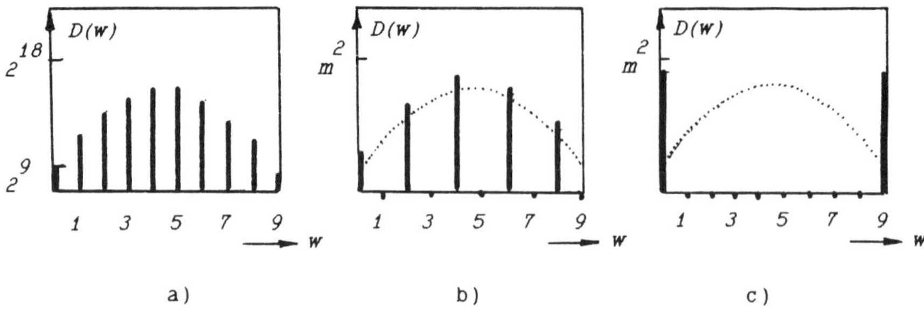

FIGURE 1
D-spectrums of regular structure sets

tional space of binary features. The DST elements number with weight w is given in this case by the equation $D(w) = 2^{9}\binom{w}{9}$; D-spectrum of even destribution has special smooth cupola-shaped form. We show this form by dotted line in further figures for comparation a D-spectrum with even one.

The second example (fig.1b) correspondes to set, contains $m = 2^{8}$ elements of (9, 8)-codes with parity control. The comparation cruve $E(w) = m^{2}\binom{w}{n}2^{-n}$ in the figure is normalized on DST size. In this case DST have no scales with odd weight; every nonzero value of the function $D(w)$ exeeds the value of function $E(w)$ twice. We see, D-spectrum essentialy represents the nature of (9, 8)-code.

The third example shows D-spectrum of the set, concentrated in two opposit vertexes of 9-dementional space of binary features. Suppose, for instance, that one half of these objects is represented by the feature vector (111110000) and another half - by the feature vector (000001111); D-spectrum of such a set has the sharp form, that is depicted in fig.1c. There are two nonzero values in opposit D-spectrum ends.

The sharp D-spectrum becames blurred around, when opposit subsets are blurred. Fig.2 illustrates this fact: every D-spectrum in fig.2 represents

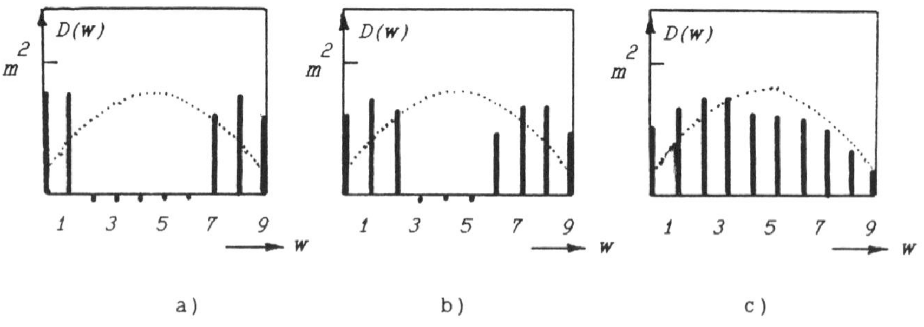

FIGURE 2
Blurred D-spectrums

the set, which is broken up into two subset: one subset around the vertex (111110000), and another - around vertex (000001111). The more subsets are blurred, the more D-spectrum is blurred. In the case fig.2a every subset is devided into two parts: vectors (*11110000) describe the elements of one subset, vectors (00000111*) - the elements of another subset (the asterisk marks variable features).

D-spectrum fig 2b corresponds to subsets (**1110000) and (0000011**); it slightly more blurred, but it still has zero-value components. D-spectrum fig 2c has no zero-value components; it corresponds to set, broken up into parts (****10000) and (00000****). The form of this D-spectrum deflects noticeably from dotted line - i.e. from D-spectrum of even destribution.

Set structure representation by D-spectrum as well as DST representation has no dependence from features representation mode and any object regulation. Moreover, D-spectrum has no influence of any features ordering (on contrary to DST representation). It reflects the set structure in the most abstract form.

2.2. Subbases and subspectrums

Every subset B of features makes a description subspace, i.e. every subset of features is subbasis of feature vector description. For each subbasis B we may build subtable of DST, which consists of shorten difference scales. For each B we have D-spectrum function $D(B, w)$ - the function is D-subspectrum of the set on subbasis B. By the definition every value of subset $D(B, w)$ may be calculated from DST components. Reverse assertion is also true: the set of D-spectrums $D(B, w)$ and whole spectrum $D(w)$ determine DST completely. Actualy only the first value $D(B, 0)$ of each D-subspectrum are requied to calculate all DST elements.

3. DIFFERENCE ALGORITHMS IN DECISION SUPPORT SYSTEMS

Classification, pattern recognition and identification of objects in the feature vector representation space are customary problems of automatic data processing for a lot of applications: medicine, geology, biology and so on. There are often extermely hard problems, which claim to use broad variaty complicated tools and methods, which claim to unite artificial and nature intellegence - for example in form of decision support sistems.

The usage of D-spectrum culculation technique complicated with computer grafic systems will make possible to pool computer and human abilities for pattern recognition applications. If we shell arm the resercher with effective tools for journey around D-spectrum and D-subspectrums space, if we shall care for convinient form of D-spectrum parameters picturing, then we shell tie the tine possibilities of human eyesight mechanizms to the dificult investigation problems.

Such tools is especialy helpfull, if D-spectrum and D-subspectrums contain enough informaition about explored set structure, if the whole complex of D-algoritms is complete one in appropriate sense. In such a case we have assurance of a way existance, on which every question about the set structure may be obtained by D-algorithms usage. This is a reason for D-algorithms potential abilities investigation.

4. ESTIMATION OF DIFFERENCE ALGORITHMS POTENTIAL ABILITIES

Difference algorithms are invariant algorithms - their results has no dependence on some feature space transformation [2]. There is a planty of heuristic criteria for invariant algorithms usage, for DST information usage in every application field. There are important questions, that arise with respect of such heuristic criteria and algorithms: what about D-algorithms potential abilities, what about completeness of DST information?

If any DST contains enough information to detect an arbitrary structure characteristic of corresponding set, then the class of D-algorithms is complete class in the following sence: every invariant algorithm may be simulated in the class of D-algorithms.

4.1. Difference algorithms imperfection

An example, that shows a lack of information in DST, is given in fig. 3, where two sets are depicted (fig. 3a, 3e). These two sets have different structures, but (in spite of that) identical D-spectrums (fig 3b) and identical D-subspectrums (fig 3c and 3d). Hence, these sets has identical DST. Hence, these sets are indiscernible by D-algorithms.

This example shows a lack of information in DST for extraction any desired structure feature, it demonstrates loss of structure information about represented set by altering representation from feature vectors form to DST form.

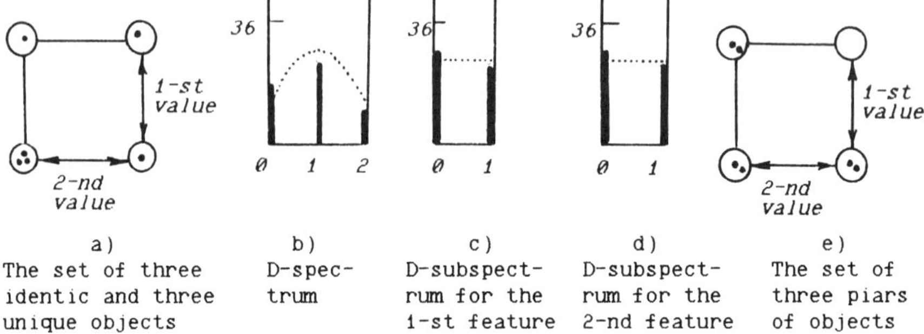

a) The set of three identic and three unique objects

b) D-spectrum

c) D-subspectrum for the 1-st feature

d) D-subspectrum for the 2-nd feature

e) The set of three piars of objects

FIGURE 3
An example of two different set structures with identic D-spectrum and identic D-subspectrums

Such sets existance entails the conclusion: in some cases D-algorithms can not detect all structure peculiarities of the set initial specification; in common case the form of D-spectrum and the forms of all D-subspectrums do not contain all information about set structure. This fact incline us to disillusion about difference algorithms sufficiency: in common case D-algorithms collection does not complete class of algorithms in the above mentioned sence. But it appears, however, that a wide class of sets exists, for which such conclusion is not true.

4.2. D-represented sets

It seems, that the inference about D-algorithm imperfaction is almost trivial, almost obvious one. Not so obvious a wide class of set existance (D-represented sets), for which complete DST contains enough information about represented set structure. If DST represents any D-represented set, then it contains enough information to get any structure property of the set. If a set belong to that class, then any task of its analysis may be fulfilled by difference algorithms.

The following assertion is true: every set, that specified by binary features and contained odd number of objects, is D-represented set. We have noted above, that odd object number set has an unique minimizing basis. The assertion is proved on constructive way - by building the procedure, that restore (from DST representation) feature vectors of initial set representation in minimizing basis. Note, that this procedure would't executed in practice (it seems better to keep original feature vectors). However, the fact of such proceedure existance has methodologicaly significant sense: it reflects wide abilities of difference algorithms. It means, that difference algorithms are usable for any structure analysis task solving. It is indeed unexpected fact: if the set has odd number n of members, it is D-represented set (including very large n), but if n is even, the set is not D-represented. If n is even, then an invariant algorithm or has or has not simulation in D-algorithm class. If n is odd, every invariant algorithm has a difference algorithm simulation.

5. CONCLUSIONS

Difference algorithms are generalization of algorithms, based on calculation of estimations [3], which are used widely from the early time of pattern recognition with computer aid. At the same time, difference algorithms are the variaty of invariant algorithms, studed deeply in the last time [2]. The result that is given in this paper shows, that the wide class of problems exist, for which D-algorithms have all necessary abilities of the more common invariant algorithms.

ACKNOWLEDGEMENTS

I whould like to bring the gratitude V.I.Kolpakov - for his contrary example, that stoped the attempts to generalize the assertion 4.2 to the even case. I whould like to bring the gratitude A.N.Domaratskiy and Yr.I.Zhuravlev for supporting of the work in various periods.

REFERENCES

[1] Zhuravlev Yu.I., Gurevitch I.B., Pattern Recognition and Image Recognition, in: Pattern Recognition, Classification, Forecasting, issue 2 (USSR, Moscow, 1989) pp.5-72.

[2] Kochetcov D.V. Pattern Recognition Algorithms Invariant on Features Space Transformation, in: Pattern Recognition, Classification, Forecasting, issue 1 (USSR, Moscow, 1989) pp. 82-113.

[3] Zhuravlev Yu.I., Nikiforov V.V., Recognition Algorithms Based on Calculation of Estimations - Cybernetics, N3, (1971) pp. 1-11.

Industrial Applications of Artificial Intelligence
J.L. Alty and L.I. Mikulich (Editors)
Elsevier Science Publishers B.V. (North-Holland)

METHODS OF ADAPTIVE LOGICAL RECOGNITION AND ITS APPLICATION

Adil V. TIMOPHEEV and Tatyana M. KOSSOVSKAYA

Department of robototechnique systems
Leningrad Avia Aparatus Institute
Leningrad, USSR

Department of Mathematics
Leningrad Shipbuilding Institute
Leningrad, USSR

To solve a series of problems in manufacture a logic-axiomatical method of adaptive recognition based on the representation of knowlege base by means of predicate calculus formulas is advised. This approach permits to build adaptive logical recognition system.

1. LOGICAL RECOGNITION SYSTEM

1.1. GENERAL DESCRIPTION

The adviced systems include: knowlege base in the form of productions - logical axioms of recognizable classes of objects; logical recognition decider providing recognition by means of logical inference retrieval; interactive systems of training and adaptation providing forming of new notions and accumulation of knowlege; dialogue monitor (linguistic processor) providing a dialogue between a user and a computer.

Recognition system operates in two regimes: regime of accumulation of information (learning regime) and regime of decision-making. In the learning regime an expert inputs all necessary notions and forms initial knowlege base. Theese knowlege may be introduced in the form of logical axioms as well as may be formed automatically by means of "show" training during which the expert presents objects of several classes to the system and indicates their names.

In the decision-making regime a manufacture recognition problem is interpretated and solved with the help of logical problem decider.

2. CLASS AXIOMS

In the learning regime logical class axioms are constructed in the form

$$\bigvee_{j=1}^{J} \mathop{\&}_{i} \mathop{\&}_{s} p_i^{a_{ijs}}(s)\,, \qquad (1)$$

where i belongs to some subsets I_j of numbers $1,\ldots,n$; s - elements (parts) of the object; p_i - predicates characterizing the object or its element; a_{ijs} - logical constants; a^c means a if c=true and not a if c=false.

Theese axioms may be built according to a training set or be given by an expert in the form of necessary and sufficient conditions of belonging to a class.

3. ADAPTATION TO TRANSFORMATIONS

In the practice, objects of every class are often distinguished only by transformations of a given agregate of transformations G . In such cases the recognition system may be expanded by adding transformation axioms in the form

$$\mathop{\&}_{i} \mathop{\&}_{s} p_i^{a_{is}}(s) \longrightarrow \mathop{\&}_{i} \mathop{\&}_{s} p_i^{b_{is}}(g(s))\,, \qquad (2)$$

where in the left and right parts of the implication i belongs to perhaps different subsets of numbers $1,\ldots,n$. Such transformation axioms provide invariance of the recognition system and its adaptation to the given transformation agregate G [1 - 6] .

4. RECOGNITION PROBLEM

The decision of the recognition problem is reduced to the automatical inference of the existence of such element s from the object S and such transformation g from the agregate G that ($g(s)=s_o$ & $A(s_o)$) from the set of transformation axioms and the full description of the object S in the terms of predicates $p_1,\ldots,p_n$. There A(s) stands for a class axiom in the form (1) , s_o - some standard object.

For this purpose the Herbrand procedure and strategies of the resolution method of Robinson [7] or the inverse method of Maslov [8] may be used. The most suitable programming languages to realize the advanced method are such as PROLOG and REFAL.

The merit of the method is possibility of logical recognition and analysis of complex production scenes containing unordered partically hidden objects. Such scenes appear in the field of view of robot vision. In such case class axioms (1) and transformation axioms (2) are built in the terms of predicates characterizing elements of a contour extraction or an image represented by a brightness matrix [3,4] .

5. APPLICATIONS

The developed approach allows to create systems of technical diagnostics. On its base an expert system of technology equipment choice is being worked out. In this case the description of machine parts are taken for class axioms and changings appearing during technological operations are taken for transformation axioms. Logical problem decider provides technologi process and equipment choice which guarantees producing of machine parts with the given characteristics.

Adaptive logical deciding rules and recognizing graphs of minimal complexity constructed in multivalued logic are considered. There are described applications of theese rules and graphs for medicine diagnostics problems, for recognition of meteorological phenomena and in the system of automatical addressing of tractor K-700 parts on the assembly line [9 - 11].

REFERENCES

[1] Kossovskaya, T.M. and Timopheev, A.V., Logic-axiomatical method of recognition and its applications, in: IFAC Proc.Ser. No.9 (Pergamon Press, 1984) pp. 523-528.

[2] Kossovskaya, T.M. and Timopheev, A.V,, Vestnik LGU, No.8 (1985) pp. 22-29.

[3] Kossovskaya, T.M., Raspoznavanie preobrazovannykh i iskazhennykh izobrazheny, in: Proc. All-Union Symp. "Zrenie organizmov i robotov", v.2 (Vilnus, 1885) pp.59-60.

[4] Timofeev, A.V., Roboty i iskusstvenny intellekt (USSR, Moscow, 1978)

[5] Kossovskaya, T.M. and Timopheev, A.V., Adaptive logical recognition algorithms for expert systems IMS, in:Proc. III Intern. Summer Seminar on IMS (Yugoslavia, Dubrovnik, 1989)

[6] Kossovskaya, T.M. and Timopheev, A.V., Logical-axiomatical method of knowlege representation and recognition for robots, in: Proc. 5-th Intern.Conf. "Art. Intell. and Inform.-Control Syst. of Robots" (CSSR, 1989)-

[7] Robinson, J.A., J. ACM, 12, No.1 (1965) pp. 21-41

[8] Maslov, S.Yu., Docl. AS USSR, v.159, No.1 (1964)pp.17-20

[9] Timofeev, A.V., Adaptivnaya sistema logicheskogo vyvoda i optimalnye opoznayushie grafy, in: Voprosy Kibernetiki (Sci.Sovet on Compl.Probl. "Cibernetics" AS USSR, 1977) pp. 33-35

[10] Timofeev, A.V., Adaptivnye robototekhnicheskie komplexy (USSR, Leningrad, 1988)

[11] Artyushkova (Kossovskaya), T.M. and Timofeev, A.V., Biologicheskaya i medicinskaya kibernetika, 4 (AS USSR, 1974) pp. 13-16

Industrial Applications of Artificial Intelligence
J.L. Alty and L.I. Mikulich (Editors)
Elsevier Science Publishers B.V. (North-Holland)

SECTION 7: DECISION MAKING SYSTEMS: CASE STUDIES

THE MODEL CREATION TECHNOLOGY WITH THE SAPFIR SYSTEM

M.B.Egorov, E.V.Kashirskaya, A.A. Utkin.

The Leningrad Institute for Informatics and Automation of the USSR Academy of Sciences.

1. INTRODUCTION.

In this paper we would like to outline the process of simulation model creation with the system SAPFIR that has been developed in the Laboratory of System Analysis of the Leningrad Institute for Informatics and Automation of the USSR Academy of Sciences.

The system SAPFIR gives the decision maker a way to create a simulation (i.e. computer program that simulates behaviour of the process investigated) and to run the program. The intended user base includes scientists and decision makers with no or limited program experience. The system requires IBM PC/XT/AT - compatible computer with 512K byte RAM and MS-DOS operating system. Implementation language is C.

The system deals with simulation of flow-type processes.

2. APPROACH AND SEQUENCE OF OPERATIONS.

The base of the SAPFIR is the Algorithmic Network Language (ANL, [1,2]) which gives a way of describing a problem field as planar graph (or network), where nodes represent operations and edges - the data involved in operations. This approach has Jay Forrester's system dynamic as its base but is different from it in many ways.

The process of creation of simulation models with SAPFIR has three stages: 1) creation of the model of a problem domain using ANL and entry of the network into the computer; 2) formulation of a simulation task by means of pointing at source variables and creation of the simulation model; 3) implementation of the model experiments.

Several simulation tasks can be formulated for the same model of a problem domain and SAPFIR can automatically create a simulation model for each of the tasks.

The flow diagram of the SAPFIR system is shown in Fig.1. The main part of the MODEL CREATION module is the EDITOR which promotes interactive input of the network. With the EDITOR it can be created as completed models as building blocks for further use.

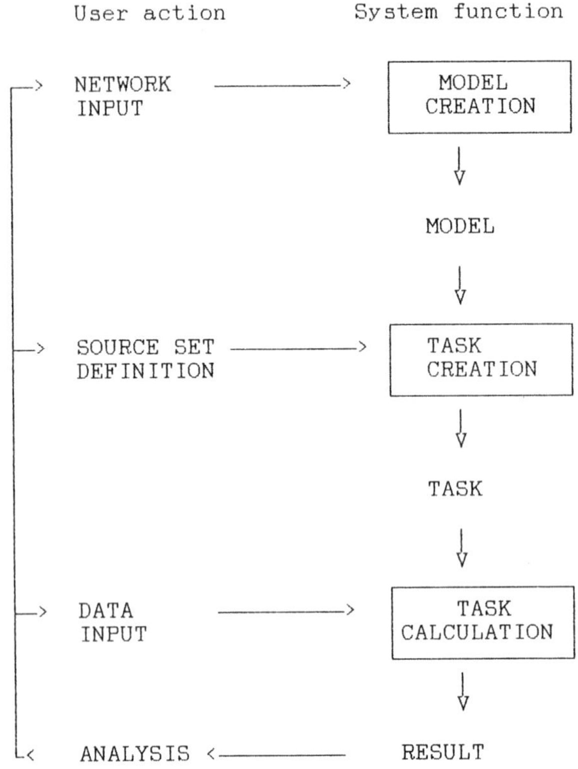

Fig.1. SAPFIR Flow Diagram.

The main part of the TASK CREATION module is the SCHEDULER which tries to synthesize the simulation program based on the network entered and information about source variables. It is obvious that not all sets of source variables allow the creation of a simulation program. SCHEDULER recognizes two cases of insoluble network: uncertainty and abundance.

The last module - TASK CALCULATION - is used to run a simulation program. A spreadsheet-like dialogue is used in this module. User-defined forms may be entered to generate a final report. Through IMPORT/EXPORT facility interaction with external packages and data bases may be achieved.

3. EXAMPLE.

To illustrate the use of the SAPFIR a simple example is presented. To create a model we first have to understand how the modelled process is going on and second draw the flow diagram of the process. Let this diagram have the form shown in the Fig.2, where x1, x2 are input parameters, x3, x4 are output parameters and remaining parameters are internal.

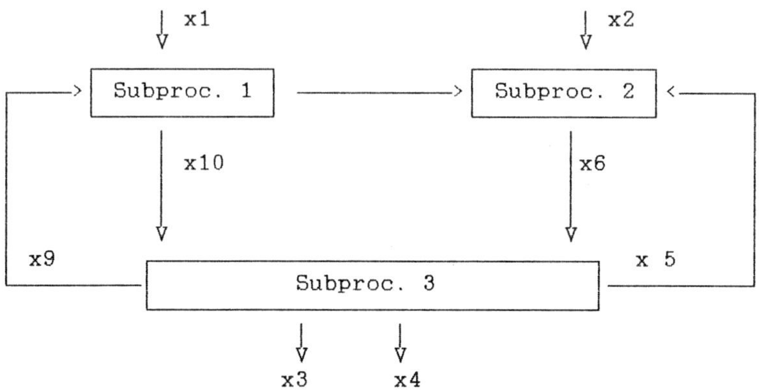

Fig.2. The sample example flow diagram.

This is the starting point for the SAPFIR system. If subprocesses blocks are already present in the SAPFIR Model Base, then the user in the MODEL CREATION mode simply loads them and then links them. If not, user should interactively define blocks. In both cases the algorithmic network is the result. When the algorithmic network is drawn, one obtains a model of a subject field that contains knowledge about variables and valid transformations of the variables.

To implement a model experiment a task should be formulated. Definition of a task consists of pointing at source variables, i.e. the system should be informed which variables are regarded as known. The next step in our example is to define x1, x2 as source variables in the TASK CREATION mode.

We can define several tasks in the model. For example, we may declare x3 and x4 as source variables. Based on the network and information about source variables the system automatically synthesizes a program that calculates remaining variables. If a message about impossibility of creation of the task is obtained, it is the user, who decides whether the set of source variables or the network itself should be changed.

When the network had been drawn are entered into computer, source variables have been defined and SAPFIR offered the result program, we may start experiments with the model using the TASK CALCULATION mode.

4. IMPLEMENTATION.

The system structure is shown in the Fig.3. The SAPFIR system itself consists of 2 major parts: the Technology Unit and the SAPFIR Virtual Machine. Related parts are the Model Base the Task Base and the Data Base.

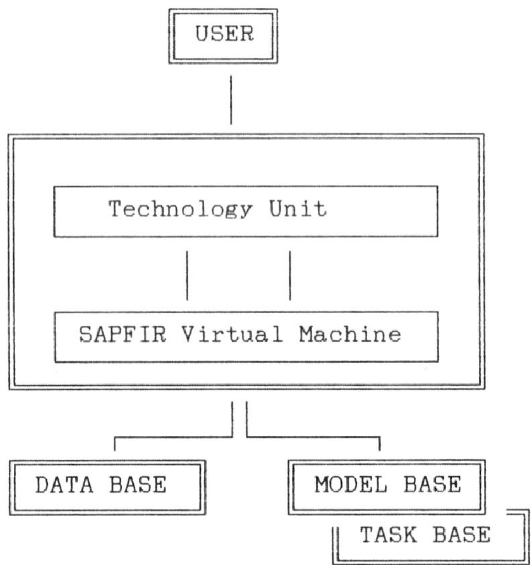

Fig.3. The System Structure.

The TECHNOLOGY UNIT (TU) consists of functions which implement modes of possible user actions to create and run simulation programs. In other words these functions define the technology of model creation in the SAPFIR from the user´s point of view. The TU programs the SAPFIR VIRTUAL MACHINE.

The SAPFIR VIRTUAL MACHINE (VM) is central part of the whole approach because it implements those functions which define a fairly permanent kernel technology of SAPFIR (network representation - scheduling of computation - run simulation program), "distinct" from the dialogue- and hardware-dependent sides of the system.

The aim of such division is to provide portability of the system among different problem domains,since each of them may require different dialogues, visual representations of network elements and so on. Another advantage of the VM is that it may be integrated with an external package. For example, Ashton-Tate's Framework may replace functions of the original TECHNOLOGY UNIT but call the same VIRTUAL MACHINE.

The MODEL BASE consists of blocks of networks which are representation of problem domains, i.e. model in the SAPFIR is equal network (or block). These networks contains information necessary to generate a TASK.

The TASK BASE contains executable simulation programs.

The DATA BASE provides necessary data for execution.

Regard a more detailed structure of the VIRTUAL MACHINE (Fig.4). From the outside point of view it consists of 5 classes of operations which encapsulate inner data structure and auxiliary operations.

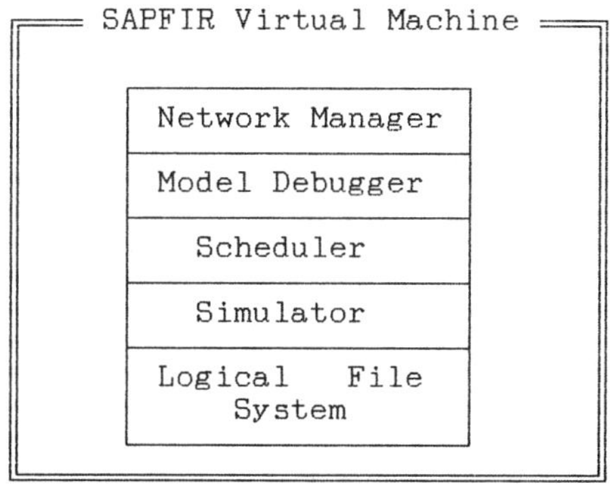

Fig.4. The Virtual Machine Structure.

The Network Manager class serves to create and manipulate network elements. The Model Debugger functions check the syntax of the network. The Scheduler functions creates executable simulation program. The Simulator functions execute the program and produce data exchange. The Logical File System provides data save/retrieval.

5. CONCLUSION.

Among main advantages of the system we may notice decreasing time for model creation; facility for "module construction" of network using blocks in model base and the possibility of several task formulation for a single model.

A number of models have been created with versions of the SAPFIR system in ecology, economy and technology, e.g. water ecosystem model, regional economy model etc.

REFERENCES

[1] Ivanischev V.V., V.E.Marley, V.P.Morozov. The Algorithmic Network Language.,Leningrad, LNIVC 1984, reprint (Russian).

[2] Complex Systems Algorithmic Simulation. Ivanischev V.V. (ed), Leningrad, LIIAN, 1989 (Russian).

Industrial Applications of Artificial Intelligence
J.L. Alty and L.I. Mikulich (Editors)
Elsevier Science Publishers B.V. (North-Holland)
1991 IFIP

DECISION SUPPORT SYSTEM FOR LARGE-SCALE DEVELOPMENT PLANNING IN CHEMICAL INDUSTRY

Barnikow,A.;Behrendt,U.;Hartmann,K.;Scharni,M.

Institute for Chemical Technology *
Academy of Sciences of the GDR
Berlin, GDR

A model-based Decision Support System (DSS) for complex technological, economic and other systems of a high dimension , which can be described by linear models is presented. The DSS aims at the determination of decision variants in industrial development planning (centralized high level decision making, development planning in bigger or smaller enterprises down to plant dispatching) in different time horizons as a result of a multi-criteria optimization. The DSS is data bank based, it consists of a data bank handler, a flexible task dependent model generator, a problem solver and a solution analyzer, which provides manifold facilities for evaluation, analysis, comparison and documentation of solutions. By these tools the DSS supports the whole process of computer aided decision making.

1. INTRODUCTION

Decision making is one of the most complex mental activities of human being. Decision situations are mostly characterized by a great variety of goals and influences, partly contradicting each other, which are connected in a complicated, often not even clearly defined manner. The idea of decision support systems was created in 1971 by Scott-Morton /1/ as interactive computer-based systems, which help the decision maker to use data and models in solving ill-structured problems, connecting by this way mental resources of human with the capabilities of computers for improving the quality of management decisions. A further improvement in decision support was the embodiment of knowledge and abilities of human experts in knowledge-based systems, the so called expert systems, which allow the computer to give intelligent advise to the user. In the author's opinion such kind of knowledge processing will become an important part of decision support systems, what can improve but not replace the model-based analysis, simulation, optimization and design of industrial process systems.

* Akademie der Wissenschaften der DDR
Institut fuer chemische Technologie
Rudower Chaussee 5, Berlin, DDR - 1199

2. WHICH PROBLEMS CAN BE SOLVED ?

DICTUM was developed for decision support in the special field of carbon based energy and chemical branches. It addresses users of centralized high level decision responsibility as well as managers in strategic planning departments of bigger or smaller enterprises.

The DICTUM system can be a powerful tool especially for simulations of /2/:

- integration of new technologies, products or feedstock into an existing structure
- influence of forecast development on feedstock supply or production demand
- system effects such as bottlenecks or at the opposite reserves
- competitive analysis of structure variations
- strategic planning
- implementation of concrete measurements for decreasing environmental pollution within a given industrial structure.

3. DATA BANKS AND LARGE-SCALE-SYSTEM GENERATION

Decision support systems operating within technological systems of high dimension and varying structures can only effectively work using a data bank based approach. Such a data bank must include all necessary information on technologies, material, energy and economic flows and also some background information. DICTUM works with data bases describing the complex technological, material, energetic, ecological and economic connections of various domains, it allows the construction and permanent modification of these data bases and can be adapted by this way to different special tasks.

In particular, the DICTUM data bank includes linear input-output element models of already existing and also new developed technologies of a special industrial domain (e.g. chemistry) with their capacities and also their verbal descriptions.

All material, energetic, economic and ecological flows described in these input-output models are involved in the section "materials" of the data bank. It contains such information like prices, enthalpy, units and different variants of the system's demand or supply.

A data bank manager supplies the necessary comfortable handling operations for appending, editing etc. and gives also information about technological connections in the whole system (e.g. which technologies are producing or consuming a certain material).

On the basis of this data bank the user can generate a

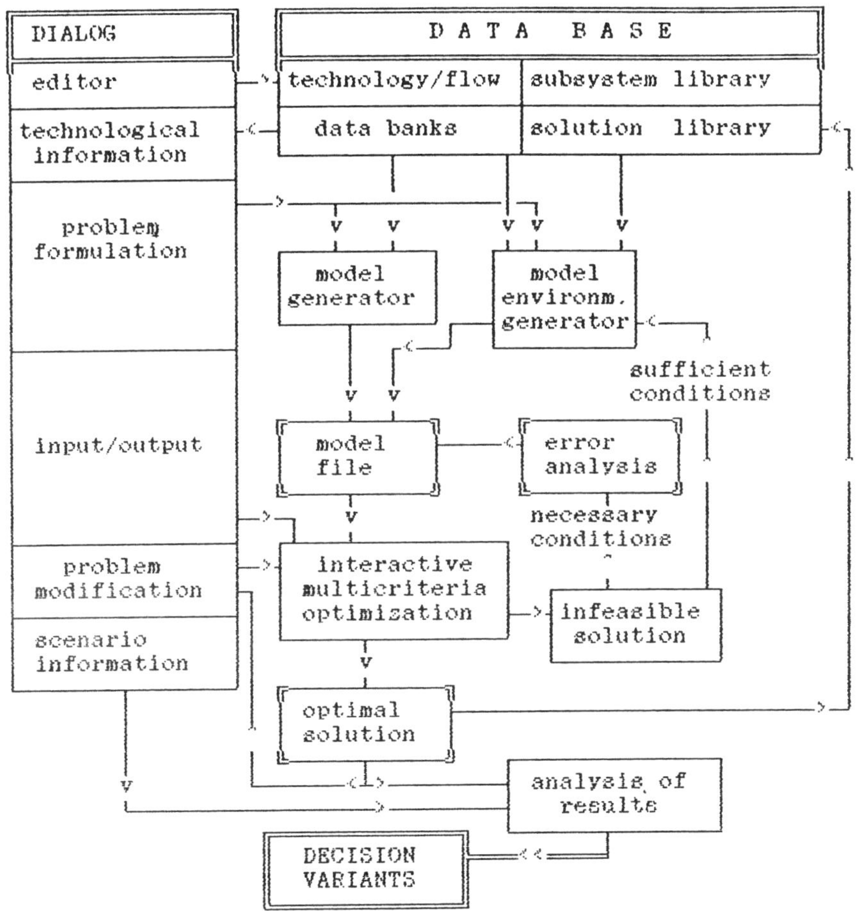

FIGURE 1 The DICTUM Communication Chart

special model of the investigated subsystem according to the concrete problem, what has to be solved in the decision making process (see fig. 1).

This generated problem-adequate substructure is described on the one hand by the technologies and flows, included from the whole data base into the concrete model and on the other hand by the constraints on technology capacities and flow demand and supply (scenario information). The selection of technologies to be included is possible by different ways:

- using standard subsystems,
- by "masks" for the technology and stream code names (according to a built up hierarchically nomenclature)
- by activating them in a user dialog, following the technological flow
- by a combination of these methods.

The scenario information (capacities and material demand or supply) can be obtained from one or several standard capacity and demand vectors included in the data bank, or can be calculated for the current task according to the real system borders based on some already solved tasks in other technological systems. The latter method of scenario generation is able to guarantee a problem description without contradictions and in this way the feasibility of the solution.

During the flexible problem generation process it is also possible to decide on the used level of aggregation. So e.g. different similar material streams can be aggregated using weight coefficients, or the user can generate systems of more aggregated technologies.

A system of economic evaluations for costs and profits, based on the actual resource use and product supply of the technological subsystem and the corresponding prices can be set up according to the concrete conditions independently of the input-output models of technologies.

One of the most important tasks of modern systems analysis apart from the determination of optimal states of existing technological systems is the definition of the best possible way of development from an existing state of technology in industry to a future state, this should also be one of the main task in long-term planning industrial systems. For the solution of such a task a model must reflect on the one hand changing ranges of products and feedstocks (which can be limited for the whole planning period, e.g. oil) and on the other hand the "history" of plants (investments, setting to work, expanding production, closing down), and also economic mechanisms of the cycle credit-investment-profit-investment.

The concept of a dynamic technological model, consisting of some period-specific models is applied in DICTUM for such investigations. Models of different time periods are coupled by investments, which increase capacity in one of the following periods, and also by feedstocks, limited for the whole simulation period (storages).

4. Simulation Process and Optimization Approaches

Usually large technological systems can be modelled as systems of linear equations or inequalities. That is due to the nessecity of aggregation and approximation for a high level representation of complex structures. For this reason in the current version of DICTUM all models are proposed to be of the linear type. Correspondingly a modified simplex method for linear programming is the only numerical method in DICTUM.

Proper optimization of technological and economical problems nowadays usually leads to multicriteria evaluation concepts. Experienced decision makers in this field are used to have their own methods for the selection and the composition of their criteria. To match the experience and habits of as much as possible decision makers on different planning levels above the single criteria optimization a representative set of multicriteria approaches (classical weighting, pairwise weighting, goal programming, preference conception) was implemented in DICTUM.

The basis of the decision support making by DICTUM is an interactive procedure. At the beginning the model, the evaluation mode, and the environment are chosen and specified. On this basis ambigeuos test situations may be simulated to find out the one or more convenient decision proposals by a dialog with the computer where the decision maker is asked for "subdecisions" on various computer-generated variants during the process.

Usually the problem is solved stepwise by a user controlled iteration process. These iterations are not of the numerical type. They concern the idea of an economical or technological high level strategic planning problem only being able to be solved on the base of testing different well designed variants and measurements by simulation runs. At each step within these iterations one complete simulation run is performed. After this certain modifications of model parameters, model environment, or evaluation parameters may be specified. At the end of this part of the dialog the new starting point for the next iteration step is formulated. In that way the decision maker finds the best technological variants matching the given technological, economical, or research problem situation.

5. The Solution Analysis and Representation

The DICTUM solutions represent concrete model simulation variants obtained by the DICTUM simulation module. They usually contain a high number of values, one for each variable, all of them being important in some way for conclusions. So, usually thousands of figures taken from different solutions are to be comparatively to each other analyzed. That's why it is absolutely necessary to have a helpful software tool for analyzing, comparing and interpreting one or more solutions.

For this special purpose a solution tracer was developed. The idea of this tool is to quantitatively show how the material streams and capacities of plants are embedded in the technological structure.

The user has to start at one point of this structure, i.e. a stream or a plant, and from here he can trace along an arbitrary technological chain. All solution components connected to each point are shown immediately on the screen.

The possibility to define and balance a block containing two or more plants enables the user to trace through a more aggregated structure including that block as one unit (additionally, such aggregated subsystems may serve a new column for computations on another aggregation level); the implementation of mathematical functions for immediate comparison of two or more solutions enlightens the variation in terms of differences or proportions; the representation of the share of producers and consumers of a given material can be given in terms of different relations, e.g. of per cent.

A special aggregation concept is realized on the base of linear combination of single values for the variables. Networks, flow sheets, outcuts, or other features with respect to the habits of the user may be composed to a "slide show".

Above this a generation of report components is possible. Here the output stream of results is driven by a set of certain filters and referring to a special table of contents. The standard filters may be modified on each step of simulation iterations. These filters are of numerical, logical, or technological type, and enable the user to select variables of bigger, smaller, or zero amounts or shadow prices, such with relevant or nonrelevant for current solution constraints, technological material groups, energetical or economical relevant streams or technologies, special interesting processes and others.

6. CONCLUSIONS

By a softwaresystem, used directly by decision makers of centralized high level decision responsibility as well as managers in strategic planning departments of bigger or smaller enterprises a new quality of decision making can be achieved. The decision making process will be considerably accelerated, the investigated technological variants embedded in a broad environment and universally evaluated. By simple changes of the data bases the effects of an implementation of the latest results of technological research in an existing structure can be tested very fast and perspektive developments can be simulated and evaluated in a variety of probable realizations. During such a decision making process solved problems are presented in an transparent way, the user does not need any knowledge in computing and can concentrate on the technologic and economic aspects of decision making.

REFERENCES

/1/ Scott-Morton, M.S.: Management Decision Systems, Harvard University 1971

/2/ Barnikow, A.; Behrendt, U.; Hartmann, K.; Scharni, M.: An Interactive Decision Support System for Energy and Chemical Industry Projects, Systems Analysis Modelling Simulation (1990) 4

Industrial Applications of Artificial Intelligence
J.L. Alty and L.I. Mikulich (Editors)
Elsevier Science Publishers B.V. (North-Holland)

THE ABILITIES OF DSS "POLINA" IN THE ANALYSIS OF MULTIPLE OBJECTIVE LINEAR PROGRAMMING PROBLEMS

I. P. POPCHEV, B. S. METEV, and I. T. YORDANOVA
Systems Research Department,
Institute of Industrial Cybernetics and Robotics,
Bulgarian Academy of Sciences,
Sofia,
Bulgaria.

ABSTRACT: This paper presents a brief review of the mathematical methods, used in DSS "POLINA", its general abilities and an example of the system application. It deals with multicriteria linear programming problems. A theoretical background of the implemented methods in "POLINA", a description and an example of its abilities are given in the paper.

1. INTRODUCTION

In the last 10-15 years an extremely intensive development of Decision Support Systems (DSS) and particularly of Multiple Criteria DSS has occurred. Multicriteria DSS are classical examples of DSS. There are three basic ways to improve these systems: by new multicriteria optimization methods, by a better user interface and by widening their "real-world" application. In the scientific literature, different descriptions of such systems are well-known, for example DIDAS [3] and VIG [2], which deal with the theoretical basis of the utilized methods and their practical implementation. The large amount of publications prove the variety of possible applications in the analysis of specific practical problems, which require explicit optimization of many criteria, as well as the use as a secondary tool in the analysis of very complex models of real processes.

2. DESCRIPTION OF THE SYSTEM

2.1. Problem Formulation

Let $x \in R^n$ and let $S \subseteq R^n$ be the feasible set in the multiple objective linear programming (MOLP) problem. The feasible region S in the decision space is defined by linear constraints. The m ($m > 1$) linear functions $f_i(x)$, $i \in I$ and $f_j(x)$, $j \in J$, are defined in S and these functions may be considered as partial criteria for optimization. The functions $f_i(x)$ should be maximized and the functions $f_j(x)$ should be minimized. The sets of indexes I and J satisfy the conditions:

$$|I| + |J| = m \quad \text{and} \quad I \cap J = 0$$

The points z with coordinates $[f_i(x), f_j(x)]$, that are images of all feasible points $x \in S$ define the feasible set $Z \subseteq R^m$ in the criterion space.

The MOLP problem considered in this paper is formulated as:

$$\text{"max"} \; \{f_i(x)\} \qquad i \in I$$

$$\text{"min"} \; \{f_j(x)\} \qquad j \in J$$

$$\underline{\text{such that}} \quad x \in S$$

Excluding the trivial case in which a point exists in the feasible region S, that simultaneously maximizes all criteria $f_i(x)$, $i \in I$ and minimizes all criteria $f_j(x)$, $j \in J$, the way to solve a multiple objective program is either using an explicit decision maker's utility function or using only implicit information about the decision maker's preferences.

2.2. Solution of the MOLP Problem

The system "POLINA" includes realizations of two methods for solving the MOLP problem. These methods belong to the reference point methods - they realize interactive procedures using a reference point z^+, which is indicated by the Decision Maker (DM) and which reflects his preferences; at each iteration the system determines a non-dominated point in the criterion space, which corresponds to the chosen reference point; the phases of decision making alternate with phases of computation.

In the first method we use ordinary Tchebycheff distance to the reference point or an analogical one. The reference point can be an arbitrary point in the criterion space.

In the second method we use the reference point, as well as, the opposite ideal point z^-. The following single criterion linear programming problem is obtained and solved in this case:

$$\min \left(d - \sum_{k=1}^{m} c_k e_k\right)$$

Such that:

(Pl)

$$\begin{array}{ll}
x \in S, & \\
d \geq b_i\,[r_i - f_i(x)\,] & i \in I \\
d \geq b_j\,[f_j(x) - r_j\,] & j \in J \\
d \geq 0 & \\
e_i(x) = f_i(x) - z^-_i & i \in I \\
e_j(x) = z^-_j - f_j(x) & j \in J \\
ek(x) \geq 0 & k = 1/m
\end{array}$$

end.

In this formulation b_i, b_j, c_k are strictly positive real coefficients, r_i, r_j are the coordinates of the reference point (an arbitrary point in R^m) and z^-_i, z^-_j are the coordinates of the opposite ideal point. The constraint $e_k(x) \geq 0$ is valid for each k and for each point $x \in S$.

2.3. Some Characteristics of the MOLP Problem Solutions Obtained Through (Pl).

The first important characteristic of the problem (Pl) is that its solutions determine only Pareto points in the criterion space Z (the weak Pareto points and the dominated points are rejected). This fact for some positions of the reference point in the criterion space is analysed in [4] and [6]. The full proof in all cases (when r is an arbitrary point) is studied in [7].

The second important characteristic of the problem (Pl) consists in the following.
Let $r^1 = (r_1^{\,1}, r_2^{\,1}, \ldots\ldots r_m^{\,1})$ and $r^2 = (r_1^{\,2}, r_2^{\,2}, \ldots\ldots r_m^{\,2})$ be two reference points and let $z^1 = (z_1^{\,1}, z_2^{\,1}, \ldots\ldots z_m^{\,1})$ and $z^2 = (z_1^{\,2}, z_2^{\,2}, \ldots\ldots z_m^{\,2})$ be the corresponding points in the criterion space obtained through (Pl). If $k \in I$ and if for r^1 and r^2 the following is true:

$$r_s^2 = r_s^1 \qquad s \in (I \cup J), \quad S \neq k$$
$$r_k^2 = r_k^1 + \delta \qquad \delta > 0$$

then:

$$z_1^2 \geq z_1^2$$

If $k \in J$, then the solution of (Pl) has a respective property. This characteristic means that after solving (Pl) with a fixed reference point r and after obtaining the solution z, for an arbitrary selected k, the reached level z_k of the k-th criterion can be improved if the new reference point is selected in an appropriate way. This characteristic for some particular cases is proved in [4], [6] and for all cases - in [7].

The system "POLINA" uses the single criterion linear programming problem (Pl) and its properties in the following way: the user indicates the point r, the system solves the problem (Pl) for this point, the vector $x^o \in S$ and the corresponding vector $z^o = [f_i(x^o), f_j(x^o)]$ are obtained. The Decision Maker has the possibility either to accept or not the point z^o as a final solution of the multicriteria problem. In the second case, if the user does not accept it, the system gives him some recommendations for the choice of the new reference point. The Decision Maker indicates this new point and the problem (Pl) is solved again. At each iteration the user "pulls" only one component of the reference point which corresponds to one of the criteria. This guarantees a subsequent improvement of these criteria, for values which don't satisfy the Decision Maker.

2.4. General Characteristics and Abilities of "POLINA"

The system "POLINA" is designed to support users, who make decisions of problems described by multicriteria linear programming models. The system offers to the Decision Maker the following possibilities:

- to input and edit the MOLP problem formulations;
- to find the ideal and the opposite ideal points of the problem;
- to check the compatibility of the problem's system of constraints;
- to check the feasibility of a point in the criterion space chosen by the user;
- to check the nondominance of a feasible point in the criterion space chosen by the user;
- to find a solution of the problem using the two interactive methods described above;
- to save the problem's formulation and the problem's results in files.

The system consists of two basic phases - preparatory and operative. The first phase includes problem definition and reduction, constraint compatibility checking, and ideal and opposite ideal points computing. The ideal and opposite ideal points computations give important information to the DM about reasonable range of decision outcomes. The operative phase deals with finding of a nondominated solution of the MOLP problem using the described methods and the realization of some additional functions, as well as, compatibility and nondominance check of a chosen point.

"POLINA" maintains an user-friendly dialogue with the Decision Maker, that helps him in the choice of the reference point and in finding of the final solution. The system recommendations are generated on the basis of the sensitivity analysis of the single criterion linear problem, which is solved at each iteration.

The system "POLINA" is implemented in C on an IBM/XT and other compatible systems. The minimum of 512 KB RAM is required.

2.5. Example

The Multicriteria DSS can be applied for different purposes. On the one hand, each problem dealing with single objective mathematical programming problems, contains a potential possibility for applying a multicriteria analysis. On the other hand, the multicriteria optimization systems have larger abilities in comparison to the standard single criterion optimization packages. For this reason they can be used in research and analysis of very complex real process models.

To illustrate the abilities of DSS "POLINA" in a practical application, we examine the problem of the machining of a 390 die-cast aluminium alloy. This problem is studied by the Reynolds Metal Company [l] and an adequate mathematical model is obtained. In [5] this model is examined and solutions of the problem are mentioned. These solutions are obtained through three methods for multicriteria optimization - Weighting Technique, Zionts-Wallenius and Compromise Programming.

The performance characteristics of the problem are selected as follows: surface roughness, surface integrity, tool life, metal removal. The Surface Roughness is equal to the height of the irregularities in the surface. It is measured in microinches. The Surface Integrity refers to the undamaged primary silicon at and immediately below the surface and it is measured in percent undamaged silicon at 0.001 in. depth below the surface. The third criterion is the Tool Life defined as the time until the tool reaches a specified wear. It is measured in minutes. The metal removal rate (MRR) is equal to the volume of metal that is machined per unit time. It is measured in in./min.

Each of these characteristics depends on the following three parameters: cutting speed v, feed rate f and the depth of cut d. The first one is defined as the speed at which the tool is moving and it is measured in surface feet/min (sfm). The second one is the rate at which the tool is pushed toward the part, and its measure is in inches per revolution (ipr). Finally, the depth of cut is the length of that part of the tool, which is doing the cut and it is measured in inches (in).

The aim in the problem is to maximize Surface Integrity(SR), Tool Life(TL) and MRR, and to minimize Surface Roughness(SR). Each of the three parameters influences in a different way each of the four criteria. For example, an increase of the feed rate f, causes the metal removal rate MRR and the surface roughness to increase also (i.e. one of the criteria changes in a desired way, the change of the other criterion is undesired). There are contradictory interactions between the criteria. For this reason an ideal solution of the defined problem does not exist.

The relations between the parameters and criteria are not linear, but they can be linearized using the natural logarithms of each of the four objectives and each of the three parameters. Then, the following functions are obtained:

$$\ln SR = 7.49 - 0.44 \ln v + 1.16 \ln (1000f) - 0.61 \ln (1000d)$$
$$\ln SI = -4.13 + 0.92 \ln v - 0.16 \ln (1000f) + 0.43 \ln (1000d)$$
$$\ln TL = 21.90 - 1.94 \ln v - 0.30 \ln (1000f) - 1.04 \ln (1000d)$$
$$\ln MRR = -11.33 + \ln v + \ln (1000f) + \ln (1000d)$$

The parameters f and d are multiplied by 1000 in order to ensure their positive logarithms (the variables in the linear programming problem must be nonnegative).

The constraints of the problem's parameters are the following:

$$600 \text{ sfm} \le v \le 1200 \text{ sfm}$$
$$0.002 \text{ ipr} \le f \le 0.018 \text{ ipr}$$
$$0.05 \text{ in} \le d \le 0.10 \text{ in.}$$

On the other hand, limiting constraints exist for some criteria:

$SR \leq 75\ \mu$ in
$SI \geq 50\%$
$TL \geq 30$min.

After applying the natural logarithm to all constraints and after accepting, that
$x_1 = \ln v$,
$x_2 = \ln (1000f)$,
$x_3 = \ln (1000d)$,
$f_1(x) = \ln SR$,
$f_2(x) = \ln SI$,
$f_3(x) = \ln TL$,
$f_4(x) = \ln MRR$,

the following MOLP problem is obtained:

$$\max \{ f_2(x), f_3(x), f_4(x) \}, \min \{f_1(x) \}$$

where
$$f_1(x) = 7.49 - 0.44x_1 + 1.16x_2 - 0.61x_3$$
$$f_2(x) = -4.13 + 0.92x_1 - 0.16x_2 + 0.43x_3$$
$$f_3(x) = 21.9 - 1.94x_1 - 0.30x_2 - 1.04x_3$$
$$f_4(x) = -11.33 + x_1 + x_2 + x_3$$

<u>such that:</u>
$$x_1 \geq 640$$
$$x_1 \leq 7.09$$
$$x_2 \geq 0.69$$
$$x_2 \leq 2.89$$
$$x_3 \geq 3.91$$
$$x_3 \leq 4.61$$
$$-0.44\ x_1 + 1.16\ x_2 - 0.61\ x_3 \leq -3.17$$
$$-0.92\ x_1 + 0.16\ x_2 - 0.43\ x_3 \leq -8.04$$
$$1.94\ x_1 + 0.30\ x_2 + 1.04\ x_3 \leq 18.50$$

The ideal point z^* of this problem is obtained using "POLINA":

$z_1^* = 2.41676$ for the vector x =(6.95804,0.69,4.61)
$z_2^* = 4.15885$ for the vector x =(7.09, 0.69, 4.36385)
$z_3^* = 3.98520$ for the vector x =(7.03163, 0.69, 3.91)
$z_4^* = 1.58050$ for the vector x =(6.83869, 1.4618, 4.61)

The opposite ideal point is:

$z_1^- = 3.67933$ for the vector x =(7.09, 1.56613, 4.1111)
$z_2^- = 3.91000$ for the vector x = (7.03163, 0.69, 3.91)
$z_3^- = 3.40000$ for the vector x = (6.83869, 1.46183, 4.61)
$z_4^- = 0.30110$ for the vector x = (7.03163, 0.69, 3.91)

The problem is solved with "POLINA" using the second method. The results can be seen in Table 1 and Table 2 - they contain the real values of the objectives and the parameters (and not the values of their natural logarithms) in the ideal point, the opposite ideal point, in the points obtained in the different iterations and in the final solution.

Table 1

objective	measure	constr.	opp.i.p.	I iter.	II iter.	III iter.	fin.sol.	idealpoint
SR	μin.	≤ 75	39.6198	13.287	14.2406	13.3926	12.019	11.209
SI	%	≥ 50	50.000	60.420	50.000	51.640	54.860	64.000
TL	min	≥ 30	30.000	30.000	45.458	43.419	40.045	53.796
MRR	in/min	none	1.3500	2.8437	2.2544	2.2290	2.1843	4.8574

Table 2

parameter	measure	constraints	I iteration	II iteration	III iteration	final sol.
v	sfm	600 ≤ v ≤1200	1029	832.98	858.34	905.15
f	ipr	0.002≤ f ≤0.018	0.0029	0.0024	0.0022	0.0020
d	in.	0.055 ≤d ≤ 0.1	0.1	0.1	0.1	0.1

The analysis of the results proves, that the points obtained at each iteration are nondominated. The procedure realized in "POLINA" may be considered as a semistructured approach for generating a sequence of improved solutions (according to the decision maker's opinion). The sequence converges to a nonextreme final solution. The points obtained in [5] through the three mentioned methods can also be obtained through the methods realized in "POLINA". The most simple way to do this is to use a reference point, which is the same as the desired one.

3. CONCLUSION

The "POLINA" system for multicriteria linear programming and decision making problems has been briefly presented in this paper. The implemented modern interactive procedures for solving MOLP problems, as well as the implemented additional functions offered to the Decision Maker are a guarantee to the successful use of the system in real practice.

4. ACKNOWLEDGEMENT

The work is supported by the Bulgarian Ministry of Science and Higher Education under the contract No 318/1987.

REFERENCES

[1] Ghiassi, M., DeVor, R.E., Dessovsky, M.I. and Kijowski, B.A., "An application of multiple criteria decision making principles for planning machining operations", *IIE Trans.* 16(2): 106-114 (1984).

[2] Korhonen, P. and Laakso, J., "A Visual Interactive Method for Solving the Multiple Criteria Problem", *European Journal of Operational Research,* Vol. 24, No2, (1986).

[3] Lewandowski, A., Kreglewski, T., Rogowski, T. and Wierzbicki, A., "Decision Support Systems of DIDAS Family (Dynamic Interactive Analysis & Support)", in: Lewandowski, A. and Wierzbicki, A. (eds.): Theory, Software and Testing Examples for Decision Support Systems,(WP-87-26,IIASA, Laxenburg, Austria,1987), pp.4-26.

[4] Metev, B. and Yordanova, I., "An Interactive Approach for MOLP Problems Analysis", International Workshop on MCDS, Helsinki, 1989, Proceedings, in print.

[5] Mitwasi, M., Connolly, A.-M., Duckstein, L., "Applying Multicriteria Decision Making Techniques for Planning Machining Operations", *Applied Mathematics and Computation,* Vol. 29, (1989), pp. 197-218.

[6] Popchev, I., Metev, B. and Yordanova, I., "A Realization of Reference Point Method Using the Tchebycheff Distance", International Conference on: Multiobjective Problems of Mathematical Programming, USSR, 1988, Proceedings, in print.

[7] Yordanova, I., "DSS with Use of MOLP Problems", Ph. D. Thesis, Sofia, (1989).

Industrial Applications of Artificial Intelligence
J.L. Alty and L.I. Mikulich (Editors)
Elsevier Science Publishers B.V. (North-Holland)

AN INTELLIGENT CAD SYSTEM FOR STRUCTURE DESIGN

W. MING, J. GUOFANG and L. SHENQIAN

CAD Laboratory,
Institute of Computing Technology,
Academia Sinica,
Beijing,
P. R. China.

ABSTRACT: With the adoption of Artificial Intelligence in the area of CAD, how to use this methodology to aid engineering design effectively and practically is becomingly increasingly important. In this paper this problem is discussed from both the characteristics of engineering design and the scope of AI techniques. Based on the discussion, an intelligent CAD system which is focussed on the structure design of a pre-processor, a kind of industrial instrument, is advanced. The system is characterised by its representation of design knowledge and its automation of engineering design. It can help the designers of pre-processors intelligently and efficiently.

1. INTRODUCTION

The term CAD (Computer Aided Design) covers the use of computers to aid designers in their design activities. Thus aids should be included which consist of specification, decomposition, synthesis, analysis, evaluation and documentation [1]. For some reasons, however, most CAD systems only emphasise the later stages of the design process providing aid for geometrical modelling, engineering analysis, drawing and so on. As a result these systems are:

1) Poor in intelligent support: the use of an application is usually restricted to solve previously solved problems

2) Complicated man-machine communication: the attention of the designers is distracted by too many minor decisions made repeatedly

3) Poor for evolutionary implementation: the extension of any new resource in the existing system is inhibited by the intricate modifications to the control logic

These problems result from the limitations inherent in conventional information processing technology. The development of Artificial Intelligence (AI) has provided ways of overcoming them. AI techniques such as knowledge representation and automatic inference have made computers more intelligent in solving problems and has reduced the gap between requirements and computer capability

The intelligent CAD system which will be discussed in this paper is targetted at the structure design of the pre-processor, a kind of industrial instrument used to collect coal gas in steel and chemical departments. During the implementation of the system some AI techniques were employed. The objectives for the system to reach are:

- provide automatic generation of the structure of the preprocessor.
- make interaction between designers and computers at a high decision level

2 Theory

2.1 Design Knowledge

For the design of pre-processor, there are three general categories of design knowledge. They are classified by the problems which they are meant to solve during design process[2].

- *Domain Knowledge* : Domain knowledge consists of information from which designers can get the means of the solution about the design of pre-processor. From the viewpoint of structure design, it is a formal scheme for describing a set of components that decide what the pre-processor is composed of and a set of rules that explain how these components are related to construct a pre-processor.
- *Control Knowledge* : Control knowledge is made of advice that intends to guide the design to progress. It defines the possible steps towards the solution and provides the proper strategies for the choice among alternatives.
- *Restrict Knowledge* : Restrict knowledge is composed of the restrictions and the requirements that must be satified during the design process.

2.2 Knowledge Representation

In order to represent the design knowledge in computer, two kinds of knowledge representation schemes are employed.

First Order Predicate Logic : First order predicate logic is used to represent domain knowledge and restrict knowledge. When represented by first order predicate logic, knowledge is classified into two parts : facts and rules. A fact is the description of attributes of a component. It is represented by 1-term or n-term atomic predicate; a rule is the description of the relationship among facts. It is represented by predicate calculus formula.

Particularly, for the implementation of automatic inference, the predicates and the predicate calculus formulae are converted into HORN clauses, a special form of first order predicate logic. For an HORN clause, it appears in one of the following forms:

rule : $A_1 \wedge A_2 \wedge \ldots \wedge A_n \rightarrow B_1$
fact : $\rightarrow B_1$
empty : $\rightarrow$
(where $n>0$, A_1, A_2, $\ldots A_n$, B_1 are atomic predicates)

The possibility for the convertion is ensured by the definition of domain knowledge and the theorem in mathematical logic.

Production System : A production system is employed to represent control knowledge. It has a simple organization which is composed of a collection of "if-then" rules. It derives a conclusion based on pattern matching between facts. The control functions carried by control knowledge can be performed by its well developed matching mechanism[3][4].

2.3 A Brief Example

To explain the knowledge representation scheme more clearly, a set of knowledge represented by HORN clauses and production rules are shown below. The knowledge is taken from the design of pre-processor. It concerns with the design of an artifact called dust-remover.

- Domain knowledge:

D1: pipe_base(y, l_1, r)∧pipe_head(x, l_2, r)∧above(x, y) →dust_remover(z, l_1+l_2, r)
D2: cylinder_pipe(x, l, r)→pipe_base(x, l, r)
D3: cylinder_pipe(y, l_1, r)∧cylinder(x, l_2, r)∧above(x, y) →pipe_base(z, l_1+l_2, r)
D4: cone_pipe(x, l, r)→pipe_head(x, l, r)
D5: prism_pipe(x, l, r)→pipe_head(x, l, r)
D6: →cylinder(1, 50, 10)
D7: →cylinder(2, 60, 20)
. . . .
Dn: →prism(n, 50, 35)

- Restrict knowledge:

R1: →dust_remover(xxx, 180, r)
R2: →dust_density(55)

- Control knowledge:

C1: IF dust_remover(x, l, r) AND more(l, 175)
THEN set(Height of Pipe_Base, >120)
C2: IF pipe_base(x, l, r) AND more(l, 100)
THEN set(Number of Cylinder_Pipe, 2)
C3: IF dust_density(x) AND more(x, 50)
THEN set(Radius of Dust_Remover, >20)

2.4 Automatic Inference

According to the classification of design knowledge, domain knowledge in fact determines a solution space for the design of pre-processor. Design results which satisfy restrict knowledge, if exists, must lie in this space. And control knowledge just plays the role of finding the results from this space. Therefore, the design knowledge becomes applicable to the formal proof procedure.

Definition of Compatibility : If S is a set of HORN clauses, and it has an explanation which makes all HORN clauses in S true, then the clause set S satisfies compatibility or, in other words, it is compatible.

Theorem of Robinson : If $A_1 \wedge A_2 \wedge \ldots \wedge A_n \rightarrow A$ and $B_1 \wedge B_2 \wedge \ldots \wedge B_m \rightarrow B$ are two HORN clauses, and A matches B_i ($A=B_i$), then the Horn clause $A_1 \wedge A_2 \wedge \ldots \wedge A_n \wedge B_1 \wedge \ldots \wedge B_{i-1} \wedge B_{i+1} \wedge \ldots \wedge B_m \rightarrow B$ succcess. ($m,n \geq 0$)

Deduction : Acting Robinson theorem on an HORN clauses set S repeatedly, if an empty clause is got, then the set S is compatible.

In terms of the definition of compability and the theorem of Robinson. the design preocss can be converted into a series of matching and replacing operations against the HORN clause set [domain knowledge, ¬restrict knowledge]. If this clause set is proven to be compatible, an explanation about it is got. This explanation is just the design solution (of course, we may fail to get it). It offers a useful way which is independent of the special problem being solved.

2.5 Some Improvements

The above inference method is effective for symbolic oriented operations. In order to use it in CAD environment where many numeric-intensive operations are involved and certain topological structures are concerned, some improvements are made.

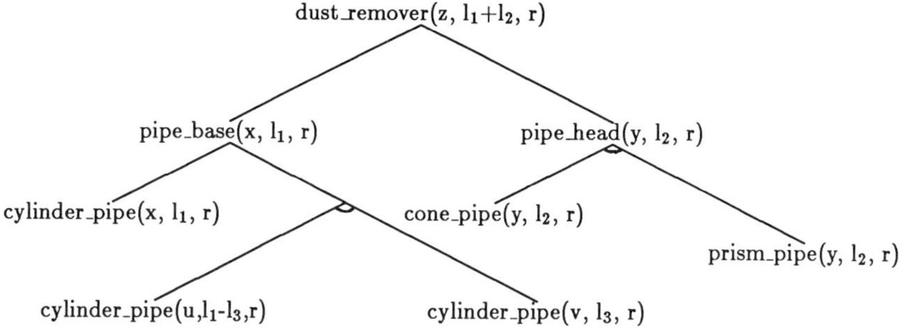

Figure 1: Dust Remover's Solution Tree

Firstly, a method which introduces the relational database system and the computing procedures into automatic inference is used.

The adoption of this method is fulfiled through the consideration of the relationship between the relational data model and computing procedure and the predicate[5]. For example, the relational data model has the following relations with the predicate:

Data model $R(A_1, A_2, \ldots A_n) \Longleftrightarrow$ Atomic predicate $R(X_1, X_2, \ldots X_n)$
Set of tuples in R $\Longleftrightarrow$ Set of true assignments to R
(where A_i is attribute, X_i is individual)

Similarly, the procedure $P(P_1, P_2 \ldots P_n)$ has the same relations with the predicate logic as the relational data model $R(A_1, A_2 \ldots A_n)$ has. Only in this case the parameter P_i is substituted for the attribute A_i and the procedure body for the set of tuples.

In the case, the relational data models and the computing procedures are viewed as the special predicates. They can participate in the automatic inference. With this strategy, when data accesses or data computions are needed during inference, the actual processes will automatically switched to the relational database system or the computing procedures. Therefore, it makes the inference mechanism avoid from matching against masses of data and from engaging in many numeric-intensive treats. The complexity of inference is reduced and the efficiency of the inference mechanism is increased.

Secondly, in terms of the classification of design knowledge, domain knowledge determines the design space of pre-processor. When all of the possible solutions in the space are considered, they can be organized into a solution tree. With the solution tree, the design process is converted into a top-down search along the tree. Each node of the tree represents a subgoal to reach. The structure of a solution tree is illustrated in Figure 1.

2.6 Design Model

Design model is the internal representation of the structure of pre-processor. It is the basis for analysis, evalution, drawing and some further processes. In this paper, an hierarchical tree model is employed. The nodes of the tree represent the components, and the branches represent the relations among components. An example is shown in Figure 2.

During design, design model is viewed as a substructure of the solution tree. It is produced while the searching operations proceed. An simple algorithm for the search is shown below.

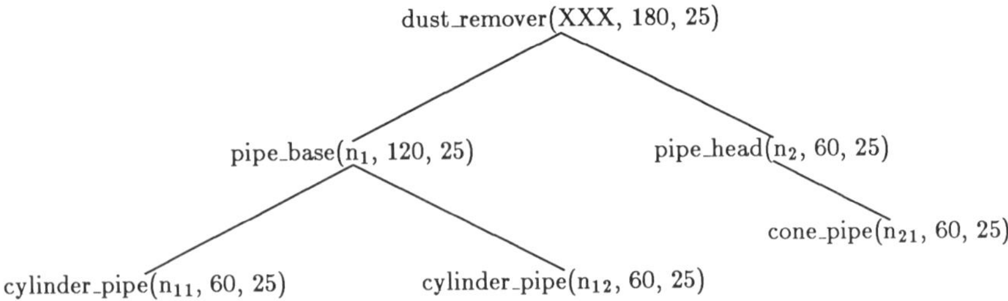

Figure 2: Dust Remover's Application Model

1. *Select a node in solution tree with certain strategy,*
2. *If no node can be selected, then goto step 7,*
3. *Replace the variables in the node with proper values,*
4. *If the node is a leaf, then query relational database, else test against restrict knowledge,*
5. *If query or test does not success, then make a backtrack,*
6. *Goto step 1,*
7. *End of searching.*

3 Implementation

The whole system consists of four subsystems and three libraries, see Figure 3. It provides the following functions:

1. Accepting designers' requirements about the design of pre-processor and finishing the design activities through inference.
2. Displaying the pre-processor's design drawings.
3. Showing the performance parameters and the analytical results corresponding to the design.
4. Offering tools for renewing, adding and modifying the contents in component library and knowledge library.

- Component acquiring subsystem and component library: Standard components are the basic elements to construct more complex components or finally pre-preocssor. The main task of component acquiring subsystem is to provide an environment for designers to describe and produce their own standard components. The data which depict the components are stored in component library.
- Knowledge acquiring subsystem and knowledge library: The knowledge acquiring subsystem's function is to collect the experience about the design of pre-processor, and store it in knowledge library in the form of rules. It is also responsible for renewing, changing, and editing these rules so as to make the system suitable for design objects in diffient application fields.
- Inference subsystem and combined-component library: Inference subsystm is the kernel of the intelligent CAD system. All inference operations take place in this part. A combined-component is a kind of mid-structure composed of standard components. It is produced during designing. All combined-components are stored in combined-component library. With combined-components, the unnecessarily repeated inference operations are avoided, and the efficiency are increased significently.

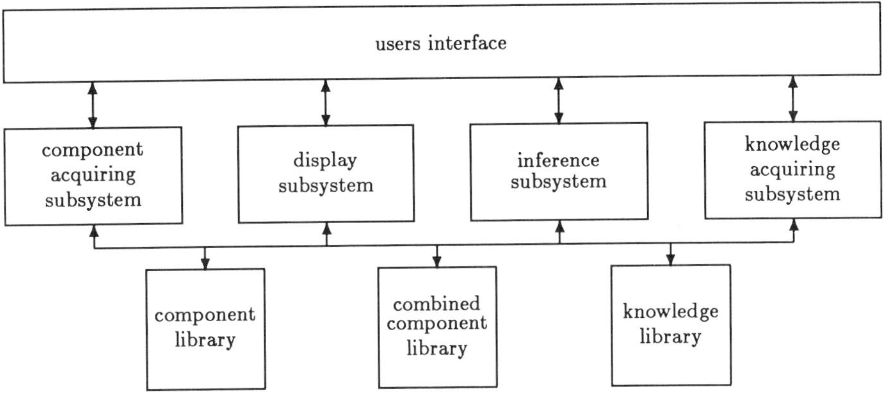

Figure 3: System's Structure

- Displaying subsystem: This subsystem is mainly used for displaying design drawings of standard components, combined-components, or finally pre-processor. Associted with model transform, the process of display is completed by a traverse along the design model.

4 Conclusion

In this paper, an approach for the adoption of AI techniques in engineering design is presented. It ensures the necessary performance for the implementation of AI based CAD systems and at the same time perserves the usual techniques of conventional information processing. The system is under development and the first result is promising. As the implementation of the system progresses, areas for further work become apparent.

1. Evaluation knowledge for design solution should be included in the system.
2. Integrity and consistency is important for the knowledge used in design.
3. System's functions should be extended to the area of manufacture in order to implement an integrated CAD/CAM system.

References

[1] T.Smithers, "AI-Based Design Versus Geometry-Based Design", *Computer-Aided Design*, Vol.21, No.3, 1989

[2] J.J.Alian, "An Intelligent CAD System", *CAD Systems*, North-Holland, 1977

[3] M.L.Maher, "Expert Systems for Structural Design", *Expert Systems in Engineering*, Springer-Varlag, 1988

[4] M.A.Rosenman, "Expert System Application in CAD", *Computer-Aided Design*, Vol.18, No.10, 1986

[5] H.S.Chen, M.Wei, "The Design and Implementation of an Intelligent CAD System", *Proceedings of the Third Pan Pacific Computer Conference*, IAP, 1989

Industrial Applications of Artificial Intelligence
J.L. Alty and L.I. Mikulich (Editors)
Elsevier Science Publishers B.V. (North-Holland)

GROUP SIMULATION EXPERT SYSTEM

I. N. KALETCHITS,
Artificial Intelligence Association,
Innovation Union AS,
Moscow,
The USSR.

ABSTRACT: This report describes the group simulation expert system of environment dynamic situations (SISS situation imitative simulation system) which allows the investigation of the processes of complex multicomponent man-machine control systems (MMS), when constructing a broad class of distributed complex systems. SISS uses numerous up-to-data results from the field of artificial intelligence. New methods of pseudoparallel undetermined situation generation process descriptions are offered.

1. INTRODUCTION

In this paper we deal with the domain dynamic situations description and simulation method for multicomponent man-machine control systems (MMS) [1]. The main component of the expert MMS are the distributed objects of control. The distinct features of these objects are the dynamic conditions of their function, their multi-factor nature, distributiveness and the multiplicity of their structures, and also their group control with an hierarchical structure. It is worth mentioning that any artificial (and natural when modelling) domain component may be transferred into a controlled object. This changes the level of control. In its turn the MMS control tasks of distributed objects are changed as the control level increases.

2. METHOD OF APPROACH

Distributed objects are mostly controlled not by one group of operators, but by several, that is why there is a problem in controlling these groups, taking into account unforeseen domain situations. Today, control systems with one or two operators and a computer as the simulation object (or the second operator) have been studied enough and understood. But this not true for large systems. The opportunity of "direct" effect by the operator group on the objects of control through the computer is necessary, i.e. we need group simulation and group control. Such simulation is important at every MMS lifecycle stage, for example at the pre-project stage (where we must analyse the domain components, where technical economical automated. control system [ACS] task and others such as exploiting and teaching). In the MMS mentioned above, control is automated only at the low levels as usual, and at the higher level the human being makes the decisions. That is why the domain effect on the control objects has its great influence on the human being making the decisions. The effect is seen particulary in extreme domain situations, when conflicts arises and unusual decisions are required. Generally, in all functions complex MMS control is planned. This means that system functions or operator ones are planned also, like practical situations in teaching systems.

With increasing system complexity the MMS becomes more important. This effect on control object and on the operators cannot usually be foreseen.

The tasks of the application and of the man may differ and even conflict. In this case, application conflict situations are more often. Therefore when simulating and. working with such systems, "extraordinary" operator control should be foreseen. It is necessary to simulate the MMS functioning in unforeseen situations in the application, which can be critical.

Contrary to existing simulation systems, the operator-customers of SISS should be given an opportunity to control the current situations simulation processes themselves.

In complex man-machine control systems it is necessary to give a full reflection of distributed objects functioning in multi-component environments, taking into account the environment effect on the object and on the operators, and to reflect in intelligible form the application information.

These requirements are provided in the given expert system through the following functional abilities. The data input into the computer is carried out by experts. Thus the simulation system combines the knowledge of many specialists in various subject fields independently. This is most useful in those cases when it is necessary to reflect the behaviour of heterogeneous domain elements and numerous operators groups in the system.

On the other hand, the actual method of representing the initial data [2] and their organization in the knowledge base possesses great expressiveness. It means that it gives deep and exact descriptions of broad knowledge about objects and other environmental phenomena in the dynamics of current events [3] .

3. RESULTS

The realization of the SISS system has provided the possibility of complex information and problems of control decisions when investigating distributed groups and control objects' behaviour in the situation of a complex, dynamically changing environment.

The system is implemented through software in a minicomputer, and is used in parallel multi-terminal conditions.

4. CONCLUSIONS

The existing simulation system SISS refers to the class of the open systems. It means that it may be set to work with various group control systems, with a broad range of dynamics of environment changes and various domain component structures. The implementation of this system and the results of experiments in domain simulation support the possibility of it being used. by both inexperienced experts and by operators.

REFERENCES

[1] Evseev, O., and Kaletchits, I., "Expert System SISS for Environment Situation Simulation and Operator Group Teaching", in: Problems of Expert Systems Design, Part 1, All-Union meeting, Theses of report (The USSR, Moscow, 1988) pp. 96-97.

[2] Kaletchits, I., "Control of Multicomponent Dynamic Situations Group Simulation Process in SISS", in: New generation computers and prospects of their usage in the National Economy, Seminar report (The USSR, Moscow, MDNTP, 1989) pp. 97-103

[3] Kaletchits, I., "Animals' Pathological Conditions Simulation by SISS", Contribution to the conference on PCs in designing and supporting decisions tasks of CMEA countries (The USSR, Suzdal, 1989) p. 25

Industrial Applications of Artificial Intelligence
J.L. Alty and L.I. Mikulich (Editors)
Elsevier Science Publishers B.V. (North-Holland)

SECTION 8: INTELLIGENT MANUFACTURING SYSTEMS: SIMULATION AND DESIGN

COMPUTER - INTELLIGENCE OPTIONS IN FLEXIBLE MANUFACTURING

R.C. MICHELINI, G.M. ACACCIA, and R.M. MOLFINO
Industrial Robot Design Research Group,
University of Genova,
Italy

ABSTRACT: Factory automation is aimed at knowledge intensive shop organizations. In this connection, computer-intelligent software implementations are considered together with mixed (causal / judgemental) processing abilities, to preserve the algorithmic efficiency with respect to deep-knowledge, while adding heuristic flexibility to the shallow-knowledge.

1. INTRODUCTION

Industrial robotics and computer integrated manufacturing issues in factory automation have led to important changes in work-organization, based on the re-introduction of the decisional aspects for controlling production processes. The efficiency of fixed automation was obtained within classical industrialization, through special-purpose equipment, and the de-skilling of online workers. The main aim was large-volume standard production with low-qualified manpower, trained according to work-division patterns, and the reduction of task-complexity down to elemental operations in fixed (optimal) execution sequences.

Currently, fixed automation is claimed to have reached a limit, for two reasons:

- market fragmentation and turbulence which limit, in time, the safe horizon, and in volume, the reliable extension of each given product type
- computer intelligence options, which provide automatic data processing capabilities (in addition to automatic material processing ones).

To achieve flexible automation, however, the manufacturing environment should utilise the technological craft of qualified operators. In fact, improvements in the efficiency of CIM-solutions is the combined result of flexibility in governing multi-agent production surroundings and of total quality management along the fabrication process. Appropriate observation loops should therefore allow on-line control of process monitoring data and modification of ongoing production, according to current product monitoring data.

Flexible on-line expert-controllers should oversee concurrent manufacturing processes and in-process diagnostics should operate within the prescriptions of quality engineering. Both these developments will heavily depend on the specialized application of artificial intelligence. Today, production engineering is indeed a very promising field for the application of such technology.

This paper deals with the implementation of flexible controllers, with embedded computer-intelligence in a knowledge-based framework with the objective of raising plant productivity with intervention [1]:

- at the *strategic* level, covering the enterprise's long horizons, by enabling large-volume throughput with highly diversified mixes, and by adapting process planning through improved exploitation of technologic investment

- at the *tactical* level, by expanding over horizons consistent with 'optimal' running performances, by enabling steady (programmed-mode) fabrication agendas and related shopfloor logistics, constrained by selected production criteria requirements;

- at the *operational* level, by dealing with occurrences, enabling transient (adaptive-mode) manufacturing scheduling, restoring production continuity in situations of unexpected events, and the exploitation of the versatility of technological equipment thus reducing idle spare resources.

The different flexibility levels, require decision-making schemata with a comparable sophistication. A set of different computer-intelligent solutions is considered, in relation to the characteristics of each information loop projected toward complex business objectives:

- employing expert simulation as a consultation aid for *strategic* planning, based on quantitative figures

- covering scheduled fabrication windows and, accordingly, programming shopfloor production control with built-in *tactical* flexibility to obtain just-in-time policies

- reacting to emergencies, thus enabling, through *operational* flexibility, the reconfiguring of the manufacturing facilities, to ensure production continuity.

2. KNOWLEDGE PROCESSING FOR FLEXIBILITY IN MANUFACTURING

Computer-based automation has proved to be an efficient instrument for increasing engineering productivity and product quality. The improvements, however, are not fully realised, unless the efficiency of the on-process decision-making opportunities are presented to the front-end operators of the plant. These potentialities are easily understood by considering trends in factory automation and distinguishing

- the *'mechanistic'* stage, - which involved a labour-intensive shop organization aiming at de-skilling front-end operators, with man-automation being based upon scientific work-organization, establishing optimal job-planning, through task-division paradigms followed by an equipment-intensive shop organization aimed at assisted automation with a pervasive diffusion of mechanistic control schemata, to assure command-planning through the closure of online feedback loops

- from the *'informational'* stage, - a measurement-intensive shop organization which exploited (in addition to material-flow automation) data-flow automation in order to obtain a work-organization with diagnostics planning, based on process supervision capabilities, followed by a knowledge-intensive shop organization, aimed at decision automation, with distributed information integration, in order to generate controls for the coordination planning of the available resources.

Without appropriate decision-making support the amount of information obtained by process and product monitoring and generated from computers, will overwhelm engineers and operators, unless the available generic data are transformed into pertinent knowledge. Engineering knowledge, particularly in the manufacturing field, is a combination of causal (science-based) principles, with judgemental (experience-based) heuristics. Artificial intelligence techniques supply unique tools to assist with decision automation of future knowledge-intensive manufacturing plants. However, it would certainly be foolish to build 'intelligent' systems based only on heuristics, with no regard for experienced engineering models, acknowledged physical principles, or governing equations, that have been tested and known for many years. The knowledge-intensive work organization has therefore to incorporate AI-findings as complementary tools that add to existing engineering methods. Thus production engineers, will be intensively involved, not only in studying ways of processing materials into useful products, but even more in investigating means for processing knowledge into effective commodities [2].

The knowledge processing required by factory automation encompasses five elemental aspects, - *acquisition, shaping, fusion, coordination* and *utilization.* Procedural efficiency depends on the various selected knowledge representation forms. In a first off-process conceptualization phase, that establishes the procedural knowledge, preliminary system-hypotheses are assessed to define the structures for the available data, with the acknowledgment of the binding relationships and of the related manipulation methods. Current approaches offer several means of doing this, for example, logic-based programming, frame-based approaches or rule-based and object-based structures. The choice for the (procedural) shallow-knowledge representation is user- and problem dependent. Combinations of different representations are also useful. In addition, the representation of deep-knowledge needs to preserve the causal structured relationships, either if they are derived from science-based principles; or from direct evidence, through experimental-based measurements. The dual nature (shallow and deep knowledge) of the representation forms should explicitly appear, in the description of the manufacturing processes.

On these premises, software for factory automation has to be developed in a multi-layer fashion, directly including the *relational, generative* and *restitution* layers [3], into simulation/emulation computer-tools for fine tuning of the control strategies, and for the off-process setting of decision sets, These computer tools can eventually expand to a *conceptualization-layer,* for the closure of learning loops charged with updating the declarative and procedural knowledge; and to an *actuation-* layer, for the closure of feedbacks on-line allowing govern-for-flexibility options. At the *relational* -layer, the procedural knowledge has formal representation; the computer-tools, at this level, supply both the simulation-environment (for the causal-based conditioning information) and the emulation-environment (for the logic-based judgemental paradigms). Then the *generative* -layer exploits the algorithmic models (mechanistic conditions, that represent the physical transformations), and the heuristic modes (plausibility bonds, corresponding to the decisional behaviour), and produces the updated current situational information of the ongoing manufacturing processes. The *restitution* -layer assures the interface for shaping the generated data into usable knowledge. Engineers do not usually have unique solutions, and different opinions toward a single problem are, of course, authorized, with good acceptability margins, in contrast to theoretically optimal solutions.

The parallelism of the algorithmic and heuristic data processing modules is an important knowledge *acquisition* and *shaping* feature, for the specialized generation of data, and for supporting decision making. In such a context, knowledge *fusion* is assured, transferring the pertinent data, generated either by simulation (mechanistic knowledge shaping) or by emulation (plausible knowledge specialization), with proper communication interfaces. Knowledge *coordination* adds sophistication in data processing, and is useful for removing procedural redundancy, with cooperative problem-solving methodologies, opening twofold prospects:

- toward an *actuation layer,* for exploiting the front-end decision sets, with specialization of the knowledge *utilization* paradigms for on-line control operations;

- toward a *conceptualization-layer,* for knowledge acquisition through learning operations, with the updating of representation patterns, by upgrading the causal models and by expanding the judgemental modes.

3. COMPUTER INTELLIGENCE TOOLS FOR FACTORY AUTOMATION

The construction of flexible-governors for factory automation exploiting new techniques in computer-intelligence has to be carried out whilst considering in parallel:

- the possibilities offered by the technological versatility of the manufacturing sections, workstations, and robotic equipment, etc.. A set of the reference functional models should be available for providing quantitative specification of the relevant material transformations;

- issues relating to the degree of judgemental freedom in the control systems, exploiting the integrated monitoring and communication devices. A set of reference behavioural modes should be detailed for investigating (with faithful simulation or emulation programs) the results of the decision logic.

In flexible manufacturing, plants typically present a horizontal lay-out, with specialized sections (tooling, machining, assembly, etc.) suitably arranged for jobshop production in order to exploit (for instance) machining-list tactics based on the technology groupings of the varying manufacturing mixes. The related functional models are conveniently developed with a modular architecture, to enable:

- a general overview on the concurrency of the multi-agent framework;
- a focus on specific operations (manufacturing or service) sequences;
- a zooming in on particular functional details, related to a work cell or to a task.

For flexible manufacturing, the controlling scheme should usually be of a hierarchic structure, with a distributed information network connecting central (factory/shop) computers to the coordination computers (that control individual manufacturing sections, in the centralized toolroom, etc.) and to peripheral computers installed within each workstation, robot, or sorting/storing cell, etc.. The specification of behavioural modes is conveniently performed via a knowledge-based architecture, to distinguish the procedural data from the declarative data [3].

Shopfloor logistics provide the critical bond for fusing functional capabilities with behavioural attributes. The manufacturing environment has a relational structure, properly formalized by product/production data-bases. and by well established criteria. The requirement is for deep-knowledge (rather than shallow-knowledge) and production engineering offers a challenging field for expert-systems based upon a mixed causal/judgemental mode, providing practical and useful applications for the advanced abstractions of Artificial Intelligence. The decision sets required for the flexible control of the shopfloor-logistics, are discussed in [4], and a set of specialized expert-programs recently developed by the Industrial Robot Design Research Group of the University of Genova-Italy, is an example of application software using computer-intelligence for the development of flexible manufacturing tools. The shopfloor operation has to adapt the parts/products distribution, and related transport operations, with the ongoing planned fabrication agenda and supplying operations, in order to improve the utilization of useful resources, using just-in-time policies.

4. CONCLUDING EXAMPLE AI-INSTRUMENTS

The previous considerations are best illustrated with a few examples. We therefore discuss below a relevant set of expert systems, with additional details being provided by the quoted papers.

Fabrication agendas provide the driving inputs; the sequences of (external) occurrences are generated according to the given schedulings of the product-mix, defined by the enterprise strategies. These cover conveniently long horizons (up to several months, depending on the product and business areas) and a toolroom manager should work out the tools/fixtures procurement and schedules, using market-pull (based on pre-programmed demands, according to market forecasts). These forecasts should be subsequently improved with push-mode constraints (in order to obtain a just-in-time delivery, modulated by clients' orders, with optimal exploitation of available resources.

The XTR-SIFIP program [4] is an expert simulator developed as a consultation instrument for production engineers. It is embedded in the NEXPERT shell, and exploits hybrid processing capabilities. Algorithmic blocks look for the provisional tools cataloguer and establish preliminary tool distribution lists consistent with the fabrication agendas. Heuristic blocks, address the updated tool catalogues, improving the resources utilization ratios, with minimal overall toolstocks. Procedural knowledge is expressed in the form of rules and frames are defined for the relational data-base. A specialized input/output module (based on a branched-menu interactive interface) simplifies the set-up operations for data entry and for result evaluation.

The final specification of the toolstock (tools assortment and procuration assessment) and toolroom management operations, is closely related to the fabrication agenda. The tool-catalogue, corresponding to 'efficient' scheduling, restricting the manufacturing strategic flexibility to subsets of 'authorised' agendas. Alternatively, 'open' toolstocks should be considered to prevent the lowering of manufacturing efficiency, and the XTR-SIFIP system can again be used with a different setting of the initial reference conditions.

Once the toolstock (described by the catalogues and provided as the output of XTR-SIFIP) conveniently matches the planned (and authorised) fabrication agenda, the shopfloor manager is charged to ensure a just-in-time supply policy. At this level, a tool dispatcher is in charge of the supply operations (programmed-mode) minimising fixed investments in conjunction with the tactics agreed by appropriate production criteria. The tool-dispatcher, in emergencies (e.g.: workstation failure, material handling miss-match, etc.) should undertake the necessary restoring actions (adaptive-mode), which allow the production to proceed by exploiting the versatility of the technological resources.

The XTD-SIFIP is a tool-tactical planner; it controls two operational requirements, that of assuring high efficiency during steady (programmed) manning conditions and that of ensuring restored operation during an emergency [6]. The expert system code is written in the language OPS 5, to exploit the speed of its inference engine. The program-mode considers different tactics, namely:

- the machining-list tactic, job-shop schedulings based on group-technology bindings;
- the product-batch tactic: flow-shop schedulings of the parts-mix, balanced among the available resources;
- the fabrication-window tactic: shopfloor control with direct tool attribution over fixed production time-spans.
- etc...

The adaptive-mode requires the on-line closure, of decisional loops. The expert-block operates stepwise, using situational updatings, as condition elements in the inference procedure. In program-mode, the decision mechanism can be moved off-line, in order to obtain high efficiency during steady operational periods of the (fabrication-window, product-batch, machining-list,etc.) selected tactic.

Once the parts/products and the related tools/fixture schedulings are selected and described in the output data-base by the XTD-SIFIP system, the actual throughput can be improved when the concurrent manufacturing processes are simultaneously allowed to run in parallel. This requires decentralisation of the control capabilities [7].

The XIM-SIFIP system is an example implementation that enables the expert integrated management of shopfloor operation, concurrently with running the tools/fixtures transporters (XT-module) and the parts/products transporters (XS-module). Decentralisation is obtained through distributed computation resources, cluster-connected via a communication layer. For material logistics, independent automated guided vehicle facilities are available and rule-based logic controls task assignment, job sequencing, traffic conditions, priority checking etc., in order to assure functional concurrency in this multi-agent environment.

For efficiency, flexible plant should normally operate by exploiting the program -mode data. The peripheral facilities need continuous communication / synchronization messages in order to control the concurrency of the manufacturing processes. The organizational requirements are incorporated at the executional layer, within the expert-blocks of the coordination computers of each manufacturing section.

The incorporation is performed beforehand, in supervisory-mode, when the relational layer is established; this initial setting has important purposes in terms of knowledge representation, providing an option for fixing the decision sets with the instantiation of the expert blocks and for specializing the conditioning environment, with the initialization of algorithmic blocks. Then the control can switch to the program-mode, and the communication layer supports the complex command / synchronization actions to assure parallel operation concurrency, updating the pertinent knowledge stored by the expert blocks of the individual manufacturing sections. The synchronization is controlled by a logical sequencer. The command strategies are conditioned by 'common interest' data, shaped through the intelligent communication layer and distributed among the coordination computers.

Finally, flexible plant controllers should be connected, at the equipment level, with the functional versatility of the individual operational devices. At this level, the X-ARS system, for instance, can be used as a consultation instrument for the selection of appropriate robotic equipment [8]. The program is essentially a structured data-base where the available industrial robot data can be stored in a frame-interconnected catalogue. The reference knowledge conveniently exploits a list of condition elements on the configuration set-ups (assessed in the joints-space), from the displacement and attitude requirements given by the user in the workspace. A library of direct and inverse kinematic transforms is available. In addition, the robot's dynamic performance can be obtained, referring to the actual nonlinear behaviour of six-degrees-of-freedom robotic manipulators and employing a library of control strategies that perform the uncoupling operations between the joints space and the workspace and set the actuators gains with full or partial compensation of the nonlinear inertial effects.

REFERENCES

[1] G.M.Acaccia, R.C.Michelini, R.M.Molfino, "Design of Intelligent Governors for the Material Handling Equipment of Automated Factories", In: T.Sata, G.Olling (Eds.), Software for Factory Automation (North-Holland,Amsterdam, pp.253-278, (1989)

[2] G.M.Acaccia, R.C.Michelini, R.M.Molfino, F.Pampagnin, G.s.Rossi, "Knowledge-based Programming Instruments for Robotised Manufacturing Facilities", Intl. J. Adv. Manufac. Technology, Vol. 3, No.3, pp.53-66, (1989).

[3] G.M.Acaccia, R.C.Michelini, R.M.Molfino, "Knowledge-based Simulators in Manufacturing Engineering", 2nd Int. Conf. Applications of Artificial Intelligence in Engineering, Boston, Aug., pp. 4-7, (1987).

[4] G.M.Acaccia, R.C.Michelini, R.M.Molfino, G.B.Rossi, "Decisional Architecture in Tool-logistics for Flexible Manufacturing", IFAC Intl. Workshop on Decisional Structures in Automated Manufacturing, Genova, 18-21 Sept. (1989).

[5] G.M.Acaccia, R.C.Michelini, R.M.Molfino, G.Raffaelli, "An Expert-Scheduler for the Toolstock Management in a CIM-environment", Intl.J. Adv. Manufac. Engineering, Vol. 1, No. 4, pp 203 -210, (1989).

[6] G.M.Acaccia, F.Campolonghi, R.C.Michelini, R.M.Molfino: 'Expert-simulation of a Tool Dispatcher for Factory Automation', Intl.J. Comput. Integ. Manuf.,Vol. 2, No. 3, 1989, pp. 131-139.

[7] R.C.Michelini, G.M.Acaccia, M Callegari, R.M.Molfino, "Integrated Management of Concurrent Shopfloor Operations", Computer-Integrated Manuf. Systems, Vol. 3, No. 1, pp.27-38, (1990).

[8] G.M.Acaccia, M.Callegari, R.C.Michelini, R.M.Molfino, P.A.Piaggio, "X-ARS: a Consultation Program for Selecting the Industrial Robots Architectures" In: J.S.Gero (Ed.), Artificial Intelligence in Engineering: Robotics & Processes (Elsevier,Amsterdam), pp. 35-58, (1988)

Industrial Applications of Artificial Intelligence
J.L. Alty and L.I. Mikulich (Editors)
Elsevier Science Publishers B.V. (North-Holland)

DEVELOPMENT OF INTELLIGENT MANUFACTURING SYSTEMS

Alexander O.POLYAKOV

Scientific-production
department of Leningrad
affiliate of Research Center,
USSR Academy of Sciences
Leningrad, USSR

The report is devoted to questions of creation real-model environment and communication languadge for high-level comlexity intelligent manufacturing system.

In 1986-1989 works were carried out for the development of a complex intelligent system for manufacturing technology design and planning [1], the particular feature of which was possible approximation of individual components and entire system modeling to the von-Neumann complexity threshold [2]. This allowed to close information flows from an object in a computer and consider a sum of their algorithmic descriptions as the description of an open-ended information object. The presence of efficiently used knowledge bases in the system permitted to consider it quite rightfully an intelligent one. Thinking over the results achieved and analysing practical aspects of engineering subsystem set functioning enabled us to arrive at a number of evaluations and rules for techniques and general trend in developing these activities [3].

Thus, let the controlled object be defined by its own information structure with separating the kernel of open-ended in a system sense functional subsystems which were separated on the basis of minimizing their external information channels while keeping a maximum of their own (basic) information interchange. The external world is set by a quantitatively unrestricted number of data inputs to the given object. The qualitative input variety is set by an observer as the design of an object he is just interested in at that research stage. Information dynamics or generation and type variation of inputs characterizing the external world are modeled in dataflow computer time, rates of which exceed many times the reality.

Since information dynamics of the object is the derivative of its own time of a real or modeled external world, such an assumption is justified. Practically this can be done in a following way: the object is formed as a set of working places for generation and analysis of manufacturing information. Working places are linked with common information environment providing information reception, expedient allocation to process associated places and its accumulation.

In the initial stage of object structuring it's already necessary to separate two information types, considering, besides the above mentioned basic information flows, also the information which regulates the content of these flows.

While the information of the first type is formed as end user-oriented documents, the second type information is actually metainformation. Separation of an information type is based on not only their different significance in manufacturing, but also on different rates peculiar to each information type existence. Recognizing the important significance of both information types in sistem operation as a whole, we come to the conclusion that system activity records should be a double-mediated information in respect to the real world.

Necessity for sufficiently free selection of working places leads to the fact that the complex automation system has no unique and constant character from the point of end-user's view. Complex automation system designers consider it more convenient to describe the system by information flows but this doesn't confine system essence because it is simultaneously a medium of documents developed in working places, a self-adopting data base, multilevel software with self-adjusting elements, etc. The test rig for accumulation of information on variable system behaviour can be made by modeling external world effect on it. The effect manifests itself in information interaction with the system at definite connection points - working places - in pace defined by information computer capabilities but not by external world requirements.

Using the object organization feutures mentioned above, it seems interesting to develope a set of information generators (demons). Rate and content of information generated by demons are controlled by some independent generators simulating external world effects.

The high object organization level will allow to develop demons generating syntactically authentic and semantically plausible information. Now we have come to a problem to install a search task with all possible combinations of rates and amounts of information from an optional number of demons at the input and with stability regions, determined by a minimum of information flow dynamics variation within the object, at the output.

The above task may be solved only based on exhaustive or task-oriented search. Here our advantage (which seems promising) is time scaling which allows to model the full range of expected input variables, i.e. to reseach information - dynamic characteristics of an object. Implementation of such demons together with varying their activity generator is a feasible task and may be executed in a following way.

Standard and automatically maintained software structure for working place requires explicit separation of programs for information exchange with a user and programs for information processing.

If the system operates in real environments the working place software is started by user actions and information exchange programs are set up for terminal input-output. User-demon activity is simulated by background run of working place software with modified information exchange programs. A user-demon is not a separate active task but a set of subroutines for a computer and executive system. Unified design of processing subroutines for working place on the basis of command interpretation maps will permit to develop demons of practically similar unification. Being connected with system maps, demons may be delivered from a need for input information generation on the random character chain level generating randomly just complete commands or command groups. The higher the complexity of working place software the simpler proper demon may be designed while retaining a plausibility extent of resulting information.

Time going modeling requires that demons before being run should be specified for developing a number of documents and, on having processed this job, they should pass message and leave the computer. While doing this, the demons themselves don't need to operate on concepts of job time and rate. It is done for them by a single super-demon - an activity allocator and time synchronizer. The super-demon, which is set by some time interval and range of rates, invokes demons, defines the required scope of their activities and decides that the due time interval is exhausted when slave run-time systems accomplish their operations. Such organization of activity allows for maximum time-divizion multiplexing of the system, obtaining a well-controlled demon set and selecting most convenient moments for information evaluation.

Algorithms of super-demon functions can be developed in different forms depending on the following reguirements: a single evaluation of particular relation of external world variables or the solution of a search task in some region of variables with the given probabilistic distributions within the region.

Generally speaking, there are no limits for both real runtime systems and demons operating jointly within the same information system, as a result of which mixed real-model environment is generated for the complex automation system. A special purpose demon may provide synchronization of the whole system (ensemble) run with time going, though it is not an obligatory condition for joint operation. The result of such a symbiosis is the demonstration of intrinsic intelligence capabilities of the system and study of capabilities increase with the system development.

However, it seems more difficult to evaluate the state and dynamics of information flows in an object of high-level system complexity. Available facilities of communication with information objects - languages, programming systems, executive systems - are not capable enough for any efficient elaboration of the set task.

An information object of a social institute type [4, 5], when being properly modeled, retains its intrinsic and particular behaviour. In connection with this communication facilities must be designed as a tool of new phenomenon study.

Leaving for convenience the term "language" we should constantly bear in mind that it can't resemble any known programming languages or belong to the group of "natural" ones. To-day it's yet impossible to answer how close may prove information object languages or if a single translator or some number of them are required for operation with various information objects. Let's imagine some characteristics of that part of communication language which is applied to the information object.

Proceeding from the object nature, one should expect that the constructive information flow concept including information generation, processing, conversion and accumulation, must be a basic element of such a language.

An important attribute of an information flow is its mediation ratio (multiplicity) of material world, the extend of connection with material and, perhaps, energy flows. Flows may generate earch other, limit, consume jointly and generate some information resources of the system. Language instructions are distinctly subdivided into two classes. The first one is intended to describe the system structure by describing flows as system parts, stations, etc. Structure-related information may be taken from available knowledge bases or by modeling hypothetical behaviour of the system.

The other class of instructions serves as a system handler. Current state evaluation and development prediction under those or other additional conditions are major manipulations here.

The set of inferences derived from accumulated knowledges about laws of functioning of the described information system type is essential for estimating design prospects of complex system automation. Unusual regularities can neither be deduced nor obtained from experience. Current state evaluation instructions applied to various time environments of various modelled systems may prove helpful in this task solution. It is necessary to have possibilities to improve state evaluations and formulate prediction laws simultaneously.

Thus, returning to the problem of design and performance optimisation of manufacturing automation systems for objects of system complexity, one can state that automated systems, though intelligent, have a limited scope of application, which is more to do with quantitative definition of significance and interaction with information flows than with qualitative issues. For instance, the Von Neumann complexity threshold now acquires a new sense; not just with respect to particularly aspects of adequate modelling requirements but as the boundary beyond which the complex system begins to function according to its own laws (which need to be examined).

REFERENCES

[1] Polyakov, A.O., "TETRAM: an Integrated System for the Automation of the Design and Planning of Manufacturing Technology", (in Russian), In: Informacionnye Problemy Avtomatizacii, Leningrad, Nauka, 1988, pp 5 - 15.

[2] Von Neumann J., "Theory of Self Reproducing Automata", Illinois U. P., (1966)

[3] Polyakov, A.O., "Problems of Increasing the Efficiency of the Design and Function of Complex Systems for the Automation of Manufacturing Processes", In: Problemy Microelektroniki i Primeneni EBM pri Razrabotke Sovremennykh Radioelectronnykh Credctv, Leningrad, Izvestiya LETI No. 409, (1989), pp 78 - 91.

[4] Boulding, K., "General Systems Theory: The Skeleton of Science", Management Science, April 1956.

[5] Johnson, R.A., Kast, F.E., and Rosenweig, J.E., "The Theory and Management of Systems", 2nd Edition, McGraw-Hill, (1967).

Industrial Applications of Artificial Intelligence
J.L. Alty and L.I. Mikulich (Editors)
Elsevier Science Publishers B.V. (North-Holland)

SCHEDULING IN THE INTELLIGENT SYSTEM AMIGO

Nick A. TSAREVSKY

Computer Center
Academy of Sciences of The USSR
Moscow, The USSR

This paper presents a description of a manufacturing works scheduling problem. It relates how the intelligent system AMIGO_FMS (Automated Modeling, Interactive Graphics and Optimization for Flexible Manufacturing Systems) assists an end user in tackling and resolving these problems. A scheme of heuristic search, used by the AMIGO, is discussed.

1. INTRODUCTION

A problem of planning some necessary actions to achieve prescribed goals is listed in a classification of typical expert tasks, [1]. The problem is to build a plan attaining the goals with possibly minimal expenditures and without violation of essential restrictions. A main property of scheduling problems is that they belong to a class of combinatorial "NP-hard" problems. In practice, attempts to solve these problems lead to huge search spaces. Artificial Intelligence techniques integrated with conventional Operation Research approaches can promise advanced problem-solving technology, which could provide satisfactory solutions to the scheduling problem.

2. BRIEF DESCRIPTION OF THE SCHEDULING SUBSYSTEM

The AMIGO Scheduling Subsystem allows the user to enter input data describing a Manufacturing Object(MO), to experiment with a numerical model of the MO, to get intermediate and final results and to improve some dynamic features of the MO. The AMIGO_FMS system is built as an application-oriented user environment and it enables the user to find compromise balanced solutions to a complex problems belonging to the realm of manufacture.

The AMIGO_FMS monitor coordinates a set of different information, optimization and numerical applied modules, gives the user a possibility of managing the succession of modules execution and to save solution variants. A user-friendly menu-driven interface is used by all AMIGO modules.

The current installation of the scheduling subsystem allows the user to handle examples of real manufacturing objects. The problem is likely to be considered as large for the scheduling module if the number of devices and/or different kinds of products reach one hundred or little more. Experiments with practical examples on an IBM PC-AT computer (10 MHz) showed an acceptable time for obtaining a result. In the example of the shop (dealing with 50 devices, 20 different products, technological successions containing in average 10 operations and with 3 months throughput program) the time of a response was approximately 3 minutes for one variant of solution.

The explanation module gives the user convincing substantial arguments, reflecting a rationality of user's choice. Initial information consists of: a) general data about each solution variant (time and cost); b) detail data about one selected by user solution. The user can analyze a Gantt chart, an equipment load diagram, queues graphs, products flow charts, an expense histogram and receive necessary reports.

The scheduling subsystem is being elaborated using a Pascal language and IBM compatible computer. Standard Pascal data structures are used to represent knowledge and facts at the application programmer level.

3. SCHEDULING PROBLEM SPECIFICATION

A main purpose of manufacture is to accomplish external orders for product output. The order's requirements can have different mathematical expression:

Problem $\mathcal{A}$ (a task with an ultimate plan horizon)

- to fulfill a production throughput program $Y = (Y_i), i\in I$, in a minimum or prescribed time $[0,T]$, where I is a set of different kinds of products;

Problem $\mathcal{B}$ (a task with cycling production deadlines)

- to fulfill a periodic program during some time interval $[0,T]$. A whole period value T (that is a minimal positive quantity) is to be computed. There is a set Q_i of orders for each product i, $i\in I$. Every q, $q\in Q_i$, is a triple

$$(Period,Phase,Portion)_{iq}, i\in I, q\in Q_i, \quad 0 \leq Phase_{iq} \leq Period_{iq}$$

where a $Period_{iq}$ is positive integer variable measured, for example, in hours. The order q means that periodically with a cycle $Period_{iq}$, beginning from a moment $t= Phase_{iq}$, the MO is to supply $Portion_{iq}$ units of product i outside the MO. That is why, the general cycle $\underline{T}$ of external orders is to be equal to a least common multiple (LCM) of all production periods:

$$\underline{T} = \text{LCM}\ \{\ Period_{iq},\ i\in I,\ q\in Q_i\ \},\qquad \underline{T} \leqslant T.$$

A manufacturing power of the MO depends on available equipment. So far as MO's equipment is concerned there are a set J of different kinds of devices and a vector of amounts of devices $M = (\ M_j),\ j\in J$.

Technological processes for production manufacturing are represented here in the form of sequences of operations; and there is a technological route SQ_i of operations O_{il} for each product i:

$$SQ_i = \{\ O_{il}\ \},\ l\in L_i,\ L_i = \{\ 1,2,\ldots,\overline{l}_i\ \},\ i\in I.$$

All parts of each product i are transported in containers and machined in the MO by homogeneous portions (or packages), $p=1,\ldots,N_i$. A package size $v(i)$ (number of parts in one container) is defined by the end user.

The unit machining time t_{ijl} and set-up time τ_{ijl} are the main operation's characteristics. Taking into account processing products by packages it is necessary to modify a time consumption of operation:

$$\tilde{t}_{ijl} = \begin{cases} t_{ijl} * v(i), & \text{if } (i,l) = (i',l'), \\ t_{ijl} * v(i) + \tau_{ijl}, & \text{if } (i,l) \neq (i',l'), \end{cases}$$

where $(i,l),(i',l')$ are current and supposed device tunings.

All jobs for the current period T have to be accomplished inside the period, that is a requirement of periodic prolongation. So, the total machining time Λ for the most labor-intensive product has an essential influence on general manufacturing period size T:

$$\Lambda = \max_{i\in I}\ \{\ \sum_{l=1}^{l=\overline{l}_i} (\ \tau_{ijl} + v(i) * t_{ijl}\ )\}$$

The final formula for the general period size is as follows

$$T = \,]\ \Lambda\ /\ \underline{T}\ [\ * \underline{T}\ ,$$

where $]\alpha[$ is a least integer which exceeds or equals to α. There is a function of integral needs in product of kind i:

$$Y_i(t) = \sum_{q\in Q_i} \sum_{\lambda=0}^{\lambda=\lambda_{iq}} Portion_{iq} * \Theta(t - Period_{iq} * \lambda - Phase_{iq}),\ t\in[0,T];$$

where $\lambda_{iq} = T/Period_{iq} - 1$; $\Theta(t)$ is a charecteristic function:

$$\Theta(t) = \{\ 0,\text{if } t<0;\ 1,\text{if } t \geqslant 0\}$$

To fulfill all orders it is necessary to provide N_i packages of product i during interval $[0,T]$:

$N_i = \,]\, Y_i / v(i) \,[$ (for problem $\mathcal{A}$)

$N_i = \,]\, Y_i(T)/v(i) \,[$ (for problem $\mathcal{B}$)

As far as the problem $\mathcal{B}$ is concerned now it is possible to compute deadlines D_p for each package p, $p=1,\dots,N_i$. Let t_k be an argument of increment of function $Y_i(t)$: $1 \leqslant k \leqslant \bar{k}_i$, and $t_k < t_{k+1}$. Then, for all i and p let's install

$$D_p = t_k, \quad \text{if} \quad m_{i(k-1)} < p \leqslant m_{ik},$$

where the sequence m_{ik} is defined as follows:

$$m_{i0} = 0, \quad m_{ik} = \,]\, Y(t_k)/v(i) \,[, \quad 1 \leqslant k \leqslant \bar{k}_i.$$

A schedule Sch defines start and finish times for all operations, a time $t_p(Sch)$ of package p completion, $p=1,\dots,N_i$, $i \in I$, and, thus, a throughput of the MO.

To complete the specification of the scheduling problem let us define their purposes. In both problems it is required to find a schedule Sch which is to provide the throughput of N_i packages of product i, $i \in I$, during the time interval $[0,T]$ under the given equipment quantity $M = (M_j), j \in J$ and technological sequences $SQ_i, i \in I$. The objective of the problem $\mathcal{A}$ is to find schedule Sch that minimizes a completion time $T(Sch)$ of the program,

$$\min_{Sch} T(Sch), \quad T(Sch) = \max_p \{ t_p(Sch) \mid p=1,\dots,N_i, i \in I \}.$$

The objective of the problem $\mathcal{B}$ is to find schedule Sch that minimizes a tardiness $Delay$

$$\min_{Sch} Delay, \quad Delay = \max_p \{ t_p(Sch) - D_p \mid p=1,\dots,N_i, i \in I \}$$

and satisfies the feasibility condition $T(Sch) \leqslant T$.
In both problems also it can take into account a day partition by shifts.

In the case when the scheduling module builds several feasible solutions it is naturally to choose the variant with a least expenditure. We ascertain an existence of "inverse" monotonic dependence between initial stocks and the $Delay$ value. (For the problem $\mathcal{B}$ stock values at moments $t=0$ and $t=T$ are to coincide.) That is why a question arises about initial stock values for the problem $\mathcal{B}$.

The AMIGO_FMS allows the user to solve in an interactive mode the generalized problems $\mathcal{A}$ and $\mathcal{B}$, concerning the streamlining of power structure, stock volumes and schedules. Additional problem variables are the vector $M = (M_j), j \in J$ components.

4. PROBLEM - SOLVING: HEURISTIC SEARCH TECHNIQUES

We now describe the scheme of search algorithm using concepts and technique of production systems,[3]. Formally, the pro-

duction system can be regarded as a triple $PS=\langle F,P,I\rangle$, [3], where F is the main memory (current problem's data), P is the knowledge base (ruleset) and I is an interpreter (solver). The interpreter is described by quadruple $I=\langle V,S,R,W\rangle$, where
- V is a process of selection active subsets F_v and P_v from the sets F and P, which will be used in an interpreter cycle;
- S is a comparison process defining a set of instantiations, i.e. the set of pairs {(rule,data)}, each rule of a pair is applicable to any datum of the pair;
- R is a conflict resolution (a planning) process, defining which of the instantiations will be implemented;
- W is an activity implementation process of the selected instantiated rule.

As far as the process of building / inference of a solution is concerned it is reduced to the following iteration process,[3]. The first rule from ordered instantiated productions, applicable to some active datum, is applied changing memory state. The process is then continued from the applicable production of highest priority. Such "verification / implementation" cycles are continued until the set of applicable rules becomes empty or will be reached the "goal".

To reduce the algorithm for the scheduling problems it is sufficiently to establish the correspondence between the variables/parameters of these problems and the formal parameters of the inference:
- F: all the knowledge and common data (technology descriptions, available devices, manufacturing program) are in the main memory. A dynamic list of schedule elements is also here. This is a "history" of packages machining. (A schedule element settles numbers of package, operation and machining device, a start and a finish times of the operation.);

-P: that is a ruleset representing knowledge about scheduling theory methods in use. The theory, [2], recommends heuristic priorities and priority rules for technological operations. The priority is a numerical value assigned to the operation. It is used to select the operation from any set of feasible operations. For example, the operations could be selected in decreasing or increasing order of the priorities. The priority rule is a numerical function, computing the priorities to operations. The production rule of the scheduling subsystem is at least a heuristic priority rule of scheduling theory;

-I: the interpreter proceeds with scheduling problem's data in way which naturally is to call simulation of manufacturing process,[2]. That is why, an intrinsic time of the MO could be assigned to each interpreter cycle and each event. (The event reflects modifications in the MO state);

-V: an active data are generated after analyzing the state of the MO. Ready operations are added to the memory by V;
-S: the characteristic feature of the problem is an absolute applicability of priority rules of scheduling theory;

-F_v: the active data on the current moment are the schedule elements corresponding to ready waiting operations (all the previous ones to which are complete) and idle devices;

-Pv: the user ordered priority rules and the active ordered productions are just the same in this case;

-R: the conflict resolution process is realized in two stages. Firstly, some priority rule is selected. Secondly, the data are chosen from the subset of instantiations corresponding to the rule. The second stage is called concourse. This procedure is a choice in a list of ready waiting operations of a sub-list of operations and an assignment of chosen operations to the set of idle devices. The concourse is carried out using operations priorities. To choose the rule an ordering of the rules is used. At first, the top rule is applied to the initial state of the MO. As far as it is applicable to all intermediate states of the MO the usage of this rule will be finished only at final state of the MO. So, all the rest rules are waiting their turn. Every rule is applied from the initial to final states of the MO and then is excluded from the ruleset;
-W: a status "schedulable" of operations which become winners in the current concourse is modified by activity to a status "in process",[2]. The intrinsic time of the MO then is moved to a nearest event and the interpreter cycle is repeated.

This process is to be continued until the MO will reach its final state and the set of active rules will be exhausted.

5. CONCLUSIONS

We have briefly considered the AMIGO_FMS Scheduling Subsystem. The scheme of algorithm for building the solution was described in terms of production systems. It is an example of a strict problem which needed an Artificial Intelligence technique for resolution. We suppose that concourse procedure and knowledge representation component of the subsystem could be further developed to handle also another kinds of complicated manufacturing scheduling problems.

REFERENCES

[1] Hayes-Roth F.,Waterman D.A. and Lenat D.B.,Eds. Building Expert Systems, (Addison-Wesley, London, 1983).

[2] Conway R.W., Maxwell W.L. and Miller L.W. Theory of scheduling, (Addison-Wesley, 1967).

[3] Popov E.V., Expert Systems, (Nauka, Moscow,1987, russ.).

[4] Tsarevsky N.A. and Terentiev A.F., The AMIGO - Interactive Graphic System for Manufacture Modeling, (Computer Center Academy of Sciences USSR, Moscow,1987, russ.)

[5] Terentiev A.F., Tsarevsky N.A., The experience in computer modeling of manufacturing systems,(Computer Center Academy of Sciences USSR, Moscow, 1990, russ.).

Industrial Applications of Artificial Intelligence
J.L. Alty and L.I. Mikulich (Editors)
Elsevier Science Publishers B.V. (North-Holland)

INTELLIGENT NEURAL NETWORKS FOR ROBOTIC CONTROL

A. D.C. HOLDEN

Computer Science and Engineering Dept., FR-35
University of Washington,
Seattle,
Washington,
USA 98195.

ABSTRACT: This paper combines the methods developed for knowledge-based systems, with the massively parallel potential of specialized hierarchies of multi-layer neural networks. Some new results are given which speed up back-propagation learning, where neural substructures are created automatically as they are needed (and are deleted, when no longer useful) to model input/output data.

The combination of knowledge based systems methods and massively parallel neural networks is useful for controlling dynamic robotic systems where a human controller can generate data, and the neural net can be trained to take over control. Back-propagation learning is too slow to be effective in large-scale systems and suffers from a tendency to seek out numerous local minima of the error function. The method given here constrains the learning process to avoid local minima and move more directly towards a condition with small errors [1, 2].

Knowledge is provided to the system in the form of a hierarchy of contexts. This hierarchy (or tree) models general situations at the upper levels, and very specific situations at the lower levels. Production Rule Sets are then used to encode human control knowledge at the lowest level and each rule-set is invoked by switching based on the decision-tree of contexts.

At the lowest level, individual rules are replaced by neural-nets which can be predesigned to replace rules, or can learn from the input/output training data for the related context. Rule replacement is direct if the rule-conditions are boolean predicates with no pattern-variables. The performance of a neural-net corresponding to a rule can be monitored as it learns. When the learning process produces a small enough error, the neural-net can replace the rule and continue learning [3, 4].

The advantages in using neural-nets to replace rules are,

(1) The neural-nets model the actual input/output data derived from human control, rather than the ideal conditions of the rules,

(2) The neural-nets extrapolate and interpolate, so that reasonable control is maintained even when the conditions demanded by a rule are not exactly satisfied, and

(3) The low-level control exerted by the neural nets would be effective in time-critical situations, because of their inherent parallelism (assuming that they were implemented in hardware).

We have implemented the above methods in a lunar-lander model [1, 5] (where the control variable was the thrust, and the other variables involved were altitude, mass, and velocity). Human control data, and a well chosen neural-net structure, produced a system which worked well. We also have modelled a simplified model of an aeroplane control [3, 4] (a two-dimensional model, where the control variables were thrust and elevator-angle). The contexts and sub-contexts are shown in Figures 1 and 2:

NORMAL FLIGHT
- TAKEOFF
  - VISUAL FLIGHT TAKEOFF
    - SHORT FIELD TAKEOFF
    - SOFT FIELD TAKEOFF
- LANDING
  - VISUAL FLIGHT LANDING
  - INSTRUMENT LANDING
- CRUISE
  - STRAIGHT AND LEVEL
  - CLIMB
  - DESCENT
  - TURN

ABNORMAL FLIGHT RECOVERY
- ENGINE FAILURE
- INSTRUMENT FAILURE
- STRUCTURAL FAILURE
- NAVIGATION FAILURE
- NON-NORMAL FLIGHT CONDITION
  - COLLISION COURSE
    - STALL
    - SPIN
    - STABLE FLIGHT OUTSIDE TOLERANCES

Figure 1 Flight Contexts

Our earlier work showed that the back-propagation learning process was fast if the input/output data being modelled was monotonic. Also, we showed that if additional redundant output ("hints") were added and used during the back-propagation training process, they could reduce the training time considerably [1, 5]. We now will show how these "hints" can be automatically added to constrain, and speed up, the learning process.

The use of hints was discovered by Suddarth [5], who noticed while creating control data for his lunar lander model, that at high altitudes he had the objective of bringing the velocity to an average value for that height, then at medium altitudes he suddenly re-set the objective to another lower average value, and then, close to the ground, he re-set the objective to a low value. When he put one additional redundant output for "desired velocity" and trained the whole network for both the thrust and the desired velocity, the training time was considerably reduced. The added constraint had the effect of moving the network weights during the training process more directly to an acceptable solution; avoiding local minima.

We have shown experimentally that, for input/output relations which are nonmonotonic, the back-propagation training time is considerably faster when a redundant output ("hint") is added for every monotonic region. The hint should be constant outside its monotonic region and coincide with the desired output in its local monotonic region. Every hint is therefore a monotonic function, and will constrain one or more of the "hidden-neurons" (neurons not on the output layer) to quickly model it, and this tends to avoid local minima.

There is evidence that, during the back-propagation training process, individual hidden neurons tend to model one of the monotonic regions of the data. Takach [6] has shown that the training time can be reduced if one hidden neuron is pre-designed so that its threshold is set to the inflection-point of one of the monotonic regions of the data and its weights pre-designed to scale the neural-net output to fit the data. For every monotonic region, a hidden neuron can then be so pre-designed, and the training time will be reduced.

PRODUCTIONS FOR ACHIEVING STRAIGHT AND LEVEL FLIGHT:
SEQUENTIAL PLAN FOR STRAIGHT-FLIGHT AND LEVEL-FLIGHT
COROUTINE PLAN FOR STRAIGHT-FLIGHT AND LEVEL-FLIGHT

PRODUCTIONS FOR ACHIEVING LEVEL-FLIGHT:
ACHIEVE L-FLIGHT
NOTICE DELTA PITCH VIA ARTIFICIAL HORIZON
NOTICE DELTA PITCH VIA W I
NOTICE DELTA PITCH VIA ALTIMETER
NOTICE DELTA PITCH VIA AIRSPEED
ELIMINATE DELTA PITCH WITH ELEVATORS
ELIMINATE DELTA PITCH WITH THROTTLE
PRODUCTIONS FOR ACHIEVING STRAIGHT-FLIGHT
ACHIEVE S-FLIGHT
NOTICE DELTA BANK VIA ARTIFICIAL HORIZON
NOTICE DELTA BANK VIA TURN COORDINATOR
NOTICE DELTA BANK VIA DIRECTIONAL GYRO
NOTICE DELTA BANK VIA MAGNETIC COMPASS
ELIMINATE DELTA BANK WITH AILERONS
ELIMINATE DELTA BANK WITH RUDDER

Figure 2 Rules for Straight and Level Flight.

The implication of the previous paragraphs is that there should be one hidden neuron for every monotonic region, that it should be pre-designed to fit the data as far as possible, and that "hints" should be added for each monotonic region.

In practice, data tends to be sparse and may be noisy. If it is noisy, a smoothing operation must be done first. If it is sparse, a low-order fit to the data can be done to interpolate, and generate more data. The pre-design method requires substantial human effort initially, whereas the use of "hints" can be done automatically. In this case, a generic neural-net with one hidden layer is used for each rule from the initial knowledge-base. The data is then scanned by the system to determine monotonic regions. A new dummy output ("hint") is generated for each monotonic region. The neural-net is then trained repeatedly using the desired output and the hints. When convergence occurs (small error) the hints are removed and training continues. At this point the network will then converge to an accurate solution.

As an example, the polynomial function y= (x+5)(x-7)(x-1) leads to three simple hints by breaking it up into regions I, II and III as shown in Figure 3.

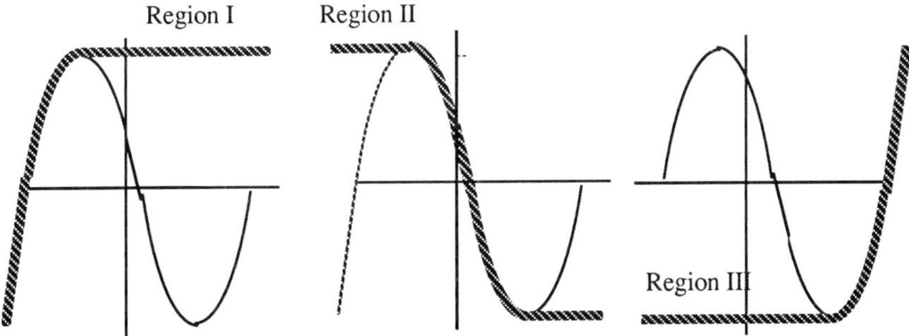

Figure 3 Regions I II and III

Two two-layer networks are created with three hidden nodes as shown in figure 4. Figure 4a) shows our hinted network with three additional dummy outputs, one for each monotonic region. Figure 4b) is a regular back-propagation network with one output node.

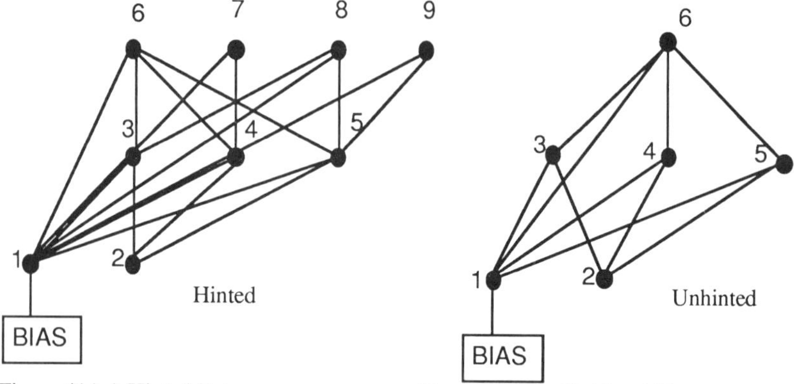

Figure 4(a) A Hinted Net
Figure 4(b) An Unhinted Net

It is difficult to accurately model an analog function with a neural net, and we find that the hints help a lot in this process. Figure 5 shows the actual function and output from both hinted and unhinted nets.

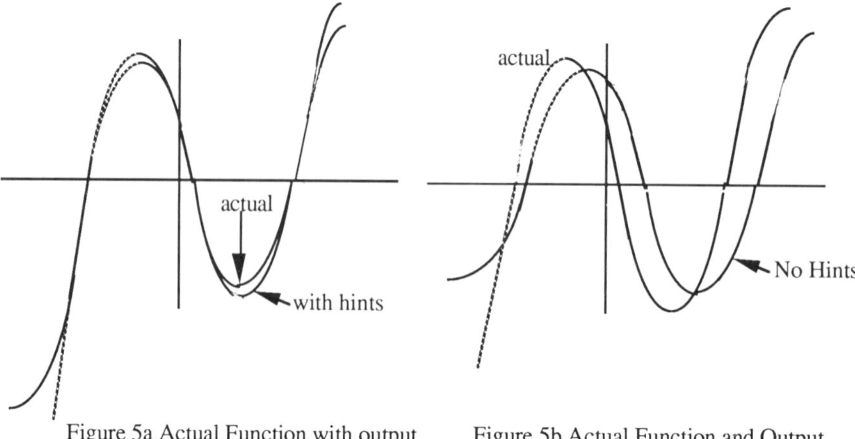

Figure 5a Actual Function with output from hinted net

Figure 5b Actual Function and Output from unhinted net

Figure 6 shows the output from the hinted net at different iteration counts. The hinted net performs much better than the unhinted net.

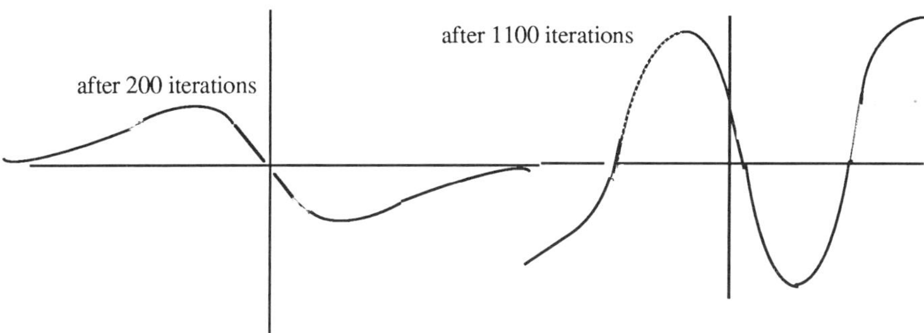

Figure 6 Hinted Net at different iteration counts

Convergence is much faster for the hinted case, as the net is much less sensitive to momentum and learning coefficient variations. This makes the hinted net more reliable and thus more easily integrated with, for example, a rule-based system.

Our experiments have shown that if all of the hints are removed in the final stages of training, much greater accuracy of modeling is achieved, for a limited number of hidden neurons, than a similar network trained without hints. To learn a multi-modal function a rule-based pre-processor is used, which suggests how to divide the training curve into monotonic sub-regions and also prepares one augmented input data file for each sub-region. Thus we have a method for automatically generating the training data for additional constraint outputs (hints) which speeds up training and leads to greater accuracy, for a neural network where the number of hidden neurons is limited.

References

[1]. Suddarth, S.C., Sutton, S.A. and Holden, A.D.C., "A Symbolic-neural Method for Solving Control Problems," Proceedings International Conference on Neural Nets, San Diego, 1988.

[2]. Suddarth, S.C. and Holden, A.D.C., "An N-Port Symbolic-Neural Method for Modelling and Controlling Systems," to be published, Journal of Man-Machine Studies.

[3]. Holden. A.D.C., "Fast Learning in Symbolic Neural Models Using External Constraints and Automatic Re-Structuring," Proceedings IEEE International Conference on Systems, Man, and Cybernetics, Cambridge, 1989.

[4]. Goldstein, I.P. and Grimson, E., "Annotated Production Systems: A Model for Skill Acquisition," AI Memo 407, AI Laboratory, M.I.T., Feb. 1977.

[5]. Suddarth, Steven C., "The Symbolic-Neural Method for Creating Models and Control Behaviors from Examples," Ph.D. Dissertation, Electrical Engineering Dept., University of Washington, Seattle, 1988.

[6]. Takach, Margarita D., "A Study of Single Hidden Layer Perceptrons", Ph.D. Dissertation, Electrical Engineering Dept., University of Washington, Seattle, 1990.

Industrial Applications of Artificial Intelligence
J.L. Alty and L.I. Mikulich (Editors)
Elsevier Science Publishers B.V. (North-Holland)

AN APPROACH TO SCHEDULING

Tomasz AMBROZIAK
Technical University of Warsaw,
Poland

1. AN ACTIVITY GRAPH

A specified number of technological processes are assumed needed to achieve a certain goal. Every process consists of elementary stringently specified activities. The set of activities which add up to a process is a partially ordered set. Every activity will be represented as a graph arc. An activity or activities is an event. Every event is represented as a graph vertex.

With this notation a set of partially ordered activities is represented as a graph G, or $G=(\mathbb{X}, \mathbb{M}, P)$ where: $\mathbb{X}$ is a set of ordinal numbers of vertices (events) in G; $\mathbb{M}$ is a set of ordinal numbers of arcs (activities) in G; P is a certain three-positioned predicate. It is assumed that $\mathbb{X}=\{x(i): i \in \mathbb{I}$, $\mathbb{I}=\{1,\ldots,i,\ldots,I\}$, $\mathbb{M}=\{m(k): k \in \mathbb{K}$, $\mathbb{K}=\{1,\ldots,k,\ldots,K\}$,or the cardinalities of the sets $\mathbb{X}$ and $\mathbb{M}$ are known.

The predicate P maps a Cartesian product $\mathbb{X} x \mathbb{M} x \mathbb{X}$ into the set $\{0,1\}$, or P: $\mathbb{X} x \mathbb{M} x \mathbb{X}$ ------> $\{0,1\}$. An arbitrary three-tuple $(x(i),m(k),x(j)) \in \mathbb{X} x \mathbb{M} x \mathbb{X}$ such that $P(x(i),m(k),x(j))=1$ is interpreted in the following way:the arc m(k) connects the vertex x(i) with the vertex x(j). If $P(x(i),m(k),x(j))=0$ the arc m(k) is said not to connect x(i) and x(j).

2. QUALITATIVE AND QUANTITATIVE DESCRIPTION OF ACTIVITIES

Facilities are assumed to be needed to perform an activity. A set $\mathbb{S}$ of facility types needed in performance of activitues is assumed to be specified,or $\mathbb{S}=\{s: s=1,\ldots ,S\}$. In addition, resources are needed to carry out activities. A set $\mathbb{P}$ of resource kinds is assumed needed, or $\mathbb{P}=\{p: p=1, \ldots,P\}$.

Assume that a mapping r of the Cartesian product $\mathbb{K} x \mathbb{S}$ into

the set $\{0,1\}$ is specified, or $r\colon \mathbb{K}\times\mathbb{S} \longrightarrow \{0,1\}$. It is true that $r(k,s)=1$ iff the s-th facility type is employed in Performing the k-th activity, otherwise $r(k,s)=1$. Consequently, for every $k\in\mathbb{K}$ the vector $r(k)$ of components $r(k,s)$ can be determined,or $r(k)=\langle r(k,1),..,r(k,s),..,r(k,S)\rangle$.
Assume that the mapping a of the Cartesian product $\mathbb{K}\times\mathbb{S}$ into the set $\mathfrak{R}^+$ is specified, or $a\colon \mathbb{K}\times\mathbb{S} \longrightarrow \mathfrak{R}^+$. The value $a(k,s)\in\mathfrak{R}^+$ determines the productivity of the s-th facility type employed in the k-th activity. Consequently, for every $k\in\mathbb{K}$ a vector $a(k)$ can be determined of components $a(k,s)$, or $a(k)=\langle a(k,1), \dots,a(k,s), \dots,a(k,S)\rangle$.
Assume also that the mapping z of the Cartesian product $\mathbb{K}\times\mathbb{P}$ into the set $\{0,1\}$ is specified, or $z\colon \mathbb{K}\times\mathbb{P}\longrightarrow\{0,1\}$. It is true that $z(k,p)=1$ iff the p-th resource is utilized in the k-th activity, otherwise $z(k,p)=0$.
Assume that the mapping n of the Cartesian product $\mathbb{P}\times\mathbb{S}$ into the set $\{0,1\}$ is specified, or $n\colon\mathbb{P}\times\mathbb{S} \longrightarrow \{0,1\}$. It is true that $n(p,s)=1$ iff, utilization of the s-th facility type entails utilization of the p-th resource, otherwise $n(p,s)=0$.
Assume that the mapping b of the Cartesian product $\mathbb{K}\times\mathbb{P}\times\mathbb{S}$ into the set $\mathfrak{R}^+$ is specified, or $b\colon \mathbb{K}\times\mathbb{P}\times\mathbb{S}\longrightarrow \mathfrak{R}^+$. The value $b(k,p,s)\in\mathfrak{R}^+$ describes the consumption norm of the p-th resource when the s-th facility type for carrying out the k-th activity. For the $k\in\mathbb{K}$ and $p\in\mathbb{P}$ a vector $b(k,p)$ with components $b(k,p,s)$ is determined, or $b(k,p)=\langle b(k,p,1), \dots,b(k,p,s), \dots,b(k,p,S)\rangle$.
Qualitative description of the set of activities is assumed to be reducible to determining for every $k\in\mathbb{K}$ the values of $a(k)$ and $b(k,p)$. Qualitative description of the set of activities is supplemented with quantitative description.
Assume that the mapping Q is specified which moves elements of set $\mathbb{K}$ into the set $\mathfrak{R}^+$, or $Q\colon \mathbb{K}\longrightarrow \mathfrak{R}^+$. The quantity $Q(k)\in\mathfrak{R}^+$ stands for the size of the k-th activity. Determining $Q(k)$ for every $k\in\mathbb{K}$ is quantitative definition of the set of activities. Let $\mathbb{Q}$ be a set of elements $Q(k)$, or $\mathbb{Q}=\{Q(k)\colon k\in\mathbb{K}\}$.

3. SCHEDULE OF A SET OF ACTIVITIES

Let $\mathbb{T}$ denote a set of times (intervals of a certain length), or $\mathbb{T}=\{t: 0 \le t < \infty\}$. It is assumed that $\mathbb{T}(k)$ such that $\mathbb{T}(k) \subseteq \mathbb{T}$ is a set of times at which the k-th activity is performed.

Let $t'(k)$ denote the time at which the k-th activity starts. It is obvious that $t'(k)=\min\{t: t\in\mathbb{T}(k)\}$. Let $tt'(k)$ denote a set of elements $t'(k)$, or $tt'=\{t'(k): k\in\mathbb{K}\}$.

The mapping u is assumed specified of the Cartesian product $\mathbb{K}x\mathbb{S}$ into the set $\Re^+$, or u: $\mathbb{K}x\mathbb{S}$ ---------> $\Re^+$. The quantity $u(k,s)\in\Re^+$ defines the amount of facilites of the s-th type utilized in performance of the k-th activity. For every $k\in\mathbb{K}$ a vector $u(k)$ of components $u(k,s)$ is determined, or $u(k)=\langle u(k,1),\ldots,u(k,s),\ldots,u(k,S)\rangle$. Let $\mathbb{U}$ be a set of elements $u(k)$, or $\mathbb{U}=\{u(k): k\in\mathbb{K}\}$.

The schedule of the k-th activity is said to be known if the numerical values are known of elements in the pair $(t'(k),u(k))$. The schedule of the set of activities is said to be known if the numerical values of elements in the pair $(tt',\mathbb{U})$ are.

4. CHARACTERISTICS OF ACTIVITIES AS A FUNCTION OF A SCHEDULE

The mapping w of the Cartesian product $\mathbb{K}x\mathbb{T}x\mathbb{S}$ into the $\Re^+$ is assumed specified, or w: $\mathbb{K}x\mathbb{T}x\mathbb{S}$ -------> $\Re^+$. The quantity $w(k,s,t)\in\Re^+$ denotes the number of facilities of the s-th type are utilized at the time t in performance of the k-th activity. For every $k\in\mathbb{K}$ and $t\in\mathbb{T}$ the vector $w(k,t)$ is determined of components $w(k,s,t)$, or $w(k,t)=\langle w(k,t,1),\ldots,w(k,t,s),\ldots,w(k,t,S)\rangle$. Let $\mathbb{W}$ be a set of elements $w(k,t,s)$, or $\mathbb{W}=\{w(k,t,s): k\in\mathbb{K}, s\in\mathbb{S}, t\in\mathbb{T}\}$ and $\mathbb{A}$, a set of elements $a(k,s)$, or $\mathbb{A}=\{a(k,s): k\in\mathbb{K}, s\in\mathbb{S}\}$.

The mapping f is assumed known that moves the Cartesian product $\mathbb{A}x\mathbb{W}$ into the set $\mathbb{Q}$, or f: $\mathbb{A}x\mathbb{W}$-----> $\mathbb{Q}$. The quantity $f(a(k,s),w(k,s,t))=Q(k)$ relates the activity size and the number of facilities employed in its implementation.

In further discussion f is assumed to take the form

$$f: \sum_{s\in\mathbb{R}(k)} \int_{t'(k)}^{t''(k)} a(k,s)w(k,s,t)dt=Q(k) \text{ where: } t''(k)=\max\{t\ t\in\mathbb{T}(k)\}$$

is the time of activity and $\mathbb{R}(k)=\{s: r(k,s)=1, s\in\mathbb{S}\}$. The dependence $w(k,s,t)$ can be specified in different ways; here it is assumed that

$$w(k,s,t)=\begin{cases} u(k,s), & t\in[t'(k), t''(k)] \\ 0, & t\notin[t'(k), t''(k)] \end{cases}$$

In the light of the above, f may be said to take the form

$$f: \sum_{s\in\mathbb{R}(k)} \int_{t'(k)}^{t''(k)} a(k,s)u(k,s)dt=Q(k)$$

With $\tau(k)$ being the time taken by the activity assume that $\tau(k)=t''(k) - t'(k)$ or $\tau(k)=Q(k)/ \sum_{s\in\mathbb{R}(k)} a(k,s)u(k,s)$.

From the latter it follows that $w(k,s,t)=w(k,s,t,t'(k),t''(k))$ or $w(k,s,t)=w(k,s,t,t'(k),u(k))$.

The mapping λ is assumed specified of the Cartesian product $\mathbb{K}x\mathbb{P}x\mathbb{T}$ into the set $\Re^+$, or $\lambda: \mathbb{K}x\mathbb{P}x\mathbb{T} \text{--------}> \Re^+$. The quantity $\lambda(k,p,t)\in\Re^+$ denotes the rate of utilizing the p-th resource in performance of the k-th activity at time t. Let $\mathbb{L}$ and $\mathbb{B}$ be sets of elements $\lambda(k,p,t)$ and $b(k,p,s)$, respectively, or $\mathbb{L}=\{\lambda(k,p,t): k\in\mathbb{K}, p\in\mathbb{P}, t\in\mathbb{T}\}$, $\mathbb{B}=\{b(k,p,s): k\in\mathbb{K}, p\in\mathbb{P}, t\in\mathbb{T}\}$.

The mapping ϕ is assumed specified of the Cartesian product $\mathbb{B}x\mathbb{W}$ into the set $\mathbb{L}$, or $\phi: \mathbb{B}x\mathbb{W} \text{-----}> \mathbb{L}$. The quantity $\phi(b(k,p,s),w(k,s,t))=\lambda(k,p,t)$ specifies the relation between the resource utilitization rate and the number of facilities used in performance of the activity.

In futher discussion ϕ is assumed to have the form

$$\phi: \sum_{s\in\mathbb{R}(k)\cap\mathbb{N}(p)} b(k,p,s)w(k,s,t)=\lambda(k,p,t) \text{ where: } \mathbb{N}(p)=\{s: n(s,p)=1, s\in\mathbb{S}\}.$$

Because $w(k,s,t)=w(k,s,t,t'(k),u(k))$ it is true that $\lambda(k,p,t)=$

$$= \sum_{s\in\mathbb{R}(k)\cap\mathbb{N}(p)} b(k,p,s)w(k,s,t,t'(k),u(k)).$$

Consequently, $\lambda(k,p,t)=\lambda(k,p,t,t'(k),u(k))$.

The mapping V is assumed specified of the Cartesian product $\mathbb{K}x\mathbb{P}$ into the set $\Re^+$, or $V: \mathbb{K}x\mathbb{P} \text{-----}> \Re^+$. The quantity $V(k,p)\in\Re^+$ denotes the consumption of the p-th resource in performance of the k-th activity. Denote by $\mathbb{L}1$ and $\mathbb{L}2$ the sets of elements $\lambda(k,p,t)$ and $V(k,p)$, respectively, or $\mathbb{L}1=\{\lambda(k,p,t): k\in\mathbb{K}, p\in\mathbb{P}, t\in\mathbb{T}\}$; $\mathbb{L}2=\{V(k,p): k\in\mathbb{K}, p\in\mathbb{P}\}$.

The mapping d is assumed specified of the set $\mathbb{L}1$ into the set $\mathbb{L}2$, or $d : \mathbb{L}1 \longrightarrow \mathbb{L}2$. The expression $d(\lambda(k,p,t))=V(k,p)$ relates the rate of resource utilization and its availability.

In further discussion d is assumed to take the form

$$d: \int_{t'(k)}^{t''(K)} \lambda(k,p,t)dt=V(k,p)$$

The mapping A is assumed specified of the Cartesian product $\mathbb{K}x\mathbb{S}$ into the set $\Re^{+}$, or $A: \mathbb{K}x\mathbb{S} \longrightarrow \Re^{+}$. The quantity $A(k,s)\in\Re^{+}$ denotes labor consumption of the s-th facility in performing the k-th activity. Denote by $\mathbb{A}$ a set of elements $A(k,s)$, or $\mathbb{A}=\{A(k,s): k\in\mathbb{K}, s\in\mathbb{S}\}$.

The mapping g is assumed specified of the set $\mathbb{W}$ into the set $\mathbb{A}$, or $g: \mathbb{W} \longrightarrow \mathbb{A}$. The dependence $G(w(k,s,t))=A(k,s)$ relates the amount of facilities utilized in performing the activity and labor consumption.

In further discussion g is assumed to have the for

$$g: \int_{t'(k)}^{t''(k)} w(k,s,t)dt=A(k,s) \text{ or } g:\int_{t'(k)}^{t''(k)} W(k,s,t,t'(k),u(k))dt=A(k,s).$$

Certain Proposition follow.

PROPOSITION 1.If- $w(k,s,t)$ is stepwise, or equal to $u(k,s)$ to $t\in[t'(k),t''(k)]$ and to zero for $t\notin[t'(k),t''(k)]$;-

$-\lambda(k,p,t,t'(k),u(k))= \sum_{s\in\mathbb{R}(k)\cap\mathbb{N}(p)} b(k,p,s)w(k,s,t)$;- $\tau(k)=t''(k)-t'(k)$

then $V(k,p)=V(k,p,u(k))$

Indeed,

$$V(k,p)= \int_{t'(k)}^{t''(k)} \sum_{s\in\mathbb{R}(k)\cap\mathbb{N}(p)} b(k,p,s)u(k,s)dt= \sum_{s\in\mathbb{R}(k)\cap\mathbb{N}(p)} b(k,p,s)u(k,s)\tau(k)=$$

$$=Q(k)\frac{\sum_{s\in\mathbb{R}(k)\cap\mathbb{N}(p)} b(k,p,s)u(k,s)}{\sum_{s\in\mathbb{R}(k)\cap\mathbb{N}(p)} a(k,s)u(k,s)}$$

From the latter dependence it follows that $V(k,p)=V(k,p,u(k))$

The similar Propositions may be proved in a similar way.

5. CHARACTERISTICS OF A SET OF ACTIVITIES AS A FUNCTION OF A SCHEDULE

The amount of facilities of the s-th type utilized for performance of a set of activities at time t is described by the formula $\sum_{k\in K} w(k,s,t,t'(k),u(k))=w(s,t,tt',\mho)$.
The labor consumption of the s-th facility type utilized in performance of a set activities is given by the formula $\sum_{k\in K} A(k,s,u(k))=A(s,\mho)$. The similar Characteristics may be defined in a similar way.

6.SOME OPTIMIZATION PROBLEMS IN SCHEDULING A SET OF ACTIVITIES

Problem 1.Determine the numerical values of elements in the pair $(tt',\mho)$ so that a criterion of the form

$$\sum_{s=1}^{S} \int_{T_0}^{T^*} [w(s,t,tt',\mho) - y(s)]^2 dt$$

take on a minimal value under the following constrains:

1. $\min_{k\in K}\{t'(k)\}=T_0$; $\max_{k\in K}\{t''(k)\}=T^*$

2. $t''(k)=t'(k) + \dfrac{Q(k)}{\sum_{s=1}^{S} a(k,s)u(k,s)}$, $\forall\ k\in K$

where $y(s)= A(s,\mho)/(T^* - T_0)$; T^*, T_0 are specified.

Problem 2.Determine the numerical values of elements in the pair $(tt',\mho)$ so that a criterion of the form

$$\sum_{s=1}^{S} \int_{T_0}^{T^*} [w(s,t,tt',\mho)]^2 dt$$

take an a minimal value under the constrains:

1. $\min_{k\in K}\{t'(k)\}=T_0$; $u(k,s) \le u^*(k,s)$, $\forall\ k\in K$, $\forall\ s\in S$

2. $t''(k)=t'(k) + \dfrac{Q(k)}{\sum_{s=1}^{S} a(k,s)u(k,s)}$, $\forall\ k\in K$

The above optimization problems are nonlinear and are hard to solve by directed methods. The above approach, however, makes it possible to formulate them as scheduling problems with various constrains and structures and solves them by approximate techniques of the graph theory.

Industrial Applications of Artificial Intelligence
J.L. Alty and L.I. Mikulich (Editors)
Elsevier Science Publishers B.V. (North-Holland)

AN APPROACH TO THE COMPUTER-AIDED STUDY OF FMS-LIKE SYSTEMS

G.M. DIMIROVSKI, O. L. ILIEV and B. R. PERCINKOVA
Electrotechnical Faculty ,
Dept. of Automation & Systems Engineering,
Cyril and Methodius University,
91000 Skopje,
Yugoslavia

ABSTRACT: A computer-assisted approach allowing convenient and simple CAD procedures to be used in FMS-like systems is described. It is aimed at the modelling, simulation and analysis of FMS functional models with respect to the design of coordination scheduling controls. It is based on the graph-network formalism and pattern/situation recognition techniques using adjoined sets of knowledge for the system studied.

1. INTRODUCTION AND BACKGROUND

The flexible automation paradigm of modern computer-integrated manufacturing systems, aimed at multi-class, high-value and low-quantity products, is a crucial one within recent developments in industrial automation [1]. Its power comes from the expanded implementation and use of a whole span of functions and versatile roles of information technology in systems control in a variety of novel computer-aided technologies [2]. The real steps forward, however, have not been just due to computerization, but rather to advanced systems engineering that has encompassed system modelling and control schemes using sophisticated decision-making, dedicated efficient information handling, and the use of uncertainty techniques and ignored missing information in the controlled objects [3-5]. In fact, a new system structure of robotized factory automation, with flexible intelligent manufacturing systems (FMS) as an essential constituent is emerging [5-7].

From the information available on the present state of knowledge and technology, however, these developments, it seems, require much more than the on-going separate basic supporting research streams of discrete-event systems, the control of large scale objects, and artificial intelligence. It is well known that distributed computing and information handling heuristically combined with engineering techniques and systems control have enabled the design and implementation of automated FMS (functionally integrating machining/ processing, material-handling and in-process storage units) regardless of current existing theories [8-12]. In fact, as has been pointed out in [7,12], in spite of considerable basic research on discrete-event systems, a large gap between the problems of developing feasible controls for FMS and the actual controlling of automated manufacturing systems still exists . Alternative and complementary methodologies are needed such as operational analysis [8-11], combined analytical and simulation modelling [11,12,15], interactive CAD techniques for design simulation and analysis [12,13] as well as applied artificial intelligence in complex system analysis [14]. Although various approaches can be derived, the generalized methodology in [15] and applied graph theory provide a sound theoretical framework for practical results. The research on discrete-event FMSs reported here has followed our previous work on interconnected discrete-time systems [16], expert typical identification using pattern-recognition [17], graphcoloring [18] employing stochastic algorithms [20], and simulation with the use of language SIMAN [21]. It can be argued that in the near future the prospects for CAD system controls that are controller-based computers rather than computer-based controllers are more likely.

2. PROBLEM FORMULATION AND SOLUTION FUNDAMENTALS

In this research, the problem of an interactive computer-assisted methodology [13,16] using graph-networks [8,15,21] and pattern-recognition techniques [3,17] for modelling, simulation and analysis of FMS-like systems with respect to the design of their coordination-scheduling control has been addressed. Some important features of an FMS need to be recalled now: the machining time for a given operation and workstation has an extremely small variance and is therefore modelled as being deterministic. The routing of processed jobs is also predetermined for a fixed failure state and a given operational decision. The evolution of the entire manufacturing system is governed by a set of deterministic, albeit complex, controlled sequence of events. Service-time ratios are close to uniform and the main performance measures (PMs) are the workstation utilization U_w and system throughput S_t.

The following premises have been assumed:

(i) in the FMS, there is a fixed finite collection of jobs J_n and fixed finite collection of manufacturing and auxiliary resources having W_m workstations;

(ii) each job $x_i \in X$, has a processing time $t_i \in T$ and no interruption takes place during its normal processing

(iii) some of jobs, x_i and x_j, cannot be processed simultaneously;

(iv) for some pair of jobs x_i, x_j there is a precedence constraint, and in the case of a constraint where p time units need to be elapsed after the end of job x_r in order job x_s to be started, a fictitious job x_f with associated $t_f = p$ can be defined;

(v) in the case of a bidirectional flow-path between two workstations, fictitious jobs x_i, x_j and four equivalency preserving, oriented path-links are introduced.

The structured conceptualization of FMS-like systems can be modelled by a graph-network represented via the following relationship

$$N=(X,\ A,\ I,\ T,\ Q).\ \ldots\ldots\ldots\ldots(1)$$

The elements in Eq.(l) represent:

- X is the set of jobs vertices x_i
- A is the set of arcs (i,j) linking two consecutive jobs;
- I is the set of integer attributes containing all subsets I_{jk} such that an oriented marking with a finite number of available markers $v_m \in N_m$ with the property $v(j)-v(i) \notin I_{jk}$ is associated with vertices set;
- T is the set of positive integers (or non-integers) t_i representing a value in time units;
- Q is a set $Q=\{(y,q)_{ji} \mid 1 \le j \le J_n,\ 1 \le i \le W_m\}$ (2)
  of pairs of operational identifier attributes [9] associated with arc sets where, given an FMS situation, (y,q) represent the average workload and service-time, respectively, for a current station and job needed to determine PMs via operational analysis theory.

As shown in [11], with the error in PMs less than 8%, one can first simulate assuming homogeneous service times $(q)_{ij} = 1$ and then iteratively investigate cases for slight deviations at one, several, or all workstations.

Such a conceptual modelling and graph-network formalism provides a computer-assisted means of modelling representations of all admissible functional situations of a given FMS and its given class of processed products. It can be shown [19] that FMS-like systems with more than one input storage and one output storage can be modelled in this way. The associated substructures defined via sets I,T and Q are aimed at special characterisation of sets of job-vertices and path-arcs, providing for parameters to be used in representing patterns and their recognition. The set of integers containing a set of markers and all their possible subsets of combined markers enables the use of chromatic-number characterization and coloring algorithms [18,20] for interconnection-strength analysis and graph structure partitioning. In addition, as shown in [17], inductive / deductive inference mechanism can be constructed provided there is available (at least one) representative attribute of a given model situation and a knowledge base having a collection of such inter-related objects.

The next stage is the design and implementation of an appropriate information base for representing the described graph-network system structure. It is easily inferred from the above definition that a careful design of an information base meeting all requirements for precise representation of the system structure, its associated items and inter-relations, is needed. According to present experience, it should follow closely the conceptualization defined by Eq.(l) and its compatible representation facility. As far as software details are concerned, there are no particular specifications and various practical implementations are feasible (one is described in Sec.3). The other vital subset of the present computer-assisted approach consists of a collection of searching and pattern-recognition algorithms that operate on the system information base. They constitute a set of operators for graph-network system analysis, starting from the structure up to FMS performance measuring indicators. Again according to present experience, since the FMS coordination-scheduling control problem is NP-complete, searching algorithms and recognition-decision schemata needed are the following (see also Figs. 1, 2):

- detection of bi-directional paths and their equivalent transformation by directed ones;
- selection of terminal vertices; selection of closed and/or complete closed subgraph structures;
- selection of loop-linked and internally/externally (or both) stable core of vertices;
- generation of equivalent tree-graph with attributes associated;
- evaluation of graphpaths and PMs; and selection of the optimized coordination-scheduling controls via situation dichotomy recognition.

3. SOFTWARE CONSIDERATIONS AND DISCUSSION

This research represents the essential part of an on-going project on two-level control systems with distributed intelligence for FMS, which employ applied AI expert support with object modelling and control decision-making functions. An additional goal adopted in this project is that all software will be developed for the IBM compatible personal computing environment. Currently, programs are written for an PC/AT machine with standard peripherals using Pascal, and are to be rewritten in C for faster processing and further experiments. In its present state, the FMS object simulation modelling and analyses program modules, and appropriate searching and recognition algorithms have been built in as test versions. Software segments for these two parts of this computer-aided technique evolve around two main programs OLBI and MIMO. Both assume the FMS-like system is represented by a graph-network model.

The first of the main programs performs an analysis of the system graph using the theory of chromatic-numbers and regular coloring of general graphs, to establish properties such as:

- average interconnection of graph vertices and, consequently, adequate influence operational identifiers;
- selection of internally and/or externally stable subgraphs (graph core) recognition as strongly interconnected subsystems; and
- recognition of loop interconnected vertices. Thus, this software module performs an

overall interconnection-strength and structure-link analysis of the system graph that is a FMS functional structure.

In Fig.1, is a system having 12 vertices and 26 arcs, with one input and two output terminals, for which 2 subgraphs with respect to interconnection strength (and 3 colors) have been selected in 3 iterations taking less than 2 seconds. This analysis can be used in conjunction with the service-time deviation estimates needed for the FMS operational analysis.

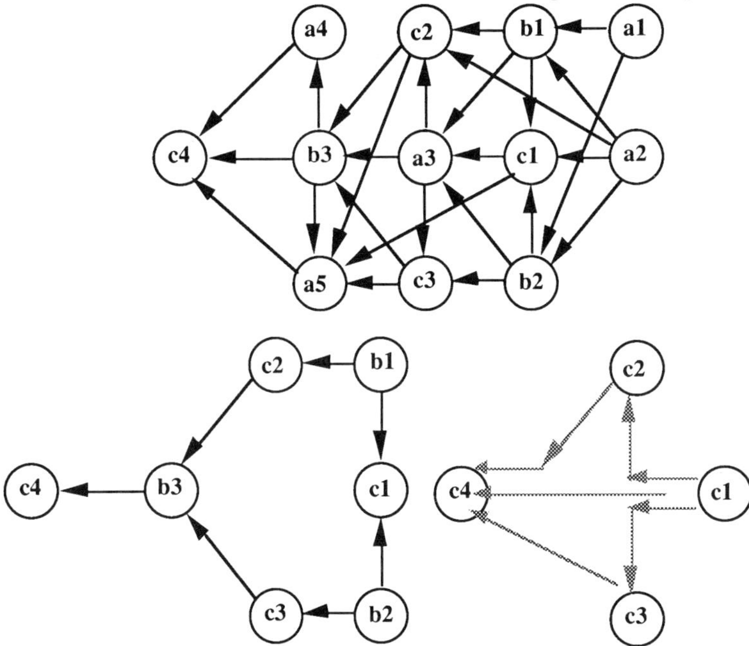

Figure 1 Iterative Interconnection Strength Analysis of a 2x1 System, and two Subgraphs (subsystem states) Recognised.

The other main program has a somewhat composite structure. It has been programmed as a three-partial program structure adequate for real complementary aims. The first one constitutes the definition phase and includes definition of system vertices and arcs including their associated (identifying and weighting) attributes. The other two partial programs are actual path-link analysis operators for two families of jobs: firstly, loop-interconnected paths and cyclic processing operations; and, secondly, alternatives of complete input/output processing operations. Both analysis operators are accompanied by graph-path evaluation analysis with respect to associated characterization attributes. However, only operator generating alternatives of complete I/O processing operations produce information for the iterative design of coordination-scheduling control sequence with respect to a chosen optimization criterion. This part of the computer-aided study of the FMS is performed via generation and subsequent analysis of equivalent tree-graphs with respect to all inputs. In Fig.2, there is a graph-network model for a 2-input/3-output system containing 4 cyclic internal operations and more than 30 complete I/O operations per input port, which has been simulated and analysed in less than one minute.

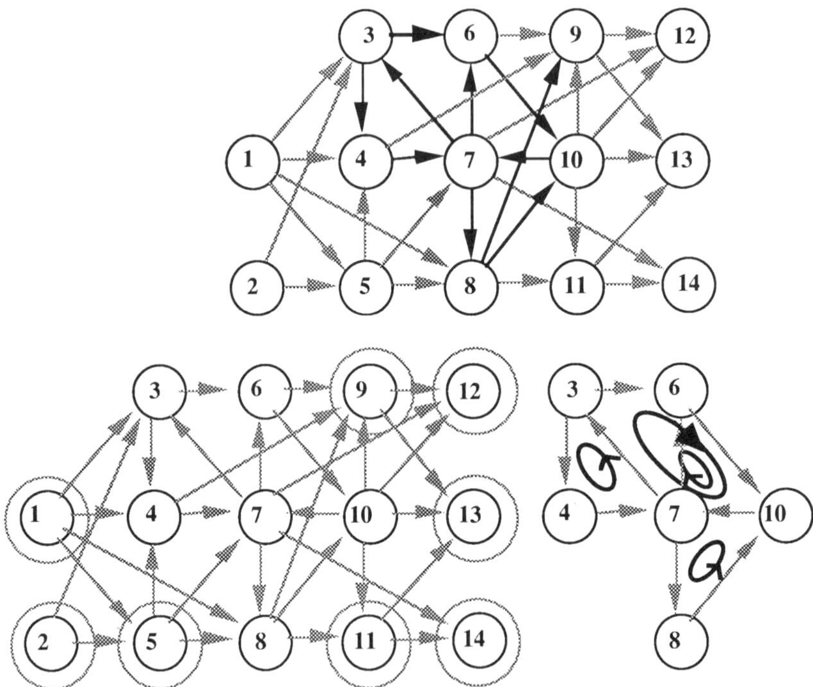

Figure 2 Iterative Structural Analysis of a 2x3 System Having 4 Cyclic and over 30 I/O Complete Operations per Input Port (Palette).

4. CONCLUSIONS

An overview comment on background developments in flexible automation and on FMS modelling and control approaches has been presented first. It has led to the problem formulation and to the outline of its solution via fundamentals in current research on an interactive CAD methodology for the study of FMS-like systems and their controls. A closer discussion with respect to software considerations as well as modest, sample illustrations have highlighted the solution techniques employed and the efficiency. Research is continuing, and it is hoped that a design procedure for feasible scheduling controls via chromatic number, equivalent tree and operational analyses is CAD implementable by means of this approach.

ACKNOWLEDGEMENT

The encouragement and a number of inspiring comments by Professor Vukobratovic are acknowledged with gratitude.

REFERENCES

[l] Ernst D. and B.Phillipson, "Modern Developments in Industrial Automation"(Pl). Preprint .lOth IFAC World Congress, Munich(FRG) 1, pp. 47-57,1987.

[2] Narita S., "The Roles of Information Technology in Systems Control" (P2). Preprint. 10th IFAC World Congress, Munich (FRG) 1, pp. 59-73, 1987.

[3] Saridies G.N., "Application of Pattern Recognition Methods to Control Systems". Trans. IEEE, AC-26, pp. 638-645,1989.

[4] Findeisen W., "Decentralized or Hierarchical Control under Consistency or Disagreement of Interests". Automatica, 18, pp.647-664, 1982.

[5] Nevins J.L., D.E.Whithey and A.C.Edsall, "Intelligent Systems in Manufacturing" (SP) Preprint. 10th IFAC World Congress, Munich (FRG) 1, pp. 130-140, 1987.

[6] Vukobratovic M., Fundamentals of Robotics (in Serbo-Croat). Tehnicka Knjiga, Beograd (YU), 1987.

[7] McLean J.R. and P.F.Brown, "The Architecture of the NBS factory Automation Research Testbed". Preprint .lOth IFAC World Congress, Munich (FRG) 1, pp. 141-146, 1987.

[8] Soldberg J.J., "A Mathematical Model of Computerized Manufacturing Systems". Proc.4th Int.Conf.on PR, Tokyo (JA), pp. 22-30, 1977.

[9] Denning P.J. and .P.Buzen, "The Operational Analysis of Queueing Network Models". Comp.Surv. 10, pp. 225-261, 1978.

[10] Buzacot J.A and J.G.Shanthikumar, "Models for Understanding Flexible Manufacturing Systems". AIIE Trans., 12, pp. 339-350, 1980.

[11] Suri R., "New Techniques for Modelling and Control of Flexible Automated Manufacturing Systems". Prepr.8th IFAC World Congres, Kyoto (JA), XIV, pp. 175-191, 1981.

[12] Burzacot J.A., "Modelling Manufacturing Systems". Preprint .9th IFAC World Congress. Budapest (HU),VI, pp. 136-141, 1984.

[13] Hollocks B., "Simulation and the Micro". J. Oper.Res. Soc., 34, pp. 331-343, 1983.

[14] Pospelov G.S., "System Analysis and Artificial Intelligence". Preprint. 8th IFAC World Congress, Kyoto(JA), XI, pp. 95-104, 1981.

[15] Zeigler B.P., M.S.Elzas, G.J.Klir and T.I.Oren (eds.), Methodology in Systems Modelling and Simulation. North Holland, Amsterdam, 1979.

[16] Dimirovski G.M.,N.E.Gough and R.M.Henry, "Computer-assisted Research of Interconnected large scale Multivariable Systems with Two-level Control" (OL). Proc. JUREMA 34 - 5th Symp. on PCS, Zagreb (YU), 1, pp. 1-10, 1989.

[17] Dimirovski G.M., B.L.Crvenkovski and D.I.Joskovski, "Expert System for Recognition and Typical Identification of Dynamic Process Models". Preprint. IFAC/IMACS/IFORS Int. Symp. on AIPAC, Nancy (FR), I, pp. 222-227, 1989.

[18] De Werra D., Chromatic Scheduling and Frequency Assignement. Res. Rep. ORWP 89/06, Ecole Polytechnique Federale, Lausanne (CH), March 1989.

[19] Iliev O.L., Simulation Modelling and Analysis of MIMO FMS-like Systems. Working Res.Rep., ZASI-ETF, Skopje, Feb. 1990.

[20] Iliev O.L and B.Percinkova, "Algorithm for Coloring General Graphs". Accepted, 14th Symp. on IT, Sarajevo(YU), March 1990.

[21] Babanovski P., G.Dimirovski, B.Percinkova and O.Iliev, "Simulation of Robotized Flexible Manufacturing Systems with the use of Language SIMAN". Accepted, 34th Yug. Conf. ETAN-RO, Zagreb, June 1990.

Industrial Applications of Artificial Intelligence
J.L. Alty and L.I. Mikulich (Editors)
Elsevier Science Publishers B.V. (North-Holland)

A TECHNOLOGICAL KNOWLEDGE MODEL IN AN FMS DESIGN SYSTEM

A. A. LESKIN and A.V. SMIRNOV
Leningrad Institute for Informatics and Automation,
USSR Academy of Sciences,
Leningrad,
The USSR.

ABSTRACT: Knowledge representation problems in intellectual CAD FMS are considered. The integrated technological knowledge model based on an object-oriented approach is developed. The design process is implemented through the use of production rules over elements of special graph-structures representing FMS virtual and physical fragments. The software of the design decision support system is described.

1. INTRODUCTION

FMS design problems deal with many alternatives involved in production process design, a multiplicity of performance criteria available, and a necessity of considering linkage to manufacturing and electronic equipment. The following tasks need to be solved when designing an FMS:

- assigning production operations for machine tools;
- generating basic production equipment composition versions;
- grouping operations and equipment items;
- arranging the equipment;
- determining effective FMS production equipment versions;
- simulation of FMS.

The solution of these problems requires a joint use of both operational research and artificial intelligence, so the technological knowledge model development is of great importance. There is no unified model representing technological knowledge. It is possible, however, to construct a family of interacting models that satisfy the requirements of the problems. The declarative knowledge is represented in object-oriented models while the procedural knowledge is represented by production rules.

2. MODELS OF DESIGNED OBJECTS

The FMS design process can be implemented as a process of evolution of the designed object model [1]. First, there is a modified structure production flowchart which consists of production operation sequences together with requirements for the equipment. Then, at another design stage, a complex of machine-tools with virtual links is designed. Finally an FMS structure is constructed along with transport and material handling facilities. The representation of the evolving model, simulating the designed object, is based upon a graph-structure consisting of a pair: a graph and a set. The elements of the set correspond to features of production operations. The graph-structure is associated with a semantic network having two types of nodes and arcs. A given object can be represented also as a frame, which makes it possible to realize an effective mechanism for prototyping the design decisions by providing the name of typical solutions and attributes to adjust it to the particular problem. Thus, the model of the designed object is the family of graph-structures, each of which can be transformed into another by special mappings. A number of the most important production system invariants is conserved under such a transformation. The process of producing an

FMS design is reduced to the realization of a basic set of operations over graph-structures: clusterization and decomposition of nodes, unions etc. [2].

Software specification of the design process is easily implemented in the framework of object-oriented technology of declarative knowledge representation.

3. MODELS OF THE FMS DESIGN PROCESS

Intellectual support for the FMS design process is carried out in the following modes: fixed scenario, interactively adjustable scenario and user's scenario. Cognitive procedures of mode identification and scenario modification are based upon the generation of a solution diagram for a particular problem. The solution diagram is defined as a path on a graph constructed on triads P_i - { X_i, M_i, Y_i } as on nodes, where M_i denotes the method, X_i and Y_i are the input and output arrays for i-th procedure, which either give a solution to some i-th subproblem or perform a matching transformation of interacting subproblems. An elementary operation of the diagram generation is a searching for a matching element P_k between the resulting nodes of backward-chaining and forward-chaining processes. The former is activated on the node-objective (sub-objective), the latter is activated on the node corresponding to data the system has.

The mechanism for finding a solution diagram for a design problem consists of the implementation of a method developed earlier, namely the method of virtual routes [1], through the use of three types of rules: instantiation, activation and termination. The instantiation operation I calls a program module R_n containing reference variables which determine the interaction of terminal nodes of "cross-processes" and controls the applicability of the procedure due to the module R_n. If the search is unsuccessful, it is repeated for another module R_m with the application of coincidence of characteristic features associated with nodes.

The rules of instantiation allow the determination of the solution diagram for the problem so that each of the rules can be presented as a set of elementary rules related to the implementation of concepts corresponding to different levels of description of facts in the problem domain:

- rules for the decomposition of design problems;
- rules for the selection of a solution method (procedure) for the sample subproblem;
- rules for the solution for the sample subproblem.

Each of these rules is based either upon generally accepted knowledge in the problem domain or upon empirical knowledge of the designer or, may be, upon heuristics used by the designer.

The activation operation A performs the data input and their matching within the framework of technological rules. If data are not in conformity, searching for a matching element is carried out. Rules for this operation are based upon knowledge in the problem area and include:

- rules relating initial data to the structure of the designed object;
- rules constraining the relationship of constructive, production and "compatibility" of elements of the designed object.

To increase the effectiveness of the activation operation two levels of description of the object area are used - conceptual and physical.

The completion operation is used for selection among alternatives to complete a design. This operation includes the following types of rules:

- rules of preferability of attribute values related to the design object;
- rules of variant selection (by Pareto method, majority selection etc.).

Thus, there are two levels of support for the design process using the production knowledge model. The planning and supervision of the solution process based upon production rules and facts are carried out at first stage. At the second stage, support based upon object-oriented technology of formal model transformations is performed.

Obtaining solutions of these design problems makes use of an integrated conceptual model in the production domain under consideration.

4. THE DESIGN DECISION SUPPORT SYSTEM AT PRELIMINARY STAGES OF FMS DESIGN

The FMS design process which is oriented to the application of design decision support systems (DDSS) technology is carried out in three stages [3].

The first stage consists in analysing the requirements and constraints and evaluation of the existence of a design decision. At the second, conceptual FMS design stage, a selection is performed among possible conceptual decision versions of design fragments related to the designed object such that further detailing at the final stage enables decisions on FMS components and parameters to be taken. Conceptual decisions for designing FMS production equipment complexes (PEC) are types of PEC components.

The third, structure-parameter synthesis stage, includes a selection of design decisions on components in accordance with production rules (Fig. 1).

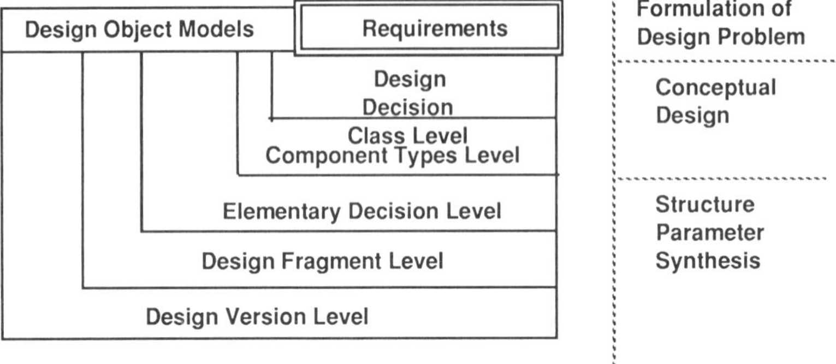

Figure 1 Design Models

The selection of design and production decisions is based upon the implementation of relationships, relating user's requirements to types of possible decision; relationships between decisions for separate FMS components; rules for matching types of conceptual decisions as well as evaluating performance indices concerning the project.

The solution of the main problems of FMS structure-parameter synthesis, (the selection of production equipment units and their arrangement over the workplace and layout) is provided by the use of discrete optimization methods using rule recommendations based upon empirical knowledge in the problem domain and upon a number of technologically justified heuristics.

The organization of the design problem solution process in DDSS requires a monitor which satisfies the requirements of the suggested method of intellectual support. The implementation of the monitor is based upon a special class of Petri-net [4]. Places in such a net are interpreted as data sets, transitions as data processing procedures; and arcs show directions of data flows. The appearance of a token in a position of the net corresponds to reception of one or more variants of an appropriate data set. The token remains in this position as long as there exists at least one variant of the data set which is suitable from the user's point of view. When a transition fires, new tokens appear in the output places. Firing takes place whenever the following conditions are realized:

- absence of tokens in output places of the token;
- presence of tokens in input places of the token;
- logical conditions for the token.

The DDSS structure realizing the above solutions is presented in Figure 2. In the first version of the system a dialogue with the user is organized by means of an hierarchical menu system. The DDSS is implemented with the use of algorithmic languages Fortran-77 and Prolog.

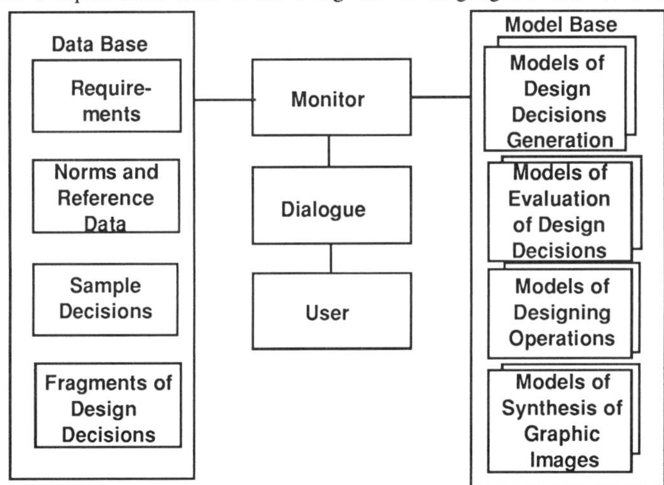

Figure 2 Design Decisions Support System

5. CONCLUSION

This approach to the implementation of production data and knowledge representation within intellectual CAD FMS is based upon the unification of the concepts of the object-oriented approach and logical programming. The in-and-out model of production knowledge satisfies the requirements of rational organization of design decision making support and can be adopted as a basis for the implementation of cognitive support for decision making.

REFERENCES

[1] Leskin, A.A., "Algebraic Models of Flexible Manufacturing Systems", (Nauka, Leningrad, 1986) (in Russian).

[2] Leskin,A.A. and Ponomarev, V.M., "Knowledge Representation in CAD FMS", Prolamat-88,(Preprints, Dresden, 1988).

[3] Ponomarev, V.M., Bogdanov, K.I., Leskin, A.A., Romanov, G.V., and Smirnov, A.V., "Computer-aided FMS Conceptual Design System", (Preprint N 45, Leningrad, 1987).

[4] Leskin, A.A., Maltsev, P.A., and Spiridonov, A.M., "Petri Nets in Simulation and Control", (Nauka, Leningrad, 1989) (in Russian).

Industrial Applications of Artificial Intelligence
J.L. Alty and L.I. Mikulich (Editors)
Elsevier Science Publishers B.V. (North-Holland)

THE MACHINE LAYOUT PROBLEM CONSIDERING TRANSPORT NETS

Peter Richter

Central Institute of
Cybernetics and Information Processes
Postfach 1298
Berlin
1086
DDR

We present an approximate algorithm that starts from a given transport net in order to find a layout for a set of modules so that the sum of the products of transport intensity and transport distance between modules is minimum, where the distance is referred to the graph metric. The algorithm heuristically solves this problem with a time effort $O(|Y|\cdot|M|\cdot(|M|+n)\cdot\log(|M|+n))$ (M=set of modules, n= transport graph's vertices, and Y=set of graph vertices envisaged to be the roots of shortest path trees).

1. INTRODUCTION

This paper deals with the Machine Layout Problem (MLP,[2]) of the layout design of Flexible Manufacturing Systems (FMS) considering transport mechanisms. If automated guidance vehicles (AGV) as material handling devices have to be used, it is worthwhile to take into consideration transport nets from the beginning of an MLP-procedure. The transport network(s) be emerge from preliminary examinations with respect to the work shop's extension, forbidden areas, and carrying as well as from analyses which have led to a rough placement of several clusters of machines resulting in a first layout of such a network. We are given a transport net transformed to the internal sparse graph representation G (V(G)=set of vertices, E(G)=set of edges, $E(G)=(E' \cup E'') \subseteq V(G)^2$, E'= stright lines, E"= circle arcs (only intended to connect E'), edge lengths $l:E(G) \longrightarrow R^+$, the set of edge sides $S=E' \times \{0,1\}$, a set of modules M (stored as polygons or at least as rectangles embracing these modules, $M=A \cup B$ (A= modules already placed, $A \cap B = \emptyset$)) and an activity relationship chart as a mapping $q:M^2 \longrightarrow R^+$ (qualitative factors (closeness rating) or quantitative factors (flow of materials, transport intensities)). The work shop's interior extension and forbidden areas are given as polygons. We denote the admissible set of the work shop's coordinates as $K \subset R^2$. The points of polygons describing forbidden areas have a unique correspondence into K. Let $w:M \longrightarrow S \times K$ be any function assigning each $b \in M$ an ordered pair w(b)=(s,(bx,by)) where (bx,by) corresponds to the reference point of module b into K and b is laid out with a given safety distance along s∈S (i.e. with w(b) and the rotation angle of b is well determined according to the angular coefficient of s). Starting from function w and graph G, a distance function $d': (w(M))^2 \longrightarrow R^+$ emerges assigning each module pair (i,j) the length d'(w(i),w(j)) of a shortest path from w(i) to w(j) in G. Of course, the points corresponding to each w(i)∈w(M) are not originally contained in V(G). In evaluating such layouts by Shortest Path Tree (SPT) algorithms (shortest paths' distances between all modules), these points have temporarily to be established as additional vertices dividing the corresponding underlying edges resulting in a new graph H.

Problem
For a graph G and a function w:M—>S X K let $C(G,w) = \sum_{(i,j)\in M} q(i,j) \cdot d'(w(i),w(j))$ be the value of w with respect to graph G and modules M. We call w "admissible" if the necessary safety distance between modules as well as between modules and edges, and between modules and the work shop is observed. We look for a function w^*:M—>S X K that suffices the objective $C(G,w^*) = \min_{\text{function } w \in M X (S X K)} \{C(G,w): w \text{ is admissible}\}$.

In contrast to the Quadratic Assignment Problem (QAP,[7]), where the modules extension is not considered and |M| places are available for the modules, the MLP is more complex due to the continuous state space and therefore, like the QAP, the MLP is NP-hard too. Thus we are well advised to look for an efficient heuristic.

2. ALGORITHM TRALAY

The algorithm determines a SPT T(G,r) in G rooted at a "suitable" vertex r∈V(G) assigning all v∈V(G) the lengths $d: V(G) \longrightarrow R^+$ of shortest paths from r to v. This procedure corresponds to the single centre problem assuming r as communication centre for all strongly communicating modules (transport intensity). As to SPT-algorithms we refer to [1], [3], [6], [8]. "Suitable" means vertices having many layout possibilities along incident edges. The set Y of such vertices should be restricted to confine time effort. This restriction can be done by interactively scanning the current graph or solving the median problem to find the |Y| best medians (minimum sum of the lengths of shortest paths to all vertices (Median Problem $O(n^2 \cdot \log n)$). Because each edge side s=((i,j),k)∈S can be assigned likewise, a shortest path distance $c: S \longrightarrow R^+$ with c(((i,j),k))= min{d(i),d(j)} as well as an occupation length $p: S \longrightarrow R^+$ caused by the modules allo-

```
                         Algorithm TRALAY

- Input of G, M, q:M² --->R+. (n=V(G),m=E(G))          O(|M|²+n+m)
- Determination of E' ⊆ E(G).                                 O(m)
- Determination of S=E' X {Ø,1}, and l:E(G)--->R+.            O(m)
- Drawing  the work shop, forbidden  areas, and G.      O(|M|+n)
- Determine a set of roots Y ⊆ V(G)
  (e.g. by the median problem).                       O(n²·log n)
- For all y∈Y DO
  BEGIN
-  |Build a SPT T(G,y).                             O(|Y|·n·log n)
-  |Determine d:V(G)--->R+.                                  "
-  |For all s∈S DO
-  |BEGIN c(s):=c((i,j),k)):=min{d(i),d(j)};p(s):=Ø;END;
-  |MAKE_HEAP(S) as to c(S);                   O(|Y|·|S|·log |S|)
-  |A:=Ø; B:=M; Cbest:=∞; wbest:=Ø;                     O(|Y|·|M|)
-  |WHILE NOT A=M do
   |BEGIN
-  ||IF B=Ø THEN
   ||BEGIN
-  |||b:∈{α,β} and α,β are determined by
   |||                                 ___                ___
   |||q(α,j)=  max    {q(i,j)};       >  q(β,j)=max{ >  q(i,j)};
   |||       (i,j)∈M²                 j∈M         i∈M j∈M\{i}
   ||END ELSE
   ||BEGIN
   ||            ___           ___
-  |||b∈B so that  > q(b,j)=max{ > q(i,j)};
   |||           j∈A        i∈B j∈A
   ||END;                                             O(|Y|·|M|²)
-  ||B:=B\{b}; A:=A U {b}; T1,T2:=Ø; p'(S):=Ø;        O(|Y|+|M|)
-  ||f:=False;
-  ||WHILE f=False DO                                 O(|Y|·|M|²)
   ||BEGIN
-  |||FIND_MIN(s,S);                           O(|Y|·|M|²·log|S|)
-  |||T1:=T1 U {s}; T2:=T2\{s};                      O(|Y|·|M|²)
-  |||Determine w(b) as to s;                                   "
-  |||IF w(b) is not admissible THEN                            "
   |||BEGIN
-  ||||Is there a drift p'(s) to overcome overlapping THEN
   ||||BEGIN
-  |||||INSERT(s,c(s)+p(s)+p'(s),S);          O(|Y|·|M|²·log |S|)
-  |||||T2:=T2 U {s};                                O(|Y|·|M|²)
   ||||END
   |||END ELSE BEGIN
-  ||||f:=True; Drawing b; p(s):=p(s)+length(b);     O(|Y|·|M|²)
   |||END
   ||END;
-  ||IF f=False THEN CYCLE (no s could be found for b);
-  ||For all t∈T1 DO if t∈T2
-  ||                THEN DECREASE_KEY(t,c(t)+p(t),S)
-  ||                ELSE INSERT(t,c(t)+p(t));
   ||                                          O(|Y|·|M|·log|S|)
   |END;
-  |IF Cbest)<C(G,w) THEN (Cbest:=C(G,w); wbest:=w);
  END;                                O(|Y|·|M|·(|M|+n)·log(|M|+n))
```

cated to S, we can embarke on a fast approach that regards the root r as the centre of strongly communicating modules and further modules b∈B are allocated in decreasing intensity order to such sides (i.e. along the edges with an admissible w(b)) that are nearest situated to the centre ("cluster development") or nearest to a certain modul("pair linking"). If we use a priority queue Q (e.g. with a binary or with a Fibonacci heap ([5], [7], [8], [11]) the following queue operations ensure least time effort: The O(|S|·log|S|)-operation MAKE_HEAP(S) establishs each s∈S into the queue Q with respect to the value c(s)+p(s) in order to enable the search for the minimum element by the O(log|S|)-operation FIND_MIN(x,S) where c(x)= min{c(s)+p(s):s∈Q} and x is deleted from the queue (Q:=Q\{x}). Additionally, we use the O(log|S|)-operations INSERT(s,y,S) and DECREASE_KEY(s,y,S) to insert a new element s∈S into the queue (Q:=Q ∪ {s}) or to reorganize the queue subject to a new decreased value y=c(s)+p(s). If some module b∈B causes overlapping with other modules already placed (w(b) not admissible) we try to use overlapping information hoping to ease the situation by calculating a drift distance p'(s) for side s to increase the occupation length p(s) by p'(s) and to restore s into the priority queue as to the value c(s)+p(s)+p'(s). Once, module b has been allocated, say to side s, all sides t∈S\{s} labelled as "temporarily changed" must be requeued with the value c(t)+p(t). If all modules are placed, i.e. an admissible mapping w has been found, the allocation graph H will be determined to evaluate the current layout (shortest paths between all M are necessary to get d'). In the manner, roughly described above, we meet approximatively our objective defined. Algorithm TRALAY was implemented as part of a layout design system LAYFMS of the design system CADFMS ([4], [9], [10]) together with approximate constructive and improvement algorithms. The algorithm given above corresponds only to the main principle.
There ere more sophisticated approaches that build a forest of t disjoint shortest path trees according to t subsets of M that have possibly emerged from preliminary examinations (cluster of modules). As we can see from the algorithm's representation above, term O(|Y|·|M|·(|M|+n)·log(|M|+n)) is the hardest one. It is realized using |Y|·|M|-times a shortest path tree algorithm for a graph H with |M|+n vertices to determine all shortest paths d'(w(i),w(j)) between all pairs $(i,j)\in M^2$. With n=|V(G)|, m=|E(G)| cosidering O(n)=O(m) for sparse graphs we get O(|M|·n·(|M|+n)·log(|M|+n)). It remains to say that, due to very fast shortest path tree algorithms ([3], [6], [8]), TRALAY is very time efficient.

3. RESULTS

TRALAY was implemented as part of a layout design system LAYFMS integrated in a design package CADFMS for flexible maufacturing systems ([4],[9],[10]). LAYFMS uses graphical symbols for layout generation and modification that were created by standard CAD-systems. After reading the binary or

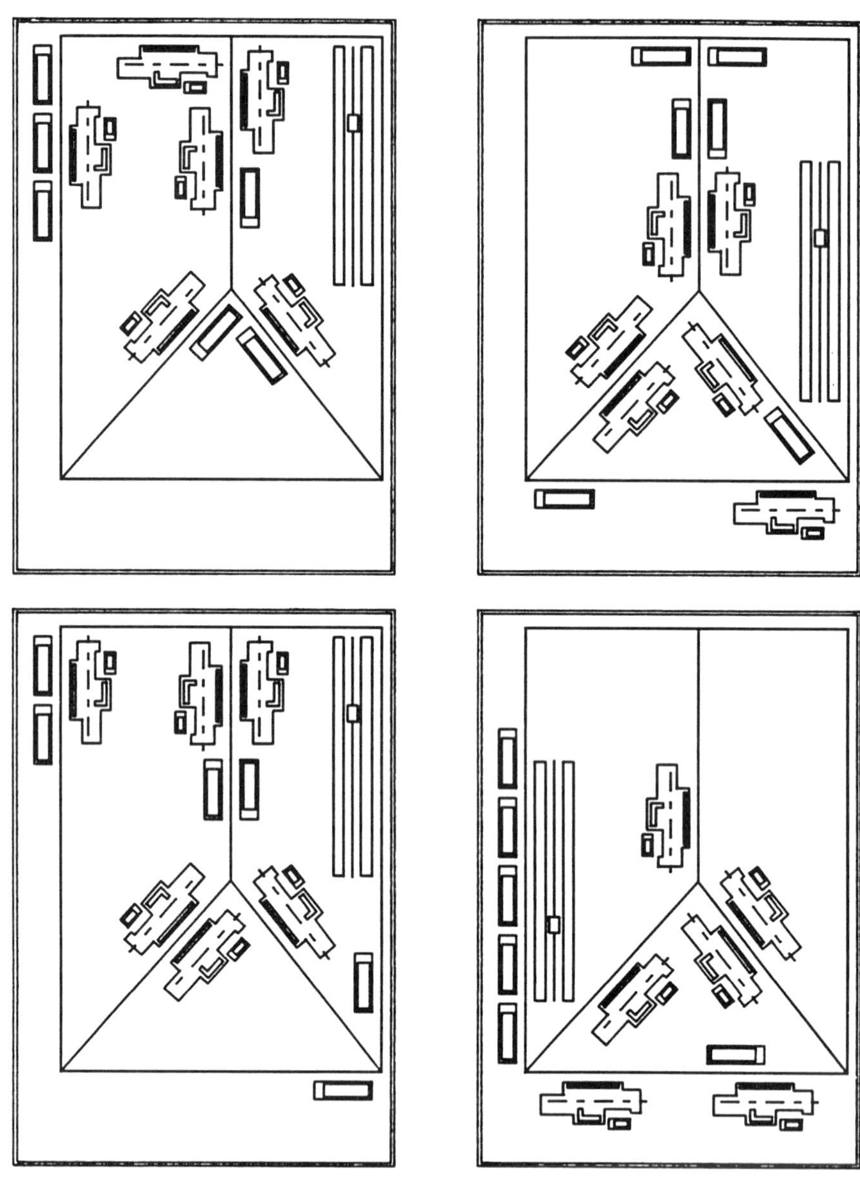

FIGURE 1
Some layouts for |M|=13 and graph G with n=6 and m=8 considering the single centre problem (the six little machines have only a small transport intensity to the bigger ones). The layout right above proved as the best one.

ascii-format picture and symbol-files a corresponding data-structure is established for drawing, deleting, rotating, moving, and coppying symbols by optimization algorithms like TRALAY. In figure 1, four different layouts generated by TRALAY are depicted. The exterior border represents the work shop's extension. The interior net represents the graph G. The layout appears immediately after the objective's input.

With a special graphical layout editor developed and integrated for LAYFMS the designer may vary and revaluate the layout again not leaving CADFMS. The outputs may be applied by standard CAD-systems.

REFERENCES

[1] Dial, R., F. Glover, F., Karney, D., Klingman, D., A Computational Analaysis of Alternative Algorithms and Labeling Techniques for Finding Shortest Path Trees, NETWORKS, Vol. 9, (1979), 215-248

[2] Francis, R.L., White, J.A., Facility Layout and Location : An Analytical Approach, Prentice Hall, Englewood Cliffs, New Jersey, 1974

[3] Gilsinn, I., Witzgall, C., A Performance Comparison of Labeling Algorithms for Calculating Shortest Path Trees; NBS Technical Note 772, U.S. Department of Commerce, (1973)

[4] Kaltwasser, J., Deul, N.,Feudel, F., Friedrich, G., Schiemangk, C., Rechnergestuetzte Projektierung von Flexiblen Fertigungssystemen in CIM Strukturen; In: Kommtech 88, 5th European Congress Fair for Technical Automation, Essen 7.-10.6.1988

[5] Mehlhorn, K., Efficiente Algorithmen, B. G. Teubner Stuttgart 1977

[6] V. Pape, V., Implementation and Efficiency of Moore-Algorithms for the Shortest Route Problem; Mathematical Programming, 7, (1974)/212-222

[7] Papadimitriou, C.H., Steiglitz, K., Combinatorial Optimization Algorithms and Complexity, Prentice Hall, INC., New Jersey, 1982

[8] Richter, P., Neue effektive Algorithmen zur Optimierung von Verbindungsstrukturen in Graphen, Dissertation A, Zentralinstitut fuer Kybernetik und Informationsprozesse Berlin, Berlin, 1989

[9] Schiemangk, C., Kaltwasser, J., The Design System CADFMS for Flexible Manufacturing Systems; In: ECE Seminar on Computer-Integrated Manufacturing (CIM), S. 25-29, Sep 1989, Botevgrad

[10] Schiemangk, C., Hofmann, J., Knauss, D., Könner, S., Mende, U., Richter, P., LAYFMS - Layout Design System for Flexible Manufacturing Systems, Workshop on Informatics in Industrial Automation, Central Institute of Cybernetics and Information Processes Berlin, Oct. 89, 277-293

[11] Vuillemin, J., A Data Structure for Manipulating Priority Queues, COMM. ACM. 21(1987) 309-314

Industrial Applications of Artificial Intelligence
J.L. Alty and L.I. Mikulich (Editors)
Elsevier Science Publishers B.V. (North-Holland)

ASSEMBLY LINE SCHEDULING: A KNOWLEDGE-BASED APPROACH

Evgeny I. ZAK

The Academy of Sciences of the USSR,
Central Economic and Mathematical Institute,
Krasikova St. 32, Moscow 117418, USSR

An integrated structure is presented of a system intended for design of well-balanced mixed-model assembly lines. The integration implies (1) combination of subproblems into a larger problem and (2) combination of formal models and an expert system.

1. INTRODUCTION

A flexible assembly system (FAS) is a computer integrated manufacturing system consisting of automatic material handling devices and work stations that can simultaneously assembly a variety of product types [1]. As a rule FAS works in so-called mixed-product assembly mode meeting both market demands and machining stage requirements.

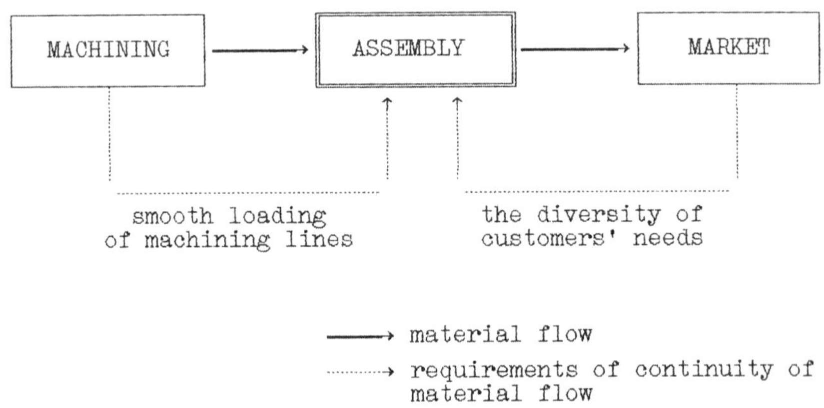

FIGURE 1. Necessity of mixed-product assembly

Mixed-model assembly is necessary to provide a continuous flow of each product. This fact is very important in the Just-In-Time (JIT) concept. Instead of assembling the same product over a long time and then switching to a different one, various products are assembled simultaneously.

An FAS balancing problem arises. It consist of four separate but related subproblems:

- selection of a set of products types to be assembled in mixed-product mode;
- single-model balancing for every selected product type;
- mixed-model balancing for a set of products;
- sequencing.

A prototype of a hybrid system, including formal model-based modules and knowledge-based modules interacting with one other will be presented below. This approach is similar to the tandem architecture methodology [3].

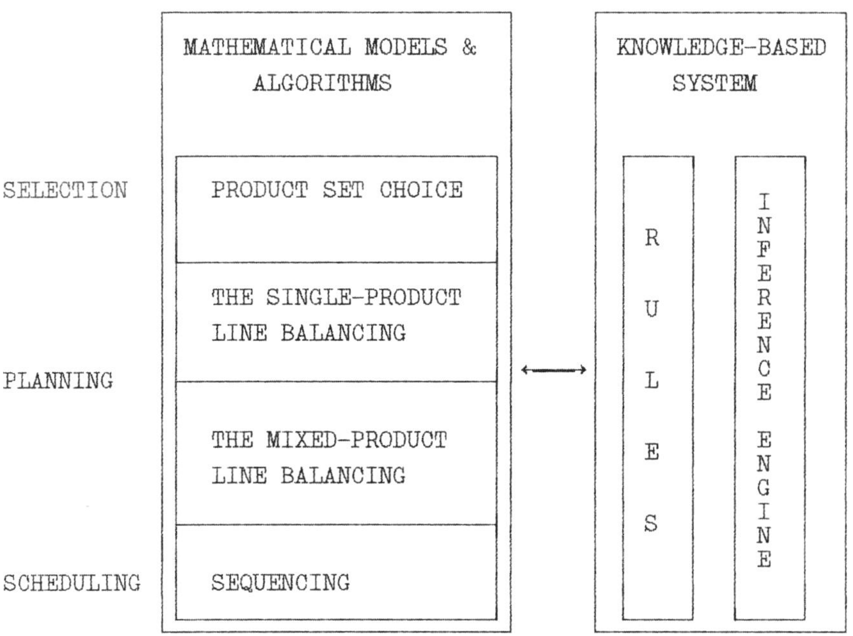

FIGURE 2. The system flowchart

2. SELECTION

The selection problem is to be solved before all the others. The selection problem can be formulated as follows. Given a potential set of products types, and process plans of assembling for each type of products including required assembly operations, machines, fixtures and ordering requirements, find a subset of the set of products types which would satisfy the market demand, provided the assembly line capacity is constrained.

The formal mathematical model is a knapsack problem. The problem is computationally hard. There are some heuristic algorithms [4].

The expert system is intended to support
- analyzing an input data for consistency;
- choosing a suitable heuristic algorithm.

The inference engine is based on forward chaining inference strategy. It operates by matching the data concerned with the IF part of a rule. If the match is successful the rule is fired.

An example of a rule:

IF total operation times of products i and j differ largely,
THEN products i and j have not to belong to the same set of products.

3. PLANNING

The planning stage incorporates single- and mixed-product balancing problem solving.

3.1. Single-model balancing

The problem has to be solved for every selected product type. The assembly line balancing problem is required to assign tasks to assembly line work stations so as to minimize the balance delay subject to certain constraints, including the cycle time.

The *cycle time* is the amount of time initially allocated to each work station within which all tasks are to be performed. In other words, an assembly line is said to be in balance when every worker's operation takes the same amount of time.

This problem in a general case was found to be computationally hard and several heuristic algorithms were proposed for solving large-scale problems. There are mathematical, procedural, and computer-based approaches (see, for example [2]) to designing well-balanced production lines.

The expert system role is the same as in the previous case.

As a result of solving the single-model balancing problem the total assembly time for each product is balanced over all stations.

3.2. Mixed-model balancing

The single-product line balancing problem must have already been solved separately for each type of product.

We deal with a variable-launch rate system, for which the cycle time is a variable depending on the type of product

$$ct_i = a_i \quad , \; i = 1,\ldots,m \; ,$$

where m is the total number of different products and a_i is the operation time of product i, $i=1,\ldots,m$. The operation times which are the same for all work stations, are balanced times (in the sense of single-product balancing) for all work stations.

We will define also the *full cycle time* t as a fixed time separating the launching of two consecutive lots of identical products:

$$t = (\; ct_i + w_i \;)\; x_i \; , \text{ for all } i \; ,$$

where x_i is the lot size for product i , and w_i is the admissible time waste. Thus products transportation from one work station to another occurs by lots of identical products over a fixed time period, a full cycle time. In our case, during a full cycle time several identical products are assembled on every work station. Imbalance in operation times can be treated by grouping identical products. The line balancing options are: to run two small products for every large one, to run three small ones for every two large ones, etc. This approach was proposed in [5] and formalized in [6, 7].

In effect, the problem is formulated as follows: It is required to synchronize the operation of every work station so that an integer number of identical products are manufactured during the full cycle time satisfying the demand, the full cycle time tending to a minimum.

The expert system interacting with this formal model evaluates the solution produced by the algorithm and allows to return to the previous stages for modifying the products set and/or the cycle times.

4. SCHEDULING

Solution of the previous problem provides balancing of the assembly line in general terms. Now we present an approach to sequencing lots of different products.

The sequencing problem is formulated as follows. Given the number of lots z_i for every product type, determine a sequence of these lots so as to provide as continuous a flow for each product as possible.

By default, the following algorithm operates. As a result of solving the previous subproblem, we have a vector $\mathbf{z} = (z_1 \ldots z_m)$ whose component z_i is the number of time periods of duration t when product i is manufactured (the number of launchings for product i). Without loss of generality assume that

$$z_1 \geqslant z_2 \geqslant \ldots \geqslant z_m .$$

Then compute the following values

$$v_{ik} = ((2k - 1)z_0/z_i + 1)/2 \quad , \ i= 1,\ldots,m \ , \quad k= 1,\ldots, z_i \ ,$$

where $z_0 = \sum_{i=1}^{m} z_i$, and k is the index denoting the lot of products.
The final ordinal launching numbers will be defined in accordance with non-decreasing sequence of v_{ik} , $i= 1,\ldots,m$; $k= 1,\ldots,z_i$.

The expert system functions are:

- if it remains after the formal algorithm has been implemented, eliminate uncertainty in the optimal decision,
- simplify problem situation,
- solve the problem for some cases.

The sample rules are shown below:

1) IF $v_{ik} = v_{jl}$ for $i,j \in \{1,\ldots,m\}$, and $k \in \{1,\ldots,z_i\}$, $l \in \{1,\ldots,z_j\}$,

   THEN some rules, concerned with the transpositions of the ordinal launching numbers, will be attracted.

2) IF the greatest common divisor, GCD, of integer numbers $z_1,\ldots,z_m$ is greater than 1 ,

   THEN it is sufficient to solve the sequencing problem for the reduced values:

   z_1 / GCD ,..., z_m / GCD.

5. CONCLUSIONS

A system prototype selects, balances, groups, and sequences products with the aim of supporting mixed-product assembly. The system consist of two kind of modules. The first kind are mathematical models and algorithms, and the second other is a rule-based knowledge system. On the one hand, formal mathematical procedures are integrated with an expert systems technology; on the other hand, different kind of problems are integrated into a system.

REFERENCES

[1] Hall, D.N., and Stecke, K.E.,"Design problems of flexible assembly systems", *Proceedings of the 2nd ORSA/TIMS Conference on Flexible Manufacturing Systems. Operations Research Models and Applications*, Elsevier, Amsterdam, 1986, 145-156.

[2] Jonhson, R.V., "Assembly line balancing algorithms: computation comparisons", *International Journal of Production Research* 19 (1981) 277-287.

[3] Kusiak, A., "Designing expert systems for scheduling of automated manufacturing", *Industrial Manufacturing* 19 (1987) 42-46.

[4] Levner, E.V., "Complexity of heuristics for knapsack type problems: a survey", *Operational Research-81, Proceedings of the 9th IFORS International Conference on Operations Research*, North-Holland, Amsterdam, 1981, part 2,317-327.

[5] Schonberger, R.J., *Japanese Manufacturing Techniques. Nine Hidden Lessons in Simplicity*, The Free Press, London, 1982.

[6] Zak, E.I., "An assembly line synchronizing model for JIT system", in: A.A.Fridman, E.V.Levner (eds.), *Mathematical Modeling in Economics and Analysis of Discrete Systems*, Central Economic and Mathematical Institute, Moscow,1988, 138-145 (in Russian).

[7] Zak, E.I., and Kardansky, L.L., "A mathematical programming approach to assembly line just-in-time scheduling", *Proceedings of the 6th International Conference of Flexible Manufacturing Systems*, International Research Institute for Management Sciences, Moscow, 1989, 110-111.

Industrial Applications of Artificial Intelligence
J.L. Alty and L.I. Mikulich (Editors)
Elsevier Science Publishers B.V. (North-Holland)

SYSTEM FOR THE DIGITAL PROCESSING OF COLOUR IMAGES ON MICROCOMPUTERS

A. Sh. GUGUSHVILI, T. G. BENASHVILI, P.D. JOKHADZE, A.G. DATIASHVILI, G.G. KSOVRELI, V.A. KUTSIAVA, T.A. TATARISHVILI and Z.A. KHOMERIKI.

Georgian Technical University,
Tbilisi,
Georgia,
The USSR.

ABSTRACT: The given system takes image input from a colour or black-and-white TV camera. It processes the video information with the help of computer programmes and displays half-tone colour video information on an RGB monitor screen in the raster of 512x512 pixels, colour codes the half-tone images and outputs to a colour printer.

1. INTRODUCTION

In order to create purposeful behaviour in robots we need to utilise artificial intelligence. The robot should have the necessary knowledge about the complex environment including technical vision. Because of this a system for digitally processing images, based upon a microcomputer which functions in real time, is of great interest.

2. DESCRIPTION OF THE SYSTEM

The system is built using home microcomputers compatible with IBM personal computers. The system structure is given in figure 1.

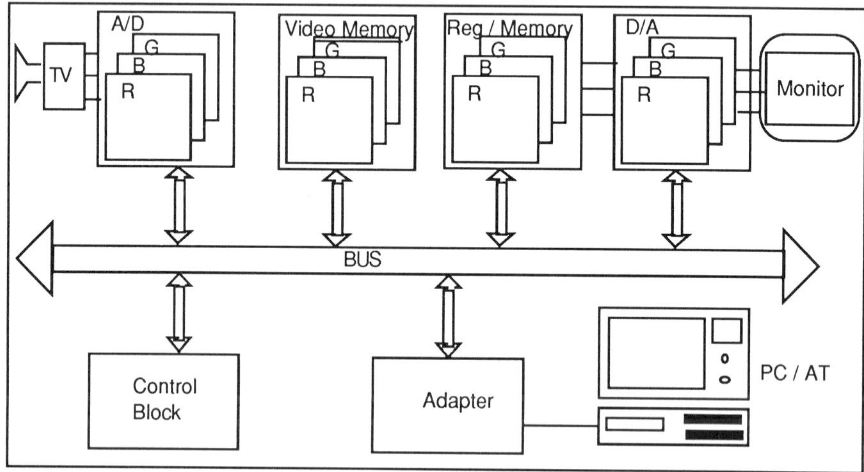

Figure 1 Structural scheme of the system of digital processing of colour images.

The image to be processed is fed into the system by means of a colour TV camera which has separate outputs for each of the channels of the main colours - R,G,B. Video signals are fed to the block of the analogue-to-digital convertor, consisting of three identical ADCs necessary for simultaneous digitalisation of the signal over all three channels. The input signal is quantised into 256 gradations, by an integrated microcircuit K1107 RB2 (a fast ADC) which has a discrimination of 8 discharges. The integral circuit K1107 RB2 is a fully parallel circuit which ensures maximum quick operation at minimum dynamic error without use of external circuit of sampling and storing device.

Output levels and signal levels of control correspond to TTl-levels. The maximum frequency of ADC transformation is equal to 20 MHz which allows coding of the input signal and a change code on the input every 50 ns. For the realization of TV Image input in a real time scale it is sufficient that the ADC operates in the system on the frequency of 12.5 MHz. Thus a digitalized value of image pixels appears on the output of the ADC every 80nz.

The stream of coded information enters from the ADC into videomemory through buffers which allow the coordination of the speed of the data stream shaping on the output of ADC with the data record time into videomemory. The latter is built on the basis of semiconductor ISIC storage RY5D which comprises a dynamic memory with 64K x 1 bit organisation. The microcircuit has an output with three conditions coordinated with TTL-levels. For storing of one frame of a colour image of 512x512 pixels the memory volume of 3x512x512x8 bit or 768 Kb is needed. The total volume of the videomemory is 4.6 Mb, which corresponds to the storage of 6 frames of colour or 18 frames of black-and-white images. The given number of frames enables us to implement elementary operations on the synthesis of dynamic images with a computer. In addition to the basic videomemory, the system provides additional memory (RAM regenerations) per frame of colour image, which enables us to keep the image on the TV monitor at the moment when the computer addresses the basic videomemory .

From image memory the data through the multiplexer are fed to the block of digital-to-analogues converters. The latter consists of three microcircuits DAC K1118 RA1 (one for each of the channels R.G.B.) and corresponding circuits of signal matching for input and output. Microcircuit K118 RA1 comprises 8-charge DAC of binary parallel code into the current with a setting time of 20 ns whlch favours their wide use in TV signals processing. Standard signals corresponding to digitalized image which feed into the TV monitor, are shaped on the outputs of DAC . For visualization of the initial image or of the results of its processing a working area of mapping of 512x512 pixels is provided on the screen of the monitor.

The system allows colour coding of a black-and-white image, which improves considerably the process of half-tone information perception on the images by the human-operator. In this stage colour coding in the system is realized by 64 colour hues.

Digital control block works out control signals for the shaping of time diagrams determining synchronous operation of separate nodes of the system. The Digital block is chiefly built on standard integral microcircuits of series 155, 531, 565.

The inside data bus of the system consists of 96 lines (32 lines per each of the R,G,B channels). For matching of the parameters of input and output signals of the system and microcomputer, a single-card adapter of external interface I41 is constructed on 1802 BBl microcircuits. The orientation chosen at development of the system for interface I41 is explained in the first place in that it is accepted as base interface of the Common nomenclature of module means. Interface I41 (the analogue of MULTIBUS, developed by lntel) is organized on the principle of the "Common Bus". Unlike earlier existing interfaces of a similar class I41 has higher speed of data exchange over the trunk and wide possibilities for the organization of multiprocessor and multicomputer operation. The standard I41 is also preferable because of the wide nomenclature of LSIC - the family of compatible 8-, 16-, 32 positional computers working in this interface and because of the considerable volume of already existing software.

Software of the system allows it to carry out the operations of image input-output, information exchange between videomemory and computer RAM image record on hard disk and its output on the monitor or the printer. The system has the possibility for implementing some functions in image processing,: separation of a fragment and its development on the image field; geometrical transformations (scaling, rotation); calculation of areas, perimeters; filtration of defects and image restoration; preparing and colour coding; drawing of histograms; three-dimensional simulation of images; statistical analysis and classification; and the synthesis of dynamic image.

Thus using of the given system for the digital processing of images as an instrument of investigations in the field of artificial intelligence would allow the increase of the quality of scientific and research works.

Industrial Applications of Artificial Intelligence
J.L. Alty and L.I. Mikulich (Editors)
Elsevier Science Publishers B.V. (North-Holland)

DECISION MAKING IN THE SYSTEM OF AUTOMATION OF MODEL CREATION "SAPFIR"

Ivanistchev V.V., Marley V.E., Morozov V.V., Tuboltzeva V.V.

The Leningrad Institute for Informatics and Automation of the USSR Academy of Sciences

Last year great attention was drown to the methods of communication with computer based on visualization of the task solving initial data [1]. In the system of automation of models creation caller SAPFIR, visualization is used for creation simulating object description [2]. The system input language is the ideographic language <I,G>, where I is the set of ideogramms, G is the language grammar.

<ideogramm>::=<block>|<simple character>

<block>::=<network>

<simple character>::= + | Δ | / | * | e | log | ln | -< |
| >- |min | max | sin | cos | asin|
|acos| = | ≠ | > | ≥ | < | ≤ | Δt

Simple characters stand for the following functions:

+	:	Z=X+Y	↑	:	$Z=X^Y$
Δ	:	Z=X−Y	e	:	$Z=e^X$
*	:	Z=X*Y	log	:	Z= log X
/	:	Z=X/Y	ln	:	Z= ln X
-<	:	Y=U*X	sin	:	Z= sin X
		Z=(1−U)*X	cos	:	Z= cos X
>-	:	Y=X+Z	asin	:	Z= arcsin X
		U=X/Y	acos	:	Z= arccos X
min	:	Z= min(X,Y)	max	:	Z= max(X,Y)

$=$	:	Z=1, if X=Y	$\neq$	:	Z=1, if X≠Y
		Z=0, if X≠Y			Z=0, if X=Y
$>$	:	Z=1, if X>Y	$\leqslant$	:	Z=1, if X⩽Y
		Z=0, if X⩽Y			Z=0, if X>Y
$<$	:	Z=1, if X<Y	$\geqslant$	:	Z=1, if X⩾Y
		Z=0, if X⩾Y			Z=0, if X<Y
Δt	:	Y(t)=Y(t-1)			

The ideografic language grammar G includes several simple rules of ideogramms composition. As a result of communication a description of the simulating object in the form of a network S is created, where nodes are the simple characters and blocks, arcs are the variables Xi,i=1,n, describing simulating object state at time t. Simple functions describe variable value changings on a shot interval Δt (simulation step). The delay operator (shift operator) transfers variables values at every step. The models created in the SAPFIR system are initially algorithmic.

The SAPFIR system is a software environment that supports three successive stages of automatic simulation technology:
1. representation of the object in the form of ideografic (algorithmic) network,
2. transformation of initial network representation to the form that allows to use one of the decision-making methods,
3. realization of decision-making methods and procedures.

Representation of an object in the form of an ideographic (algorithmic) network S is a heuristic procedure. Transformation of the initial model representation (algorithmic network) into a programme form P is made after formulating the task of calculation in the form of:

$$Z : \langle X_{inp} \longrightarrow X_{out} \rangle$$

where

X_{inp} is a set of model input variables,

X_{out} is a set of model output variables.

The latest version of the SAPFIR system contains several decision-making procedures:
1. iterative procedure,
2. procedure of inverse analysis of the task on the base of the network parallel-level form (PLF),
3. procedure of network conversion,
4. procedure of embedding in the model some control procedures for local model blocks and variables.

The first three methods are intended to solve the task ω that is formulated by the user in the form

$$\omega : \langle U_{inp} \xrightarrow{C_r} U_{out} \rangle$$

U_{inp} is a set of control variables, $x_i \in U_{inp}$, $U_{inp} \subseteq X_{inp}$;

U_{out} is a set of criterial variables, $x_i \in U_{out}$, $U_{out} \subseteq X_{out}$;

Usually, $U_{inp} \subset X_{inp}$ and $U_{out} \subset X_{out}$;

C_r is a mapping, executed by the programme P, that connects values of control and criterial variables at the simulation step.

The iterative method is a traditional method of input variable value selection, providing desirable changing of criterial variables:

$$\tilde{U}_{out}(k) = C_r(\tilde{U}_{inp}(k)) ,$$

$$C_{com}(\tilde{U}_{out}(k), \tilde{U}^*_{out}) = \{\Delta x^*_i(k)\}_{x_i \in U_{inp}} ,$$

$$\{\Delta x_i(k+1)\}_{x_i \in U_{inp}} = \Xi (\{\Delta x^*_i(k)\}_{x_i \in U_{out}}) ,$$

$$\tilde{U}_{inp}(k+1) = \Sigma(\tilde{U}_{inp}(k), \{\Delta x_i(k+1)\}_{x_i \in U_{inp}}) ,$$

where:

$\tilde{U}_{inp}(k)$, $\tilde{U}_{out}(k)$ are subsets of numerical values of control and criterial variables at the simulation step number k ;

C_{com} is comparison of desirable and obtained criterial variables values at the simulation step number k ;

$\Delta x^*_i(k)$ is the difference between desirable and obtained criterial variables values ;

Ξ is a heuristic procedure of determining the criterial variables value increment. $\Delta x_i(k+1)$, $x_i \in U_{inp}$

The method of inverse analysis transforms the network into the parallel-level form with the further use of the procedure for substantiation of the control variable giving changes that provide the criterial variables changes in the direction given(decrease, increase).

In comparison with the iterative method the method of inverse analysis supports the heuristics procedure Ξ. The method is illustrated by the example: the network is shown on fig.1. The cone of solubility for variable X17 is built on the base of parallel-level form. With the help of increment axioms for network operators (nodes) [2], the procedure of spreading the criterial variable sign increment from the lowest level to zero level on the parallel-level form is built. In conformity with received recomendations, the user determines the control variable values for the next simulation step. The user may block some variables at any level. It means that the value of blocked variables will not be changed. Fig.2 illustrates the process of the variable X17 approaching to the desirable value.

The method of network conversion uses the property of network solubility with different sets of input variables. Putting the criterial variable in the input set one gets the opportunity to find conditions when the criterial variable attains a desirable value. The sphere of network conversion method applicability is considered.

The method of embedding in the model the control procedures now exists as a set of soluted practical tasks.

The SAPFIR system is developed for the nonprogramming user, it increases labour productivity 3-6 times. The system is realized on the base of several PC Iskra-226, Iskra-1030, IBM-PC/XT/AT, IBM-PS/2-30, IBM-PS/2-80.

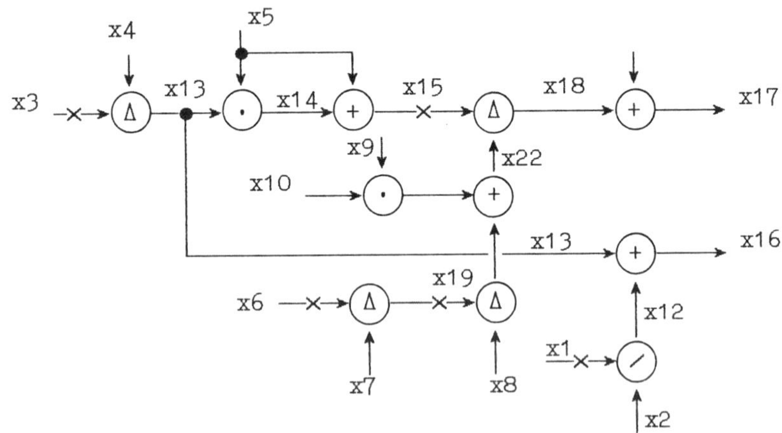

Fig.1. Algorithmic network.

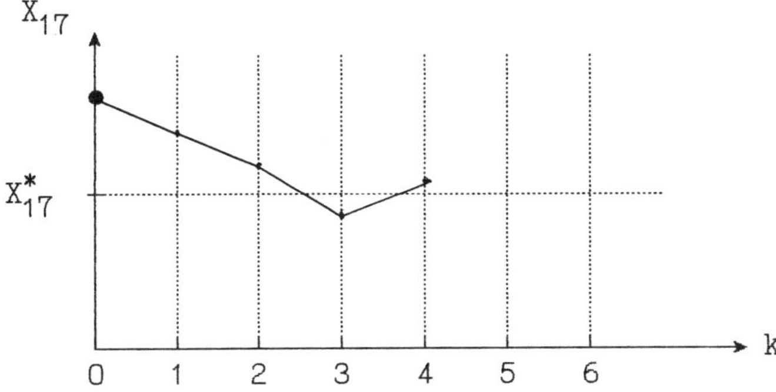

Fig. 2. The result given by the procedure of inverse analysis.

REFERENCES

[1] Zenkin A.A. Interactive computer grafic in theoretic reseaches. Technical Cybernetics, № 5, 1987.

[2] Ivanistchev V.V. Automation of Flow Systems Simulation. L, Science, 1988.

Industrial Applications of Artificial Intelligence
J.L. Alty and L.I. Mikulich (Editors)
Elsevier Science Publishers B.V. (North-Holland)

TECHNOMOD: INTERACTIVE INTEGRATED SYSTEM - THE SHELL FOR GEOMETRIC MODELLING AND SOLUTION OF PHYSICAL PROBLEMS AND OBJECTS ON IBM PC XT/AT

A.I. Boldyrev, O.V. Mihailov, V.G. Moroz

TECHNOSOFT, Kiev USSR

The interactive uzer-friendly menu-driven shell system TECHNOMOD performs finite element analysis for planar and axisymmetric cases. TECHNOMOD consists of modules (modelling, mesh generation, initial and boundary conditions, problem solving, visualisation). They can be substituted by other modules, used independently and transformed and tailored to the end-user wishes.

Formalization of decision making at any stage in the design - simulation process in integrated CAD/CAM systems is possible for very simple or predetermined situations only. It is very difficult in generalise. Therefore systems design is concentrated on the development of convenient and effective interactive facilities allowing the end user to make most of the decisions.

This article addresses the class of interactive shell systems for CAD/CAM. There are a lot of such systems on mainframes. Among them are Integraph, Medusa, Anvil, Nastran and Patran systems. AutoCAD, RoboCAD, VersaCAD, CADD, FastCAD, Cosmos and others have been developed for the IBM PC XT/AT or compatibles. Their main demerit is the solution of only one task in the integrated design - the simulation process in CAD/CAE and execution of only drawing or finite element analysis (FEM). There are different causes for this situation. Among them is the resource - consuming nature of these tasks. At present due to new processor chips such as the Intel 386/20, 25, 33 Mhz the power of the PC now approaches that of workstations and superminis. High quality graphical input - output devices are standard for the modern PC. So the PC is transformed into a CAD/CAE workstation. It enables all facilities of integrated mainframe software for geometry modelling and FEM to be realised at low cost. Therefore development of shell - environments for designing "turn - key" systems to customer order is very timely.

Two main aspects are discussed in this work, i.e., integration of all design - simulation steps and an effective user - computer interface, in particular graphic interfaces with icons, menu and multiwindows are used.

TECHNOMOD is compatible with widespread AutoCAD systems at the level of files in DXF format and geometric model internal representation.

The developed shell - system TEHNOMOD is aimed at the mechanical and building industry. It allows the design different 2-D constructions and investigates them under the influence of different loads.

The set of operations include:

1. 2-D region geometry modelling for any form of mechanical parts, construction, etc.

The main structure element and notions for any form model are

- boundary element connection nodes;
- boundary element;
- boundary element splitting;
- subregion;
- region.

Boundary element connection nodes a point with x,y coordinates in the definition field connect two element ends. Straight lines and arcs are boundary elements. Boundary element and splitting is a set of points spread out on boundary element and split into straight lines. The splitting may be even or uneven. The system automatically splits boundary elements by user-defined parameters. The contour of a (sub) region is a closed set of boundary elements. Any subregion is defined as a contour.

2-D multiconnective region is defined as a union of uniconnective subregions. This structure characterizes the topology of a 2-D multiconnective region. Geometry modelling step allows the determination of the topology and geometry of an object. Its logical structure is eqvivalent to a graph with a set of vertexes (nodes of boundary element connection) and connections among them a set of graph arcs (boundary elements). Uniconnective subregions in logical model are presented as subsets which allow correction of both topology and geometry at any step.

2. To make a mesh generation with triangular elements with predetermined density for different zones and subregions of an object.

Mesh generation is made automatically using the information after the geometry modelling step. Optimization of mesh nodes coordinates and their order is carried out for later effective calculations.

After mesh generating the FEM model is created with nodes, edges and triangles as elements.

3. To control initial and boundary conditions in graphics mode (meanings and directions of loads, shifts, etc) for different tasks solutions. During the loading process a user chooses nodes, edges or triangular elements and inputs some numerical values. There is a possibility of structure element labelling (boundary element, closed contour, subregion) for further the processing of initial and boundary conditions. If the need occurs, a user can correct data or use stored information.

4. To solve the elastic loading task. there are some variants of strained - deformed state:

- axisymmetrical;
- planestrained;
- planedeformed.

The global system matrix of rigidity is stored in a compact form. In the case of memory lack a linear equation system can be solved step-by-step.

Solution of the elastic task results in a horizontal and vertical moving of nodes and of stress values.

5. To display intermediate and final results:
   - geometry model;
   - triangle mesh;
   - results of loading process;
   - solution results (stress and shift values).

Results can be presented in
- isolines;
- equilevel map where regions of some levels are flooded with "clear" colours from standard system palettes.
- equilevel map with user-defined "mixed" colour palette.

Any part of the image can be zoomed for more detailed view of the analysed function.

6. To save data on hard disk and use them in future.

7. To print intermediate and final results. The software is realized in C on the IBM PC/XT/AT or compatibles with EGA card and core memory of 640Kb. The volume of EXE module is 580Kb.

TECHNOMOD consists of plug-in modules (geometry modelling, mesh generation, initial and boundary conditions control, problem solving, visualization) that allows the change of any module and tuning of the system to customer requirements.

If the user has developed this module himself he has to arrange compatibility with the TECHNOMOD - module. In other case its necessary to develop a special block.

At present TECHNOMOD is undergoing essential enhancement of its capabilities, namely:
- 3-D geometry modelling;
- 3-D mesh generation;
- increase in quantity of solvable physical tasks (including 3-D);
- using DBMS for solution libraries, reference information and different modules.

Industrial Applications of Artificial Intelligence
J.L. Alty and L.I. Mikulich (Editors)
Elsevier Science Publishers B.V. (North-Holland)

AN APPROACH TO THE DESIGN OF DISTRIBUTED CONTROL SYSTEMS FOR FMS

I.P. Belyakova

Leningrad Institute for Informatics and Automation
USSR Academy of Sciences
Leningrad, USSR

The paper presents an approach to the development of software for distributed control systems. The approach is based on the object-oriented methodology using the message passing for inter-object communication. The paper describes the main concepts, the implementation on different computers and the human-computer interface of such systems

1. INTRODUCTION

Contemporary production control systems are based on a distributed architecture[1]. As a rule, production equipment is allocated into cells according to common subtask. Each cell is controlled by a computer. All such subsystems connected via a network form a production control system. Such systems include many software components that interact with each other and run in parallel. Their design, testing and maintenance are very complex tasks requiring constant human attention and should provide an access to each software component for monitoring and controlling. The application of distributed systems is limited because there are few such programming tools.

The object-oriented approach provides great possibilities to the designer of distributed systems. Several projects such as EDEN[2], ARGUS[3], NEXUS[4] have been carried out for experimental investigations of new languages and systems of the general application. These languages and systems are not in wide use, but there are experimental versions.

The present paper describes an approach, developed at LIIAN for FMS. It allows a programmer to simplify the building, testing and maintenance of distributed control systems. Object-oriented programming is the basis of this approach. The approach includes: the decomposition of systems into part - objects; encapsulation of data and functions; a type object definition . The object is considered as an active autonomous component with several inputs and outputs for parallel interaction with other objects. The interaction is performed in a text form according to a set of interobject protocols.

The approach uses no special languages for system design, and requires no special operating environment for realization. We have developed out several experimental systems for production control, for its distributed data base and simulation of FMS.

2. CONCEPTS

The hardware of the distributed control systems (DCS) includes a set of computer nodes - subsystems $\{SS_i\}$, $i=1,...,I$, connected via a communication network. Each subsystem SS_i controls a group of manufacturing equipment (CNC machines and robots, warehouses and transport) or other subsystems $\{D_j^i\}$, $j=1,...,J_i$. The subsystems may be controlled by supervisor-operator.

The software of subsystem SS_i is built as a set of autonomous software components $\{O_m^i\}$, $m=1,...,M_i$, called controlled and control objects . There are objects for each manufacturing device D_j^i or subsystem SS_i, including a human-operator. These objects perform interface functions. In addition the subsystem contains purely software objects to perform application tasks . As a result the software structure of the subsystems reflects work environment and function possibilities

Objects are active components, running concurrently. Each object O_m^i of subsystem SS_i has a unique name N_m^i. It can perform a certain set of functions $\{F_l^m\}$, $l=1,....,L_m^i$, activated by another object, by an external device subsystem or by itself. During the function execution it can invoke functions in other object of its own subsystems or remote ones. The components have no common variables.

Inter-object communication is based on message passing. For this aim each object has a set of special containers $\{T_v^m\}$, $v=1,...,V_m^i$, called terminal files (TF), one set - for connection with a control object and another - for a controlled object. Each inter-object connection has its own TF. There are several types of messages: command message, reply message, data message . All messages are lines of text, the format of the messages depends on their type .

For example, the command message has the following structure:

```
Command::= <Object_name>:<Function_name>(<Parameters>);
Object_name::={[Subsystem_name/]}<Object_name>;
Function_name::=F1|F2|......
Parameters::={[Argument,]}.
```

The control objects send command messages through TF to invoke a function in the controlled object. The controlled object performs the function and sends a reply message as a result through the same TF. There is a set of the certain reply messages $\{M_t^1\}$, $t=1,....,T_1^m$, for each function F_{1m}, that reflect controlled object's status. A certain rule corresponds to each reply message and describes control object's behaviour in that case. The communication involves more complicated dialog than question-answer. Certain protocols are associated with each function and describe the sequence of message exchange . So object communication is according to the protocol.

The object can receive command messages from the other objects simultaneously. Messages arriving at the object's TFs, while the object is processing commands from an object , wait for their turn. When the controlled object gets no commands in all TF it is blocked until receiving a message .

Objects of different subsystems interact by means of special communication objects, that execute multiplexing massages from several objects sending them via communication channels and demultiplexing them from channel to objects.

3. IMPLEMENTATION

The approach was implemented on several types of computers and operating systems (OS): - ELECTRONICA - 79 (PDP11-34), OS -DEMOS (UNIX); - ELECTRONICA - 60 (LSI-11), special real time systems; - ISKRA - 1030 (IBM PC XT/AT), C-EXECUTIVE and a specially built-in window manager.

An object is realized as one or several cycle program processes in one of the operating environments . C language was used for the programming of objects. The object includes hierarchical data structures, which define links with other objects, attributes of terminal files, attributes of functions and protocols, performed by object and invoked by others, attributes of replies and rules. The object contains a set of functions, procedures for protocols and rules.

The objects are controlled by a shell-interpreter, which performs the receipt of messages, their interpretation and sending reply messages. Different data structures may be used as a TF, from usual files up to windows, that depends on OS possibilities. Synchronizing access to TF is executed by means of operating system tools or special mechanisms .

The structures of individual subsystems are rather identical. They include several objects of general use. There are the communication object, providing intersubsystem interaction, the operator - object, providing interface with a human-operator, the data base management object, which enables communication with a data base. For new systems only design and development of special application objects and objects providing interface with special equipment are required. For FMS of shop-floor level the set of application objects may include the object-dispatcher and object of statistical processing.

Using the C language enhances portability of program systems. The approach is practically independent of hardware and OS. To move systems on other OS it is necessary only to rewrite procedures for sending and receiving messages for the existing mechanism in this OS. New equipment included into a system requires the design of the interface objects and modification of data structures in objects connected with the new one. Usually a set of commands and functions of the subsystem become wider.

4. OBJECT-ORIENTED HUMAN INTERFACE

A human interface with distributed systems allowing users to imagine the system structure and to access individual software components is a very important not only during the stage of testing and debugging, but during the working cycle. It is a whole lot easier when a human-operator can see the structure of the subsystem and what every subsystems and its components are doing at any moment. The object-oriented structure of systems provides the basis of the convenient interface with an operator. Windows are most useful from this viewpoint, because the objects communicate via windows by means of text line that made it possible to display the content of these windows on the screen for monitoring, checking and interaction with a human-operator.

We have developed the environment and common use objects that allows the designer easily to use the described inter-object and inter-operator interface. The operating system is based on C-EXECUTIVE type OS expanded by a window manager and synchronization mechanism. The screen structure reflects the structure components of a subsystem and their functions and links. In the system objects can asynchronously interact with a human-operator, accepting his command (data), executing them and sending reply messages. The system can display to the operator the sequence of inter-object messages for any air of objects in a dynamic manner. The operator may check the status of any object in this subsystem or remote ones and correct it.

5. CONCLUSION

The approach based on modular programming using autonomous objects provides great possibilities for the complex system development . The structure of systems and objects allows the application of computer-aided software design. Proposals to use the text form of communication between objects approaches an inter-human communication and in addition, allows the users to check and to correct the state of the dynamic system

REFERENCES

[1] Yoshinao Arai, Seiji Hata and i.e., Production control system of microcomputer hierarchical structure for FMS. Proc. 1st Intern.conf on Flex. Manufact.Syst.(Brighton, UK., 20-22 Oct., 1982) pp. 259-265.
[2] Almes, G.T., Black, A.P., Lazowska, E.D. and Noe, J.D., The Eden System: A technical Review. IEEE Trans. Software Eng., vol SE-11, no.1, (1985) pp. 43-59.
[3] Liskov, B., On linguistic Support For Distributed Programs. IEEE Trans. Software Eng., vol SE-8, (1982) pp 203-210.
[4] Tripathi, A., Ghonami, A. and Schmitz, T., Object management in the NEXUS distributed operating system. Proc. Intern. conf.Compcon Spring 87.

Industrial Applications of Artificial Intelligence
J.L. Alty and L.I. Mikulich (Editors)
Elsevier Science Publishers B.V. (North-Holland)

SYNTHESIS OF ADAPTIVE ROBOT CONTROL SYSTEMS UNDER UNCERTAINTY CONDITIONS

V.M. KUNTSEVITCH

V.M. Glushkov Institute of Cybernetics,
Academy of Sciences of Ukrainian SSR,
Kiev,
The USSR.

ABSTRACT: For most real control problems uncertainty is typically present with respect to the properties (parameters) of the control processes themselves as well as with respect to the environment acting on them. Only adaptive control systems which help to implement the control processes proper can operate efficiently under such conditions. The paper investigates a game approach to the solution of control problems under uncertainty conditions.

1. INTRODUCTION

For most real control problems and, in particular, for industrial technology and robotics process control problems, uncertainty is typically present with respect to the properties (parameters) of the control processes themselves as well as with respect to the environment acting on them. Therefore, only adaptive control systems which help to implement the control processes proper, and the study of controlled plant properties can contribute to operating efficiently under such conditions.

Until recently, most work on adaptive control systems has used only stochastic uncertainty models according to which a probabilistic character is assigned to all uncertain constants (processes) in the mathematical model of the control process. However, there are a wide group of control problems for which such an approach is unacceptable for a number of reasons. In this connection a game approach to the solution of control problems under uncertain conditions which makes it possible to have guaranteed results has found increasing application in the last few years. Guaranteed estimates in solving the problem of parametric identification have played an important part in the use of such an approach to formulate unknown-plant parameter control problems.

2. OBTAINING GUARANTEED ESTIMATES IN THE PARAMETRIC IDENTIFICATION PROBLEM.

A general scheme for the construction of guaranteed estimates of the vector L is exemplified in this paper by a class of controlled plants without memory which are described, at discrete time moments, by equations of the form

$$Z_n = \Phi (U_n , L , F_n) , \qquad n = 1 , 2 , 3 ,.... \qquad (1)$$

where U_n , Z_n are vectors of "input" and "output" respectively, F_n is a vector of uncontrolled disturbances (noise) for which its A-Priori estimate

$$F_n \in S \qquad \forall \ n > 0 \qquad (2)$$

is specified, S is a specified convex constrained set, L , a vector of constant but unknown parameters with A-Priori estimate

$$L \in \aleph_0 \qquad (3)$$

is a specified convex constrained set, $\aleph_0$ is a specified non-linear vector-function (by argument L) in this general case.

Let at the nth step for L there be an estimate

$$L \in \aleph_n \qquad (4)$$

From (1) taking into account (2) after measuring values Z_{n+1} and U_{n+1} there follows the estimate

$$L \in \overline{\aleph}_{n+1} = \{ L: Z_{n+1} - \Phi(U_{n+1}, L, F_n) = 0 \} \qquad (5)$$

Then from (4) and (5) for L we obtain A-Posteriori estimates

$$L \in \aleph_{n+1} = \overline{\aleph}_{n+1} \cap \aleph_n$$

Constructive algorithms for the implementation of the operation of intersection of sets were developed first of all for a class of systems (1) linear by parameters, also when obtaining upper bounds of sets $\aleph_{n+1}$ and for some classes of non-linear parameter systems.

The recurrent procedure for reconstructing a sequence of estimates (5) is naturally extended to the class of dynamic systems by difference equations of the form

$$X_{n+1} = \Phi (X_n , U_n , L , F_n), \quad n = 0, 1, 2, ... \qquad (6)$$

where X_n is the system state vector and the rest of the designations have the same meaning as in (1).

From the principle viewpoint the equations are solved by simultaneous construction of estimates of the state vectors and parameters for systems of the form (6) in the case when the state vector X_n is inaccessible to direct measurement and the equation of measurement (observation) has the form

$$Y_n = H (X_n , V_n) \qquad (7)$$

where V_n is a vector of noise for which its A-Priori estimate

$$V_n \in W \quad \forall \ n \geq 0 \qquad (8)$$

is specified, W is a specified constrained set, $H(.)$ is a specified vector function.

3. SYNTHESIS OF OPTIMAL CONTROL

The solution of the simplest class of control problems when for the system (6) some function of specified losses are of the form

$$\omega_n = \omega (X_{n+1} , U_n) = \omega [\Phi (X_n , U_n , L , F_n) U_n] \quad (9)$$

must be minimised by specifying the choice of control U_n at each nth step. Since the variable F_n and L in (9) are unknown and only their estimates (2) and (5) are specified for them, it is evident that such a problem is ill-defined and the definition should be completed in some manner. To obtain the guaranteed result the optimal control is searched for from the solution of the problem

$$\min_{U_n} \max_{\substack{F_n \in S \\ L \in \aleph_n}} \{ \omega [\Phi (X_n , U_n , L , F_n) U_n] \}, \quad n = 0, 1, 2, ... (10)$$

The difference between the adaptive control system and the non-adaptive one evidently consists in the fact that for the non-adaptive control system the problem for all $n \geq 0$ is solved using only A-Priori estimate $\aleph_0$. If this estimate is sufficiently rough the final result of control appears to be unsatisfactory. There are methods for solving problems of type (10).

Industrial Applications of Artificial Intelligence
J.L. Alty and L.I. Mikulich (Editors)
Elsevier Science Publishers B.V. (North-Holland)

SOME PROBLEMS AND METHODS OF PRE-DESIGN SIMULATION OF AUTOMATED SHOPS

E.N. KHOBOTOV

The problems of the development and use of computer integrated manufacturing (CIM) systems are of great importance at present. In many cases CIM applications are created as flexible manufacturing systems (FMS) of various types and purposes. This is mainly related to the fact that FMS are highly efficient computer-controlled production systems which make it possible to reduce appreciably the time necessary for the introduction and assimilation of new products, to raise considerably labour efficiency in medium-size and small-lot production, to reduce shop areas, and also to raise the quality of produce.

These properties of FMS permit them to create via their integration an advanced CIM of high effectiveness. However current FMS are rather expensive, and the introduction of them at sites unprepared for the use of FMS, together with drawbacks in their own design, may lead to unjustified financial expense. For the effective use of FMS and the creation of a modern CIM on this basis, the efficiency of the systems to be introduced should be coordinated with the adjacent production sectors and FMS for all the kinds of articles worked. Under these conditions only, as well as under correct scheduling and control of the work of each of the systems and the shop as a whole, one may use effectively the considerable capabilities of various FMS and CIM.

In this connection, an important role is played by the methods of the pre-design simulation of work of individual FMS and of automated shops composed of such systems. Models of equipment choice for an automated shop are constructed using choice models of the composition of the individual FMS [1,2,3], which are presumed to be included in the shop's composition.

Such models are constructed under the following assumptions.

For each workpiece forming part of any article which is planned for production in the shop under known design:

- the types of equipment on which all the articles and parts composing each article can be worked;

- techological route of working of each article and part (it is supposed that each article or part could be produced along the unique route);

- average size of the lots of articles of all types;

- average frequency of occurrence of each lot of articles in the production plan for the shop.

Under these assumptions, the problem of choice of equipment consists of a proper choice of the architecture of the form of the FMS system, the composition of the shop and the inter-operation transport mechanisms connecting and maintaining these FMS, and also the capacities of storage of parts and blanks in the shop. The structure of the shop and the individual manufacturing systems composing it are chosen so as to reduce, under the restrictions imposed by the cost of the shop's equipment, the time of working of parts and articles to maximize the efficiency of the shop for a given range of products, to extend production capabilities of the shop and also to guarantee an acceptable output in case of failure of some part of the equipment.

To solve such problems of pre-design simulation choice, models of equipment of the shop are proposed that enable one to choose its composition and structure in accordance with the above-mentioned requirements.

The models proposed consist of the optimisation and simulation subsystem. The optimisation system enables one to readily obtain estimates of the shop equipment composition and the most profitable listed range of parts manufactured. Then the estimates obtained are corrected using the simulation models .

A coordinated use of the optimisation and simulation models markedly reduce the time of simulation, improve its quality and to offer the designer a set of varied arrangements of the shop from which he can select the most suitable one.

REFERENCES

[1]. Khobotov E.N. "Principles of Constructing Systems of the Pre-design Simulation of FMS": Abstracts of papers presented to the VI Inter. Conf. on Flexible Manufacturing Systems, M., MNIIPU, 1989.

[2]. Khobotov E.N. "On an Approach to the Development of Methods of the Pre-design Simulation of Certain types of Flexible Production Systems", In: "Present State and Prospects of Flexible Manufacturing Systems". M., MNIIPU - MTSNTI, 1989.

[3]. Kalachev V.N., and Khobotov E.N. "Models of Choosing the Optimum Structure of some Types of Flexible Production Systems", In: "Present State and Prospects of Flexible Manufacturing Systems". M., MNIIPU - MTSNTI, 1986.

Industrial Applications of Artificial Intelligence
J.L. Alty and L.I. Mikulich (Editors)
Elsevier Science Publishers B.V. (North-Holland)

PRINCIPLES OF INTELLIGENT PROCESS PLANNING SYSTEM DESIGN

P. N. BELYANIN, I .V. BOBROVA, A . GONZALEZ-SABATER

Research Institute of Aviation,
Technology and Industrial Engineering,
Moscow,
The USSR.

ABSTRACT: The problems and methods for the design of computer-aided process planning systems through the use of artificial intelligence principles and techniques are described in this paper

1. INTRODUCTION

The suggested methodology for the creation of CAPP (Computer Aided Process Planning) systems covers practically all types of technology and has been evaluated through the development of CAPP systems for the basic manufacturing processes of machining and assembly.

The main principles of CAPP subsystem design and development consist of the determination and formalization of technology planning laws which provide high levels of automation of the planning process itself and software versatility.

An absence of process planning decisions in the input data is fundamental for the CAPP systems we are considering. Only information from design plans and specifications of a part (product) are used as input data. The description in a specially developed problem-oriented language is sent to the system for the generation of planning decisions. It generates individual planning decisions and, eventually, a manufacturing process on a basis of a process knowledge base containing knowledge about production technology laws and process planning logic.

2. THE KNOWLEDGE BASES

The major problem for such poorly formalized a knowledge domain such as technology lies in the generation and structuring data of the knowledge base.

Knowledge that should be formalized for a CAPP system may be divided into three categories: process knowledge, knowledge about planning processes, and knowledge about human-computer interfaces.

A process knowledge base is comprised of:

- technology laws,
- planning goals with their decomposition into local subgoals,
- a formalized description of the production environment which affects the plan
- methods for the accumulation and correction of process knowledge.

The planning process knowledge base depends significantly on an accepted conceptual model of planning. The structural-modular concept of thinking (reasoning) of a professional is considered in this paper. It follows the scheme:

initial situation - its structural and generalized model - limited set of generalized decisions - selection of generalized decision - generation of detailed decision.

The knowledge base on planning processes contains definitions and initial situation analysis methods, classification relations for initial situations, methods of formation of manufacturing process structure, optimization methods, and ways of completion of generalized structures, with respect to a full process description.

The multiplicity of factors in the planning processes and the insufficient formalization of a number of manufacturing situations, presupposes the participation of a user planner in this process. To support this, a knowledge base module for an intelligent interface was created which provides human-computer interaction within a single man-machine complex.

This module comprises a problem-oriented language for initial situation descriptions, a means for a self-forming operational environment for problem solution, forms for the presentation of information which the user exchanges with the system when solving problems, and methods for dialogue organization.

The heterogeneity of the laws, requirements, and restrictions, etc, inherent in conventional technology led to a need for the utilization of various knowledge presentation forms and the construction of a mathematical mode. Then, computational procedures provide simultaneous operation of these forms in single process planning system modes.

For this purpose at the first stage of knowledge base development a well defined system of concepts and their attributes was established as well as a structure of the concepts and possibility of their presentation in simple objects of the selected system of concepts characterizing the data domain and conceptual model of planning.

3. FRAME STRUCTURE

Knowledge about the plan (manufacturing process) structure and individual planning decisions at the intension level have a well defined hierarchical nature and in this connection a system of frames for the description of planning decision structures and their characteristics was developed.

For CAPP in Machining, the system has the following forms:

$$T = < Q_i (C_i, \{B_i^j\}_j, <P_k^i = \{a_k, \{r_k^n\}_n, \{e_k^m\}_m, \{n_k, t_k, s_k\}\}>_k)>_i ,$$

where T - manufacturing process frame,
Q_j- operation frame
P_k machining pass frame
C_i - equipment, $B\{_i^j\}_j$ - bases
a_k - machined surface
$\{r_k^n\}_n$ - dimensional characteristics,
$\{e_k^m\}_m$ - tool package
$\{n_k, t_k, s_k\}$ - machining conditions

In the construction of the frame system, generated objects are determined, attributes of classification and ordering of sets and their elements are established, intersections of relations, their nesting ability and stages of generation are determined. The operation Q_i is represented by a frame

$$Q_i <=> \{ M_a^{ij}(A_i = \underset{j}{U} a_i), M_c^i (C_i), M_b^{ij} (B_i = \underset{j}{U} b_j), R_1(A_i), R_2(B_i) \}$$

A manufacturing operation is a generated planning decision of the 2nd kind since it is composed of two generated planning decisions of the 1st kind. A set of base surfaces and a group of A_i surfaces are machined during the given operations (1st kind decisions are formed from input data). The manufacturing operation description frame has two procedure references $R_1(A_i)$ and $R_2(B_i)$ to these planning decisions formation. As they are derived, the appropriate slots in manufacturing process frame are filled.

Technology laws necessary for process planning are represented by production rules system like:

$$A \dashrightarrow B,\ (A \dashrightarrow C) \dashrightarrow (B \dashrightarrow D) \qquad (1)$$

To check the consistency and completeness of the system under given data domain conditions a special type calculus was created that includes T - a basic element set, P - a syntactically correct expressions from T, A - a set of a priori true expressions, F - an inference rule set (formal and/or semantic) allowing expansion of the axiom set at the cost of other expressions.

For example, in formalising the planning process of machining technology, a set of machined surfaces, equipment and tools T=A U C U J was assumed as a set of basic elements. The syntactic rules are identical to predicate calculus syntactic rules and the inference rules F contain propositional calculus inference rules (for deducible formulae proof a method of solution functions is used).

Complex technology concepts generated in the system such as bases, operations, passes and routes are presented as deducible formulae. Statements containing the conditions of existence for major relations: order, compatibility and predetermination, were selected as axioms. Similar models were derived in the construction of knowledge bases for assembly process planning .

Structural properties common to all products and determining assembly process content were selected in this case. These properties mainly depend on the interactions of parts within a product and the process of assembly planning is based on the analysis of these interactions.

4. THE PROCESS PLANNING TASK

The process planning task was formulated as the task of process knowledge base (PKB) management. Control algorithms forming the content of the knowledge base on planning processes constitute meta-knowledge with respect to the PKB and contain a means of analysis and classification of initial situations, and methods of initiating appropriate PKB sections.

Descriptions of information contained in the part and billet drawings were adopted as the initial situation for planning processes of parts machining. As to the assembly processes, we used information from assembly drawings. Initial situation descriptions are realized in terms of the problem-oriented language used for PKB.

Developed classification relations make it possible to divide the initial description of the part (product) into multiple objects, to create topological structures and place them into one of the known classes or formulate a new class and determine its parameters.

A set of possible decisions with the use of an oriented graph apparatus and frame systems describing a set of different structural elements of technology is constructed on the basis of topological classes.

During the construction of possible planning decisions their redundancy appears. It has the form of different alternatives. To solve these alternatives a system of preference criteria was created. In the process of decision making there may appear an insufficiency of information for formal decision-making. In order to increase the level of decision making automation, the rules for defining the best alternative under incomplete information conditions were established. However besides automatic decisions, a dialogue with the user is forseen in this case as well as automatic evaluation of the acceptability of its propositions. After selection of one or more variants of the manufacturing process structure, its expansion takes place. It is implemented at this stage using analytical models. In the end, the decision process (process planning) is represented by the following system of decision functions

$$F = <F_1, ..., F_n >$$

each F_i function is a tuple of special type functions

$$F_i = <Q_1, P_1, Q_2, ...P_{n-1}, Q_n >$$

Where Q_i - a function of the plan state definition at the ith-step of decision,
$P_i (Q_i, Q_j)$ - functions of pass providing transformation of Q_1 state into Q_i .$P(Q_i ,Q_j)$ contain production type (1) or an analytical dependence as well as meta-rules providing selection of specific rules or chains of rules, or analytical formulae.

The considered decision functions use four procedure classes: classification, ordering, structurisation and calculation procedures. Classification procedures use basic relations of equivalency and predetermination.

Ordering procedures are the most complex and important. From the point of view of process planning these procedures provide the formation of ordered sets of initial bases, registration schemes of machined surfaces, the set of which determines formation of variants of manufacturing process structures and optimization.

Generation of the manufacturing process structure without reference to the limited set of type schemes is the most significant practical achievement of this study. It allowed us to bring the degree of automation of creative task solutions in process planning to a qualitatively new level.

Structurisation procedures are used for the creation of complex objects out of simple ones. It is precisely these procedures that provide the transformation of frames and their interaction. Calculation procedures have an analytical nature and are used for machining process planning when the calculation of operation dimensions tool parameters, tool movement trajectory operating conditions, etc. are required.

5. CONCLUSIONS

Developed CAPP systems possess high levels of automation of the planning process itself, invariance to the planning objects and can be easily integrated with computer aided design and management systems. Developed systems properties provide their high effectiveness in respect to prevalent CAPP systems.

At present computer-aided planning of manufacturing processes has received wide acceptance. It implements a question-answer dialogue mode together with the automation of retrieval in classifiers for unified planning decisions with subsequent correction.

Low levels of automation of the planning process itself and the necessity for the development of a complex system for classification and coding of products and technologies, represent the main drawbacks of the mentioned computer-aided planning systems.

In addition, in connection with the use of planning decisions as the input data, the linguistics of these computer-aided planning systems use technological concepts; this significantly complicates or makes possible integration with computer-aided design and preparation of control programs. Their linguistics contains simple geometric elements (lines, points, surfaces,etc.).

The fundamental possibility of creating technology on the basis of design plans and specifications without human intervention was realised in developed CAPP systems at the expense of a thorough study and formalisation of the knowledge base on planning processes. However, the possibility of interaction with the user in the process of decision making was forseen and implemented taking into account the multiplicity of factors of technological problems.

The considered approach to the synthesis of CAPP built with the use of artificial intelligence principles and methods has been implemented in CAPP systems for machining a wide range of machine elements developed and operating since 1985.

Industrial Applications of Artificial Intelligence
J.L. Alty and L.I. Mikulich (Editors)
Elsevier Science Publishers B.V. (North-Holland)

SECTION 9: INTELLIGENT MANUFACTURING: CASE STUDIES

AN EXPERT SYSTEM FOR SELECTION OF DISPATCHING SYSTEMS TO BE USED IN FLEXIBLE AUTOMATION OF PRODUCTION

W. ZEBROWSKI

Institute for Organization of Production Systems,
Warsaw University of Technology,
Warsaw,
Poland.

ABSTRACT: The paper contains a description of a prototype expert system EXDOSYP based on the use of induction synthesis, intended to define the structure of the dispatching system to be used and to determine a complex of problems to be solved while implementing flexible automation of production processes.

1. INTRODUCTION

The procedure for constructing a dispatching system for flexibly automated production is associated with the necessity to decompose the existing enterprise management system so as to divide it into a number of functional subsystems of a less complex nature.

One of main shortcomings encountered in the design processes and the modernization of enterprises as associated with the implementation of flexible production process automation, is the subjectivity of the selection criteria used in selecting the dispatching systems.

There are the various dispatching systems and methods of solving problems associated with production processes used in production enterprises. Often the selection of such systems and methods is devoid of well grounded reasons. In selecting them only some minor factors are being taken into account and some other ones, of relatively great importance for each particular case, are neglected.

The design of a dispatching system for production processes is associated with the need for achieving full informational, engineering and organisational integration of all subsystems involved. The scope of the application of each particular system and its potentialities are highly dependent on the number, class and type of flexible production cells (work centres, machine groups, shops, departments etc.) available, the nature of production processes involved, control techniques adopted and the computer hardware and software facilities available at an enterprise.

The commonly used principles of designing production control systems, which can be defined as "tailoring to measure", result eventually in petrification ("stiffening") of design procedures and consequently cause difficulties when attempts are made to further improve or modernize such systems. This constitutes an essential obstacle in aiming at standardization and unification of designs and modular integration of individual components of control systems.

The experience gained hitherto in countries where flexible automation of production processes has already reached a relatively high level [1] shows that there is a need to standardize and unify the designs of individual components of control systems.

Both in the theory and practice of operator control, a number of methods of solving the problems associated with modelling correctly the run of the production process have been developed. These methods, means and organizational principles constitute an operative production process control system consisting, amongst other things, of the following:

- short-term planning,
- validation of short-term planning,
- ordering,
- dispatching,
- record keeping.

Fundamental to design standardization is work aimed at rationalising matching models of components of operative control, while duly taking into account the need of proper identification of manufacturing conditions enabling the implementation of dispatching systems. It seems reasonable to assume that artificial intelligence methods and intelligent computer systems may be very helpful in the rational use of standard models under actual manufacturing conditions.

2. FACTORS INFLUENCING THE SELECTION OF DISPATCHING SYSTEMS AND THEIR MODELS

During the selection of an appropriate dispatching system and its model the following factors are of vital importance:

- the engineering features of products being, or to be, manufactured (product mix, subassemblies, specific labour demands, size, weight, number of operations etc.)
- the type of production flow (mass, batch, job-lot etc.),
- the scale and stability of production output,
- the unification degree of parts and subassemblies,
- the organizational structure of production facilities, including number and size of flexible production cells,
- the degree of automation and degree of integration in information processing.

So, for example, when manufacturing products of high complexity with large number of parts and subassemblies, it is more purposeful to use a decentralized production control system. In the case of small lot production it is also common to use decentralized control systems, whereas mass production is characteristized by centralized systems.

The higher the quantity and stability of production output, the more purposeful seems to be use of a centralized (integrated) control system. For large production enterprises and production departments characterized by a complex production structure it is usually more effective to use autonomous (decentralized) control systems. Workpiece oriented specialization of work centres (machine groups) and departments gives some reasons to use a centralized (integrated) production control system.

One of possible ways to solve the problem of system and model selection is to develop an expert (advisory) system employing inductive synthesis to generate the decision rules based on collected knowledge in the form of a collection of already existing design solutions. Such rules will allow further decisions to be taken in situations when no actually existing examples are available.

3. THE STRUCTURE OF THE PROTOTYPE EXPERT SYSTEM EXDOSYP

In developing the prototype expert system EXDOSYP a specific tool system [2] has been used. The definition of the EXDOSYP, in the notation required, is shown in Fig. 1 below.

The main EXDOSYP Module calls sequentially all the remaining modules according to backward-chaining principles. For the sake of simplicity the list of resultant values for individual modules #_KBM_2, #_KBM_3 etc. is not included within the definition shown in Fig. 1.

Consider as an example, the structure of #_KBM_2 module. This is the Planning Models Selection Module. According to the classification adopted [3,4] eight types of production planning models have been distinguished. They are as follows:

- production planning model - planning by cyclograms (MODEL 1),
- production planning model - cyclic planning (MODEL 2)
- production planning model - one-month gap phasing in production of individual parts (MODEL 3)
- production planning model - one-month gap phasing in production of sets of parts (MODEL 4)
- production planning model - planning according to scheduled time-units (MODEL 5)
- production planning model - planning according to actual products stock (MODEL 6)
- production planning model - planning according to W-I-P stock on hand (MODEL 7)
- production planning model --planning according to mini-max principle (MODEL 8).

```
MEMO        [                          EXDOSYP
PROTOTYPE ADVISORY SYSTEM ENABLING RATIONAL SELECTION OF
DISPATCHING SYSTEMS TO BE USED UNDER CIRCUMSTANCES OF FLEXIBLE
AUTOMATION OF PRODUCTION PROCESSES]

#_KBM_2     [ PLANNING MODELS SELECTION MODULE ]
#_KBM_3     [ SYSTEM'S TECHNICAL MEANS SELECTION MODULE ]
#_KBM_4     [ RECORD KEEPING METHODS SELECTION MODULE ]
#_KBM_5     [ REGULATION METHODS SELECTION MODULE ]
#_KBM_6     [ DISPATCHER CONTROL METHODS SELECTION MODULE]
RESULT      [ ]
DONE

            Definitions for Knowledge Base EXDOSYP

      #_KBM_1 #_KBM_2 #_KBM_3 #_KBM_4 #_KBM_5 RESULT

1:       *       *       *       *       *     DONE

            Examples for Knowledge Base EXDOSYP
```

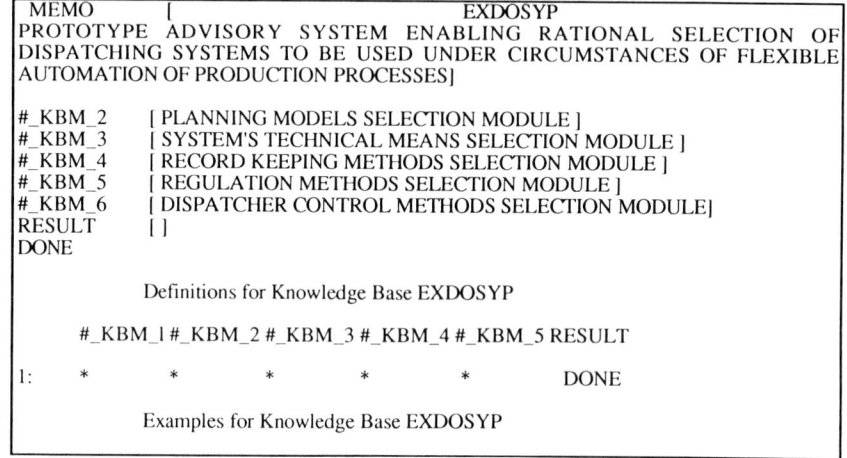

Figure 1 Definitions and examples for the EXDOSYP Main Module

One of rules employed by that module allows selection of appropriate modules from the above depending on such factors as production stability, production continuity, production repetitiveness, disturbances in production runs and market values of products. In Fig. 2 we shown the definition of the #_KBM_2 module as well as the appropriate decision rules.

The factors (#_STABIL, #_CONTIN, #_REPEAT, #_DISTUR, #_VALUE) appearing in the above definition and decision rules have been treated as separate modules. An example of the definition and rule for the #_STABIL module is shown in Fig. 3.

The selection of a particular planning model determines the relevant recommendations concerning:

- creation of planning standards in terms of time-schedules, organizational and production engineering measures and operative aspects,
- analysis of production plan feasibility in terms of time, production engineering and economic limitations, if any,
- methods for determining the optimum production plan,
- methods for determining resource demand necessary to accomplish the production

plan tasks,

#_STABIL	#_REPEAT	#_CONTIN	#_DISTUR	#_VALUE	MODNAME
yes	yes	yes	yes	yes	MODEL_1
no	no	no	no	no	MODEL_2
					MODEL_3
					MODEL_4
					MODEL_5
					MODEL_6
					MODEL_7
					MODEL_8

Definitions for Knowledge Base _KBM_2

```
#_STABIL ??
  yes:#_CONTIN??
              yes: ------------------------------------------------------------MODEL_1
               no:#_DISTUR??
                    yes:#_VALUE??
                               yes:-------------------------------------------- MODEL_3
                                 no:------------------------------------------- MODEL_4
                     no:------------------------------------------------------- MODEL_2
   no:#_REPEAT??
         yes:#_DISTUR??
                yes:---------------------------------------------------------- MODEL_4
                  no:#_VALUE??
                      yes:---------------------------------------------------- MODEL_5
                       no:---------------------------------------------------- MODEL_4
          no:#_DISTUR??
             yes:#_VALUE??
                  yes:-------------------------------------------------------- MODEL_7
                   no:-------------------------------------------------------- MODEL_8
             no:-------------------------------------------------------------- MODEL_6
```

Rule for knowledge base _KBM_2

FIGURE 2 Definitions and one of rules for the # KBM 2 Module

- calculation of economic and process indices,
- methods of determining time-schedules for auxiliary services.

Using the #_KBM_3 Module it is possible to get recommendations concerning selection of one from among of 24 typical structures for a dispatching system.

By consulting the module #_KBM_4 i.e. (for selection of record keeping methods) it is possible to obtain recommendations concerning:

- creation of and keeping up-to-date information files,
- methods of keeping records on production in progress i.e. on the accomplishment of production tasks by individual production cells and creation of models depicting dynamic image of production.

The module #_KBM_5 provides appraisements concerning:

- methods and techniques of comparing actual (dynamic image) and planned production progress according to given indices,

- methods of assigning optimum production tasks per day/shift,
- methods of assigning tasks per day/shift for auxiliary services.

The decision rules generated for the #_KBM_6 module provide information concerning:

- check-up on adequate provision of all resources being necessary to accomplish production tasks,
- check-up on condition of equipment and decisions taken in emergency cases.

The data base, which can be regarded as one of elements of the EXDOSYP System, contains information concerning, amongst others, the following:

- assortment of manufactured products/goods,
- the planned production output during individual planning periods,
- the production structure in terms of constructional features of products,
- the production processes,
- the organizational structure of the whole enterprise, including numbers of specialized and automated workplaces as well as those incorporated into production lines, numbers and characteristic features of flexible production cells,
- the standard parameters concerning labour demand for individual products,
- the standard parameters concerning workplaces etc.

```
ESTAB [IS THE PRODUCTION OF THAT PRODUCT OF STABILIZED
         NATURE ?]
Sl [yes]
S2 [no]
S3 [Ascertain as per information contained in data
    base]
RSTAB
yes
no
#dbsS
                    Definitions of Knowledge  Base  _STABIL
1: FSTAB??
2: Sl-------------------------------------------yes
3: S2-------------------------------------------no
4: S3-------------------------------------------#dbsS
                        Rule for knowledge base _STABIL
```

Figure 3 Definitions and a rule for the #_STABIL Module

Each knowledge base module has at its disposal appropriate access to the data base through specialized programs. It is a rule that whenever the system can take a decision on the basis of data contained in the data base the user is informed about the resultant decision. In cases, however, when the data required are not present in the data base or a given specialized program gives an unsatisfactory result, the user himself must take a relevant decision.

The correctness of drawing conclusions and the minimization of conversational processing at the main module level are ensured, among others, by the use of global variables.

The current prototype EXDOSYP employs standard ways of conversational processing through the tool. Reporting about the progress and results of consultations are ensured by an appropriate standard option of the tool. It is hoped to extend the system in the future to generate documentation pertaining to a specific dispatching system being selected in the course of consultations as the most suitable one for particular manufacturing conditions.

4. CONCLUSIONS

The studies already carried out give sufficient reasons to state that inductive methods are very useful in the creation of such advisory systems due to the simplicity in the form of the knowledge acquired which, in fact, is a collection of exemplary solutions chosen from amongst already existing ones. Some restrictions are imposed by use of the ID3 algorithm which does not allows the creation of other than rather simple decision rules. Although this can be advantageous in some situations, in cases, however, where there are a large number of factors influencing the decisions to be taken, it does not give a warranty that a rational rule can be obtained and requires the use of the match method. Versions of similar systems intended for practical industrial use are to be written in specialized artificial intelligence languages.

5. REFERENCES

[1] Santarek K., and Strzelczak S., "Flexible Manufacturing Systems", WNT, Warsaw, 1989 (in Polish)

[2] Wes Thomas, rev. by W. Hapgood "1St-Class.Manual", Programs in Motion Inc., Wayland,MA, USA, 1987

[3] Wloczewski J., "Production Planning in Industrial Enterprise", IWZZ, Warsaw, 1988, (in Polish)

[4] Zebrowski W., "Selection of the Production Control Systems and Scheduling Models with Expert System Tool application", III-rd International Scientific Conference SYPRO'90 (in course of issue, in Polish)

Industrial Applications of Artificial Intelligence
J.L. Alty and L.I. Mikulich (Editors)
Elsevier Science Publishers B.V. (North-Holland)

REAL TIME PRODUCTION CONTROL SYSTEM PRODUS-85

O. V. EVSEEV
Department of Control Processes,
Intelligent Automation,
Institute of Electronics,
Machine Building,
Moscow,
The USSR.

ABSTRACT: Production systems when applied to discrete processes in real time control need to take into account the following factors: the distribution of parallel working objects which the system is to interact with; control law dependence on the behaviour of processes in time; the necessity of dynamic focusing and adjustment of the system's attention in changing situations; the low action speed of production systems which must be improved to satisfy the restrictions of real time. These factors determine the structural, information, logic and language peculiarities of the Production Real Time Control System PRODUS-85.

1. INTRODUCTION

Artificial intelligence models provide a satisfactory base for a significant simplification of real time complex process control systems and for qualitative improvement of their control and monitoring functions. These possibilities are realized in a real time production control system PRODUS-85 [1]. This system is a shell and an operational medium for supporting a broad class of intelligent control, monitoring, decision-making and diagnostic systems. At present PRODUS-85 is used for CAM control components design in various CAD/CAM systems. It has direct adaptive interfaces with control equipment and operator displays, as well as with CAD and technological planning computers.

According to the principle of domain-independence, the system should satisfy the requirements:

1. orientation towards the control objects' structure and to the laws or rules of control and monitoring algorithms, diagnostics and dialogue;

2. the ability to re-apply and modify applied functions in the course of duty;

3. the ability of simultaneous interaction with many external objects and several computing, control and decision making processes. Production systems are the most suitable approach for realizing these properties.

2. INFORMATION, LOGIC AND LANGUAGE OF THE SYSTEM

2.1. Base

If control algorithms are considered as the set of "situation-action" rules, then the Information Base of the control production system should describe the structure and current condition of control objects, work place, the status of external program systems, and the control process state as well. PRODUS-85 is based on the "object-attribute-meaning" principle. Its conceptual scheme has a network structure and allows the description of any object or/and concept complex in subsets/classes of arbitrary structure and hierarchy. Integer real symbol attributes (parameters) are compared to objects. Objects, attributes and their meanings may have natural language names. To describe a controlled complex every external local object is compared to the Base object and a set of parameters representing its state and a corresponding set of input/output orders are defined. Objects, designating subsets, may represent local subsystems, and consist of a number of similar control objects.

Since the control and decision making rules are expressed more naturally by dependencies of time events in many cases, then facts in the control Production System Base should overlap in time. In PRODUS-85 such overlap exists automatically for all facts with a pre-history storage depth set by the user.

2.2. If-parts logic

The if-parts of rules are better represented in frames of logic with quantifiers, which allow aggregation of similar productions with the same type of object control. This fact together with the temporal nature of the rule conditions mentioned above, gives proof of the following production system control peculiarity, realized in PRODU5-85. Not only "truth", "lie", but also two sets are considered to encompass the meanings of production condition logic expressions: the Base objects' sets for which this expression is true, and a set of moments or time interval in which the expression is true. These additional data should be transferred to then-parts of rules for actions with objects and for control purposes as well.

Modal quantified predicate arithmetic temporal logic serves as a formal language for registering the if-parts of rules into PRODUS-85. It allows us to express a partial order of events and their relative position on the time scale for separate objects and their complexes. One of the most widely used expressions in this logic has formally the following form:

$$¥\, x \notin X: Q\,(\,R(p(x)\,,\,A),\,T(t))$$

Here x - is the Base object or concept; X - is the name of Base objects' subset; ¥ - is one of four quantors; "for fixed x", "for any x of X", "there are some x in subset X", "there is at least one x in X".

The Distinction between the last two quantors is necessary because they have different operational semantics. The procedure for testing statements with these quantors are different and the test results are also different: in one case it is a subset, in another - a single object. Set X can be any subset of Base objects or subset of objects, for which any other statement is true. E.g.:"there is at least one x among those, for which statement No. 3 is true". The expression p(x) notes a parameter (attribute) of object x or parameter of order, received by the system from object x; A - is an argument to be compared with value p(x); R - is a relation between p(x) and A, which is tested under comparison; T(t) is an interval of time $T(t) = (t_1\,,\,t_2\,)$, at which the truth of statement is tested. This interval is counted from starting point t. The expression R(p(x),A) is called a fact. Symbol Q denotes one of three time logic predicates: "fact R appears at interval T,' "fact R is kept at interval T", "fact R disappears at interval T".

Two time scales are used in logic. The absolute scale begins at system start time and finishes at the current one. Starting point t of time interval T can be situated in any given place of the absolute scale. The relative scale can be fixed to the truth interval of any chosen predicate. When using such a scale the starting point of interval T can be placed at the earliest moment of time at which any given predicate became true, or the starting point can be placed at the latest moment of time, at which such predicate was true. Interval T bounds can take any value.

Such logic differs, for instance, from Camp's time logic [2] mainly in the fact that we use one operator "at interval" instead of two operators "after" and "before". This one operator's expressiveness is not however weaker. Logic allows in the external language to bind the facts in time (events). For example: "event R appears or disappears or is kept before or after the appearance or disappearance of event S", "the event appears or disappears simultaneously with S", "the event has just appeared or disappeared", "the event had disappeared or appeared 10 sec before S appeared or disappeared", "the event appears or disappears not earlier than 20 sec after S", "the fact is still being kept up to the present moment", "the fact appears, disappears or is kept at interval (5 sec, 100 sec), counted from the appearance or disappearance of S" etc.

2.3. Rule Actions and Conflicts

Rule actions in the control production system together with operations of the Base condition transformation involve output orders and messages to external objects, which can operate simultaneously and independently. That is why in the control production system the mechanism of conflict resolution should operate as follows:

- At every interpretation process step, several non-conflicting rules, describing the system's reaction to the influence of various external objects must fire in the general case.
- The settlement of conflicts in its essence must fit the general definite physical separation needed for carrying out control.

For these purposes in PRODUS-85 priorities can be determined among rules and privileges for one rules' subset over another one can be set.

2.4. Dynamic change of attention focusing

When an unfavourable situation or emergency occurs in the controlled process, the system must immediately refocus its attention to analysis or compensate detected deflections, and interrupt the current process of rule interpretation. To do this a production emergency call mechanism is used in PRODUS-85.

Any production can be marked as an "emergency". Then it will fire immediately after determining the truth of its "if-part" and thus by its own actions will interrupt the current if-parts matching process for other rules. Several emergency rules, set one by one, should immediately focus the system's attention only on reasoning about the situations of importance. The work of the others (no emergency) should be postponed.

Today we are carrying out experimental research on a pseudo-recursive version of the production system, which allows the usage of recursion in the rule language. It allows us to express rules, the actions of which recursively call other subsets of rules. When carrying out the recursive call, the cut of the current reasoning process takes place, and the system begins to work only with called rules. On finishing this work or on reaching the certain condition of the Base, the recursion return to the interrupted processes to continue reasoning. The recursive depth is restricted by the stack.

The recursive production language is not only a suitable means of focusing the system's attention, but it also contributes to the effective laconicism of production models. Auxiliary concepts and objects do not occur in the Base. The rule if-part dimension is reduced. The evident usage of the principle of reducing tasks to subtasks becomes possible. The emergency and recursive calls combination provides for quick reaction in extreme situations.

2.5. Interaction with External Objects

Messages or orders are sent from external objects to the system in an asynchronous way at unforeseen moments. That is why, simultaneously with the rule interpretation process in the control production system, a process of receiving data in a special buffer must be continuous. In the buffer, PRODUS-85 data are being stored until the previous Base condition is fully analysed, all necessary reactions are worked out, and until all inferences are over. Only then should the stored data be transferred to the Base.

3. GENERATION AND OPTIMIZATION OF APPLIED CONTROL SYSTEMS

There is a need to speed up the rather slow interpretation process of the real time production systems by using special production activation means or preliminary problem-oriented optimizing of the set production algorithm. In PRODUS-85 these functions are carried out by the Base and production program generator, translating models of knowledge about the problem application of the system from the external language of the user to the internal data structure.

The generator processes the Base conceptual scheme description and the texts of rules, in a language similar to natural language. All the Base object attributes necessary for describing its condition are extracted from texts of rules. The addressing system of attributes is formed, and the reservation of memory is made. If-parts of rules are translated to frame structures, filled with numerical if-codes most suitable for interpretation. Then-parts are automatically translated first to procedures in FORTRAN, then their objective code is built. The rule activation scheme is also built.

The activation process includes dynamic activation and deactivation of separate conditions (atoms), their conjunction forming if-parts of productions. If any fact received from external input (or as a result of rules firing), is put into the Base, then all the production atoms not contradictory to this fact are activated, and all contradictory atoms are deactivated. Simultaneously some activated atoms can be marked as true, and all deactivated ones marked as false. Operations of assuming such values are subset by the generator into rules actions and into procedures of information input into the Base.

For the atoms to be activated a special procedure is applied, which in the course of interpretation consumes information about the dynamic changes of the Base and which is aware beforehand of the atoms' subsets to be activated according to the corresponding changes. Atoms testing the Base objects with a changed state are activated; if they contain quantors or arguments being computed. Productions are activated and their if-parts are matched for the Base current state, only if all its atoms are active.

Data controlling such activation processes are automatically extracted from initial production texts at the stage of generation. A fast activation algorithm with linear computation complexity is used in the course of interpretation. It is based on a supergraphs application as a knowledge representation minimal description model [3]. During generation, extraction of the rules, which increases their reaction time, is also performed. For the activation scheme described we can extract internal representation of all the non-quantified atoms that become true or false after a certain rule firing or after receiving input data into the Base. For all operations on the Base attribute changes, only non-quantified atoms possessing the address to them, can be extracted from action-parts as well. As a result we have a set of productions, equal to the initial one, but with less matchings and addressing to the Base.

The operation of activation may overlap in time with the user. In this case, if rules initiate any environmental processes, then atoms waiting for responses from corresponding objects should be activated after some time, determined by the fast actions of environment processes. Before that, one should regard such atoms as false and not examine all productions they are involved in. Rules for such activations have the following form: "If Rule 27 acts, then fact F can appear only after 20 minutes".

The generation also finds conflicting rules - those and only those rules, which can be simultaneously active and contain only non-contradictory atoms, and also carry out some contradictory operations, i.e. appropriate various meanings of one and the same Base object attribute or retrieve various orders for one and the same external object.

PRODUS-85 is implemented in FORTRAN and Assembler. The response time is 1 second. The system is oriented to the control of four machining FM Systems and in these applications they carry out the following applied functions:

task input from technological planning computer and CNC-programs from CAD levels;
loading/unloading at the FMS input/output;
control of preparatory operations for technological bases, setting and completing of pallet hardware, reorientation and dispalleting;
connection to the data base;
guided vehicles and storing operation control;
control of machine-tool adjustment and of machining of pallet components;
dialogue with personnel;
process monitoring and preliminary diagnostics.

REFERENCES

[1] Evseev, O.V., "Control Production System for FMS", in: Izvestia AS. Techn. Cybernetics (USSR, 1987), No. 5, pp.93-112 .

[2] Valiev,M.K.,"Time Dependences in Database", in: Izvestia AS. Techn.Cybernetics, (USSR, 1985), No. 1.

[3] Evseev, O.V., "Supergraphs for Representing Knowledge in Minimal Description Models, in: Problems of Artificial Intelligence and Recognition of Images, V. 1, Artificial intelligence, Institute of Cybernetics after Glushkov, AS of the Ukraine (Kiev, USSR, 1984), pp. 66-67

Industrial Applications of Artificial Intelligence
J.L. Alty and L.I. Mikulich (Editors)
Elsevier Science Publishers B.V. (North-Holland)

INTELLIGENT TECHNOLOGICAL DESIGN SYSTEMS

KOLCHIN, A.F., ZYKOVA, S.A., POZDNEEV, B.M.
CAD Department
MOSSTANKIN
Moscow, USSR

The results and the experience of the work of the CAD Department of MOSSTANKIN in the field of the applying artificial intelligence tools and methods to technological design tasks are presented in the paper.

I. INTRODUCTION

Integrated engineering manufacture requires automation and information access in its three main stages: product design, technological manufacturing training and product production.
Technological manufacturing training is one of the most important components of the process of technological design, but is a complex object for automation. Existing local systems of technology design and technological training for different kinds of manufacturing (lathe and milling, extrusion and etc.), do not allow effective simulation of a through route of machining because of the authonomy of system design, the absence of structural variable tecnological information etc.
The principles of construction and functioning of the intelligent design system applied to the production of typical engineering components (skafts, flanges and so on) are expounded in the 2nd section of the paper.
The second project described in section 3 is devoted to research into the general principles of constructing the consultation system for the development of manufacturing process (the route of the machining is already chosen) for producing rotational parts. Special attention is paid to the problem of data analysis in a system of this kind.
Further directions of the research are presented in the 4th section.

2. AN INTELLIGENT SYSTEM FOR THE DESIGN OF TECHNOLOGIES (ISDT)

2.I. The main tasks solving by the ISDT

Experience shows that design parameters are corrected after the accomplishment of the process of construction for about 50% of the parts in order to raise the level of validity of manufacturing. The process of coordination of parts construction and the technological departments is of the iterational type and takes a lot of time (weeks, even months).

The process of working out the structure of these parts in order to reach the necessary level of validity of their manufacturing is conducted, as a rule, without any analysis of the machining route and without taking into account the technological capabilities of the main operations (scrap-free blanking of the initial material, sheet presswork, heat treatment, welding, protection covering).
In order to solve the problem, the Intelligent System for the Design of Technologies (ISDT) [2] is created. The main goal of the ISDT is to integrate the work of the design and process control departments of the enterprise. The ISDT must ensure, firstly, expert support in the design stage, namely, the process of working out the structure of the parts in order to reach the necessary level of the validity of their manufacturing, secondly, the choice of the enlarged route of the machining that takes into account the rational use of all technological machining methods existing at the main enterprise and at the partner enterprises. Special demands are produced for information and hardware - software consistency of the ISDT and CAD designers on the one hand and the ISDT and technological preparing of manufacturing CAD of the individual types of machining on the other.

2.2. Processing and implementation of the ISDT

The system provides a rational choice for the route of machining taking into consideration the technological capabilities of methods and machining techniques existing in the knowledge base.
The following factors are used as criteria of optimisation:
- Metal capacity;
- Energy capacity;
- Difficulty capacity;
- Cost production;
- Main equipment cost.

The input to the system consists of structured information of the produced part (the basis for the choice of the alternative routes) and their optimisation according to the given criteria.
The system provides the implementation of enlarged technological design during three steps. The first step is the choice of the necessary stages for production providing subsequent transformation of the input material into a part (scrapfree blanking of the initial material, forming, size processing, heat processing, protection covering). Different variants of the use of various initial metals (hot-drown rolled metal, forging, casting, powders and ets.) can be modelled at that stage.
At the second stage the enlarged technological routes derived from the methods and ways of machining, are generated taking into consideration the chosen stages of production.
In the final step of design the enlarged evaluation of the resource capacity of the alternative routes of machining and the choice of the best of them are implemented.
In the first version of the system the first step is

implemented as a dialogue procedure. It is necessary to note that the other two steps implement the wellknown solution strategy "generate and test". However in the given version of the system these tasks are divided because of the absence of heuristics used for the evaluation of the solutions. The knowledge is acquired and formed in the process of the work of the first part and used in the second one. That is why the step of generation of technological routes has been implemented in the production shell "INTEREXPERT", and the last step has been implemented as a dialogue procedure.
The most important component for further development of the system is the knowledge acquisition stage that forms facts and production rules for the knowledge base used at the second and the third steps. The method of "thinking aloud" and repertory grids are used.
The testing of the system for parts of electrical engines and electrical appliances has proved the effectiveness of the system and its ability to adapt and extend. It is hoped to develop the system in order to reach the level of designing separate blocks and products as a whole.

3. DATA ANALYSIS IN THE INTELLIGENT TECHNOLOGICAL SYSTEM

3.I. The Intelligent System for the Generation of Technological Processes (ISGTP)

Parts of the body-rotation type produced at one of the enterprises of mechanical engineering have been subdevided into several groups (about 200 groups), each group contains from several dozen to several hundred parts, differing in their names, sizes, etc; this subdivision is based on the principle of the uniformity of the technological process for the parts within a single group. The construction of the general technological process for each group (for each part of a group the process is adapted according to the concrete parameters of the part) demands considerable intellectual effort and time (2-3 months).
For the automation of the development of the general technological process, an Intelligent System for the Generation of the Technological Processes (ISGTP) is planned. It is expected that several initial technological processes will be created by expert-technologists and put in the system, the others will be generated by the ISGTP itself.
Since there are no stable connections between the development of the concrete technological process and the knowledge used and there exist only a few parts for solution of the problem for technological process construction that allow pure formalization, it seems useful that the task should be solved through generalization of the experience available using analogies combined with the pure formalization. The multitude of types of knowledge used, the goals of knowledge processing, and strategies of tasks solving, demand various models of knowledge representation and processing.
These factors lead to the concept of a hybrid complex system

with compulsory elements of machine learning, the ability to the analyse existing knowledge, the possibility of selfmodification based on experience and its analysis of new information. The system would have a rich interface, the dialogue would be conducted in a language which is close to natural one.
The terminal product of the system – the program of the general technological process for a certain group of parts given to the terminal user – is implemented with the help of the production language OPS5. The average program consists of about 300 OPS5 rules, the run time is nearly 20 minutes (for the PC Macintosh Plus). One of the programs of this type has been created and it is described in [3].

3.2. Data analysis in ISGTP

The following items can be shared out as the most significant aspects of data analysis in the ISGTP:
- data analysis on unredundancy;
- data analysis on completeness in the sense of their sufficiency for the concrete task (certain class of the tasks) solution;
- the search for contradictions and their analysis.

The analysis on nonredundancy includes finding (and elimination) of repeating identical elements of the data base and also, if the corresponding directive exists the direct conclusions from the data. Logical mechanisms are used – particularly, the resolutions method.
The analysis on completeness in the sense of their sufficiency for the concrete task (certain class of the tasks) solution is also performed by means of mathematical logic and covers logical methods of solution only. This type of analysis needs in formation on the characteristics of the goals – according to this information the minimal set of data needed for a given achievement is formed. Then by means of pattern-matching it is found if this set of data exists in the data base at the present moment; if not the lacking data are determined. The machine learning module responsible for data base supplement and necessary modifications carries out the elicitation for the missing knowledge (if it is possible).
The search for contradictions and their analysis – data analysis on contradiction, or inconsistency – is of great interest. The following main types of contradictions (discrepancies) are distinguished:
- fatal contradictions (discrepancies);
- contradictions (discrepancies) of development.

Fatal contradictions are logical contradictions; fatally contradicted elements can not remain in the base without certain modifications. Once revealed, these contradictions require one of the following actions:
- the removal of one of the considered elements;
- the removal of all the considered elements;
- the modification of one of the considered elements;

- the modification of all the considered elements.
The contradictions of the development represent the contradictions of the data base elements which are not corresponding to each other, say because of their insufficient definition (determination).
The finding of contradictions of development give rise to one or several hypothesis [I] which are not the logical consequences of the considered data base elements and serve, therefore, as a starting point for the development of the data base and the reason and basis for hypothesis formation.
The revealing of contradictions is performed by means of logical methods. While classifying contradictions heuristic methods as well as dialog with a user are used.
The non-traditional part of the data analysis mechanisms - the revealing and classification of contradictions and the choice of the strategy of contradiction processing seem to be the important elements of the system, since they makes it possible to process knowledge that is unsufficiently determined and appeares inevitably, for example, as a result of deriving knowledge from the experts and also to eliminate the discrepancies and to enlarge the existing data base with the help of the hypothesis formation.

4. CONCLUSIONS AND THE FURTHER WORK

The experience of the creation of the intelligent technological systems reveals the necessity for the following main directions of research:
- the detection, classification and representation of the diverse technological knowledge and decision support methods;
- the creation of conceptual models of technological tasks on different levels;
- the determination of peculiarities of the information support blocks (knowledge acquisition, machine learning, data analysis, etc.) in the integrated intelligent technological system.

REFERENCES

[I] Hajek, P., Havranek T., Mechanizing Hypothesis Formation : Mathematical Foundations for a General Theory (Springer-verlag, Berlin, Haidelberg, New York, I978)

[2] Solomencev,Y.M., Didenko,V.P., Maxin, Y.A., Pozdneev,B.M., The concept of organization and functioning of computer aided expert system for mechanical engineering design. In: Proceedings of All-Union Conference "CAD-Informatics: Computer-Aided Design Machines and Technologies", Moscow, USSR, I989, pp. 28 -37 (in Russ.)

[3] Kolchin,A.F., Zykova,S.A., The Intelligent tecnological design system. In: Proceedings of IV-th All-Union Conference by Computer-Aided Design and Constraction in Machin-Bulding, Minsk, I989, Vol.2, pp. IOO-IO2 (in Russ.)

Industrial Applications of Artificial Intelligence
J.L. Alty and L.I. Mikulich (Editors)
Elsevier Science Publishers B.V. (North-Holland)

AN INTELLIGENT SYSTEM FOR SUPPORT FOR THE EARLY STAGES OF VLSI CIRCUIT DESIGN AND ITS KNOWLEDGE REPRESENTATION LANGUAGE

V. KOROLYOV and L. GARUSTOVITCH

Institute for Engineering Cybernetics,
Surganova 6,
Minsk 220605,
The USSR.

V. VASHKEVITCH AND A. ASTREIKO,
Minsk Radioengineering Institute,
P. Brovky 6,
Minsk 220600,
The USSR.

O. SAMTSOV,
Pritytskogo 72,
Minsk, 220134,
The USSR.

ABSTRACT: This paper presents an intelligent system intended to assist its users at the early stages of the design of arithmetic units of VLSI circuits. The project is viewed as a constituent part of a more general one, aimed at implementing new expressive knowledge representation languages with an extendable variety of knowledge processing operations. This variety includes operations of both logical inference and the running of programmes.

1. INTRODUCTION

In this report the main aspects of an application concerning an intelligent system for the support of the early stages of VLSI circuits design is described. The main task of this project are:

1. Developing a new knowledge representation language that has highly expressive capabilities. This language was named Semantic Code (SC). Its texts are homogeneous semantic networks of a special kind.

2. Fixing the set of mechanisms, or operations, for parallel processing of the knowledge base, represented in the form of

the texts of the SC language. Below they will be named as SC-operations. The SClanguage together with a set of SC-operations was named by the authors the Abstract SC-Machine (ASCM). ASCM determines in full the level of logical organization of the intelligent system, described in this paper.

3. Software implementation of ASCM.

4. Filling the knowledge base of the intelligent system in the SC language.

Below the main aspects of the project are presented in more detail.

2. SYNTAX AND SEMANTICS OF THE SEMANTIC CODE

It has been commonly acknowledged that fundamentally new formal models and knowledge representation languages are needed for intelligent systems, oriented at serious practical applications in different fields of knowledge. A language for filling a knowledge base of such a system should easily represent complex hierarchical structures and perform a large number of knowledge processing operations, including both logical inference and running of programmes. The Semantic Code (SC) language, being developed by the authors, seems to meet these demands in general.

The set of elements of all text, written in SC language, or SC-text, may be divided into a set of SC-nodes and a set of SC-arcs. Structure of any SC-text is similar to the structure of an oriented graph with a single difference any SC-arc may be drawn not only between two SC-nodes, but also between an SC-node and an SC-arc.

Each element of SC-text has certain semantic interpretation. Each SC-arc is a sign of connection "A set of elements (marked by the beginning of SC-arc) - an element of this set (marked by the end of this SC-arc)". Each SC-node is interpreted either as an element of the field of knowledge, represented by SC-text, or as an element of the formal theory that describes logical structure of this field of knowledge. In the second case SC-node may designate a logical relation, quantifier, logical sentence, SC-programme.

Any element of field of knowledge, represented in SC, may be an object, relation, symmetrical or asymmetrical connection (any connection is an element of n-ary relation, where $n>1$; in SC there is an important structural difference between symmetrical and asymmetrical connections), attribute (that is, semantic role of an element in an asymmetrical connection), or a set or structure. Such a variety of structural types of elements makes it expedient to divide the set of SC-nodes into seven structural types. This classification embraces as well SC-nodes that take part in description of formal theory of any field of knowledge. For example, SC-nodes that designate logical relations or quantifiers, belong to the structural type of relations. SC-nodes (that designate logical sentences) may belong to different structural types such as structures (if the sentence designated is conjunction of atomary sentences), symmetrical connections (for disjunctory sentences) or asymmetrical connections (for implications).

The set of all the elements of SC-text may also be divided into a set of SC-constants and a set of SC-variables. SC-variables are found in logical sentences with quantifiers and are bounded by quantifiers of existentiality, generality and modal quantifiers (Seldom, Often and several others). During knowledge processing SC-variable may be bounded with some SC-constant or some other SC-variable.

Among SC-constants several important subsets may be marked out. One of them is a subset of indefinite SC-constants. Any such constant during knowledge processing may be identified with some other constant, and after that they may be glued together. Another one is a subset of stationary informational objects. All its elements are SC-nodes. They include numerical, textual and some other SC-constants. In contrast to other SC-nodes, they may have inner contents.

Another highly important subset of SC-constants is a set of basic constants. SC-text, describing logical structure of the formal theory of any field of knowledge, cannot be deciphered without information about semantics of all the basic constants. They include quantifiers, logical relations (OR, AND, NOT, Implication), signs of SC-programmes and signs of their specifications, signs of several commonly used relations over numbers and characters. All basic constants are SC-nodes. In any fragment of SC-text, describing the formal theory of some field of knowledge, all SC-nodes, belonging to the structural types of relations and attributes, are basic constants.

3. ABSTRACT SC-MACHINE

Any field of knowledge is represented in SC language in the form of single large SC-text that describes data to be processed, generalized information (rules, regularities, procedures) and tasks that are to be solved. While tasks are solved, information, represented in SC language is being processed. New information is being generated on the basis of rules and regularities, described in the knowledge base; new information may be also received from the user. Knowledge processing in SC results in a changing configuration of SC-text. SC-nodes and SC-arcs may be generated, removed or glued together. These changes are brought by a finite quantity of SC-operations.

Semantic Code language together with a set of SC-operations is formally interpreted as the Abstract SC-Machine (ASCM). ASCM includes SC-memory, in which information is presented in SC language, and the set of SC-operations, transforms SC-memory in parallel and asynchronous way. Each SC-operation is characterized by general conditions and general results of its fulfillment. SC-operation is being fulfilled in such a moment when and over such a fragment of SC-memory where conditions for its fulfillment are discovered. SC-operations may interact only through common SC-memory.

The number of basic constants in SC is theoretically unlimited.This makes it possible to try to include different mechanisms of knowledge processing into the set of SC-operations. This is the most important peculiarity of the presented knowledge representation language. It is noteworthy to mention here that projects based upon Prolog and other languages of logic programming have disclosed limited capabibilities of inference in Horne clauses. Yet more powerful mechanisms of knowledge processing can't be included into operational semantics of these languages in a natural way.

The set of SC-operations includes the following classes.

1. SC-operations of dialogue with the user (including SC-operations of input and output).

2. SC-operations of logical inference (including SC-operations: of associative search of information; of transforming tasks into subtasks; SC-operations that disclose semantics of logical relations, etc).

3. SC-operations of running SC-programmes and of calling external programmes, written in other languages.

4. SC-operations over informational objects.

5. SC-operations over relations and sets.

6. SC-operations for "garbage collection".

4. AN INTELLIGENT SYSTEM BASED UPON THE ABSTRACT SC-MACHINE

Upon the basis of the concept of ASCM different knowledge representation languages, oriented at applications in particular fields of knowledge, may be developed. At the same time, testing of this concept upon different fields of knowledge is the only possible way to disclose the optimal set of problem-independent SC-operations.

If the set of problem-independent SC-operations is disclosed and implemented, it is necessary only to fill the knowledge base in the form of SC-text in order to create an intelligent system for a particular application. In such SC-text two components may be marked out: the problem-independent and problem-oriented ones. The former include SC-nodes (first of all - relations and attributes) that may be used for formalization of other fields of knowledge. The latter include SC-nodes and SC-arcs, used only for formalization of given field of knowledge.

Automated design of integrated circuits has become the first area for practical testing of ASCM. First experience of the application of knowledge processing techniques in this area has shown that they can be used effectively for solving separate tasks at the early stages of design. In order to automate the whole design these techniques are to be harmonously combined with more traditional ones for processing large amount of numerical information [1]. A knowledge representation language, based upon SC and having appropriate system of SC-operations and problem-oriented component, may be naturally used for these purposes.

The authors are involved in a project for an intelligent system that supports the early stages of design of arithmetical units of VLSI circuits. The knowledge base of this system is desscribed in SC language. It consists of two basic parts. Each of them constitutes its own formal theory. One of them is the problem theory, describing several alternative ways of designing adders. Its knowledge base makes it possible for the system to partition the adder, which is being designed, into sections, to choose for every section its mode of implementation, to perform primary evaluation of parameters of the adder and to formulate the task for another CAD system to shape the structural description of the adder at the level of library elements. Another one is the problem-independent theory of dialogue between the system and the user. All acts of interaction between them and all acts of transformation of the database of the problem theory, or the problem database, by the system in process of solving the task are reflected in the database of the theory of dialogue where they are designated by special SC-nodes. Any SC-operation after being fulfilled leaves its "track" in the database of the theory of dialogue. The variety of such "tracks", left by SC-operations, fulfilled in process of solving some task, forms the protocol of the process of solving this task. It makes it possible to arrange the following modes of dialogue between the user and the system.

1. The user formulates the task and the system solves it and gives to the user the final answer (in the form of structural scheme); if the user asks the system to explain the answer, the system displays the protocol of the process of solving the task.

2. The system solves the task and displays the protocol; the user may interfere at some point by formulating a subtask in which he may introduce changes into the problem database and order the system to solve the initial task from the point of interruption taking into account these changes; thus final solution emerges as a man-machine dialogue.

3. The user may ask the system to teach him to design adders, then formulate a task and solve it, using the system; the system solves this task itself, compares its own solution with one achieved by the user and displays comments upon his decisions.

In future the knowledge base of the system and the set of SC-operations for knowledge processing are to be extended. It should make it possible for the system to design not only adders but also multipliers and some other units. Also the system should be able to recognize, store and use the users' decisions that may improve its performance.

This system is being programmed in programming language C. In future its internal language SC is to be implemented in hardware in the form of highly parallel multiprocesor system with reconfigurable structure of communication channels between its processing elements (similar to the approach, described in [2]).

5. CONCLUSIONS

Knowledge engineering techniques are effective in CAD if used for solving appropriate tasks that can't be solved satisfactory by means of traditional algorithmic techniques. In the present project the main stress is put upon wide capabilities of dialogue between the user and the intelligent system at the stage of choosing general structural scheme of the circuit being designed. The set of problem-independent knowledge processing operations, revealed and formalized for this intelligent system, are to be confirmed and expanded in process of further testing of Abstract SC-Machine both in CAD and in other fields of knowledge.

ACKNOWLEDGEMENTS

The authors should like to thank: Dr. V.Golenkov, the head of the Laboratory of Artificial Intelligence in Minsk Radioengineering Institute and Institute of Engineering Cybernetics, for his guidance in the project; experts A.Yurovsky and E. Revinsky from Research and Production Association "Integral" (Minsk, USSR) for their participation in filling the knowledge base of the system; and all those engaged in programming SC-operations for first results in practical implementation of the project.

REFERENCES

[1] Fujita, T., Knowledge Base and Algorithm for VLSI Design, in: Proc. Int. Symp. Circuits and Systems, Kyoto June 5-7 1985, v.2 pp. 877-880.

[2] Sapaty, P.S., A wave language for parallel processing of semantic networks, in: Computers and Artificial Intelligence (Bratislava, Checkoslovakia) v.5 (1986) N4 pp.289-314.

Industrial Applications of Artificial Intelligence
J.L. Alty and L.I. Mikulich (Editors)
Elsevier Science Publishers B.V. (North-Holland)

THE ADAPTIVE-INTELLIGENT CONTROL OF ROBOTS AND TECHNOLOGICAL EQUIPMENT FOR INTELLIGENT MANUFACTURING

A.V.TIMOFEJEV
Leningrad Institute of Aviation Instrument Making

ABSTRACT: The paper presents methods for the adaptive-intelligent control of robots and other technological equipment under conditions of process information deficiency. Flexible algorithms for programming and sensor correction of movements compensated by uncertainty factors are proposed. Robust and adaptive control algorithms which compensate for uncontrolled disturbances and which ensure the desired character of transient processes have been synthesized. A description of the results of the application of the proposed methods to adaptive Flexible Manufacturing Systems (FMS) for powder metallurgy and laser treatment is presented.

Keywords: Adaptive-intelligent control; self-tuning regulators; Identification, sensors, industrial robots; flexible manufacturing.

1. INTRODUCTION

The application of adaptation and artifical intelligence methods is one of the effective ways of increasing the reliability of FMS. It requires the synthesis of robust adaptive-intelligent algorithms for processing sensor information and for the control of the FMS [1-7].

2. AIMS AND PROBLEMS OF ADAPTIVE-INTELLIGENT CONTROL

The dynamics of a large class of robots and other FMS technological equipment can be described by a system of differential equations [1,4-10]

$$A\,(q,1)\,q^{(r)} + b\,(q,q.....q^{(r-1)},1) + V = U, \qquad (1)$$

where q is a vector of generalised coordinates of dimension m
q^j is its jth-derivative with respect to time t,
j=l,...,r, ,1- p parameter vector of the motors, actuators and functional elements,
U a control vector, vector of dimension m,
V a vector of time-independent disturbances of dimension m.

The control coordinates and parameter limitations are usually represented as

$$\underline{C}_{ij} < q_i^{(j)} < \bar{C}_{ij} \;\ldots\ldots\ldots\ldots\ldots\; j = 0,1,....,r, \qquad (2)$$

$$|U_i(t)| < C_{ui} \;\ldots\ldots\ldots\ldots\ldots\; i = 1,2,.....,m, \qquad (3)$$

$$1 \in Q_1 \qquad ||V(t)|| < C_v \qquad (4)$$

The control aim consist in the synthesis of the Programmed Movement (PM) of q_p (t) which satisfies the limitations of (2). For the solution of the problem it is sufficient to calculate a programmed movement q_p (t), t $[t_0, t_T]$, satisfying boundary conditions, and to synthesize the intelligent control algorithms for realisation of the PM. The PM and control synthesis are complicated by the unknown obstacles P in the operation area and due to the parameter uncertainty l and disturbances V. The uncertainty class is determined by many P_l, Q_V and C_V parameters.

3. ADAPTIVE ALGORITHMS FOR CONSTRUCTION AND OPTIMISATION OF PM

PM is synthesized on the basis of the method of parameterisation [6,7] which allows boundary conditions to be satisfied in advance. In conformity with this method the PM is formed as follows

$$q_p(t) = a_0(t) + \sum_{j=1}^{N} W_j a_j(t), \quad t_0 \le t \le t_T \qquad (5)$$

where $W = | w_j |_{j=1}^{N}$ - N - a vector of unknown parameters

$a_0(t), a_1(t), \ldots, a_N(t)$ - pre-set m-measured basic functions, which satisfy the following conditions:

-PM satisfies the boundary conditions with any parameter chosen;
-functions $a_j(t)$ can be differentiated r times, are linearly independent within $[t_0, t_T]$ and are simple in realisation.

Specific methods for choosing basic functions from the class of polynomials and others are considered in a number of works [6,7].

The analytical synthesis of PM for the determination of the parameters $W_1, \ldots, W_N$ can be done allowing for the limitations (2) and obstacles P in the operation area. By substituting (5) in (2) we obtain a system of linear inequalities. Recurrent finitely converging algorithms (PFCA) can be used for the solution of these inequalities [7]. The boundary conditions and adaptability to obstacles P are advantages of this method.

The integral functional of quality for the optimisation of PM takes the form

$$J[q_p(.)] = \int_{t_0}^{t_T} \sum_{j=1}^{r} q_p^{(j)T} L_j q_p^{(j)} dt \qquad (6)$$

Where L_j are positively determined m x m matrices.

PM is calculated in the form of (6) with registration of the limitations of (2) [6,7].

4. ALGORITHMS OF STABILIZATION OF THE PROGRAMMED MOVEMENT

The aim of the robot and equipment control of an FMS is to guarantee transient processes (TP) with pre-set characteristics, e.g. their exponential character with respect to each coordinate. The synthesis of control is achieved in conformity with the principle of the high speed control of PM [7]. The result is the following algorithm for stabilising PM.

$$U = A(q,l)\,[q_p^{(r)} + \ldots + G_{r-1} e^{(r-1)} + \ldots + G_0 e] + b(q,q,\ldots,q^{(r-1)},l), \quad e = q - q_p \qquad (8)$$

By substituting (8) into (1) a linear differential equation of the closed-loop system with these the pre-set parameters $G_0, G_1, \ldots, G_{r-1}$ is obtained [4-7].

5. ROBUST AND ADAPTIVE-INTELLIGENCE CONTROL ALGORITHMS

For the realisation of control (8) the 1 vector of parameters is needed, which is not only unknown but also is subject to unpredictable changes in a given set of Q 1 , therefore in practice a certain evaluation $\hat{l}$ of the unknown Vector l has to be formed and substituted into (8). The resultant algorithm for robust control is obtained for which evaluation [3,4-7] is correct.

$$\| E(t) \| < C \ \| E(t_0) \| \exp[-d\,(t - t_0)\,] + C(C_0\, d^{-1} \| l - \hat{l} \| + d^{-1} C_v), \quad (9)$$

where $E(t) = | e^{(i)}(t) |_{i=0}^{r-1}$,C, C_0 , d - positive numbers

Hence it appears from (9) that the occurrence of PM performance is essentially limited by the level of parameter disturbances $\hat{l} - l$ and time independent disturbance C_v . The effective methods of compensation for $l - \hat{l}$ and V to improve the quality of TP are:

- -self-tuning of parameters
- -identification l and V,
- -sensor-intellectual correction of PM q_p (t).

6. OPTIMAL ALGORITHMS FOR SELF-TUNING AND IDENTIFICATION

The control performance criterion form the basis of the synthesis of adaptation algorithms. As an example of such a criterion are the inequalities (Timofejev, 1976-1980).

$$F(\bar{l}, t) = S - \| U - A(q,\bar{l})\, q^{(r)} - b(q, ..., q^{(r-1)}, l) \|^2 > 0, \quad (10)$$

where s is a positive number determining the accuracy of the implementation of PM. Inequalities of such type are called [4,5] estimatory. The adaptation algorithms are synthesized as the algorithms for solving such inequalities. The discrete and continuous algorithms for self-tuning and identification of unknown parameters are suggested in a number of works [4-7].

One of the most efficient adaptation algorithms the gradient algorithm, uses the algorithm in the form

$$\hat{l}_{k+1} = \hat{l}_0 + \sum_{j=1}^{k} f_j \operatorname{grad} F(\hat{l}_j, t'_j), \ k=1,2,... \quad (11)$$

whose parameters f_j are chosen taking into account the optimality criterion

$$\| l - \hat{l}_{k+1} \| = \min_{f_j}, \ j=1,2,...,k,$$

where t'_j is the first moment when conditions set by the inequalities (10) are not satisfied under $l = \hat{l}_j$, $t = t_j$; $t_{j+1} = t'_j + y$, y is an upper-bound estimate for the computation time at the every step of the algorithm (11). This optimal adaptation algorithm has two important properties;

- the adaptation time is less or equal py;
- at the last step of the algorithm $k \leq p$ the exact identification of the vector of unknown parameters l takes place (provided there are no disturbances).

7. THE INSTRUMENTAL MEANS OF DESIGN FOR MULTI-PROCESSOR ADAPTIVE CONTROL SYSTEMS

The design of systems of robust and adaptive control for the robots and FMS equipment and their microprocessor realization is a complex and time-consuming problem. For its solution it is advantageous to make use of interactive means of design which allow the automation of the synthesis and analysis of such systems. The description of these means and the technology for the computer-aided design of systems of robust and adaptive control for robots and technological FMS equipment is given in a number of works [7-9]. Interactive techniques and computer-aided design approaches have been used to advantage in the calculation, simulation and realisation of specific systems of robust and adaptive control for various types of manipulators, transport and measuring robots[4-9]. The a practical results show that under a large level of the uncontrollable parametric disturbances the adaptive-intelligent control systems provide the required quality

8. REFERENCES

[9]. Timofejev, A.V., Gusev, S.V., Vukobratovich, V.A., Yurevich, E.I., 1983, Algorithms of adaptive control of robot movement. Mechanism and Machine Theory, Pergamon Press, Y. 18,4, pp 279-281.

[10].Timofejev, A.V., Guliaev, G.A., Zotov, Y.K., 1986, Computer-aided design of multimicroprocessing control for FMS. Information control problems in manufacturing technology Robots and FMS. 5-th IFAC/IFIP/IMACS Symposium, USSR,Suzdal, Preprints, Published for the IFAC, 470-474.

[11] Timofejev, A.B.,Dolidze, R.T., Godun, A.V., Adaptive Control of powder metallurgy and laser working Equipment. Workshop on Evaluated Control Strategies in Industrial Applications. IFAC Symposium,USSR, Tbilisi, Abstracts, Pergamon Press, pp 84-86.

AUTHOR INDEX

SUBJECT INDEX